BRITISH WRITERS

BRITISH WRITERS

JAY PARINI

Editor

RETROSPECTIVE SUPPLEMENT I

CHARLES SCRIBNER'S SONS

GALE GROUP

THOMSON LEARNING

New York • Detroit • San Diego • San Francisco
Boston • New Haven, Conn. • Waterville, Maine
London • Munich

Charles Scribner's Sons
an imprint of The Gale Group
27500 Drake Rd.
Farmington Hills, MI 48331-3535

Library of Congress Cataloging-in-Publication Data

British Writers Retrospective Supplement I / Jay Parini, editor.
    p. cm.
    Includes bibliographical references and index.
    ISBN 0-684-31227-1 (alk. paper)
      1. English literature—Bio-bibliography. 2. English literature—History and criticism. 3. Authors, English—Biography. I. Parini, Jay.

    PR85 .B688 Suppl. 8
    820.9—dc21
    [B]   001049628

Acknowledgments

Acknowledgment is gratefully made to those publishers and individuals who permitted the use of the following materials in copyright:

W. H. AUDEN Auden, W. H. From *Another Time*. Faber & Faber Limited, 1940. Reproduced by permission of Faber & Faber Ltd.—Auden, W. H. From *The Age of Anxiety: A Baroque Eclogue*. Random House, 1947. Copyright, 1946, 1947, by W. H. Auden. All rights reserved. Reproduced by permission—Auden, W. H. From "A Summer Night," "Consider," "For the Time Being," "In Memory of Ernst Toller," "The Seven Stages," "Voltaire at Ferney," in *Collected Poems*. Edited by Edward Mendelson. Vintage Books, 1991. Copyright © 1976, 1991 by The Estate of W. H. Auden. All rights reserved. Reproduced by permission.

SAMUEL BECKETT Beckett, Samuel. From "Endgame," "Footfalls," "Happy Days," "Krapp's Last Tape," "Not I," "Play," "The Unnamable," "Waiting for Godot," in *The Complete Dramatic Works*. Faber & Faber, 1986. This collection © Samuel Beckett 1986. Reproduced by permission of Faber & Faber Ltd.

CHARLOTTE BRONTË Barker, Juliet. From The Brontës. Weidenfeld and Nicolson, 1994. Copyright © 1994 Juliet R. V. Barker. All rights reserved. Reproduced by permission.

WILLIAM GOLDING Golding, William. From "Crosses," "Egypt From My Inside," "The English Channel," "Fable," "The Ladder and the Tree," in *The Hot Gates and other occasional pieces*. Faber and Faber, 1965. © 1965 by William Golding. All rights reserved. Reproduced by permission of Faber & Faber Ltd.—Kermode, Frank. From Modern Essays. Fontana Books, 1971. Copyright © Frank Kermode 1970. Reproduced by permission—Golding, William. From "A Moving Target," "An Affection for Cathedrals," "Belief and Creativity," "My First Book," "Surge and Thunder," in *A Moving Target*. Faber and Faber, 1982. © William Golding 1982. Reproduced by permission of Faber & Faber Ltd.

SEAMUS HEANEY Heaney, Seamus. From "Blackberry-Picking," "Digging," "Death of a Naturalist," in *Death of a Naturalist*. Faber & Faber, 1966. © Seamus Heaney 1966. Reproduced by permission of Faber & Faber Ltd.—Heaney, Seamus. From "The Forge," "Requiem for the Croppies," in *Door into the Dark*. Faber & Faber, 1969. © 1969 by Seamus Heaney. Reproduced by permission of Faber & Faber Ltd.— Heaney, Seamus.

From "North," in *North*. Faber & Faber Ltd., 1975. © Seamus Heaney 1975. All rights reserved. Reproduced by permission of Faber & Faber Ltd.— Heaney, Seamus. From *Field Work*. Faber & Faber, 1979. © 1976, 1979 by Seamus Heaney. Reproduced by permission of Faber & Faber Ltd.— Heaney, Seamus. From "Clearances," in *The Haw Lantern*. Faber & Faber, 1987. © Seamus Heaney 1987. All rights reserved. Reproduced by permission of Faber & Faber Ltd.— Heaney, Seamus. From "Field of Vision," "Fosterling," "Glanmore Revisited," "Seeing Things," in *Seeing Things*. Faber & Faber, 1991. Copyright © 1991 by Seamus Heaney. All rights reserved. Reproduced by permission of Faber & Faber Ltd.—Heaney, Seamus. From "A Brigid's Girdle," "A Sofa in the Forties," "The Rain Stick," "Weighing In," in *The Spirit Level*. Faber & Faber, 1996. © Seamus Heaney, 1996. All rights reserved. Reproduced by permission of Faber & Faber Ltd.—Heaney, Seamus. From "Bann Valley Eclogue," "Castalian Spring," "Sonnets from Hellas," in *Electric Light*. Faber and Faber, 2001. © Seamus Heaney, 2001. All rights reserved. Reproduced by permission of Faber & Faber Ltd.

SAMUEL JOHNSON Boswell, James. From *Life*. Edited by R. W. Chapman. Oxford, 1980. Reproduced by permission.

BEN JONSON Eliot, T. S. From *The Sacred Wood: Essays on Poetry and Criticism*. Methuen & Co. Ltd., 1920. Reproduced by permission of Faber & Faber Ltd.

JOHN KEATS Trilling, Lionel. From *The Opposing Self: Nine Essays in Criticism*. The Viking Press, 1955. Copyright 1955 by Lionel Trilling. Reproduced by permission—*Studies in Romanticism*, v. 29, Fall, 1990. Copyright 1990 by the Trustees of Boston University. Reproduced by permission.

HAROLD PINTER Bensky, Lawrence M. From "An Interview with Harold Pinter," in *Writers at Work: The Paris Interviews, Third Series*. Edited by George Plimpton. The Viking Press, 1967. Copyright © 1967 by The Paris Review, Inc. All rights reserved. Reproduced by permission—Esslin, Martin. From *The Peopled Wound: The Plays of Harold Pinter*. Methuen & Co. Ltd., 1970. Reproduced by permission—Pinter, Harold. From "A Night Out," "A Slight Ache," "The Birthday Party," "Introduction: Writing for the Theatre," "The Room," in *Plays: One*. Eyre Methuen Ltd., 1976. © 1962, 1964 by Harold Pinter. This collection © 1976 by H. Pinter Ltd. Reproduced by permission—Pinter, Harold. From "The Caretaker," "Introduction: Writing for Myself," "The Lover," in *Plays: Two*. Eyre Methuen Ltd., 1977. This collection © 1977, 1979 by H. Pinter Ltd. Reproduced by permission—Pinter, Harold. From "The Basement," "The Homecoming," in *Plays: Three*. Eyre Methuen Ltd., 1978. Reproduced by permission—Cohn, Ruby. From "The Economy of Betrayal," in *Harold Pinter: A Casebook*. Edited by Lois Gordon. Garland Publishing, 1990. © 1990 Lois Gordon. All rights reserved. Reproduced by permission—Billington, Michael. From "Early Stages," "Hackney Lad," "Memory Man," "Moonlit Nights," "Party Manners," "Power Play," "Preface," "Private Worlds," in *The Life and Work of Harold Pinter*. Faber and Faber, 1996. © Michael Billington, 1996. Reproduced by permission—*American Theatre*, v. 11, March, 1994. Copyright © 1993, Theatre Communications Group. Reproduced by permission—*BBC European Service*, March 3, 1960. Reproduced by permission—*The Listener*, v. 82, November 6, 1960. Reproduced by permission—*Theatre Quarterly*, n. 16, Novermber, 1974–January, 1975. Reproduced by permission.

ALEXANDER POPE Spence, Joseph. From *Observations, Anecdotes, and Characters of Books and Men, Volume 1*. Edited by James M. Osborn. Oxford at the Clarendon Press, 1966. © Oxford University Press 1966. Reproduced by permission.

VIRGINIA WOOLF Woolf, Virginia. From *A Room of One's Own*. Harcourt, Brace and Company, 1929. Copyright, 1929, by Harcourt, Brace and Company, Inc. Reproduced by permission—Woolf, Virginia. From "The Leaning Tower," in *Collected Essays, Volume 2*. The Hogarth Press, 1966. © Leonard Woolf 1966. Reproduced by permission—Woolf, Virginia. From a letter in *The Letters of Virginia Woolf, Volume III: 1923–1928*. Edited by Nigel Nicolson and Joanne Trautmann. Harcourt Brace Jovanovich, 1977. Copyright © 1977 by Quentin Bell and Angelica Garnett. Reproduced by permission—Woolf, Virginia. From a letter in *The Letters of Virginia Woolf, Volume IV: 1929-1931*. Edited by Nigel Nicolson and Joanne Trautmann. Harcourt Brace Jovanovich, 1978. Copyright © 1978 by Quentin Bell and Angelica Garnett. Reproduced by permission—Woolf, Virginia. From a letter in *The Letters of Virginia Woolf, Volume VI: 1936-1941*. Edited by Nigel Nicolson and Joanne Trautmann. Harcourt Brace Jovanovich, 1980. Copyright © 1980 by Quentin Bell and Angelica

Garnett. Reproduced by permission— Woolf, Virginia. From "1920" and "1922," in *The Diary of Virginia Woolf, Volume II: 1920-1924*. Edited by Anne Olivier Bell. The Hogarth Press, 1978. © Quentin Bell and Angelica Garnett 1978. Reproduced by permission—Woolf, Virginia. From "1925" "1926" and "1930," in *The Diary of Virginia Woolf, Volume III: 1925–1930*. Edited by Anne Olivier Bell. The Hogarth Press, 1980. © Quentin Bell and Angelica Garnett 1980. Reproduced by permission—Woolf, Virginia. From "1931" and "1933," in *The Diary of Virginia Woolf, Volume IV: 1931-1935*. Edited by Anne Olivier Bell. The Hogarth Press, 1982. © Quentin Bell and Angelica Garnett 1982. Reproduced by permission—Woolf, Virginia. From "1938" and "1940," in *The Diary of Virginia Woolf, Volume V: 1936–1941*. Edited by Anne Olivier Bell. The Hogarth Press, 1984. © Quentin Bell and Angelica Garnett 1984. Reproduced by permission—Woolf, Virginia. From "A Sketch of the Past," "Am I a Snob?," in *Moments of Being*. Edited by Jeanne Schulkind. The Hogarth Press, 1985. © Quentin Bell and Angelica Garnett 1985. Reproduced by permission—Woolf, Virginia. From "Character in Fiction," "Revolving Lights," in *The Essays of Virginia Woolf: Volume III, 1919–1924*. Edited by Andrew McNeillie. The Hogarth Press, 1988. © Quentin Bell and Angelica Garnett 1988. Reproduced by permission— Bell, Vanessa. From a letter in *Selected Letters of Vanessa Bell*. Edited by Regina Marler. Pantheon Books, 1993. Copyright © 1993 by Regina Marler. All rights reserved. Reproduced by permission—Woolf, Virginia. From "Modern Fiction," "Montaigne," "The New Biography," "Poetry, Fiction, and the Future," in *The Essays of Virginia Woolf: Volume IV, 1925–1928*. Edited by Andrew McNeillie. The Hogarth Press, 1994. © Quentin Bell and Angelica Garnett 1994. Reproduced by permission.

W. B. YEATS. Yeats, W. B. From *Letters on Poetry from W. B. Yeats to Dorothy Wellesley*. Oxford University Press, 1964. Reproduced by permission—Yeats, W. B. From "Byzantium," "The Circus Animals' Desertion," "Coole Park," "Coole and Ballylee, 1931," "A Dialogue of Self and Soul," "Lapis Lazuli," "Long-Legged Fly," "Meditations in Time of Civil War: Ancestral Houses," "The Municipal Gallery Revisited," "My Descendants," "Nineteen Hundred and Nineteen," "Preface to the pamphlet 'On the Boiler'," "The Road at My Door," "Sailing to Byzantium," "The Tower," "Under Ben Bulben," "What Then?," in *The Poems*. Edited by Richard J. Finneran. Macmillan Publishing Company, 1983. Copyright © Anne Yeats 1983. All rights reserved. Reproduced by permission.

Editorial and Production Staff

Project Editor
PAMELA PARKINSON

Contributing Editors
MATTHEW MAY
KEN WACHSBERGER

Copyeditors
JANET BYRNE
TONY COULTER
MELISSA DOBSON
MARCIA MEANS

Proofreader
CAROL HOLMES

Indexer
LAURIE ANDRIOT

Permission Researcher
UMA KUKATHAS

Production Manager
EVI SEOUD

Buyer
STACY MELSON

Associate Publisher
TIMOTHY J. DEWERFF

Publisher
FRANK MENCHACA

Contents

Introduction

In *British Writers, Retrospective Supplement I*, we offer substantial reconsiderations of twenty major British and Irish authors, ranging over the centuries from Christopher Marlowe, the great Elizabethan playwright, to well-known contemporary writers, such as Seamus Heaney and Harold Pinter. In each article, the critic looks back at the whole career of an author who has made a significant impact on literary history, offering close readings, supplying biographical data, and sifting the most recent critical responses to these writers. These revaluations are meant to amplify and extend earlier articles on these authors that appeared in this series.

In the original set of *British Writers*, published between 1979 and 1984, seven volumes appeared, treating the lives and works of significant poets, novelists, playwrights, essayists and autobiographers from the Anglo-Saxon era to the present. This set was followed by half a dozen supplemental volumes where authors were discussed who, for various reasons, had been thus far neglected.

The intention throughout the series has been to provide lucid, informative essays aimed at the general reader. Most of the critics writing for this supplement, as in the previous volumes, are college teachers, scholars, and writers. As anyone glancing through this collection will notice, the critics are held to the highest standards of writing and sound scholarship. Their work often rises to a high level of craft and critical vision as they introduce a writer of some importance in the history of British, Irish, or Anglophone literature. A certain amount of biographical context for the work of each author is offered so that readers can appreciate the historical ground that provided the texts under review with air and light, soil and water. The essays each conclude with a select bibliography intended to direct the reading of those should want to pursue the subject further.

Among the poets considered in this volume are Alexander Pope, William Blake, John Keats, Percy Bysshe Shelley, W.B. Yeats, W.H. Auden, and Seamus Heaney. Each has been a defining poet of his era, and the articles in this volume explore their work in careful, often inspired, fashion.

Thomas Hardy, Samuel Johnson, and Robert Louis Stevenson each wrote poetry, but their work is largely considered in the context of their work in prose. Hardy, of course, is almost equally valued as both poet and novelist, and the essay on his work here looks carefully at his contribution to each field. Johnson was perhaps the greatest critic of all time in English, and his career is reconsidered in a sweeping essay that examines his editorial and critical as well as his imaginative writing—in poetry, drama, and prose.

Writers of fiction discussed here are Daniel Defoe, Henry Fielding, Robert Louis Stevenson, James Joyce, and Virginia Woolf. The task of reconsidering such major careers in relatively brief space was no mean feat, yet our contributors have succeeded admirably, focusing their attention on the major works, offering close readings and critical revaluations of literary careers that continue to have a major impact on the writing of fiction.

The playwrights covered in this volume include Marlowe (also a poet), Ben Jonson (also a poet and critic), J.M. Synge, Samuel Beckett, and Harold Pinter. Each of these writers had a profound impact on the course of English and Irish drama, and their achievements are considered in detailed, comprehensive articles.

This volume of *British Writers* represents an important revaluation of major British and Irish authors. The articles included here will be useful to students and general readers in search of well-informed, clearly written, intelligent essays that reflect on the life and work of significant authors.

JAY PARINI

Chronology

CHRONOLOGY

CHRONOLOGY

CHRONOLOGY

CHRONOLOGY

The Grand Remonstrance censuring royal policy passed by eleven votes

William Wycherley born

1642 Parliament submits the nineteen Propositions, which King Charles rejects as annihilating the royal power

The Civil War begins

The theaters close

Royalist victory at Edgehill; King Charles established at Oxford

Deaths of Sir John Suckling and Galileo

1643 Parliament concludes the Solemn League and Covenant with the Scots

Louis XIV crowned king of France

Charles Sackville, earl of Dorset, born

1644 Parliamentary victory at Marston Moor

The New Model army raised

Milton's *Areopagitica*

1645 Parliamentary victory under Fairfax and Cromwell at Naseby

Fairfax captures Bristol

Archbishop Laud executed

Edmund Waller's *Poems*

1646 Fairfax besieges King Charles at Oxford

King Charles takes refuge in Scotland; end of the First Civil War

King Charles attempts negotiations with the Scots

Parliament's proposals sent to the king and rejected

Richard Crashaw's *Steps to the Temple*

1647 Conflict between Parliament and the army

A general council of the army established that discusses representational government within the army

The Agreement of the People drawn up by the Levelers; its proposals include manhood suffrage

King Charles concludes an agreement with the Scots

George Fox begins to preach

John Wilmot, earl of Rochester, born

1648 Cromwell dismisses the general council of the army

The Second Civil War begins

Fairfax defeats the Kentish royalists at Maidstone

Cromwell defeats the Scots at Preston

The Thirty Years' War ended by the treaty of Westphalia

Parliament purged by the army

Thomas Herrick's *Hesperides*

1649–1660 **Commonwealth**

1649 King Charles I tried and executed

The monarchy and the House of Lords abolished

The Commonwealth proclaimed

Cromwell invades Ireland and defeats the royalist Catholic forces

Death of Richard Crashaw

Richard Lovelace's *Lucasta*

1650 Cromwell defeats the Scots at Dunbar

Henry Vaughan's *Silex Scintillans* (first part)

Death of Descartes

1651 Charles II crowned king of the Scots, at Scone

Charles II invades England, is defeated at Worcester, escapes to France

Thomas Hobbes's *Leviathan*

William Harvey's *Essays on the Generation of Animals*

1652 War with Holland

1653 The Rump Parliament dissolved by the army

A new Parliament and council of state nominated; Cromwell becomes Lord Protector

Walton's *The Compleat Angler*

1654 Peace concluded with Holland

War against Spain

1655 Parliament attempts to reduce the army and is dissolved

Rule of the major-generals

1656 Sir William Davenant produces *The Siege of Rhodes*, one of the first English operas

Abraham Cowley's *Davideis*

1657 Second Parliament of the Protectorate

Cromwell is offered and declines the throne

Death of Richard Lovelace

CHRONOLOGY

1658   Death of Oliver Cromwell
      Richard Cromwell succeeds as Protector

1659   Conflict between Parliament and the army

1660   General Monck negotiates with Charles II
      Charles II offers the conciliatory Declaration of Breda and accepts Parliament's invitation to return
      Will's Coffee House established
      Sir William Davenant and Thomas Killigrew licensed to set up two companies of players, the Duke of York's and the King's Servants, including actors and actresses
      Daniel Defoe born
      Pepys's *Diary* begun

1660–1685   **Reign of Charles II**

1661   Parliament passes the Act of Uniformity, enjoining the use of the Book of Common Prayer; many Puritan and dissenting clergy leave their livings

1662   Peace Treaty with Spain
      King Charles II marries Catherine of Braganza
      The Royal Society incorporated (founded in 1660)

1664   War against Holland
      New Amsterdam captured and becomes New York
      Molière's *Tartuffe*
      Heinrich Schütz's *Christmas Oratorio*
      John Vanbrugh born

1665   The Great Plague
      Newton discovers the binomial theorem and invents the integral and differential calculus, at Cambridge

1666   The Great Fire of London
      Bunyan's *Grace Abounding*
      Molière's *Le Misanthrope*
      London Gazette founded

1667   The Dutch fleet sails up the Medway and burns English ships
      The war with Holland ended by the Treaty of Breda
      Milton's *Paradise Lost*
      Thomas Sprat's *History of the Royal Society*
      Jonathan Swift born

      Death of Abraham Cowley

1668   Sir Christopher Wren begins St. Paul's Cathedral (completed 1710)
      Triple Alliance formed with Holland and Sweden against France
      Dryden's *Essay of Dramatick Poesy*

1670   Alliance formed with France through the secret Treaty of Dover
      Pascal's *Pensées*
      The Hudson's Bay Company founded
      William Congreve born

1671   Milton's *Samson Agonistes* and *Paradise Regained*

1672   War against Holland
      Wycherley's *The Country Wife*
      Joseph Addison born
      Richard Steele born
      King Charles issues the Declaration of Indulgence, suspending penal laws against Nonconformists and Catholics

1673   Parliament passes the Test Act, making acceptance of the doctrines of the Church of England a condition for holding public office

1674   War with Holland ended by the Treaty of Westminster
      Death of John Milton
      Death of Robert Herrick
      Death of Thomas Traherne

1676   George Etherege's *The Man of Mode*

1677   Aphra Behn's *The Rover* (1st part)
      Baruch Spinoza's *Ethics*
      Jean Racine's *Phèdre*
      King Charles's niece, Mary, marries her cousin William of Orange

1678   Fabrication of the so-called popish plot by Titus Oates
      Bunyan's *Pilgrim's Progress*
      Dryden's *All for Love*
      Marie de La Vergne de La Fayette's *La Princesse de Clèves*
      Death of Andrew Marvell
      George Farquhar born

1679   Parliament passes the Habeas Corpus Act
      Rochester's *A Satire Against Mankind*

1680   Death of John Wilmot, earl of Rochester

CHRONOLOGY

CHRONOLOGY

Death of Charles Sackville, earl of Dorset

1707 Farquhar's *The Beaux' Stratagem*

Act of Union joining England and Scotland

Death of George Farquhar

Henry Fielding born

1709 The *Tatler* founded (1709–1711)

Nicholas Rowe's edition of Shakespeare

Samuel Johnson born

Marlborough defeats the French at Malplaquet

Charles XII of Sweden defeated at Poltava

1710 South Sea Company founded

First copyright act

George Berkeley's *Treatise Concerning the Principles of Human Knowledge*

1711 Swift's *The Conduct of the Allies*

The *Spectator* founded (1711–1712; 1714)

Marlborough dismissed

David Hume born

1712 Pope's *The Rape of the Lock* (Cantos 1–2)

Antonio Vivaldi's Concertos, Op. 3

Jean-Jacques Rousseau born

1713 War with France ended by the Treaty of Utrecht

The *Guardian* founded

Swift becomes dean of St. Patrick's, Dublin

Addison's *Cato*

Ann Finch's *Miscellany Poems, on Several Occasions*

Laurence Sterne born

1714–1727 Reign of George I

1714 Pope's expended version of *The Rape of the Lock* (Cantos 1–5)

1715 The Jacobite rebellion in Scotland

Pope's translation of Homer's *Iliad* (1715–1720)

Death of Louis XIV

Louis XV crowned King of France

1716 Death of William Wycherley

Thomas Gray born

1717 Pope's *Eloisa to Abelard*

David Garrick born

Horace Walpole born

1718 Quadruple Alliance (Britain, France, the Netherlands, the German Empire) in war against Spain

1719 Defoe's *Robinson Crusoe*

Death of Joseph Addison

1720 Inoculation against smallpox introduced in Boston

War against Spain

The South Sea Bubble

Defoe's *Captain Singleton* and *Memoirs of a Cavalier*

1721 Tobias Smollett born

William Collins born

1722 Defoe's *Moll Flanders, Journal of the Plague Year*, and *Colonel Jack*

Sir Richard Steele's *The Conscious Lovers*

1724 Defoe's *Roxana*

Swift's *The Drapier's Letters*

1725 Pope's translation of Homer's *Odyssey* (1725–1726)

1726 Swift's *Gulliver's Travels*

Voltaire in England (1726–1729)

Death of Sir John Vanbrugh

1727–1760 Reign of George II

Handel's *Coronation Anthem*

1728 Gay's *The Beggar's Opera*

Pope's *The Dunciad* (Books 1–2)

Oliver Goldsmith born

1729 Bach's *St. Matthew Passion*

Swift's *A Modest Proposal*

Edmund Burke born

Deaths of William Congreve

Death Sir Richard Steele

1731 Navigation improved by introduction of the quadrant

Pope's *Moral Essays* (1731–1735)

Franklin begins publishing *Poor Richard's Almanac*

Death of Daniel Defoe

William Cowper born

1732 Death of John Gay

William Hogarth's *A Harlot's Progress*

1733 Pope's *Essay on Man* (1733–1734)

Lewis Theobald's edition of Shakespeare

1734 Voltaire's *Lettres philosophiques*

1737 Edward Gibbon born

1738 Johnson's *London*

1739 Hume's *Treatise on Human Nature*

CHRONOLOGY

1740 War of the Austrian Succession, 1740–1748 (King George's War in America, 1744–1748)

George Anson begins his circumnavigation of the world (1740–1744)

Frederick the Great becomes king of Prussia (1740–1786)

Richardson's *Pamela* (1740–1741)

James Boswell born

1742 Bach's *Goldberg Variations*

Fielding's *Joseph Andrews*

Edward Young's *Night Thoughts* (1742–1745)

Pope's *The New Dunciad* (Book 4)

1744 Johnson's *Life of Mr. Richard Savage*

Death of Alexander Pope

1745 Second Jacobite rebellion, led by Charles Edward, the Young Pretender

Death of Jonathan Swift

1746 The Young Pretender defeated at Culloden

Collins's *Odes on Several Descriptive and Allegorical Subjects*

Jonathan Edwards's *A Treatise Concerning the Religious Affections*

1747 Richardson's *Clarissa Harlowe* (1747–1748)

Franklin's experiments with electricity announced

Voltaire's *Essai sur les moeurs*

1748 War of the Austrian Succession ended by the Peace of Aix-la-Chapelle

Smollett's *Adventures of Roderick Random*

Hume's *Enquiry Concerning Human Understanding*

Montesquieu's *L'Esprit des lois*

1749 Bach's *The Art of the Fugue*

Johann Wolfgang von Goethe born

Fielding's *Tom Jones*

Johnson's *The Vanity of Human Wishes*

Bolingbroke's *Idea of a Patriot King*

1750 The *Rambler* founded (1750–1752)

1751 Gray's *Elegy Written in a Country Churchyard*

Fielding's *Amelia*

Smollett's *Adventures of Peregrine Pickle*

Denis Diderot and Jean le Rond d'Alembert begin to publish the *Encyclopédie* (1751–1765)

Richard Brinsley Sheridan born

1752 Frances Burney and Thomas Chatterton born

Charlotte Lenox's *The Female Quixote*

1753 Richardson's *History of Sir Charles Grandison* (1753–1754)

Smollett's *The Adventures of Ferdinand Count Fathom*

1754 Hume's *History of England* (1754–1762)

Death of Henry Fielding

George Crabbe born

1755 Lisbon destroyed by earthquake

Fielding's *Journal of a Voyage to Lisbon* published posthumously

Johnson's *Dictionary of the English Language*

1756 The Seven Years' War against France, 1756–1763 (the French and Indian War in America, 1755–1760)

William Pitt the elder becomes prime minister

Johnson's proposal for an edition of Shakespeare

1757 Robert Clive wins the battle of Plassey, in India

Gray's "The Progress of Poesy" and "The Bard"

Burke's *Philosophical Enquiry into the Origin of Our Ideas of the Sublime and Beautiful*

Hume's *Natural History of Religion*

William Blake born

1758 The Idler founded (1758–1760)

1759 Capture of Quebec by General James Wolfe

Johnson's History of Rasselas, Prince of Abyssinia

Voltaire's Candide

The British Museum opens

Sterne's The Life and Opinions of Tristram Shandy (1759–1767)

Death of William Collins

Mary Wollstonecraft born

Robert Burns born

1760–1820 **Reign of George III**

CHRONOLOGY

1760 James Macpherson's *Fragments of Ancient Poetry Collected in the Highlands of Scotland*
William Beckford born

1761 Rousseau's *Julie, ou la nouvelle Héloïse*
Death of Samuel Richardson

1762 Rousseau's *Du Contrat social* and *émile*
Catherine the Great becomes czarina of Russia (1762–1796)

1763 The Seven Years' War ended by the Peace of Paris
Smart's *A Song to David*

1764 James Hargreaves invents the spinning jenny

1765 Parliament passes the Stamp Act to tax the American colonies
Johnson's edition of Shakespeare
Walpole's *The Castle of Otranto*
Thomas Percy's *Reliques of Ancient English Poetry*
Blackstone's *Commentaries on the Laws of England* (1765–1769)

1766 The Stamp Act repealed
Swift's *Journal to Stella* first published in a collection of his letters
Goldsmith's *The Vicar of Wakefield*
Smollett's *Travels Through France and Italy*
Lessing's *Laokoon*
Rousseau in England (1766–1767)
Germaine de Staël born

1768 Mozart's *Bastien und Bastienne*
Sterne's *A Sentimental Journey Through France and Italy*
The Royal Academy founded by George III
First edition of the *Encyclopaedia Britannica*
Maria Edgeworth born
Death of Laurence Sterne

1769 David Garrick organizes the Shakespeare Jubilee at Stratford-upon-Avon
Sir Joshua Reynolds's *Discourses* (1769–1790)
Richard Arkwright invents the spinning water frame
Elizabeth Griffith's *The Delicate Distress*

Napoleon Bonaparte born

1770 Boston Massacre
William Billings's *The New England Psalm Singer*
Burke's *Thoughts on the Cause of the Present Discontents*
Goldsmith's *The Deserted Village*
Death of Thomas Chatterton
William Wordsworth born

1771 Arkwright's first spinning mill founded
Benjamin Franklin begins *The Autobiography*
Death of Thomas Gray
Death of Tobias Smollett
Walter Scott born

1772 Samuel Taylor Coleridge born

1773 Boston Tea Party
Anna Laetitia Aikin's *Poems*
Goldsmith's *She Stoops to Conquer*
Goethe's *Götz von Berlichingen*

1774 The first Continental Congress meets in Philadelphia
Goethe's *Sorrows of Young Werther*
Joseph Priestly discovers oxygen
Death of Oliver Goldsmith
Robert Southey born

1775 Burke's speech on American taxation
American War of Independence begins with the battles of Lexington and Concord
Johnson's *Journey to the Western Islands of Scotland*
Richard Brinsley Sheridan's *The Rivals* and *The Duenna*
Beaumarchais's *Le Barbier de Séville*
James Watt and Matthew Boulton begin building steam engines in England
Birth of Jane Austen
Birth of Charles Lamb
Birth of Walter Savage Landor
Birth of Matthew Lewis

1776 American Declaration of Independence
Gibbon's *Decline and Fall of the Roman Empire* (to 1788)
Adam Smith's *Inquiry into the Nature & Causes of the Wealth of Nations*
Thomas Paine's *Common Sense*

Death of David Hume

1777 Maurice Morgann's *Essay on the Dramatic Character of Sir John Falstaff*

Sheridan's *The School for Scandal* first performed (published 1780)

General Burgoyne surrenders at Saratoga

1778 The American colonies allied with France

Britain and France at war

Captain James Cook discovers Hawaii

Deaths of William Pitt, first earl of Chatham, of Jean Jacques Rousseau, and of Voltaire

William Hazlitt born

1779 Johnson's *Prefaces to the Works of the English Poets* (1779–1781); reissued in 1781 as *The Lives of the Most Eminent English Poets*

Sheridan's *The Critic*

Samuel Crompton invents the spinning mule

Death of David Garrick

1780 The Gordon Riots in London

1781 Charles Cornwallis surrenders at Yorktown

Jean Antoine Houdon's *Voltaire*

Immanuel Kant's *Critique of Pure Reason*

Rousseau's *Confessions* published posthumously (to 1788)

Friedrich von Schiller's *Die Räuber*

1782 Frances Burney's *Cecilia*

William Cowper's "The Journey of John Gilpin" published in the *Public Advertiser*

Choderlos de Laclos's *Les Liaisons dangereuses*

Ignatius Sancho's *Letters of the Late Iganatius Sancho, an African*

1783 American War of Independence ended by the Definitive Treaty of Peace, signed at Paris

William Blake's *Poetical Sketches*

George Crabbe's *The Village*

William Pitt the younger becomes prime minister

Marie-Henri Beyle (Stendhal) born

1784 Beaumarchais's *Le Mariage de Figaro* first performed (published 1785)

Death of Samuel Johnson

1785 Warren Hastings returns to England from India

James Boswell's *The Journey of a Tour of the Hebrides, with Samuel Johnson, LL.D.*

Cowper's *The Task*

Edmund Cartwright invents the power loom

Thomas De Quincey born

Thomas Love Peacock born

1786 William Beckford's *Vathek* published in English (originally written in French in 1782)

Robert Burns's *Poems Chiefly in the Scottish Dialect*

Mozart's *The Marriage of Figaro*

Death of Frederick the Great

1787 The Committee for the Abolition of the Slave Trade founded in England

The Constitutional Convention meets at Philadelphia; the Constitution is signed

William Bligh and crew begin voyage to Tahiti in the H.M.S. *Bounty*

Jefferson's *Notes on the State of Virginia*

Thomas Taylor's translation of *Concerning the Beautiful* (Plotinus)

1788 The trial of Hastings begins on charges of corruption of the government in India

The Estates-General of France summoned

U.S. Constitution is ratified

George Washington elected president of the United States

Giovanni Casanova's *Histoire de ma fuite* (first manuscript of his memoirs)

The *Daily Universal Register* becomes the *Times* (London)

George Gordon, Lord Byron born

1789 The Estates-General meets at Versailles

The National Assembly (Assemblée Nationale) convened

The fall of the Bastille marks the beginning of the French Revolution

CHRONOLOGY

The National Assembly draws up the Declaration of Rights of Man and of the Citizen

First U.S. Congress meets in New York

Blake's *Songs of Innocence*

Jeremy Bentham's *Introduction to the Principles of Morals and Legislation* introduces the theory of utilitarianism

Erasmus Darwin's *The Botanic Garden*

Gilbert White's *Natural History of Selborne*

1790 Congress sets permanent capital city site on the Potomac River

First U.S. Census

Burke's *Reflections on the Revolution in France*

Blake's *The Marriage of Heaven and Hell*

Edmund Malone's edition of Shakespeare

Wollstonecraft's *A Vindication of the Rights of Man*

Death of Benjamin Franklin

1791 French royal family's flight from Paris and capture at Varennes; imprisonment in the Tuileries

Anti-Jacobin riots at Birmingham

Bill of Rights is ratified

Paine's *The Rights of Man* (1791–1792)

Boswell's *The Life of Johnson*

Burns's *Tam o' Shanter*

The *Observer* founded

Mozart's *Requiem*

1792 The Prussians invade France and are repulsed at Valmy

September massacres

The National Convention declares royalty abolished in France

Washington reelected president of the United States

New York Stock Exchange opens

Samuel Rogers's *Pleasure of Memory*

Mary Wollstonecraft's *Vindication of the Rights of Woman*

Percy Bysshe Shelley born

1793 Trial and execution of Louis XVI and Marie-Antoinette

France declares war against England

Reign of Terror begins

The Committee of Public Safety (Comité de Salut Public) established

Eli Whitney devises the cotton gin

William Godwin's *An Enquiry Concerning Political Justice*

Blake's *Visions of the Daughters of Albion and America*

Olaudah Equiano's *The Interesting Narrative of the Life of Olaudah Equiano*

Wordsworth's *An Evening Walk* and *Descriptive Sketches*

1794 Execution of Georges Danton and Maximilien de Robespierre

Paine's *The Age of Reason* (1794–1796)

Blake's *Songs of Experience*

Ann Radcliffe's *The Mysteries of Udolpho*

Erasumus Darwin's *Zoonomia*

Death of Edward Gibbon

1795 The government of the Directory established (1795–1799)

Hastings acquitted

Landor's *Poems*

Goethe's *Wilhelm Meister*

Death of James Boswell

John Keats and Thomas Carlyle born

1796 Napoleon takes command in Italy

Edward Jenner performs first smallpox vaccination

Coleridge's *Poems on Various Subjects*

Matthew Lewis's *The Monk*

Watson's *Apology for the Bible*

Death of Robert Burns

1797 The peace of Campo Formio: extinction of the Venetian Republic

XYZ Affair

John Adams elected second president of the United States

Mutinies in the Royal Navy at Spithead and the Nore

Thomas Bewick's *History of British Birds*

Blake's *Vala, Or the Four Zoas* (first version)

Ann Radcliffe's *The Italian*

CHRONOLOGY

Scott's *The Lady of the Lake*
Southey's *Curse of Kehama*
Germaine de Staël's *De l'Allemagne*
Elizabeth Gaskell born

1811–1820 **Regency of George IV**
1811 Luddite Riots begin
Coleridge's *Lectures on Shakespeare*
  (1811–1814)
Austen's *Sense and Sensibility*
Schubert's first *Lieder*
Shelley's *The Necessity of Atheism*
John Constable's *Dedham Vale*
William Makepeace Thackeray born
1812 Napoleon invades Russia; captures
  and retreats from Moscow
United States declares war against
  England
Henry Bell's steamship *Comet* is
  launched on the Clyde river
Madison reelected president of the
  United States
Byron's *Childe Harold* (Cantos 1–2)
The Brothers Grimm's *Fairy Tales*
  (1812–1815)
Hegel's *The Science of Logic*
Birth of Charles Dickens
Birth of Robert Browning
1813 Wellington wins the battle of Vitoria
  and enters France
Austen's *Pride and Prejudice*
Byron's *The Giaour* and *The Bride of
  Abydos*
Shelley's *Queen Mab*
Southey's *Life of Nelson*
1814 Napoleon abdicates and is exiled to
  Elba; Bourbon restoration with
  Louis XVIII
Treaty of Ghent ends the war
  between Britain and the United
  States
Jane Austen's *Mansfield Park*
Byron's *The Corsair* and *Lara*
Scott's *Waverley*
Wordsworth's *The Excursion*
1815 Napoleon returns to France (the
  Hundred Days); is defeated at
  Waterloo and exiled to St. Helena
U.S.S. *Fulton*, the first steam war-
  ship, built
Scott's *Guy Mannering*

Schlegel's *Lectures on Dramatic Art
  and Literature* translated
Wordsworth's *The White Doe of Ryl-
  stone*
Anthony Trollope born
1816 Byron leaves England permanently
The Elgin Marbles exhibited in the
  British Museum
James Monroe elected president of
  the United States
Austen's *Emma*
Byron's *Childe Harold* (Canto 3)
Coleridge's *Christabel, Kubla Khan: A
  Vision, The Pains of Sleep*
Benjamin Constant's *Adolphe*
Goethe's *Italienische Reise*
Peacock's *Headlong Hall*
Scott's *The Antiquary*
Shelley's *Alastor*
Rossini's *Il Barbiere di Siviglia*
Death of Richard Brinsley Sheridan
Charlotte Brontë born
1817 *Blackwood's Edinburgh* magazine
  founded
Austen's *Northanger Abbey* and *Per-
  suasion*
Byron's *Manfred*
Coleridge's *Biographia Literaria*
Hazlitt's *The Characters of Shake-
  speare's Plays* and *The Round Table*
Keats's *Poems*
Peacock's *Melincourt*
David Ricardo's *Principles of Political
  Economy and Taxation*
Deaths of Jane Austen and Ger-
  maine de Staël
Branwell Brontë and Henry David
  Thoreau born
1818 Byron's *Childe Harold* (Canto 4), and
  Beppo
John Evelyn's *Diary*
Hazlitt's *Lectures on the English Poets*
Keats's *Endymion*
Peacock's *Nightmare Abbey*
Scott's *Rob Roy* and *The Heart of Mid-
  Lothian*
Mary Shelley's *Frankenstein*
Percy Shelley's *The Revolt of Islam*
Emily Brontë born
Karl Marx born
Ivan Sergeyevich Turgenev born

1819   The *Savannah* becomes the first steamship to cross the Atlantic (in 26 days)

Peterloo massacre in Manchester

Byron's *Don Juan* (to 1824) and *Mazeppa*

Crabbe's *Tales of the Hall*

Géricault's *Raft of the Medusa*

Hazlitt's *Lectures on the English Comic Writers*

William Hone's *The Political House that Jack Built*

Arthur Schopenhauer's *Die Welt als Wille und Vorstellung (The World as Will and Idea)*

Scott's *The Bride of Lammermoor* and *A Legend of Montrose*

Shelley's *The Cenci*, "The Masque of Anarchy," and "Ode to the West Wind"

Wordsworth's *Peter Bell*

Queen Victoria born

Mary Ann Evans (George Eliot) born

1819–1820   Washington Irving's *The Sketch Book of Geoffrey Crayon, Gent*

1820–1830   Reign of George IV

1820   Trial of Queen Caroline

Cato Street Conspiracy suppressed; Arthur Thistlewood hanged

Monroe reelected president of the United States

Missouri Compromise

The *London* magazine founded

Keats's *Lamia, Isabella, The Eve of St. Agnes, and Other Poems*

Hazlitt's *Lectures Chiefly on the Dramatic Literature of the Age of Elizabeth*

Charles Maturin's *Melmoth the Wanderer*

Scott's *Ivanhoe* and *The Monastery*

Shelley's *Prometheus Unbound*

Anne Brontë born

1821   Greek War of Independence begins

Liberia founded as a colony for freed slaves

Byron's *Cain, Marino Faliero, The Two Foscari*, and *Sardanapalus*

John Constable's *Hay Wain*

De Quincey's *Confessions of an English Opium-Eater*

Hazlitt's *Table Talk* (1821–1822)

Scott's *Kenilworth*

Shelley's *Adonais* and *Epipsychidion*

Death of John Keats

Death of Napoleon Bonaparte

Charles Baudelaire born

Fyodor Dostoyevsky born

Gustave Flaubert born

1822   The Massacres of Chios (Greeks rebel against Turkish rule)

Byron's *The Vision of Judgment*

Peacock's *Maid Marian*

Scott's *Peveril of the Peak*

Shelley's *Hellas*

Death of Percy Bysshe Shelley

Matthew Arnold born

1823   Monroe Doctrine proclaimed

Byron's *The Age of Bronze* and *The Island*

Hazlitt's *Liber Amoris*

Lamb's *Essays of Elia*

Scott's *Quentin Durward*

1824   The National Gallery opened in London

John Quincy Adams elected president of the United States

The *Westminster Review* founded

Beethoven's Ninth Symphony first performed

James Hogg's *The Private Memoirs and Confessions of a Justified Sinner*

Landor's *Imaginary Conversations* (1824–1829)

Scott's *Redgauntlet*

Death of George Gordon, Lord Byron

1825   Inauguration of steam-powered passenger and freight service on the Stockton and Darlington railway

Bolivia and Brazil become independent

Hazlitt's *The Spirit of the Age*

Alessandro Manzoni's *I Promessi Sposi* (1825–1826)

Felix Mendelssohn's String Octet

1826   André-Marie Ampère's *Mémoire sur la théorie mathématique des phénomènes électrodynamiques*

CHRONOLOGY

James Fenimore Cooper's *The Last of the Mohicans*
Disraeli's *Vivian Grey* (1826–1827)
Scott's *Woodstock*

1827 The battle of Navarino ensures the independence of Greece
Josef Ressel obtains patent for the screw propeller for steamships
Beethoven's Quartet, Op. 131
Heinrich Heine's *Buch der Lieder*
Thomas Hood's *Other Poems*
Death of William Blake

1828 Andrew Jackson elected president of the United States
Birth of Henrik Ibsen
Birth of George Meredith
Birth of Dante Gabriel Rossetti
Birth of Leo Tolstoy

1829 The Catholic Emancipation Act
Robert Peel establishes the metropolitan police force
Greek independence recognized by Turkey
Balzac begins *La Comédie humaine* (1829–1848)
Hector Berlioz's *Symphonie Fantastique*
Eugène Delacroix's *Sardanapalus*
Peacock's *The Misfortunes of Elphin*
J. M. W. Turner's *Ulysses Deriding Polyphemus*

1830–1837 Reign of William IV

1830 Charles X of France abdicates and is succeeded by Louis-Philippe
The Liverpool-Manchester railway opened
Tennyson's *Poems, Chiefly Lyrical*
Death of William Hazlitt
Christina Rossetti born

1831 Michael Faraday discovers electromagnetic induction
Charles Darwin's voyage on H.M.S. *Beagle* begins (1831–1836)
The Barbizon school of artists' first exhibition
Nat Turner slave revolt crushed in Virginia
Peacock's *Crotchet Castle*
Stendhal's *Le Rouge et le noir*
Edward Trelawny's *The Adventures of a Younger Son*

1832 The first Reform Bill
Samuel Morse invents the telegraph
Jackson reelected president of the United States
Disraeli's *Contarini Fleming*
Goethe's *Faust* (Part 2)
Tennyson's *Poems, Chiefly Lyrical*, including "The Lotus-Eaters" and "The Lady of Shalott"
Death of Johann Wolfgang von Goethe
Death of Sir Walter Scott
Death of George Crabbe
Lewis Carroll born

1833 Robert Browning's *Pauline*
John Keble launches the Oxford Movement
American Anti-Slavery Society founded
Lamb's *Last Essays of Elia*
Carlyle's *Sartor Resartus* (1833–1834)
Pushkin's *Eugene Onegin*
Mendelssohn's *Italian Symphony* first performed

1834 Abolition of slavery in the British Empire
Louis Braille's alphabet for the blind
Balzac's *Le Père Goriot*
Gogol's *Dead Souls* (Part 1, 1834–1842)
Death of Samuel Taylor Coleridge
Death of Charles Lamb
William Morris born

1835 Hans Christian Andersen's *Fairy Tales* (1st ser.)
Robert Browning's *Paracelsus*
Samuel Butler born
Alexis de Tocqueville's *De la Democratie en Amerique* (1835–1840)

1836 Martin Van Buren elected president of the United States
Dickens's *Sketches by Boz* (1836–1837)
Landor's *Pericles and Aspasia*

1837–1901 Reign of Queen Victoria

1837 Carlyle's *The French Revolution*
Dickens's *Oliver Twist* (1837–1838) and *Pickwick Papers*
Disraeli's *Venetia* and *Henrietta Temple*
Death of Alexander Pushkin

1838   Chartist movement in England
National Gallery in London opened
Elizabeth Barrett Browning's *The Seraphim and Other Poems*
Louis Daguerre takes first photographs
Dickens's *Nicholas Nickleby* (1838–1839)
Robert Schumann's *Kinderszenen, Kriesleriana*

1839   Louis Daguerre perfects process for producing an image on a silver-coated copper plate
Faraday's *Experimental Researches in Electricity* (1839–1855)
First Chartist riots
Opium War between Great Britain and China
Carlyle's *Chartism*

1840   Canadian Act of Union
Queen Victoria marries Prince Albert
Charles Barry begins construction of the Houses of Parliament (1840–1852)
William Henry Harrison elected president of the United States
Robert Browning's *Sordello*
Mikhail Lermontov's *A Hero of Our Time*
Thomas Hardy born
Death of Frances Burney

1841   New Zealand proclaimed a British colony
James Clark Ross discovers the Antarctic continent
Punch founded
John Tyler succeeds to the presidency after the death of Harrison
Carlyle's *Heroes and Hero-Worship*
Dickens's *The Old Curiosity Shop*

1842   Chartist riots
Income tax revived in Great Britain
The Mines Act, forbidding work underground by women or by children under the age of ten
Charles Edward Mudie's Lending Library founded in London
Dickens visits America
Robert Browning's *Dramatic Lyrics*
Macaulay's *Lays of Ancient Rome*

Tennyson's *Poems*, including "Morte d'Arthur," "St. Simeon Stylites," and "Ulysses"
Wordsworth's *Poems*
Death of Stendhal

1843   Marc Isambard Brunel's Thames tunnel opened
The Economist founded
Carlyle's *Past and Present*
Dickens's *A Christmas Carol*
Sören Kierkegaard's *Fear and Trembling*
John Stuart Mill's *Logic*
Macaulay's *Critical and Historical Essays*
John Ruskin's *Modern Painters* (1843–1860)
Death of Robert Southey

1844   Rochdale Society of Equitable Pioneers, one of the first consumers' cooperatives, founded by twenty-eight Lancashire weavers
James K. Polk elected president of the United States
Elizabeth Barrett Browning's *Poems*, including "The Cry of the Children"
Dickens's *Martin Chuzzlewit*
Disraeli's *Coningsby*
Turner's *Rain, Steam and Speed*
Gerard Manley Hopkins born
Death of William Beckford

1845   The great potato famine in Ireland begins (1845–1849)
Disraeli's *Sybil*
Richard Wagner's *Tannhäuser*
Death of Thomas Hood

1846   Repeal of the Corn Laws
The *Daily News* founded (edited by Dickens the first three weeks)
Standard-gauge railway introduced in Britain
The Brontës' pseudonymous *Poems by Currer, Ellis and Acton Bell*
Frederick Douglass's *Narrative of the Life of Frederick Douglass an American Slave*
Lear's *Book of Nonsense*

1847   The Ten Hours Factory Act
James Simpson uses chloroform as an anesthetic

CHRONOLOGY

Anne Brontë's *Agnes Grey*
Charlotte Brontë's *Jane Eyre*
Emily Brontë's *Wuthering Heights*
Bram Stoker born
Tennyson's *The Princess*
Giuseppe Verdi's *Macbeth*

1848 The year of revolutions in France, Germany, Italy, Hungary, Poland
Marx and Engels issue *The Communist Manifesto*
The Chartist Petition
The Pre-Raphaelite Brotherhood founded
Zachary Taylor elected president of the United States
Anne Brontë's *The Tenant of Wildfell Hall*
Dickens's *Dombey and Son*
Elizabeth Gaskell's *Mary Barton*
Macaulay's *History of England* (1848–1861)
Mill's *Principles of Political Economy*
Thackeray's *Vanity Fair*
Death of Emily Brontë

1849 Bedford College for women founded
Arnold's *The Strayed Reveller*
Charlotte Brontë's *Shirley*
Ruskin's *The Seven Lamps of Architecture*
Death of Anne Brontë
Death of Maria Edgeworth

1850 The Public Libraries Act
First submarine telegraph cable laid between Dover and Calais
Millard Fillmore succeeds to the presidency after the death of Taylor
Elizabeth Barrett Browning's *Sonnets from the Portuguese*
Carlyle's *Latter-Day Pamphlets*
Dickens's *Household Words* (1850–1859) and *David Copperfield*
Emerson's *Representative Men*
Hawthorne's *The Scarlet Letter*
Charles Kingsley's *Alton Locke*
The Pre-Raphaelites publish the *Germ*
Robert Louis Stevenson born
Tennyson's *In Memoriam*
Thackeray's *The History of Pendennis*

Richard Wagner's *Lohengrin*
Death of Wordsworth; *The Prelude* is published posthumously
Death of Honoré de Balzac

1851 The Great Exhibition opens at the Crystal Palace in Hyde Park
Louis Napoleon seizes power in France
Gold strike in Victoria incites Australian gold rush
Elizabeth Gaskell's *Cranford* (1851–1853)
Melville's *Moby Dick*
Meredith's *Poems*
Ruskin's *The Stones of Venice* (1851–1853)

1852 The Second Empire proclaimed with Napoleon III as emperor
David Livingstone begins to explore the Zambezi (1852–1856)
Franklin Pierce elected president of the United States
Arnold's *Empedocles on Etna*
Harriet Beecher Stowe's *Uncle Tom's Cabin*
Thackeray's *The History of Henry Esmond, Esq.*

1853 Crimean War (1853–1856)
Arnold's *Poems*, including "The Scholar Gypsy" and "Sohrab and Rustum"
Charlotte Brontë's *Villette*
Elizabeth Gaskell's *Crawford and Ruth*

1854 Frederick D. Maurice's Working Men's College founded in London with more than 130 pupils
Battle of Balaklava
Dickens's *Hard Times*
John Mitchel's *Jail Journal*
Theodor Mommsen's *History of Rome* (1854–1856)
Tennyson's "The Charge of the Light Brigade"
Thoreau's *Walden*
Florence Nightingale in the Crimea (1854–1856)
Births of Oscar Wilde and James George Frazer

1855 David Livingstone discovers the Victoria Falls

Robert Browning's *Men and Women*
Elizabeth Gaskell's *North and South*
Franz Liszt's *Faust* Symphony
Olive Schreiner born
Tennyson's *Maud*
Thackeray's *The Newcomes*
Trollope's *The Warden*
Whitman's *Leaves of Grass* (first version)
Death of Charlotte Brontë

1856 The Treaty of Paris ends the Crimean War
Henry Bessemer's steel process invented
James Buchanan elected president of the United States
Flaubert's *Madame Bovary*
Henry Rider Haggard born

1857 The Indian Mutiny begins; crushed in 1858
Joseph Conrad is born
The Matrimonial Causes Act
Charlotte Brontë's *The Professor*
Elizabeth Barrett Browning's *Aurora Leigh*
Baudelaire's *Les Fleurs du Mal*
Dickens's *Little Dorritt*
Elizabeth Gaskell's *The Life of Charlotte Brontë*
Thomas Hughes's *Tom Brown's School Days*
Trollope's *Barchester Towers*

1858 Carlyle's *History of Frederick the Great* (1858–1865)
George Eliot's *Scenes of Clerical Life*
Morris's *The Defense of Guinevere*
Trollope's *Dr. Thorne*

1859 Charles Darwin's *The Origin of Species*
Dickens's *A Tale of Two Cities*
Arthur Conan Doyle born
George Eliot's *Adam Bede*
Fitzgerald's *The Rubaiyat of Omar Khayyám*
Meredith's *The Ordeal of Richard Feverel*
Mill's *On Liberty*
Samuel Smiles's *Self-Help*
Tennyson's *Idylls of the King*
Death of Thomas De Quincey

Death of Thomas Babington Macaulay

1860 Abraham Lincoln elected president of the United States
The *Cornhill* magazine founded with Thackeray as editor
James M. Barrie born
William Wilkie Collins's *The Woman in White*
George Eliot's *The Mill on the Floss*

1861 American Civil War begins
Louis Pasteur presents the germ theory of disease
Arnold's *Lectures on Translating Homer*
Dickens's *Great Expectations*
George Eliot's *Silas Marner*
Meredith's *Evan Harrington*
Francis Turner Palgrave's *The Golden Treasury*
Trollope's *Framley Parsonage*
Peacock's *Gryll Grange*
Death of Prince Albert

1862 George Eliot's *Romola*
Meredith's *Modern Love*
Christina Rossetti's *Goblin Market*
Ruskin's *Unto This Last*
Trollope's *Orley Farm*
Turgenev's *Fathers and Sons*

1863 Thomas Huxley's *Man's Place in Nature*
Death of William Makepeace Thackeray

1864 The Geneva Red Cross Convention signed by twelve nations
Lincoln reelected president of the United States
Johannes Brahms's Piano Quintet in F minor
Robert Browning's *Dramatis Personae*
John Henry Newman's *Apologia pro vita sua*
Tennyson's *Enoch Arden*
Trollope's *The Small House at Allington*

1865 Assassination of Lincoln; Andrew Johnson succeeds to the presidency
Arnold's *Essays in Criticism* (1st ser.)

Carroll's *Alice's Adventures in Wonderland*
Dickens's *Our Mutual Friend*
Sir Samuel Ferguson's *Lays of the Western Gael*
Meredith's *Rhoda Fleming*
A. C. Swinburne's *Atalanta in Calydon*
William Butler Yeats born
Death of Elizabeth Gaskell

1866   First successful transatlantic telegraph cable laid
George Eliot's *Felix Holt, the Radical*
Elizabeth Gaskell's *Wives and Daughters* (posthumously)
Beatrix Potter born
Swinburne's *Poems and Ballads*
Death of Thomas Love Peacock

1867   The second Reform Bill
Arnold's *New Poems*
Bagehot's *The English Constitution*
Carlyle's *Shooting Niagara*
Dostoyevsky's *Crime and Punishment*
Marx's *Das Kapital* (vol. 1)
Johann Strauss's *On The Beautiful Blue Danube*
Trollope's *The Last Chronicle of Barset*
Giuseppe Verdi's *Don Carlos*
Death of Charles Baudelaire

1868   Gladstone becomes prime minister (1868–1874)
Johnson impeached by House of Representatives; acquitted by Senate
Ulysses S. Grant elected president of the United States
Christopher L. Sholes patents the typewriter
Robert Browning's *The Ring and the Book* (1868–1869)
Collins's *The Moonstone*
John Bigelow publishes complete version of Franklin's *The Autobiography*

1869   The Suez Canal opened
Girton College, Cambridge, founded
Arnold's *Culture and Anarchy*
Mill's *The Subjection of Women*
Tolstoy's *War and Peace*
Trollope's *Phineas Finn*

1870   The Elementary Education Act establishes schools under the aegis of local boards
Dickens's *Edwin Drood*
Disraeli's *Lothair*
Morris's *The Earthly Paradise*
Dante Gabriel Rossetti's *Poems*

1871   Trade unions legalized
Newnham College, Cambridge, founded for women students
Carroll's *Through the Looking Glass*
Darwin's *The Descent of Man*
Meredith's *The Adventures of Harry Richmond*
Swinburne's *Songs Before Sunrise*
John Millington Synge born

1872   Max Beerbohm born
Samuel Butler's *Erewhon*
George Eliot's *Middlemarch*
Grant reelected president of the United States
Hardy's *Under the Greenwood Tree*
Charles Lever's *Lord Kilgobbin*
Nietzsche's *The Birth of Tragedy*

1873   Arnold's *Literature and Dogma*
Mill's *Autobiography*
Pater's *Studies in the History of the Renaissance*
Rimbaud's *Une Saison en enfer*
Trollope's *The Eustace Diamonds*

1874   Disraeli becomes prime minister
Cézanne's *A Modern Olympia* (completed)
Hardy's *Far from the Madding Crowd*
James Thomson's *The City of Dreadful Night*

1875   Britain buys Suez Canal shares
Tchaikovsky's Piano Concerto No. 1
Thomas Eakins's *Gross Clinic*
Trollope's *The Way We Live Now*

ca. 1875   Alexander Graham Bell, with the assistence of Thomas Watson, devises an apparatus for transmitting sound by electricity

1876   F. H. Bradley's *Ethical Studies*
George Eliot's *Daniel Deronda*
Henry James's *Roderick Hudson*
Meredith's *Beauchamp's Career*
Morris's *Sigurd the Volsung*
Trollope's *The Prime Minister*

1877   Rutherford B. Hayes elected president of the United States after Electoral Commission awards him disputed votes

Johannes Brahms's First and Second Symphonies

Henry James's *The American*

Tolstoy's *Anna Karenina*

1878   Electric street lighting introduced in London

Hardy's *The Return of the Native*

Swinburne's *Poems and Ballads* (2d ser.)

Edward Thomas born

1879   Somerville College and Lady Margaret Hall opened at Oxford for women

The London telephone exchange built

Gladstone's Midlothian campaign (1879–1880)

Robert Browning's *Dramatic Idyls*

Ibsen's *A Doll House*

Meredith's *The Egoist*

1880   Gladstone's second term as prime minister (1880–1885)

James A. Garfield elected president of the United States

George Eastman invents dry, rolled film and the hand-held camera

Thomas Edison invents the light bulb

Robert Browning's *Dramatic Idyls Second Series*

Disraeli's *Endymion*

Dostoyevsky's *The Brothers Karamazov*

Hardy's *The Trumpet-Major*

Lytton Strachey born

Death of Gustave Flaubert

Death of Mary Ann Evans (George Eliot)

1881   Garfield assassinated; Chester A. Arthur succeeds to the presidency

Henry James's *The Portrait of a Lady* and *Washington Square*

Joachuim Maria Machado de Assis's *Memórias póstumas de Brás Cubas*

Renoir's *Luncheon of the Boating Party*

Dante Gabriel Rossetti's *Ballads and Sonnets*

P. G. Wodehouse born

Death of Fyodor Dostoyevsky

Death of Benjamin Disraeli

1882   Triple Alliance formed between German empire, Austrian empire, and Italy

Leslie Stephen begins to edit the *Dictionary of National Biography*

Married Women's Property Act passed in Britain

Britain occupies Egypt and the Sudan

Births of James Joyce and Virginia Woolf

Deaths of Anthony Trollope and Christina Rossetti

1883   Uprising of the Mahdi: Britain evacuates the Sudan

Royal College of Music opens

T. H. Green's *Ethics*

Ralph Iron's (Olive Schreiner) *The Story of an African Farm*

Nietzsche's *Thus Spake Zarathustra* (to 1885)

Stevenson's *Treasure Island*

Deaths of Karl Marx and Ivan Sergeyevich Turgenev

1884   The Mahdi captures Omdurman: General Gordon appointed to command the garrison of Khartoum

Grover Cleveland elected president of the United States

The *Oxford English Dictionary* begins publishing

The Fabian Society founded

Hiram Maxim's recoil-operated machine gun invented

Louis Pasteur inoculates against rabies

Mark Twain's *Huckleberry Finn*

1885   The Mahdi captures Khartoum: General Gordon killed

Haggard's *King Solomon's Mines*

Marx's *Das Kapital* (vol. 2)

Meredith's *Diana of the Crossways*

Pater's *Marius the Epicurean*

D. H. Lawrence born

1886   The Canadian Pacific Railway completed

CHRONOLOGY

Gold discovered in the Transvaal
Ronald Firbank born
Henry James's *The Bostonians* and
   The Princess Casamassima
Georges Seurat's *Sunday on the
   Island of La Grande Jatte*
Stevenson's *The Strange Case of Dr.
   Jekyll and Mr. Hyde*

1887   Queen Victoria's Golden Jubilee
Rupert Brooke born
Anton Bruckner's *Te Deum*
Haggard's *Allan Quatermain* and *She*
Hardy's *The Woodlanders*
Giuseppe Verdi's *Othello*

1888   Benjamin Harrison elected president
   of the United States
Henry James's *The Aspern Papers*
Kipling's *Plain Tales from the Hills*
Rimsky-Korsakov's *Scheherazade*
Births of T. E. Lawrence and T. S.
   Eliot
Death of Gerard Manley Hopkins

1889   Yeats's *The Wanderings of Oisin*
Eiffel Tower completed
Vincent Van Gogh's *The Starry Night*
Deaths of Robert Browning and
   Matthew Arnold

1890   Morris founds the Kelmscott Press
Agatha Christie born
Dickinson's *Poems by Emily Dickin-
   son* (posthumously)
Frazer's *The Golden Bough* (1st ed.)
Henry James's *The Tragic Muse*
Morris's *News From Nowhere*
Richard Strauss's *Death and Transfig-
   uration*
Jean Rhys born

1891   George Gissing's *New Grub Street*
Hardy's *Tess of the d'Urbervilles*
Wilde's *The Picture of Dorian Gray*

1892   Grover Cleveland elected president
   of the United States
Conan Doyle's *The Adventures of
   Sherlock Holmes*
Shaw's *Widower's Houses*
Wilde's *Lady Windermere's Fan*
Birth of J. R. R. Tolkien
Birth of Rebecca West
Death of Alfred, Lord Tennyson

1893   George Moore's *Modern Painting*

Wilde's *A Woman of No Importance*
   and *Salomé*
Louis Sullivan's *Transportation Building* at World's Columbian Exhibition in Chicago

1894   Kipling's *The Jungle Book*
George Moore's *Esther Waters*
Marx's *Das Kapital* (vol. 3)
Audrey Beardsley's *The Yellow Book*
   begins to appear quarterly
Gauguin's *The Day of the God*
Shaw's *Arms and the Man*
Death of Robert Louis Stevenson

1895   Trial and imprisonment of Oscar
   Wilde
William Ramsay announces discov-
   ery of helium
The National Trust founded
Radio is born when Guglielmo Mar-
   coni transmits electric signals
   through the air from one end of his
   house to the other
Conrad's *Almayer's Folly*
Hardy's *Jude the Obscure*
Wells's *The Time Machine*
Wilde's *The Importance of Being
   Earnest*
Yeats's *Poems*

ca. 1985   Loie Fuller's *La Danse du Feu*

1896   William McKinley elected president
   of the United States
Failure of the Jameson Raid on the
   Transvaal
Housman's *A Shropshire Lad*
Two of Thomas Traherne's manu-
   scripts discovered in a London
   bookstall
Death of William Morris

1897   Queen Victoria's Diamond Jubilee
Conrad's *The Nigger of the Narcissus*
Havelock Ellis's *Studies in the Psy-
   chology of Sex* begins publication
Henry James's *The Spoils of Poynton*
   and *What Maisie Knew*
Kipling's *Captains Courageous*
Stèphane Mallarmè's *Un Coup de
   Dés*
Shaw's *Candida*
Stoker's *Dracula*
Wells's *The Invisible Man*

1904   Roosevelt elected president of the
United States
Russo-Japanese war (1904–1905)
Construction of the Panama Canal
begins
The ultraviolet lamp invented
The engineering firm of Rolls Royce
founded
Barrie's *Peter Pan* first performed
Cecil Day Lewis born
Chekhov's *The Cherry Orchard*
Conrad's *Nostromo*
Antoni Gaudí's Casa Batlló begun
Henry James's *The Golden Bowl*
Kipling's *Traffics and Discoveries*
Georges Rouault's *Head of a Tragic
Clown*
G. M. Trevelyan's *England Under the
Stuarts*
Puccini's *Madame Butterfly*
First Shaw-Granville Barker season
at the Royal Court Theatre
The Abbey Theatre founded in
Dublin
Graham Greene born

1905   Russian sailors on the battleship
Potemkin mutiny
After riots and a general strike the
czar concedes demands by the
Duma for legislative powers, a
wider franchise, and civil liberties
Albert Einstein publishes his first
theory of relativity
The Austin Motor Company founded
Bennett's *Tales of the Five Towns*
Claude Debussy's *La Mer*
E. M. Forster's *Where Angels Fear to
Tread*
Henry Green born
Matisse's *The Open Window*
Richard Strauss's *Salome*
H. G. Wells's *Kipps*
Wilde's *De Profundis*

1906   Liberals win a landslide victory in
the British general election
The Trades Disputes Act legitimizes
peaceful picketing in Britain
Captain Dreyfus rehabilitated in
France

J. J. Thomson begins research on
gamma rays
Reginald Fessenden transmits first
radio broadcast
The U.S. Pure Food and Drug Act
passed
Samuel Beckett born
Churchill's *Lord Randolph Churchill*
William Empson born
Galsworthy's *The Man of Property*
Charles Ives's *The Unanswered Question*
Kipling's *Puck of Pook's Hill*
Shaw's *The Doctor's Dilemma*
Yeats's *Poems 1899–1905*

1907   Exhibition of cubist paintings in
Paris
Henry Adams's *The Education of
Henry Adams*
W.H. Auden born
Henri Bergson's *Creative Evolution*
Conrad's *The Secret Agent*
Daphne du Maurier born
Firbank's *A Disciple from the Country*
Forster's *The Longest Journey*
Christopher Fry born
André Gide's *La Porte étroite*
Shaw's *John Bull's Other Island* and
Major Barbara
Synge's *The Playboy of the Western
World*
Trevelyan's *Garibaldi's Defence of the
Roman Republic*

1908   Herbert Asquith becomes prime
minister
David Lloyd George becomes chancellor of the exchequer
William Howard Taft elected president of the United States
The Young Turks seize power in
Istanbul
Henry Ford's Model T car produced
Bennett's *The Old Wives' Tale*
Pierre Bonnard's *Nude Against the
Light*
Georges Braque's *House at L'Estaque*
Chesterton's *The Man Who Was
Thursday*
Jacob Epstein's *Figures* erected in
London
Forster's *A Room with a View*

CHRONOLOGY

Death of Bram Stoker

1913 Second Balkan War begins

Henry Ford pioneers factory assembly technique through conveyor belts

Guillaume Apollinaire's *Alcools*

Epstein's *Tomb of Oscar Wilde*

New York Armory Show introduces modern art to the world

Alain Fournier's *Le Grand Meaulnes*

Freud's *Totem and Tabu*

D. H. Lawrence's *Sons and Lovers*

Mann's *Death in Venice*

Proust's *Du Côté de chez Swann* (first volume of *À la recherche du temps perdu*, 1913–1922)

Barbara Pym born

Ravel's *Daphnis and Chloé*

Igor Stravinsky's *The Rite of Spring*

1914 The Panama Canal opens (formal dedication on 12 July 1920)

Irish Home Rule Bill passed in the House of Commons

Archduke Franz Ferdinand assassinated at Sarajevo

World War I begins

Battles of the Marne, Masurian Lakes, and Falkland Islands

Joyce's *Dubliners*

Shaw's *Pygmalion* and *Androcles and the Lion*

Gertrude Stein's *Tender Buttons*

Yeats's *Responsibilities*

Wyndham Lewis publishes *Blast* magazine and *The Vorticist Manifesto*

1915 The Dardanelles campaign begins

Britain and Germany begin naval and submarine blockades

The *Lusitania* is sunk

Hugo Junkers manufactures the first fighter aircraft

Poison gas used for the first time

First Zeppelin raid in London

Brooke's *1914: Five Sonnets*

Norman Douglas's *Old Calabria*

D. W. Griffith's *The Birth of a Nation*

Gustav Holst's *The Planets*

D. H. Lawrence's *The Rainbow*

Wyndham Lewis's *The Crowd*

Maugham's *Of Human Bondage*

Picasso's *Harlequin*

Sibelius's Fifth Symphony

Death of Rupert Brooke

1916 Evacuation of Gallipoli and the Dardanelles

Battles of the Somme, Jutland, and Verdun

Britain introduces conscription

The Easter Rebellion in Dublin

Asquith resigns and David Lloyd George

becomes prime minister

The Sykes-Picot agreement on the partition of Turkey

First military tanks used

Wilson reelected president president of the United States

Henri Barbusse's *Le Feu*

Griffith's *Intolerance*

Joyce's *Portrait of the Artist as a Young Man*

Jung's *Psychology of the Unconscious*

Moore's *The Brook Kerith*

Edith Sitwell edits *Wheels* (1916–1921)

Wells's *Mr. Britling Sees It Through*

1917 United States enters World War I

Czar Nicholas II abdicates

The Balfour Declaration on a Jewish national home in Palestine

The Bolshevik Revolution

Georges Clemenceau elected prime minister of France

Lenin appointed chief commissar; Trotsky appointed minister of foreign affairs

Conrad's *The Shadow-Line*

Douglas' *South Wind*

Eliot's *Prufrock and Other Observations*

Modigliani's *Nude with Necklace*

Sassoon's *The Old Huntsman*

Prokofiev's *Classical Symphony*

Yeats's *The Wild Swans at Coole*

Death of Edward Thomas; *Poems* published posthumously

1918 Wilson puts forward Fourteen Points for World Peace

Central Powers and Russia sign the Treaty of Brest-Litovsk

CHRONOLOGY

Execution of Czar Nicholas II and
 his family
Kaiser Wilhelm II abdicates
The Armistice signed
Women granted the vote at age thir-
 ty in Britain
Rupert Brooke's *Collected Poems*
 (posthumously)
Gerard Manley Hopkins's *Poems*
 (posthumously)
Joyce's *Exiles*
Lewis's *Tarr*
Sassoon's *Counter-Attack*
Oswald Spengler's *The Decline of the
 West*
Strachey's *Eminent Victorians*
Béla Bartók's *Bluebeard's Castle*
Charlie Chaplin's *Shoulder Arms*

1919 The Versailles Peace Treaty signed
J. W. Alcock and A. W. Brown make
 first transatlantic flight
Ross Smith flies from London to
 Australia
National Socialist party founded in
 Germany
Benito Mussolini founds the Fascist
 party in Italy
Sinn Fein Congress adopts declara-
 tion of independence in Dublin
Eamon De Valera elected president
 of Sinn Fein party
Communist Third International
 founded
Lady Astor elected first woman
 Member of Parliament
Prohibition in the United States
John Maynard Keynes's *The Econom-
 ic Consequences of the Peace*
Eliot's *Poems*
Maugham's *The Moon and Sixpence*
Eric Satie's *Socrate*
Shaw's *Heartbreak House*
The Bauhaus school of design,
 building, and crafts founded by
 Walter Gropius
Amedeo Modigliani's *Self-Portrait*
Doris Lessing born

1920 The League of Nations established
Warren G. Harding elected president of the United States

Senate votes against joining the
 League and rejects the Treaty of
 Versailles
The Nineteenth Amendment gives
 women the right to vote in the
 United States
White Russian forces of Denikin and
 Kolchak defeated by the Bolshe-
 viks
Karel Čapek's *R.U.R.*
Galsworthy's *In Chancery* and *The
 Skin Game*
Sinclair Lewis's *Main Street*
Katherine Mansfield's *Bliss*
Matisse's *Odalisques* (1920–1925)
Ezra Pound's *Hugh Selwyn Mauberly*
Paul Valéry's *Le Cimetière Marin*
Yeats's *Michael Robartes and the
 Dancer*
Death of Olive Schreiner

1921 Britain signs peace with Ireland
First medium-wave radio broadcast
 in the United States
The British Broadcasting Corpora-
 tion founded
Braque's *Still Life with Guitar*
Chaplin's *The Kid*
Aldous Huxley's *Crome Yellow*
Paul Klee's *The Fish*
D. H. Lawrence's *Women in Love*
John McTaggart's *The Nature of Exis-
 tence* (vol. 1)
Moore's *Héloïse and Abélard*
Eugene O'Neill's *The Emperor Jones*
Luigi Pirandello's *Six Characters in
 Search of an Author*
Shaw's *Back to Methuselah*
Strachey's *Queen Victoria*

1922 Lloyd George's Coalition government
succeeded by Bonar Law's Conservative government
Benito Mussolini marches on Rome
 and forms a government
William Cosgrave elected president
 of the Irish Free State
The BBC begins broadcasting in
 London
Lord Carnarvon and Howard Carter
 discover Tutankhamen's tomb
The PEN club founded in London

The *Criterion* founded with T. S.
  Eliot as editor
Kingsley Amis born
Eliot's *The Waste Land*
A. E. Housman's *Last Poems*
Joyce's *Ulysses*
D. H. Lawrence's *Aaron's Rod* and
  England, My England
Sinclair Lewis's *Babbitt*
O'Neill's *Anna Christie*
Pirandello's *Henry IV*
Edith Sitwell's *Façade*
Kurt Schwitters begins *Ursonate*
  (completed 1932)
Gertrude Stein's *Geography and Plays*
Virginia Woolf's *Jacob's Room*
Yeats's *The Trembling of the Veil*

1923   The Union of Soviet Socialist
  Republics established
French and Belgian troops occupy
  the Ruhr in consequence of Ger-
  many's failure to pay reparations
Mustafa Kemal (Ataturk) proclaims
  Turkey a republic and is elected
  president
Warren G. Harding dies; Calvin
  Coolidge becomes president
Stanley Baldwin succeeds Bonar
  Law as prime minister
Adolf Hitler's attempted coup in
  Munich fails
Time magazine begins publishing
E. N. da C. Andrade's *The Structure
  of the Atom*
Brendan Behan born
Bennett's *Riceyman Steps*
Churchill's *The World Crisis*
  (1923–1927)
Henry Cowell's *Aeolian Harp*
J. E. Flecker's *Hassan* produced
Nadine Gordimer born
Paul Klee's *Magic Theatre*
D. H. Lawrence's *Kangaroo*
Rainer Maria Rilke's *Duino Elegies*
  and *Sonnets to Orpheus*
Arnold Schoenberg's *Suite*, Op. 25
Jean Sibelius's *Sixth Symphony*
Picasso's *Seated Woman*
William Walton's *Façade*

1924   Ramsay MacDonald forms first
  Labour government, loses general

election, and is succeeded by Stan-
  ley Baldwin
Calvin Coolidge elected president of
  the United States
Early sound film, *Hawthorne*, shown
  in New York
Noël Coward's *The Vortex*
Forster's *A Passage to India*
Fernand Léger's *élément Méchanique*
Mann's *The Magic Mountain*
Pablo Neruda's *Twenty Love Poems
  and a Song of Despair*
Shaw's *St. Joan*
Death of Joseph Conrad

1925   Reza Khan becomes shah of Iran
First surrealist exhibition held in
  Paris
Louis Armstrong organizes his Hot
  Five
Jean Arp's *Lunar Frog*
Alban Berg's *Wozzeck*
Chaplin's *The Gold Rush*
John Dos Passos's *Manhattan Trans-
  fer*
Theodore Dreiser's *An American
  Tragedy*
Sergei Eisenstein's *Battleship
  Potemkin*
F. Scott Fitzgerald's *The Great Gatsby*
André Gide's *Les Faux Monnayeurs*
Hardy's *Human Shows and Far Phan-
  tasies*
Huxley's *Those Barren Leaves*
Kafka's *The Trial*
O'Casey's *Juno and the Paycock*
Virginia Woolf's *Mrs. Dalloway* and
  The Common Reader
Constantin Brancusi's *Bird in Space*
Shostakovich's *First Symphony*
Sibelius's *Tapiola*
Gertrude Stein's *The Making of Amer-
  icans*
Death of Sir Henry Rider Haggard

1926   George Antheil's *Ballet méchanique*
Isaac Babel's *Red Calvary*
Walter Gropius's Bauhaus complet-
  ed
Ford's *A Man Could Stand Up*
Gide's *Si le grain ne meurt*
Hemingway's *The Sun also Rises*
Kafka's *The Castle*

D. H. Lawrence's *The Plumed Serpent*
T. E. Lawrence's *Seven Pillars of Wisdom* privately circulated
Maugham's *The Casuarina Tree*
O'Casey's *The Plough and the Stars*
Puccini's *Turandot*
Death of Ronald Firbank

1927 General Chiang Kai-shek becomes prime minister in China
Trotsky expelled by the Communist party as a deviationist; Stalin becomes leader of the party and dictator of the Soviet Union
Charles Lindbergh flies from New York to Paris
Philo T. Farnsworth transmits first television image
J. W. Dunne's *An Experiment with Time*
Freud's *Autobiography* translated into English
Buckminster Fuller's Dymaxion House
Albert Giacometti's *Observing Head*
Ernest Hemingway's *Men Without Women*
Fritz Lang's *Metropolis*
Wyndham Lewis's *Time and Western Man*
F. W. Murnau's *Sunrise*
Proust's *Le Temps retrouvé* posthumously published
Stravinsky's *Oedipus Rex*
Virginia Woolf's *To the Lighthouse*

1928 The Kellogg-Briand Pact, outlawing war and providing for peaceful settlement of disputes, signed in Paris by sixty-two nations, including the Soviet Union
Herbert Hoover elected president of the United States
Women's suffrage granted at age twenty-one in Britain
Alexander Fleming discovers penicillin
Bertolt Brecht and Kurt Weill's *The Three-Penny Opera*
Eisenstein's *October*
Huxley's *Point Counter Point*
Christopher Isherwood's *All the Conspirators*

D. H. Lawrence's *Lady Chatterley's Lover*
Wyndham Lewis's *The Childermass*
Matisse's *Seated Odalisque*
Munch's *Girl on a Sofa*
Shaw's *Intelligent Woman's Guide to Socialism*
Mikhail Sholokov begins publishing *And Quiet Flows the Don* (completed 1940)
Anton Webern's Symphony
Rebecca West's *The Strange Necessity*
Virginia Woolf's *Orlando*
Yeats's *The Tower*
Death of Thomas Hardy

1929 The Labour party wins British general election
Trotsky expelled from the Soviet Union
Museum of Modern Art opens in New York
Collapse of U.S. stock exchange begins world economic crisis
Robert Bridges's *The Testament of Beauty*
Max Ernst's *La Femme 100 Têtes*
William Faulkner's *The Sound and the Fury*
Robert Graves's *Goodbye to All That*
Hemingway's *A Farewell to Arms*
Ernst Junger's *The Storm of Steel*
Hugo von Hoffmansthal's *Poems*
Henry Moore's *Reclining Figure*
Georgia O'Keeffe's *Black Cross, New Mexico*
J. B. Priestley's *The Good Companions*
Erich Maria Remarque's *All Quiet on the Western Front*
Shaw's *The Applecart*
R. C. Sheriff's *Journey's End*
Edith Sitwell's *Gold Coast Customs*
Thomas Wolfe's *Look Homeward, Angel*
Virginia Woolf's *A Room of One's Own*
Yeats's *The Winding Stair*
Second surrealist manifesto; Salvador
Dali joins the surrealists
Epstein's *Night and Day*

Mondrian's *Composition with Yellow Blue*

1930 Allied occupation of the Rhineland ends

Mohandas Gandhi opens civil disobedience campaign in India

The *Daily Worker*, journal of the British Communist party, begins publishing

J. W. Reppe makes artificial fabrics from an acetylene base

John Arden born

Auden's *Poems*

Coward's *Private Lives*

Ruth Crawford Seeger's *Study in Mixed Accents*

Eliot's *Ash Wednesday*

Freud's Civilization and its Discontents

Wyndham Lewis's *The Apes of God*

Maugham's *Cakes and Ale*

Harold Pinter born

Ezra Pound's *XXX Cantos*

Evelyn Waugh's *Vile Bodies*

Deaths of D. H. Lawrence and Sir Arthur Conan Doyle

1931 The failure of the Credit Anstalt in Austria starts a financial collapse in Central Europe

Britain abandons the gold standard; the pound falls by twenty-five percent

Mutiny in the Royal Navy at Invergordon over pay cuts

Ramsay MacDonald resigns, splits the Cabinet, and is expelled by the Labour party; in the general election the National Government wins by a majority of five hundred seats

The Statute of Westminster defines dominion status

Ninette de Valois founds the Vic-Wells

Ballet (eventually the Royal Ballet)

Coward's *Cavalcade*

Dali's The *Persistence of Memory*

John le Carré born

Hugh MacDiarmid's *First Hymm to Lenin*

O'Neill's *Mourning Becomes Electra*

Anthony Powell's *Afternoon Men*

Antoine de Saint-Exupéry's *Vol de nuit*

Walton's *Belshazzar's Feast*

Edgard Varèse's *Ionisation*

Virginia Woolf's *The Waves*

1932 Franklin D. Roosevelt elected president of the United States

Paul von Hindenburg elected president of Germany; Franz von Papen elected chancellor

Sir Oswald Mosley founds British Union of Fascists

The BBC takes over development of television from J. L. Baird's company

Basic English of 850 words designed as a prospective international language

The Folger Library opens in Washington, D.C.

The Shakespeare Memorial Theatre opens in Stratford-upon-Avon

Faulkner's *Light in August*

Huxley's *Brave New World*

F. R. Leavis' *New Bearings in English Poetry*

Boris Pasternak's *Second Birth*

Ravel's *Concerto for Left Hand*

Rouault's *Christ Mocked by Soldiers*

Waugh's *Black Mischief*

Yeats's *Words for Music Perhaps*

Death of Lytton Strachey

1933 Roosevelt inaugurates the New Deal

Hitler becomes chancellor of Germany

The Reichstag set on fire

Hitler suspends civil liberties and freedom of the press; German trade unions suppressed

George Balanchine and Lincoln Kirstein found the School of American Ballet

Paul Hindemith's *Mathis der Maler*

Lowry's *Ultramarine*

André Malraux's *La Condition humaine*

Olivier Messiaen's *L'Ascension*

Orwell's *Down and Out in Paris and London*

CHRONOLOGY

Gertrude Stein's *The Autobiography of Alice B. Toklas*

Arnold Toynbee's *A Study of History*

1934 The League Disarmament Conference ends in failure

The Soviet Union admitted to the League

Hitler becomes Führer

Civil war in Austria; Engelbert Dollfuss assassinated in attempted Nazi coup

Frédéric Joliot and Irene Joliot-Curie discover artificial (induced) radioactivity

Einstein's *My Philosophy*

Fitzgerald's *Tender Is the Night*

Graves's *I, Claudius* and *Claudius the God*

Toynbee's *A Study of History* begins publication (1934–1954)

Waugh's *A Handful of Dust*

Agatha Christie's *Murder on the Orient Express*

1935 Grigori Zinoviev and other Soviet leaders convicted of treason

Stanley Baldwin becomes prime minister in National Government; National Government wins general election in Britain

Italy invades Abyssinia

Germany repudiates disarmament clauses of Treaty of Versailles

Germany reintroduces compulsory military service and outlaws the Jews

Robert Watson-Watt builds first practical radar equipment

Karl Jaspers's *Suffering and Existence*

Ivy Compton-Burnett's *A House and Its Head*

Alban Berg's *Violin Concerto*

Eliot's *Murder in the Cathedral*

Barbara Hepworth's *Three Forms*

George Gershwin's *Porgy and Bess*

Greene's *England Made Me*

Isherwood's *Mr. Norris Changes Trains*

Malraux's *Le Temps du mépris*

Yeats's *Dramatis Personae*

Klee's *Child Consecrated to Suffering*

Benedict Nicholson's *White Relief*

Death of T. E. Lawrence

1936 Edward VII accedes to the throne in January; abdicates in December

1936–1952 Reign of George VI

German troops occupy the Rhineland

Ninety-nine percent of German electorate vote for Nazi candidates

The Popular Front wins general election in France; Léon Blum becomes prime minister

Roosevelt reelected president of the United States

The Popular Front wins general election in Spain

Spanish Civil War begins

Italian troops occupy Addis Ababa; Abyssinia annexed by Italy

BBC begins television service from Alexandra Palace

Auden's *Look, Stranger!*

Auden and Isherwood's *The Ascent of F-6*

A. J. Ayer's *Language, Truth and Logic*

Djuna Barnes's *Nightwood*

Walter Benjamin's "The Work of Art in the Age of Mechanical Reproduction"

Chaplin's *Modern Times*

Faulkner's *Absalom, Absalom!*

Greene's *A Gun for Sale*

Huxley's *Eyeless in Gaza*

Keynes's *General Theory of Employment*

F. R. Leavis's *Revaluation*

Federico García Lorca's *The House of Bernarda Alba*

Mondrian's *Composition in Red and Blue*

Dylan Thomas's *Twenty-five Poems*

Wells's *The Shape of Things to Come* filmed

Rebecca West's *The Thinking Reed*

Frank Lloyd Wright's *Falling Water*

1937 Trial of Karl Radek and other Soviet leaders

Neville Chamberlain succeeds Stanley Baldwin as prime minister

China and Japan at war

Frank Whittle designs jet engine

Picasso's *Guernica*

Shostakovich's Fifth Symphony
Magritte's *La Reproduction interdite*
Hemingway's *To Have and Have Not*
Malraux's *L'Espoir*
Orwell's *The Road to Wigan Pier*
Priestley's *Time and the Conways*
Tolkien's *The Hobbit*
Virginia Woolf's *The Years*
Death of James M. Barrie

1938　Trial of Nikolai Bukharin and other
　　　　Soviet political leaders
　　　Austria occupied by German troops
　　　　and declared part of the Reich
　　　Hitler states his determination to
　　　　annex Sudetenland from Czecho-
　　　　slovakia
　　　Britain, France, Germany, and Italy
　　　　sign the Munich agreement
　　　German troops occupy Sudetenland
　　　Antonin Artaud's *The Theatre and Its
　　　　Double*
　　　Chester F. Carlson makes his first
　　　　dry-copy, which led to modern
　　　　xerographic printing
　　　Edward Hulton founds *Picture Post*
　　　Cyril Connolly's *Enemies of Promise*
　　　du Maurier's *Rebecca*
　　　Faulkner's *The Unvanquished*
　　　Greene's *Brighton Rock*
　　　Hindemith's *Mathis der Maler*
　　　Leni Riefenstahl's *Olympia*
　　　Jean Renoir's *La Grande Illusion*
　　　Jean-Paul Sartre's *La Nausée*
　　　Yeats's *New Poems*
　　　Anthony Asquith's *Pygmalion* and
　　　　Walt Disney's *Snow White*

1939　German troops occupy Bohemia and
　　　　Moravia; Czechoslovakia incorpo-
　　　　rated into Third Reich
　　　Madrid surrenders to General Fran-
　　　　co; the Spanish Civil War ends
　　　Italy invades Albania
　　　Spain joins Germany, Italy, and
　　　　Japan in anti-Comintern Pact
　　　Britain and France pledge support
　　　　to Poland, Romania, and Greece
　　　The Soviet Union proposes defen-
　　　　sive alliance with Britain; British
　　　　military mission visits Moscow
　　　The Soviet Union and Germany sign
　　　　nonaggression treaty, secretly pro-

viding for partition of Poland
　between them
Germany invades Poland; Britain,
　France, and Germany at war
The Soviet Union invades Finland
New York World's Fair opens
Brecht's *Galileo*
Eliot's *The Family Reunion*
Isherwood's *Good-bye to Berlin*
Joyce's *Finnegans Wake* (1922–1939)
MacNeice's *Autumn Journal*
Flann O'Brien's *At Swim-Two Birds*
Powell's *What's Become of Waring?*
Seamus Heaney born
Death of William Butler Yeats

1940　Churchill becomes prime minister
　　　Italy declares war on France, Britain,
　　　　and Greece
　　　General de Gaulle founds Free
　　　　French Movement
　　　The Battle of Britain and the bomb-
　　　　ing of London
　　　Roosevelt reelected president of the
　　　　United States for third term
　　　Betjeman's *Old Lights for New
　　　　Chancels*
　　　Brecht's *The Good Woman of Setzuan*
　　　Angela Carter born
　　　Chaplin's *The Great Dictator*
　　　Disney's *Fantasia*
　　　Greene's *The Power and the Glory*
　　　Hemingway's *For Whom the Bell Tolls*
　　　C. P. Snow's *Strangers and Brothers*
　　　　(retitled *George Passant* in 1970,
　　　　when entire sequence of ten nov-
　　　　els, published 1940–1970, was enti-
　　　　tled *Strangers and Brothers*)
　　　George R. Stibitz demonstrates first
　　　　complex computer
　　　Richard Wright's *Native Son*

1941　German forces occupy Yugoslavia,
　　　　Greece, and Crete, and invade the
　　　　Soviet Union
　　　Lend-Lease agreement between the
　　　　United States and Britain
　　　President Roosevelt and Winston
　　　　Churchill sign the Atlantic Charter
　　　Japanese forces attack Pearl Harbor;
　　　　United States declares war on
　　　　Japan, Germany, Italy; Britain on
　　　　Japan

Auden's *New Year Letter*
James Burnham's *The Managerial Revolution*
F. Scott Fitzgerald's *The Last Tycoon*
Huxley's *Grey Eminence*
Shostakovich's *Seventh Symphony*
Tippett's *A Child of Our Time*
Orson Welles's *Citizen Kane*
Virginia Woolf's *Between the Acts*
Deaths of James Joyce and Virginia Woolf

1942 Japanese forces capture Singapore, Hong Kong, Bataan, Manila
German forces capture Tobruk
U.S. fleet defeats the Japanese in the Coral Sea, captures Guadalcanal
Battle of El Alamein
Allied forces land in French North Africa
Atom first split at University of Chicago
William Beveridge's *Social Insurance and Allied Services*
Albert Camus's *L'étranger*
Joyce Cary's *To Be a Pilgrim*
Camilo José Cela's *La Familia de Pascual Duarte*
Dmitri Shostakovich's *Leningrad Symphony*
Edith Sitwell's *Street Songs*
Waugh's *Put Out More Flags*

1943 German forces surrender at Stalingrad
German and Italian forces surrender in North Africa
Italy surrenders to Allies and declares war on Germany
Cairo conference between Roosevelt, Churchill, Chiang Kai-shek
Teheran conference between Roosevelt, Churchill, Stalin
Eliot's *Four Quartets*
Henry Moore's *Madonna and Child*
Sartre's *Les Mouches*
Vaughan Williams's *Fifth Symphony*
Death of Beatrix Potter

1944 Allied forces land in Normandy and southern France
Allied forces enter Rome
Attempted assassination of Hitler fails

Liberation of Paris
U.S. forces land in Philippines
German offensive in the Ardennes halted
Roosevelt reelected president of the United States for fourth term
Education Act passed in Britain
Pay-as-You-Earn income tax introduced
Beveridge's *Full Employment in a Free Society*
Jorge Luis Borges's *Ficciónes*
Cary's *The Horse's Mouth*
E. E. Cummings's *1 X 1*
F. A. Hayek's *The Road to Serfdom*
Huxley's *Time Must Have a Stop*
Maugham's *The Razor's Edge*
Sartre's *Huis Clos*
Edith Sitwell's *Green Song and Other Poems*
Graham Sutherland's *Christ on the Cross*
Trevelyan's *English Social History*

1945 British and Indian forces open offensive in Burma
Yalta conference between Roosevelt, Churchill, Stalin
Mussolini executed by Italian partisans
Roosevelt dies; Harry S. Truman becomes president
Hitler commits suicide; German forces surrender
The Potsdam Peace Conference
The United Nations Charter ratified in San Francisco
The Labour Party wins British General Election
Atomic bombs dropped on Hiroshima and Nagasaki
Surrender of Japanese forces ends World War II
Trial of Nazi war criminals opens at Nuremberg
All-India Congress demands British withdrawal from India
De Gaulle elected president of French Provisional Government; resigns the next year
Betjeman's *New Bats in Old Belfries*
Britten's *Peter Grimes*

Orwell's *Animal Farm*
Charlie Parker records "Koko" and "Now's The Time"
Russell's *History of Western Philosophy*
Sartre's *The Age of Reason*
Edith Sitwell's *The Song of the Cold*
Waugh's *Brideshead Revisited*

1946 Bills to nationalize railways, coal mines, and the Bank of England passed in Britain
Nuremberg Trials concluded
United Nations General Assembly meets in New York as its permanent headquarters
The Arab Council inaugurated in Britain
Frederick Ashton's *Symphonic Variations*
Britten's *The Rape of Lucretia*
Martha Graham's *Cave of the Heart*
Barbara Hepworth's *Pelagos*
David Lean's *Great Expectations*
Robert Matta's *Being With*
O'Neill's *The Iceman Cometh*
Roberto Rosselini's *Paisà*
Dylan Thomas's *Deaths and Entrances*

1947 President Truman announces program of aid to Greece and Turkey and outlines the "Truman Doctrine"
Independence of India proclaimed; partition between India and Pakistan, and communal strife between Hindus and Moslems follows
General Marshall calls for a European recovery program
First supersonic air flight
Britain's first atomic pile at Harwell comes into operation
Edinburgh festival established
Discovery of the Dead Sea Scrolls in Palestine
Princess Elizabeth marries Philip Mountbatten, duke of Edinburgh
Auden's *Age of Anxiety*
Camus's *La Peste*
Chaplin's *Monsieur Verdoux*
Lowry's *Under the Volcano*

Jackson Pollock's *Full Fathom Five*
Priestley's *An Inspector Calls*
Raymond Queneau's *Excercises in Style*
Edith Sitwell's *The Shadow of Cain*
Waugh's *Scott-King's Modern Europe*

1948 Gandhi assassinated
Czech Communist Party seizes power
Pan-European movement (1948–1958) begins with the formation of the permanent Organization for European Economic Cooperation (OEEC)
Berlin airlift begins as the Soviet Union halts road and rail traffic to the city
British mandate in Palestine ends; Israeli provisional government formed
Yugoslavia expelled from Soviet bloc
Columbia Records introduces the long-playing record
Truman elected of the United States for second term
John Cage's *Sonatas and Interludes*
Greene's *The Heart of the Matter*
Huxley's *Ape and Essence*
Leavis's *The Great Tradition*
James Hillier patents the electron microscope
Andrew J. Moyer's discoveries lead to industrial penicillin production
Olivier Messiaen's *3 Talas*
Pound's *Cantos*
Priestley's *The Linden Tree*
Pierre Schaeffer produces first musique concrète recordings
Waugh's *The Loved One*

1949 North Atlantic Treaty Organization established with headquarters in Brussels
Berlin blockade lifted
German Federal Republic recognized; capital established at Bonn
Konrad Adenauer becomes German chancellor
Mao Tse-tung becomes chairman of the People's Republic of China fol-

lowing Communist victory over the Nationalists

Simone de Beauvoir's *The Second Sex*

Cary's *A Fearful Joy*

Arthur Miller's *Death of a Salesman*

Orwell's *Nineteen Eighty-four*

1950 Korean War breaks out

Nobel Prize for literature awarded to Bertrand Russell

Heinrich Böll's *Traveler, if You Come to Spa...*

R. H. S. Crossman's *The God That Failed*

T. S. Eliot's *The Cocktail Party*

Fry's *Venus Observed*

Doris Lessing's *The Grass Is Singing*

C. S. Lewis' *The Chronicles of Narnia* (1950–1956)

Wyndham Lewis's *Rude Assignment*

George Orwell's *Shooting an Elephant*

Carol Reed's *The Third Man*

Isaac Bashevis Singer's *The Family Moskat*

Dylan Thomas's *Twenty-six Poems*

ca. 1950 Agatha Christie's *Mousetrap*

1951 Guy Burgess and Donald Maclean defect from Britain to the Soviet Union

The Conservative party under Winston Churchill wins British general election

The Festival of Britain celebrates both the centenary of the Crystal Palace Exhibition and British postwar recovery

Electric power is produced by atomic energy at Arcon, Idaho

W. H. Auden's *Nones*

Beckett's *Molloy* and *Malone Dies*

Benjamin Britten's *Billy Budd*

Camilo José Cela's *La Colmena*

Greene's *The End of the Affair*

Langston Hughes's *Montage of a Dream Deferred*

Akira Kurosawa's *Rashomon*

Wyndham Lewis's *Rotting Hill*

Anthony Powell's *A Question of Upbringing* (first volume of *A Dance to the Music of Time*, 1951–1975)

J. D. Salinger's *The Catcher in the Rye*

David Smith's *Hudson River Landscape*

C. P. Snow's *The Masters*

Igor Stravinsky's *The Rake's Progress*

1952– **Reign of Elizabeth II**

At Eniwetok Atoll the United States detonates the first hydrogen bomb

The European Coal and Steel Community comes into being

Radiocarbon dating introduced to archaeology

Michael Ventris deciphers Linear B script

Dwight D. Eisenhower elected president of the United States

Beckett's *Waiting for Godot*

Charles Chaplin's *Limelight*

Ralph Ellison's *Invisible Man*

Ernest Hemingway's *The Old Man and the Sea*

Eugène Ionesco's *The Chairs*

Arthur Koestler's *Arrow in the Blue*

F. R. Leavis's *The Common Pursuit*

Lessing's *Martha Quest* (first volume of *The Children of Violence*, 1952–1965)

C. S. Lewis's *Mere Christianity*

Thomas's *Collected Poems*

Amos Tutuola's *The Palm-Wine Drunkard*

Evelyn Waugh's *Men at Arms* (first volume of *Sword of Honour*, 1952–1961)

Angus Wilson's *Hemlock and After*

1953 Constitution for a European political community drafted

Julius and Ethel Rosenberg executed for passing U.S. secrets to the Soviet Union

Cease-fire declared in Korea

Edmund Hillary and his Sherpa guide, Tenzing Norkay, scale Mt. Everest

Nobel Prize for literature awarded to Winston Churchill

General Mohammed Naguib proclaims Egypt a republic

James Baldwin's *Go Tell It on the Mountain*

Beckett's *Watt*

Joyce Cary's *Except the Lord*

Robert Graves's *Poems 1953*

1954 First atomic submarine, *Nautilus,* is launched by the United States

Dien Bien Phu captured by the Vietminh

Geneva Conference ends French dominion over Indochina

U.S. Supreme Court declares racial segregation in schools unconstitutional

Nasser becomes president of Egypt

Nobel Prize for literature awarded to Ernest Hemingway

Kingsley Amis's *Lucky Jim*

Brendan Behan's *The Quare Fellow*

John Betjeman's *A Few Late Chrysanthemums*

William Golding's *Lord of the Flies*

Frank B. Colton develops first oral contraception: Enovid

Christopher Isherwood's *The World in the Evening*

Koestler's *The Invisible Writing*

Iris Murdoch's *Under the Net*

C. P. Snow's *The New Men*

Karlheinz Stockhausen's *Kontra-Punkte*

Thomas's *Under Milk Wood* published posthumously

Tolkien's *Lord of the Rings* (to 1955)

1955 Warsaw Pact signed

West Germany enters NATO as Allied occupation ends

The Conservative party under Anthony Eden wins British general election

Cary's *Not Honour More*

Willem de Kooning's *Woman as Landscape*

Greene's *The Quiet American*

Jasper John's *Green Target*

Philip Larkin's *The Less Deceived*

F. R. Leavis's *D. H. Lawrence, Novelist*

Le Corbusier's Notre-Dame-du-Haut Chapel completed

Vladimir Nabokov's *Lolita*

Patrick White's *The Tree of Man*

1956 Nasser's nationalization of the Suez Canal leads to Israeli, British, and French armed intervention

Uprising in Hungary suppressed by Soviet troops

Khrushchev denounces Stalin at Twentieth Communist Party Congress

Eisenhower reelected president of the United States

Anthony Burgess's *Time for a Tiger*

Allen Ginsberg's *Howl and Other Poems*

Golding's *Pincher Martin*

Naguib Mahfouz's *Palace Walk* (Book I of the Cairo Trilogy)

Murdoch's *Flight from the Enchanter*

John Osborne's *Look Back in Anger*

Snow's *Homecomings*

Edmund Wilson's *Anglo-Saxon Attitudes*

1957 The Soviet Union launches the first artificial earth satellite, *Sputnik I*

Eden succeeded by Harold Macmillan

Suez Canal reopened

Eisenhower Doctrine formulated

Parliament receives the Wolfenden Report on Homosexuality and Prostitution

Nobel Prize for literature awarded to Albert Camus

Beckett's *Endgame* and *All That Fall*

Lawrence Durrell's *Justine* (first volume of *The Alexandria Quartet,* 1957–1960)

Ted Hughes's *The Hawk in the Rain*

Naguib Mahfouz's *Palace of Desire* (Book II of the Cairo Trilogy) and *Sugar Street* (Book III of the Cairo Trilogy)

Murdoch's *The Sandcastle*

V. S. Naipaul's *The Mystic Masseur*

Eugene O'Neill's *Long Day's Journey into Night*

Osborne's *The Entertainer*

Harold Pinter's *The Room*

Muriel Spark's *The Comforters*

White's *Voss*

1958 European Economic Community established

Khrushchev succeeds Bulganin as Soviet premier

CHRONOLOGY

Charles de Gaulle becomes head of France's newly constituted Fifth Republic

The United Arab Republic formed by Egypt and Syria

The United States sends troops into Lebanon

First U.S. satellite, *Explorer 1*, launched

Nobel Prize for literature awarded to Boris Pasternak

Beckett's *Krapp's Last Tape*

Merce Cunningham's *Summerspace*

John Kenneth Galbraith's *The Affluent Society*

Greene's *Our Man in Havana*

Murdoch's *The Bell*

Eduardo Paolozzi's *Japanese War God*

Pasternak's *Dr. Zhivago*

Snow's *The Conscience of the Rich*

1959 Fidel Castro assumes power in Cuba

St. Lawrence Seaway opens

The European Free Trade Association founded

Alaska and Hawaii become the forty-ninth and fiftieth states

The Conservative party under Harold Macmillan wins British general election

Brendan Behan's *The Hostage*

William S. Burroughs's *Naked Lunch*

Alexander Calder's *Big Red*

Eliot Carter's *String Quartet* No. 2

Odysseus Elytis's *To Áxion estí*

Golding's *Free Fall*

Günter Grass's *The Tin Drum*

Graves's *Collected Poems*

Koestler's *The Sleepwalkers*

Pinter's *The Birthday Party*

Robert Raushenberg's *Monogram*

Snow's *The Two Cultures and the Scientific Revolution*

Spark's *Memento Mori*

Charles Townes invents the maser and the laser

1960 South Africa bans the African National Congress and Pan-African Congress

The Congo achieves independence

John F. Kennedy elected president of the United States

The U.S. bathyscaphe *Trieste* descends to 35,800 feet

Publication of the unexpurgated *Lady Chatterley's Lover* permitted by court

Auden's *Hommage to Clio*

John Barth's *The Sot-Weed Factor*

Luciano Berio's *In Circles*

Betjeman's *Summoned by Bells*

Elias Canetti's *Crowds and Power*

Louise Nevelson's *Royal Tide V*

Pinter's *The Caretaker*

Claude Simon's *La Route des Flandres*

Snow's *The Affair*

David Storey's *This Sporting Life*

1961 South Africa leaves the British Commonwealth

Sierra Leone and Tanganyika achieve independence

The Berlin Wall erected

The New English Bible published

Beckett's *How It Is*

Greene's *A Burnt-Out Case*

Koestler's *The Lotus and the Robot*

Murdoch's *A Severed Head*

Naipaul's *A House for Mr Biswas*

Osborne's *Luther*

Spark's *The Prime of Miss Jean Brodie*

White's *Riders in the Chariot*

1962 John Glenn becomes first U.S. astronaut to orbit earth

The United States launches the spacecraft *Mariner* to explore Venus

Algeria achieves independence

Cuban missile crisis ends in withdrawal of Soviet missiles from Cuba

Adolf Eichmann executed in Israel for Nazi war crimes

Second Vatican Council convened by Pope John XXIII

Nobel Prize for literature awarded to John Steinbeck

Edward Albee's *Who's Afraid of Virginia Woolf?*

Francis Bacon's *One of three studies for a Crucifixion*

Beckett's *Happy Days*

l

CHRONOLOGY

Benjamin Britten's *War Requiem*
Anthony Burgess' *A Clockwork Orange* and *The Wanting Seed*
Aldous Huxley's *Island*
Isherwood's *Down There on a Visit*
Lessing's *The Golden Notebook*
Marshall McLuhan's *The Gutenberg Galaxy*
Nabokov's *Pale Fire*
Mary Quant introduces the miniskirt
Aleksandr Solzhenitsyn's *One Day in the Life of Ivan Denisovich*
John Tavener's *3 Holy Sonnets*
Derek Walcott's *In a Green Night*
Andy Warhol's *210 Coca-Cola Bottles*
William Carlos Williams's *Patterson* (begun 1946)

ca. 1962   Joseph Cornell's *Eclipse series*

1963   Britain, the United States, and the Soviet Union sign a test-ban treaty
Britain refused entry to the European Economic Community
The Soviet Union puts into orbit the first woman astronaut, Valentina Tereshkova
Paul VI becomes pope
President Kennedy assassinated; Lyndon B. Johnson assumes office
Nobel Prize for literature awarded to George Seferis
Britten's *War Requiem*
John le Carré's *The Spy Who Came in from the Cold*
John Fowles's *The Collector*
David Hockney's *Picture emphasizing stillness*
Allen Jones's *Hermaphrodite*
Philip King's *Genghis Khan*
Murdoch's *The Unicorn*
Thomas Pynchon's *V.*
Wole Soyinka's *A Dance of the Forests* (published)
Spark's *The Girls of Slender Means*
Storey's *Radcliffe*
John Updike's *The Centaur*

1964   Tonkin Gulf incident leads to retaliatory strikes by U.S. aircraft against North Vietnam
Greece and Turkey contend for control of Cyprus

Britain grants licenses to drill for oil in the North Sea
The Shakespeare Quatercentenary celebrated
Lyndon Johnson elected president of the United States
The Labour party under Harold Wilson wins British general election
Nobel Prize for literature awarded to Jean-Paul Sartre
Saul Bellow's *Herzog*
Stan Brakhage's *Dog Star Man* (completed)
Burgess's *Nothing Like the Sun*
John Furnival's *Tour de Babel Changées en Ponts*
Golding's *The Spire*
Isherwood's *A Single Man*
Stanley Kubrick's *Dr. Strangelove*
Larkin's *The Whitsun Weddings*
Naipaul's *An Area of Darkness*
Peter Shaffer's *The Royal Hunt of the Sun*
Snow's *Corridors of Power*
Death of Brendan Behan

1965   The first U.S. combat forces land in Vietnam
The U.S. spacecraft Mariner transmits photographs of Mars
British Petroleum Company finds oil in the North Sea
War breaks out between India and Pakistan
Rhodesia declares its independence
Ontario power failure blacks out the Canadian and U.S. east coasts
Nobel Prize for literature awarded to Mikhail Sholokhov
Robert Lowell's *For the Union Dead*
Norman Mailer's *An American Dream*
Osborne's *Inadmissible Evidence*
Pinter's *The Homecoming*
Spark's *The Mandelbaum Gate*
Stockhausen's *Mikrophonie II*
Death of T. S. Eliot

1966   The Labour party under Harold Wilson wins British general election
The Archbishop of Canterbury visits Pope Paul VI

Florence, Italy, severely damaged by floods

Paris exhibition celebrates Picasso's eighty-fifth birthday

Julio Cortàzar's *Hopscotch*

Fowles's *The Magus*

Greene's *The Comedians*

Allan Kaprow's *Assemblage, Environments & Happenings*

Osborne's *A Patriot for Me*

Rhy's *Wide Sargasso Sea*

Paul Scott's *The Jewel in the Crown* (first volume of *The Raj Quartet*, 1966–1975)

White's *The Solid Mandala*

1967 Thurgood Marshall becomes first black U.S. Supreme Court justice

Six-Day War pits Israel against Egypt and Syria

Biafra's secession from Nigeria leads to civil war

Francis Chichester completes solo circumnavigation of the globe

Dr. Christiaan Barnard performs first heart transplant operation, in South Africa

China explodes its first hydrogen bomb

Anthony Caro's *Prairie*

Bob Dylan's *Times they are A-Changin'*

García Márquez's *One Hundred Years of Solitude*

Golding's *The Pyramid*

Heaney's *Death of a Naturalist*

Hughes's *Wodwo*

Isherwood's *A Meeting by the River*

Naipaul's *The Mimic Men*

Kenzaburo Oé's *The Silent Cry*

Tom Stoppard's *Rosencrantz and Guildenstern Are Dead*

Orson Welles's *Chimes at Midnight*

Angus Wilson's *No Laughing Matter*

1968 Violent student protests erupt in France and West Germany

Warsaw Pact troops occupy Czechoslovakia

Violence in Northern Ireland causes Britain to send in troops

Tet offensive by Communist forces launched against South Vietnam's cities

Theater censorship ended in Britain

Robert Kennedy and Martin Luther King, Jr., assassinated

Richard M. Nixon elected president of the United States

Booker Prize for fiction established

Luciano Berio's *Sinfonia*

Durrell's *Tunc*

Graves's *Poems 1965–1968*

Peter Handke's *Kaspar*

B.S. Johnson's *You're Human Like the Rest of Them*

Miës van der Rohe's Neu Nationalgalerie completed

Osborne's *The Hotel in Amsterdam*

Snow's *The Sleep of Reason*

Solzhenitsyn's *The First Circle* and *Cancer Ward*

Spark's *The Public Image*

1969 Humans set foot on the moon for the first time when astronauts descend to its surface in a landing vehicle from the U.S. spacecraft *Apollo 11*

The Soviet unmanned spacecraft *Venus V* lands on Venus

Capital punishment abolished in Britain

Colonel Muammar Qaddafi seizes power in Libya

Solzhenitsyn expelled from the Soviet Union

Nobel Prize for literature awarded to Samuel Beckett

Angela Carter's *The Magic Toyshop*

Fowles's *The French Lieutenant's Woman*

Eva Hesse's *Expanded Expansion*

P. H. Newby's *Something to Answer For*

Georges Perec's *La Disparition*

Storey's *The Contractor*

1970 Civil war in Nigeria ends with Biafra's surrender

U.S. planes bomb Cambodia

The Conservative party under Edward Heath wins British general election

CHRONOLOGY

Nobel Prize for literature awarded
  to Aleksandr Solzhenitsyn
Durrell's *Nunquam*
Gordimer's *A Guest of Honor*
Hughes's *Crow*
F. R. Leavis's and Q. D. Leavis's
  Dickens the Novelist
Toni Morrison's *The Bluest Eye*
Joyce Carol Oates's *The Wheel of Love*
Bernice Rubens's *The Elected Member*
Snow's *Last Things*
Spark's *The Driver's Seat*

1971 Communist China given Nationalist
  China's UN seat
Decimal currency introduced to
  Britain
Indira Gandhi becomes India's
  prime minister
Nobel Prize for literature awarded
  to Heinrich Böll
Bond's *The Pope's Wedding*
Gavin Bryars's *Jesus' Blood Never
  Failed Me Yet*
Raymond Federman's *Double or
  Nothing*
Ian Hamilton Finlay's *Poems to Hear
  and See*
Eugenio Montale's *Satura*
Naipaul's *In a Free State*
Pinter's *Old Times*
Spark's *Not to Disturb*

1972 The civil strife of "Bloody Sunday"
  causes Northern Ireland to come
  under the direct rule of Westmin-
  ster
Nixon becomes the first U.S. presi-
  dent to visit Moscow and Beijing
The Watergate break-in precipitates
  scandal in the United States
Eleven Israeli athletes killed by ter-
  rorists at Munich Olympics
Nixon reelected president of the
  United States
John Berger's *G*
Bond's *Lear*
Alex Comfort's *The Joy of Sex*
Peter Handke's *A Sorrow Beyond
  Dreams*
Pinter's *Monologue*
Snow's *The Malcontents*
Wole Soyinka's *The Man Died*

Stoppard's *Jumpers*
Eudora Welty's *The Optimist's
  Daughter*

1973 Britain, Ireland, and Denmark enter
  European Economic Community
Egypt and Syria attack Israel in the
  Yom Kippur War
Energy crisis in Britain reduces pro-
  duction to a three-day week
Nobel Prize for literature awarded
  to Patrick White
Stan Cohen and Herb Boyer prove
  that DNA cloning is feasible
Bond's *The Sea*
Joseph Brodsky's *Selected Poems*
J. G. Farrell's *The Siege of Krishnapur*
Edward Gorey's *Amphigorey*
Greene's *The Honorary Consul*
Lessing's *The Summer Before the Dark*
Murdoch's *The Black Prince*
Thomas Pynchon's *Gravity's Rain-
  bow*
Shaffer's *Equus*
White's *The Eye of the Storm*
Death of J.R.R. Tolkien

1974 Miners strike in Britain
Greece's military junta overthrown
Emperor Haile Selassie of Ethiopia
  deposed
President Makarios of Cyprus
  replaced by military coup
Nixon resigns as U.S. president and
  is succeeded by Gerald R. Ford
Betjeman's *A Nip in the Air*
Bond's *Bingo*
Louise Bourgeois's *Destruction of the
  Father*
Durrell's *Monsieur* (first volume of
  The Avignon Quintet, 1974–1985)
Gordimer's *The Conservationist*
Larkin's *The High Windows*
Stanley Middleton's *Holiday*
Pinter's *No Man's Land*
Solzhenitsyn's *The Gulag Archipelago*
Spark's *The Abbess of Crewe*

1975 The U.S. *Apollo* and Soviet *Soyuz*
  spacecrafts rendezvous in space
The Helsinki Accords on human
  rights signed
U.S. forces leave Vietnam

King Juan Carlos succeeds Franco as Spain's head of state

Nobel Prize for literature awarded to Eugenio Montale

Death of Sir P. G. Wodehouse

John Ashbery's *Self-portrait in a Convex Mirror*

Christo begins *The Pont Neuf Wrapped* (completed 1985)

E. L. Doctorow's *Ragtime*

Ruth Prawer Jhabvala's *Heat and Dust*

E. O. Wilson's *Sociobiology*

1976 New U.S. copyright law goes into effect

Israeli commandos free hostages from hijacked plane at Entebbe, Uganda

British and French SST Concordes make first regularly scheduled commercial flights

The United States celebrates its bicentennial

Jimmy Carter elected president of the United States

Byron and Shelley manuscripts discovered in Barclay's Bank, Pall Mall

Bob Cobbing's *Bill Jubobe*

Richard Dawkins's *The Selfish Gene*

Heaney's *North*

Hughes's *Seasons' Songs*

Koestler's *The Thirteenth Tribe*

David Storey's *Saville*

Spark's *The Take-over*

White's *A Fringe of Leaves*

Death of Agatha Christie

1977 Silver jubilee of Queen Elizabeth II celebrated

Egyptian president Anwar el-Sadat visits Israel

"Gang of Four" expelled from Chinese Communist party

First woman ordained in the U.S. Episcopal church

After twenty-nine years in power, Israel's Labour party is defeated by the Likud party

Fowles's *Daniel Martin*

Hughes's *Gaudete*

Paul Scott's *Staying On*

1978 Treaty between Israel and Egypt negotiated at Camp David

Pope John Paul I dies a month after his coronation and is succeeded by Karol Cardinal Wojtyla, who takes the name John Paul II

Former Italian premier Aldo Moro murdered by left-wing terrorists

Nobel Prize for literature awarded to Isaac Bashevis Singer

Greene's *The Human Factor*

Hughes's *Cave Birds*

Murdoch's *The Sea, The Sea*

Kenzaburo Oé's *Teach Us to Outgrow Our Madness* (published in Japanese in 1969)

1979 The United States and China establish diplomatic relations

Ayatollah Khomeini takes power in Iran and his supporters hold U.S. embassy staff hostage in Teheran

Rhodesia becomes Zimbabwe

Earl Mountbatten assassinated

The Soviet Union invades Afghanistan

The Conservative party under Margaret Thatcher wins British general election

Nobel Prize for literature awarded to Odysseus Elytis

Penelope Fitzgerald's *Offshore*

Golding's *Darkness Visible*

Heaney's *Field Work*

Hughes's *Moortown*

Lessing's *Shikasta* (first volume of *Canopus in Argos, Archives*)

Naipaul's *A Bend in the River*

Pinter's *Betrayal*

Spark's *Territorial Rights*

White's *The Twyborn Affair*

Death of Jean Rhys

1980 Iran-Iraq war begins

Strikes in Gdansk give rise to the Solidarity movement

Mt. St. Helen's erupts in Washington State

British steelworkers strike for the first time since 1926

More than fifty nations boycott Moscow Olympics

Ronald Reagan elected president of the United States

Burgess's *Earthly Powers*

Golding's *Rites of Passage*
Heaney's *Preoccupations*
Tom Phillips's *A Humument*
Pinter's *Family Voices*
Shaffer's *Amadeus*
Storey's *A Prodigal Child*
Angus Wilson's *Setting the World on Fire*

1981   Greece admitted to the European Economic Community

Iran hostage crisis ends with release of U.S. embassy staff

Twelve Labour MPs and nine peers found British Social Democratic party

Socialist party under François Mitterand wins French general election

Rupert Murdoch buys *The Times* of London

Turkish gunman wounds Pope John Paul II in assassination attempt

U.S. gunman wounds President Reagan in assassination attempt

President Sadat of Egypt assassinated

Nobel Prize for literature awarded to Elias Canetti

Rushdie's *Midnight's Children*
Spark's *Loitering with Intent*
Wislawa Szymborska's *Sounds, Feelings, Thoughts*

1982   Britain drives Argentina's invasion force out of the Falkland Islands

U.S. space shuttle makes first successful trip

Yuri Andropov becomes general secretary of the Central Committee of the Soviet Communist party

Israel invades Lebanon

First artificial heart implanted at Salt Lake City hospital

John Arden's *Silence Among the Weapons*
Bellow's *The Dean's December*
Gao Xingjian's *Signal Alarm*
Greene's *Monsignor Quixote*
Thomas Keneally's *Schindler's Ark*

1983   South Korean airliner with 269 aboard shot down after straying into Soviet airspace

U.S. forces invade Grenada following left-wing coup

Widespread protests erupt over placement of nuclear missiles in Europe

The £1 coin comes into circulation in Britain

Australia wins the America's Cup

Nobel Prize for literature awarded to William Golding

J. M. Coetzee's *Life and Times of Michael K.*

Gao Xingjian's *Bus Stop*
Hughes's *River*
Murdoch's *The Philosopher's Pupil*
Alice Walker wins Pulitzer Prize for fiction with *The Color Purple*
Death of Rebecca West

1984   Konstantin Chernenko becomes general secretary of the Central Committee of the Soviet Communist party

Prime Minister Indira Gandhi of India assassinated by Sikh bodyguards

Reagan reelected president of the United States

Toxic gas leak at Bhopal, India, plant kills 2,000

British miners go on strike

Irish Republican Army attempts to kill Prime Minister Thatcher with bomb detonated at a Brighton hotel

World Court holds against U.S. mining of Nicaraguan harbors

Anita Brookner's *Hotel du Lac*
Golding's *The Paper Men*
Heaney's *Station Island*
Milan Kundera's *The Unbearable Lightness of Being*
Lessing's *The Diary of Jane Somers*
Pinter's *One for the Road*
Spark's *The Only Problem*

1985   United States deploys cruise missiles in Europe

Mikhail Gorbachev becomes general secretary of the Soviet Communist party following death of Konstantin Chernenko

Riots break out in Handsworth district (Birmingham) and Brixton

Republic of Ireland gains consultative role in Northern Ireland

State of emergency is declared in South Africa

Nobel Prize for literature awarded to Claude Simon

Margaret Atwood's *The Handmaid's Tale*

Keri Hulme's *The Bone People*

A. N. Wilson's *Gentlemen in England*

Lessing's *The Good Terrorist*

Richard Long's *A Hundred Sticks Placed on a Beaver Lodge*

Murdoch's *The Good Apprentice*

Fowles's *A Maggot*

1986 U.S. space shuttle *Challenger* explodes

United States attacks Libya

Atomic power plant at Chernobyl destroyed in accident

Corazon Aquino becomes president of the Philippines

Giotto spacecraft encounters Comet Halley

Nobel Prize for literature awarded to Wole Soyinka

Final volume of *Oxford English Dictionary* supplement published

Amis's *The Old Devils*

Clark Coolidge's *Solution Passage*

Ishiguro's *An Artist of the Floating World*

A. N. Wilson's *Love Unknown*

Powell's *The Fisher King*

1987 Gorbachev begins reform of Communist party of the Soviet Union

Stock market collapses

Iran-contra affair reveals that Reagan administration used money from arms sales to Iran to fund Nicaraguan rebels

Palestinian uprising begins in Israeli-occupied territories

Nobel Prize for literature awarded to Joseph Brodsky

Burgess's *Little Wilson and Big God*

Drabble's *The Radiant Way*

Jas H. Duke's *Poems of War and Peace*

Golding's *Close Quarters*

Andy Goldsworthy's *Clearly Broken Pebbles Sratched White*

Heaney's *The Haw Lantern*

Toni Morrison's *Beloved*

Penelope Lively's *Moon Tiger*

1988 Soviet Union begins withdrawing troops from Afghanistan

Iranian airliner shot down by U.S. Navy over Persian Gulf

War between Iran and Iraq ends

George Bush elected president of the United States

Pan American flight 103 destroyed over Lockerbie, Scotland

Nobel Prize for literature awarded to Naguib Mafouz

Amis's *Difficulties with Girls*

Peter Carey's *Oscar and Lucinda*

Greene's *The Captain and the Enemy*

Rushdie's *Satanic Verses*

1989 Ayatollah Khomeini pronounces death sentence on Salman Rushdie; Great Britain and Iran sever diplomatic relations

F. W. de Klerk becomes president of South Africa

Chinese government crushes student demonstration in Tiananmen Square

Communist regimes are weakened or abolished in Poland, Czechoslovakia, Hungary, East Germany, and Romania

Lithuania nullifies its inclusion in Soviet Union

Nobel Prize for literature awarded to José Cela

Second edition of *Oxford English Dictionary* published

Amis's *London Fields*

Drabble's *A Natural Curiosity*

Ishiguro's *The Remains of the Day*

Murdoch's *The Message to the Planet*

David Nash's *Red Shrine*

Death of Samuel Beckett

1990 Communist monopoly ends in Bulgaria

Riots break out against community charge in England

Nelson Mandela released from prison in South Africa

Civil war breaks out in Yugoslavia; Croatia and Slovenia declare independence

Bush and Gorbachev sign START agreement to reduce nuclear-weapons arsenals

President Jean-Baptiste Aristide overthrown by military in Haiti

Dissolution of the Soviet Union

A. S. Byatt's *Possession*

Derek Walcott's *Omeros*

1991 Allied forces bomb Baghdad following Iraqi invasion of Kuwait

Boris Yeltsin assumes presidency of Russia

Nobel Prize for literature awarded to Nadine Gordimer

Pat Barker's *The Regeneration Trilogy*

Ben Okri's *The Famished Road*

Pinter's *Party Time*

Death of Graham Greene

1992 U.N. Conference on Environment and Development (the "Earth Summit") meets in Rio de Janeiro

Prince and Princess of Wales separate

War in Bosnia-Herzegovina intensifies

Bill Clinton elected president of the United States in three-way race with Bush and independent candidate H. Ross Perot

Nobel Prize for literature awarded to Derek Walcott

Heaney's *Seeing Things*

Michael Ondaatje's *The English Patient*

Barry Unsworth's *Sacred Hunger*

Death of Angela Carter

1993 Czechoslovakia divides into the Czech Republic and Slovakia; playwright Vaclav Havel elected president of the Czech Republic

Britain ratifies Treaty on European Union (the "Maastricht Treaty")

U.S. troops provide humanitarian aid amid famine in Somalia

United States, Canada, and Mexico sign North American Free Trade Agreement

Nobel Prize for literature awarded to Toni Morrison

Roddy Doyle's *Paddy Clarke Ha Ha Ha*

Pinter's *Moonlight*

1994 Nelson Mandela elected president in South Africa's first post-apartheid election

Jean-Baptiste Aristide restored to presidency of Haiti

Clinton health care reforms rejected by Congress

Civil war in Rwanda

Republicans win control of both houses of Congress for first time in forty years

Prime Minister Albert Reynolds of Ireland meets with Gerry Adams, president of Sinn Fein

First women ordained priests in Church of England

Nobel Prize for literature awarded to Kenzaburo Õe

Amis's *You Can't Do Both*

James Kelman's *How Late It Was, How Late*

Naipaul's *A Way in the World*

1995 Britain and Irish Republican Army engage   in diplomatic talks

Barings Bank forced into bankruptcy as a result of a maverick bond trader's losses

United States restores full diplomatic relations with Vietnam

NATO initiates air strikes in Bosnia

Death of Stephen Spender

Israeli Prime Minister Yitzhak Rabin assassinated

Microsoft founder, Bill Gates, is world's richest individual with 12.9 billion dollars

Timothy McVeigh bombs federal building in Oklahoma City

Nobel Prize for literature awarded to Seamus Heaney

Pat Barker's *The Ghost Road*

Death of Sir Kingsley Amis

1996 IRA breaks cease-fire; Sein Fein representatives barred from Northern Ireland peace talks

Prince and Princess of Wales divorce

Cease-fire agreement in Chechnia; Russian forces begin to withdraw

Boris Yeltsin reelected president of Russia

Bill Clinton reelected president of the United States

Nobel Prize for literature awarded to Wislawa Szymborska

British government destroys approximately 100,000 cows suspected of infection with Creutzfeldt-Jakob, or "mad cow" disease

Pinter's *Ashes to Ashes*

Graham Swift's *Last Orders*

1997 China resumes rule of Hong Kong

Diana, Princess of Wales, dies in an automobile accident

Unveiling of first fully-cloned adult animal, a sheep named Dolly

Peter Carey's *Jack Maggs*

Arundhati Roy's *The God of Small Things* wins Booker McConnell Prize for fiction

1998 United States renews bombing of Bagdad, Iraq

Independent legislature and Parliaments return to Scotland and Wales

Ted Hughes, Symbolist poet and husband of Sylvia Plath, dies

Tony Cragg's *Envelope*

Ian McEwan's *Amsterdam* wins Booker McConnell Prize for fiction

Nobel Prize for literature awarded to Jose Saramago

1999 King Hussein of Jordan dies

United Nations responds militarily to Serbian President Slobodan Milosevic's escalation of crisis in Kosovo

J. M. Coetzee's *Disgrace* wins Booker McConnell Prize for fiction

Nobel Prize for literature awarded to Gunter Grass

Jared Diamond's *Guns, Germs, and Steel*

Pinter's *Celebration*

Anita Desai's *Fasting, Feasting*

2000 Penelope Fitzgerald dies

J. K. Rowling's *Harry Potter and the Goblet of Fire* sells more than 300,000 copies in its first day

Oil blockades by fuel haulers protesting high oil taxes bring much of Britain to a standstill

Slobodan Milosevic loses Serbian general election to Vojislav Kostunica

Death of Scotland's First Minister, Donald Dewar

Nobel Prize for literature awarded to Gao Xingjian

George W. Bush, son of former president George Bush, becomes president of the United States after Supreme Court halts recount of closest election in history

Death of former Canadian Prime Minister Pierre Elliot Trudeau

Human Genome Project researchers complete map of the genetic code of a human chromosome

Vladimir Putin succeeds Boris Yeltsin as president of Russia

British Prime Minister Tony Blair's son Leo is born, making him the first child born to a sitting prime minister in 152 years

Margaret Atwood's *The Blind Assassin* wins Booker McConnell Prize for fiction

Kazuo Ishiguro's *When We Were Orphans*

Trezza Azzopardi's *The Hiding Place*

2001 In Britain, the House of Lords passes legislation that legalizes the creation of cloned human embryos

British Prime Minister Tony Blair wins second term

In the United States, terrorists attack World Trade Center and Pentagon with hijacked airplanes, resulting in the collapse of the World Trade Center towers and the deaths of thousands

Ian McEwan's *An Atonement*

Rushdie's *Fury*

Peter Carey's *True History of the Kelly Gang*

Death of Eudora Welty

List of Contributors

SCOTT ASHLEY. Sir James Knott Research Fellow in history at the University of Newcastle Upon Tyne. He has published on medieval and modern literary history and is currently researching the relationship between elite and popular culture in the middle ages. **J. M. Synge**

CHARLES ROBERT BAKER. Poet, short story writer, and essayist. Author of *What Miss Johnson Taught, Christmas Frost, A Peacock in a Pecan Tree,* and several literary biographies in the Scribner's *American Writers* series. Mr. Baker lives in Dallas, Texas. **Ben Jonson**

SUSAN BALÉE. Writer and educator. Ph.D. in English from Columbia University. Dr. Balée has published numerous articles on American and British literature in *The Hudson Review, Victorian Literature and Culture, Nineteenth-century Contexts,* and other journals. She is the author of *Flannery O'Connor: Literary Prophet of the South* (Chelsea, 1994), the first published biography of the Southern writer. Dr. Balée teaches creative writing at the annual Suncoast Writers' Conference in Florida and the Philadelphia Writers' Conference. She lives in Wyncote, Pennsylvania, with her husband and two children. **Percy Bysshe Shelley**

FRED BILSON.Lecturer in English, lingustics, and computer studies. Currently works supporting dyslexic students at the University of Glamorgan, Trefforest, South Wales. Bilson is completing a doctorate on the sound structure of natural languages.**Jonathan Swift**

DANIEL BRAYTON. Professor of literature at Middlebury College in Vermont. Brayton received his doctorate in English from Cornell in 2001, having specialized in Renaissance drama, utopian literature, and literary and cultural theory. His article, "Angling in the Lake of Darkness: Possession and the Politics of Discovery in King Lear," is forthcoming in *English Literary History* (ELH). He is currently working on a book about Shakespeare and early modern geographical discourse. **Christopher Marlowe**

SANDIE BYRNE. Fellow in English at Balliol College, Oxford. Her publications include works on eighteenth and nineteenth-century fiction and twentieth-century poetry. **Daniel Defoe**

RICHARD DAVENPORT-HINES Historian and biographer. Fellow of the Royal Historical Society, and a past winner of the Wolfson Prize for History and Biography. He also serves on the Committee of the London Library. Publications include *Dudley Docker* (1985), *Sex, Death and Punishment* (1990), *The Macmillans* (1992), *Vice* (1993), *Auden* (1995), *Gothic* (1998), and *The Pursuit of Oblivion: A Global History of Narcotics 1500–2000* (2001). He has also reviewed books for numerous newspapers and magazines, including the *New York Times.* **W. H. Auden**

JANE GOLDMAN. Senior Lecturer in English and American Literature at the University of Dundee, Scotland. Author of *The Feminist Aesthetics of Virginia Woolf: Modernism, Post- Impressionism and the Politics of the Visual* (Cambridge University Press, 1998); editor of *The Icon Critical Guide to Virginia Woolf* (Icon, 1997); coeditor of *Virginia Woolf Out of Bounds: Selected Papers from the Tenth Annual Conference on Virginia Woolf* (Pace University Press, 2001); coeditor of *Modernism: An Anthology of Sources and Documents* (Edinburgh University Press and Chicago University Press, 1998). She is currently writing *Image to Apocalypse: 1910–1945* for Palgrave. **Virginia Woolf**

BARBARA HARDY. Educator, critic, and writer. Author of *Thomas Hardy: Imagining Imagination, Dylan Thomas: An Original Language,* and *Svern Blidg: Collected and New Poems.* Hardy also contributes reviews to the *Daily Telegraph,* the *Spectator,* and the *Times Literary Supplement.* **Thomas Hardy**

CLAIRE HARMAN. Freelance writer. Coordinating Editor of the literary magazine *PN Review* in the 1980s. She published her first biography, of Sylvia Townsend Warner, in 1989. Her biography of the eighteenth century novelist Fanny Burney appeared in 2000 and she is currently engaged in writing a life of Robert Louis Stevenson, whose *Essays and Poems* and *Selected Stories* she has edited for Everyman Editions. She has also edited Sylvia Townsend Warner's *Collected Poems* and *Diaries* and reviews regularly in the British literary press. She lives in Oxford, England. **Robert Louis Stevenson**

HENRY HART. Mildred and J.B. Hickman Professor of Humanities at the College of William and Mary. Hart has published critical studies of Seamus Heaney, Robert Lowell, and Geoffrey Hill as well as two volumes of poetry. His most recent book is a biography, *James Dickey: The World as a Lie* (St. Martin's Press). **Seamus Heaney**

JAMES A. W. HEFFERNAN. Professor of English and Frederick Sessions Beebe Professor in the Art of Writing at Dartmouth College. Heffernan has recently delivered twenty-four lectures on Joyce's *Ulysses* for the Teaching Company of Springfield, Virginia, which has issued them on videotape and audiotape. His books include *Wordsworth's Theory of Poetry* (1968), *The Re-Creation of Landscape: A Study of Wordsworth, Coleridge, Constable, and Turner* (1985), *Museum of Words: The Poetics of Ekphrasis from Homer to Ashbery* (1993), and—as co-author—*Writing: A College Handbook*, fifth edition (2001). **James Joyce**

BRIAN HENRY. Assistant Professor of English at the University of Georgia. Coeditor of *Verse* and Senior Editor at Verse Press. Author of *Astronaut*, a book of poetry published in the United States, England, and Slovenia. Editor of the forthcoming *On James Tate* (University of Michigan Press) and *The Verse Book of New American Poets* (Verse Press). Author of numerous critical essays and reviews for such publications as the *Times Literary Supplement*, *The Kenyon Review*, and *The Yale Review*. **John Keats**

PETER KEMP. Writer and editor. Fiction Editor and Chief Fiction Reviewer of the *London Sunday Times*. Publications include *Muriel Spark* (1974), *H.G. Wells and the Culminating Ape* (1982, revised 1996) and *The Oxford Dictionary of Literary Quotations* (edited, 1997). **William Golding**

MELISSA KNOX. Writer. Author of *Oscar Wilde: A Long and Lovely Suicide* (Yale University Press, 1994) and *Oscar Wilde in the 1990s* (Camden House, 2001). She has published essays on Thomas De Quincey, Oscar Wilde, Anaïs Nin, and William Butler Yeats. She lives in Germany. **Harold Pinter**

GREVEL LINDOP. Emeritus Professor of Romantic and Early Victorian Studies at the University of Manchester, England. Publications include *The Opium-Eater: A Life of Thomas De Quincey*; *A Literary Guide to the Lake District*; and four volumes of poems, most recently *Selected Poems* (2000). He is General Editor of *The Works of Thomas De Quincey* (2000–2002) and Director of the Temenos Academy, an educational foundation concerned with the spiritual dimension of the arts. **William Blake**

ANTONIA LOSANO. Professor of English at Middlebury College in Vermont. Losano teaches 19th century literature and women's studies. Her recent publications include an essay on women's exercise videos and an article on the Victorian travel writer Marianne North. She is currently at work on a book project on the intersections of women's writing and women's painting in the 19th century. **Brontë Sisters**

CHRISTOPHER MACLACHLAN. Senior Lecturer in the School of English, University of St. Andrews, Scotland. Research interests include Scottish and eighteenth-century literature. MacLachlan has published essays on Burns, Hume, John Buchan and Muriel Spark, and edited Matthew Lewis's Gothic novel *The Monk* for Penguin Classics. An anthology of eighteenth-century Scottish verse is forthcoming and he is preparing a new edition of travel writings by Robert Louis Stevenson. **Henry Fielding**

NEIL POWELL. Poet, biographer, editor, and lecturer. His books include five collections of poetry—*At the Edge* (1977), *A Season of Calm Weather* (1982), *True Colours* (1991), *The Stones on Thorpeness Beach* (1994), and *Selected Poems* (1998)—as well as *Carpenters of Light* (1979), *Roy Fuller: Writer and Society* (1995), and *The Language of Jazz* (1997). He lives in Suffolk, England and is working on a biography of George Crabbe. **W. B. Yeats**

LYDIA RAINFORD. Lecturer in English at Merton College, Oxford. Having completed a doctoral thesis on feminist literary theory, she is now working on a book about visual memory in modern literature. Rainford has published journal articles on women's writing, Modernism and Samuel Beckett, and is currently coediting a book entitled *Literature and Visual Technologies*. **Samuel Beckett**

DAVID WOMERSLEY. Fellow and Tutor in English Literature at Jesus College, Oxford. Womersley has written widely on many aspects of eighteenth-century English literature, and his study of Gib-

bon's reputation, *Gibbon and 'The Watchmen of the Holy City'*, will be published by Oxford University Press in 2002. His current research interests center on Pope, the Scriblerians, and Whig writing of the late seventeenth and early eighteenth centuries.
Alexander Pope

W. H. AUDEN

(1907–1973)

Richard Davenport-Hines

W. H. AUDEN felt ill unless he wrote every day. Even if his output seemed trashy or mediocre, he was impelled to try to integrate his thoughts. But he was not a self-indulgent, casual scribbler; all his acts were self-disciplined and purposive. Nothing about his career was in miniature. "The minor artist," he said in 1947, "keeps to one thing, does it well, and keeps on doing it . . . [but] never risks failure. When he discovers his particular style and vision, his artistic history is over." Major artists, he reckoned, were either people like Dante and Marcel Proust, who spent a lifetime preparing one masterpiece, or those who were committed to perpetual development. "The moment such an artist learns to do something, he stops and tries to do something else, something new—like Shakespeare, or [Richard] Wagner, or Picasso" (*Lectures on Shakespeare*, 2000, p. 166). As he realized, he belonged in the Wagner and Picasso category. He was seldom satisfied with his achievements: he constantly rejected his previous work and ideas as specious and tinkered with the wording of his published poems through the years. His determination to change and improve, the versatility of his vocabulary and technique, and the richness of his intellectual powers surpass those of other twentieth-century poets, including T. S. Eliot, Thomas Hardy, William Butler Yeats, Robert Frost, and Wallace Stevens.

Auden, supremely, was a poet, though he wrote plays, opera libretti, and superbly insightful reviews and essays (of which a sample was published in his prose collection *Forewords and Afterwords*, 1973). He was first and foremost in love with language. In the poem "In Memory of W. B. Yeats" (as published in *Another Time*, 1940) he wrote:

> Time that is intolerant
> Of the brave and innocent,
> And indifferent in a week
> To a beautiful physique,
>
> Worships language and forgives
> Everyone by whom it lives.

The varieties of poetic meter were a joy to him, yet his technical skill was never arid; it was used to express a profusion of ethical ideas and a wealth of personal feeling, with which his contemporaries could not vie. At a time in the early 1920s when the psychoanalyst Sigmund Freud's name was seldom heard in Britain, the adolescent Auden studied Freudian theories and incorporated psychoanalytical ideas into his poetry. Auden's elegy "In Memory of Sigmund Freud" is a justly celebrated part of his oeuvre. He read and used concepts from other psychologists, notably W. H. R. Rivers, the author of *Instinct and the Unconscious* (1920) and a major influence on the lives of the English poets Wilfred Owen, Siegfried Sassoon, and Robert Graves. Auden was the first poet to incorporate, deliberately and formally, the ideas of twentieth-century psychology in his work. He observed that "art, as a rule, is practiced by people with a highly developed consciousness and highly developed tensions, with a nostalgia for the innocence of unconsciousness" (*Lectures on Shakespeare*, p. 97). This was certainly applicable to him.

Auden was an encyclopedic poet whose most ambitious works tried to integrate world history, natural phenomena, spiritual experiences, and intimate personal feelings into an intellectually systematic and emotionally coherent entirety. Psychology, then, was not primary in his poetic ideas. He was stupendously responsive to the influence of other poets. "In Memory of W. B. Yeats" is his eloquent tribute to a master whose influence he came to repudiate with vigor. Auden liked to accumulate, classify, and analyze facts and to make sense of large, chaotic amounts of information. He had a series of intellectual father figures whose work was similarly polymathic, including the English savant turned California mystic Gerald Heard and Wolfgang Kohler, one of the originators of Gestalt psychology who fled from Nazi Germany to New York. Auden had a greedy appetite for prose fiction. Images from Proust's novel *A la recherche du temps perdu* (*Remembrance of Things Past*) appear in his sonnet "Who's Who" and in section 3 of "The Quest."

Short stories by Henry James, such as "The Jolly Corner" and "The Private Life," contributed to the final stanzas of part 8 of "The Quest" and to "Nones"—a debt he acknowledged in his somewhat overblown poem, "At the Grave of Henry James." There are also references to detective heroes (such as Bulldog Drummond and Sherlock Holmes) dotted through his work. He had a quirky pictorial sense and took inspiration for poems from such painters as Pieter Brueghel and Giovanni Bellini. His remark in 1961 that the single piece of literature that had given him most pleasure that year was an article entitled "Cleaning Shrimps" printed in *Scientific American* typified his love of recondite or specialist literature. He drew on mining manuals, military biographies, history books, anthropology, political theory, newspapers, and much else for his ideas. After 1940, he used mainly theologians as a source for his poetry, because, after a period of ambivalence about Christianity, he returned to the church in that year and became (to the dismay of many old admirers and to the incomprehension of many later readers) a Christian poet.

EARLY LIFE

WYSTAN Hugh Auden was born on 21 February 1907, in York, England, the third and youngest son of George Augustus Auden, a physician, and Constance Rosalie Bicknell, who before her marriage had trained as a nurse with the intention of becoming a medical missionary. In 1908 Dr. Auden was appointed as the school medical officer in Britain's largest industrial city, Birmingham, and his family moved to a pleasant suburb, Solihull. Dr. Auden was a practical reformer who became a pivot in the administrative machinery that alleviated Birmingham's misery, illness, and dirt. Later he was professor of public health at Birmingham University. He was an unselfish, affectionate, and self sufficient man with great intellectual curiosity, and a profound humanitarian. He became a learned contributor to the *Journal of Mental Science* and as early as 1912 investigated the condition in children now known as dyslexia. Auden's mother, by contrast, was intense, excitable, and domineering; an intelligent but not an easy woman, she was often ill. She was a devout member of the Church of England and attended a controversially ritualistic congregation that used incense, candles, music, and other accoutrements of worship associated with Roman Catholicism. At the age of six Auden became a boat boy, dressed in a red cassock and white linen cotta, carrying the boat of incense grains to the altar. As a choirboy he learned to sight-read music and noticed the difference in the metrical values of words when they were spoken or sung. This was the beginning of his conscious interest in language.

His father's study contained books on medicine, archaeology, and the classics. Auden learned from his parents to value knowledge and education and developed an interest in medicine, disease, and theology. He was mentally precocious and physically backward, myopic, clumsy, untidy, dirty, and greedy about food and drink. Books delighted him, and he became a voracious reader. As a small child he invented a private dream landscape of limestone countryside that was devoid of human beings but filled with lead mines, slag heaps, narrow-gauge tramlines, and hard, impersonal mining machinery. His mother was emotionally demanding and too vigilantly attentive for his liking; he came to prefer machines to people, for inanimate objects expected no response and wanted nothing back. In later life he hinted that his difficulty in truly believing in and understanding the existence of other people resembled mild autism. For much of his life, he felt profoundly, even terrifyingly isolated. Indeed, at times it seemed that his adult sexual cravings expressed his need for physical confirmation of the existence of other people.

He shared with one of his brothers a streak of emotional masochism—a tendency to examine his conscience and deplore his own motives until he was anguished—that sometimes resembled self-hatred. Overall, though, he had a secure, privileged, and enriching childhood for which he came to feel warm and appropriate gratitude. Though the tensions between his parents were disruptive, he suffered no traumas as a boy. He came to feel, however, that the creative or intelligent child must devise, or patiently wait for, reasons to become neurotic, that neuroses gave direction, focus, and even protection to a young life and could be likened to guardian angels. Even as a child he had a smattering of Freudian ideas at a time when psychoanalysis was almost unknown in England, and he reimagined his parents into mythical symbols or fractured deities.

Auden began attending a boarding school, St. Edmund's, in Surrey in 1915. Another pupil at the school was the future novelist Christopher Isherwood, who was intermittently his lover until 1939, his literary collaborator, and his lifelong friend. As an adult, Auden considered that children were born honest and had to learn frivolity and insincerity before they could become serious or responsible about other people. It was at St. Edmund's, particularly in Isherwood's company, that he learned to be frivolous: he made witty remarks and, using his stock of mispronounced semiscientific jargon, mischievously provided other boys with their first stupendous and startling information on sex. With Isherwood he developed private jokes and an intimate coded language of their own.

In 1920 he went to Gresham's School, a progressive boarding school in Holt, Norfolk, where science had an unusual prominence in the curriculum. The headmaster was a pompous unmarried teetotaler who was so anxious about masturbation that he had all the boys' trouser pockets sewn up. Auden despised the headmaster's pious discipline and was repelled by the commonplace religious preaching at Gresham's, where great questions of faith were reduced to the mean, dispiriting level that supported school rules. Gradually he ceased to believe in Christianity.

At first Auden intended to be a mining engineer, but in 1922 he befriended an older boy, Robert Medley, who later became his lover and subsequently a distinguished painter and accomplished art teacher. They were walking together one Sunday afternoon in a plowed field when Medley casually asked if Auden wrote poetry. In that moment it came to Auden, like a revelation, that to write poetry was what he wanted. The discovery was overmastering. He accepted his vocation immediately. Typically, he started studying poetry books from the school library and began writing his own derivative or imitative efforts. Thomas Hardy soon supplanted his first poetic influence, William Wordsworth. The best of Auden's early work celebrated his favorite derelict landscapes and the mechanical debris that littered them; "The Traction-Engine" is an example. Altogether his intellectual maturity and literary ambition were prodigious.

In 1925 Auden matriculated at the most aristocratic of Oxford colleges, Christ Church. His scholarship in natural sciences partly paid his fees, but he transferred to a course in politics, philosophy, and economics. Then Isherwood persuaded him to change course again: he was finally admitted to the English school in 1926. Famously, at his first interview with his new tutor in English, he announced his intention to be a great poet. He became a prominent figure in student life, famous for his mannerisms, exuberant jokes, vivid gossip, bossiness over his friends' love lives, enthusiasm for psychoanalysis, and leftist political commitment. His favorite Oxford walks were characteristic: past the gasworks and the municipal garbage dump. He collected around him a set of gifted young mutineers, but his brilliance isolated him in his relationships. Unlike most student poseurs, there was a dazzling self-discipline underneath. Auden was devoting his life to intellectual efforts to analyze and dominate his circumstances. He wanted to synthesize human and natural experience in his poetry.

Of course, he continued to write poetry in profusion. T. S. Eliot's *The Waste Land* (1922) became an important poetic influence on him; he followed Eliot's example too slavishly and bombastically for a time. It led his writing into self-assured obscurity and accentuated his tendency to prescriptive urgency. He emancipated himself from Eliot by intense study and emulation of Yeats's poetry and then the poetry of Robert Graves. Together with another promising young poet, Cecil Day-Lewis, he edited an anthology entitled *Oxford Poetry* (1927). It is crucial that during the 1920s English literary criticism, as an intellectual discipline, came of age. Auden scrutinized books and articles as they appeared. In 1926, for example, he read *Science and Poetry* by I. A. Richards and incorporated its ideas into his creative campaign. All his major poetry, and even his few cheerful minor verses, throughout his life derived from his reading and thought.

THE YOUNG POET

FINALLY, in August 1927, Auden wrote a poem, "The Watershed," in a poetic idiom uniquely his own. The poem describes a narrow tract of high ground with meager soil surrounded by dismantled mines. A few months later, in 1928, he wrote another poem, "The Secret Agent," in the tone that became known as "Audenesque." These poems seemed threatening, ambiguous, and disorienting; their language is terse and cryptic. Their daunting originality and implicit menace thrilled early readers, even when the meanings were inaccessible. Auden, indeed, teased and intimidated his friends with ruthless diagnoses of their emotional ills. He instructed his young poetic protégé Stephen Spender, who became his occasional lover, that art was born out of humiliation; Spender suspected that Auden's secret fantasy of a poet was as a surgeon in white coat and rubber gloves. Auden's icy clinical intellectual outlook conflicted with his gregariousness: he was a hilarious mimic, loved clowning and dressing up, and was full of uproarious jokes.

After a period of adventurous sexual activity, Auden attempted celibacy in 1927. His readings of Freud and other psychological theorists suggested that homosexuality was indicative of arrested sexual development. Homosexuality was also a serious legal offense in Britain until partial decriminalization in 1967, a fact that resulted in Auden and Isherwood frequently calling themselves, both frivolously and warily, crooks. In 1927 or 1928 Auden underwent a form of psychoanalysis. His analyst may have been Margaret Marshall, an intense, clownish, lewd woman who treated Auden's elder brother John for depression and disastrously married him. At this time, Auden, probably through Marshall's influence, became impressed by the ideas of Émile Coué, a popular French psychologist. Coué had coined a famous phrase for his adherents to repeat twenty times each morning and evening: "Day by day, in every way, I am getting better and better." Auden practiced these techniques of self-mastery and self-improvement.

After graduating (with an undistinguished degree) from Oxford in 1928, he went to live in Berlin for a year. This was in itself a stark contrast to most creatively inclined people of his generation, who chose Paris. But he was bored by French culture, and Italy under Benito Mussolini's fascist government was intolerable. Germany attracted him because, as a hungry schoolboy during the war, whenever he took an extra slice of bread with margarine, a patronizing schoolmaster would sneer that he was undermining the war effort. He accordingly associated Germany with forbidden pleasures. In Berlin he met and became the lover of an older man, John Layard, an anthropologist with a history of emotional disturbance. Indeed, Layard shot himself in the head but survived after being found by Auden.

Layard had been a patient of an American psychologist, Homer Lane, a charismatic figure who was perhaps something of a sham. Lane's idea was to liberate the forces of an individual's subconscious without applying censorship or moral restraints. He believed that to act out one's impulses was to become happy and virtuous; emotional or physical repression was a denial of one's nature and produced neurosis or physical illness. The cure for an illness, or for emotional torment, was to indulge one's wishes. Lane's beliefs indicated, for example, that one would contract syphilis not by sleeping around but by sleeping around and feeling guilty about it afterward. This philosophy had more important consequences than leading Auden to have a lot of sex in Berlin. He developed theories of sexuality that owed much to Freud and attributed homosexuality to bad nurturing: these beliefs were unfair to his mother, harsh on himself, and have been discredited by discoveries during the 1990s about the genetic component in the homosexual disposition. Auden had become engaged to marry a woman nurse before he left for Berlin; sure now of his sexual preferences, he broke off the engagement on returning to England in 1929.

For a year he worked as a private tutor in London. During the period 1930–1932 he taught at a private school, Larchfield Academy, in Scotland and then, from 1932 until 1935, at the Downs School in Herefordshire. He was an eccentric, vivid schoolteacher who enjoyed the comedy, community, and gossip of school life. For some boys he seemed inspirational. His affinity with certain pupils suggested an immaturity in his outlook.

His work first reached a wider readership when the text of his theatrical charade, *Paid on Both Sides,* was published in 1930 by a critical magazine edited by T. S. Eliot, *Criterion.* He likened this short play to a parable of English middle-class professional life of 1907–1929, for it recounted a feud perpetuated by a hate-ridden mother; both he and Isherwood then harbored grudges against their mothers for having complicated their upbringing and sexuality. As befits a charade to be performed by friends, it is comic and incongruous in places, with jazz music from the back of the stage representing the groans of a captured spy. It is an exciting, confusing piece of writing, with passages of real suspense and sadness but above all with a language of prodigious richness. There are cryptic, compelling images of derelict ironworks, mortgaged manors, Scotland Yard investigators, a handsome raider who terrorizes remote districts, a dockside barmaid failing to communicate by telephone, old wounds, old feuds, and a God-figure called "watcher in the dark" (*Plays and Other Dramatic Writings, 1928–1938*, 1988, p. 16).

The charade is important because of its chorus commenting on the action. Unlike the choruses in the plays of previous dramatists dating back to Shakespeare and the ancient Greeks, Auden's chorus possesses privileged information withheld from characters in the play and, in particular, knows about connections, tensions, and motives that bind them together. As a result, the characters, in contrast to the chorus, seem doomed never to understand their circumstances or experience. The patterns are invisible and the meanings lost to them. This technique had been used before in novels; Auden all his life was an omnivorous reader, and he borrowed ideas and images with a zestful promiscuity. The chorus in *Paid on Both Sides* was, among other things, a way of depicting onstage the human unconscious. Faber and Faber, the London publishing house where T. S. Eliot worked, republished the charade under the title *Poems* later in 1930, together with thirty short, untitled poems.

Auden's early poetry expresses a dynamic, even violent force that arouses fear. Human pretensions, energies, technical skills, hopes, and emotions are all negligible, for the protagonists of his poems seem as powerless as the characters in his charade. In many early poems he looks down from a great height with numbed, distant observation. Western civilization and capitalism are depicted as sick. "Consider this," he began the poem "Consider," from 1930, "as the hawk sees it or the helmeted airman." The poem is addressed to a "supreme Antagonist, / More powerful than the great northern whale," the inner self thriving on anxiety and repression, which attacks people and kills their capacity for love, until everywhere its victims are "seized with immeasurable neurotic dread." The supreme antagonist has always recruited agents from among the repressed and guilty, handsome young men and spiteful village women, but now, as Western capitalism falters, with its "silted harbours, derelict works," there was everywhere raised "a prodigious alarm." Financiers, academics, clergymen, seekers after happiness—they are all warned, "It is later than you think." They could not get away, "Not though you pack to leave within an hour, / Escaping humming down arterial roads." It was their doom "After some haunted migratory years / To disin-

tegrate on an instance in the explosion of mania / Or lapse for ever into a classic fatigue" (*Collected Poems*, 1991, pp. 61–62). The reference to arterial roads—the English equivalent of freeways, which were just being built as traffic arteries through industrial districts and commuter suburbs—shows another characteristic of young Auden's images. He and friends who wrote like him—Day-Lewis, Spender, and Louis MacNeice—were dubbed "the pylon poets" because of their references to new technology, such as power stations and electricity pylons.

While Auden worked as a schoolmaster, he prepared an extraordinary new book expressing the mood of an English boarding-school adolescent, with a taste for secret confidences and ardent friendships, a yearning for heroism, and disgust for pompous authority. The book originated from a scholarly article by his former lover John Layard, published in the *Journal of the Royal Anthropological Institute* in 1930, on the subject of ritual epilepsy among the islanders of the New Hebrides. Layard examined beliefs in sorcerers with the ability to fly, known as "flying tricksters." Auden's book *The Orators: An English Study* (1932), was intended as a criticism of the Romantics' view of personality and the fascist idealization of young male heroes, but it contained severe, if coded, self-criticism. It is a mélange of wonderful poems mixed with scrappy, elliptical notes and prose of a high order. It is zestful and sometimes amusingly hectic, but the section entitled "The Journal of an Airman" is paranoid, guilt-ridden, isolated, and desperate. Delusions, persecution mania, and other disturbing emotions recur throughout the book; there is also a running metaphor representing homosexuality in terms of aviation. Auden adapted the religious language and references of his boyhood for secular ends. The theme of a martyred, self-sacrificing leader in *The Orators* is essentially Christian; Anglican responses are parodied in part 2 of the "Argument" section; and there are allusions to Christ before the Resurrection, gargoyles, modernist bishops, and similar matter. Despite his rejection of Christianity, Auden could not get away from its imaginative grasp.

THE POET AND TWO VISIONS

ON a warm evening in the summer of 1933 Auden was sitting on the lawn after dinner with three colleagues at the Downs School. He had not used alcohol or drugs. More than thirty years later he published an account of what happened:

We were talking casually about everyday matters when, quite suddenly and unexpectedly, something happened. I felt myself invaded by a power which, though I consented to it, was irresistible and certainly not mine. For the first time in my life I knew exactly—because, thanks to the power, I was doing it—what it means to love one's neighbor as oneself.

(*Forewards and Afterwords*, p. 69)

This surge of feeling and perception—a mystical experience that he called a vision of agape—transformed his life. He continued: "I recalled with shame the many occasions on which I had been spiteful, snobbish, selfish, but the immediate joy was greater than the shame, for I knew that, so long as I was possessed by this spirit, it would be literally impossible for me deliberately to injure another human being." His mystical feelings receded gently over the next two days, but their effects were enduring.

"Among the various factors which several years later brought me back to the Christian faith in which I had been brought up, the memory of this experience and asking myself what it could mean was one of the most crucial, though, at the time it occurred, I thought I had done with Christianity for good" (*Forewords and Afterwords*, p. 70). That same month of June 1933 he wrote a poem beginning "Out on the lawn I lie in bed," later entitled by him "A Summer Night," which celebrated this experience. Its sixteen stanzas of undiluted joy and calm convey what it might mean to love one's neighbor. The opening stanzas speak of colleagues, lovers, friends, and the seers who have influenced him. This time it is the moon, rather than a helmeted airman, that looks down from a superior height. Although there is modern technology in the poem, it is reconciled with religion and art and is not antagonistic or isolated:

> She climbs the European sky,
> Churches and power-stations lie
>   Alike among earth's fixtures:
> Into the galleries she peers
> And blankly as a butcher stares
>   Upon the marvellous pictures.
>   (*Collected Poems*, p. 118)

Then Auden moves from the personal to the political with references to violence in Eastern Europe;

hungry, wretched crowds; and the coming revolutionary climax. But the final stanza brings calm, reconciliation, and forgiveness. His new outlook was made explicit in a book review written later in 1933: "The first criterion of success in any human activity, the necessary preliminary, whether to scientific discovery or to artistic vision, is intensity of attention or, less pompously, love" ("A Review of *The Book of Talbot*, by Violet Clifton," *Prose and Travel Books in Prose and Verse*, 1997, p. 43).

In the ensuing years, Auden wrote a wonderful variety of poems exploring the themes of love. These include his cabaret songs of 1936, the elegiac "Funeral Blues" (well known from the film *Four Weddings and a Funeral*), and the more deliriously happy "Jam Tart." These songs were intensely personal. Auden found that he could express his most intimate feelings, without sounding mawkish or self-centered, if they were sung in the soprano voice of his friend Hedli Anderson. One of the most beautiful of his love poems, "Lullaby," shows joy at the beauty of his lover and gratitude for the sexual pleasure, but sadness at the transitory and unfaithful nature of their feelings. This "Lullaby," which derived from an earlier version drafted after his vision in 1933, contains the frank confession that the poet, too, is incapable of fidelity, falling for a succession of idealizations or dream figures but too self-centered and guilt-ridden to sustain lasting love. "O Tell Me the Truth About Love" is a more optimistic, jaunty lyric. Though his love poetry is eloquent and versatile and appeals to the experience of many readers, it was in some respects only theoretical. When, in the early 1930s, he finally had his first experience of being in love—as opposed to engaging in cheerful and affectionate sex—it was with an adolescent schoolboy who could scarcely respond as an equal in intellect or experience.

From 1932 Auden began contributing to literary periodicals with such titles as *New Verse*. He used prose to develop new ideas and beliefs, which he then would incorporate into poetry to test the validity of his arguments and challenge the authenticity of his feelings. After 1932 his poetry began appearing in influential anthologies with such titles as *New Signatures*. He himself compiled a total of twenty-two poetic anthologies of the works of others during his lifetime; *The Poet's Tongue* (1935) not only was the most original of his early anthologies but also was a symptom of a new departure in his working life. It was collaborative: his coauthor was a headmaster friend.

In 1935 Auden began trying to write in communities rather than creative isolation. He renounced school teaching and went to work in London as a mildly subversive member of the General Post Office's documentary film unit, where his colleagues included the painter William Coldstream and the producer John Grierson. He wrote a technically brilliant script for a documentary film, *Night Mail,* and lyrics for a song in a similar film, *Coal Face.* With his glee at disguises and clowning, he played the part of Father Christmas in a third production, *The Calendar of the Year.* In this period he wrote two plays, *The Dog Beneath the Skin* (1935) and *The Ascent of F6* (1936), which were produced at the experimental Group Theatre under the direction of Rupert Doone, the brilliant but difficult partner of Auden's boyhood lover Robert Medley. Christopher Isherwood worked as an equal collaborator on the plays, and their friend Benjamin Britten wrote music for their lyrics. These shared acts of creation in the film unit and the theater helped Auden shed some of the isolated inwardness of his early poetry. This is perhaps reflected in the affection evident in his more enduring work of 1935, such as "August for the People . . ." (dedicated to Isherwood) and "On This Island." The plays of 1935–1936 examined the psychological wounds in both individuals and communities. Although they contain compelling scenes, ambitious ideas, and bewitching language, they had a mixed reception and have not endured in the theatrical repertoire. A final Auden/Isherwood play, *On the Frontier* (1938), was least successful.

It was to Auden's credit that he was uncomfortable in metropolitan literary society, and despite his passionate friendships with Isherwood, Spender, and others, he shirked membership in literary cliques. In 1932 he contributed to a critical magazine called *Scrutiny* edited by F. R. Leavis, an academic who taught English at the University of Cambridge and adulated the work of D. H. Lawrence. Auden had been impressed by Lawrence's ideas since his undergraduate reading but purged himself of the influence after 1934. Leavis and his followers treated this as apostasy, and thereafter *Scrutiny* was unrelenting in its denunciations of Auden's work. Often the poet was accused of immaturity in his ideas or feelings, which was an oblique but recognizable attack on his sexuality. The critical hostility of *Scrutiny,* though petty and vicious, damaged Auden's reputation in Britain, especially after 1945.

In the mid-1930s Auden was convinced that artists with ability must resemble newspaper reporters and collaborated in an idiosyncratic but successful book of reportage. He and his friend Louis MacNeice visited Iceland together for two months during the summer of 1936, and subsequently published a mixture of prose and poetry about their visit, *Letters from Iceland* (1937). This record of a happy holiday, crammed with odd and amusing facts about the country, is redolent of the men's gaiety while they were away. Auden's long poem "Letter to Lord Byron" is the climax of the volume: it is a witty, chatty exercise with ingenious rhymes and iconoclastic ideas. Another characteristic piece is "Last Will and Testament," written jointly by the two men. This is a fast-moving list of bequests to friends, enemies, and public figures (living and dead) with all the in-jokes and intimacies that Auden loved. It ends with a prayer; henceforth all Auden's plays and long poems ended with a prayer, although they were not directed to a deity until 1941.

Despite the irrepressible high spirits of the book, Auden had an experience in Iceland of searing unpleasantness, which provided a counterpart vision of violence to his earlier, transforming vision of love. He visited a whaling station and published a photograph of the flensing of a whale by steam winch, with the gory detritus on the slipway. In boyhood he had had a craze for whales, which he thought the "most beautiful" of animals. "It combines the fascination of something alive, enormous, and gentle, with the functional beauties of modern machinery." He watched a seventy-one-ton whale being torn to pieces by steam winches and cranes. In the background a canary chirped, and the radio played silly tunes while blood stained the bay deep crimson for fifty yards. When the lunch bell clanged, the whalers stuck their spades in the carcass and went off to eat. "It gave one an extraordinary vision of the cold controlled ferocity of the human species" (Chapter 11 of *Letters from Iceland; Prose and Travel Books,* p. 288).

This was an important day in Auden's life. He referred to the whaling station briefly in his poem about vision and observation, "Letter to William Coldstream," and to whale killing in "Grub First, Then Ethics." But his experience on this occasion aroused a profounder and more enduring preoccupation. On several occasions he referred to a

Charles Addams cartoon that he had seen in an American magazine during the 1940s. It showed a silent and motionless crowd watching a little man, armed with a bourgeois umbrella, struggling for his life with a huge octopus that had clambered out of a manhole cover in a teeming New York street. Two men with briefcases are walking past the onlookers without craning their heads. "It doesn't take much to collect a crowd in New York," one of them says. While the lone individual struggles for existence, the spectators watch indifferently, and the passersby exist only negatively.

Auden's great poetic expression of such incidents is in his captivating poem describing Brueghel's painting of the mythical story of Icarus, who flies with artificial wings too near the sun, so that the wax melts and he falls into the Aegean Sea. As Auden describes the scene in "Musée des Beaux Arts," neither the plowman nor the sailors in Brueghel's painting notice, or can be bothered to notice, the boy plunging from the sky. They are too busy with unimportant things or too inattentive. He returned again to this idea in "Memorial for the City" his great poem treating the crematorium chimney, atrocities, and bombed cities of Hitler's Germany.

Before his vision of uncontrolled human ferocity in Iceland, Auden had been showing increasing concern about the rise of European dictators. In his "Ode to John Warner" he had referred sarcastically to Mussolini in Italy, Józef Pilsudski in Poland, and Adolf Hitler in Germany as charmers, though Josef Stalin in Soviet Russia was exempt from his anathemas. Hitler and Mussolini, in company with Winston Churchill and Franklin D. Roosevelt, woo the electors in "A Bride in the '30's." In his sprightly but macabre "James Honeyman," a neurotic scientist devises a lethal new poison gas for the coming war. Auden became increasingly active in left-wing politics from a sense of duty—a desire to reduce human suffering and injustice—but also to cure his feelings of emotional isolation. His propagandist poems vary in quality: "A Communist to Others" is too long and overbearing, for example.

Auden made a tremendous impact on eager young British and American intellectuals of the 1930s. He seemed to speak in language they could admire about their own most urgent concerns. They studied what he wrote with solemn and careful intensity and took his meanings seriously. He became an arbiter of how to think and behave.

A stanza in "Voltaire at Ferney" is largely autobiographical:

> Cajoling, scolding, scheming, cleverest of them all,
> He'd led the other children in a holy war
> Against the infamous grown-ups, and, like a child,
>   been sly
> And humble when there was occasion for
> The two-faced answer or the plain protective lie,
> But, patient like a peasant, waited for their fall.
> (*Complete Poems*, p. 250)

Despite his celebrity as a cultural icon of young dissent, he went in 1937 to Buckingham Palace to receive the King's Gold Medal for Poetry. His status as a cult figure, however, made him increasingly uncomfortable.

He also went to Spain, in 1937. He had volunteered to drive an ambulance for the democratic Republican forces fighting the fascists in the Spanish Civil War, although once in Barcelona he was diverted into futile radio broadcasting. He remained convinced of the evil of fascism but was quickly disillusioned by the brutality and political corruption of the Republicans and returned to England abruptly within two months. He was especially shocked and distressed by the closure of Barcelona's churches and the harassment of priests. Despite his rejection of Christianity sixteen years earlier, he discovered that churches still felt important to him. He kept this insight to himself, at first. Back in England he was restrained in his comments on the Spanish Republican cause, although his admirers did not seem to notice, partly because of his most politically explicit poem, "Spain."

This longish poem became a rallying cry for committed young people in Britain and told them that political action could be an expression of love and achieve a just society. But it was fractured in its arguments and glib, with a particularly phony phrase about poets exploding like bombs, and it had some of the flashy opportunism of a party hack's writings. The poem was famously, if unfairly, criticized for its amorality by George Orwell, and Auden was never satisfied with its sacrifice of truth to expedience. He made some drastic alterations and in later life repudiated it. It is excluded from his *Collected Poems* and most easily consulted in *Another Time*. In 1937, though, "Spain" confirmed his position as the most famous British writer of his generation.

In 1938 Auden and Isherwood traveled together in China, which had been invaded by Japanese forces a few years earlier. This resulted in their joint book, *Journey to a War* (1939), containing a sonnet sequence "In Time of War" in which Auden successfully canceled the ethical anomalies of "Spain." The twenty-seven sonnets, followed by a longer "Commentary," arguably constitute Auden's greatest achievement of the 1930s. "In Time of War" is an attempted synthesis of human nature written with ruthless audacity and unblinking vision in an epoch of tyranny and violence. It traces the history of humankind from the expulsion from Eden through the rise of organized religion to the mechanized age and its neuroses. One of its most perceptive readers, Lincoln Kirstein, the founder of the New York City Ballet, felt the sequence was almost hateful in its refusal to take or give comfort. Auden confronted the deteriorating human disaster, spurned all offers of bogus moral impunity, and, with irresistible logical force, examined the ethical responsibility of the times. He discarded forever the quasi-medical diagnostics of his earlier poetry and shifted toward a new ethical basis. The rich complexity of "In Time of War," like that of *The Orators*, defies succinct summary. After leaving China, Auden wrote several important or accessible poems during late 1938 and early 1939, including "Rimbaud," "A. E. Housman," "Edward Lear," and "Epitaph on a Tyrant."

AUDEN'S MARRIAGES AND LOVES

IN 1935 Auden married Erika Mann, the daughter of the great German novelist Thomas Mann. He scarcely knew her, and undertook the marriage, at Isherwood's suggestion, so as to provide her with a British passport and the means to escape Nazi persecution. Mann was a lesbian; the couple never lived together or consummated their marriage, but neither did they divorce. In 1946–1947 Auden enjoyed a fulfilling love affair with an American woman, Rhoda Jaffe; later, in moods of lonely dejection, he proposed marriage to a young American widow, Thekla Clark, in 1952 and to the New York German intellectual Hannah Arendt in 1970. Auden's only real marriage, contracted in 1939, was not, however, recognizable in law.

It was the sequel of his decision to shift continents and change nationality. He and Isherwood left England in January 1939 for New York with the intention of becoming U.S. residents and citizens. Many of his admirers felt personally betrayed by the departure of someone regarded as a chief spokesman of young, left, and anti-fascist men and women—especially after the outbreak of war in Europe nine months later. Subsequently, in 1940, a few scurrilous journalists and obscure politicians tried to brand Auden as a coward.

Two poems written soon after Auden reached New York show his outlook at this time. He was bent on gratitude and convinced that mysterious Absolutes controlled human existence. His elegy to Yeats, "In Memory of W. B. Yeats," concludes, "In the prison of his days / teach the free man how to praise" (*Collected Poems*, p. 249). Shortly afterward, in another elegy, "In Memory of Ernst Toller," commemorating a German playwright who had committed suicide, Auden observed:

> We are lived by powers we pretend to understand:
> They arrange our loves; it is they who direct at the
> end
> The enemy bullet, the sickness, or even our hand.
>   (*Collected Poems*, p. 250)

He felt in this new way because he had found a new love. In the spring of 1939 he met an eighteen-year-old college boy, Chester Kallman (1921–1975), the highly intelligent, wayward, and handsome blond son of a Brooklyn dentist. Auden's love of Kallman enabled him for the first time to appreciate the value of unique individuals rather than generalized humanity. Although he was intensely aware of Kallman as an individual rather than a subject for poetic or allegorical rhapsodies, he nevertheless interpreted this mischievous youth as a sacred being. Kallman's alarming weaknesses of temperament were impossible to ignore, so Auden decided that a person's misfortunes and mistakes should be regarded as potentially unique opportunities and strengths. He and Kallman exchanged some form of private vows together during a "honeymoon" in New Mexico in the summer of 1939. The poetic manifestation of their involvement together was a series of visionary love poems, such as "Like a Vocation" and "The Prophets," written that summer.

Kallman had considerable artistic sensibility and wrote poems himself, but he was irredeemably self-centered and sponged off Auden for most of his life. Auden later came to feel that with the arrogance of the artist he had moved from trying to create a world of language into the forbidden task of trying to re-create a human being, that he had tried to annex Kallman's free will into his own. This raised such anxieties between them that they both began behaving badly toward each other. When Kallman told Auden in 1941 that the sexual acts in their relationship must end and complained of his possessive interference, Auden attacked him during the night: Kallman awoke to find Auden's hands around his throat. Auden interpreted this incident as showing the potential for Nazism in everyone and continued his adoring admiration of the younger man with a passion that could seem perverse or stubborn to outsiders. They continued as intimate friends, for many years sharing apartments in New York City and summer homes in Europe. They collaborated in writing the libretto for Igor Stravinsky's opera of *The Rake's Progress*, which was first staged in 1951. Subsequently they wrote libretti for operas by Hans Werner Henze and Nicolas Nabokov. Their relationship was intellectually enriching but could seem emotionally destructive, especially as Kallman degenerated into alcoholism and increasingly desperate entanglements with younger men.

Auden could always write fluently about his beliefs but often quickly outgrew them. This happened with his political views of the 1930s and with the religious ideas developed in *The Prolific and the Devourer* (1993), a book drafted in 1939 but only published posthumously. In this he interpreted the Gospels to depict Jesus as a scientist, an economist, and a historian who foresaw the development of mechanized society. He tried to persuade himself that human instincts craved enlightenment and clung to the idea that historical trends were progressive and deterministic, that things got better. But these illusions became impossible for him in December 1939, after he went to a cinema in the Yorkville district of New York, where the largely German-American audience chanted "Kill the Poles" during a newsreel about the war in Europe. He waited over a decade before writing this incident in one of his most magnificent and important shorter poems, "The Shield of Achilles."

He had been revolted to find that he had a talent for rousing political meetings to mindless enthusiasm, and he decided that he was as tainted as the Yorkville louts. This feeling was reinforced by his quick dislike of his poem written at the outbreak of World War II, "September 1, 1939." Like "Spain," it was received well by readers, who were moved by the language but were less fastidious about his arguments. Although it was excluded from his *Collected Poems*, the poem is printed in *Another Time* and in anthologies, where it can indeed seem overly emphatic, smug, and false. This indictment cannot be leveled at his "New Year Letter," which was published together with his impressive and perhaps more accessible sonnet sequence "The Quest," about individual types facing an existential choice, in *The Double Man* (1941). "New Year Letter" is an urbanely formal and didactic epistle of rhymed octosyllabic couplets followed by eighty-five pages of erudite and impish notes. It develops a rich metaphysical argument about history, evolution, and eternity. The paradoxes and antagonisms are wittily deployed in this epic work assessing the history of human ideas and indicting the state of mid-twentieth-century thought. Its language and learning are authoritative; there is an authenticity and modesty lacking in his earlier propandist poems.

Auden wrote at least one love song in this period, of almost unbearably poignant beauty, "If I Could Tell You," but his harking on the duty to rejoice in such poems as "In Sickness and in Health" and "Atlantis" can seem too preachy. He emerged from this rather strained phase of his creativity after replacing the primacy of Freudian psychoanalytical and Marxist political ideas with the existential Christianity of the nineteenth-century Danish philosopher Søren Kierkegaard. Under Kierkegaard's influence, Auden discarded his more conceited fantasies about his artistic vocation and praised, rather than dreaded, the power of the Absolute in the world. Having reacted against his own ideas in *The Prolific and the Devourer*, he henceforth disliked humanized religion stripped of the mystique of God.

German Protestant theologians exiled in the United States became his friends, notably Paul Tillich and Reinhold Niebuhr; he became convinced that Christianity and social justice were mutually related. During the war years he wrote two long poems of Christian psychology. "For the Time Being," later subtitled "A Christmas Oratorio," describes the Christmas story in nine episodes through a mixture of chorus, narrative, dialogues, songs, and prose. It has a covert subtext about the collapse of his relations with Kallman and the saving of the emotional remnants. There are amusing incongruities and delectable ironies: the Roman troops on their way to massacre the innocents talk in camp slang, and Herod laments the need for the massacre in the phrases of a fretful, overworked liberal rationalist. Auden now insisted on a frivolous rather than a stern tone when discussing momentous subjects. He partly represents himself in the character of Joseph, who hangs out in bars. Auden's narrator declares, "To choose what is difficult all one's days / As if it were easy, that is faith" (*Collected Poems*, p. 365).

"For the Time Being" teems with vivid and exciting religious ideas. Crucial lines in the chorale speak of human imperfection, divine forgiveness, and redemption:

> Though written by Thy children with
> A smudged and crooked line,
> The Word is ever legible,
> Thy meaning unequivocal,
> And for Thy Goodness even sin
> Is valid for a sign.
>
> (*Collected Poems*, p. 374)

Auden is exultant when he writes of the Incarnation. The final narration and chorus move through irony and anxiety to a concluding affirmation.

"The Sea and the Mirror" was Auden's next long poem. It presents the Christian conception of art and traces the kinship between perfect divine love and imperfect human love through verse and prose monologues spoken by characters taken from Shakespeare's *The Tempest*. The variety of characters enabled Auden to express different versions of his temperament and opinions in their contrasting speeches. He used a comparable method of self-portraiture in his highly revealing and shocking poem "A Household," in which the three protagonists are all versions of himself.

AUDEN AS AN AMERICAN

AUDEN contemplated applying for U.S. citizenship as early as 1938, made his application in 1940, and received his citizenship in 1946. He had previously served his host country in an official capacity. For several months during 1945 he worked on a research team employed by the Morale Division of the U.S. Strategic Bombing Survey investigating the effects of Allied bombings on the inhabitants of German cities. He took the responsibilities of his citizenship seriously and, among other tasks, sat on a grand jury. Initially, he supported himself by teaching as much as by his writing. Auden gave courses on creative writing at the Writers' School run by the League of American Writers in New York in 1939–1940 and then taught for a time at St. Mark's School in Massachusetts. Afterward he taught at the University of Michigan in Ann Arbor (1941–1942), Swarthmore College (1944), Bennington College (1946), and Barnard College (1947).

The first major work that Auden published after the war was *The Age of Anxiety: A Baroque Eclogue* (1947). It won him a Pulitzer Prize, although it is the least satisfactory of the eight major poetic sequences written after his move to the United States. It is a theatrically constructed book-length sequence of prose and poetry in which four lonely people in New York go on a bar crawl. Parts of the book seem hackneyed, though it contains important philosophical ideas and exciting language. Among the proliferating ideas in *The Age of Anxiety*, two can be stressed. The section entitled "The Masque" begins with an observation that was central to Auden's thinking at this time. It also constituted a severe personal criticism, tantamount to self-hatred, of his conduct in the early 1940s, when he returned to Christianity and considered himself married to Kallman. He thought he had been posturing and bogus:

> Only animals who are below civilization and the angels who are beyond it can be sincere. Human beings are, necessarily, actors who cannot become something before they have first pretended to be it; and they can be divided, not into the hypocritical and the sincere, but into the sane who know they are acting and the mad who do not.
>
> (*Collected Poems*, p. 518)

This is a terrifying insight. Auden also wrote, in the section entitled "The Seven Ages," of "that state of prehistoric happiness which, by human beings, can only be imagined in terms of a landscape bearing a symbolic resemblance to the human body" (*Collected Poems*, p. 484). This idea soon came to dominate his imaginative life.

AUDEN AS A CHRISTIAN POET

AUDEN still wrote short, individual poems, which were beautifully accessible, such as "The Fall of Rome" and the first of "Five Songs," which opens,

"Deftly, admiral, cast your fly." In 1945 he and married friends bought a holiday shack on Fire Island, off the Long Island coast, where he spent several summers. From 1948 until 1957, each spring and summer, he rented a house in the coastal village on Forio on Ischia, an island in the Bay of Naples in the Mediterranean. Both islands were developing as favored gay resorts; he celebrated each of them in poems written during 1948, "Pleasure Island" and "Ischia." After 1948 he fell into the pattern of wintering in New York, where he made money writing freelance prose and devoted his Italian visits to composing poetry. He once joked that English might be the language spoken in heaven but in the earthly paradise, all speech and song was Italian.

Italy provided his sea change into something rich and strange. It fulfilled his need (prefigured in *The Age of Anxiety*) of a carnal landscape—that is, of great good places (in Henry James's phrase) symbolizing the human body and connoting elemental happiness. He was seeking ways to celebrate humanness in tones that were modest, restrained, and unpretending. He wanted to express his joy in the personal and the intimate without the overpowering scale and tone that he had come to dislike in some of his earlier work. Italian landscape seemed human in its connotations for Auden: it was palpable, not mythical, but it could convey the absolute. "In Praise of Limestone," the exquisitely lyrical poem that he wrote during his 1948 visit to Italy, was explicit in comparing Italian landscape to a mother's body and expressed joy in the created world rather than indulging in fantasies of transcendence.

The poem marked an important new phase in his ideas about the human body. It enabled him to proceed by the then unfashionable device of taking the human body as the subject for private celebration. The flesh was not only common to all humans but also central to the transubstantiation that Christians believed took place as the wine and bread became the body of Jesus in the act of Communion. The flesh had sacred meaning, with its promise of salvation. Auden's Italian visit of 1948 thus transformed his poetic imagination more profoundly than his move to the United States. It mattered as much as his vision of 1933 and more than his visit to the Iceland whaling station. Edward Mendelson, Auden's literary executor and shrewdest interpreter, has written of this phase of the poet's development with particular authority. He has demonstrated that, for Auden, the human body acted independently of conscious human wishes and was immune to the frailties of human character. There need be no efforts to reconcile its senses and its reason. The body was unaware of either culture or inhibitions, yet influenced them both. It had no intellectual vices and no credulity or stupidity, and it could not hate.

Auden often worried about seeming pompous. To prove to himself that although he was developing new ideas of great magnitude in his poetry, he was not becoming too serious, shortly after writing "In Praise of Limestone" he determined to celebrate the playfulness of the human body in a more immediate sense. "The Platonic Blow, by Miss Oral" is a long, detailed, and graphic account of his favorite sexual act.

Auden averred that the presuppositions of Christian dogma could not be proved but must be believed as an act of faith. Such faith provided the means to evaluate one's experiences. He insisted that Christians had three duties: to God, to their neighbor, and to Nature. He reckoned himself to be neither revolutionary nor reactionary but a counterrevolutionary working against the trends of his time. Thus he rejected the notions that birth or environment determined human character and that humankind could be liberated by knowledge. He upheld the right of every natural body to health and play. He regarded as "un-Christian" any "understanding of God as retributive justice, where success is good and failure means wrong, and where there is no need for forgiveness" (*Lectures on Shakespeare*, p. 312). He mustered his religious beliefs in a sequence of eight poems written intermittently from 1949 to 1954 about the Crucifixion and its aftermath.

Auden was an obsessively punctual man and titled each poem after prayer services held by the church at precise times of days. "Horae Canonicae," as the seven parts are collectively known, is too full of shame to be called devotional and too bitter to be called ceremonious. Shame and guilt are crucial to their mood. The sequence was written after Doomsday, in the aftermath of the nuclear bombings of Nagasaki and Hiroshima, in the Cold War period, when the talk was of bigger bombs, more destructive bombs, and larger stockpiles of bombs and when expertise, genius, devotion, and billions of dollars were at the service of collective paranoia and aggression. It was a period when the apocalypse seemed imminent. Auden insistently remembers the victim in "Horae Canonicae": the sequence is in places sublime but allows no consolation or comfort. One phrase may hint at its power. In the section entitled "Vespers," after describing the foundations of "arcadias, utopias, our dear old bag of a democracy," Auden writes: "For without a cement of blood (it must be human, it must be innocent) no secular wall will safely stand" (*Complete Poems*, p. 639). This, literally, was what he believed.

In addition to "Horae Canonicae," Auden wrote a sequence of poems in 1952–1953 collectively entitled "Bucolics," celebrating his delight in winds, woods, mountains, lakes, and other natural features of the earth. He was patient, generous, and shrewd in his advice to aspirant poets. As judge of the Yale Series of Younger Poets from 1947 to 1962, he chose for publication the first volumes of such talents as Adrienne Rich, John Ashbery, and John Hollander. Auden served from 1956 to 1961 as Professor of Poetry at Oxford University, where he experienced paranoia and panic at actual or anticipated hostility from his former compatriots, the British. His poem about this experience, "There Will Be No Peace," is a powerful evocation of his feelings of persecution, although it is disfavored by many literary critics. "Poetry is not magic," he argued in one of his Oxford lectures, "Writing." "In so far as poetry, or any other of the arts, can be said to have an ulterior purpose, it is, by telling the truth, to disenchant and disintoxicate" (*The Dyer's Hand*, 1962, p. 27).

LATE WORK

AUDEN had gone to Italy in 1948 to write such poems as "Horae Canonicae," and when the sequence was finished, he was ready to move on. Unexpectedly, in 1958, he won an Italian literary prize; the proceeds he partly spent on buying a small house, set among fruit trees, in the Austrian village of Kirchstetten. He relinquished the Italian phase of his life in "Good-Bye to the Mezzogiorno." Kirchstetten's proximity to Vienna enabled him to visit the Opera House there. Sometimes he stood in the garden at Kirchstetten with tears of gratitude in his eyes.

There is a reticence and occasional dullness about the poems he wrote during his Oxford professorship, but from 1961 to 1966 he enjoyed a creative revival exemplified by his sequence of poems

"Thanksgiving for a Habitat." The first of these to be written was "On Installing an American Kitchen in Lower Austria"; he later retitled it "Grub First, Then Ethics." From 1962 to 1964 he wrote additional serene, grateful, and observant poems celebrating the functions and characteristics of the rooms of his house at Kirchstetten. These were not angry or confrontational poems, though there is no timidity in their ideas; rather they are frank and happy. The book in which they were published, *About the House* (1965), was condemned as smug or cozy by some reviewers, but Auden was convinced that his work was improving. Certainly, by 1964, he had recovered from the qualitative lapse of the late 1950s. "Thanksgiving for a Habitat" was the last of his great poetic sequences and the most underrated but emphatically not the weakest.

Auden continued to meet with prejudice. In 1963 *Time* magazine prepared a cover story about him, which was abandoned at a late stage because the managing editor refused to honor a homosexual. His private life and health were also deteriorating. He and Kallman spent less time together after 1963, although they continued to share their summers in Austria. Auden accordingly felt lonelier. In 1971, for example, he wrote an eloquent and un-self-pitying poem, "Loneliness," and the more ominously titled "Talking to Myself," which looked forward to his death. Kallman spiraled downward into acute alcoholism, lost his looks, and had an increasingly obsessive, masochistic, and unhappy sex life. The wreck of his lover anguished and demoralized Auden. Lecturing on the drunkenness of Sir John Falstaff in Shakespeare's plays, he had said that alcohol "destroys the sense of time and makes one childlike and able to return to the innocence one enjoyed before one had sex" (*Lectures on Shakespeare*, p. 111). Perhaps this was why he, too, drank excessively; "The Garrison" mentions his taste for vodka martinis. Starting in 1965, when he was not yet sixty, his life became increasingly grim, and his social, if not his literary, skills began deteriorating.

Speaking in 1947 of Shakespeare's final plays, Auden had laid out the rules for the late work of great writers:

There must be no sign of a wish either for popularity or for an artistic perfection that is designed to reap critical acclaim. Late works also have a kind of obscurity that is different from that of a young artist. . . . The writer of late works is sometimes shocking out of his indifference as to whether he shocks or not. . . . The work's strangeness must be intentional or because the author doesn't care. Nor is there a wish in late works for big, spectacular, purple effects. There *is* an enormous interest in particular kinds of artistic problems lovingly worked out for themselves.

(Lectures on Shakespeare, pp. 270–271)

It is a measure of the man's constancy that he fulfilled these standards with his own late work.

The misuse of the phrase "We must love one another or die" from "September 1, 1939" in an emotive television advertisement from Lyndon Johnson's 1964 presidential campaign seemed shocking and contemptible to Auden and made him cut many early propagandist poems, or phrases about power politics, from future editions of his books. But as demonstrated by his great historical poem about the end of British imperial rule in India in 1947, "Partition," he never ceased to be a poet concerned with political power and social justice. His rich, elegant, disenchanting poem "Rois Fainéants" refers both to his own international celebrity on the poetry-reading circuit and to doomed rock stars with shoulder-length hair who are surfeited with substances and sex by their recording companies because they are intended to die young.

There are other impressive poems—reflective and meandering but always lexicographically rigorous—from the late period. He preserved his sense of wonder, and he strove to recover from suffocating gloom by insisting on his sense of gratitude, as in "Thank You, Fog." Twenty years earlier Auden had said that a writer in his closing phase should lovingly work out problems for their own sake and not worry about seeming strange. "A Bad Night" was his attempt to distract himself from insomnia by writing a poem full of bizarre and obscure words. At this period of his life he could still be droll, patient, endearing, and vitalized by his global humanistic outlook.

In 1972 Auden returned to live in Oxford, where he felt ill and unhappy. He spent the summer of 1973 in Kirchstetten. On his return journey, he stopped for a night in Vienna to give a poetry reading and died afterward in his sleep, on 29 September, of heart failure. "I don't believe people die until they've done their work, and when they have, they die," he had told a New York lecture audience in 1947. "People, as a rule, die when they wish to" (*Lectures on Shakespeare*, p. 296).

SELECTED BIBLIOGRAPHY

I. COLLECTED WORKS. *Collected Shorter Poems, 1927–1957* (London and New York, 1966); *Collected Longer Poems* (London, 1968; New York, 1969); *The English Auden: Poems, Essays and Dramatic Works, 1927–1939*, ed. by Edward Mendelson (London, 1977; New York, 1978); *Plays and Other Dramatic Writings by W. H. Auden, 1928–1938*, ed. by Edward Mendelson (Princeton, 1988); *Collected Poems*, ed. by Edward Mendelson (New York, 1991); *W. H. Auden and Chester Kallman: Libretti and Other Dramatic Writings by W. H. Auden, 1939–1973*, ed. by Edward Mendelson (Princeton, 1993); *Juvenilia: Poems 1922–1928*, ed. by Katherine Bucknell (Princeton, 1994); *As I Walked Out One Evening: Songs, Ballads, Lullabies, Limericks and Other Light Verse*, ed. by Edward Mendelson (New York and London, 1995); *Prose and Travel Books in Prose and Verse*, ed. by Edward Mendelson (Princeton, 1997), the first of four volumes of prose and travel books, including works from 1926 to 1938.

II. POETRY, PROSE POEMS, AND DRAMATIC WORKS. *Poems* (London, 1930; New York, 1934), includes *Paid on Both Sides*, a charade in verse; *The Orators: An English Study* (London, 1932; New York, 1967); *The Dance of Death: A Play in Three Acts* (London, 1933); *The Dog Beneath the Skin; or, Where Is Frances?* (London and New York, 1935), with Christopher Isherwood; *The Ascent of F6: A Tragedy in Two Acts* (London, 1936; New York, 1937), with Christopher Isherwood; *Look, Stranger!* (London, 1936), published in the United States as *On the Island* (New York, 1937); *Letters from Iceland* (London and New York, 1937), with Louis MacNeice; *On the Frontier*, with Christopher Isherwood (London, 1938; New York, 1939); *Journey to a War* (London and New York, 1939), with Christopher Isherwood.

Another Time (New York and London, 1940); *The Double Man* (New York, 1941), published in the United Kingdom as *New Year Letter* (London, 1941); *For the Time Being* (New York, 1944; London, 1945); *The Age of Anxiety: A Baroque Eclogue* (New York, 1947; London, 1948); *Nones* (New York, 1951; London, 1952); *The Shield of Achilles* (New York and London, 1955); *Homage to Clio* (New York and London, 1960); *About the House* (New York, 1965; London, 1966); *City Without Walls, and Other Poems* (London, 1969; New York, 1970); *Epistle to a Godson, and Other Poems* (New York and London, 1972); *Thank You, Fog: Last Poems* (New York and London, 1974).

III. PROSE. *The Enchafèd Flood; or, The Romantic Iconography of the Sea* (New York, 1950; London, 1951); *The Dyer's Hand and Other Essays* (New York, 1962; London, 1963); *Secondary Worlds* (New York and London, 1968), the T. S. Eliot memorial lectures delivered by Auden at Eliot College, University of Kent, October 1967; *Forewords and Afterwords*, ed. by Edward Mendelson (New York and London, 1973); *Auden as Didymus: The Poet as Columnist Anonymous*, ed. by John Deedy (Mount Vernon, N.Y., 1993); *The Prolific and the Devourer*

(Hopewell, N.J., 1993); *Lectures on Shakespeare,* ed. by Arthur Kirsch (Princeton, 2000).

IV. ANTHOLOGIES COMPILED BY AUDEN. *Oxford Poetry,* coedited with Cecil Day-Lewis (London, 1927); *The Poet's Tongue,* coedited with John Garrett (London, 1935); *The Viking Book of Aphorisms,* coedited with Louis Kronenberger (New York, 1966); *A Certain World: A Commonplace Book* (New York, 1970; London, 1971).

V. INTERVIEWS. May Cameron, "Author! Author! England's White-Haired Literary Boys, W. H. Auden and Christopher Isherwood, Talk of China and Themselves," *New York Post,* 9 July 1938; Maurice Cranston, "Poet's Retreat," *John O'London's Weekly* 57 (6 February 1948); Maurice Dolbier, "Interviewing a Poet at the Breakfast Table," *Providence (Rhode Island) Journal,* 20 January 1952, sec. 6; "Poets Do Better, One of Them Says," *Los Angeles Times,* 16 March 1954; Polly Platt, "W. H. Auden," *American Scholar* 36 (spring 1967); Mary Jane Fortunato and William Packard, "Craft Interview: W. H. Auden," *New York Quarterly* 1 (winter1970), reprinted in William Packard, ed., *The Craft of Poetry: Interviews from the New York Quarterly* (New York, 1974); Jon Bradshaw, "Holding to Schedule with W. H. Auden," *Esquire* 73 (January 1970); Alan Levy, "In the Autumn of the Age of Anxiety," *New York Times,* 8 August 1971, sec. 6; Daniel Halpern, "Interview with W. H. Auden," *Antaeus* 5 (spring 1972); Michael Andre, "A Talk with W. H. Auden," *Unmuzzled Ox* 1 (summer 1972); "Remembering and Forgetting: W. H. Auden Talks to Richard Crossman About Poetry," *Listener* (London) 89 (22 February 1973); Michael Newman, "W. H. Auden: The Art of Poetry," *Paris Review* 57 (spring 1974), reprinted in George Plimpton, ed., *Writers at Work: The Paris Review Interviews* (New York, 1989); Walter Kerr, "An Unpublished Interview (1953)," *Harvard Advocate* 108, nos. 2–3 (1975); Marvin Cohen, "An Interview with W. H. Auden," *Arts in Society* 12 (fall/winter 1975); Suresh Raichura and Amritjit Singh, "A Conversation with W. H. Auden," *Southwest Review* 60 (winter 1975).

VI. BIBLIOGRAPHIES. B. C. Bloomfield and Edward Mendelson, *W. H. Auden: A Bibliography 1924–1969* (Charlottesville, Va., 1972); Edward Mendelson, "W. H. Auden: A Bibliographical Supplement," in *The Map of All My Youth: Early Works, Friends, and Influences,* ed. by Katherine Bucknell and Nicholas Jenkins (Oxford and New York, 1990); Edward Mendelson, "Interviews, Dialogues, and Conversations with W. H. Auden: A Bibliography," in *The Language of Learning and the Language of Love: Uncollected Writing, New Interpretations,* ed. by Katherine Bucknell and Nicholas Jenkins (Oxford and New York, 1994); "Published Letters by W. H. Auden: A Bibliography," in *In Solitude, for Company: W. H. Auden After 1940,* ed. by Katherine Bucknell and Nicholas Jenkins (Oxford and New York, 1995).

VII. BIOGRAPHICAL STUDIES. Stephen Spender, *W. H. Auden: A Tribute* (London, 1975); Humphrey Carpenter, *W. H. Auden: A Biography* (Boston, 1981); Howard Griffin, *Conversations with Auden* (San Francisco, 1981); Charles H. Miller, *Auden, an American Friendship* (New York, 1983); Dorothy J. Farnan, *Auden in Love* (New York, 1984); Alan Ansen, *The Table Talk of W. H. Auden* (Princeton, 1990); Thekla Clark, *Wystan and Chester: A Personal Memoir of W. H. Auden and Chester Kallman* (New York, 1996); Richard Davenport-Hines, *Auden* (New York, 1995).

VIII. CRITICAL STUDIES. Monroe Spears, *The Poetry of W. H. Auden: The Disenchanted Island* (New York, 1963); Samuel Hynes, *The Auden Generation: Literature and Politics in England in the 1930s* (London, 1976; New York, 1977); Randall Jarrell, *Kipling, Auden & Co.: Essays and Reviews, 1935–1964* (New York, 1980); Edward Mendelson, *Early Auden* (New York, 1981); Lucy McDiarmid, *Auden's Apologies for Poetry* (Princeton, 1990); Katherine Bucknell and Nicholas Jenkins, eds., *Auden Studies:* vol. 1, *The Map of All My Youth: Early Works, Friends, and Influences* (New York and Oxford, 1990), vol. 2, *The Language of Learning and the Language of Love: Uncollected Writing, New Interpretations* (New York and Oxford, 1994), vol. 3, *In Solitude, for Company: W. H. Auden after 1940, Unpublished Prose and Recent Criticism* (New York and Oxford, 1995); John Fuller, *W. H. Auden: A Commentary* (Princeton, 1998); Edward Mendelson, *Later Auden* (New York, 1999).

SAMUEL BECKETT

(1906–1989)

Lydia Rainford

SAMUEL BARCLAY BECKETT was born at Cooldrinagh in Foxrock, County Dublin, Ireland on Good Friday, 13 April 1906. He was the second-born of two sons of Protestant, middle-class parents, his father a self-made businessman. Samuel proved to be an excellent pupil at school, thriving at both sport and academic work. He went on to study Modern Languages at Trinity College, Dublin, and in 1927, after gaining the top marks in his B.A. final examination, he left on an exchange to teach English at the École Normale Supérieure in Paris. During his two-year stay he met and befriended the Irish novelist James Joyce. He also published his first creative writing, in 1929, in the literary review *transition*: a short story, called "Assumption," and an essay on Joyce's *Work in Progress* (eventually to become *Finnegan's Wake*), entitled "Dante . . . Bruno. Vico . . . Joyce." His links with the literary circles in Paris earned him commissions to translate texts for several reviews and small magazines. In 1930 he won a poetry competition for his poem *Whoroscope,* and completed a critical work on the French writer *Proust.*

Beckett returned to Dublin in 1930, when he was elected to the newly created post of Lecturer in French and assistant to the Professor of Romance Languages at Trinity College. However, he could not tolerate life as an academic, and resigned after only four terms. Beckett's family, in particular his mother, were horrified at this act of irresponsibility, but Beckett now determined to make his way as a writer. He traveled for a time in Europe, where he began his first, never-to-be-finished novel, *A Dream of Fair to Middling Women,* then continued to write poems, stories, and translations while living with his parents in Dublin. His father died unexpectedly in the summer of 1933, and this event, combined with his general feelings of aimlessness, threw Beckett into a deep depression. He began to suffer anxiety attacks and from various physical ailments so, at the advice of his doctor, he moved to London to undergo psycho-

analysis. He lived there from 1933 to 1935, during which time he attended the lectures of C. G. Jung, saw the publication of his collection of short stories, *More Pricks Than Kicks* (1934), and gathered material for his next novel, *Murphy* (1938).

Beckett moved to Paris in 1936, and except for a period during the war, made a home there for the rest of his life. In 1937 he began an affair with the woman who became his lifelong partner, Suzanne Deschevaux-Dumesnil. Although he was not always faithful to her, they had a close relationship, and he married her in 1961. Suzanne was instrumental in furthering Beckett's writing career because, unlike the author, she was willing to hawk his manuscripts around to different publishers. She also took on teaching and sewing work when funds ran low, which, considering the small allowance given to Beckett by his family, was fairly often.

World War II broke out in 1939, and France fell to Germany in 1940. Beckett continued to live in Paris and in 1941 he joined the Resistance, translating and handling information for a local intelligence cell. After the war he was awarded the Croix de Guerre for this work. In 1942 Beckett's intelligence cell was betrayed to the Nazis, and Suzanne and Beckett fled Paris only hours before the Gestapo broke into their apartment. They traveled south, and spent the rest of the war living in seclusion in a village called Roussillon. Here he completed the novel *Watt,* which failed to find publication until 1953.

When Liberation came, Beckett and Suzanne moved back to Paris and, in spite of the deprivations brought by rationing and inflation, Beckett returned to writing. The following years proved extremely fertile in this regard, in part because of his decision to write in French. Between 1946 and 1950 Beckett wrote four novels, two plays, four long stories, and a piece of art criticism. These included the works which brought his breakthrough as a writer: the play *En attendant Godot*

(*Waiting for Godot*) and his *Trilogy* of novels. The publication in 1951 of the first two of these novels, *Molloy* and *Malone Meurt (Malone Dies)*, established his reputation in France, and the success of the first productions of *Waiting for Godot* from 1953 to 1955 brought him worldwide fame. However, there were also sadnesses in these years, with the deaths of his mother in 1950, and his beloved brother, Frank, in 1954.

The next two decades were ones of great activity, as Beckett visited many countries, directing and advising on productions of his plays. Beckett was sociable if not gregarious, and he formed lasting friendships with the artists and performers he met. However, he shied away from any publicity, and when he was awarded the Nobel Prize for Literature in 1969 he briefly went into hiding to escape intrusion from the press. For the most part he lived an ascetic existence with Suzanne in Paris and Ussy sur Marne, continuing to write poems, plays, and prose into old age. He died a few months after Suzanne on 22 December 1989.

AIMS AND INFLUENCES

IT is a difficult thing to write about the influences on Beckett's work. As an excellent scholar and linguist, he had an extensive knowledge of European literature and culture, and his notebooks and diaries are full of interesting phrases and ideas that he picked up from his reading. However, if Beckett draws on these in his writing, it is usually to negate them. Beckett believed that our experience of the world is essentially chaotic, and none of our modes of understanding can explain it. His early works parody the tendency of humans to rely on imposed systems and patterns in their attempt to find an order and meaning for their experience; so literary and philosophical references in these works are only made to reveal the inadequacy of their claims to "truth." This is particularly true of the frequent references to Cartesian philosophy, whose rational method was a point of both fascination and suspicion for Beckett. From the *Trilogy* onwards, allusions are so deeply embedded that to pursue, for example, a specifically philosophical interpretation of the text is to play into the hands of Beckett's attempts to undermine such closed methods of comprehension. This resistance to allusion extends to biographical references. While his works frequently draw on his own experience—memories of his childhood, French and Irish landscapes, feelings of grief or guilt—the experience is so abstracted into literary form that attempts to trace the specifics of original prompts become pointless.

Having said this, there was one influence which cannot be downplayed, and that is the writing of James Joyce. Joyce was a close friend and mentor to Beckett, and it was his experimental fiction that most inspired Beckett's decision to become a writer. Both men sought to redefine the forms in which experience was narrated in literature. However, where Joyce did this by including in his narratives every thought of his characters, every possible etymology and allusion, Beckett worked by stripping away what he considered excess content. He described this difference in an interview with Israel Shenker in 1956: "The more Joyce knew the more he could. He's tending towards omniscience and omnipotence as an artist. I'm working with impotence, ignorance" (*New York Times*, 5 May 1956, p. 3).

Elsewhere Beckett writes of wanting to tear language apart "to get at the things (or the Nothingness) behind it," and of dissolving the "terrible materiality of the word surface" (*Disjecta*, 1983, pp. 171–172). While these statements sound destructive, even nihilistic, they are tied to what, paradoxically, was an ambitious and inventive artistic project: to find a way of conveying the elements of lived experience that lie beyond the comfort of prefabricated forms and ideas. These elements would include unpredicted events, unthinkable emotions, and the gaps between physical and mental sensations or present and remembered time—all of which are in their very nature somewhere between "things" and "nothingness." But what preoccupied Beckett most was the "thing" or "nothing" beyond life: the space or void after death or before birth, which defines and haunts our lives but cannot be known within the terms of life. Time and again Beckett stripped back and reformed his modes of expression in an attempt to capture the sense of this "nothingness." Time and again he would feel he had failed, and would have to start again. Yet this failure was a necessary part of his effort of invention, and he described it in his *Three Dialogues* (1965) with Georges Duthuit in 1949, in a formulation which neatly summarizes the aims of his art: "The expression that there is nothing to express, nothing with which to express, nothing from which to express, no power to express, no desire to express, together with the obligation to express" (*Disjecta*, p. 139).

BECKETT'S EARLY WORKS

BECKETT'S early works were preoccupied with attempts to disrupt literary and philosophical conventions. His early poem *Whoroscope* (1930) rewrites Descartes's dictum, "Cogito ergo sum" ("I think therefore I am"), as "Fallor ergo sum" ("I make mistakes therefore I am"), and *More Pricks Than Kicks* (1934) and *Murphy* (1938) are full of erudite allusions and parodies.

More Kicks Than Pricks is a collection of comic stories that revolve around Belacqua Shuah, a difficult hero who lives his life at one remove. Belacqua is rather fittingly named after a character in Dante's *Purgatorio*, who having repented to God belatedly is obliged to spend a period equal to his lifetime waiting in Antepurgatory, the entrance to Purgatory, before he is allowed to enter and atone for his sins. The Belacqua of Beckett's book is similarly idle, and is denied access to the Absolute in all his mock-intellectual quests.

The first story in the collection, "Dante and the Lobster," is the most obvious case in point as it works as a mock-epic version of Dante's poem. Belacqua, who is studying *The Divine Comedy*, engages in a mock-epic battle with his lunch (he burns and "vanquishes" his toast, he struggles to find the right piece of "alive" and "stenching" cheese); then he makes a mock-epic descent into the Underworld (his aunt's basement), where a lobster is boiled alive for his dinner. Belacqua is horrified at the thought of this cruel punishment of a live creature, but comforts himself with the thought that "it's a quick death, God help us all" (*More Pricks Than Kicks*, 1970, p. 14, p. 21). At this point the narrative voice, which has remained sympathetic to Belacqua's perspective until now, suddenly retorts, "It is not."

This sudden intervention, which forms the last words of the chapter, throws the authority of the preceding action, and the reader's judgment of it, into crisis. Belacqua, who we have safely identified as the hero of the narrative, has his heroic status brutally undercut, and we are left without a focalizing point through which to understand events. Nor can we trust the narrative voice as omniscient, because two chapters later it reveals itself to be a "sometime friend" of Belacqua who has given up trying to track the hero's movements

(p. 39). Final judgment is suspended, and the narrative is left in an Antepurgatorial void.

Beckett repeats these suspensions throughout the collection of stories. Every time a degree of textual knowledge becomes possible, every time a picture of the world begins to be composed, it is negated by a chance intervention or event. Belcqua loses two wives through twists of fate before dying unexpectedly during a minor medical operation. Even then the narrative does not close with him, but continues in a chapter about his remains, entitled "Draff" ("draff" is the remains of malt left after the brewing process, which farmers feed to swine).

Beyond his obvious delight in unexpected turns of plot and language, Beckett's motive here is clearly to question the neat conclusions that are conventionally made in fiction. His refusal of closure even extends to the text's intolerance of unifying metaphors. The chapter entitled "A Wet Night" contains a gentle parody of the closing moments in Joyce's story "The Dead," from *Dubliners*. Where Joyce uses the snow falling in Dublin as a devastating metaphor for the loss and paralysis which pervades the city, Beckett echoes the metaphor in bathetic fashion by commenting that the rain "fell upon the bay, the littoral, the mountains and the plains, and notably upon the Central Bog it fell with a rather desolate uniformity" (*More Pricks Than Kicks*, p. 87).

The point here is not to show up the inadequacy of Joyce's technique, but to underscore the form and tone that Beckett feels is most fitting to the worldview he is presenting; or, rather, problematizing. If humanity's experience of the world is chaotic and confused, and its attempts to impose order frequently fail, then why should its fictional version create a false sense of coherence? *More Pricks Than Kicks* reflects the incoherence of its hero's life through its deliberately incoherent form.

The target of interrogation in *Murphy* is philosophical rather than literary coherence. The eponymous hero of the novel is in many ways an ironic reflection of Beckett, because like the author during this period, he lives an impoverished life in London. Like Belacqua, Murphy is never more than half-engaged with the world around him, and resists the efforts of his girlfriend, Celia, to force him into paid employment. However, the resistance is for a reason, because he is engaged in a methodical exploration of the different realms of his consciousness.

Murphy considers himself in Cartesian terms as being "split in two, a body and mind" (*Murphy*, 1963, p. 76). He lives by the teachings of Descartes's follower, Arnold Geulincx, whose dictum—"Ubi nihil vales, ibi nihil velis" ("Where you are worth nothing, there you should want nothing")—taught that man lacks the power to control the actions of the external world, but is free within his own mind. Murphy attempts to cut himself off from the actual world and retreat into the deepest recesses of his mind, to a "zone of darkness" where he can float "as a mote in the dark of absolute freedom" (p. 79). He fails, however, to achieve a properly reasoned and ascetic detachment from the world and his body, since he is constantly distracted by his passions and physical appetites, in particular his "deplorable susceptibility to Celia" (p. 124). The comedy of the novel stems from the fact that Murphy has mistaken his freedom *from* will for freedom *of* will, so his attempts to gain systematic knowledge always end in disaster. His categorization of jokes and biscuits; his experiment in psychology with a waitress; even his work in a mental asylum, which he hopes will provide sanctuary from the "colossal fiasco" of the real world: all are brought down by the accidents and contingencies of his lived experience (p. 123). The final grand irony of the novel comes when Murphy does achieve the freedom he craves, but only through his accidental death by the "superfine chaos" of escaped gas (p. 173).

Beckett took his literary and philosophical debunking to its logical conclusion in his next novel, *Watt*, which was written between 1941 and 1944, but not published until 1953. That it took so long to find a willing publisher is not surprising, as at times its narrative verges on the unreadable. *Watt* follows the eponymous hero from a station, to his work in service at the house of a Mr. Knott. Here he meets various other servants, learns the complexities of feeding Mr. Knott and emptying his chamber pot, then leaves to make way for another servant. Beyond these facts little is learnt, for the narrative is invaded by Watt's exhaustive efforts to conduct rational inquiry according to logical rules. No trivial detail is deemed unworthy of this attention. Pages are devoted to the careful listing of all the possible combinations of bringing the dog together with the bowl of Mr. Knott's leftovers; a similarly long section lists every relation and ailment of the local Lynch family, and even to describe Watt walking takes a lengthy paragraph that catalogues each individual leg movement.

The resulting experience for the reader is somewhere between high comedy and screaming boredom. The book is still recognizably in the tradition of Irish authors such as Jonathan Swift and Laurence Sterne, who employed the progressive, rationalist ideas of their time parodically to halt the progress of their narratives. However, Beckett pushes this ruse almost to the point of madness. So infinite is the scope for minute description and digression that its narrative cannot close in the conventional sense, and has to be abandoned. *Watt* ends with an "Addenda" of material that, a footnote claims, only failed to be incorporated in the main body of the narrative because of "fatigue and disgust" (*Watt*, 1963, p. 247). The novel interrogates its conventions of knowing and narrating until they have literally worn out.

POST-WAR PROSE: BECKETT'S BREAKTHROUGH

WATT was written during the World War II, and much of it was completed while Beckett was in hiding from the Gestapo in Roussillon. It is possible to read the prevalent sense of monotony in the novel as stemming from the boredom Beckett must have felt at this time, waiting for liberation and engaged in grinding manual labor. However, the real impact of this period, and Beckett's full realization of the horrors that had taken place in the war, only begins to be traceable in his work of the immediate post-war period.

Beckett produced an astounding amount of writing between 1946 and 1950, including the works that brought his breakthrough after years of obscurity: the novel *Trilogy* and the French text of *Waiting for Godot*. This extraordinarily fertile period followed what Beckett described to friends and critics as a "revelation" of the path he should subsequently follow in his work. This path is clearly the way of "impoverishment," the exploration of "impotence" and "ignorance" which he alluded to later in his interviews concerning Joyce. As such it extends the "decreative" and anti-epistemological aims of his pre-war novels and stories. However, the visions and journeys of the writing of this period are considerably darker than the largely comic early works. They are not only concerned with mental angst but with physical deprivation and torment. The heroes now wander like vagrants in alien, depopulated landscapes, and the forces which determine their worlds are not simply indifferent and arbitrary, as they were in *More Pricks Than Kicks* and *Murphy*, but hostile and sadistic. Beckett's portrayal of the "nothingness" behind human language and systems becomes infused with a sense of unthinkable suffering and emptiness which modern writers and thinkers have come to represent consciousness "after Auschwitz."

Nevertheless, to historicize Beckett's writing in this period is not to explain it completely. The biggest change in his work after the war lay in his shifting focus to an internalized mode of narrative—in particular through his use of monologue—which enabled him to explore the contingencies and uncertainties of subjective consciousness in a more integrated form. Beckett also began to write predominantly in French, and although he was extremely fluent, the inevitable strangeness of writing in his second language proved fruitful in conveying the experience of being an unknowing or unknowable subject. The sense of rootlessness and uncertainty in the stories he wrote in 1956—"La Fin" (The End), "L'Expulsé" (The Expelled), "Premier Amour" (First Love), "Le Calmant" (The Calmative), and the whimsical novel *Mercier et Camier (Mercier and Camier)*—seems to rest in their sense that the language they are using is somehow alienated from the experience they are describing. But it was not until his *Trilogy* of novels—*Molloy, Malone Meurt (Malone Dies)* and *L'Innommable (The Unnamable)*—written between 1947 and 1950, that Beckett fully exploited this effect. The *Trilogy* goes so far in interrogating the form and narration of experience that the recognizable novelistic "content" of life histories and events ceases to have any significance. All that matters is a few fundamental questions: Who is writing or speaking? Why are they writing or speaking? And to what end(s) is their narrative written or spoken?

Molloy is divided into two long chapters, each of which is apparently narrated by a different character. In the first part, Molloy tells us that he is in his mother's room, having been brought there in some kind of vehicle. Now he sits and writes for a man who comes every week, pays him, and collects the pages. Molloy does not know how long he has been in the room, or what has happened to his mother, but he proceeds to describe the journey he made to find her before his last collapse. Molloy frequently digresses from his story, as his mind is elderly and prone to wandering. The progress of his narrated journey is similarly dis-

tracted: he loses his way, he loses his bicycle (his prop for his bad leg), and having lost his temper, he kicks and bludgeons a man he meets in a forest. Eventually he loses his capacity to walk, and falls prostrate in a ditch, which is where his narrative ends.

The narrator of the second chapter is called Moran and seems, at first, to be the opposite of Molloy. Where Molloy is chaotic, indifferent and decrepit, Moran is correct and fastidious. Moran is writing a report about his work as an "agent." He describes how he was sent by Gaber, the messenger of his "organisation," on a mission to find Molloy. He seems half-familiar with Molloy, associating him with "a gallery of moribunds. Murphy, Watt, Yerk, Mercier, and all the others" he has dealt with in the past (*Trilogy*, 1979, p. 126). However, as soon as he sets out on his quest he begins to suffer a Molloy-like fate: one of his legs becomes paralyzed, he has to send for a bicycle, and while stranded in the wilderness he bludgeons a man to death whose face "vaguely resembled [his] own"(*Trilogy*, p. 139). Eventually he is ordered home, but his progress back is slow because he becomes increasingly decrepit. He finds his house deserted and disordered.

These plot summaries give little sense of the nature of the narratives, which are not concerned for the most part with events. Molloy's narrative is full of darkly comic deliberations over his declining body, and while Moran attempts to stick to facts, his journey leaves him feeling "dispossessed of self" and unable to focus (*Trilogy*, p. 137). Yet it is clear from even these bare bones of plot there are peculiar parallels between the two halves of the novel. Both Molloy and Moran are impelled in some way to go on their journey and to write about it. Each of the monologues and each of the narrated journeys is circular in movement. Both protagonists cause death and become more and more decrepit throughout the story. Neither finds the person they are seeking. More strangely, the two characters seem, eventually, to collapse into each other, and even into other Beckettian heroes.

The mystery of who these people are, and why and wherefore they wander and write, is increased by the fact that the texts are monologues. There is no authoritative narrative voice, so as readers we are as blind to what is determining events as the protagonists. There are many subtextual clues as to what is going on. Molloy's quest could be read psychoanalytically as being an infantile search for the mother, and as Moran's wayward doppelgänger in the second narrative, he could represent the unconscious of Moran's repressed self. There are many embedded references to rationalist philosophy, which might imply that the heroes are on a quest for self-knowledge. And the names of Moran's bosses may be significant. "Youdi" (from the Arabic *yahudi*) is the colloquial French word for Jew, and echoes the Old Testament God, Yahweh. "Gaber" may suggest Gabriel, God's messenger. This would hint at why Molloy and Moran cannot comprehend their directives, for the ways of God "passeth all understanding." Yet none of these interpretations is more convincing than the others, so like the heroes' journeys, they end up at deathly and unfathomable destinations.

Such are the number of interpretative dead ends that we may assume that Beckett is deliberately throwing us red herrings. Rather than seeking explanations, we might, then, ask why there are no explanations. One of Molloy's sly asides might give us an answer. At one point, having described his physical disabilities, he half-resists explaining why he spent so long in one place: "But why should I? In order to establish beyond all question that I could not do otherwise? For that is the conclusion I would come to, fatally" (*Trilogy*, p. 48).

The syntax of this final sentence, and the wordplay on "fatally," suggests that his inability to go, or to get anywhere if he does, is bound up with the inevitably fatal conclusion to all human effort. Making reference to Geulincx's theories of the free mind, and to Ulysses' epic sea quest, Molloy seems to be consoled by the fact that because his boat "bears me from no fatherland away, [it] bears me onward to no shipwreck." The heavy irony here not only undermines Cartesian rationalism, it takes a sideswipe at all those grand aesthetic quests of literary modernism, including Joyce's. The narrative wanderings of Beckett's heroes are rootless and pointless, and the only place they can be sure of reaching is the no-place of their own deaths. By acknowledging this, at least grand hopes for meaning will not be shipwrecked.

And yet the characters still wander, still write. Indeed, the obligation to continue writing is all that is left at the end of both characters' wanderings. Beckett's formulation in the *Three Dialogues* that there is "nothing to express . . . together with the obligation to express" haunts the whole of his

novel, and is finally (fatally) its only conclusion. Faced with the inevitable non-progress towards death, all anyone can do is write and invent—and try to trace the course of this non-progress. In some profound sense there is nothing else to be done.

Having destroyed all paths to explanation in *Molloy*, this idea of obligatory invention is all that is left to ponder in *Malone Dies* and *The Unnamable*. Considering the poverty of its sentiments, it proves surprisingly fertile ground.

Malone lies immobile and dying in a room. His death is imminent, but while he waits, he decides to tell himself stories. The stories he tells, he determines, will have "no ugliness or beauty or fervour in them any more, they will be almost lifeless, like the teller" (*Trilogy*, p. 166). The almost lifeless stories and their almost lifeless author manage to keep going for nearly a hundred pages. In the process, plots are spun and characters are invented but no narrative or identity lasts for very long. Malone begins with a tale of a young man called Saposcat, who seems to become an old tramp called Macmann; then Malone digresses into a tale about a certain Lemuel. Midway through this story, Malone's narrative dries up, suggesting that he has died.

The ever-changing cast is at once a symptom of Malone's fading powers and the only thing that is keeping him alive. There is no point, coherence, or consistency to any of the life histories he tells, including his own life history. Malone's identity blurs with that of his invented characters and with the characters of previous Beckett novels: he owns the same possessions as Molloy; he makes oblique allusions to other Beckett plots; and he speaks collectively of "the Murphys, Merciers, Molloys, Morans and Malones" (p. 217). Yet, as long as this list continues, as long as he makes them and himself up, death and silence do not take place: "Live and invent. I have tried. Invent. It is not the word. Neither is live. No matter. I have tried" (*Trilogy*, p. 179).

This is not to say that death does not actually happen, but that it cannot happen within narrative; it cannot be described in words. Even when Malone stops inventing, we cannot be sure that he has died, because our knowledge of his existence or nonexistence is completely dependent on his narrative.

It is at this point that all the dead ends of *Molloy* and *Malone Dies*, and Beckett's declarations about "nothingness" and "impoverishment" come into focus. For Beckett is clearly attempting to express an unspeakable paradox. Words, narrative, are futile, and express nothing, because they cannot shed light on the one thing worth expressing, and for which all expressions are destined: the death of the one who expresses. And yet while they are failing in this expression, they fill up the profound emptiness that the speaker or writer feels at the prospect of death, perhaps even kidding them into imagining they are killing time. Through their inability to grasp death, words provide a very necessary distraction from the unthinkable fact of human mortality. This is why there is always an "obligation to express."

However, Beckett does not rest with this paradox. In *The Unnamable,* he goes on to explore its flip side, if such a thing is possible. The narrator in the last book of the *Trilogy* does not know where he is or who he is, goes nowhere and has no sense of time: "Where now? Who now? When now? Unquestioning. I, say I. Unbelieving. Questions, hypotheses, call them that. Keep going, going on, call that going, call that on" (*Trilogy,* p. 267). He cannot be dead, because he is still speaking, but neither is he conventionally alive. His bodily existence seems to have fallen away, and he relies on his "delegates" to tell him stories of the world of men, which he relates in his narrative. These delegates are a further set of moribunds, and, once again, The Unnamable's identity seems to blur with theirs. The only difference to former characters of the *Trilogy* is that they are not simply decrepit or dying, but almost non-existent. Basil is arbitrarily renamed Mahood, and then Worm. At first he seems to have a single leg, then only a torso, then, as Worm, he becomes "nothing but a shapeless heap" (p. 328). In fact, Worm is unborn, not yet "humanized," "life trying to get in, no, trying to get him out" (p. 131, p. 135).

The question that *The Unnamable* appears to be asking is, if narrative cannot delay death, and cannot speak of it directly, can it, strictly speaking, express life either? If words are only a distraction from the fate of the speaker, are they not also inadequately placed to describe his beginnings and his present existence? The complete disorientation of the narrative in this novel, the preoccupation with being unable to be born and unable to die, or even to know the difference between these two states, would seem to answer this question in the negative. The experience narrated in *The Unnamable* is merely that of language being spoken: "Two holes and me in the middle, slightly choked. Or a single one, entrance and exit, where the words swarm and jostle like ants, hasty, indifferent, bringing nothing, taking nothing away, too light to leave a mark" (*Trilogy,* p. 326).

Words "buzz" and "murmur" somewhere between eating and excreting, birth and death, but never capture or coincide with this journey. He cannot control or possess his words and they cannot capture him. This is why the Unnamable can never rightfully narrate his "own" self: "I seem to speak, it is not I, about me, it is not about me" (p. 267). At the end of the novel he is still on the threshold, waiting "before the door that opens on [his] own story" (p. 382). It will, of course, never open, because the conclusion of Beckett's narrative is that nothing can be revealed. And yet this lack of revelation also means that there is no conclusion, no end to the narrative. Coming from nothing and going to nothing, undead and unalive, all words can do is continue to distract. Even if it is hardly bearable, the obligation remains: "you must go on, I can't go on, I'll go on."

BECKETT'S EARLY DRAMA

IF Beckett's most enduring preoccupation is with the failure of humanity's systems and patterns to find meaning, his fascination with the endless possible reinvention of the form of these systems and patterns also never fades. On the level of artistic form, this is most apparent in Beckett's drama. Beckett initially turned to writing for the theater as a relief from the tortures of writing his vexed postwar prose. His first full-length play, *Eleutheria* written in 1947, explored the familiar Beckettian theme of freedom, but was for the most part a parody of different dramatic genres, ranging from melodrama and boulevard comedy to absurdist farce. It is an uneven and underdramatized work, and Beckett withdrew it from public circulation before it was produced or published. *Waiting for Godot* was first produced in the failing Théâtre de Babylone in Paris in 1953. Having slowly gained audience numbers and notoriety among Parisian theatergoers, it was translated and produced across Europe. It took a further two years to find financial backing and actors in England and America, and even then the play met with mixed responses: critics in London panned, then raved about the 1955 production, and in 1956 it flopped in Miami before finding success on Broadway. This slow-burning momentum has gathered ever since, so that now *Waiting for Godot* is perhaps the best-known play of the twentieth century. However, in terms of Beckett's dramatic innovations it was just the beginning. For the next thirty years he continued to strip away most of the dead wood of conventional theater and cross-fertilized its forms with those of other arts and media. The result of his efforts was some of the most startling and enduring images—two men and a tree; a woman buried up to her neck; figures in urns and ashbins—and some of the most perfectly cadenced dialogue in modern theater. Simply put, Beckett's theater changed the rules of what could and should count as "drama."

Waiting for Godot is a play founded on repetitions. It rehearses the excruciating bind of having to continue to exist without anything happening, and without knowing why or for what one is there. Or to be more specific, and less metaphysical, the play depicts the excruciating bind of two men who are confined to a particular time and place, waiting for someone who never arrives.

Vladimir and Estragon, two friends who live like vagrants, find themselves beside a tree on a country road. Estragon suggests they leave, but Vladimir says this is not possible because they are "waiting for Godot" (*Complete Dramatic Works*, p. 15). Vladimir is not sure where, when, or why exactly they are meeting him, and he fails to materialize. However, other people do arrive: First, Pozzo, a verbose and self-important man, and his servant, Lucky, who Pozzo whips and keeps with a rope around his neck. Then a Boy arrives, who says he is Godot's messenger. He informs Vladimir and Estragon that Godot won't be coming today but "surely tomorrow" (p. 49). Alone again and dejected, Vladimir suggests to Estragon that they should go, and Estragon contemplates hanging himself from the tree. They do neither, and remain on stage as the first act ends. The action of the second act is all but identical to the first: four or five leaves are on the tree; Pozzo (blind) and Lucky (dumb) return but do not recognize Vladimir and Estragon; a Boy (it is uncertain whether he is the same boy) brings the same message from Godot. After another failed suicide they decide to go, but do not move.

The puzzle, and the brilliance, of *Waiting for Godot* is that it repeatedly gestures towards so many influences and explanations without being defined by any of them. Allusions to vaudeville, and echoes of J. M. Synge's poet-beggar figures and of the symbolist dramas of Maurice Maeterlinck or

W. B. Yeats, are conjoined with a reflexive meta-theatrical joke: audiences and characters alike are waiting for something to happen. One can read the play through its embedded references to Bishop Berkeley's dictum, "Esse est percipi" ("To be is to be perceived"), for the two protagonists are most concerned that Godot should know they have been *seen* by his messenger boy. Or one can read it through Vladimir's continual worry over the reliability of the Apostles' accounts of the Crucifixion: lacking certain knowledge of their situation, the two tramps cannot know if, like the two thieves, they are to be "saved" or "damned." All such interpretations may illuminate, but do not "explain" the action of the play, because the whole point of the play's repetitive structure is that no revelation or conclusion—no Godot—is forthcoming.

Such dead ends and half-allusions in Beckett's prose *Trilogy* lead to a depiction of the sheer endurance of the human effort to write and invent. Here, the echoes and repetitions work to reveal a similar endurance, but one that, in keeping with the theatrical context, roots its inventiveness in physical and spoken acts. Vladimir and Estragon are forever waiting, caught in an endless physical presence, and an endlessly present time; on stage and in time. Yet this presence is one which they cannot trust in, cannot experience as the "here and now," because it is constantly interrupted by the anticipation, or dread, of what might come in the future, and the uncertainty of what has happened in the past. Their pointless banter, ritualized games and physical clowning are all "habits," mere distractions that deaden the radical uncertainty of their predicament, but as such, they are very necessary habits—even only as comic relief. Moreover, in performing these acts and rituals together, they can be temporarily relieved of the responsibility of their terrible unknowingness. Even if being perceived (and thus being) in this way does not prevent the feeling of it being unbearable, it enables, forces them to go on. This is why Vladimir and Estragon cannot leave each other, and nor can Pozzo and Lucky (in spite of the cruelty of their relation), and also why Beckett reportedly once said that his play was all about "symbiosis."

Symbiosis persists in Beckett's next stage play, but the diversionary repetitions and rituals are in terminal decline. Written in French as *Fin de partie*, and first performed in 1957, *Endgame* revolves around Hamm and Clov, one white-faced the other red-faced, making the final moves of an elaborate chesslike game. As in *Waiting for Godot,* their situation is uncertain. They are in a room surrounded by a deserted, barren landscape. The cause of this sterility is not known, but when Clov looks out of the window with his telescope, all he sees is "Zero" and "Grey" (p. 106). Considering when the play was written, it is tempting to think of some postnuclear setting, and Hamm's name might also suggest a Biblical Flood (Hamm was one of Noah's sons). But the lack of landscape could just as well be a meta-theatrical joke, because after all there is nothing to see through stage set windows. Indeed, self-conscious theatricality is in the air. The handkerchief draped over Hamm's head is raised and dropped like the stage curtain. Hamm and Clov banter and set up one-liners as if they are in an improvisation competition:

CLOV: What is there to keep me here?
HAMM: The dialogue.
    (*Complete Dramatic Works,* p. 121)

A "ham" is, of course, also a colloquial term for a bad actor, and Hamlet one of the great tragic roles. Hamm sees himself as a leading man, and spends much of the play gearing up for his "last soliloquy," but his blindness and senile ranting more closely resemble King Lear than the Danish prince. As both actor and chess piece he is clinging onto his position long after he should have relinquished his throne.

Survival is the root of the play, but not in any triumphant sense of the word. Hamm and Clov are both clinging onto "this . . . this . . . thing," even though they have both had more than enough (p. 94). They are like Vladimir and Estragon, or Pozzo and Lucky several acts after *Waiting for Godot* ends. They are utterly sick of each other, yet wholly dependent upon each other, because there is nothing else and no one else beyond—not even the prospect of a Godot figure. The only other human figures in the play are Hamm's parents, Nagg and Nell, and a small boy who Clov spies through the window near the end of the play. Nagg and Nell are mere remainders of people, trapped in ashbins and crying like infants for their "pap." The little boy may just be a figment of Clov's imagination. Hamm tries to conjure tales of past activities and acquaintances but they trail off into confusion. Everything is running down and running out. And there will be no second act, so no possibility of change.

The players are left with virtually no room for maneuvering, yet in some strange way this forces the exaggeration of their efforts. In fact, the excess and "staginess" of Hamm and Clov's performances is precisely what indicates the desperation of their circumstances. Beckett is following through the logic of the prose *Trilogy* and *Waiting for Godot* to its end, tracing the futile but endlessly inventive effort of humans to compose some order out of the chaos that surrounds them. As a representation of the final moments of this effort, *Endgame* presents its last pathetic flounderings. The real tragedy of humanity is that faced with meaninglessness and death, it can only "cry in darkness" and "remain" (pp. 133 and 134).

The "remains" in *Krapp's Last Tape* (1959) endure through more mechanical means. Beckett had already exploited sound effects in a play for radio, *All That Fall* (1957), but *Krapp* was one of the first times Beckett employed new, traditionally non-theatrical media in his work for the stage. The tape recorder at the heart of the play has a disruptive effect on audience expectations of plot and character because the snatches of old recordings we hear interrupt, distort, and replicate the time of the play's action and the personality of its protagonist.

The action of the play is simple. Krapp, a solitary old man, eats bananas, paces about his room, listens to a tape he recorded on his thirty-ninth birthday, and records his thoughts now, thirty years later. Krapp uses the tape machine as a kind of externalized memory device, revisiting meticulously catalogued "moments" in order to compare his present self with his younger self. He seems to be trying to order his life experience, and seeking to reconcile the conflicting sides of his character—intellectual, spiritual, emotional, libidinal—but the evidence his tapes give him hinder his efforts. For while the recordings show up the dreary repetitiveness of his singular life across the years, they also fail to reveal any continuity in his thoughts and motivations. A moment of intellectual "fire" and "revelation" which the younger Krapp treasured is of no significance to the old Krapp; and old Krapp returns obsessively to a moment of lyrical intimacy with a woman that the younger Krapp discarded (*Complete Dramatic Works,* p. 220). Even sitting at the end of his life, Krapp is unable to experience his own self in its entirety, for his current feelings impel him to edit the material he listens to.

This uncanny sense of the dislocation of the self, or selves, is most comically evident in Krapp's pause over the word "viduity." Used casually by the younger Krapp, in his reflection over his mother's death, the old Krapp no longer has any idea what it means. When he looks up the word in the dictionary the definition, "Being—or remaining—a widow—or widower," causes him to pause confusedly: "Being—or remaining?" emphasizes the peculiar, but very real, difference between the two states, (p. 219). To "be" a widow does not mean one will remain one, just as to "be" Krapp does not mean that he will remain the same Krapp. And yet at the same time to "be" *is* to "remain," to be left behind when others die, like Krapp's mother after her husband, Krapp after his mother, or the aging Krapp after his youthful self has declined. Krapp is increasingly aware that his position now, as a decrepit old man, is one of "remaining." The longer he listens to his tapes the more they serve as a cruel reminder of what has been lost, a marker of how he has widowed himself.

THE DRAMA OF THE 1960s—
MOVING TO MINIMALISM

THE significance of the recorded moments in *Krapp's Last Tape* stems as much from the different shades of light and dark, from the varying tones of voice, as from the actual "meaning" of what is said. Beckett had been obsessed by the unity of form and content in writing since his early criticism, but in his work for the theater, shape and structure take on a whole new importance. In addition to the different sounds and patterns of language, Beckett pinpoints cadences of speech, and exploits a range of nonverbal signifiers—lights, music, movements, the physical geography of the actors, gestures, facial expressions—which mold the sense of the dramatic action. As a director of his own plays, Beckett spent a literally painful amount of time perfecting the tiniest modulations of voice or gesture in his actors, and throughout the 1960s and 1970s the plays became increasingly reliant on these elements. Critics have frequently read this formal development as Beckett's attempt to perfect his "literature of the unword." Yet such interpretations need to be qualified, as they risk suggesting that Beckett finally leaves language behind and finds some kind of alternative refuge in the truth of purely physical or visual communication. In fact, only the thirty-five

second-long *Breath* and two of the late television plays bypass words completely. It seems more accurate to think of his effort as being to ensure that neither verbal nor nonverbal forms are preeminent. Words are still important, though not as content-laden, directly referential signifiers. Rather, as with the physical and technical aspects of theater, they are suggestive, expressive, forming patterns without claiming full and final "meaning." The tensions created by this interaction of different strains enable Beckett's desired dissolution of the "terrible materiality of the word surface."

This is true of Beckett's 1961 play *Happy Days*, which works through conflicts between levity and weight, and light and dark. Winnie, the heroine, sits buried up to her waist, then up to her neck, in a mound of earth, in a desolate, harshly lit landscape. Her only company is her husband, Willie, who sits unresponsive and almost out of sight, behind the mound. Like so many of Beckett's characters, she is subject to tyrannical directions; this time in the form of a bell, which rings to signal when she must wake and when she must sleep. In the face of this horrifying situation, Winnie remains impossibly optimistic. She chatters away to Willie, she sings "her" song and she selects and uses various objects—toothbrush, toothpaste, hairbrush, mirror—from her handbag. The only object she does not use is a gun, which, once removed from the bag, sits ominously beside her on the mound.

There is no naturalistic explanation for Winnie's predicament. However, this does not mean the situation is nonsensical. For below the "word surface" there are significant patterns of association. Winnie thinks of herself as a creature of the air, as "the thrush, or the bird of dawning, with no thought of benefit, to oneself or anyone else." She imagines that were it not for the mound of earth, she would float away, "like gossamer" (*Complete Dramatic Works*, pp. 151–152). While directing the 1979 production of *Happy Days* at the Royal Court Theatre, Beckett described Winnie as "a bird with oil on her feathers," and told the actress Billie Whitelaw to "give a kind of pecking quality" to the way Winnie picks up the objects from her bag. This is not to say that Winnie is literally a bird. She is obviously a familiar type of middle-aged woman: nostalgic and stoical, with a strong sense of propriety. Yet the bird analogy indicates the pull of directions that determines the play. Regardless of the precise reason for Winnie's entrapment, she is straining to lift herself up, to transcend the gathering force of the earth, and perhaps the grave. The tension between the great weight bearing upon her and her aspiration to fly represents a struggle for freedom.

Having said this, it is difficult to reach conclusions about the moral or ideological significance of the play's struggle. The audience is not witnessing a simple oppositional conflict, for while we may admire Winnie's spirit, and even see her as a symbol of human courage in the face of adversity, there is nothing defiant about her flutterings. In fact, the longer we witness Winnie's efforts to remain buoyant, the more they seem part of her constraint. As they are repeated, her "on/off" smiles and clichéd phrases begin to seem less her own, less a sign of genuine optimism, than a forced, half-conscious routine. It is as if she is aware of something existing beyond the bell and the light—the freedom, perhaps of "eternal dark" she once mentions—but is even more frightened of this than of her gradual decline (p. 166). Ultimately Winnie's loquaciousness, like her endless toothbrushing and bag searching, is a form of displacement activity which tries desperately to ward off the silence and darkness which are rapidly encroaching upon her. The words mean little in themselves, but beneath the "word surface" they speak volumes about the pathological compulsion of humans to continue in spite of the void.

If the bright light in *Happy Days* is purgatorial, in *Play* (1964) it is infernal; a "Hellish half-light," as one of the protagonists calls it (*Complete Dramatic Works*, p. 312). Three characters—a man (M) and two women (W1 and W2)—sit in darkness in identical gray urns, with only their heads protruding. A spotlight provokes them into speech, at first in chorus, and then individually. The speakers seem unaware of each other, but as they speak, it gradually becomes apparent that they are connected through the events they are relating: the sordid story of the man's betrayal of his wife (W1), and his affair with the other woman (W2). These events took place before the "change" took place, and they found themselves in urns. Now they are condemned to repeat their different versions of their little melodrama over and over again, the light dictating when they can and cannot speak.

Play was written in English in 1962–1963, and first performed in German, in Germany, in 1963. Within Beckett's dramatic oeuvre, it marks a point of transition. Its staging, situation, and language

all share resemblances with earlier plays—the figures in urns are reminiscent of Nagg and Nell in their dustbins in *Endgame,* and the purgatorial setting and clichéd language of the characters echo *Happy Days*—but the technical precision and the tight, almost musical structure of the dialogue anticipate Beckett's late minimalist drama. The sequential movement of light and speech, flowing rapidly between different urns, distances the audience from the action to the point where it seems at times like a composition of images and sounds. Yet in spite of this, the play does not simply operate on an abstract level. The form is still grounded in the different emotions and reactions of the characters; they even address the light as if it has an inner life and, like them, is caught in the endless spiral of repetition and decline.

By the end of the 1960s, Beckett's drama had found its way to the same residual, "unnamable" experience as his prose *Trilogy* had examined. Theatrical content had been reduced to the point where what is being spoken, what is speaking it, and to whom it is speaking is barely determinable. The sheer labor of continuing to perform in the face of this is excruciating. W2 in *Play* says it is "Like dragging a great roller, on a scorching day" (p. 315). Nevertheless, the performance continues, just as the Unnamable continued to "go on," like the tiny flickering moment between the light growing and fading in *Breath* (1969), or like the characters in *Come and Go* (1967), who are individually doomed but caught in a seemingly endless moment, linked together like rings.

LATE PLAYS—FIGMENTS AND FRAGMENTS

GIVEN that Beckett's late drama functions in the uncanny space between being and not being, it is not surprising that it displays a preoccupation not only with the moments preceding death, but with ghosts, phantoms, memories, disembodied voices, and all that remains after life. The most startling and literal example of this is in *Not I*, which was written and performed in 1972. The protagonist of the play is an illuminated mouth, called simply Mouth, which speaks into the darkness of the stage and auditorium. Mouth's stream of words can be heard from the moment the house lights go down to when they come up again, but they are only intelligible while the curtain is raised and the audience's attention is directed fully at the horrifying spectacle of the disembodied orifice. The only interruption to this focus comes from an equally anonymous "Auditor," which stands downstage and occasionally raises its arms "in a gesture of helpless compassion" (*Complete Dramatic Works*, p. 375).

The impact of this play is on a visceral rather than intellectual level. The shock of Mouth on the visual and aural senses of the audience thwarts their attempts to understand what is happening: by the end of the performance they feel as helpless as the Auditor. However, the thematic concerns of the play are very close to *The Unnamable*. Mouth seems to be female rather than male, but she shares the Unnamable's space of narration, physically absent or dead apart from the hole that spews forth language. She does not know where she is or who she is, or was, before "all went out," but she is nevertheless compelled to describe this confusion. The flow of language is uncontrollable, like a basic bodily function without the body:

> . . . sudden urge to . . . tell . . . then rush out stop the first she saw . . . nearest
> lavatory . . . start pouring it out . . . steady stream . . . mad stuff . . . half the vowels wrong. . . .
> (*Complete Dramatic Works*, p. 382)

This is strongly reminiscent of the Unnamable's "two holes and me in the middle," and like him, Mouth resists referring to herself in the first person. Her narrative veers between describing a life of great loneliness and neglect, and describing the state of nonbeing, but neither thread of narrative converges to form a present-tense "I." Indeed, at points, where the realization dawns on Mouth that she may be referring to herself, the flow of words falters, and she cries, insistently, "what? . . who? . . no! . . she!" Mouth's speech is never still enough to be present, and comes from somewhere before and beyond the personal. It is "all dead still but for the buzzing" (p. 379), the white noise of the merest existence, one point away from degree zero.

Not I is probably Beckett's most nerve-racking play, but his later period of drama also explores near-nothingness in other, more lyrical forms. *Footfalls* (1976) dramatizes the torment of a ghostly figure who does not know where she "began" (*Complete Dramatic Works*, p. 401). *That Time* (1976), considered by Beckett as "a brother to *Not I*," focuses on another disembodied protagonist—the head of an old man—but this time he listens rather than speaks. The old man listens to three voices, which are his own narrating different periods of his solitary life: middle age (voice A), old age (voice C), and youth (voice B). In this sense, there are resemblances to *Krapp's Last Tape*, but whereas the earlier play recorded deliberate, "voluntary" memory, the flow of narrative here emulates the dreamlike feel of involuntary memory; a free association of images and locations washing in and out of consciousness.

The moments before death are treated in a more singular fashion in *Rockaby* (written in 1980, performed in 1981). In this play a "prematurely" old woman, dressed in an ornate black frock, rocks, or is rocked, in her rocking chair, while an untraceable voice narrates the gradual winding down of her life:

> till in the end
> the day came
> in the end came
> close of a long day
> when she said to herself
> whom else
> time she stopped
> *time she stopped*
> going to and fro
> (*Complete Dramatic Works*, p. 435)

It is uncertain whether the voice is her own, a detached commentator's or the ghost of memory. Although the voice seems to be referring to the present action, it speaks in the past tense, and towards the end of the play there is a syntactical ambiguity which suggests that the voice could be talking about the old woman's mother; for she too "rocked / all the years / all in black / best black." When the line "time she stopped" occurs, the old woman joins in with the voice, but otherwise she listens to it, apparently for comfort, asking for "more" every time the narrative comes to a halt. Gradually the old woman's request becomes fainter, until, at the end of the play, her head inclines onto her chest, implying she has died.

The extraordinary beauty of this play comes from the way the voice's narrative ebbs and flows, falling back onto a refrain only to find new variations. The modulations of voice move with the rocking chair, whose rhythms draw out the woman's dying moments, as if obeying her will to carry on living. The overall effect is of the final fight for breath: a sudden gasp of air, with its accompanying flood of consciousness, images, memories, followed by a slow decline into stillness. The last burst of movement brings not an acceptance of death exactly, but a startling dismissal of life—"fuck life," spits the voice—as if the effort of breathing is just too much to make any more

The minimalist nature of Beckett's late plays means that they stretch the possibilities of theatrical performance to their limits. Ambiguity of place, space, and time are relatively easy for an audience to accommodate, but the reduction of action to a set of movements or sequence of linguistic motifs can be almost unendurable. Arguably, some of Beckett's later dramas for the stage are too static. While the shock of the ranting Mouth in *Not I* might root audiences to the action, the smiling head of *That Time* is perhaps too subtle a visual focus in a space as large as the theater. Beckett's late plays operate in the ethereal realms of memory, dreams, and imagination, and thus seem to require a more interior space than the theater can provide.

This is presumably why Beckett turned to television in his last plays. The little box gave him both the scale and technical sophistication he needed to conduct his final explorations of the mind. *Ghost Trio* (1976), *. . .but the clouds. . .* (1976), and *Nacht und Traüme* (1984) stand out as his most groundbreaking experiments in the medium. These plays rehearse familiar Beckettian ideas—a man waiting in a room for a woman who never arrives, or a man methodically trying to reconstruct a memory—but the televisual context alters the tone radically. Beckett employs different camera shots and angles to slowly piece together a collage of impressions, and uses continual fade-outs to suggest a lack of conclusion or resolution. Each play is structured around a faint snatch of music, a few lines of a poem or a remembered image. The music and poetry are themselves echoes from other great lyrical works: Beethoven's Fifth Piano Trio; Yeats's poem *The Tower*; Schubert's Lied, *Nacht und Traüme*. The overall effect is both intimate and elusive. The physicality of the theater disappears completely, and what we are left with in each case is a delicate sketch of the spectral quality of human longing, grief, and love—all indefinable feelings, which haunt us nevertheless.

The elegiac beauty of these pieces is no doubt due in part to the medium, but could also perhaps be due to Beckett writing them in great old age: *Nacht und Traüme* was completed when he was seventy-six. Whatever the reason, this is some of his most moving and forgiving work, not just revealing the cruel uncertainties of speaking and "being" in time, but mourning its losses and dwelling lovingly on what remains behind.

LATE PROSE

No trace anywhere of life, you say, pah, no difficulty there, imagination not dead yet, yes, dead, good, imagination dead imagine.

(*Complete Short Prose*, 1995, p. 182)

As in drama, so in prose. As this quotation from the 1965 prose text, *Imagination Dead Imagine*, makes clear, Beckett's concern in his late prose was with the fragments and figments of imaginary forms which persist beyond life or at the point of death. His writing in prose after the *Trilogy* rehearses the same uncertainties of time, place, and identity that were voiced in *The Unnamable*, but goes ever further in its exploration of the different possibilities of expression. Just a selection of the titles of these late, brief pieces—*Texts for Nothing, Imagination Dead Imagine, Enough, Lessness, Fizzles, Stirrings Still*—conveys the twin poles of reduction and elaboration which Beckett is working around. There is less and less content, less concern with "what" is being narrated, but an ever-increasing focus on "how" narration happens. By the time Beckett wrote the texts often referred to as his late prose trilogy—*Company* (1979), *Ill Seen Ill Said* (1982), and *Worstward Ho* (1983)—he had distilled his narrative to the point where it simply rehearses and queries the processes of its own production.

Company narrates someone (the first person) imagining somebody else (the second person), who hears a voice in the dark (the third person). The text revolves around the different listeners and speakers as a way of asking where the narrative voice exists. *Ill Seen Ill Said*, like *Rockaby*, repeats the routine of an old lady who watches and is watched. And *Worstward Ho* progresses through the merest alterations and movements of language. Beginning with an injunction, "On. Say on," and ending with a statement of the impossibility of continuing, "Nohow on," the text's sentences move between the variations of language which emerge from the basic situation of there being an imagined voice:

On. Say on. Be said on. Somehow on. Till nohow on. Said nohow on.

> . . . All of old. Nothing else ever. Ever tried. Ever failed. No matter. Try again. Fail again.
> Fail better.
>   (*Worstward Ho*, in *Nohow On*, 1989, p. 101)

The narrative comes into being, then fades away again, without ever quite wearing out. Every time it threatens to end it falls back onto the refrain, "Said nohow on," which urges it to make one more impossible effort.

In his late prose Beckett leaves little to be said, especially by critics, because there are no more meanings or references to be extracted. What remains are the echoes of voice, the cadences of endless linguistic variations, the trace elements of the act of creative writing. As a final expression of the "nothingness" and necessity of expression, it could be said to "fail better" than his previous experiments in narrative form.

SELECTED BIBLIOGRAPHY

I. COLLECTED WORKS. Poetry: *Collected Poems 1930–1978* (London, 1984). Prose: *No's Knife: Collected Shorter Prose 1945–1966* (London, 1967) (*Collected Shorter Prose, 1945–1980* (London, 1984); *The Complete Short Prose, 1929–1989* (New York, 1995). Plays: *Collected Shorter Plays* (London, 1984); *The Complete Dramatic Works* (London, 1986).

II. POETRY. *Whoroscope* (Paris, 1930), repr. in *Collected Poems 1930–1978* (London, 1984); *Echo's Bones and Other Precipitates* (Paris, 1935), repr. in *Collected Poems 1930–1978* (London, 1984); *Poems in English* (London, 1961); *Poèmes* (Paris, 1968); *Poems in English and French* (London, 1977); *Poèmes suivi de Mirlitonnades* (Paris, 1978); *Comment dire* (Paris, 1989), trans. as *What Is the Word*, in *As the Story Was Told: Uncollected and Late Prose* (London, 1990).

III. PROSE. *More Pricks Than Kicks* (London, 1934; repr. London, 1970); *Murphy* (London, 1938; repr. 1963).

Molloy (Paris, 1951), trans. by Patrick Bowles and Samuel Beckett (Paris, 1955); *Malone meurt* (Paris, 1951), trans. as *Malone Dies* (London, 1958); *L'Innommable* (Paris, 1953), trans. as *The Unnamable*, in *Trilogy (Molloy, Malone Dies, The Unnamable)* (London, 1959; repr. London, 1979); *Watt* (Paris, 1953; repr. London, 1963); *Nouvelles et textes pour rien* (Paris, 1955); *From an Abandoned Work*, in *Trinity News*, Vol.111, no. 4 (1956), repr. London, 1958 and in *No's Knife* (London, 1967).

Comment c'est (Paris, 1961), trans. as *How It Is* (London, 1964); *Imagination morte imaginez* (Paris, 1965), repr. in *Têtes-mortes* (Paris, 1967) and trans. as *Imagination Dead Imagine* (London, 1965), trans. repr. in *No's Knife* (London, 1967); *Assez* (Paris, 1966), repr. in *Têtes-mortes* (Paris, 1967); *Bing* (Paris, 1966), repr. in *Têtes-mortes* (Paris, 1967) and, trans. as *Ping*, in *No's Knife* (London, 1967); *Têtes-mortes* (Paris, 1967); *Sans* (Paris, 1969), trans. as *Lessness* (London, 1970).

Mercier et Camier (Paris, 1970), trans. as *Mercier and Camier* (London, 1974); *Le Dépeupleur* (Paris, 1970), trans. as *The Lost Ones* (London, 1972); *Premier Amour* (Paris, 1970), trans. as *First Love* (London, 1973); *Au loin un oiseau* (New York, 1973), trans. as *Afar a Bird*, in *For to End Yet Again and Other Fizzles* (London, 1976); *Still* (Milan, 1974, repr. London, 1975), repr. in *For To End Yet Again and Other Fizzles* (London, 1976); *Pour finir encore et autres foirades* (Paris, 1976), trans. as *Fizzles* (London, 1976); *For To End Yet Again and Other Fizzles* (London, 1976); *All Strange Away* (New York, 1976); *Company* (London, 1979).

Mal vu mal dit (Paris, 1981), trans. as *Ill Seen Ill Said* (London, 1982); *Worstward Ho* (London, 1983); *Stirrings Still* (New York and London, 1988); *Nohow On*, collects *Company, Ill Seen Ill Said*, and *Worstward Ho* (London, 1989).

As the Story Was Told: Uncollected and Late Prose (London, 1990); *Dream of Fair to Middling Women* (London and Paris, 1992), unpublished novel written in 1932.

IV. PLAYS. *En attendant Godot* (Paris, 1952), trans. as *Waiting for Godot* (London, 1956); *All That Fall* (London, 1957); *Fin de partie, suivie de Acte sans paroles* (Paris, 1957), trans. as *Endgame, A Play in One Act, Followed by Act Without Words, a Mime for One Player* (London, 1958); *Krapp's Last Tape*, in *Krapp's Last Tape and Embers* (London, 1959); *Embers*, in *Krapp's Last Tape and Embers* (London, 1959).

Happy Days (London, 1962); *Words and Music*, in *Evergreen Review*, vol. 6 (1962), repr. in *Play and Two Short Pieces for Radio* (London, 1964); *Acte sans paroles II*, in *Dramatische Dichtungen*, Vol. 1 (Frankfurt, 1963), repr. in *Comédie et actes divers* (Paris, 1966) and trans. as *Act Without Words II*, in *Eh Joe and Other Writings* (London, 1967); *Cascando*, in *Dramatische Dichtungen*, Vol. 1 (Frankfurt, 1963), repr. in *Comédie et actes divers* (Paris, 1966) and trans. as *Cascando* in *Play and Two Short Pieces for Radio* (London, 1964); *Play*, in *Play and Two Short Pieces for Radio* (London, 1964); *Come and Go* (London, 1967); *Eh Joe*, in *Eh Joe and Other Writings* (London, 1967); *Film*, in *Eh Joe and Other Writings* (London, 1967); *Breath*, in *Gambit*, vol. 4, no. 15 (1969), repr. in *Breath and Other Short Plays* (London, 1972).

Not I (London, 1973), repr. in *Ends and Odds* (London, 1977); *Theatre I and Theatre II*, in *Ends and Odds* (London, 1977); *Rough for Radio I*, in *Stereo Headphones 7* (spring 1976), repr. as *Radio I* in *Ends and Odds* (London, 1977); *Rough for Radio II* (New York, 1976), repr. as *Radio II* in *Ends and Odds* (London, 1977); *That Time* (New York, 1976), repr. in *Ends and Odds* (London, 1977); *Footfalls* (London, 1976), repr. in *Ends and Odds* (London, 1977);

Ghost Trio, in *Journal of Beckett Studies* 1 (winter 1976), repr. in *Ends and Odds* (London, 1977); *. . . but the clouds . . .* (1976), repr. in *Ends and Odds* (London, 1977); *A Piece of Monologue,* in *The Kenyon Review,* New Series, vol. 1, no. 3 (summer 1979), repr. in *Rockaby and Other Short Pieces* (New York, 1981; repr. London, 1982).

Rockaby, in *Rockaby and Other Short Pieces* (New York, 1981; repr. London, 1982); *Ohio Impromptu,* in *Rockaby and Other Short Pieces* (New York, 1981; repr. London, 1982); *Catastrophe,* in *Catastrophe et autres dramaticules* (Paris, 1982), trans. as *Catastrophe* (London, 1984); *What Where,* in *Ohio Impromptu/Catastrophe/What Where* (New York, 1983), repr. in *Collected Shorter Plays* (London, 1984); *Quad,* in *Collected Shorter Plays* (London, 1984); *Nacht und Träume,* in *Collected Shorter Plays* (London, 1984).

Éleuthéria (Paris, 1995) unpublished play written 1947, trans. as *Eleutheria* (New York, 1995).

V. CRITICISM. "Dante . . . Bruno. . . . Vico . . . Joyce," in *Our Exagmination Round His Factification for Incamination of Work in Progress* (Paris, 1929; repr. London, 1961); *Proust* (London, 1931), repr. with *Three Dialogues: Samuel Beckett and Georges Duthuit* (London, 1965); *Disjecta. Miscellaneous Writings and a Dramatic Fragment,* ed. by Ruby Cohn (London, 1983).

VI. PRODUCTION NOTEBOOKS. James Knowlson, ed., *Happy Days: Samuel Beckett's Production Notebook* (London and Boston, 1985); *The Theatrical Notebooks of Samuel Beckett,* 4 volumes (London, 1992, 1993, 1999), Vol. 1, *Waiting for Godot,* ed. by Dougald McMillan and James Knowlson, Vol. 2, *Endgame,* ed. by S. E. Gontarski, Vol. 3, *Krapp's Last Tape,* ed. by James Knowlson; Vol. 4, *The Shorter Plays,* ed. by S. E. Gontarski.

VII. BIOGRAPHIES. Deirdre Bair, *Samuel Beckett: A Biography* (London and New York, 1978); Enoch Brater, *Why Beckett* (London, 1989); Lois Gordon, *The World of Samuel Beckett, 1906–1946* (New Haven, 1996); James Knowlson, *Damned to Fame: The Life of Samuel Beckett* (London, 1996).

VII. CRITICAL STUDIES. John Fletcher, *The Novels of Samuel Beckett* (London, 1964); Martin Esslin, ed., *Samuel Beckett: A Collection of Critical Essays* (Englewood Cliffs, N. J., 1965); Raymond Federman, *Journey to Chaos: Samuel Beckett's Early Fiction* (Berkeley and Los Angeles, 1965); Martin Esslin, *The Theatre of the Absurd* (Harmondsworth, U.K., 1968); Hugh Kenner, *Samuel Beckett: A Critical Study* (Berkeley, 1968).

Raymond Federman and John Fletcher, *Samuel Beckett: His Works and His Critics* (Los Angeles, Berkeley, and London, 1970); Lawrence E. Harvey, *Samuel Beckett, Poet and Critic* (Princeton, 1970); Davis Hesla, *The Shape of Chaos: An Interpretation of the Art of Samuel Beckett* (Minneapolis, 1971); Ruby Cohn, *Back to Beckett* (Princeton, 1973); Hugh Kenner, *A Reader's Guide to Samuel Beckett* (London, 1973); Katherine Worth, ed., *Beckett the Shape Changer* (London and Boston, 1975); John Pilling, *Samuel Beckett* (London, Henley, and Boston, 1976); Clas Zillia-cus, *Beckett and Broadcasting: A Study of the Works of Samuel Beckett for and in Radio and Television* (Åbo, Finland, 1976); Vivian Mercier, *Beckett/Beckett* (New York, 1977); Richard Admussen, *The Samuel Beckett Manuscripts: A Study* (Boston, 1979); Barbara Reich Gluck, *Beckett and Joyce: Friendship and Fiction* (Lewisburg, Pa., and London, 1979); Lawrence Graver and Raymond Federman, eds., *Samuel Beckett: The Critical Heritage* (London and Boston, 1979); James Knowlson and John Pilling, *Frescoes of the Skull: The Later Prose and Drama of Samuel Beckett* (London, 1979).

Ruby Cohn, *Just Play: Beckett's Theater* (Princeton, 1980); Maurice Blanchot, "Where Now? Who Now?" in *The Siren's Song: Selected Essays* (Brighton, 1982); Charles R. Lyons, *Samuel Beckett* (Basingstoke, U.K., London, and New York, 1983); Rubin Rabinovitz, *The Development of Samuel Beckett's Fiction* (Urbana and Chicago, 1984); S. E. Gontarski, *The Intent of Undoing in Samuel Beckett's Dramatic Texts* (Bloomington, 1985); Linda Ben-Zvi, *Samuel Beckett* (Boston, 1986); Enoch Brater, ed., *Beckett at 80: Beckett in Context* (New York and Oxford, 1986); Peter Gidal, *Understanding Beckett* (Basingstoke and London, 1986); James Acheson and Arthur Kateryna, eds., *Beckett's Later Fiction and Drama: Texts for Company* (Basingstoke, U. K., and London, 1987); Enoch Brater, *Beyond Minimalism: Beckett's Late Style in the Theater* (New York and Oxford, 1987); Alan Friedman, Charles Rossman, and Dina Scherzer, eds., *Beckett Translating: Translating Beckett* (University Park, Pa., 1987); Harold Bloom, *Samuel Beckett's Molloy, Malone Dies, The Unnamable* (New York, 1988); Steven Connor, *Samuel Beckett: Repetition, Theory, and Text* (Oxford, 1988); Dougald McMillan and Martha Fehsenfeld, *Beckett in the Theatre* (London, 1988); Rosemary Pountney, *Theatre of Shadows: Samuel Beckett's Drama 1956-76* (Gerrards Cross, U.K.,1988); Nicholas Zurbrugg, *Beckett and Proust* (Gerrards Cross, U.K., 1988); Robin J. Davis and Lance St. John Butler, *"Make Sense Who May": Essays on Samuel Beckett's Later Work* (Gerrards Cross, U.K., 1989); Jonathan Kalb, *Beckett in Performance* (Cambridge, 1989).

Linda Ben-Zvi, *Women in Beckett: Performance and Critical Perspectives* (Urbana and Chicago, 1990); Lance St. John Butler and Robin J. Davis, *Rethinking Beckett: A Collection of Critical Essays* (Basingstoke, U. K., and London, 1990); P. J. Murphy, *Reconstructing Beckett: Language for Being in Samuel Beckett's Fiction* (Toronto, 1990); John P. Harrington, *The Irish Beckett* (Syracuse, N.Y., 1991); John Pilling and Mary Bryden, eds., *The Ideal Core of the Onion: Reading Beckett Archives* (Reading, 1992); Rubin Rabinovitz, *Innovation in Samuel Beckett's Fiction* (Urbana, 1992); Eyal Amiran, *Wandering and Home: Beckett's Metaphysical Narrative* (University Park, Pa., 1993); Marius Buning and Lois Oppenheim, eds., *Beckett in the 1990s* (Amsterdam and Atlanta, 1993); S. E. Gontarski, ed., *The Beckett Studies Reader* (Gainesville, Fla., 1993); Anna McMullan, *Theatre on Trial: Samuel Beckett's Later Drama* (New York and London, 1993); Christopher

Ricks, *Beckett's Dying Words* (Oxford, 1993); Lois Oppenheim, *Directing Beckett* (Ann Arbor, 1994); John Pilling, ed., *The Cambridge Companion to Beckett* (Cambridge, 1994); Richard Begam, *Samuel Beckett and the End of Modernity* (Stanford, 1996); Mel Gussow, *Conversations with (and About) Beckett* (London, 1996); James Acheson, *Samuel Beckett's Artistic Theory and Practice: Criticism, Drama, and Early Fiction* (Basingstoke, 1997); Mary Bryden, *Samuel Beckett and the Idea of God* (Basingstoke and New York, 1998).

Paul Davies, *Beckett and Eros: The Death of Humanism* (Basingstoke and New York, 2000); Lois Oppenheim, *The Painted Word: Samuel Beckett's Dialogue with Art* (Ann Arbor, 2000); David Pattie, *The Complete Critical Guide to Samuel Beckett* (New York, 2001).

WILLIAM BLAKE

(1757–1827)

Grevel Lindop

WILLIAM BLAKE WAS born on 28 November 1757 in the Soho district of London, where his father kept a small shop selling gloves, stockings, and haberdashery. Since the art and poetry of Blake's adult life would flow from his powerful sense of spiritual vision, it is disappointing that we know almost nothing about the religious life of his parents. Probably, like many London tradespeople, they were Dissenters—devout, Bible-reading Protestants who remained outside the established Church of England because they believed that its clergy and rituals came between the individual soul and God, and who disliked the Church's support for monarchy and aristocracy. Even this, however, is guesswork based partly on Blake's own later views. All we know for certain is that even as a child William Blake revealed an almost overwhelming faculty of imaginative vision, and an immense talent for drawing. When he was four years old he once screamed with fright because he "saw God put his head to the window." Once "his mother beat him for running in & saying that he saw the prophet Ezekiel under a tree in the fields" and on other occasions he saw "a tree filled with angels" and angelic figures amongst haymakers in a meadow (Bentley, *The Stranger from Paradise*, p. 19).

Blake's education was unconventional. His mother probably taught him to read, and he is said to have attended school only briefly, because he would not tolerate the beatings that were then a normal feature of the classroom. Since he drew constantly and with great ability, he was sent at the age of ten to Pars's Drawing School, where he learned figure-drawing (mainly from plaster casts of Greek and Roman sculpture) and began to collect prints—engraved reproductions of paintings by Old Masters such as Raphael and Michelangelo, whose then unfashionable work became for him a lifelong enthusiasm. At fourteen he went on to a seven-year apprenticeship with an engraver, James Basire, who taught him the craft by which he would afterwards live.

Engravers were regarded as skilled craftsmen rather than artists. Their job was to take paintings or drawings by professional artists, and copy them on to metal plates from which they could be printed either for sale as pictures, or for use as book illustrations. Blake had aspirations to become more than a mere copier, and attended drawing classes at the Royal Academy in the hope of eventually becoming a professional painter. But since he had little money and no wealthy patron, this ambition remained unfulfilled.

EARLY WORKS

IN 1782 Blake married a London girl, Catherine Boucher. She was intelligent, though uneducated (Blake himself taught her to read, write, and draw), and it was to be a long and happy marriage. At about the same time came Blake's first publication, a seventy-page pamphlet called *Poetical Sketches* (1783). Its printing, for private circulation rather than sale, was paid for by a clergyman, the Rev. A. S. Mathew, whose home was a center for literary and artistic gatherings where Blake was known for reading his poems and sometimes singing them to music of his own composition.

Poetical Sketches shows a strange mixture of styles and subjects, with flashes of poetic brilliance and many small but daring experiments in poetic form. According to Mathew's somewhat apologetic preface, some of the poems were written when Blake was still a child. We do not know which ones, except that "How sweet I roam'd . . ." was written before he was fourteen. There are shapely and harmonious "songs" with echoes of Shakespeare; there is crude Gothic horror (as in the unrhymed ballad of "Fair Elenor"); there is a fragment of poetic drama (*Edward III*) imitating Shakespeare's Histories. Other poems show Blake alert to the first stirrings of Romanticism, drawing inspiration from the fake-medieval poems of Thomas Chatterton and the prose poetry of James

Macpherson's pseudo-Celtic Ossian. "To the Muses" suggests that Blake believes British poetry to be almost dead, forsaken by the Muses:

> How have you left the antient love
>   That bards of old enjoy'd in you!
> The languid strings do scarcely move!
>   The sound is forc'd, the notes are few!
>   (p. 417)[1]

Blake seems determined to find new inspiration. He demonstrates it most promisingly in poems that view nature with almost religious awe, seeing spiritual beauty and energy everywhere and combining sharp visual imagery with a daring choice of rhythms and line endings that defies the end-stopped neatness of eighteenth-century convention. In "To the Evening Star" Blake addresses the star as "fair hair'd angel of the evening" and urges it to:

> Let thy west wind sleep on
> The lake; speak silence with thy glimmering eyes,
> And wash the dusk with silver.
>
>   (p. 410)

The four poems on the seasons treat the times of year as dynamic titans, and "Winter" is portrayed as a cruel, steel-clad, scepter-wielding tyrant king: clearly Blake's first vision of the figure who will become one of his greatest creations, the Urizen of the later poems.

Grateful though he must have been for Mathew's generosity in funding *Poetical Sketches*, Blake made little effort to distribute it and even mocked Mathew and his circle in a satirical prose fragment written around 1784. *An Island in the Moon*, as it is known (the outer pages and original title are lost), gives a farcical account of a group of absurd characters—philosophers like Sipsop the Pythagorean and Quid the Cynic, scientists like Inflammable Gass and Obtuse Angle, scholars like Etruscan Column the Antiquarian, and prim, religious ladies like Miss Gittipin and Mrs. Nannicantipot. They argue, squabble, shout, and sing, competing for attention and engaging in surrealistic debate, offering us a parodic view of a second-rate eighteenth-century intellectual salon in full cry.

Besides showing that Blake could write sharp satire, *An Island in the Moon* offers two other revelations. First, when Miss Gittipin demands, "Pray, Mr Obtuse Angle, sing us a song," the mathematician responds by singing an untitled poem ("Upon a holy Thursday, their innocent faces clean . . .") which anyone who knows Blake's mature work will recognize as "Holy Thursday" from *Songs of Innocence* (1789). Mrs. Nannicantipot responds by singing "Nurse's Song," and Quid follows with "The Little Boy Lost," after which, for a while, "nobody could sing any longer" (p. 463). The appearance of three *Songs of Innocence* in this crazy context is startling enough; but it is followed—after a gap where, frustratingly, some pages have been lost—by a character, perhaps Quid, announcing plans for the production of splendid books: " 'Then,' said he, 'I would have all the writing Engraved instead of Printed, and at every other leaf a high finish'd print—all in three Volumes folio—& sell them a hundred pounds apiece. They would print off two thousand.' 'Then,' said she, 'whoever will not have them will be ignorant fools & will not deserve to live' " (p. 465). Apparently Blake had not only started writing the poems which would form *Songs of Innocence*, but was also thinking about producing his own engraved and decorated books.

Serious experiments leading to Blake's unique "illuminated books" began in 1788–1789, a highly creative period which produced four remarkable works. One, *Tiriel*, was never engraved or printed, and exists only as a manuscript and a set of eight pen-and-wash drawings, perhaps originally intended as the basis for an illustrated book of the kind projected in *An Island in the Moon*. Why Blake abandoned *Tiriel* we do not know. It is a powerful work, brief but epic in style, about the downfall of a tyrant king who is also a cruel father. The echoes of Shakespeare's *King Lear* are obvious as the blind and aged Tiriel curses his children and sets out to wander alone through wild country, but Tiriel's troubles, far more than Lear's, are self-created. Grasping and egoistic, preoccupied with self-pity and revenge, he has no love for anyone. In his wanderings he comes to "the vales of Har," a curious enclosed land where Har and his sister Heva, an aged but childlike pair, live a life of insipid triviality, cared for by their mother Mnetha: "Playing with flowers and running after birds they spent the day, / And in the night like infants slept, delighted with infant dreams" (p. 277). Their world is perhaps the world of an

---

[1] All page references refer to the *Complete Poetry and Prose*, ed. by David V. Erdman (rev. ed., New York, 1982), unless otherwise noted.

Adam and Eve who have failed to gain experience or to confront life, remaining instead in an Eden which has become their prison. Tiriel conceals his identity, but after further wanderings and bitter encounters with other members of his family he returns to Har and Heva. Tiriel dies, after revealing that he is the son of Har and with his last words blaming Har for the emotional damage that has made him the miserable being he has been.

Tiriel is a confusing and somewhat incoherent work, but then it exists only as an abandoned draft. It shows clearly that Blake was concerned already with what would become his recurrent themes: spiritual blindness; compassion and cruelty; oppression in the nation and in the family. It also shows his power to create symbolic figures that are memorable in themselves and suggest many meanings. Is Tiriel a caricature of the current English monarch, mad King George III, or is he every unjust ruler and every cruel father? Is it significant that Mnetha's name recalls that of Mnemosyne, the Greek goddess of memory and mother of the Muses? Is Blake deliberately rewriting *King Lear* or, indeed, the classical Greek drama of the blinded, wandering King Oedipus? The questions cannot be answered, but the poem challenges us to explore all these possibilities and more, and to find our own emotional responses to these disturbing, dreamlike characters and events. *Tiriel* is the first in a series of works by which Blake will challenge all our assumptions about reading and imagining, and will force us to explore ourselves as well as his meanings.

About the same time Blake produced two tiny books (*There Is No Natural Religion* and *All Religions Are One*), each made up of pages not much larger than postage stamps, asserting the importance of the "Poetic Genius" or creative principle in each person. Each of these little books consists of a series of numbered propositions like those in a philosophical treatise. In addition, *There Is No Natural Religion* establishes a pattern that was to become important for Blake, for it is written in two contrary "series." The first series shows the inadequacy of ideas of education and knowledge that exclude the "Poetic or Prophetic" (p. 3); the second series asserts the importance of exploration, aspiration, and above all of "see[ing] the Infinite in all things" (p. 3). The two parts of the book thus argue against, and supplement, one another. It was a pattern which would recur in Blake's work, and one of the ways in which he

ensured that his work could never be reduced to a single, static meaning, but would remain unstable, argumentative, and alive.

There Is No Natural Religion and *All Religions Are One* are important in another way, for they are Blake's first "illuminated books," in which he used the unique method of design and printing which would characterize all his greatest works. The method, which Blake later claimed was taught to him in a dream by his beloved brother Robert, who had died in 1787, is known as "relief etching." It involved writing and drawing directly onto a copper plate, using a pen or brush dipped into an acid-resistant varnish. Instead of laboriously copying a preexisting design with an engraving tool, as conventional engraving required, the new method allowed Blake to decorate his page and write his text as spontaneously as if he were working on paper. Once the writing and drawing were complete, the plate was put into acid, which would "bite" away any copper not covered by the varnish. Thus the lines drawn by Blake would be left standing up as ridges on the plate. Carefully inked and run through a small hand-turned printing press with a sheet of paper, the plate would leave a fine clear impression that could be printed again as often as necessary. The impressions could then be colored with watercolor, and details could be added or changed in pen-and-ink. The result was a supply of richly colored pages, each an individual work of art, which could be made up into books. Since an engraved plate prints in reverse, any text had to be written backwards; but "mirror-writing" was a skill taught to all apprentice engravers, and Blake became steadily more skilled at it until his reverse calligraphy was beautiful as well as clear.

THE BOOK OF THEL *AND* SONGS OF INNOCENCE

IN 1789 Blake produced two of his finest Illuminated Books, which are also among his greatest poetical works. One was *The Book of Thel*, which, in a pastoral setting, depicts a young shepherdess hesitating on the brink of existence. We may think of her as an unborn spirit about to enter the world of material birth, as a child on the verge of adolescence, or more specifically as a virgin about to enter the realm of sexual experience: as so often, Blake leaves this for our own interpretation. Thel questions the meaning of life and agonizes over the fact that it seems to lead only to death: "O life of this our spring! why fades the lotus of the water? / Why fade these children of the spring? born but to smile & fall" (p. 3).

In her quest she interrogates four creatures (a "Lilly," a cloud, a worm, and a clod of clay) that seem to symbolize constituents of nature (plant, atmosphere, animal, and mineral) as well as the four elements of water, air, fire, and earth. Each of these beings, in its own poignant way, advocates trust and submission to the ecological and spiritual cycles whereby each gives itself, without resentment, for the good of others. But Thel cannot accept this. Clay, the earthly mother figure, grants her a vision of life in the world, but Thel perceives only darkness and suffering, summed up in a series of anguished questions pointing to the vulnerable and constricted nature of human life:

Why cannot the Ear be closed to its own destruction?
Or the glistning Eye to the poison of a smile! . . .
Why a tender curb upon the youthful burning boy!
Why a little curtain of flesh on the bed of our desire?

(p. 6)

Horrified at what she hears, Thel "fled back unhinderd till she came into the vales of Har" (perhaps the same Har whom we encountered in *Tiriel*, though Blake could not expect his readers to know that earlier, unpublished poem). She has rejected existence, seeing only its dark sides. The poem leaves us to decide whether or not she has done the right thing.

Blake's other and even greater achievement in 1789 was *Songs of Innocence*. Most readers encounter Blake's *Songs* in the later, two-part work, *Songs of Innocence and of Experience*. It is worth remembering that *Songs of Innocence* was originally published alone, as a freestanding work celebrating the spontaneous joy, trust, and integrity of early childhood. Whether Blake always intended to pair this with its troubled and skeptical counterpart, *Songs of Experience*, we do not know. The contrasting first and second "series" of *There Is No Natural Religion*, a book that contains two contrary views, might lead us to guess that a two-part structure had always been part of his plan. But there is no real evidence either way. Since Blake was by 1789 running a small book- and print-shop with a friend, and children's books were coming into fashion for the first time, it may be that initially *Songs of Innocence* was intended simply as an attractive book for children.

If so, it is a remarkably rich and complex one, despite its surface simplicity. *Songs of Innocence* contains a multitude of voices: male and female, black and white, adult and child. The keynote of them all is a happy confidence, whether in the most idyllic circumstances ("Laughing Song" or "The Shepherd") or the most terrible (as in "The Chimney Sweeper," where the child laborer, who has been "sold" by his father and must sleep "in soot" after a long day of dangerous work, concentrates on comforting a companion and finds hope in his dream of an angel with "a bright key" who will set the boys free from their sufferings). Yet the poems are not complacent. The last line of "The Chimney Sweeper," "so if all do their duty they need not fear harm" (p. 10), comforting for a child audience, may contain a veiled threat for the adult who reads it. Surely the adult's task is to intervene and press for change: reformers stressed that it was a sacred duty for citizens to prevent such exploitation, and Blake does nothing to conceal the horror of the sweeper's plight. But the child's innocence gives him an inner freedom: he can still dream, and he can still love.

Such poems are fraught with multiple meanings and ironies. Interpreting them, readers are forced to confront their own values and question their own ways of reading and thinking. Such complexities are evident in "The Little Black Boy," an implicit protest against slavery (which Blake loathed) that never mentions slavery as such, and even begins by seeming to accept the stereotypes of "black" and "white" so common in eighteenth-century England. Yet the poem progressively undermines the assumptions that make prejudice and slavery possible. "We are put on earth a little space," the boy sings, "That we may learn to bear the beams of love" (p. 9). All bodies are clouds that shade us during life from the blazing intensity of God's love. There is confidence in his assertion that in heaven the white boy may be less used than he to such love, and may need his protection; and a painful irony in his suggestion that, when all differences have been removed, the white boy may "then" love him. Blake does not conform neatly to modern political categories, but he does fundamentally challenge all the assumptions of his time about what it means to be human. His sheer concern for goodness and common humanity shines through the simple wording and the surprisingly subtle logic, as with so many other poems in *Innocence*.

Pain and danger are not lacking from the world of Innocence. But for those who share an Innocent vision, all is ultimately resolved in harmony. Humanity and nature are one in God ("I a child and thou a lamb, / We are called by his name," p. 9); "Old John with white hair" (p. 8), watching the playing of the children in "The Ecchoing Green," regains for a while the innocent joy of his own childhood; and all the lost children are found. In "Introduction" the poet portrays himself as a rural piper, inspired by the vision of a child on a cloud. In the final poem, "The Voice of the Ancient Bard," the poet has become a prophet, Biblical or Celtic, a bearded sage who summons the young to "come hither, And see the opening morn, / Image of truth new born"(p. 31). It is an optimistic vision: *Songs of Innocence* shows us the world as a Garden of Eden, flourishing in the hearts of individuals even where an unjust society fails to embody it outwardly. It suggests that each person preserves—and not only in childhood—some contact with a time before evil and cynicism entered consciousness. It was a vision Blake would always retain, but would never again present in such purity.

THE FRENCH REVOLUTION *AND* THE MARRIAGE OF HEAVEN AND HELL

1789 was a momentous year not only for Blake but for European history, for on 14 July the French revolution broke out. Blake was in sympathy with the initially democratic aims of the Revolution and believed, like many radicals of the time, that it marked the beginning of a new age, when visionary ideals of liberty and justice might at last become earthly realities. In fact the Revolution led to serious limitations of freedom in Britain as the government, fearful that revolutionary ideas might spread from France, censored the press and prosecuted political dissidents. In continental Europe the Revolution precipitated a series of wars that would rage almost unbroken until 1815. After 1789 Blake's work, responding to this changed world, became more openly revolutionary, but also grimmer, the radiant vision of Innocence challenged by the fire and darkness of Experience.

1791 produced two very different but equally revolutionary works. One was *The French Revolution*, intended as the first Book of "A Poem in Seven Books," of which the other six were apparently never written. The poem survives in a single copy, typeset in ordinary letterpress and without illustra-tions, produced for the London publisher Joseph Johnson. Johnson, a well-known radical who published, among other innovative writings, the works of Thomas Paine, had evidently planned to publish Blake's new poem but cancelled the project at an early stage. Whether this was through fear of government censorship or because, on consideration, he found Blake's work too unconventional, is not known. *The French Revolution* in the form that exists is an immensely vivid account, in epic style, of the Revolution's early days, focusing on the horrors of the Bastille, France's state prison, and on the debate in the French assembly, the Estates-General, between conservatives and revolutionaries. Blake's depiction of the seven prisoners in the Bastille, each one an emblem symbolizing a different aspect of the wretchedness caused by tyranny, is horrifically vivid. "In the tower nam'd Darkness," for example:

was a man
Pinion'd down to the stone floor, his strong bones
   scarce cover'd with sinews; the iron rings
Were forg'd smaller as the flesh decay'd, a mask of
   iron on his face hid the lineaments
Of ancient kings, and the frown of the eternal lion
   was hid from the oppress'd earth.

(p. 287)

And the speeches of Orleans, champion of democracy, contain some of Blake's most powerful and inspiring poetry:

. . . go, merciless man! enter into the infinite labyrinth
   of another's brain
Ere thou measure the circle that he shall run. Go, thou
   cold recluse, into the fires
Of another's high flaming rich bosom, and return
   unconsum'd, and write laws.
If thou canst not do this, doubt thy theories, learn to
   consider all men as thy equals,
Thy brethren, and not as thy foot or thy hand, unless
   thou first fearest to hurt them.

(p. 294)

Sadly, the poem breaks off before the destruction of the Bastille, which Blake might have treated in unforgettable style. *The French Revolution* is a powerful fragment and shows that Blake saw the revolution, and all history, as involving not merely individuals but also spiritual forces which made every event on earth part of a huge drama both psychological and cosmic, a perspective which would increasingly become central to his work.

The other major work of 1790 was *The Marriage of Heaven and Hell*, which is not only a hugely provocative satire on conventional religion and morality, but also one of Blake's finest self-published "illuminated books." Flames curl from the margins of the pages as if the book itself were on fire; angels, devils, vegetation, and flying figures proliferate between the lines of the text. With biting irony and relentless satire, Blake questions every assumption of his time about good and evil, heaven and hell.

Part of the stimulus for the book came from his close study of the writings of Emmanuel Swedenborg (1688–1772), a Swedish visionary whose teachings had aroused considerable interest in England, and whose ideas had recently led to the founding of a "New Jerusalem Church" in London. Swedenborg had taught that the Bible should be understood not literally but symbolically, as a series of metaphors and parables rather than as fact or history—a view that Blake found thoroughly congenial. Swedenborg also claimed that he had been taken by angels to visit Heaven and Hell, and gave a detailed account of his journeys in *Heaven and Its Wonders, and Hell* (1758). Blake seems initially to have been excited by Swedenborg's work, hoping that it might offer a more imaginative, compassionate, and spiritually direct alternative to the narrow teachings prevalent in the ordinary churches and chapels of the day, but by 1790 he had become disillusioned with Swedenborg who, he says, "has not written one new truth" and, worse, "has written all the old falsehoods" (p. 43). Blake parodies Swedenborg's visits to heaven and hell with his own ridiculous and grotesque cosmic journeys, in which he learns wisdom from devils and demonstrates the narrow-minded prejudice and pomposity of angels.

The most important insight of the *Marriage* is that "Without Contraries is no progression. Attraction and Repulsion, Reason and Energy, Love and Hate, are necessary to Human existence" (p. 34). Again Blake is pitting conflicting opposites against each other, and one result here is a challenge to reinterpret the notions of "good" and "evil." "Good," Blake proclaims, "is the passive that obeys reason. Evil is the active springing from Energy" (p. 34). With this startling vision of reality, in which "goodness" is a mere keeping of rules and "evil" another name for creativity, Blake enjoys mocking pious assumptions in the most shocking way. "As I was walking among the fires of hell," he tells us, "delighted with the enjoyments of Genius, which to Angels look like torment and insanity, I collected some of their proverbs" (p. 35), and he gives us seventy of these "Proverbs of Hell," a collection of astonishing aphorisms, by turns startling, beautiful, deeply disturbing, and simply wise. Like the poems in *Songs of Innocence* they reward reflection, revealing more depth and meaning the longer we consider them. "The tygers of wrath are wiser than the horses of instruction" (p. 37) seems a straightforward endorsement of righteous indignation; "Prisons are built with stones of Law, Brothels with bricks of religion" (p. 36) suggests both social protest and subtler psychological reflections on repression. "The most sublime act is to set another before you" (p. 36) appears to champion an ideal of unselfishness; yet "sooner murder an infant in its cradle than nurse unacted desires" (p. 38) suggests an inhuman degree of selfishness—unless the "infant[s]" to be killed are in fact the "desires" which one would otherwise, in a telling metaphor, "nurse." The proverbs frequently contradict each other. As "Proverbs of Hell," they represent the thoughts people dare not think, for whatever reason: the inconvenient, the uncomfortable, the embarrassing, the socially unacceptable, or personally inadmissible. They force us to think and they allow us to take nothing for granted.

Besides questioning notions of morality, the *Marriage* questions the nature of our world and our perception of it. As one of the "proverbs" says, "A fool sees not the same tree that a wise man sees" (p. 35), and a basic concern of the *Marriage* is the idea that our world is shaped, and often severely limited, by our perceptions. At one point Blake asks, "How do you know but ev'ry Bird that cuts the airy way / Is an immense world of delight, clos'd by your senses five?" (p. 35).

And he asserts that "If the doors of perception were cleansed every thing would appear to man as it is, infinite. For man has closed himself up, till he sees all things thro' narrow chinks of his cavern" (p. 39). Religion, he tells us, began with the visions of: ancient Poets [who] animated all sensible objects with Gods or Geniuses, calling them by the names and adorning them with the properties of woods, rivers, mountains, lakes, cities, nations, and whatever their enlarged and numerous senses could perceive. . . . Till a system was formed, which some took advantage of, & enslav'd the vulgar . . . thus began priesthood" (p. 38).

The object of *The Marriage of Heaven and Hell* is, it seems, to "cleanse" the "doors of perception" by breaking established patterns of thought about society, religion, morality, and the perceptual structure of our world itself, so that human experience on every level may be freed from habit and enriched by a restoration of creativity. It is Blake's highly individual response to the opening of an age of revolution.

POLITICAL PROPHECIES

BLAKE'S project of attempting to share his inspired, spiritual vision of the world with the few people willing to buy his astonishing illuminated books continued in a group of politically flavored works produced in the early 1790s. Two of these, *America* and *Europe*, are explicitly subtitled "A Prophecy"; the other, *Visions of the Daughters of Albion*, is also clearly a "prophetic" work in the sense of being the urgent utterance of a poet who feels himself spiritually inspired with an urgent mission to awaken his audience to vital truths. All three poems connect creativity and spiritual vision with revolutionary, democratic politics; and all three are among the greatest masterpieces of Blake's graphic design.

Visions of the Daughters of Albion (1793) confronts a wide spectrum of issues about which Blake felt passionately, from slavery and the oppression of women, to false ideas of sexuality and destructive philosophies of sensory perception. The range of concerns is implied by the title: the *Daughters of Albion* are the women of England, who are, in Blake's view, "enslav'd"; whilst the word *Visions* points to the question of how we see the world, and the poem's frontispiece illustrates the three main characters brooded over by a sun glaring like a fiery eye between clouds which form an ominous eye-socket. The poem is full of references to light, the sun, vision, and perception. Its main emphasis, however, is on the position of women. Blake was aware of the work of Mary Wollstonecraft: he had illustrated her *Original Stories from Real Life* (1791) and certainly knew her *Vindication of the Rights of Woman* (1792). The view of women put forward in Blake's poem is too contradictory to be labeled "feminist," but it certainly focuses on the rights, freedoms, sufferings, and sexuality of women with unprecedented directness.

Its narrative is relatively simple. Oothoon, like Thel in the earlier poem, is a young woman on the verge of experience: in this case, it seems, of sexu-al experience in particular. Like Thel she questions a flower (a "bright Marygold") and the flower encourages her to commit herself:

Pluck thou my flower, Oothon the mild
Another flower shall spring, because the soul of
   sweet delight
Can never pass away.

                     (p. 46)

Oothoon flies "in wing'd exulting swift delight" over the ocean to join her lover, Theotormon: not a difficult feat, for in an elemental pattern that again recalls *The Book of Thel*, Oothoon is not only a maiden but also a cloud, whilst Theotormon is both a young lover and the ocean. On her journey, however, Oothoon is attacked and raped by the brutal slave-owner Bromion (thunder). Bromion follows up his attack by abusing her as a "harlot" and boasting of his tyranny over his slaves:

Stampt with my signet are the swarthy children of the
   sun:
They are obedient, they resist not, they obey the
   scourge:
Their daughters worship terrors and obey the
   violent[.]

                     (p. 46)

Oothoon's lover Theotormon, though apparently more powerful than Bromion, shows no compassion for her. Now that she has been raped he despises her, and is riven with jealousy. He keeps Oothoon and her attacker "Bound back to back" and instead of comforting her, broods on his own resentment and jealousy. The remaining three-quarters of the poem consist of the lamentations of the characters. Theotormon is self-pitying and egoistic (Blake's illustrations show him with folded arms clutching his bowed head in a grotesquely contorted posture indicating complete withdrawal); Bromion is violent, materialistic, and cynical; but Oothoon, clearly speaking for Blake, is selfless, loving, and tireless in her attempts to arouse the other characters to the possibilities of love, forgiveness, and new life.

Oothoon's language is passionate and lyrical throughout, and moves dizzyingly from one topic to another. Sometimes she praises diversity: "How can the giver of gifts experience the delights of the merchant? / How the industrious citizen the pains of the husbandman?" (p. 48). Sometimes she denounces the miseries of loveless and legally binding marriage: "she who burns with youth, and knows no fixed lot, is bound / In spells of law to one she loathes: and must she drag the chain / Of life in weary lust!" (p. 49).

At other points she attacks the dully materialistic concepts of perception common in eighteenth-century philosophical thought:

> They told me that the night & day were all that I
>   could see;
> They told me that I had five senses to enclose me up.
> And they inclos'd my infinite brain into a narrow
>   circle . . .
> Till all from life I was obliterated and erased.
>
>   (p. 47)

Her most powerful lines are reserved for the praise of free love and a criticism of jealousy:

> I cry, Love! Love! Love! happy happy Love! Free as
>   the mountain wind!
> Can that be Love, that drinks another as a sponge
>   drinks water?
> That clouds with jealousy his nights, with weepings
>   all the day: . . .
> Such is self-love that envies all! a creeping skeleton
> With lamplike eyes watching around the frozen
>   marriage-bed.
>
>   (p. 50)

Her most startling lines, however, are those where she demonstrates her total lack of jealousy by offering to entrap other companions for her jealous lover, Theotormon:

> [S]ilken nets and traps of adamant will Oothoon
>   spread,
> And catch for thee girls of mild silver, and of furious
>   gold;
> I'll lie beside thee on a bank & view their wanton play
> In lovely copulation bliss on bliss with Theotormon[.]
>
>   (p. 50)

Blake undoubtedly intended the lines to shock. Some readers have taken them as rhetorical overstatement intended to show how unimaginably far Oothoon feels herself from any sense of sexual possessiveness; others have thought that they show Oothon herself as partly corrupted by the selfishness of the poem's emotionally limited male characters. Others have assumed that Blake is simply indulging in naive sexual fantasy and unconvincingly attributing it to his heroine. A different view again is offered if we remember the poem's elemental symbolism. On that level of meaning, if Oothoon is cloud and Theotormon sea, she is describing the refraction of sunlight and moonlight by the clouds on to the glittering surface of the sea: a natural part of the living cosmic cycle. It is worth remembering that the word "copulation" is first used by Oothoon when she speaks of looking at "the morning sun": "there" (she says) "my eyes are fix'd / In happy copulation" (p. 50), clearly meaning a "coupling" of eye with vision rather than a sexual encounter. Or, again, does Blake see all such encounters as in some sense erotic or sexual? As so often, he challenges us but provides no final answer.

America a Prophecy (1793) celebrates the American Revolution of "Washington, Franklin, Paine, & Warren, Gates, Hancock & Green" (p. 52) for its fight against the tyranny of "Albion's Angel," representing the power of the British monarchy—for as in the earlier and clumsier *French Revolution*, Blake sees revolution as a spiritual force inspiring the colonists to act together for freedom. The poem is a major step forward in Blake's myth-making, for it introduces Orc, the spirit of revolution, who is shown in the poem's symbolic "Preludium" as an imprisoned youth breaking his chains and seizing the mysterious "daughter of Urthona" in a sexual embrace which will lead to a burgeoning of new life. In the main body of the poem Orc reappears to inspire revolution:

> Red rose the clouds from the Atlantic in vast wheels
>   of blood
> And in the red clouds rose a wonder o'er the Atlantic
>   sea;
> Intense! Naked! A Human fire fierce glowing, as the
>   wedge
> Of iron heated in the furnace; his terrible limbs were
>   fire
> With myriads of cloudy terrors banners dark and
>   towers
> Surrounded; heat but not light went thro' the murky
>   atmosphere.
>
>   (p. 53)

Britain's failing attempts to crush the revolution recoil on Britain herself: "Sick'ning lay Londons Guardian, and the ancient miter'd York / Their heads on snowy hills, their ensigns sick'ning in the sky" (p. 57); and, forming a link with *Visions*, Blake shows the revolution as bringing renewed freedom for women:

For the female spirits of the dead pining in bonds of
  religion;
Run from their fetters reddening, & in long drawn
  arches sitting:
They feel the nerves of youth renew, and desires of
  ancient times.
Over their pale limbs as a vine when the tender grape
  appears.

(p. 57)

Opposing Orc, Urizen, the spirit of tyranny, now
becomes a fully fledged character also. A white-
haired parody of God the Father as conventionally
imagined, surrounded by clouds and snows,
Urizen owes much to Blake's earlier representations of the tyrant kings, "Winter" (in *Poetical
Sketches*) and Tiriel. Here, he "emerg'd his leprous
head / From out his holy shrine . . . his jealous
wing wav'd o'er the deep: / Weeping in dismal
howling woe he dark descended howling" (p. 57)
in his attempt to stop the spread of revolutionary
change by pouring "His stored snows . . . and his
icy magazines." He manages to prevent a revolution in Europe, but only for a few years: "Angels
and weak men twelve years should govern o'er the
strong, / And then their end should come, when
France receiv'd the Demons light" (p. 57). For Blake
views the French Revolution as a continuation of
the American struggle. It is noticeable that the
forces of conservatism are typified as "Angels" and
Orc as "the Demon." Blake is still using the
provocative reversals of *The Marriage of Heaven and
Hell*, associating creativity and liberation with
"Hell" and timid conformism with "Angels."

The last of this trilogy of political prophecies,
Europe a Prophecy (1794), is also the most obscure.
Whereas *America* and the earlier *French Revolution*
had shown human beings, including known historical figures, inspired, aided, or opposed by
titanic spiritual forces, *Europe*, though sharing the
same political concerns, seems to be set throughout in a dreamlike spiritual realm. The dominant
figure now is a female, Enitharmon, who is an
emotional tyrant rather than a military one, determined to keep humanity enslaved by ideological
means. Her principal means of control is guilt: she
commands her envoys to inculcate a sense of
shame and inferiority, a joyless travesty of religion
and a culture of manipulation:

Go! tell the human race that Woman's love is Sin!
That an Eternal life awaits the worms of sixty winters
In an allegorical abode where existence hath never come:

Forbid all Joy, & from her childhood shall the little
  female
Spread nets in every secret path.

(p. 62)

Rather than being misogynistic, the last two
lines probably echo the protests of Mary Wollstonecraft's *Vindication* (chapter 5) at the manner
in which girls were taught from an early age to
adopt "a system of cunning and lasciviousness" to
please, and manipulate, men.

Having sent out her agents, Enitharmon sleeps
for eighteen hundred years (approximately the
period from the beginning of the Christian era to
Blake's own time) while Europe lies crushed by
these oppressive values and by more obvious
kinds of deprivation:

Enitharmon laugh'd in her sleep to see (O woman's
  triumph)
Every house a den, every man bound; the shadows
  are fill'd
With spectres, and the windows wove over with
  curses of iron:
Over the doors Thou shalt not, & over the chimneys
  fear is written:
With bands of iron round their necks, fasten'd into
  the walls
The citizens: in leaden gyves the inhabitants of
  suburbs
Walk heavy: soft and bent are the bones of the
  villagers[.]

(p. 64)

Enitharmon is awakened at last by the turmoil
of the American Revolution; she weeps, while her
son, the fiery Orc, leaves for France to inspire
fresh democratic uprisings.

Such a bare outline gives little idea of the many
cryptic episodes, unidentified mythological figures, and confusing chronology of the poem.
Europe gives the impression that Blake is trying
to pack too much meaning into too little space,
and asking the reader to accept too much on
trust. But if *Europe* is unsatisfying as a text, it
nonetheless contains some of Blake's finest
graphic work, from the famous frontispiece,
which shows God (or Urizen?) beginning his creation by inscribing the boundaries of the universe with a pair of golden compasses, through
many richly colored integral illuminations on the

text plates, to a series of full-page designs of stark power showing the effects of famine, poverty, fear, and political tyranny. The designs do not clarify the obscurity of the text, but they offer ample compensation.

SONGS OF INNOCENCE AND EXPERIENCE

BLAKE completed five remarkable years of creativity by revisiting *Songs of Innocence* and adding its counterpart, *Songs of Experience*. The new work that resulted, *Songs of Innocence and of Experience* (1794), is his masterpiece and one of the highest achievements of Romantic poetry. Resting on the creative opposition of contraries, it is an astonishingly rich work, at once simple and complex, contradictory and unified. Its unifying forces include a finely integrated language of graphic imagery, where the poems are surrounded by delicate designs of flames, flowers, vines, interlaced trees, pastoral scenes, and groups of adults and children. Blake gave the book a new title page showing Adam and Eve, in aprons of leaves, cast out from paradise and pursued by flames. The book also has (for the first time) a subtitle: "shewing the Two Contrary States of the Human Soul" (p. 7). Both picture and words indicate clearly that "Innocence" and "Experience" are, amongst other things, the fallen and unfallen states of human consciousness, conceived by Blake not as phases in a Biblical myth, but as immediate modes of awareness which we have all shared.

Certain poems from *Innocence* were moved over into *Experience*, among them "The Little Girl Lost" and " . . . Found," "The School Boy," and "The Voice of the Ancient Bard." Two new "bardic" poems ("Introduction" and "Earth's Answer") were added to *Experience*, so that the Bard, a sober prophetic figure, now typifies the poet in the world of Experience, as the pastoral figure of the piper typifies the poet in Innocence. Two more deeply pessimistic poems about lost children were added to *Experience*, so that a sequence of six poems on this theme now runs through the book as a whole.

Such structuring suggests that Blake had found elements of foreboding and constraint within the original *Songs of Innocence* and used them as starting points for his depiction of the "contrary state," the painful, complex, dangerous, and at times despairing state of Experience. But whether his creation of the two-part work of 1794 was a sudden inspiration or the fulfillment of a long-cherished plan, we cannot know.

Blake allowed opposites to coexist in a conflicting unity by writing new poems for *Experience* that directly confront particular *Songs of Innocence*. Thus the innocent "Chimney Sweeper" with his dreams and touching confidence in angels is now balanced by "THE Chimney Sweeper" of *Experience*, who tells us, with bitter social criticism, that his hypocritical parents have gone to church, where they "praise God & his priest & King / Who make up a heaven of our misery" (p. 23). The "Nurse's Song" of *Innocence*, with its carefree indulgence of childhood play, is sourly mirrored by *Experience*'s "NURSES Song," where a nurse regards the children (now themselves older and more secretive) with envy and cynicism.

Other paired poems do not share the same title, but have equally obvious links. "The Lamb" and "The Tyger," "The Divine Image" and "The Human Abstract" clearly challenge one another. But such relationships shade off into less obvious ones. "The Ecchoing Green," the quintessential landscape of Innocence, may be seen as opposed either by "The Garden of Love" where "A Chapel was built in the midst, / Where I used to play on the green" (p. 26), or by "London," surely the poem which sums up most fully the grim landscape of Experience. In fact the *Songs* offer an endless network of contrasts, parallels and thematic patterns for the reader to explore, and a multitude of different voices to listen to. Of all works of Romantic poetry, the *Songs* are perhaps the most open to the interplay of difference and diversity.

Blake never offers a verbal definition of Innocence or Experience. Rather he allows us to develop a vision of the two states from the poems themselves. Innocence is trustful, loving, and confident, and sees the world through the radiance of a divine vision in which there can be no ultimate wrong. Experience, on the other hand, is dominated by an awareness of pain and conflict, of problems that have no likely solution, and of bitter feelings that cannot be resolved. Its vision is discontented and often political. Many of the most powerful *Songs of Experience* are mysterious poems over whose meanings readers have always argued. "The Tyger," for example, with its pounding rhythms and fiery visual imagery, is probably Blake's most widely known poem, yet it remains a challenge to interpretation. The "tyger," presented as a creature forged in a fiery workshop, drawing into its nature the myth of Prometheus ("What the hand dare seize the fire?") and the war in heaven as recounted in Milton's *Paradise Lost* ("When the stars threw down their spears / And water'd heaven with their tears . . .," p. 24), may be seen as depicting the nature of evil, questioning the nature of God, confronting human anger, celebrating social revolution, or suggesting countless other meanings. The poem itself consists of fifteen unanswered questions. It haunts its readers partly because its "meaning" can never be resolved. As so often, Blake's evident purpose is to challenge thought and stimulate mental vision, thereby sharing something of his own dauntingly beautiful imaginative world.

THE URIZEN BOOKS

BLAKE'S bookselling venture with James Parker had long ago collapsed, and he was now making his living exclusively from engraving, generally copying other artists' designs for book illustrations, but occasionally receiving commissions to design and engrave his own illustrations, as in 1794, when he was commissioned to design and engrave the illustrations for a lavish new edition of Edward Young's meditative poem *Night Thoughts*. Such projects came to him rarely, and though he was known as an excellent (though individualistic) engraver and designer, he remained poor.

Nonetheless he remained as determined as ever to articulate his personal myth, and in 1794–1795 produced four illuminated poems that together express his most complete cosmic vision. The first and most important of the four is *The First Book of Urizen* (1794), which, in a bitter parody of the Biblical creation-story, tells of how Urizen separates himself egoistically from Eternity, determined to become a self-centered individual and to create a self-contained world that he can control. The account, written in short, Bible-style verses, is at once a satire on the conventional conception of the creator-God, an attack on the mechanistic "reason" which dominated eighteenth-century science and philosophy, a mockery of tyrannical monarchy, and an account of the emergence of the isolated modern self. These, however, are mere interpretations. Blake presents the events simply as vision:

Lo, a shadow of horror is risen
In eternity! Unknown, unprolific,
Self-clos'd, all-repelling: what demon

Hath form'd this abominable void,
This soul-shuddering vacuum? Some said
"It is Urizen." But unknown, abstracted,
Brooding, secret, the dark power hid.
(p. 70)

Urizen's goal is to find "a joy without pain" by controlling life, death, nature, and himself. Instead he produces chaos and conflict, and in a vain attempt to prevent the disaster from spreading, Los, another of the "Eternals" (for Blake imagines Eternity as a community of free human energies) attempts to place limits on Urizen and his world. Los, like a metalworker, forges a confining shape for Urizen, who gradually takes shape in a process that grotesquely resembles the development of a human fetus in the womb:

From the caverns of his jointed Spine
Down sunk with fright a red
Round Globe, hot burning, deep,
Deep down into the abyss;
Panting, Conglobing, Trembling,

Shooting out ten thousand branches
Around his solid bones.
(pp. 75–76)

The process also has similarities to eighteenth-century ideas about the formation of planets and stars, for what is being created is not only the isolated modern self but the Newtonian conception of the universe as a sterile space filled with meaningless lumps of moving matter. Urizen represents all aspects of the modern consciousness as Blake understood it.

Los, however, is not immune from the process of degeneration. Pitying Urizen, he finds himself divided (for "Pity divides the Soul"). His feminine portion—the pitying part of himself—splits off, to become Enitharmon, the first female. A family tragedy begins to unfold, as Los embraces Enitharmon and she gives birth to Orc, the fiery boy whom we recognize from the earlier political Prophecies. Los becomes jealous of his son and soon, in a parody of the Biblical story of Isaac, is offering him as a human sacrifice to Urizen.

The depths and multiple meanings of *The First Book of Urizen* are impossible to summarize and are best absorbed simply by repeated readings of the text itself. The poem must be taken, receptively, as a vision first and foremost, with attempts at interpretation coming later once the poem's remarkable images have taken a hold on the mind. Hasty attempts to "decode" the poem only render it more obscure, and impede its emotional power as an appalled yet compassionate vision of the state of human consciousness as Blake perceives it. And ideally it should be seen with the rich, somber colors and titanically powerful designs provided by Blake.

The three other "Urizen" books, all of them shorter and all published by Blake in 1795, merely extend and enrich the myth, as if viewing it from different angles. *The Song of Los* emphasizes the political consequences of Urizen's domination; *The Book of Ahania* gives an unexpected glimpse of Urizen as he was before his self-imposed separation from the other Eternals, in the happy times when he was a divine farmer, his task "On the human soul to cast / The seed of eternal science" (p. 89). *The Book of Los*, recapitulating material from *The First Book of Urizen*, also adds sad reflections on an ideal past when no human quality was regarded as a sin "and none impure were deem'd" (p. 90)—a state now lost owing to Urizen's devotion to a philosophy of law, blame, and control.

Blake's project in producing this personal myth seems so extraordinary that it may be worth reflecting that readers of the 1790s (though very few bought Blake's books) may have found it less odd than we do. Mythological epics full of unfamiliar characters with bizarre names were plentiful in the 1790s. Readers could choose among Robert Southey's Indian *Curse of Kehama* (featuring such characters as Kailyal, Ereenia, and Nealliny) or his Welsh-American *Madoc* (with Aeglyvarch, Coanocotzin, and Yuhidthiton), James Macpherson's *Ossian* (Sul-Malla, Duth-carmor); Sir William Jones's translations of Hindu poetry (Peitamber, Yudishteir) and many others. Much of this work is now little read; Blake's has survived better.

VALA *AND* MILTON

WHILE working on his illustrations for Young's *Night Thoughts*, perhaps in 1796, Blake seems to have decided to develop the material of the *Urizen* books into a full-scale epic under the title of *Vala*, later changed to *The Four Zoas*. The poem was to be in nine "Nights," a structure borrowed from *Night Thoughts*, and it was written mainly on the backs of sheets of drawings and proofs of the *Night Thoughts* illustrations. Blake worked on the poem at intervals until at least 1807 but never finished it to his satisfaction. A huge spiritual drama of fall and resurrection, *Vala* takes much of its basic narrative from the *Urizen* books, but expands it to include new "characters." Vala herself is a figure of female power, perhaps in part representing Nature, and the human consciousness is now represented by four figures, the "Four Zoas" of Blake's revised title. These are Urizen (associated especially with the faculty of reason); Luvah (emotion); Tharmas (the body and its senses); and Urthona (imagination). The Zoas also correspond to the four traditional elements, the points of the compass, and the four living creatures seen in the vision of the Prophet Ezekiel (see Ezek. 1). *Vala* goes beyond the Urizen books by describing not only the fall of human consciousness, but also its redemption, its triumphant return to a state of freedom, integration, and creativity. The radiant vision of Night the Ninth, when all aspects of being are redeemed into a new paradisal state, is immensely moving:

> The Sun has left his blackness & has found a fresher
> morning,
> And the mild moon rejoices in the clear & cloudless
> night,
> And man walks forth from midst of fires: the evil is
> all consumed,
> His eyes behold the Angelic spheres arising night &
> day;
> The stars consum'd like a lamp blown out, & in their
> stead, behold
> The Expanding Eyes of Man behold the depths of
> wondrous worlds!
>
> (p. 406)

In 1800 Blake's career underwent a temporary diversion when he moved with his wife to the seaside village of Felpham in Sussex at the inducement of a wealthy patron and minor poet, William Hayley. Blake appreciated both Felpham's beauty and Hayley's good intentions, but both were to reveal a darker side. Hayley's idea of helping Blake was to keep him busy with copy engraving and the painting of miniature portraits, and to deter him from working on his own visionary art and poetry. Relations became strained and Blake decided to return to London. Worse still, before he left the village, a chance quarrel with a drunken soldier who had wandered into Blake's garden led to Blake's being charged with sedition on the soldier's maliciously false evidence. Blake returned to London in 1803 facing the terrible prospect of a political trial, which could lead to prison or worse. He was acquitted, the soldier's evidence being self-contradictory and obviously false, but the experience must have been traumatic.

Yet his time at Felpham had not been wasted. It became the starting-point for another long poem, *Milton*, which Blake began to engrave in 1804. *Milton* centers on a mystical experience which Blake seems to have had in his garden at Felpham, in which he saw descending from heaven both the spiritual figure of a virgin, Ololon, and his own great poetic predecessor, John Milton, who had returned to earth to find reconciliation with the feminine which he had despised and rejected during his life. This encountering of male and female principles merged into a vision of "Jesus the Saviour" uniting mankind to inaugurate the Resurrection and Judgement of the world. Blake found his sense of his own poetic mission renewed, and gained new insights into both time and nature. *Milton* contains Blake's most magnificent celebrations of the natural world and also extraordinary passages describing "a moment in each day that Satan cannot find" (p. 136), a moment "less than the pulsation of an artery" which is, nevertheless, "equal in its period & value to Six Thousand Years" (p. 127)—that is, to the whole duration of the created world. Unpacking the imaginative significance of a mystical experience that may have lasted only for a split-second, *Milton* follows no conventional narrative sequence and defeats any attempt to read it as linear "autobiography." It should be read first for its many superb lyrical passages, around which a fuller understanding of the text will gradually develop. It must be said that Blake is not a poet for hasty reading, or for a single reading. The reader who returns from time to time over many years will come to understand him with increasing depth and delight, but will never exhaust the richness of meaning and the sense of discovery which each new encounter will bring.

JERUSALEM *AND THE LAST YEARS*

BLAKE was now settled again in London, in one of the small apartments where he and his wife would spend the rest of their lives. He had a modest reputation as a gifted artist and engraver, a few loyal patrons who bought his books and paintings, and a thin trickle of work: enough to keep body and soul together, but little more. He had a small suc-

cess with his illustrations to Robert Blair's poem *The Grave* (1808) which, radical or not, he dedicated with a loyal and charming poem to the queen; and he produced his splendid panoramic engraving of Chaucer's *Canterbury Pilgrims*: though in both cases he was robbed of most of his profits by a crooked publisher, Robert Cromek. In 1809 he held a retrospective exhibition of his paintings in the family haberdashery shop, now owned by his brother James. But the exhibition was a failure, and Blake did not again try to find a broad public.

His last major poetic work, *Jerusalem*, seems to have been in preparation from 1804 until 1820. Though using passages salvaged from *Vala* it is, like *Milton*, very much a spiritual and psychological drama rather than an epic narrative. The hero now is Los, the creative imagination, who struggles both against his own "spectre"—the self-doubt, skepticism, anger, and depression which threaten to swamp faith and imagination inwardly—and against external forces of destructive criticism, political tyranny, and false religion. The poem attempts to imagine the redemption of humanity, visualized as a sleeping giant, Albion (a traditional poetic name for Britain), who must reunite with his spiritual form or female "emanation," Jerusalem. The imagination for Blake is a sacred, spiritual force, and important passages of the poem are devoted to re-imagining Britain as a sacred territory, where each place corresponds both to a human emotional state and to a Biblical location. Blake's ultimate goal seems to be the complete visionary integration of humanity and the world in a spiritual consciousness that will in itself constitute redemption and resurrection.

Like *Milton*, *Jerusalem* presents the reader with formidable problems that only time, patience, and curiosity will solve. Yet its essential vision is summed up in the opening stanzas of the lyric that opens *Jerusalem*'s chapter 2, where Blake sees London districts transformed by his own bright spiritual vision:

> The fields from Islington to Marybone,
> To Primrose Hill and Saint Johns Wood:
>   Were builded over with pillars of gold,
> And there Jerusalem's pillars stood.
>
> Her Little-ones ran on the fields
> The Lamb of God among them seen
>   And fair Jerusalem his Bride
> Among the little meadows green.

(p. 171)

With its one hundred elaborately decorated plates, *Jerusalem* is Blake's most ambitious illuminated book. He finished it in 1820, late in life, at a time when he had to accept that worldly success had passed him by. Only five copies were printed. Blake published no more poetry: the verses known as "Auguries of Innocence" which sum up his vision so effectively—

> To see a World in a Grain of Sand
> And a Heaven in a Wild Flower,
> Hold infinity in the palm of your hand
> And Eternity in an hour
> (p. 490, p. 493)

—were left, with many other mysterious and powerful poems, in an unpublished notebook. But he continued to produce major graphic works, illustrating *The Pastorals of Virgil* (1818), *The Book of Job* (1826), and Dante's *Divine Comedy* (1824–1827). He also acquired, from about 1824, disciples: a group of young artists led by Samuel Palmer and Edward Calvert, who regarded Blake with profound respect and treated him as a spiritual mentor as well as a teacher of art.

Blake died on 12 August 1827, "singing," as one of his pupils recalled, "of the things he saw in Heaven." Remembered at first only by a few friends and connoisseurs, Blake's work was brought to public attention by Alexander Gilchrist's pioneering *Life of William Blake* (1863) and steadily gained admirers. An immense amount of scholarship during the twentieth century made available the sources, contexts and meanings of Blake's work, and changes in literary taste rendered the indeterminacy and obscurity of Blake's work more acceptable, whilst his moral, political and religious opinions came to seem less startling. Nonetheless Blake's poetry remains challenging: sometimes piercingly direct, sometimes profoundly obscure, it continues to question all our ways of reading and responding. Blake's enterprise was to open the reader's eyes to a vision of humanity and the world as a sacred, creative multiplicity-in-unity, flooded with a divine love which is to be found in the heart of every person. He succeeded more than almost any other writer in conveying something of the notoriously incommunicable vision of the mystic; the unique forms taken by his poems and pictures are the necessary vehicle of that enterprise.

SELECTED BIBLIOGRAPHY

I. COLLECTED WORKS. *The Poetical Works of William Blake, Lyrical and Miscellaneous*, ed. by William Michael Rossetti (London, 1874); *The Works of William Blake, Poetic, Symbolic, and Critical*, 3 vols., ed. by Edwin J. Ellis and W. B. Yeats (London, 1893); *The Poems of William Blake*, ed. by John Sampson (London, 1913); *The Prophetic Writings of William Blake*, 2 vols., ed. by D. J. Sloss and J. P. R. Wallis (Oxford, 1926); *Poetry and Prose of William Blake*, ed. by Geoffrey Keynes (London and New York, 1927); *The Portable Blake*, ed. by Alfred Kazin (New York, 1946); *Complete Writings of William Blake*, ed. by Geoffrey Keynes (London and New York, 1957; many times repr.); *The Complete Poetry and Prose of William Blake*, ed. by David V. Erdman, commentary by Harold Bloom (New York, 1965; rev. ed. 1982, many times repr.); *William Blake: The Complete Poems*, ed. by Alicia Ostriker (Harmondsworth, U.K., 1977); *William Blake's Writings*, 2 vols., ed. by G. E. Bentley, Jr., (Oxford, 1978); *Blake: The Complete Poems*, ed. by W. H. Stevenson (rev. ed., London, 1989); *William Blake: The Illuminated Books*. Vol. 1, *Jerusalem*, Vol. 2, *Songs of Innocence and of Experience*, Vol. 3, *The Early Illuminated Books*, Vol. 4, *The Continental Prophecies*, Vol. 5, *Milton a Poem*, Vol. 6, *The Urizen Books*, general editor David Bindman (London and Princeton, 1991–1995).

II. INDIVIDUAL WORKS PUBLISHED BY WILLIAM BLAKE[2]. *There Is No Natural Religion* [1788]; *All Religions Are One* [1788]; *The Book of Thel* (1789); *Songs of Innocence* (1789); *The Marriage of Heaven and Hell* [1790]; *America a Prophecy* (1793); *Europe a Prophecy* (1794); *For Children: The Gates of Paradise* [1793]; *Visions of the Daughters of Albion* (1793); *Songs of Innocence and of Experience* (1794); *The First Book of Urizen* (1794); *The Book of Ahania* (1795); *The Book of Los* (1795); *The Song of Los* (1795); *Milton a Poem* (1804); *Jerusalem* (1804).

III. WORKS PUBLISHED FOR BLAKE BY OTHERS. *Poetical Sketches*, privately printed for A. S. Mathew (London, 1783); *The French Revolution*, printed by Joseph Johnson (London, 1791).

IV. BIOGRAPHIES. Alexander Gilchrist, *The Life of William Blake, "Pictor Ignotus"* (London, 1863); Mona Wilson, *The Life of William Blake* (London, 1927); Jacob Bronowski, *William Blake, 1757–1827* (London, 1943; rev. as *William Blake and the Age of Revolution*, London and New York, 1965); G. E. Bentley, Jr., ed., *Blake Records* (Oxford, 1969); G. E. Bentley, Jr., *Blake Records Supplement* (Oxford, 1988); Peter Ackroyd, *Blake* (London, 1995); G. E. Bentley, Jr., *The Stranger from Paradise: A Biography of William Blake* (New Haven and London, 2001).

V. BIBLIOGRAPHY. G. E. Bentley, Jr., and Martin K. Nurmi, eds., *A Blake Bibliography* (Minneapolis, 1964).

VI. CRITICAL STUDIES. Algernon Charles Swinburne, *William Blake: A Critical Essay* (London, 1868); Arthur

---

[2] Undated works have date in square brackets; otherwise dates are taken from title pages, and may not represent true date of completion; all works were published in London.

Symons, *William Blake* (London, 1907); Joseph Wicksteed, *Blake's Vision of the Book of Job* (London and New York, 1910); S. Foster Damon, *William Blake: His Philosophy and Symbols* (Boston and London, 1924).

Margaret Ruth Lowery, *Windows of the Morning: A Critical Study of William Blake's "Poetical Sketches, 1783"* (New Haven and London, 1940); Mark Schorer, *William Blake: The Politics of Vision* (New York, 1946); Northrop Frye, *Fearful Symmetry: A Study of William Blake* (Princeton, 1947); Bernard Blackstone, *English Blake* (Cambridge, 1949); Geoffrey Keynes, *Blake Studies: Notes on His Life and Works in Seventeen Chapters* (London, 1949).

David V. Erdman, *Blake: Prophet Against Empire: A Poet's Interpretation of the History of His Own Times* (Princeton, 1954; rev. 1969); Stanley Gardner, *Infinity on the Anvil: A Critical Study of Blake's Poetry* (Oxford, 1954); A. L. Morton, *The Everlasting Gospel: A Study In the Sources of William Blake* (London, 1958); Anthony Blunt, *The Art of William Blake* (New York, 1959); Robert F. Gleckner, *The Piper and the Bard: A Study of William Blake* (Detroit, 1959).

Peter F. Fisher, *The Valley of Vision: Blake as Prophet and Revolutionary* (Toronto, 1961); George Mills Harper, *The Neoplatonism of William Blake* (Chapel Hill, 1961); H. M. Margoliouth, *William Blake* (Oxford, 1961); Harold Bloom, *Blake's Apocalypse: A Study in Poetic Argument* (Garden City, N.Y., 1963); Harold Bloom, "William Blake," in *The Visionary Company: A Reading of English Romantic Poetry* (New York, 1963); Jean H. Hagstrum, *William Blake, Poet and Painter: An Introduction to the Illuminated Verse* (Chicago, 1964); E. D. Hirsch, Jr., *Innocence and Experience: An Introduction to Blake* (New Haven and London, 1964); Desiree Hirst, *Hidden Riches: Traditional Symbolism from the Renaissance to Blake* (London, 1964); S. Foster Damon, *A Blake Dictionary: The Ideas and Symbols of William Blake* (Providence, R.I., 1965; rev. ed., New Haven and London, 1988); Alicia Ostriker, *Vision and Verse in William Blake* (Madison, 1965); John Beer, *Blake's Humanism* (Manchester, 1968); Kathleen Raine, *Blake and Tradition*, 2 vols. (London and Princeton, 1968); John Beer, *Blake's Visionary Universe* (Manchester, 1969); Alvin H. Rosenfeld, ed., *William Blake: Essays for S. Foster Damon* (Providence, 1969).

David V. Erdman and John E. Grant, eds., *Blake's Visionary Forms Dramatic* (Princeton, 1970); Morton D. Paley, *Energy and the Imagination: A Study of the Development of Blake's Thought* (Oxford, 1970); John Adlard, *The Sports of Cruelty: Fairies, Folk-Songs, Charms, and Other Country Matters in the Work of William Blake* (London, 1972); Stuart Curran and Joseph Anthony Wittreich, Jr., *Blake's Sublime Allegory: Essays on* The Four Zoas, Milton *and* Jerusalem (Madison, 1973); David Wagenknecht, *Blake's Night: William Blake and the Idea of Pastoral* (Cambridge, Mass., 1973); Donald Ault, *Visionary Physics: Blake's Response to Newton* (Chicago, 1974); Anne K. Mellor, *Blake's Human Form Divine* (Berkeley, 1974); Edward Larrissy, *William Blake* (Oxford, 1975); Joseph Anthony Wittreich, Jr., *Angel of Apocalypse: Blake's Idea of Milton* (Madison and London, 1975); Susan Fox, *Poetic Form in Blake's Milton* (Princeton, 1976); G. E. Bentley, Jr., *Blake Books* (Oxford, 1977); David Bindman, *Blake as an Artist* (Oxford, 1977); W. J. T. Mitchell, *Blake's Composite Art: A Study of the Illuminated Poetry* (Princeton, 1978).

Zachary Leader, *Reading Blake's Songs* (London, 1981); David Bindman, *William Blake: His Art and Times* (London, 1982); Morris Eaves, *William Blake's Theory of Art* (Princeton, 1982); Nelson Hilton, *Literal Imagination: Blake's Vision of Words* (Berkeley, 1983); Morton D. Paley, *The Continuing City: William Blake's Jerusalem* (Oxford, 1983); Robert N. Essick, *William Blake and the Language of Adam* (Oxford, 1989).

Vincent A. De Luca, *Words of Eternity: Blake and the Poetics of the Sublime* (Princeton, 1991); Jon Mee, *Dangerous Enthusiasm: William Blake and the Culture of Radicalism in the 1790s* (Oxford, 1992); E. P. Thompson, *Witness Against the Beast: William Blake and the Moral Law* (Cambridge, 1993); Joseph Viscomi, *Blake and the Idea of the Book* (Princeton, 1993).

THE BRONTË SISTERS
Charlotte, Emily, and Anne

Antonia Losano

THE BRONTË FAMILY BIOGRAPHY

PERHAPS THE MOST astonishing fact about the Brontë family is that it produced *three* remarkably creative women writers: Charlotte, Emily, and Anne. Living in a rural parsonage in the north of England, the three sisters wrote unprecedented novels and poetry that stunned and often shocked their contemporaries. Two of their novels—*Jane Eyre* and *Wuthering Heights*—remain among the most famous English novels of all time.

The unusual, sad, and often outrageous events in the family biography have attracted readers as much as the quality of their literary output. Where Brontë biography is concerned, it is very difficult to tell fact from legend. Early biographers told of a half-mad father, an alcoholic and wastrel brother, a repressively religious aunt, a Gothic landscape, and childhoods spent in almost complete isolation. While much of this is exaggeration, much is in fact true—the three sisters *did* have an unusual childhood and extremely tragic lives. The early history of the family begins with Patrick Brontë, an Irish clergyman working in Yorkshire in the northern part of England. In January of 1812 he met Maria Branwell, then twenty-nine years old, the daughter of a successful grocer and tea merchant. The two became engaged in August and were married in December. The couple's courtship took place amid a turbulent historical backdrop: in 1812 Napoleon invaded Russia, while Britain faced riots at home and war against France and the United States.

Maria and Patrick Brontë's first child, named Maria after her mother, was born in 1814. The following year saw the famous Battle of Waterloo, the final defeat of Napoleon, and the end of decades of war between England and France; 1815 also saw the birth of the Brontës' second daughter, Elizabeth. In 1816 Charlotte was born, and in 1817 the long-awaited first son, Branwell, was born. In 1818 Emily was born, and Anne, the last child, was born in 1820.

In 1820 Patrick was appointed as minister to the parish of Haworth in Yorkshire, and the Brontë family—now with six children—moved to Haworth parsonage, where they would remain. (The Haworth parsonage is now a remarkable museum of Brontë history, manuscripts, and memorabilia.) In 1821 the mother of the Brontë children died, leaving the six siblings to the sole care of their father. The tragedy was heightened by the fact that her illness was terribly expensive and left the family deeply in debt. Never wealthy, the Brontës were now in need of the kind of education that would allow the children to earn their own livings. For young middle-class women of the period this meant training to become a teacher or a governess, the only respectable occupations for a middle-class woman who did not marry—and, without money to provide his daughters with dowries, Patrick suspected that his daughters would have few offers of marriage.

Becoming a governess in the nineteenth century meant learning to draw, play the piano, and teach French and Italian, as well as acquiring a smattering of other knowledge that would help young girls to become "accomplished" but not educated in the sense we consider necessary today. (Education as we understand it now was largely the prerogative of male children only.) Toward this end, in 1824 the four eldest daughters—Maria, Elizabeth, Charlotte, and Emily—were enrolled in a school for clergymen's daughters. The children were considerably unhappy there, as Charlotte's fictionalized school "Lowood" in *Jane Eyre* attests. It was while at the school that Maria contracted consumption, a name given to various diseases in the period but most frequently applied to the chronic pulmonary form of tuberculosis, which was the leading cause of death during the nineteenth century. In Maria's case, however, some recent scholars believe her actual illness to have been typhus rather than tuberculosis. Consumption was regularly associated with creative genius (the poet John Keats died of it), and was imagined at the time to be hereditary, although it was in fact contagious and struck most often in crowded dwelling places or among those subject to poor hygiene and nutrition. Thus the school was largely responsible for Maria's death in 1825 at age eleven. Charlotte later fictionalized Maria's death in the character of Helen Burns, Jane's friend at Lowood school in *Jane Eyre*. Almost immediately after Maria's death Elizabeth, the next eldest daughter, also became ill; she died three months later at the age of ten. Patrick Brontë flew to remove Charlotte and Emily from the school. They never returned.

The loss of two sisters was a profound shock to the three younger girls—especially the loss of the two *elder* sisters who, even though young, had served as maternal figures for Charlotte and Emily since the death of their mother. Charlotte now went from the relatively sheltered position of middle child to the responsibilities of the eldest; this had immeasurable impact upon her personality. The repercussions of these early losses permeate all the sisters' writings; the combined loss of the Brontë sisters' mother and their two eldest sisters seems to account for the fact that nearly all the heroines in the novels of Charlotte, Emily, and Anne are motherless, and many are entirely orphaned. Jane Eyre is an orphan; every character in Emily's *Wuthering Heights* loses at least one parent, generally the mother; Helen Graham in Anne's *The Tenant of Wildfell Hall* grows up with her aunt and uncle, and her young son becomes fatherless during the course of the novel. Additionally, a constant theme in the sisters' fiction is the desperate search for love and family—a search for belonging and connectedness. In *Jane Eyre*, for example, Charlotte portrays the enormous joy that the orphan Jane feels at finally discovering that she has a family of cousins:

Glorious discovering to a lonely wretch! This was wealth indeed!—Wealth to the heart!—a mine of pure, genial affections. This was a blessing, bright, vivid, and exhilarating;—not like the ponderous gift of gold; rich and welcome enough in its way, but sobering from its weight. I now clapped my hands in sudden joy—my pulse bounded, my veins thrilled.

(p. 339)

Possibly because of the desperate desire for affection seen in the sisters' literature, early biographers of the Brontë family painted Haworth as a lonely, secluded place, surrounded by wild moorlands and eerie graveyards. The children were said to have been forced into almost complete isolation. In reality, however, Haworth was a busy industrial town, and the Brontë family was exposed to the social and cultural life of the area. Similarly, popular legend—set in motion by Elizabeth Gaskell in her early biography of Charlotte Brontë—reports Patrick Brontë to have been ferocious and reclusive after the death of his wife, alternately ignoring and terrorizing his children. Other biographers paint Aunt Branwell, who came to live with the children after their mother's death, as a gloomy and strict religious zealot, terrifying the children with threats of damnation. The evidence of family friends and letters suggests otherwise, however. Patrick was evidently an extremely busy professional man, who made what time he could for his many children and encouraged them to become religious and educated. He was, after all, a clergyman with professional and social duties that brought him and his children into the public world; he might have been aloof, but he was probably not the ogre early biographers liked to imagine. Similarly, the image of Aunt Branwell as a religious tyrant has been largely reconsidered.

If the Brontë sisters did not have the miserable childhood that early biographers depicted, the children *were* unique in their precocious literary endeavors and in their evident disinterest (especially on the part of Emily) in the lively social world around them. It seems they *chose*, rather than were forced, to remain separate from the public world; they were happiest within the confines of the parsonage and the broad reaches of their own imaginations. After the deaths of Maria and Elizabeth, the period 1825–1829 saw the remaining sisters back at home, educating themselves with assistance from their father, his library, and various tutors. They studied the Bible, Greek and Latin classics, Aesop's fables, *The Arabian Nights,* Sir Walter Scott's novels, and others. It was during this period that they produced the earliest known examples of written work.

The enormous literary talents of the Brontë sisters did not come out of nowhere. Their father was himself an aspiring writer and local literary celebrity. He published several volumes of poems and stories during his lifetime, as well as volumes of essays and sermons in his later life. He did not, however, actively encourage any of his children to write, though he seems to have been inadvertently the cause of their earliest literary endeavors. In

1826, Patrick brought home a box of toy soldiers as a gift for his son. Each of the four Brontë children took a soldier as his or her special character and together the children created a series of plays and stories around their soldiers. These stories eventually were written down and became the basis of an enormous quantity of juvenilia, which in turn provided inspiration for the novels eventually written by the three sisters. In these early stories the soldiers traveled to Africa, where they fought with the natives and eventually founded Glasstown and an extensive empire. The children created complex imaginary lands called Gondal (created by Emily and Anne) and Angria (Charlotte's and Branwell's imaginary country). The collected juvenilia from this period are fascinating and extensive; the worlds have a complete social structure, with kings and heads of state, wars, romances, intrigue, and treachery. The children were much influenced by history and contemporary politics, often naming characters in their countries after political figures. The children were also influenced by the rise of imperialism in their time, as England began to bring more and more of the globe under colonial rule. The African setting allowed the Brontës to create lush and exotic settings, exhibiting the siblings' interest in the discourse of Orientalism, the western interest in Asian and Indian cultures (Gondalan and Angrian characters often have foreign names like Zenobia, Zamorna, and Quashia). The Eastern-influenced settings are radically un-English and abound with fairies, magicians, and other supernatural beings (associated at the time with Eastern countries), as the following quote from one of Charlotte's early tales suggests:

[The genii sit] upon thrones of pure and massive gold in the midst of an immense hall surrounded by pillars of fine & brilliant diamond the pavement sparkles with amethyst jasper & saphire a large & cloudlike canopy hangs over the heads of the geni all studded with bright rubies from which a red clear light streams irradiating all around with its burning glow & forming a fine contrast to the mild flood of glory which pours from the magnificent emerald dome & invests every thing with a solemn shadowy grandeur [which] reminds you that you are gazing on the production of a mighty imagination.

(quoted in Barker, p. 161)

After many years at home, during which Gondal and Angria flourished, Charlotte, at age fourteen, was sent to school again in 1831—this time to Roe Head, to complete her education and fit her for a teaching position. In 1835 Charlotte took up her first post as a teacher at Roe Head. Emily joined her as a student there but remained only three months; after suffering intensely from illness, melancholia, and homesickness, Emily returned home, and continued writing her stories.

In 1837 Queen Victoria took the throne, and the Victorian Age officially began. The Brontë sisters are most frequently classified as Victorian writers, but as this brief biography has shown, they lived much of their formative years during a different cultural moment, and their writing shows numerous influences of Romantic era writing—Gothic, impassioned, socially radical—as well as a recognition that a new era was dawning.

In the same year that Victoria became queen it was Anne's turn to leave the Haworth nest, and she joined Charlotte at Roe Head to become educated as a governess. She took her first post in 1839 but was dismissed because she couldn't control her boisterous pupils. She then served as governess to the Robinson family from 1841 to 1845. Here she became a valued friend of her charges and appeared content enough in her position to remain with the Robinsons during holidays. This success was short-lived, however; at Anne's suggestion her brother Branwell became tutor to the Robinson's son, with disastrous results. Branwell became involved in an affair with Mrs. Robinson, which horrified Anne ("sick of mankind and their disgusting ways" she wrote in the back of one of her books during the period) and forced her to give up her position. Branwell was fired shortly afterwards and returned home to embark upon a distressing career of alcohol and drug addiction.

Charlotte remained at Roe Head until 1839 and then became a governess in private families. In 1842 she traveled with Emily to study languages in Brussels; they returned at the end of the year because of Aunt Branwell's death. Charlotte, with a taste for travel that her sisters lacked, returned to Brussels in 1843. There she fell in love with a married professor named Constantin Georges Romain Heger, but Monsieur Heger did not return her affections. She returned home heartbroken, but soon found ample solace in writing.

LITERARY ENDEAVORS

A REMARKABLY close family, the Brontës benefit from critical consideration as a unit. Their literary output certainly should (and will) be viewed separately, but the intense intimacy between the three sisters means that their lives, and their work, can profitably be viewed as integrally connected. They lived and wrote as a tightly knit group, not in isolation.

Their first published work was a thin volume of poems. Charlotte in a later work tells the story of how in 1845 she "accidentally" came upon a journal filled with poetry by Emily; convinced "that these were not common effusions, nor at all like the poetry women generally write," Charlotte persuaded the intensely private Emily to agree to publication. Although she consented, Emily was reportedly furious and never forgave Charlotte for the intrusion into her fantasy world. The resultant volume contained poems by all three sisters and was published under the pseudonyms "Currer, Ellis, and Acton Bell," names under which the sisters continued to publish. The volume sold only two copies, but its publication inspired each of the sisters to begin working on a novel. In addition, the logistics of steering the slim volume through publication—negotiating with publishers and editors, thinking through marketing, collecting reviews and the like—gave Charlotte, who had organized it entirely, what she called a "wonderful zest to life."

The year 1846 saw the sisters at work on *Wuthering Heights* (Emily), *Agnes Grey* (Anne), and *The Professor* (Charlotte). The three volumes were written in close collaboration; many of the novels' passages were read aloud, and plot or stylistic concerns were aired freely at the family supper table. All three sisters drew heavily on the Gondal and Angria stories as well as personal experiences and current social issues.

The sisters intended their novels to be published together, in the three-volume format that was the popular standard of the time. The manuscripts made the rounds of publishers for nearly a year before sparking interest. During this time Charlotte had already begun working on her second novel, *Jane Eyre*, and Anne had begun *The Tenant of Wildfell Hall*. Eventually *Wuthering Heights* and *Agnes Grey* found a publisher in Thomas Cautley Newby, but Charlotte's *The Professor* was not wanted. (It was not published until 1857, two years after her death.) Even Emily and Anne were forced to pay for the publication of their novels themselves; these appeared together in 1847 under the names Ellis and Acton Bell. Reviewers were quick to jump on *Wuthering Heights*, alter-

nately praising it to the skies and lambasting it for blasphemy. *Agnes Grey* was virtually ignored.

Charlotte, after *The Professor* failed to secure publication with Newby, dispatched the novel to Smith, Elder & Co. William Smith Williams, the firm's reader, approved of the novel but decided that it wouldn't sell. The firm sent a letter declining to publish it but added that they would be happy to see any future work by the same writer. This cheered Charlotte immensely, and she raced to finish *Jane Eyre*, sending it to Smith, Elder & Co. a mere two weeks after receiving their letter. When *Jane Eyre*, by "Currer Bell," was published in 1847, it gathered much attention. The majority of reviews were extraordinarily positive, and the public's demand for the novel was enormous; the first edition sold out in only three months. It was quickly adapted for the stage; in February of 1848 *Jane Eyre: The Secrets of Thornfield Manor* was produced at the Victoria Theatre in London.

When critics began to compare the works of the Bells, however, critical tone changed slightly. The Brontë sisters hold a place of such honor in the literary canon that it is difficult to believe the shock and outrage that greeted their first publications. *Jane Eyre* and *Wuthering Heights* were accused of brutality, coarseness, and immorality (even by reviewers who admitted to admiring their energy and imaginative power). When Anne's second novel, *The Tenant of Wildfell Hall*, appeared soon after in 1848, the critics were even more convinced that its detailed depiction of the debauchery of an abusive alcoholic proved that the Bell family had an obsession with the coarse and the brutal. Even the most positive reviews of all three sisters' novels commented upon the distasteful or radical nature of their subject matter.

Since the Brontë sisters are now placed among the foremost women writers, it is ironic that during the early years of publication an enormous number of the reviews spent considerable time worrying over the *gender* of the Bell writers. Their pseudonyms—Acton, Currer, and Ellis Bell—preserved the sister's initials but made their names gender-neutral. Reviewers of the first volume of poems had assumed the Bells to be a family of brothers; when the novels appeared, new surmises were formed. Many critics insisted that Currer Bell, at least—the writer of *Jane Eyre*—was female. A reviewer in 1848 wrote,

The name and sex of the writer are still a mystery. . . . However, we, for our part, cannot doubt that the book is written by a female, and as certain provincialisms indicate, by one from the North of England. Who, indeed, but a woman could have ventured, with the smallest prospect of success, to fill three octavo volumes with the history of a woman's heart? . . . Mr. Rochester, the hero of the story, is as clearly the vision of a woman's fancy, as the heroine is the image of a woman's heart.

(*The Christian Remembrancer,* January 1848)

The same reviewer, however, admits that the public's hypothesis that Currer Bell was a man is justified, for

a book more unfeminine, both in its excellences and defects, it would be hard to find in the annals of female authorship. Throughout there is masculine power, breadth and shrewdness, combined with masculine hardness, coarseness, and freedom of expression. . . . The love-scenes glow with a fire as fierce as that of Sappho, and somewhat more fuliginous. There is an intimate acquaintance with the worst parts of human nature, a practised sagacity in discovering the latent ulcer, and a ruthless rigour in exposing it, which must commend our admiration, but are almost startling in one of the softer sex.

Critics at the time often confused the three writers, and many readers assumed that Currer, Ellis, and Acton were all the same person, and a *man.* (Later critics put forth the hypothesis that all the novels were written by Branwell Brontë, which is both unsound and chronologically impossible.) Eventually Charlotte and Anne were forced to make a visit to London to see the heads of Smith, Elder & Co. to prove that they were in fact separate and female individuals. (Emily refused firmly to make the trip, and the publishers had to take her existence on faith.) Only in 1850, after the deaths of Emily and Anne, did the public become acquainted with the real identity and gender of the Bells. Even Patrick Brontë was unaware that his daughters had been writing and publishing until one day, about a year after the publication of *Jane Eyre,* when Charlotte gently broke the news to him that his daughters were making their fame and fortune as novelists.

While the Brontë sisters were having exciting adventures in publishing, the Brontë brother was literally drinking himself to death. In 1848 Branwell died, leaving his sisters sad and bitter about his wasted life. His debauchery and excesses had an enormous impact upon his family. Close on the heels of Branwell's death, Emily herself finally succumbed to the consumption she had been resolutely fighting; she died on 29 December of 1848. And, incredibly, not six months later, on 28 May 1849, Anne too died.

The deaths of her three remaining siblings in such a short space of time left Charlotte devastated. She pulled herself together and completed her next novel, *Shirley,* which was published in 1849. She then supervised the republication of her sisters' first novels in 1850, contributing the "Biographical Notice of Ellis and Acton Bell," in which she revealed that the Bells were in fact three sisters. Charlotte published her last novel, *Villette,* in 1853. The final years of her life were busy and sociable; after the deaths of her siblings she mixed with the world, becoming acquainted with famous authors of the day, particularly Elizabeth Gaskell, and becoming something of a celebrity herself. In 1854 she marred Arthur Nicholls, her father's curate. The marriage was by all accounts an extremely happy one, but of short duration: Charlotte Brontë died on 31 March 1855, probably from complications during pregnancy. The newspapers announced, "Currer Bell is Dead!" and Mrs. Gaskell began collecting materials for the first biography of Charlotte, published in 1857.

MAIN THEMES IN THE BRONTËS' WORKS

WHILE the work of each sister contains its own unique concerns, there are several themes shared by all three writers. Most importantly, all three sisters evince an intense interest in the emotional and intellectual development of women in an era that tended to repress and oppress women. Thus Charlotte, in *Jane Eyre, Shirley,* and *Villette,* creates heroines who are vocal in their independence. Similarly, in *Wuthering Heights,* Catherine and later her daughter, Cathy, are represented as powerful women, even if ultimately powerless against the patriarchal social structure that confines them. Helen Graham in Anne's *The Tenant of Wildfell Hall* is an independent professional woman (one of the first real working women in English literature), painting for a living and determined to raise her son by herself.

Perhaps the most famous single articulation of the Brontë sisters' commitment to feminist themes comes from *Jane Eyre:*

It is in vain to say human beings ought to be satisfied with tranquility: they must have action; and they will make it if they cannot find it. Millions are condemned to a stiller doom than mine, and millions are in silent revolt against their lot. Nobody knows how many rebellions besides political rebellions ferment in the masses of life which people the earth. Women are supposed to be very calm generally: but women feel just as men feel; they need exercise for their faculties, and a field for their efforts as much as their brothers do; they suffer from too rigid a restraint, too absolute a stagnation, precisely as men would suffer; and it is narrow-minded in their more privileged fellow-creatures to say that they ought to confine themselves to making puddings and knitting stockings, to playing on the piano and embroidering bags. It is thoughtless to condemn them, or laugh at them, if they seek to do more or learn more than custom has pronounced necessary for their sex.

(p. 115)

The "silent revolt" Jane speaks of here is a constant feature of Brontë novels; all the heroines are to some degree or another, and with different degrees of silence, in revolt against the accepted lot of women in the mid-nineteenth century.

Another central concern for the Brontës is the influence of landscape on individual character. The two houses in Emily's *Wuthering Heights*—Thrushcross Grange and Wuthering Heights itself—become central "characters" in the novel, each possessing its peculiar temperament and exerting a powerful influence upon the inhabitants. The Heights, and the landscape that surrounds it, reflects the passionate intensity of Heathcliff himself. Similarly, though with less persistence, Charlotte also concerns herself with setting. In *Jane Eyre*, Mr. Rochester's house Thornfield represents his character; Ferndean, where Jane and Rochester come together at the end of the novel, represents the melding of their two personalities into a new and peaceful setting.

Anne puts a slightly critical spin on the issue of setting. One might expect, at the outset of *Tenant of Wildfell Hall*, that the old derelict hall of the title would prove to be haunted, or at least vaguely mysterious. But in the world of Anne's novel, Wildfell Hall remains steadfastly un-Gothic; there is no ghostly laughter in the attic, no howling winds, no romantic dark passageways. The house is simply uncomfortable and cold, and we see Anne offering a critique of her sisters' Romantic imaginations by choosing realism over Gothic imagination.

The visual arts also pervade the sisters' work. The Brontë children began drawing lessons in 1834 and continued to paint and sketch throughout their lives. They illustrated many of their juvenile stories of Gondal and Angria, and many sketches and paintings of the sisters survive. Branwell's dream was to become a professional painter (some biographers believe he may have gone to London to study painting), and Charlotte herself wished to become a visual artist before her eyesight became too weak and she turned her full attention to writing. The family possessed numerous engravings of famous pictures and books of pictures. Among the most important influences upon the Brontës were the sublime paintings of the Romantic painter John Martin. In all the Brontë sisters' novels, the visual and the visual arts play a key role: the heroine of *The Tenant of Wildfell Hall* is a professional painter; Agnes Grey is skilled in drawing (as befits a governess); and Jane in *Jane Eyre* first attracts Rochester's attention because her portfolio of amateur artwork is so wildly unusual.

Finally, social critique motivates all the Brontë novels. Many of the Brontë novels can be classed with the so-called "social problem novels" (also called the "condition of England" novels), which include Mrs. Gaskell's *Mary Barton* and *North and South*, Dickens' *Hard Times*, Disraeli's *Sybil*, and others. These novels offer realistic representations of the major social issues (poverty, pollution, factory conditions, women's rights, child labor, dehumanization of the workers) arising from the rapid industrialization in nineteenth-century England. Anne Brontë's novels *Agnes Grey* and *The Tenant of Wildfell Hall* fit into this category: the first considers the plight of the governess while the second depicts the devastations of alcoholism and the absolute powerlessness of women within marriage. Emily's *Wuthering Heights* is regularly read as a powerful portrait of social revolution, but Charlotte's *Shirley* gains most from a consideration in light of social issues. Early critics of the novel, comparing *Shirley* with *Jane Eyre* or *Villette*, found the lack of romance in *Shirley* profoundly troubling. More recent critics, however, have recognized *Shirley* to be an immensely rich and satisfying social critique.

It is no accident that two Brontë novels, *Agnes Grey* and *Jane Eyre*, feature governess heroines; the plight of the governess was a volatile topic beginning in the 1840s. Governesses were often the daughters of middle- or upper-class families who had suffered financial losses, and hence were forced to send their daughters out into the working world. A series of wars and colonial emigration also meant that there were fewer men in England, and more spinsters who needed some way of making a living. In an era when a real "lady" did not work, becoming a paid member of the labor force meant demeaning oneself and being stripped of class privileges. It also meant becoming vulnerable to market conditions, which steadily worsened for governesses during the 1840s and 1850s as an economic depression sent more and more young women into the governess market and hence drove salaries down. Living with a wealthy family, and forced to work where once she might have been the mistress of her own household, the governess was prey to numerous hardships. A report from the mid-1840s revealed that, statistically speaking, there were more governesses in mental institutions in England than women of any other profession or walk of life.

A scene from *Jane Eyre* shows how the elite treated their governesses. In the parlor at Thornfield, the wealthy Blanche Ingram tells the assembled company:

"Mary and I have had, I should think, a dozen at least in our day; half of them detestable and the rest ridiculous, and all incubi—were they not, mama?"

"My dearest, don't mention governesses: the word makes me nervous. I have suffered a martyrdom from their incompetency and caprice. I thank Heaven I have now done with them!"

Mrs. Dent here bent over to the pious lady, and whispered something in her ear; I suppose from the answer elicited, it was a reminder that one of the anathematized race was present.

"Tant pis!" said her ladyship, "I hope it may do her good!" Then, in a lower voice, but still loud enough for me to hear, "I noticed her; I am a judge of physiognomy, and in hers I see all the faults of her class."

(p. 186)

The "anathematized race" of governesses, as Jane here calls them, was forced to endure many such comments from wealthy mothers. Charlotte and Anne, having been governesses themselves, knew first-hand the potential brutality with which governesses could be treated.

ANNE BRONTË

THE youngest member of the family, Anne Brontë was only twenty months old when her mother died. Educated mostly at home, Anne exhibited early on a tendency to religious melancholy. Her persona was evidently meek and quiet: Branwell described her as "nothing, absolutely nothing . . . next door to an idiot" (Gérin, 1961, p. 82), and Charlotte offers a not quite as negative but equally problematic assessment of Anne. We have almost no letters or private papers belonging to Anne, so our biographical beliefs about her are reliant in larger part upon Charlotte, who had a low opinion of Anne's work. Yet Charlotte was a poor reader of her sister's fiction, misunderstanding Anne's motivations and her prose. Readers are only now beginning to adequately reassess Anne's work.

Anne transformed some of her experiences as a governess into the short novel *Agnes Grey* (1847), one of the first English novels to have a plain and ordinary young woman as the heroine. Agnes has no special "spark," no beauty, no wit, not even an enormous amount of piety. Yet the novel succeeds as a biting exposé of the tribulations of a governess as it traces Agnes's traumatic experiences in two households, and her eventual engagement to a country curate, Mr. Weston, who like the heroine is entirely quotidian, neither wealthy nor wild nor passionately intense. The critic George Moore called *Agnes Grey* "the most perfect prose narrative in English literature" for its subtle and subdued style.

Anne's second and final novel, *The Tenant of Wildfell Hall* (1848), is considerably less subdued but equally subtle, particularly in narrative structure. Like *Wuthering Heights, The Tenant of Wildfell Hall* is a framed narrative. The hero, Gilbert Markham, tells the story of his meeting with the reclusive Helen Graham, the new mysterious "tenant" of the dilapidated hall. After such a potentially romantic and Gothic beginning the story becomes a powerful social critique. Helen is in fact hiding out from her abusive and alcoholic husband, Arthur Huntingdon, and the central part of the novel which Gilbert's narrative frames is Helen's diary of the gradual decline of her marriage. After she has told her story, the frame narrative resumes; Helen and Gilbert fall in love, but as she is still married the lovers must part. Eventually Helen's husband dies from alcoholism, and she and Gilbert are at last free to declare their love and marry.

The novel was received with much shock and condemnation because of the painful details of Arthur Huntingdon's debauchery and abuse. Even Charlotte, after Anne's death, wrote that the "choice of subject was an entire mistake." Charlotte may have been dismayed by *Tenant* because the character of the profligate, alcoholic, and sexually promiscuous Arthur Huntingdon was thought to be based on the character of Branwell Brontë. Readers at the time considered the novel to be excessively brutal and overly realistic, even pornographic in its treatment of the drunken escapades of Huntingdon and his friends. Anne Brontë, however, defended her decision to write "from the life" in a preface to the second edition of the novel:

My object in writing the following pages was not simply to amuse the Reader; neither was it to gratify my own taste, nor yet to ingratiate myself with the Press and the Public: I wished to tell the truth, for truth always conveys its own moral to those who are able to receive it. . . . I would fain contribute my humble quota towards [reforming society]; and if I can gain the public ear at all, I would rather whisper a few wholesome truths therein than much soft nonsense. . . .

I may have gone too far, in which case I shall be careful not to trouble myself or my readers in the same way again; but when we have to do with vice and vicious characters, I maintain it is better to depict them as they really are than as they would wish to appear. To represent a bad thing in its least offensive light is, doubtless, the most agreeable course for a writer of fiction to pursue; but is it the most honest, or the safest? Is it better to reveal the snares and pitfalls of life to the young and thoughtless traveller, or to cover them with branches and flowers? Oh, reader! if there were less of this delicate concealment of facts–this whispering, "peace, peace," when there is no peace, there would be less of sin and misery to the young of both sexes who are left to wring their bitter knowledge from experience.

(pp. 29–30)

Anne's novels were critiques not only of social norms of her time, but also subtle comments on her sisters' works. As mentioned earlier, she refused to turn Wildfell Hall (which has the same initials as Wuthering Heights, it should be noted) into a monument of Gothic trauma; even while living in a ruin the heroine of *Tenant* insists upon good fires and clean linen. Anne resolutely domesticates the potentially romantic space rather than allowing its Gothic or mysterious potentials to emerge. Likewise, instead of allowing the wild and debauched Arthur Huntingdon to become the novel's romantic hero, Anne makes it clear that his womanizing (no different from Rochester's) is morally offensive, and kills him off. Anne evidently found very little in Rochester or Heathcliff appealing, and her novels make this clear.

The romantic hero Anne supplies for her heroine is equally problematic. Gilbert Markham, though he is sympathetic in many ways, and appears to be deeply in love with our heroine, reveals one terrifying thing about himself. At one point in the novel, enraged with (mistaken) jealously, Gilbert violently strikes another man (whom he believes to be Helen's lover but is in fact Helen's brother) in the head with a cane, and leaves him on the side of the road for dead. The man does not in fact die, but this insight into Gilbert's character should give the reader pause: Anne seems to be hinting rather forcefully that this man Helen marries in the end is *not* the Prince Charming he represents himself to be, or the man we as readers want him to be. Her novel refuses to offer the reader an intense romantic fantasy of the sort we find in *Jane Eyre;* instead, we are offered a painful and problematic critique of masculine character and female vulnerability.

EMILY BRONTË

IT says volumes about Emily Brontë that there exists no record of Emily ever making friends with a person outside the family. As the dreamy sister, she appears to have taken the fantasy worlds of Gondal and Angria most seriously. Yet she was emotionally, morally, and even physically intensely powerful: Charlotte wrote that Emily was "stronger than a man, simpler than a child, her nature stood alone" (*Biographical Notice,* 1850). Charlotte also called her sister "wild," "vigorous," and "possessed of a secret power and fire that might have kindled the veins of a hero." In fact, critics often suggest that the character of Mr. Rochester in *Jane Eyre* was in part modeled on Emily herself, rather than upon any of the men in Charlotte's life. Tales of Emily's masculine behavior are scattered throughout the Brontë family history: Emily was the only Brontë child, for example, whom Patrick taught to fire his pistol; Emily once separated two ferocious fighting dogs with her bare hands; after being bitten by a rabid animal, she seared her own wound with hot tongs from the fire.

Although all three sisters wrote poetry, Emily is the only one of the sisters who is generally acknowledged as a successful poet. Many of Emily's poems (such as "The Prisoner: A Fragment," "R. Alcona to J. Brenzaida," and "Remembrance") were written as part of the Gondal saga, and abound with political intrigue, rebellion, and war. Other lyrics, unconnected with the fantasy world of Gondal, offer Emily's personal vision of the radical power of imagination to transcend ordinary experience. Like Catherine and Heathcliff in *Wuthering Heights*, the speakers of Emily's poems are on fire for something beyond the confines of convention. An early poem, "I'm happiest when most away," (1838) reads:

I'm happiest when most away
I can bear my soul from its home of clay
On a windy night when the moon is bright
And the eye can wander through worlds of light—

When I am not and none beside—
Nor earth nor sea nor cloudless sky—
But only spirit wandering wide
Through infinite immensity.

(Lloyd-Evans)

The speaker here, as in almost all Emily's poems, exhibits a passionate and absolute solitude, but a very Romantic desire for spiritual connection to some greater force. Both the form of the poem—the simple quatrains and the reliance upon dashes—and the commitment to shedding the self ("when I am not") in order to access the "infinite immensity," suggest strong similarities with the American poet Emily Dickinson, who began writing some twenty years later. Both writers rely on hymnlike stanzas and achieve a haunting, visionary tone.

Another poem, "Riches I hold in light esteem," demonstrates what the critic Margaret Reynolds aptly terms the "lawless self-sufficiency" of Emily's poems (Leighton and Reynolds, p. 198):

Riches I hold in light esteem
And Love I laugh to scorn
And lust of Fame was but a dream
That vanished with the morn—

And if I pray, the only prayer
That moves my lips for me
Is—"Leave the heart that now I bear
And give me liberty."

(Lloyd-Evans)

The standard quatrain stanza and the regular *abab* rhyme scheme of ballad stanza are here put to radical use to express precisely irregular sentiments: the rejection of social convention (as represented by Fame, Love, or Riches) and the embracing of Liberty. The quiet declaration of "*if* I pray" also raises the crucial issue of religion in Emily's work.

As in her prose, Emily's poems contain a charged and sensuous representation of nature. The natural world might often be decaying or dead, but it is nevertheless a powerful force, and the speaker feels a certain masochistic pleasure in her encounter with this power, as in the following poem:

The night is darkening round me,
The wild winds coldly blow,
But a tyrant spell has bound me
And I cannot, cannot go.

The giant trees are bending
Their bare boughs weighed with snow
And the storm is fast descending
And yet I cannot go.

Clouds beyond clouds above me,
Wastes beyond wastes below,
But nothing drear can move me,
I will not, cannot go.

The shift in the final line from "cannot" to "will not" go shows much of the force of Emily's poetry; the speakers are intensely self-willed, rejecting convention and safety. The "tyrant spell" that binds the speaker in the first stanza is revealed to be none other than the speaker's own will.

The unbending strength of the individual will is also the main subject of Emily's only novel, *Wuthering Heights*. The novel straddles Romanticism and emergent Victorianism; it fuses romance and realism. It is simultaneously a ghost story, a revenge tragedy, a local history, a passionate romance, and a powerful social commentary. Structured as a frame narrative, the novel is begun by the outer narrator Lockwood who arrives to live in Thrushcross Grange. The nearest neighboring house is Wuthering Heights, a lonely and forsaken place. Lockwood's first violent meeting with the inhabitants sparks his curiosity, which motivates the rest of the narrative; gradually the story of Wuthering Heights and the Grange is told to him by Nelly Dean, the housekeeper who has witnessed the entire saga.

Many years before, Nelly explains, Mr. Earnshaw, owner of the Heights and father of Catherine Earnshaw and Hindley, brought home a street urchin to raise with his own children. This child is Heathcliff, a lower-class boy of passionate and ferocious nature. Catherine's brother Hindley mistreats Heathcliff and refuses (after Mr. Earnshaw's death) to educate or civilize Heathcliff, who grows up wild and uncouth and is forced into a servile position in the household. Nevertheless, Heathcliff and Catherine become passionately attached; the unusual intensity of their connection motivates much of the narrative. Catherine tells Nelly Dean, apropos of her upcoming engagement to her neighbor at the Grange:

"I've no business to marry Edgar Linton than I have to be in Heaven; and if the wicked man in there [Hindley, her brother] had not brought Heathcliff so low, I shouldn't have thought of it. It would degrade me to marry Heathcliff now; so he shall never know how I love him: and that, not because he's handsome, Nelly, but because he's more myself than I am. Whatever our souls are made of, his and mine are the same; and Linton's is as different as a moonbeam from lightning, or frost from fire. . . .

My great miseries in this world have been Heathcliff's miseries, and I watched and felt each from the beginning: my great thought in living is himself. If all else perished, and *he* remained, I should still continue to be; and if all else remained, and he were annihilated, the universe would turn to a mighty stranger; I should not seem a part of it. My love for Linton is like the foliage in the woods: time will change it, I'm well aware, as winter changes the trees. My love for Heathcliff resembles the eternal rocks beneath: a source of little visible delight, but necessary. Nelly, I *am* Heathcliff! He's always, always in my mind: not as a pleasure, any more than I am always a pleasure to myself, but as my own being."

(pp. 73, 74–75)

Tragically, Heathcliff hears only the first of this speech, and thinking Catherine would be "degraded" to marry him, runs away and is absent for three years. During this time Catherine marries Linton, loving him with a mild affection. Heathcliff returns, wealthy and educated but with the same wildness of character, and evinces a new determination to destroy the Earnshaws and Linton for separating him from Catherine and mistreating him as a youth. His destructive power is enormous, succeeding in ruining the lives of nearly every member of the Heights and Grange and eventually contributing to Catherine's death. The novel continues through a second generation, following the tumultuous life of Catherine's daughter, Cathy, who becomes an inhabitant of the Heights, now in Heathcliff's possession. As the novel ends, Heathcliff has exhausted his desire for revenge and is courting death as the only means of becoming reunited with Catherine, whose ghost he perceives to be calling to him. At his death there is the promise of his spiritual reconnection with Catherine; on earth there is the promise of reuniting the Grange and the Heights through the happy marriage of Cathy and Hareton, the son of Catherine's brother, Hindley.

The novel is most famous for the intensity, violence, and radical passion of Heathcliff's nature, and for the profound connection between Heathcliff and Catherine. Heathcliff remains one of the most famous romantic antiheroes in literature. He is undeniably "evil" in the traditional sense of the word, and many readers hold him in disgust. Yet Heathcliff is also undeniably the most compelling and complex character in the novel, and as such also becomes the subject of pity and even attraction. Critical debates over the character of Heathcliff resemble debates over the character of Satan in Milton's *Paradise Lost:* how can an evil figure be so compelling? Does the author mean for us to condemn or admire him? Even Charlotte, generally loud in her admiration for Emily's work, wrote in 1850, "Whether it is right or advisable to create beings like Heathcliff, I do not know." She then added, "I scarcely think it is." But Heathcliff cannot be ignored, and even disapproving readers and critics have tended to admire Heathcliff as a potent figure for social rebellion: as a lower-class character, Heathcliff destroys what he perceives as the unfeeling, staid, and passionless upper classes. The intensity of the bond between Catherine and Heathcliff also is itself a criticism of the dull and proper affection that motivates Edgar or other traditionally respectable people in the narrative. In *Wuthering Heights* Emily offers a truly radical view of individualism, class mobility, and passion.

CHARLOTTE BRONTË

CHARLOTTE, the only Brontë child left alive after 1848, had more years in which to write, and hence has the largest literary output of the three sisters. Charlotte also—perhaps simply because she lived the longest, but also perhaps because of her character—was the sister who saw the most of the world. Her wider scope is revealed in her novels, in which the heroines tend to be infected with wanderlust; as Jane Eyre says, "I remembered that the real world was wide, and that a varied field of hopes and fears, of sensations and excitements, awaited those who had courage to go forth into its expanse, to seek real knowledge of life amidst its perils" (p. 74).

Jane Eyre, Charlotte's first published novel, is the first-person narrative of an unconventional young girl who grows up an outcast in her aunt's household, eventually is sent to school, and from there journeys into the world as a governess. Jane's first position is at Thornfield, the home of Mr. Rochester—a dark, brooding, wealthy man with a brusque manner and a secret in his past. Thornfield proves as mysterious as its owner: Jane hears strange laughter coming from the upper stories and sees a terribly ghostly figure in her bedchamber at night. The unthinkable (in terms of the social structure of the time) happens, and Rochester falls in love with his employee Jane. But at the very moment of their wedding Rochester's secret is revealed: he is already married to a West Indian Creole woman named Bertha Mason, who has gone mad and is being kept by Rochester in the attic at Thornfield—the very woman whose cackling laughter and terrible face have already alarmed Jane.

Jane flees the temptation to become Rochester's mistress and heads out alone into the world. Starving and sick, she falls in a faint at the steps of Moor House, in which live St. John Rivers, a clergyman, and his sisters, Mary and Diana. The Rivers family nurses Jane (now calling herself Jane Elliott to avoid detection) back to health, and St. John offers Jane work as a teacher in the rural school. Eventually Jane's identity is discovered, and news comes that her uncle has died, leaving her a large fortune. It is also revealed that the Rivers siblings are Jane's cousins; Jane divides her fortune with her newly found family, and, after hearing Rochester's voice calling mysteriously to her from across the moors, sets off to find him. Upon arriving at Thornfield she finds the house burned to the ground and Rochester missing; in the fire—started by Bertha—Rochester has lost an arm and his eyesight in a failed attempt to save Bertha. Jane finds Rochester in his new home, and the two are blissfully reunited; the last chapter begins, famously, with the line "Reader, I married him."

While the broad outlines of the novel make its affiliation with the romance and the Gothic novel quite clear, the novel is also a powerful argument for the equality of women and the equality of class. Before their first declarations of love, Jane rebels against her employer's treatment of her, saying to him:

"I tell you I must go!" I retorted, roused to something like passion. "Do you think I can stay to become nothing to you? Do you think I am an automaton?—a machine without feelings? and can bear to have my morsel of bread snatched from my lips, and my drop of living water dashed from my cup? Do you think, because I am poor, obscure, plain, and little, I am soulless and heartless? You think wrong!—I have as much soul as you,—and full as much heart! And if God had gifted me with some beauty, and much wealth, I should have made it as hard for you to leave me, as it is now for me to leave you. I am not talking to you now through the medium of custom, conventionalities, nor

even of mortal flesh:—it is my spirit that addresses your spirit; just as if both had passed through the grave, and we stood at God's feel, equal,—as we are!"

(pp. 265–266)

Jane's vehement declarations of equality and her robust anger at injustice through the novel drew shocked indignation from many critics. The most famous review of *Jane Eyre,* by the painter Lady Elizabeth Eastlake in the *Quarterly Review* (December 1848), condemned the novel for being dangerous and sacrilegious precisely because Jane rebelled against her lot in life. Some religious thought at the time insisted that one was born into one's proper sphere—as a passive woman, or an oppressed working class man—and one should remain there. As Lady Eastlake writes, "It pleased God to make Jane an orphan, friendless, and penniless—yet she thanks nobody, least of all Him."

Matthew Arnold, the Victorian poet, shared Eastlake's assessment of Charlotte's work; in a letter discussing *Villette* he wrote that Charlotte's mind was filled with "nothing but hunger, rebellion and rage"—a very negative assessment for a Victorian woman. Arnold insisted that "Miss Brontë has written a hideous, undelightful, convulsed, constricted novel . . . one of the most utterly disagreeable books I have ever read." Later critics, however, admired rather than disapproved the radical nature of novel, seeing in Jane's anger a biting social commentary and an admirable protest against the plight of women in the nineteenth century. Virginia Woolf, writing in 1925 on the continuing appeal of *Jane Eyre,* speaks of the "genius, the vehemence, the indignation of Charlotte Brontë." Critics in the late twentieth century took Woolf's assessment further and have placed *Jane Eyre* in the forefront of the literary canon. In addition, the emergence of feminist literary criticism in the 1970s and 1980s encouraged a reassessment of all the Brontës' works, which are now seen as central to both the women's literary tradition and English literature as a whole. The "hunger, rebellion and rage" that dismayed Arnold is now considered positive intensity rather than unfeminine behavior.

The figure of Bertha Mason, Rochester's first wife, is particularly important to the early feminist arguments about the novel. In a groundbreaking book, *The Madwoman in the Attic* (1979), the critics Sandra Gilbert and Susan Gubar argue that many women's texts offer a figure that functions as an alter ego for the "good" heroine; the alter ego expresses the anger, violence, or discontent that the proper heroine cannot display. In *Jane Eyre*, Bertha serves this purpose for Jane, symbolically representing all that Jane must repress. With the publication of Gayatri Spivak's essay "Three Women's Texts and a Critique of Imperialism" in 1985, another crucial—though hitherto submerged—aspect of Bertha Mason emerged into the critical debate. Spivak considers Jean Rhys's novel *Wide Sargasso Sea* in conjunction with *Jane Eyre*; Rhys's work, written in 1966, "revises" *Jane Eyre* by telling the story of Rochester's first wife before she arrives at Thornfield. Rhys and Spivak brought Bertha's *race* and colonial heritage at last into the foreground and considered the impact of imperialism in *Jane Eyre*. Bertha's West Indian background, once acknowledged, opens up *Jane Eyre* to postcolonial readings. The novel, critics now argue, uses the figure of the non-English woman as a bestial counterpoint to the white Jane, who represents the upright, moral, pure woman of England. Thus Brontë herself—by portraying Bertha as sexually impure, insane, and savage—participates in the racism and imperial mindset of many of her contemporaries.

On the other hand, other critics argue that Brontë is also, perhaps simultaneously, offering a critique of imperialism through her image of Bertha. In other words, Charlotte means to generate not disgust but sympathy for Bertha; Bertha is meant to foreground just how cruelly the colonizer (in the figure of Mr. Rochester) treats the colonized (Bertha). By making Jane and Bertha structurally similar (they are both outcasts, both Mr. Rochester's dependents, both his wives, etc.), Brontë also suggests the political connection between colonized individuals and women. Both groups are dominated by the white, English male. *Jane Eyre* offers a narrative in which one group, at least, can escape masculine, imperialist domination and achieve independence.

The novel celebrates Jane's eventual complete control over her own destiny. Even the syntactic structure of the famous line, "Reader, I married him"—not "we were married," or "he married me"—grammatically represents Jane's position as acting subject, rather than object, at the end of the novel. Rochester's blindness, and his need for Jane to lead him around and describe the visible world to him, is often read as symbolic castration, further enhancing Jane's control. Jane's lover—once a powerful, wealthy man who employed her—must become helpless, blind, and weak, so that Jane will not become a passive wife under masculine domination.

Charlotte's third novel, *Shirley*, is her most "realist" novel, interested in labor relations and class difference. It contains no Gothic houses or secret attic chambers, and it is the only one of Charlotte's novels to be written in the third person. Charlotte herself called the novel "unromantic as Monday morning." The story is set in Yorkshire just after the Napoleonic wars and details the horrors of the depressed wool industry at a time of high tension between workers and mill owners. Rather than trace the development of a single, powerful consciousness (as in *Jane Eyre*), *Shirley* follows the social, political, and emotional lives of several characters. One hero, the mill owner Robert Moore, introduces the newest labor-saving devices into his mill, ignoring the protests of his workers, who rebel. They attempt to destroy the mill and eventually attempt to assassinate Robert himself. In an attempt to repair his fortunes, Robert proposes to Shirley Keeldar, an heiress. She refuses him, eventually marrying his brother Louis, who has been a tutor in her family. By marrying "beneath her," Shirley incurs the wrath of her family, but her independent, spirited character overcomes all opposition. Robert eventually marries Caroline Helstone, the novel's other heroine. In the passive, confined, and unhappy figure of Caroline, Charlotte makes a powerful protest against the limited opportunities available to women in the period.

In *Villette* we see the re-emergence of many of Charlotte's interests in women's teaching and in female independence and power. The narrator of the novel, Lucy Snowe, shares much with Jane Eyre: both are orphans, both are forced to make their livings as educators (Lucy goes to work not as a governess but in a school), and both are ferociously independent. She says early in the novel, "Thus, there remained no possibility of dependence on others; to myself alone could I look" (p 32). Lucy is, however, even more wild and restless than Jane Eyre. Lucy Snowe is at war with herself as well as with society and convention. She is represented wandering several times in the novel out into a storm, and storms become representative of her own rebellious nature.

During the central part of the novel Lucy Snowe travels to Brussels (which Brontë renames Villette) to teach. She details her strained relations with the proprietress of the school, Madame Beck, as well as her intense loneliness and a desire for emotional affection so profound that at one point in the novel she becomes ill and suffers a nervous breakdown. Eventually she becomes attracted to a dominating professor, Paul Emanuel. After a number of fiery and argumentative encounters (reminiscent of those between Jane and Rochester), the two declare their love for one another. Their love has many obstacles, not least that he is Catholic and she is Protestant. At the end of the novel Monsieur Emanuel buys for his beloved a small house and school for her to run, then travels abroad. While he is away Lucy's endeavor flourishes, and she becomes a contented working woman. The final page of the novel shows Lucy seated at her window, watching a growing storm and waiting for her lover's boat to arrive. She writes:

The skies hang full and dark—a rack sails from the west; the clouds cast themselves into strange forms—arches and broad radiations; there rise resplendent mornings—glorious, royal, purple as monarch in his state; the heavens are one flame; so wild are they, they rival battle at its thickest—so bloody, they shame Victory in her pride. I know some signs of the sky; I have noted them ever since childhood. . . .

That storm roared frenzied for seven days. It did not cease till the Atlantic was strewn with wrecks: it did not lull till the deeps had gorged their full of sustenance. . . .

Here pause—pause at once. There is enough said. Trouble no quiet, kind heart; leave sunny imaginations hope. Let it be theirs to conceive the delight of joy born again fresh out of great terror, the rapture of rescue from peril, the wondrous reprieve from dread, the fruition of return. Let them picture union and a happy succeeding life.

(p. 474)

The ending offers not the romantic fantasy *Jane Eyre* gave us, but a more powerful vision of solitary female independence. It has always seemed quite clear to readers that Paul Emanuel dies in a shipwreck, although Lucy steadfastly refuses to tell us. We never know exactly what happens, but these final paragraphs are telling. The storm—itself an emblem of Lucy in the novel—appears to be triumphantly wrecking ships with a violence Lucy describes as beautiful and exciting. Charlotte suggests that it is Lucy herself, for all her love of Monsieur Paul, who stops him from returning to marry her, and remove her from the independence that remains the most important characteristic of all the Brontë heroines. Lucy Snowe stands

as the most radical example of the kind of woman the Brontës invented, and were themselves: independent, powerful, and utterly unconventional.

BIBLIOGRAPHY

THE BRONTË FAMILY

I. JOINT PUBLICATIONS. *Poems* by Currer, Ellis, and Acton Bell (London, 1846); Juliet Barker, ed., *The Brontës: Selected Poems* (London, repr. 1993).

II. LETTERS. Clement Shorter, *The Brontës: Life and Letters* (London and New York, 1908); T. J. Wise and A. Symington, eds., *The Brontës: Their Lives, Friendships, and Correspondence*, 4 vols. (Oxford, 1932, repr. 1980).

III. BIOGRAPHIES. Francis Leyland, *The Brontë Family*, 2 vols. (London, 1886); Mrs. Ellis H. Chadwick, *In the Footsteps of the Brontës* (London, 1914; repr. New York 1971); Fannie Ratchford, *The Brontës' Web of Childhood* (New York, 1941); Phyllis Bentley, *The Brontës and Their World* (London, 1969); Brian Wilks, *The Brontës* (London and New York, 1975); Juliet Barker, *The Brontës* (London and New York, 1994).

IV. CRITICAL STUDIES. Tom Winnifrith, *The Brontës and Their Background: Romance and Reality* (London, 1973); Miriam Allott, ed., *The Brontës: The Critical Heritage* (London and Boston, 1974); Terry Eagleton, *Myths of Power: A Marxist Study of the Brontës* (London and New York, 1975); Christine Alexander and Jane Sellars, *The Art of the Brontës* (Cambridge and New York, 1995); Susan Meyer, *Imperialism at Home: Race and Victorian Women's Fiction* (Ithaca, N.Y., 1996).

CHARLOTTE BRONTË

I. FIRST EDITIONS. *Jane Eyre* (London, 1847); *Shirley* (London, 1849); *Villette* (London, 1853); *The Professor* (posthumous, London, 1857).

II. MODERN EDITIONS. Victor Neufeldt, ed., *The Poems of Charlotte Brontë: A New Text and Commentary* (New York, 1985); Christine Alexander, ed., *An Edition of the Early Writings of Charlotte Brontë, 1826–1832* (London and New York, 1987); *Jane Eyre*, Norton Critical Edition (New York, 1971, rev. 1987); *Jane Eyre*, Oxford World's Classics (Oxford, 1998); *Shirley*, Oxford World's Classics (Oxford, 1998); *The Professor*, Oxford World's Classics (Oxford, 2001); *Villette*, Oxford World's Classics (Oxford, 2001).

III. LETTERS AND MANUSCRIPTS. Christine Alexander, *A Bibliography of the Manuscripts of Charlotte Brontë* (Westport, Conn., 1982); Margaret Smith, *The Letters of Charlotte Brontë, 1829–1847*, 2 vols. (Oxford, 1995).

IV. BIOGRAPHIES. Elizabeth Gaskell, *Life of Charlotte Brontë* (London, 1857); Augustine Birrell, *The Life of Charlotte Brontë* (London, 1887); Rebecca Fraser, *The*

Brontës: Charlotte Brontë and Her Family (New York, 1988); Lyndall Gordon, Charlotte Brontë: A Passionate Life (New York, 1994; London, 1995).

V. CRITICAL STUDIES. Elizabeth Rigby, Lady Eastlake, "Jane Eyre and Vanity Fair," in Quarterly Review (December 1848); Virginia Woolf, "Jane Eyre and Wuthering Heights," in The Common Reader (New York and London, 1925); Robert Bernard Martin, The Accents of Persuasion (London, 1966); Miriam Allott, ed., Charlotte Brontë: Jane Eyre and Villette: A Casebook (London, 1973); Sandra M. Gilbert and Susan Gubar, The Madwoman in the Attic (New Haven, Conn., 1979); Christine Alexander, The Early Writings of Charlotte Brontë (Oxford, 1983); John Maynard, Charlotte Brontë and Sexuality (Cambridge, U.K., and New York, 1984); Gayatri Spivak, "Three Women's Texts and a Critique of Imperialism," in Critical Inquiry 12 (autumn 1985); John Kucich, Repression in Victorian Fiction: Charlotte Brontë, George Eliot, and Charles Dickens (Berkeley, Calif., 1987); Mary Poovey, Uneven Developments: The Ideological Work of Gender in Mid-Victorian England (Chicago, 1988); Janet Gezari, Charlotte Brontë and Defensive Conduct (Philadelphia, 1992); Susan Fraiman, Unbecoming Women: British Women Writers and the Novel of Development (New York, 1993); Sally Shuttleworth, Charlotte Brontë and Victorian Psychology (Cambridge, U.K., and New York, 1996); Heather Glen, ed., New Casebooks on Jane Eyre (1997).

EMILY BRONTË

I. FIRST EDITIONS. Emily Brontë and Anne Brontë, Wuthering Heights and Agnes Grey (London, 1847).

II. MODERN EDITIONS. C. W. Hatfield, ed., The Complete Poems of Emily Jane Brontë (New York, 1941); Wuthering Heights, Norton Critical Edition (New York, 1989); Barbara Lloyd-Evans, ed., The Poems of Emily Brontë (London, 1992); T. J. Wise and John Alexander Symington, eds., The Poems of Emily Jane Brontë and Anne Brontë (Oxford, 1934); Angela Leighton and Margaret Reynolds, Victorian Women Poets: An Anthology (Oxford and Cambridge, Mass., 1995); Wuthering Heights, Oxford World's Classics (Oxford, 1998).

III. BIOGRAPHIES. Charlotte Brontë, Biographical Notice of Ellis and Acton Bell, in Wuthering Heights, 2d ed. (London 1850); John Hewish, Emily Brontë: A Critical and Biographical Study (London and New York, 1969); Winifred Gérin, Emily Brontë: A Biography (Oxford, 1972); Edward Chitham, A Life of Emily Brontë (Oxford and New York, 1987).

V. CRITICAL STUDIES. Anne Smith, ed., The Art of Emily Brontë (London, 1976); Margaret Homans, Women Writers and Poetic Identity: Dorothy Wordsworth, Emily Brontë, and Emily Dickinson (Princeton, N.J., 1980); Stevie Davies, Emily Brontë (Hemel Hempstead, U.K., 1988); Lyn Pykett, Emily Brontë (Basingstoke, U.K., 1989); U. C. Knoepflmacher, Wuthering Heights (Cambridge, U.K.,

and New York, 1989); Irene Tayler, Holy Ghosts: The Male Muses of Emily and Charlotte Brontë (New York, 1990); Alison Milbank, Daughters of the House: Modes of the Gothic in Victorian Fiction (New York, 1992); Martha Nussbaum, "Wuthering Heights: The Romantic Ascent," in Philosophy and Literature 20 (October 1996); Lin Haire-Sargeant, "Sympathy for the Devil: The Problem of Heathcliff in Film Versions of Wuthering Heights," in Barbara Tepa Lupack, ed., Nineteenth-Century Women at the Movies: Adapting Classic Women's Fiction to Film (Bowling Green, Ohio, 1999); Hayley Mitchell, Readings on Wuthering Heights (1999); Michelle Masse, "'He's More Myself Than I Am': Narcissism and Gender in Wuthering Heights," in Peter Rudnytsky, ed., Psychoanalyses/Feminisms (Albany, N.Y., 2000).

ANNE BRONTË

I. FIRST EDITIONS. Wuthering Heights and Agnes Grey (London, 1847); The Tenant of Wildfell Hall (London, 1848).

II. MODERN EDITIONS. T. J. Wise and John Alexander Symington, eds., The Poems of Emily Jane Brontë and Anne Brontë (Oxford, 1934); Edward Chitham, ed., The Poems of Anne Brontë: A New Text and Commentary (Totowa, New Jersey, 1979); Agnes Grey, Oxford World's Classics (Oxford, 1998); The Tenant of Wildfell Hall, Oxford World's Classics (Oxford, 1998).

III. BIOGRAPHIES. Winifred Gérin, Anne Brontë (London, 1976); Edward Chitham, A Life of Anne Brontë (Oxford and Cambridge, Mass., 1991).

IV. CRITICAL STUDIES. P. J. M. Scott, Anne Brontë: A New Critical Assessment (London and Totowa, N.J., 1983); Jan Gordon, "Gossip, Diary, Letter, Text: Anne Brontë's Narrative Tenant and the Problematic of the Gothic Sequel," in English Language History 51 (winter 1984); N. M. Jacobs, "Gender and Layered Narrative in Wuthering Heights and The Tenant of Wildfell Hall," in Journal of Narrative Technique 16 (fall 1986); Elizabeth Langland, Anne Brontë: The Other One (Totowa, New Jersey, 1989); Robert Liddell, Twin Spirits: The Novels of Emily and Anne Brontë (London, 1990); Arnold Bell, The Novels of Anne Brontë: A Study and Reappraisal (Braunton, Devon, U.K., 1992); Elizabeth Langland, "The Voicing of Feminine Desire in Anne Brontë's The Tenant of Wildfell Hall," in Antony Harrison and Beverly Taylor, eds., Gender and Discourse in Victorian Literature (De Kalb, Ill., 1992); Elizabeth Berry, Anne Brontë's Radical Vision: Structures of Consciousness (Victoria, B.C., 1994); Maria Frawley, Anne Brontë (London and New York 1996); Laura Berry, "Acts of Custody and Incarceration in Wuthering Heights and The Tenant of Wildfell Hall," in Novel: A Forum on Fiction 30 (fall 1996); Elizabeth Rose Gruner, "Plotting the Mother: Caroline Norton, Helen Huntingdon, and Isabel Vane," in Tulsa Studies in Women's Literature 12 (fall 1997).

DANIEL DEFOE

(1660–1731)

Sandie Byrne

CANONICAL WRITER (SCANDALMONGER, pamphleteer, travel-writer, journalist); wealthy merchant (bankrupt, life-long debtor); respected political commentator (spy, Whig polemicist, Tory polemicist, satirist, jailbird); "True-Born Englishman" and Gentleman with connections to the aristocracy (of Yeoman stock; possibly descended from Dutch émigrés); Humanitarian (anti-Catholic, pro-slavery); Daniel Defoe (Foe, later Dafoe, Defooe, De Fooe; a.k.a. Eye Witness, T. Taylor, Andrew Morton, Heliostrapolis, Secretary to the Emperor of the Moon). Just as his writing interweaves fiction into nonfiction, and vice versa, and sometimes passes off the one as the other, so Defoe's life is a tissue of contradictions and misinformation. Even his birth is mysterious: while those of his sisters, Mary and Elizabeth, are recorded in the Parish Register, Daniel's is not (possibly because the Register at the time recorded only baptisms rather than births).

Defoe was perhaps what Moll Flanders calls an "amphibian Creature"; "a Tradesman forsooth, that was something of a Gentleman too that would carry a sword to the play and not carry the mark of his apron or his tradesman's hat, or even countenance, outside the shop" (*Moll Flanders,* ed. by G. A. Starr, London, 1973, p. 104). Defoe himself attempted to blur these social distinctions, writing in *The Compleat Tradesman (1725–1727),* "Trade is so far here from being inconsistent with a gentleman, that, in short, trade in England makes gentlemen, and has peopled this nation with gentlemen" (vol. 1, chapter 22).

He was born the third child and first son to James and Alice Foe in 1660, the year in which the Commonwealth ended, and King Charles II was restored to the throne. The Defoe family came from the farming region near Peterborough, but James was a well-to-do merchant, a tallow chandler (a dealer in tallow, from which candles were made) who lived with his family at St. Giles, Cripplegate, London. The family was Puritan and Cromwellian, and had lived through a period when both these attitudes were in the ascendant. This ended with the Restoration, of both the king and of Anglicanism—giving rise to the fear that the old, pre-Protestant style of religion would return, either through the king, who had married a Catholic, or through his brother and heir, another Catholic. The climate of the times was one of suspicion and fear. The "Clarendon Code" (named after Edward Hyde, the Chancellor) ensured that Dissenters could hold neither public nor church office, and imposed heavy penalties for participation in any form of non-Anglican worship. Defoe's parents were so convinced that their Bibles would be confiscated that they set the family to the task of copying them out in shorthand.

As a young child, Daniel survived the Great Plague (1665), which he was to reconstruct from childhood memories in *A Journal of the Plague Year,* (1722) and the Great Fire of London (1666). His mother died when he was ten and the following year he was sent to the Reverend James Fisher's school for Dissenters' children in Dorking, after which, since his religion debarred him from the universities, he attended Charles Morton's Academy, also set up for the benefit of Nonconformists, in Newington Green, near London. Although socially and politically disadvantageous, this education was wider and more liberal than any he could have received from Oxford or Cambridge at that time, since the established universities still followed a curriculum based around grammar and rhetoric, and the acquisition of Greek and, especially, Latin, while the Dissenting Academies allowed the study of new and unorthodox texts. At Newington, Defoe was able to study natural philosophy (science), astronomy, geography, and history, thus laying the foundations of a broad and eclectic knowledge that he was to plunder in his writing. Morton also held classes in "eloquence," and made his pupils produce letters on a variety of subjects as if to rulers, ambassadors, and foreign agents, so Defoe was able to perfect early in life his facility for writing in almost any required style and on any given subject. Defoe may have been intended for the ministry, but seems to have decided against that course by the time he graduated in 1679. His teacher, Charles Morton, eventually escaped religious persecution by emigrating to America, where he became vice-president of Harvard.

Defoe seems to have entered business around 1681, operating as a hose-factor (wholesaler of hosiery) and probably dealing in other commodities, from his father's premises. In 1683 he was courting Mary Tuffley, to whom he sent a manuscript anthology of pieces which were (presumably) favorites of his or which he felt were appropriate reading for a young woman. The "Historical Collections or Memoires of Passages and Stories Collected from Severall Authors" included a number of stirring or morally improving anecdotes of the lives of (among others) Alexander the Great, Julius Caesar, and Augustus. The couple married a year later, Mary bringing to the marriage a substantial dowry (£3,700), which Defoe invested in setting up his own premises—warehouse and offices below, and dwelling above—in a prosperous part of London. Eight years later he declared bankrupcy, and he was never again entirely clear of debt for the rest of his life. He was imprisoned in the Fleet Prison in October and November 1692, and in the King's Bench Prison in February 1693. Having negotiated terms with his creditors, he found work as a manager-trustee for one of the licensed lotteries of the day. Sometime after, in about 1695, he added the "De" to his name. From 1695 to 1699 he was an accountant to the commissioners of Glass Duty (i.e., the tax on windows), and invested in a brick and tile works in Tilbury, which failed in 1703.

The failures of his business interests seem not to be the result of any lack of enthusiasm or talent on Defoe's part. His writings about trade and mercantile adventures are lively and engaged, and show his pride in being too shrewd to be caught by the many knaves and frauds he describes as ready to entrap the unwary. His bankruptcy was probably brought about in part by the precariousness of the market for such luxury goods as he dealt in—from hose to brandy to civet (derived from cats' urine for the production of perfumes)—and speculated on (for example, a diving bell for the discovery of sunken treasure), and from his

investment in the high-risk area of marine insurance. One cause, however, was his involvement in politics, or more precisely, rebellion. He was a supporter of Charles II's illegitimate son, the duke of Monmouth, for whose cause and against James II he fought in 1685. After a decisive defeat at the Battle of Sedgemoor, Monmouth was captured and executed, and suspected supporters of the rising were hunted down, imprisoned, or barbarously executed. Until the General Pardon of May 1687, therefore, Defoe would have had to remain in hiding, and it is likely that he spent much of the time abroad, partly in pursuit of business interests, until the "Glorious Revolution" resulted in the accession of William of Orange and his queen, Mary. In 1688, Defoe was among those who rode out to meet the army of William III, as he was to become, on its way to London, and he remained a staunch supporter of William, defending him in a number of pamphlets.

The extent of Defoe's political activities, open and clandestine, and his exact relationship with William III and the earl of Oxford, for whom he is said to have established a network of spies, is not known, nor can we be certain of whether Defoe was the author of a number of political treatises published at this time. His first full-length political pamphlet was *Reflections upon the Late Great Revolution* (1689) and his first full-length book was *An Essay upon Projects* (1697), a work which, among other things, promotes the character of the "projector," whom we might now call entrepreneur or capitalist, and whom we might associate with Defoe himself. The projector is an enabler and improver, and Defoe proposes schemes for the improvement of a number of social practices and institutions: changes in banking and lotteries; the humane treatment of bankrupts; the establishment of a military academy to provide for a standing army; the creation of an academy of letters, and of an academy for women.

The long poem *The True-Born Englishman* (1701), an attack on the myth of racial "purity" cited in support of the xenophobic contemporary attitudes, especially those directed against the Dutch future William III, was a best seller, but the satirical pamphlet *The Shortest Way with the Dissenters* (1703), imitated rather too well the kind of hysterical tirade against Dissenters by fanatical Anglicans, and led to Defoe's conviction in July 1703 for seditious libel, for which he was sentenced to pay a fine of two hundred marks, stand in the pillory three times, and give sureties of good behavior for seven years. He was released from Newgate Gaol in November on the intervention of the Secretary of State, Robert Harley, first earl of Oxford, and entered into the service of the moderate Tory Harley as a political journalist and sampler of public opinion. During his imprisonment, Defoe wrote his mock-Pindaric ode, "Hymn to the Pillory," which he is said to have read aloud whilst pilloried himself. It shows how much of a realist he had become: "Actions receive their tincture from the times, / And as they change are virtues made of crimes" (The Shakespeare Head Edition of the *Novels and Selected Writings of Daniel Defoe*, 14 vols., 1927–1928, p. 150).

This pragmatism may have served Defoe well when the moderate Harley moved from Whiggism to join the Tory administration, and, after a period in power from 1710, fell with the disgraced Tories in 1715. Defoe was able to transfer his services to the new ministry. Or perhaps he had become, as Maximillian Novak suggests, a "Court Whig," following a moderate form of Whiggism loyal to a monarch who was seen as protecting English interests and liberties (*Daniel Defoe: Master of Fictions*, 2001, p. 120).

In 1704, Defoe established his pro-government periodical *A Review of the Affairs of France: Purg'd from the Errors and partiality of News-Writers and Petty-Statesmen, of all Sides* (later, *A Review of the State of the British Nation*), which he single-handedly produced two or three times a week until 1713, becoming one of the most influential opinion-makers in the country. During 1706–1710, he traveled in Scotland on behalf of Harley and the Lord Treasurer, Godolphin, as an unofficial agent in the negotiation of the Act of Union between England and Scotland that came into effect in 1707, and gathering material for his *History of the Union of Scotland and England* (1709). Writing to Harley from Scotland, he boasts of his success as a confidential agent:

I am perfectly unsuspected as corresponding with anybody in England. I converse with Presbyterian, Episcopal-Dissenter, papist, and Non-Juror, and I hope with equal circumspection. I flatter myself you will have no complaints of my conduct. I have faithfull emissaries in every company and I talk to everybody in their own way. To the merchants I am about to settle here in trade. . . . With the lawyers I want to purchase a house and land to bring my family and live upon it (God knows where the money is to pay for it). Today I am going into

partnership with a Member of Parliament in a glass-house, tomorrow with another in a salt work. . . . I am all to everyone that I may gain some.

(*Letters of Daniel Defoe*, ed. by George Harris Healey, Oxford, 1955, pp. 158–59)

Back in England, he was arrested again for debt in March 1713 and again for seditious libel the following April, on charges resulting from the literal interpretation of three satirical pamphlets. Defoe published a furious tirade against the law that had thus falsely imprisoned him, and was committed to the Queen's Bench Prison for contempt of court. He was released after publication of apologies in two editions of the *Review* and the payment of a fine. The pattern was to be repeated shortly after, when Defoe was charged with seditious libel for suggesting that one of the regents of George, Elector of Hanover (now George I of England), Lord Annesley, was a Jacobite, then eventually agreed to work for the new, Whig, Secretary of State, Townshend. He continued to defend his mentor Harley, however, even after the latter was sent to the Tower of London on a charge of High Treason in 1715.

Defoe was taking the waters medicinally in Derbyshire in 1712, and his health may have been uncertain from then on. Worry about debt and the possibility of imprisonment could not have helped matters, yet he continued to be a prolific writer. By the early 1720s he either controlled or wrote for nine newspapers and periodicals and had made his name as a public poet and pamphleteer; a propagandist.

In the last years of his life, the specters of old debts returned to haunt him, and he was forced to go into hiding from a creditor of fifty years before. He died on April 1731, of "a lethargy" (probably a stroke) in lodgings in Ropemaker's Alley, Moorfields. He was buried in the Dissenters' cemetery in Bunhill Fields, but his gravestone can be seen in Stoke Newington District Library in the East End of London.

REPUTATION

MUCH of Defoe's work was published anonymously or pseudonymously, making attribution of his voluminous output (probably over 560 works) sometimes difficult, but he did put his name, or initials, to some of his writing, and many others have subsequently been prepared to do it for him. His best-known work, *The Life and Strange Surpriz-*

ing Adventures of Robinson Crusoe, of York, Mariner (1719) (hereafter, *Robinson Crusoe*) was almost unmentioned in literary criticism of the eighteenth century, though his political and other pamphlets attracted attention from the first. As a novel, *Robinson Crusoe* was beneath the quills of serious literary scholars or even that of Alexander Pope, who, though usually quick to pierce the pretentiousness of any writer, skimmed Defoe in a few lines. (See Joseph Spence, *Observations, Anecdotes and Characters of Books and Men,* ed. By James Osborn, 2 vols., Oxford, 1966, vol. 1, p. 213.) Jonathan Swift, of course, pilloried those prolific writers whom he considered hacks in *Gulliver's Travels* (1726).

Defoe did have enemies in his lifetime, as well as many who disagreed with his religion, politics, and opinions. His writing, morals, and antecedents were attacked in works such as *The True-Born-Hugonot: Or, Daniel Defoe: a Satyr* (1703), and even fellow Dissenters sometimes questioned his right to speak for them, as well as the manner in which he did so, as in John Howe's *Some Consideration of a Preface to an Enquiry, Concerning the Occasional Conformity of the Dissenters* (1701).

An early biographer was William Shiells, whose "Life of the Author" was prefaced to *Daniel Defoe's Voyage Round the World* (1787), and Samuel Johnson was an admirer, but the first important life and bibliography came with George Chalmers' expanded edition of his 1785 work. By 1793 Andrew Kippis could acknowledge (in *Biographia Britannica,* ed. by Andrew Kippis, Joseph Towers, et al., London, 1793) that Defoe had been neglected: "full justice was far from being done to his reputation . . . for a considerable time after his decease" but "the world has at last become sensible of his great and various talents" (vol. 5, p. 74). As Novak points out (*Daniel Defoe,* p. 2), the installation of Defoe in the Temple of Fame was not only on the basis of the quality of his writing, but also on the quality of his life, which was required to be saintly. Defoe was accordingly made a hero of Whig principles, a sufferer for Dissenting religion, and a pioneer of free trade principles. As Novak puts it: "Not until William Minto's debunking biography (*Daniel Defoe,* London, 1879) . . . did the bubble burst" (p. 2).

Anonymity served Defoe well in some ways, but anonymous and pseudonymous publication made the canon of Defoe's work hard to establish, and recent scholarship has been concerned with the issues of whether Defoe was the author of works traditionally attributed to him, and of the basis on which past generations of scholars (and booksellers) had made those attributions. Defoe himself, in his *Appeal to Honour and Justice* (1715), complained that whenever any unpopular pamphlet or tract appeared, "I am immediately charg'd with being the Author, and very often the first Knowledge I have had of a Books being publish'd, has been from being abus'd for being the Author of it, in some Pamphlet publish'd in Answer to it" (p. 25).

Defoe's offering of his novels as "histories" and "memoirs" recounted by their protagonists, and subsequent booksellers' and publishers' being deceived by or colluding with this fiction, makes the establishment of provenance more difficult. *Memoirs of a Cavalier,* for example, was published in 1720 without Defoe's name. The publisher of the second, 1750, edition, James Lister, identified the Cavalier as Andrew Newport (who had in fact been a child at the time when the Cavalier was fighting under Gustavus Adolphus), and advertised the book as "Memoirs of the Honourable Col. Andrew Newport, a Shropshire Gentleman." The sixth edition, in 1784, did refer to Defoe, but only as someone who had published the Memoirs "from the original Manuscript," keeping intact the fiction of his being a mere editor or transmitter of the tale. The seventh edition, of 1792, dropped Defoe again, and reverted to the Newport attribution.

A further complication is the existence of a number of rewritten and bowdlerized texts, such as *The History of Mademoiselle de Beleau; or, The New Roxana* (1775) and *The History of Laetitia Atkins, vulgarly called Moll. Flanders* (1776), both published by Francis Noble, who, recognizing that Defoe's name was marketable, included it on each of the rewritten novels and in a fictitious introduction to *Laetitia Atkins.* He wasn't alone. Defoe complained, "My Name's the Hackney Title of the Times" (*An Elegy on the Author of the True-Born Englishman,* 1704, vol. 1, p. 70), an emblematic or generic name, like Merlin or Robin Hood, adopted by or given to generations of figures participating in its iconic status.

P. N. Furbank and W. R. Owens made the case for discounting many of the attributions in their book *The Canonisation of Daniel Defoe,* but a counterargument was advanced by Maximillian Novak in a long article for the *Huntingdon Library Quarterly* in which he finds textual authority for many of the conventional attributions. Defoe seems to anticipate the complexity of his bibliography, and the powerful but divergent cases made by bibliographers and textual critics, in his *Appeal to Honour and Justice,* in which he says that there was "no purpose to oppose" the attribution of works to his authorship, since "One Man will swear to the Style; another to this or that Expression; another to Way of Printing; and all so positive. . . ." (p. 46).

POETRY

MOST of Defoe's poetry is lampooning or satirical, and his strongest influences were likely to have been the "wits" such as Marvell, Rochester, and Dryden, as well as Milton, Cowley, Waller, and Aphra Behn. In his *The Pacificator* (1700), a long poem that enacts the politics of his contemporary poets, he compares himself to William Congreve, master of comedy and lampoon. Two of his earliest published works were the poems *A New Discovery of an Old Intreague* (1691) and "To the Athenian Society" (1692), and one of his most popular and frequently reprinted works during his lifetime was the long poem *The True-Born Englishman* (1701). Although Defoe received revenue from ten legal editions of the poem, many more were pirated and sold at less than the official price. The poem was a riposte to *The Foreigner,* which Defoe described as:

a vile abhor'd Pamphlet, in very ill Verse, written by one Mr Tutchin, and call'd THE FOREIGNERS: in which the Author . . . fell personally upon the King himself, and then upon the *Dutch* Nation; and after having reproach'd his Majesty with Crimes, that his worst Enemy could not think of without Horror, he sums up all in the odious Name of FOREIGNER.

This fill'd me with a kind of Rage against the Book; and gave birth to a Trifle which I could hope should have met with so general an Acceptation as it did, I mean, *The True-Born Englishman.*

> (*Appeal to the Honour and Justice . . . ,*
> Shakespeare Head edition, p. 195)

The poem argues that the very language of the English contains the trace of their mixed heritage, and makes a nonsense of claims of purity:

From this amphibious Ill-born Mob began
That vain ill-natur'd thing, an Englishman.
The Customs, Sirnames, Languages, and Manners,
Of all these Nations are their own Explainers:

Whose Relicks are so lasting and so strong,
They ha' left a *Shibboleth* upon our Tongue;
By which with easy search you may distinguish
Your *Roman-Saxon-Danish-Norman* English.
(in *Poems on Affairs of State,* ed. by Frank Ellis,
New Haven, 1963–1975, vol. 6, p. 270)

Like most of Defoe's poems, *The True-Born Englishman* sustains its witty abuse in loosely rhymed iambic couplets.

Other poems on political subjects included *Legion's Memorial,* a protest against the imprisonment of five legitimate petitioners to Parliament, and *A New Satyr on the Parliament,* both written in 1701. Defoe's tone is Hobbesian: he speaks of the "Tincture in the Blood" which would make all men "be Tyrants if they cou'd," even elected Members of Parliament; that is, that self-interest puts all men in competition with one another, so that strong government is needed to enforce control and civilized interaction. The Biblical allusion in this poem's signature, "Our Name is Legion and we are many," would not have been lost on Parliament, and would have had a strong flavor of Revolution (*Legion's Memorial,* 1701; in Shakespeare Head Edition, p. 91). Later that year, *A New Satyr on the Parliament* accused the Commons of corruption:

But you, although your Powers depend
    On every Plowman's Vote,
Beyond the Law that Power extend,
To ruine those you should defend,
    And sell the Power you bought.
    (in *Poems on Affairs of State,* vol. 6, p. 324)

One of his more impudent poems commemorates one of his more impudent deeds, his turning of the intended humiliation of being put in the pillory into a triumph. Surrounded by supporters, and therefore protected from the stones, mud, and excrement usually thrown at the pilloried offender, Defoe quoted from and watched his friends sell copies of the pamphlet for which he was condemned, *The Shortest Way with the Dissenters.* In his poem, *A Hymn to the Pillory,* he imagines himself as a martyr, made an example of to all outspoken, honest men, standing in the place that should have belonged to those who sent him there— "And he who for no Crime shall on thy Brows appear / Bears less Reproach than they who plac'd 'em there"—with a paper pinned to his hat advertising the reason for his martyrdom:

Tell them 'twas because he was too bold,
And told those Truths, which shou'd not ha' been
  told.
Extoll the Justice of the land
Who Punish what they will not understand.
Tell them he stands Exalted there
For speaking what we wou'd not hear;
And yet he might ha' been secure,
Had he said less, or wou'd he ha said more.
              ("A Hymn to the Pillory," in
The Shakespeare Head Edition, lines 138–151)

Subsequently, in December of 1701, Defoe was to consolidate and theorize his views on the power and prerogatives of Parliament in a pamphlet, *The Original Power of the Collective Body of the People of England, Examined and Asserted*, asserting that the House of Commons could hold power only as representatives of the electorate (property-owning men, since this was before Parliamentary reform), and were subject to the law. The rights and powers of the people derived from property, as did the monarch's. If a man owned all of the land of Britain, he would rule Britain. The freeholders of Britain voted for its Members of Parliament and entered into a contract with them. If the Commons broke that contract, it, and their power, was dissolved.

FICTION

ROBINSON Crusoe (1719) has traditionally been accepted as the earliest novel in English, though John Bunyan's *Pilgrim's Progress* (1678) may have a better claim, and Samuel Richardson's *Pamela*, published nine years after the death of Defoe, truly established the genre. While acknowledging that there are a number of texts which might have a better claim to that title, Max Novak (in "Defoe as an Innovator of Fictional Form," in John Richetti, ed., *The Cambridge Companion to the Eighteenth-Century Novel*, p. 42) nonetheless asserts that Defoe wrote under the impression that what he was doing was entirely new, and that Defoe's readers believed that they were experiencing something new. Defoe advertised the newness of his forms assertively in his introductions, whilst simultaneously claiming that they are made necessary by the public's reprehensible demand for novelty. He claims that *The Family Instructor* (vol. 1, 1715) is entirely new and may thus appear odd, but if any condemn its new methods, they should not blame the author but:

their own more irregular Tempers, that must have every thing turned into new Models; must be touch'd with Novelty, and have their Fancies humour'd with the Dress of a thing; and if it be what has been said over and over a thousand times, yet if it has but a different colour'd Coat, or a new Feather in its Cap, it pleases and wins upon them, whereas the same Truths written in the divinest Stile in the World, would be flat, stale and unpleasant without it. (vol. 1, p. 2.)

In the second part, published three years later, Defoe refers to Novelty as "the modern Vice of the reading Palate" (vol. 3, p. iii).

Critics have drawn a line of descent for the early novels of Defoe, Fielding, and Richardson from autobiography, didactic works, and pre-novelistic discourses such as the Romance and Elizabethan prose fiction, but Novak suggests that the "new species" of writing created by Defoe developed from his journalism. Defoe's accounts of events he had not necessarily witnessed were imbued with vivid description and a sense of immediacy, and his *Review* contained not only factual reportage but also illustrative and allegorical fictional pieces. Just as his nonfiction writing was often fictitious in detail, so his fiction was glossed as factual. While *Robinson Crusoe* resembles an autobiography transmitted through an intermediary, and *A History of the Plague Year* a "real" or serious history, the testimonies of Roxana or Moll Flanders resemble the "secret histories" of well-known personages lightly encoded to protect the scandalmonger from accusations of libel.

Defoe's novels are characteristically offered as autobiography or observed fact, yet the author, masquerading as editor—a recorder of someone else's story, though also sometimes witness to part of it—provides commentary on and spurious authentication for the texts through both extra-narrative material and direct address. Sometimes, we might feel, Defoe protests too much, as when the preface to the first edition of *Memoirs of a Cavalier* runs through the whole gamut of "Credit," "Truth," "History," "Facts," and "Authentick Particulars" in its justification, of itself as a "plain but honest Account," and flatters the reader by including them among "all Men of Sense and Judgment" who will give credence to it (pp. 3–4); or when the narrator of *The Storm* (1704) vows that he is "resolv'd to use so much Caution" in his relation that he will "transmit nothing to Posterity without authentick Vouchers, and such Testimony as no reasonable Man will dispute" (p. 33). Yet the major novels are not primarily didactic in purpose. Nor, however, are they just novels. They are also commentaries on human nature in general and in eighteenth-century England in particular; imaginative works in which well-developed characters convey their immediate experience of a recognizable world, but also volumes of spiritual and ideological instruction; Defoe the journalist's discourses on diverse aspects of contemporary life, and Defoe the social prophet's visions of the future.

As Novak points out, Defoe blends realistic and plausible material with the marvelous and allegorical in a way that was later to define the novel. For Novak, the variety of structures—spiritual autobiography, traveler's narrative, fantasy of utopian self-sufficiency, political and economic allegory—are unified under the realist surface of the novel, but provide a multilayered text which lends itself to myriad and complex readings (p. 49). Defoe, presenting the novel as both true and authentic "history," as many of the novels are described, and allegorical satire, indicates that it works on at least two levels. If the realistic and the implausible were mixed, so also were the original and plagiarized. Defoe cheerfully plundered historical and anecdotal fact as well as fiction for his characters, plots, and settings. A number of fictional castaways existed before Crusoe (in, for example, Grimmelhausen's *Simplicismus* and Gracian's *El Criticon*), and at least one non-fictional, Alexander Selkirk, who was marooned for five years on Juan Fernandez.

Whether or not they were original in our sense of the word, the new fictions were popular. The insights they offered into the mind and motivations of a central protagonist, often provided through a first-person narrative; their racy, fast-moving plots; their casts of worthies and grotesques; the opportunities they afforded for armchair travel; and their vivid descriptive passages, littered with the things which were littering the lives of the enlarging mercantile classes; all these made the novels both entertaining and informative. Whereas Richardson and Fielding found it necessary to claim that their novels were also morally instructive, and required their more scandalous protagonists to repent of their ways, Defoe did not always require his thieves, prostitutes, and deceivers to proclaim the dying wish that they had chosen the path of virtue. He knew well that it too often led to starvation.

For the author of a number of serious works of religious and moral instruction, Defoe is remarkably unjudging of his cast of immoral and irreligious heroes and heroines whose lives of roguery and deceit, surprisingly, do not reap the wages of sin. Both Roxana and Moll offer their lives as warnings of the fate of women who err, and constantly pay lip service to their past "wickedness," but the narrative voice does not condemn them, and the reader is not entirely convinced of their moral development. While Roxana describes herself as a vessel of vice, she also wonders whether she feels real remorse or simply what she calls "Storm-Repentance," that is, merely a regret which is the consequence of misery, rather than penitence growing from the dictates of conscience. It is not too difficult to imagine either Moll or Roxana, struck by a new run of bad luck, easily shedding her reformed persona and reverting to crime. By the middle decades of the eighteenth century, however, both suffering and penitence were required of an erring protagonist, particularly an erring female protagonist. Booksellers concurred with Goldsmith's sentiments that:

> When lovely woman stoops to folly,
>   And finds too late that men betray,
> What charm can soothe her melancholy,
>   What art can wash her guilt away?
> The only art her guilt to cover,
>   To hide her shame from every eye,
> To give repentance to her love
>   And wring his bosom—is to die.
>   (*The Vicar of Wakefield*, 1766, ed.
>   A. Friedman (Oxford, 1981)

Accordingly, several editions of *Roxana* were, as John Mullan notes, furnished with suitable endings involving deathbed confession and true repentance (*Roxana*, ed. by John Mullan, Oxford, 1996, intro., p. vii).

In his journalism, Defoe deplores the rising crime in the England of the first quarter of the eighteenth century, and both anatomizes and condemns the careers of master thieves such as Jonathan Wild and Jack Shepherd, but in his fiction he traces the origins of the life of crime, often in misfortune and injustice, and anatomizes the society which makes crime the only available alternative to abject poverty. When Colonel Jack finds his first wife, whom he divorced for her infidelity, among the transported felons on his plantation, after poverty has led her to prostitution, theft, and discovery, and learns that hardship has reformed her, he remarries her, an unusual, possibly unique step for an eighteenth-century hero, who would have been expected to put conventional social over Christian morality.

As Mullan points out, the lives of Defoe's protagonists harden them against human feelings; they are far from exhibiting the sensibility of the virtuous heroes and heroines of Richardson and others' "sentimental" novels (pp. xiv–xv). Defoe's characters are wanderers in a commercialized and commodified world, and they can rarely afford the luxury of conscience, close relationships, family ties, or strong feelings, which might bind them or leave them vulnerable. Community and family roots give way to itinerant pursuit of "fortune," or flight from retribution; bonds of blood and affection give way to temporary associations of expediency; duty and responsibility give way to contract; sympathy and altruism to pragmatism. Even the stability of the name is lost, as characters frequently change or disguise both first name and patronymic. This could be reflective of the optimism of a time when trade and industry were opening society and enabling the English working classes to become both geographically and socially mobile, to leave behind old identities and remake themselves; but more often the loss of old stabilities comes with no lasting compensation. The fortunes which are made are as easily lost. The social travelers and fortune hunters never seem to secure the treasure trove that will enable them to settle down to happy-ever-after, but remain castaways or refugees who merely give up or are flung out from the chase.

ROBINSON CRUSOE

PUBLISHED in Defoe's 59th year, *Robinson Crusoe* (1719) has gained the status of myth, and Crusoe himself has become an archetype. Writing at the bicentenary of the book's publication (later collected in *The Common Reader,* London, 1925), Virginia Woolf suggested that it "resembles one of the anonymous productions of the race itself rather than the effect of a single mind" (p.125). If Crusoe had not existed, it would have been necessary to invent him. He is a perfect emblem of the resourceful and self-determining autonomous individual—independent of social comforts and constraints alike—outfacing the worst that nature

can do: Marlborough man. Yet he is also a model of specifically bourgeois individualism; a capitalist. As Ian Watt puts it in his *The Rise of the Novel* (London, 1957, p. 160), Defoe is also "economic man." Even if its story is one of individual resourcefulness and character, however, a mythic or archetypal tale cannot be a study in a unique personality or psychology. *Robinson Crusoe* could equally be read as an allegory, an emblematic spiritual autobiography in the Puritan tradition—a reading which has its fullest realization in J. Paul Hunter's *The Reluctant Pilgrim: Defoe's Emblematic Method and Quest for Form* (Baltimore, 1966).

If the novel is a record of the soul's journey to enlightenment and spiritual fulfillment, it does not neglect more secular goals. Defoe's religion was real, but also realist, and quite consonant with material ambitions. Crusoe not only wrests his own destiny from adversity through effort rather than meekly accepting his ordained station, he also applies himself to making his destiny profitable. This is partly through his own labor, and we can see the pleasure Crusoe takes in creating his shelf, his bread, his utensils with his own hands: "It might be truly said, that now I work'd for my Bread; 'tis a little wonderful, and what I believe few People have thought much upon, (viz.) the strange multitude of little Things necessary. . . ." (ed., J. Donald Crowley, Oxford, 1983, p. 118);

"No Joy at a Thing of so mean a Nature was ever equal to mine, when I found I had made an Earthen Pot that would bear the Fire. . . ." (p. 121)

It is also, however, through exploitation of others' labors, as is evident in his dealings with Friday and his detailed and anxious enquiries into the state of his Brazilian plantation when he calls at Lisbon (pp. 279–284). *Robinson Crusoe* was published into a European society characterized by what we would now call emergent capitalism. France had introduced paper currency; John Law's theories were influencing ideas about economics; and venture capitalism in the form of speculation in shares—of foreign as well as domestic enterprises—led to a highly active stock market and, inevitably, the first crash. The South Sea Company attracted so much speculation that its stock initially soared to the then fantastic sum of £1000 in June 1720, but by September of the same year, the value had plummeted to £180. Fortunes were lost, and the company directors forfeited their estates.

As a good journalist, Defoe was relentlessly curious and a compiler of facts, figures, statistics, and episodes and anecdotes worthy of reporting. Like a good journalist, and like a good capitalist, Crusoe surrounds himself, literally or imaginatively, with "things": artifacts and ornaments; provisions and stores; tools and weapons; facts and figures; lists and statistics. Much of the novel reads like a traveler's notebook and catalogue. When Crusoe makes his house, his pot and his oven, his boat, or teaches Friday, or orders his business affairs, we are given a multitude of facts and details in a plain, unelaborated, unfanciful style. The symbolism is minimal; the language is referential and empirical rather than literary.

Crusoe's cataloguing of minutiae makes him a good narrator in as much as his stockpiled facts furnish the narrative with a wealth of detail about the setting for his adventures and the experiencing of them. As T. S. Eliot might have said, however, we could feel that Crusoe had the experience, but missed the emotion. He gives us very little sense of what it felt like to be shipwrecked, or even what it tastes and smells like; there is little scope for imaginative empathy or the enjoyment of vicarious powerful emotion. Eighteenth-century novels did not create complex, unique characters whose psychological make-up they then explore. The protagonists of Defoe's works are eyewitnesses whose viewpoint must remain as unwavering and objective as possible if we are to trust their accounts.

One small bar to such trust is created by the inconsistencies scattered through the novel. Writing at speed, Defoe makes errors of continuity. Crusoe removes his clothes in order to swim to the ship, but is soon filling his pockets with ship's biscuits; his ink supply is failing, but then is restored; he runs out of salt, but has plenty when he teaches Friday to eat salt meat; his young billy goat transforms into a nanny.

If Robinson Crusoe the character is a successful capitalist, *Robinson Crusoe* the book has been a highly profitable commodity for capitalist booksellers and publishers since its first appearance. Four authorized editions were printed within less than four months of publication, and a further unauthorized edition and a newspaper serialization rapidly followed. It was to become perhaps the best-selling novel of all time, certainly one of the most enduring. Yet the sale of the manuscript only made Defoe £10 and it, together with its author, was attacked by the contemporary critic Charles Gildon, in *The Life and Strange Surprising Adventures of D—— De F——*, as designed against the public good; as a populist, subversive, and possibly dissenting book.

Defoe's sequels to *Robinson Crusoe, Farther Adventures* (1720) and *Serious Reflexions* (1720), are less lively and fresh than the original. In *Farther Adventures,* Crusoe's Governorship of the colony fails, and he wanders through Asia, in the remote but, disappointing, known world. Having enjoyed inhabiting Crusoe's imaginary microcosm much as we enjoyed playing house in tree or tent, or under a table, as children, we perhaps feel a loss when Crusoe tells us: "I have now done with my Island, and all manner of Discourse about it; and whosoever reads the rest of my Memorandums, wou'd do well to turn his Thoughts entirely from it, and expect to read of the Follies of an old Man . . ." (Shakespeare Head Edition, p. 79).

Serious Reflexions is a collection of essays on themes from *Robinson Crusoe* such as isolation and solitude, religion and providence.

Imitation "Robinsoniads" and more subtle homages to the novel have proliferated since the eighteenth century, beginning with *The Hermit* in 1727, and including such works as Johann Wyss's *The Swiss Family Robinson* (1812–1813) and more recent and challenging adaptations such as Michel Tournier's *Vendredi où les limbes du Pacifique* (1969) and J. M. Coetzee's *Foe* (1986).

MEMOIRS OF A CAVALIER
AND CAPTAIN SINGLETON

FOLLOWING the success of the first volumes of *Robinson Crusoe,* Defoe published *Memoirs of a Cavalier* in May 1720. Where Crusoe narrates his own story, the Cavalier is a characteristic figure of Defoe's fiction, the eyewitness. Known only by the initials of his son, "L. K.," on the covering note ostensibly sent with the manuscript, and his place and date of birth (Shropshire, 1608), he can serve as a real person, if we care to imagine him as such, or as no one, a seeing eye. The *Memoirs* give a perspective on the English Civil War which had ended at the time of Defoe's birth, and enable Defoe, though a staunch Dissenter, to provide a critical view of the Cavalier forces and the Anglican clergy, by making its hero participate in the Thirty Years' War between Sweden and Austria before fighting under Prince Rupert for Charles I.

As well as providing a history book, the *Memoirs* serves as travel guide and catalogue of worthies. The Cavalier describes the particulars of appearance, yet seems to look through them to provide readers also with resumés of character and motivation. In France:

I saw the Cardinall; there was an Air of Church Gravity in his Habit, but all the Vigor of a General, and the Sprightliness of a vast Genius in his Face; he affected a little Stiffness in his Behaviour, but managed all his Affairs with such Clearness, such Steddiness, and such Application, that it was no Wonder he had such Success in every Undertaking.

Here I saw the King, whose Figure was mean, his Countenance hollow, and always seemed dejected, and every Way discovering that Weakness in his Countenance that appeared in his Actions.

If he was ever sprightly and vigorous it was when the Cardinal was with him; for he depended so much on every Thing he did, that he was at the utmost Dilemma when he was absent, always timorous, jealous, and irresolute.

(ed., James T. Boulton, Oxford, 1991, pp. 21–22)

The novel also gave Defoe the opportunity to exercise the talent for describing battle scenes perfected in his journalist days, and to move in and out of focus, shifting his perspective from the Cavalier's limited, local observations, to the larger picture, and the viewpoint of the national and international.

Defoe's *The Life, Adventures, and Pyracies of the Famous Captain Singleton* (June 1720) is also semifactual, and followed an account in the *Review* of the life of a real pirate, Captain Avery, from which much of the plot is borrowed. Bob Singleton, kidnapped in infancy and sent to sea, pursues a lawless and amoral career through Madagascar, Africa, the West Indies, the Indian Ocean, and the China Seas, and having accumulated a fortune, returns home to marry. Singleton makes the typical journey of the Defoe protagonist from error (or sin) to riches, to recognition of the emptiness of material rewards, to penitence (however transitory or expedient) and spiritual insight or contentment. He acknowledges the worthlessness of the fortune in gold and ivory he has with such pains acquired by the middle of the story; it is "like Dirt under my Feet; I had no Value for it, no Peace in the Possession of it, no great Concern about me for the leaving of it" (ed., Shiv K. Kumar, Oxford, 1990, p. 265). He reflects that "this Scene of my

Life may be said to have begun in Theft, and ended in Luxury; a sad Setting out, as worse a Coming home" (p. 277). A Quaker, William, is the catalyst by which Singleton's conscience and moral sense—absent through his deficient upbringing without tuition and example—come into being, and, through his marriage to William's sister, Singleton is able to settle down to a respectable future. Not in his own person, however, but in permanent disguise. There is a typically Defoean list of conditions:

Why first, says I, you shall not disclose your self to one of your Relations in *England* but your Sister, no not to one.

Secondly, we will not shave off our Mustachoes or Beards . . . nor leave off our long Vests, that we may pass for *Grecians* and Foreigners.

Thirdly, That we shall never speak *English* in publick before any body, your Sister excepted.

Fourthly, That we will always live together, and pass for Brothers.

(p. 277)

MOLL FLANDERS

JUST as Captain Singleton was kidnapped as a child, so Moll Flanders—in *The Fortunes and Misfortunes of the Famous Moll Flanders* (1722)—is similarly bereft of parents, her mother being transported to Virginia for theft soon after her birth. She repeats the pattern of abandonment in the way she leaves her own children, which is often related by a throwaway line. Brought up in respectability and piety in the house of the mayor of Colchester, Moll is seduced, and embarks on a roller-coaster life of marriages and illicit relationships, children born and abandoned, fortune and destitution, an unusual autonomy (for a woman of the time) and incarceration in Newgate. Convicted of theft and transported to Virginia together with one of the men she has married, Jemy, an ex-highwayman, Moll discovers that she has inherited a plantation, and becomes both prosperous and respectable. Like many of Defoe's characters, Moll follows her homing instinct back to England, where she contemplates an old age in which she will be penitent for her former wickedness. She stays "Moll," though, even though it is not her real name, but a nickname with overtones of the gangster's moll, or prostitute.

Moll enters the exchange system of the eighteenth century not as a projector or a merchant, but as a commodity; she learns early in the novel that her body is regarded as an object for sale, or hire, and we observe her learning a confusing lesson about the relationship between love and money. Her first suitor leaps up from her on hearing a noise: "professing a great deal of Love for me, but told me it was all an honest Affection, and that he meant no ill to me; and with that he put five Guineas into my Hand, and went away down Stairs. I was more confounded with the Money than I was before with the Love" (ed., G. Starr, London, 1973, pp. 24–25). Later, he swears that he does not intend to abuse but to marry Moll, as soon as he comes into his estate, and that he will maintain her honorably "if *I* would grant his Request" (p. 67), in token of which he gives her a purse of a hundred guineas, and promises to give her another for each year until he marries her (p. 31).

Although Defoe reiterates that Moll as well as her lover has pleasure in her "wickedness," we get little sense of sensual satisfaction in her sexual encounters, and her narrative represents the transaction as one of exchange, in which she has given away all that was of value in her. Nonetheless, it is herself that she blames: "thus I finish'd my own Destruction at once, for from this Day, being forsaken of my Virtue, and my Modesty, I had nothing of Value left to recommend me, either to God's Blessing, or Man's Assistance."

In the course of the novel, Moll acquires and loses many objects of value—coins, jewels, bolts of silk, watches—some given in exchange for services rendered, some from kindness, and some stolen, and she begins to judge others and, even herself, in terms of what they can and will give. Society becomes a chain of give and/or take. In Virginia, she gives her son (by her brother) a keepsake that she hopes will have sentimental value for him - a watch she had stolen "from a Gentlewoman's side" (p. 338). His love for her is measured by the income from the plantation and gifts he gives her. She even falters in her pleasure in being reunited with Jemy: "I was if I had been in a new World, and began secretly now to wish that I had not brought my *Lancashire* Husband from *England* at all" (p. 335).

A respectable way of life is one more thing that Moll acquires, but she is still the self-interested survivor of old, gladdened by the news that her brother/husband is dead "because now I could appear as I was in a marry'd Condition," and instinctively concealing of her wealth: "[her son] happen'd to be there just when my Cargo from *England* came in, which I let him believe belong'd all to my Husband's Estate, not to me" (p. 427).

A JOURNAL OF THE PLAGUE YEAR

THOUGH a work of historical fiction, *A Journal of the Plague Year* (1722) could be read as reportage and may be the combined product of Defoe's recollections of the plague which ravaged London in 1664–1665 during his infancy, the memories of his family (including his uncle, Henry Foe, under whose initials the work was published), official documents, publications such as Thomas Decker's *Wonderfull Yearre* (1603), and Defoe's powerful imagination. When it was published, in 1722, another outbreak was a real and terrifying possibility. It was active in France, less than 25 miles from the south of England, and had killed between forty and sixty thousand people in Marseilles in 1720. The Continental outbreaks were followed avidly by English newspapers, and led to Sir Robert Walpole's deeply unpopular Quarantine Act of 1721. Defoe supported some measures of the Act, such as the quarantine of ships, but opposed the wholesale quarantine of infected centers of population. Characteristically, Defoe combines journalistic compilation of facts and statistics with vivid description; varies his perspective from the long view of the detached recorder to the involved and emotive narrow focus on the individual; and follows rational consideration of the causes of the epidemic with a relation of the signs and portents, comets, dreams, cloud shapes, apparitions, and ghosts which presaged it. After waves of terror followed by waves of complacency on the part of the city, and resolution and irresolution on the part of the narrator, the plague arrives. Defoe narrates the stories of London people: aldermen and charlatans, doctors and quacks, heroes, and ordinary, terrified people. The stories are sometimes edifying and sometimes appalling. He sets one such exemplary anecdote in the neighborhood of his own early youth, carefully giving it the detail of verisimilitude:

For example, in Coleman-Street, there are abundance of Alleys, as appears still; a House was shut up in that they call *Whites*-Alley, and this House had a back Window, not a Door into a Court, which had a passage into Bell-Alley; a Watchman was set by the Constable, at the Door of this House [to enforce the quarantine of its inhabitants] and there he stood, or his Comrade Night and Day while the Family went all away in the Evening, out at that Window into the Court, and left the poor Fellows warding, and watching, for near a Fortnight.

Not far from the same Place, they blow'd up a Watchman with Gunpowder, and burnt the poor Fellow dreadfully, and while he made hidious Crys, and no Body would venture to come near to help him; the whole Family that were able to stir, got out at the Windows one Story high; two that were left Sick, calling for Help . . .

(ed., Louis Landa, Oxford, 1972, p. 48)

ROXANA

IN Defoe's last novel, *Roxana; or, the Fortunate Mistress* (1724), "Roxana," unlike Moll, gives away her virtue in order to survive, but, also unlike Moll, her price rises, and she prostitutes herself in exchange for fame and fortune. Roxana struggles with her conscience when her maid, Amy, suggests that she should submit to their landlord in exchange for food, and comes to the approved conclusion: "without question, a Woman ought rather to die, than to prostitute her Virtue and Honour, let the Temptation be what it will." Nonetheless, though she refuses to enter into an open transaction, she professes herself so overcome by the kindness of the landlord in voluntarily and freely giving her not only food but goods, free rent, and money, that she does live with him as though in marriage. Real marriage, at this stage, is out of the question, as he has a wife, and later, because Roxana has found a better way of life. She tells Sir Robert Clayton, who recommends her to marry, that:

I knew of no State of Matrimony, but what was, at best, a State of Inferiority, if not of Bondage; that I had no Notion of it; that I liv'd a Life of absolute Liberty now; was free as I was born, and having a plentiful Fortune, I did not understand what Coherence the Words *Honour* and *Obey* had with the Liberty of a *Free Woman*; that I knew no Reason the Men had to engross the whole Liberty of the Race, and make the Women, notwithstanding any disparity of Fortune, be subject to the Laws of Marriage, of their own making.

(ed., John Mullan, Oxford, 1998, pp. 170–171)

Though this confident manifesto is preempted by the qualifying claim, "had I taken his Advice, I had been really happy" (p. 170), we feel that this may only be a nod at conventionality. Roxana is making a declaration of independence in the only way available for a woman; she will be like a man: "seeing Liberty seem'd to be the Men's Property, I wou'd be a *Man-Woman;* for as I was born free, I wou'd die so" (p. 171). It seems that, brought into poverty by a man (her husband, a brewer, who is bankrupt), she will look to men for restitution—using their ridiculous desperation for sexual gratification, and becoming predator rather than victim. She even rejects marriage to a Prince, and achieves wealth, status, and fame. Finally, she even achieves her long-held ambition to have a title, in marrying a rich merchant who purchases a baronetcy and eventually makes her a Countess. She escapes poverty and dependence, but she cannot escape biology; she has twelve children, and her daughters are her undoing. Like Moll in her long voyage through life, Roxana has seemed to drop her children by the wayside without much thought, but one of them, Susan, tracks her down, just as she is established as a wealthy, titled, married woman. She reflects in a manner chilling to modern sensibility: "It is true, I wanted as much to be deliver'd from her, as ever a Sick-Man did from a Third-Day Augue; and had she dropp'd into the Grave by any fair Way, *as I may call it;* I mean had she died by any ordinary Distemper, I shou'd have shed but very few Tears for her" (p. 302). Exactly what happens is unclear; perhaps Amy murders Susan, but it is Roxana who is depicted with a guilty conscience that inflicts fits of trembling and images of horror. Significantly, the novel ends not with Roxana penitent and content, but with "a dreadful Course of Calamities" and Roxana may regret her actions in that they have caused her pain, but she does not repent of them in the Christian sense. She reflects that "the Blast of Heaven seem'd to follow the Injury done the poor Girl, by us both; and I was brought so low again, that my Repentance seem'd to be only the Consequence of my Misery, as my Misery was of my Crime" (p. 330).

NONFICTION

DEFOE's journalism and wide-ranging experience both of the world of learning and the real world of corruption, compromise, and the makeshift made him a vivid, engaging, and pithy writer on almost all subjects. He was also a humanitarian who argued persuasively for reform. *The Poor Man's Plea* (1698) appeals to Conscience to end the association of poverty with vice in the minds of the more fortunate, and for the equal and judicious application of the law to all, rich and poor.

Poor Man speaks of:

Cobwebb Laws, in which the small flies are catch'd, and great ones break through. My Lord-Mayor has whipt about the poor Beggars and a few scandalous Whores have been sent to the House of Correction; some Ale-house-keepers and Vintners have been Fin'd for drawing Drink on the Sabbath-day, but all this falls upon us of the Mob, the poor *Plebeii,* as if all the Vice lay among us. . . . *The Man with a Gold Ring, and Gay Cloths,* may Swear before the Justice, or at the Justice; may reel home through the open Streets, and no man take any notice of it; but if a poor man gets drunk or swear an oath, he must to the Stocks without Remedy.

(Shakespeare Head Edition, pp. 6–7)

Defoe was unusual in his day for his advanced views on the education of women, whom he saw as equally capable of intellectual and moral development as men. He states his position rationally and unequivocally in *An Essay upon Projects* (1967) (ed. by Joyce Kennedy, Michael Seidel, and M. E. Novak, New York, 1999):

The soul is placed in the body like a rough diamond, and must be polished, or the luster of it will never appear: and it is manifest that as the rational soul distinguishes us from brutes, so education carries on the distinction and makes some less brutish than other. . . . But why then should women be denied the benefit of instruction? If knowledge and understanding had been useless additions to the sex, God Almighty would never have given them capacities, for He made nothing needless. Besides, I would ask such what they can see in ignorance that they should think it a necessary ornament to a woman? or how much worse is a wise woman than a fool? or what has the woman done to forfeit the privilege of being taught? Does she plague us with her pride and impertinence? Why did we not let her learn, that she might have had more wit? Shall we upbraid women with folly when it is only the error of this inhuman custom that hindered them being made wiser? (p. 108)

A TOUR THRO' THE WHOLE ISLAND OF GREAT BRITAIN

THOUGH Defoe spent much of his life in travel, his base was always London, and though he is best known for a work set far from city and English life, he missed no opportunity to eulogize the capital to the reading public at large as the jewel of

"the most flourishing and opulent country in the world" (*Tour,* ed. by Pat Rogers, Oxford, 1986, p. 43). His *Tour Thro' the Whole Island of Great Britain* (1724–1726) describes London as the "great centre of England," worthy of being placed at the center of his great work, and asserts that "nothing in the world does, or ever did, equal it, except old Rome in Trajan's time" (p. 286). The monuments and buildings are all beautiful or fine or magnificent, and if the churches are not as lavishly ornamented as those on the Continent, that is all the better: "The churches in London are rather convenient than fine, not adorned with pomp and pageantry as in Popish countries, but, like the true Protestant plainness, they have made very little of ornament either within them or without" (p. 302). The 400,000-word *Tour,* written as a series of "letters," is a eulogy to Great Britain, a boost to morale at home and an advertisement of strength to Europe. Defoe admits that he has not described Britain's deficiencies, though he could have made the description of the towns and landscape a satire on its populace: "The author says, that indeed he might have given his pen a loose here, to have complained how much the conduct of the people diminishes the reputation of the island, on many modern occasions, and so we could have made his historical account a satire upon the country, as well as upon the people" (p. 44).

He refrains, however, because this is a patriotic, not an objective account, and "they are ill friends to England, who strive to write a history of her nudities, and expose, much less recommend her wicked part to posterity" (p. 44).

The Britain of the *Tour* is flourishing, fertile, abundantly over-flowing with crops, buildings of note, and, above all, trade, the wellspring of prosperity. The beauties that chiefly excite Defoe are not the crags, peaks, and lakes that were to attract the tourists of the Romantic sublime in the next century, but industrial buildings and the evidence of industry in the populace. At Blackstone Edge, near Halifax, Defoe notes approvingly:

these people are full of business; not a beggar, not an idle person to be seen, except here and there an almshouse, where people ancient, decrepit, and past labour, might perhaps be found; for it is observable, that the people here, however laborious, generally live to a great age, a certain testimony to the goodness and wholesomeness of the country . . . but helped and established by their being constantly employed, and, as we call it, their working hard. (p. 491)

As they mount a hill, the day clears, and:

the sun shining, we could see that almost at every house there was a tenter [frame for stretching cloth], — and almost on every tenter a piece of cloth, or kersie, or shalloon, for they are the three articles of that country's labour; from which the sun glancing, and, as I may say, shining (the white reflecting its rays) to us, I thought it was the most agreeable sight that I ever saw. . . . [L]ook which way we could . . . it was all the same; innumerable houses and tenters, and a white piece upon every tenter. (p. 492)

Defoe goes into the visible signs of the manufacturing process in great detail, from the fetching of the wool, to the washing, carding, spinning, fulling, dyeing, weaving, dressing, tenting, and marketing of the cloth.

Defoe's monumental *Tour* stresses the changed and changing nature of England—socially, architecturally, economically—and his sense of the mutability of things and the instability of his age and his own fortunes was well-founded: "No man has tasted differing fortunes more / And thirteen times I have been rich and poor" (*Review*, Vol. 8, preface). He lived through the reigns of seven monarchs (counting William-and-Mary as one), two official changes of the nation's faith, several governments, innumerable scandals, a great plague, and a great fire which transformed the capital from a warren of alleys and stews, of highly combustible lathe-and-plaster houses, almost touching at their upper stories, into a neo-classical city of symmetrical stone façades and open squares.

Alexander Pope, in his *Dunciad* depicts Defoe looking down from the pillory "unabashed." In spite of all that he did and all that he saw, we feel that Defoe remained precisely that.

SELECTED BIBLIOGRAPHY

I. COLLECTED WORKS. The Shakespeare Head Edition of the *Novels and Selected Writings of Daniel Defoe*, 14 vols. (Oxford, 1927–1928); *Selected Writings of Daniel Defoe*, ed. J. T. Boulton, 2nd ed. (Cambridge, 1975); *The Versatile Defoe*, ed. Laura Ann Curtis (London, 1979).

II. EDITIONS OF THE MAJOR WORKS PUBLISHED IN DEFOE'S LIFETIME.[1]

An Essay upon Projects (1697); *The Poor Man's Plea* (1698). *The True-Born Englishman* (1701); *The Shortest-Way with the Dissenters* (1702) in *A True Collection of the Writings of the Author of The True-Born Englishman*, 2 vols. (1703–1705); *The Consolidator: or, Memoirs of Sundry Transactions from the World in the Moon* (1705); *A True Relation of the Apparition of one Mrs Veal* (1706); *Jure Divino: a Satyr* (1706); *The History of the Union of Great Britain* (1709); *The Family Instructor* (1715); *An Appeal to Honour and Justice, Tho' it be of His Worst Enemies* (1715); *Letters by a Turkish Spy* (1718); *The Life and Strange Surprizing Adventures of Robinson Crusoe, of York, Mariner* (1719). *The Farther Adventures* (1720); *Memoires of a Cavalier: Or, a Military Journal of the Wars in Germany, and the Wars in England; from the Year 1632, to the Year 1648* (1720); *The Life, Adventures and Piracies of the Famous Captain Singleton* (1720); *Serious Reflections . . . of Robinson Crusoe* (1720); *Life and Adventures of Mr Duncan Campbell* (1720); *The Fortunes and Misfortunes of the Famous Moll Flanders* (1722); *Religious Courtship* (1722); *The History of Peter the Great* (1722); *Due Preparations for the Plague* (1722); *A Journal of the Plague Year* (1722); *The History of the Remarkable Life of the truly Honourable Colonel Jacque* (1722); *The Fortunate Mistress (Roxana)* (1724), pub. as *Roxana; or, the Fortunate Mistress. Being a History of the Life and Vast Variety of Fortunes of Mademoiselle de Beleau* (1742); *A Tour Thro' the Whole Island of Great Britain*, 3 vols. (1724–1726); *A New Voyage Round the World* (1724); *A History of the Pirates* (1724–1728); *The Compleat English Tradesman* (1725–1727); *The Four Voyages of Capt. George Roberts* (1726); *A General History of the Principal Discoveries and Improvements in Useful Arts* (1726); *The Political History of the Devil: As Well Ancient as Modern* (1726); *System of Magick* (1726); *An Essay on the History and Reality of Apparitions* (1727); *A New Family Instructor* (1727); *Conjugal Lewdness: Or, Matrimonial Whoredom* (1727); *Augusta Triumphans* (1728); *A Plan of the English Commerce* (1728).

III. PUBLISHED AFTER DEFOE'S DEATH. *The Compleat English Gentleman*, ed. Karl Bülbring (London, 1890); *A Tour Thro' the Whole Island of Great Britain*, extended to four volumes (1742); *The Novels and Miscellaneous Works of Daniel Defoe*, 20 vols. (1840–41).

IV. USEFUL MODERN EDITIONS. *A Review . . .*, facsimile edition, ed. Arthur Wellesley Secord, 22 vols. (1938); *A Tour Thro' the Whole Island of Great Britain*, ed. G. D. H. Cole, 2 vols. (London, 1927; rev. ed. 1963); *A Tour Thro' the Whole Island of Great Britain*, abridged and illus. edition, eds P. N. Furbank, W. R. Owens and A. J. Coulson (New Haven, 1991); *Memoires of a Cavalier*, facsimile edition, intro. Malcolm Bosse (London, 1972).

Paperback editions: Oxford University Press (Oxford World Classics Series) publish useful paperback editions, with annotations and introductions, of *Robinson Crusoe*, ed. J. Donald Crowley (London, 1972); *Moll Flanders*, ed. George A. Starr (London, 1973); *Roxana*, ed. John Mullan (London, 1996); *A Journal of the Plague Year*,

[1] Much of Defoe's fiction was published anonymously and attribution is not always certain. See the works cited under Bibliographical Studies.

ed. Louis Landa (London, 1969); *Memoirs of a Cavalier,* ed. John Mullan (London, 1991); *Captain Singleton,* ed. Shiv K. Kumar (London, 1990).

Penguin (Penguin Classics) publish similarly useful annotated paperback editions of *Robinson Crusoe,* ed. Angus Ross (Harmondsworth, 1963); *A Journal of the Plague Year,* eds. Anthony Burgess and Christopher Bristow (Harmondsworth, 1966); *Moll Flanders,* ed. David Blewitt (London, 1989); *Roxana,* ed. David Blewitt (London, 1989); *A Tour Thro' the Whole Island of Great Britain,* abridged edition, ed. Pat Rogers (Harmondsworth, 1971).

WW Norton publish paperback editions of the texts together with complete and excerpted criticism, of *Robinson Crusoe,* ed. Michael Shinagel (New York, 1994); *Moll Flanders,* ed. Edward H. Kelly (New York, 1973); *A Journal of the Plague Year,* ed. Paula R. Backscheider (New York, 1992).

Useful anthology including verse by Defoe: *Poems on Affairs of State: Augustan Satirical Verse, 1660–1714,* ed. Frank Ellis, 7 vols (New Haven, 1963–1975).

V. JOURNALS. *Athenian Mercury,* contributor; ed. John Dunton (1691–97); *A Review of the Affairs of France . . .,* wrote single-handedly (1704–13); *Mercator* (1713); *Mercurius Politicus,* editor (1716–1720); *Weekly Journal,* contributor; ed. Nathaniel Mist (1717); *The Manufacturer* (1720); *The Director,* editor (1720–1721).

V. LETTERS. George Harris Healey, ed., *The Letters of Daniel Defoe* (Oxford, 1955).

VI. BIBLIOGRAPHIES. Of Defoe's writing: John Robert Moore, *A Checklist of the Writings of Daniel Defoe,* 2nd ed. (Hamden, Conn., 1971); Spiro Peterson, *Daniel Defoe: A Reference Guide 1731–1924* (Boston, 1987); P. N. Furbank and W. R. Owens, *The Canonisation of Daniel Defoe* (London, 1988); *Defoe De-attributions: A Critique of J. R. Moore's Checklist* (London, 1994); Maximillian Novak, "The Defoe Canon: Attribution and De-attribution," in *Huntingdon Library Quarterly* 59 (1997).

Of criticism: John Stoler, *Daniel Defoe: An Annotated Bibliography of Modern Criticism, 1900–1980* (New York, 1984);

VII. BIOGRAPHIES. Walter Wilson, *Memoirs of the Life and Times of Daniel Defoe* (London, 1830); John Robert Moore, *Daniel Defoe: Citizen of the Modern World* (Chicago, 1958); F. Bastian, *Defoe's Early Life* (London, 1981); Paula R. Backscheider, *Daniel Defoe: His Life* (Baltimore, 1989); Maximillian E. Novak, *Daniel Defoe: Master of Fictions* (Oxford, 2001).

VIII. CRITICAL STUDIES. Maximillian E. Novak, *Economics and the Fiction of Daniel Defoe* (Berkeley and Los Angeles, 1962); Maximillian E. Novak, *Defoe and the Nature of Man* (Oxford, 1963); George A. Starr, *Defoe and Spiritual Autobiography* (Princeton, 1965); J. Paul Hunter, *The Reluctant Pilgrim: Defoe's Emblematic Method and Quest for Form* (Baltimore, 1966); George A. Starr, *Defoe and Casuistry* (Princeton, 1971); James R. Sutherland, *Daniel Defoe: A Critical Study* (Cambridge, Mass., 1971); Pat Rogers, ed., *Defoe: The Critical Heritage* (London, 1972); John J. Richetti, *Defoe's Narratives: Situations and Structures* (Oxford, 1975); Michael Boardman, *Defoe and the Uses of Narrative* (New Brunswick, N.J., 1983); Maximillian E. Novak, *Realism, Myth, and History in Defoe's Fiction* (Lincoln, Nebr., and London, 1983); Geoffrey Still, *Defoe and the Idea of Fiction* (London, 1983); Laura

HENRY FIELDING

(1707–1754)

Christopher MacLachlan

HENRY FIELDING IS not only one of the founders of the novel in English but also a successful and highly readable novelist in his own right. Though he was not actually the first to write long fiction in English, his place as one of the two leading English novelists of the eighteenth century remains undisputed; any discussion about his reputation mostly concerns his standing in relation to his great contemporary and rival, Samuel Richardson. Setting this aside for later consideration, it is right to begin by stressing that in themselves Fielding's novels are entertaining and readable and full of interesting and often attractive characters, lively and humorous action, and much detail relating to their setting in time and place.

Fielding gives us a vivid picture of eighteenth-century England, a picture at times as graphic and memorable as any of those of his contemporary, the painter William Hogarth. The visual and dramatic aspects of Fielding's comedy and his ability to write expressive dialogue have meant that his books have been adapted successfully for the cinema and television, so reaching an ever-expanding public. Yet his novels also show careful literary craftsmanship; a fund of learning and; as, modern critics have shown, a deep and serious concern with moral and religious themes.

LIFE

FIELDING was born the eldest of seven children on 22 April 1707 at Sharpham Park, Somerset, in the southwest of England. His father, Edmund, was a soldier who rose to the rank of general. As an officer, Fielding's father had the status of a gentleman, and he also had aristocratic connections, though never the income to sustain high social pretensions. Fielding's mother, Sarah Gould, the daughter of a judge, had an upper-class background too. Fielding was brought up believing in his social status, and, despite the poverty and struggle to make a living he met with in later life, he never doubted that he was a gentleman by birth.

In 1718 Fielding's mother died, and soon after his father married a Roman Catholic widow. This caused a great row with the Gould family, especially over the care of Henry and his siblings (including Sarah Fielding, born 8 November 1710, who was also to become a novelist). In 1719 Henry was sent to the most famous English boarding school, Eton College, where he not only acquired the education in classical Latin and its literature that was the mark of a gentleman and which was to permeate his later writings but also made a number of influential friends who would help his adult career. Perhaps the main significance for Fielding of his going to Eton, which marked the breakup of the family life he had known in Somerset, was the sense of being thrust out into the world and forced to make the best of it, a fate that befalls the heroes of his two best novels.

In 1728 Fielding went to the University of Leiden in the Netherlands and began studying law, but by the following year his father was no longer able to supply him with money, and Fielding returned to London with very limited prospects. As a young gentleman without an income or the hope of an inheritance, because of his father's financial entanglements, he had few options, since his rank meant that he could not stoop to any sort of trade or mercantile occupation without losing caste. Literature offered one of the few possibilities of making a living for a young man of general education but no professional qualifications.

Throughout the eighteenth century the theater offered the ambitious the kind of hope of wealth and fame now represented by the idea of a chart-topping record. Anyone who could persuade one of the London theater managers to produce a play that won the approval of theatergoers enough to be performed more than a few times would earn a significant sum. Fielding had, in fact, had his first play, *Love in Several Masques: A Comedy* (1728), put on before he went to Leiden. It was overshadowed, however, by the success earlier in the season of

John Gay's ballad opera *The Beggar's Opera* and of *The Provoked Husband,* a comedy by Colley Cibber. When Fielding came back to London in 1729, he tried again to write a successful play.

A major factor in the success of *The Beggar's Opera* was its political satire; Gay's characters were recognized easily as low-life imitations of government figures, notably the man increasingly referred to as the prime minister (not out of respect or approbation), Robert Walpole, the leader of the Whig party, who since 1722 had been the real ruler of the country, controlling Parliament through his use of government appointments. His Tory opponents, frustrated by Walpole's success in Parliament, waged a vigorous war of words against him outside it. The 1720s and 1730s were a great age of satire in England, highlighted by such works as Jonathan Swift's *Gulliver's Travels* (1726) and a series of neoclassical verse masterpieces by Alexander Pope.

Into this political battle Fielding was inevitably drawn, as virtually nothing could be written without attracting political reading. Fielding himself, with his aristocratic pretensions, easily sided with the Tory opposition, gathered around some of the great English landowners, against the government Whigs, who were usually seen as representing the interests of the new merchant class centered on the commerce of the City of London. From 1728 until 1737, then, Fielding's efforts went into the writing of more than twenty stage pieces, some full-length plays but many the short so-called after-pieces performed after a play to close the evening's entertainment. He had several hits and increasingly became the leader of the theatrical attack on Walpole and his ministers.

In 1734 he married Charlotte Cradock, with whom he had three children. Two of them died young, and Charlotte herself died in 1744. Long before that Fielding's dramatic career was over, the victim of Walpole's revenge on the theaters in the form of the Licensing Act of 1737, which closed unlicensed theaters, including the one Fielding worked for, and required all plays to be submitted for approval to a government officer, the Lord Chamberlain (a form of censorship not removed until 1968). Fielding's first reaction was to resume his study of the law, qualifying in 1740, but his attempts to make a living as a lawyer were unsuccessful, perhaps because in the previous year he also became editor of an opposition newspaper, *The Champion.*

In 1740, however, occurred the event that was to change Fielding's literary career and lead to his greatest success, for it was in that year that Samuel Richardson published his first novel, *Pamela; or, Virtue Rewarded,* the story, told in letters and journals mostly by the servant girl Pamela herself, of her resistance to sexual harassment by her master, which in the end so convinces him of her virtue that he falls in love with her and makes her his wife. The success of Richardson's novel was immediate and immense. He had combined a story that interested and excited readers with an outcome that met with the approval of moralists and clergymen, and the intimate detail in which he had made his heroine express herself made her seem as real to his readers as some film and television characters do to audiences today.

Fielding, however, reacted strongly against the idea that all a girl had to do to rise in the world was to deny herself to a rich young man so that he would be driven to marry her. He saw this as a trade-off of virtue for social advancement. Six months after the appearance of *Pamela,* Fielding anonymously published his first reply to it in *An Apology for the Life of Mrs. Shamela Andrews* (1741), which parodies the form and content of Richardson's novel, twisting Pamela's motives into those of a girl of easy virtue who tricks her doting young master into a marriage that will bring her material reward and a cover for continuing liaisons with other men.

Richardson was furious, but nevertheless Fielding returned to the attack with his first full-length novel, *The History and Adventures of Joseph Andrews and of His Friend Mr. Abraham Adams* (1742). Joseph is the brother of Pamela, who also must resist the lustful attentions of a superior, in this case, his mistress. *Joseph Andrews,* however, goes beyond the parody of *Pamela* to a deeper exploration of the rewards of virtue in this world and the place of Christian morality in it, mainly through the character of Parson Abraham Adams, who accompanies Joseph on most of his adventures.

There is some evidence that by this time Fielding had accepted money from Walpole to cease his attacks upon him, but in any case Walpole fell from power just before the publication of *Joseph Andrews.* In 1743 Fielding published a collection of verse and prose under the title *Miscellanies,* including a satirical fantasy entitled *A Journey from This World to the Next* and a short novel, *The Life of Mr. Jonathan Wild the Great.* He continued to be active in journalism and, in 1745, began a new periodical called the *True Patriot,* opposing that year's Jacobite Rebellion, an attempt to replace the Hanoverians as the ruling dynasty by their deposed predecessors, the Stuarts. The rebel army, mainly consisting of Scottish clansmen, marched to within two hundred miles of London. Some echoes of the confusion they caused are evident in the background of Fielding's novel *The History of Tom Jones, a Foundling* (1749), but then they retreated and were finally defeated in the Scottish Highlands. This did not prevent Fielding's beginning another pro-Hanoverian periodical, the *Jacobite's Journal,* in 1747. In the same year he surprised everyone by marrying Mary Daniel, who had been his first wife's maid, and thus ironically his life imitated the plot of *Pamela.* Fielding had five children by his second wife.

Richardson himself published *Clarissa,* his second and greatest novel, in 1747–1748. Fielding generously acknowledged his rival's achievement. He himself was at that time working on *Tom Jones,* which appeared in 1749 and immediately became the center of attention, recognized by many as the vivid and entertaining novel it is regarded as today but also attacked by others for the sympathetic way in which it presents its eponymous hero's misdemeanors. Nevertheless, *Tom Jones* not only confirmed Fielding's position as a major writer but also, along with *Clarissa,* ensured that the novel would be regarded as a major literary form in English and soon would dominate all others.

Fielding himself, however, already had begun a new career before his masterpiece was in print. In 1749 he was made a magistrate in the county of Middlesex, which includes London, and from then until near the end of his life Fielding was dedicated to fighting crime and tackling the social evils that caused it. Along with his half-brother, John, he organized the first London police force, the famous Bow Street Runners, and tried to pursue enlightened principles in the trial and sentencing of offenders. In 1751 he published *An Enquiry into the Causes of the Late Increase of Robbers* and in 1753 *A Proposal for Making an Effectual Provision for the Poor.* While it would be wrong to claim Fielding had modern ideas about crime and society, it is fair to say that he was ahead of his time in addressing the social problems he encountered as a magistrate.

At the same time he did not neglect literature. In 1751 he also published his last novel, *Amelia,* a work that has never attracted more than grudging admiration. Its titular heroine is thought to be a tribute to Fielding's own wife, and the theme of the novel, the gradual reformation of Amelia's husband, who, despite his love for his wife, causes her much trouble and concern because of his thoughtlessness and lack of principle, can be seen as the author's criticism of himself for failing to treat his beloved first wife as she deserved. The seriousness of the novel's meaning, however, does not compensate for its subdued tone and lack of the humor and incident so abundant in *Joseph Andrews* and *Tom Jones.*

But *Amelia* was not the last of Fielding's writings, for in 1752 he began yet another periodical, the *Covent-Garden Journal,* but by 1754 years of work and injudicious eating and drinking had ruined Fielding's health. He resigned his magistracy and left England for the south in search of a warmer climate. He sailed to Portugal, but hardly had he reached Lisbon before death overtook him on 8 October. He left behind the journal of his voyage there, a remarkably sardonic account of his last weeks of life, published in 1755, the year after his death.

PLAYS

FIELDING'S plays are now little read or performed, but a brief word about them is useful in preparation for discussion of his novels. Writing plays provided Fielding with an income during the first part of his life, and had it not been for the ending of his theatrical career by the Licensing Act of 1737 he probably would not have become a novelist at all. He learned from the theater the need and the skill to please an audience.

His first play, *Love in Several Masques,* shows something of the novice playwright's anxiety to impress. It crowds in a wide range of the characters and devices conventional in English comedy of the eighteenth century. Fielding's comedy has three pairs of lovers as well as a fop; a pedant; an interfering servant; an old uncle, who tries to force his niece to marry against her will; and his middle-aged but lecherous wife, who attempts a secret assignation with one of the young heroes. As the title promises, there is a scene of mistaken identity at a masked ball. There is also much use of forged letters and letters that fall into the wrong hands, and the plot is wound up by means of a mock duel. The diction of the play is often high-flown—the lovers occasionally break into verse—and the dialogue is studded with what are intended to be witty remarks. The play ends with a song. Cramming all this in means that the characters are reduced to little more than caricatures and the action is often difficult to follow. The play shows Fielding's alertness to what audiences expected but also a very conventional approach for its time.

Fielding's awareness of theatrical convention took a more interesting direction in his later plays, which are notable for their mockery of dramatic styles and language. One of his greatest successes was *The Life and Death of Tom Thumb, the Great* (1730, revised in the following year as *The Tragedy of Tragedies*), a burlesque tragedy in blank verse that ends with a mass slaughter of its characters, including the killing of the ghost of Tom Thumb.

Many of his other theatrical pieces, unlike *Tom Thumb,* are rehearsal plays, that is, plays in which the audience joins actors playing the parts of a playwright and his friends (or critics) in watching a rehearsal of a play he has written. This structure, of course, allows Fielding to voice his own satirical comments on the action of the play within the play and bring out its secondary meanings, often political. The most successful of these rehearsal plays was probably *Pasquin: A Dramatick Satire upon the Times* (1736), in which two plays are rehearsed: the first, a comedy called "The Election," has scenes in which voters take bribes from both parties but the election is decided by the mayor in favor of the politician who has offered him more; the second play is another verse tragedy in which Queen Common-Sense is overcome by Queen Ignorance.

Perhaps the most remarkable of Fielding's plays is one of his last and possibly the direct cause of Walpole's attack on the theaters. The oddly titled *Historical Register for the Year 1736* (first performed in 1737) is another rehearsal play, but here Fielding abandons the pretence of continuous action and, in effect, presents a series of comic scenes linked by commentary from the playwright character in conversation with his patron, Lord Dapper, and the critic Sourwit. The most telling scene is a mock auction in which bids are invited for such things as a piece of patriotism, a bottle of courage, and a clear conscience. Bidding is briskest for "a considerable quantity of influence at court," but nobody wants "three grains of modesty" or "a little common sense." The satire here is plain and clearly anticipates the morality of the later novels, but equally evident is the play's anticipation of the structure of modern review and television comedy consisting of loosely linked sketches. The further development of this form in the eighteenth century was cut short by Walpole, but it prefigures Fielding's achievement in shaping the comic novel in English.

SHAMELA *AND* JOSEPH ANDREWS

THE heart of *Shamela* is what is claimed to be a set of the authentic letters that Samuel Richardson transformed into *Pamela.* In fact, says Fielding, the letter writer's name is really Shamela, not Pamela, and far from being a virtuous maid assailed by a lusty master, she is a scheming fortune hunter who in her letters boasts about the devices she uses to entrap her master into marrying her. She is encouraged by her fellow servants; by her lover, Parson Williams; and even by her mother, to whom most of her letters are written. Having captured her prize, she then announces that she is coming to London to exploit her new wealth and fashionable status.

Shamela is quite short; in modern editions it does not exceed forty pages, and many of these are taken up by prefatory matter before the letters of Shamela herself. In this Fielding was ridiculing the way Richardson surrounded the text in later editions of *Pamela* with prefaces and letters and appendixes, in which he reproduced fulsome praise of his novel and its moral teaching. Such praise is imitated in Parson Tickletext's letter lauding *Pamela* at the beginning of *Shamela,* answered by the first letter from Parson Oliver, which deplores the way people have been taken in by Richardson's novel and offers to set the record straight by publishing her actual letters under her real name, Shamela. In the course of this letter Fielding firmly states his fundamental objection to *Pamela*:

> The instruction which it conveys to servant-maids is, I think, very plainly this: to look out for their masters as sharp as they can; the consequences of which will be, besides neglect of their business, and the using all manner of means to come at ornaments of their persons, that if the master is not a fool, they will be debauched by him; and if he is a fool, they will marry him, neither of which, I apprehend, my good friend, we desire should be the case of our sons.

Richardson had suppressed the surname of Pamela's master, always referring to him as "Mr.

B." Fielding gleefully expanded the initial and named him Squire Booby. He also turns Pamela's acquaintance with Mr. B's curate, Parson Williams, into Shamela's previous affair with him, by whom she has already had a child. He turns Williams into a casuistical hypocrite who argues that repentance absolves sin and preaches the doctrine of salvation by grace, not good works. In this respect *Shamela* anticipates Fielding's discussion of religion in his later novels.

As well as attacking the social, moral, and religious positions discernible in *Pamela,* Fielding's mockery also extends to matters of style. The absurdity of Richardson's epistolary method, which he claimed led to what he called "writing to the moment," is memorably ridiculed by Shamela as she tells of one of Squire Booby's assaults on what she calls her "vartue": "Mrs. Jervis and I are just in bed, and the door unlocked; if my master should come—Odsbobs! I hear him just coming in at the door. You see I write in the present tense, as Parson Williams says." Fielding also clearly differentiates between the style and spelling of Shamela and the much more elaborate and supposedly educated prose of the letters by Williams.

Such obvious awareness of stylistic matters has the effect of drawing attention to the contrivance of the writing of the book in a way that undermines Richardson's pose as the mere editor of Pamela's letters. Allied with this recognition of the text as constructed by an author is Fielding's sense of it as belonging to a literary and cultural context. Even in the short space of *Shamela* this is brought home by the frequent references to other texts, not only *Pamela,* of course, but also many contemporary works, particularly the recent overweening autobiography of Colley Cibber, *Apology for the Life of Colley Cibber, Comedian* (1740), and sermons and other writings by the Methodist George Whitefield, and to key works of morality like the anonymous *Whole Duty of Man* (1658), of which Shamela owns a copy "with only the duty to one's neighbour torn out." (*Shamela,* Letter XII. Shamela Andrews to Henrietta Maria Honora Andrews) Whereas Richardson seems to desire readers to become absorbed in the feelings and experiences of Pamela, judging them for themselves, Fielding seems constantly to invite his readers to engage in dialogue not only with himself but also with a wide range of sources and analogues to his text, representing a whole cultural tradition.

Yet for all that there are so many serious implications in *Shamela,* and a definite moral purpose, it remains a very humorous work. Shamela herself, though we cannot approve of her, is a lively and amusing character. Fielding does not make her a monster; on the contrary, he makes her only too believable as a young woman out for what she can get. Indeed, his point is that she is more believable than the paragon of virtue readers saw in Pamela. Nevertheless, Shamela is clearly a negative picture, an example of what to avoid. In *Joseph Andrews,* Fielding tries to present portraits of human goodness, though these are contrasted with many characters who lack virtue.

Joseph, the brother of Pamela, is a servant in the household of Sir Thomas Booby, uncle of the hero of Richardson's novel. After the death of Sir Thomas, Joseph attracts the amorous attention of his widow. His resistance to her leads to his dismissal, and he leaves London for his parents' house in the country. On the way he meets up with his friend, Parson Abraham Adams, an honest but rather naive man who tries to live by the Christianity he preaches and is frequently taken in by selfish and cynical people. Joseph and Adams travel together, encountering a series of adventures that illustrate their virtues and good intentions and the lack of them in most of the people they meet. They join up with Joseph's betrothed, the beautiful but lowly born Fanny Goodwill, and have to spend a lot of time defending her from the lustful attacks of various men, including the effete gentleman Beau Didapper. At last they reach their destination, only to find that Lady Booby, with Pamela and her new husband, is also in the vicinity. Startling revelations about Joseph's parentage first make it seem that Fanny is his sister, but then he is discovered to be the long-lost son of a gentleman. Assured of a comfortable income, he marries Fanny and settles down to a life of unexpected happiness on his own estate.

Like *Shamela, Joseph Andrews* is a novel that draws attention to its bookishness. Fielding turns against the literary ventriloquism of Richardson's epistolary method and that of Daniel Defoe's first-person narrative (as in *Robinson Crusoe,* 1719) and presents his story through the medium of a prominent narrator, who, far from disguising his role, draws frequent attention to it. The text is divided into books and chapters, whose beginnings and endings are marked by the narrator's interventions. The second book of the novel even begins with a chapter on chapter divisions, and the whole work opens with an elaborate preface in which Fielding offers both a discussion of the kind of fiction he has written and a definition of the humor it contains.

Some of this theorizing might be taken to be defensive, an attempt to forestall objections to the manner and contents of the work; at the same time Fielding shows a desire to relate the novel, a new and not yet respectable form of literature, to accepted literary traditions and concepts. His definition of *Joseph Andrews* as a "comic epic-poem in prose" clearly tries to attach it to both comedy and epic as cognate forms, and his frequent use of mock-heroic descriptions in the novel itself should bring to mind the classics being used as yardsticks, including Homer and Vergil, not to mention the masterly mock-heroic satire of John Dryden and Pope.

In still more pointed ways does *Joseph Andrews* present its intertextuality. Its title page advertises the novel as "Written in Imitation of the Manner of Cervantes, Author of *Don Quixote*." There are a number of ways in which the novel imitates the Spanish masterpiece written by Miguel de Cervantes. Structurally, *Don Quixote* (1605, 1615) is an episodic story held together by its main characters, its general themes, and its narrative voice. Fielding exploits all these devices. His two main characters, Joseph Andrews and his friend Parson Abraham Adams, while they are not simple parallels to Don Quixote and his servant, Sancho Panza, are obviously a contrasted pair of men, one young and the other old, who between them represent different outlooks and expectations of life and who can be used to discuss the world from differing viewpoints as they move through it. Adams has something of the Don's innocence and inability to see the world as it is; Joseph has the openness and enthusiasm of youth. Both characters commit themselves, often violently, to opposing wrongdoing and injustice and are often rewarded with pain and humiliation.

The Quixotic theme of the ironic gap between the high ideals of those who try to live by moral standards and the treatment they receive in a world of knaves and weak hypocrites is very evident in *Joseph Andrews;* so, too, is the suggestion that however naive and mistaken about people Parson Adams may be, his hope that they may be better than they really are is somehow more attractive than the disillusioned realism of the

worldly. Joseph and Adams are touchstone characters; the reader judges others in the novel by the way they react to them, and through them Fielding conveys his morality more successfully than by the direct statements of his narrator.

The other major text *Joseph Andrews* refers to is, of course, the Bible. The Old Testament associations of the names of the main characters are evidently significant. Joseph's defense of his honor against the lust of his mistress, Lady Booby, must be seen as not just a comic inversion of his sister Pamela's story but also an allusion to the story of the biblical Joseph when he was a trusted servant in the house of the Egyptian captain Potiphar (Genesis 39). In Potiphar's absence Joseph has to resist the attentions of his wife. Spurned by him, she accuses Joseph to Potiphar when he returns. Joseph as a type of wronged innocence suggests that in the scenes in which Joseph Andrews fights off Lady Booby, Fielding was not just making fun of the sexual double standard of his day. Modern critics have perhaps been too ready to share Lady Booby's astonishment that a young man should talk seriously of defending his honor.

Abraham Adams obviously shares the names of two biblical figures. As a son of Adam he can be taken to represent humanity in general, though, as the first man, he may combine both primal innocence and original sin. At times his ignorance of the world suggests the first, but Fielding is careful not to make him unhumanly faultless. His other name links him to the Jewish patriarch of the Book of Genesis, and one important aspect of the parson's character is his role as a father and family man. This implies that part of Fielding's objection to *Pamela* was the way it focused moral debate on the experiences of the young and single, neglecting questions to do with more adult responsibilities. It is because these questions take us out into the world at large that so much of *Joseph Andrews* is set on the road, where a variety of moral dilemmas may be encountered.

There is a strong connection between *Joseph Andrews* and the Bible in terms of structure and method, and here perhaps the New Testament is more relevant than the Old Testament. In illustrating his moral ideas by a set of episodes, almost self-contained accounts of incidents on his heroes' journey, Fielding imitates the didactic method of the Gospels, with their many parables that show morality in action and invite the reader to draw conclusions. Rather daringly, Fielding invokes divine precedent for the kind of fiction he writes and for its intentions.

The parallel with the New Testament is quite obvious at several points in the novel; for example, in the episode in book 2, chapter 14, involving the worldly Parson Trulliber, who treats his pigs with more care than his fellowmen. There is a clear allusion here to the Gadarene swine in Mark 5:11–13 or to the pigs in the story of the Prodigal Son in Luke 15:11–32. The most definite biblical parallel in the novel, however, is in book 1, chapter 12. Joseph has been robbed, stripped of his clothes, and thrown into a ditch, where he is found by a passing stagecoach. Each of the passengers in the coach gives a reason for not helping Joseph, and it is left to the postilion, "a lad who hath been since transported for robbing a henroost," to give Joseph his coat and take him on board. Fielding certainly expected his readers to see the resemblance between this story and the parable of the Good Samaritan in Luke 10:30–37.

The action of the postilion, which remains virtuous even if he himself does not always seem so, at least not in the eyes of the law, leads to consideration of the underlying morality of *Joseph Andrews*. In chapter 17 of book 1, Adams converses with another clergyman, Mr. Barnabas, about the nature of religion. Barnabas attacks the ideas of George Whitefield and his fellow founder of Methodism, John Wesley, as threats to the wealth and comfort of the church. Adams replies that he at first agreed with the Methodists in their opposition to the church's worldly wealth but turned against them when they espoused

the detestable doctrine of faith against good works. . . . For can any thing be more derogatory to the honour of God, than for men to imagine that the all-wise being will hereafter say to the good and virtuous "Notwithstanding the purity of thy life, notwithstanding that constant rule of virtue and goodness in which you walked upon earth, still as thou did'st not believe every thing in the true orthodox manner, thy want of faith shall condemn thee"?

He adds that it has always been his opinion "that a virtuous and good Turk, or heathen, are more acceptable in the sight of their creator, than a vicious and wicked Christian, though his faith was as perfectly orthodox as St Paul's himself."

Judging by the rest of the novel and by things said in both *Shamela* and *Tom Jones*, Adams here speaks for Fielding himself, both in his opposition to the idea that belief alone is necessary to make a good Christian and in his declaration that true virtue is a matter of behavior and action, not niceties of doctrine. It is not what you are but what you do, especially to and for other people, that makes you a virtuous person in Fielding's eyes. In a very fundamental way he saw in the novel as a form an excellent means for conveying just this kind of moral outlook. Character in action is at the heart of the novel. It is also, of course, a feature of drama, but there the author himself cannot appear (although in many of his plays Fielding, by using the rehearsal device, tries to incorporate his own spokesmen in the action). In the novel, however, the author can act as narrator, directing the reader's attention and leading him to desired conclusions.

But in addition to the suitability of the structure of the novel for Fielding's moral purpose, there is also the advantage that the novel can claim to present a clear picture of ordinary life in much greater detail and fullness than any other literary or, indeed, artistic form. Something approaching the density of context in which real moral problems are faced can be reproduced in a novel, where actions and their consequences can be described at length; characters can be shown confronting more than one problem or situation; and questions of consistency of response, the implications of what someone decides to do, especially for other people, and the uncertainties of the outcomes of actions all can be explored.

Fielding's idea of virtue is dynamic, not static; it is a matter of becoming, not being. The journey structure of *Joseph Andrews* is not just a plot device; it is also a life metaphor. Virtue is not a possession but the sum of the responses made to the situations and people we meet in life. This means that a person's moral status is not fixed but may vary according to how he or she responds to people and situations. Nobody can be assured of his or her virtuousness without constant exertion, and even the best of us can make mistakes. To think otherwise is, for Fielding, the height of affectation and hypocrisy, and throughout his novels he makes particular targets of characters who believe that their social or professional position guarantees them moral superiority. He is far more forgiving of poor and needy people who cannot afford the luxury of a satisfied conscience.

It is because Fielding saw virtue as a process, not a state, that he was so annoyed by *Pamela*, which tended, in its description of how a young woman defended her virginity from her master, to make goodness seem something that could be preserved, as though it were an object in itself. This is probably an unfair way of reading Richardson's novel, and there are certainly important things to be said on behalf of his sympathetic approach to the right of even a servant girl to have control over her body and her life. For Fielding, however, the narrowing of the word "virtue" to mean sexual chastity seemed to make it an all-or-nothing matter, reducing ethical discussion to absolute choices. If a girl's virtue were of supreme value, worth more to her than life itself, as Pamela seems to imply, what happened if she lost it? Could she ever be virtuous again?

Not only did this seem an absurd and inhuman position to Fielding, it was also contrary to experience. Life went on for those who made moral errors and even for their victims, for the most part. Morality had to be able to cope with this reality and offer help and encouragement to people, not divide them into the saved and the damned. Richardson had focused his study of "virtue rewarded" on the experience of virtually one character in one situation; by expanding the scope of *Joseph Andrews* to include a wide range of characters of all ages and conditions and facing them with an equally wide range of decisions to make, not only in their personal lives but also in relation to their place in society, often represented by some of its institutions, such as the law and the church, Fielding made sure the English novel would have a moral purpose of the broadest and most inclusive kind.

TOM JONES

FIELDING'S greatest novel opens in Somerset, the county of his own birth and childhood in the southwest of England. There we meet Mr. Allworthy, the widowed and childless owner of a country estate centered on his significantly named house, Paradise-hall, where he lives with his unmarried sister, Bridget. One night, as he is retiring, he discovers that a baby has been left in his bed. To the surprise of his servants, he orders the baby to be cared for while he investigates his origins. Suspicion falls on Jenny Jones, the servant of the village schoolteacher, Partridge. When called before Allworthy, who, as the leading landowner, is also the local magistrate, she fails to give a satis-

factory account of herself and is dismissed from the parish. Instead of sending the baby to an orphanage, Allworthy, with the acquiescence of his sister, adopts the boy himself, naming him Tom Jones.

Shortly afterward Bridget Allworthy marries Captain Blifil and gives birth to a son. The sudden death of the captain, however, leaves young Blifil, like Tom, in the care of Allworthy, who arranges for both boys to be brought up in his house, employing two tutors, a clergyman named Thwackum and a philosopher called Square. Tom grows up to be a wild but open-hearted young rascal, but Blifil turns into a devious, selfish hypocrite, who, envious of Tom's popularity and high spirits, takes every opportunity to betray his misdemeanors to the two tutors and to blacken his character with Allworthy.

Nevertheless, apart from Thwackum and Square, who are completely taken in by Blifil's hypocritical flattery, most people prefer Tom. This includes one of Allworthy's neighbors, Squire Western, a boorish fellow who lives for hunting and drinking and also his beautiful daughter, Sophia. Although Tom has enjoyed the favors of the village girls, he soon falls in love with Sophia and she with him, but her father would never consent to her marrying a penniless bastard. Blifil, seeing the affection between Tom and Sophia, is jealously attracted to her too, and, as Allworthy's heir, his suit finds much more favor with Western.

Suddenly, Allworthy falls very ill and seems likely to die. The household is overcome by anxiety, none more so than the emotional Tom, but when Allworthy makes an unexpected recovery, Tom swings to the opposite extreme and, drinking joyfully to his foster father's health, becomes very drunk. While he is in this state, a messenger arrives for Blifil with news of his mother's death. Blifil takes care to report this in such a way as to make Tom's reaction seem unfeeling and later convinces Allworthy that Tom's drunken celebrations were in expectation of the squire's death and a rich inheritance from him. Blifil now brings forward a number of other accusations and grievances against Tom, and the result is that Allworthy loses faith in him and dismisses him from his house.

Tom sets out into the world with very little idea of what to do or where to go. He decides to go to sea, but falling in with a group of soldiers who are marching to oppose the Jacobite rebels in the north he joins them instead. On the way he meets

Partridge, who refuses to believe Tom has lost all favor with Allworthy and thinks it will be to his advantage to attach himself to the lad. Fielding thus reproduces the arrangement of *Joseph Andrews* in bringing together as companions the young titular hero of the novel with an older man, although, unlike Parson Adams, Partridge is a physical and moral coward. In this novel it is the young man, Tom Jones himself, who represents benevolence and a commitment to virtuous action. It is Tom who goes to the aid of a woman about to be raped and takes her to an inn, where the gratitude of this Mrs. Waters turns into warmer feelings for her handsome rescuer.

Meanwhile, Squire Western's brutal efforts to make Sophia agree to a match with Blifil have driven her to escape from home and set out for London, coincidentally following the same route as Tom. Pursued by her father, she arrives at the very inn where Tom is in bed with Mrs. Waters and leaves before he knows it, so that she is now ahead of him. He finds her pocketbook, containing a large banknote, and begins following her to return it. Reaching London, Sophia goes to her aunt, Lady Bellaston, unaware that she is a fashionably immoral woman. When Tom appears with the pocketbook, Lady Bellaston conceals her knowledge of Sophia's presence and seduces him. She also encourages the rakish Lord Fellamar to court Sophia for her inheritance. Fortunately, Squire Western arrives and saves his daughter but renews his insistence that she marry Blifil.

Tom, meanwhile, having paid a call on a lady, is attacked in the street by her jealous husband and wounds him in a duel. He is imprisoned and, when the man is reported to have died, seems likely to be hanged. He is visited in prison by Mrs. Waters, who, learning his identity, reveals that she is, in fact, Jenny Jones. Tom seems to have added incest to adultery and murder, but now at last the truth of his birth is revealed. Mrs. Waters goes to Mr. Allworthy, who also has arrived in London, and tells him that Tom is his own sister's son. It emerges that Blifil has known this since the time of Bridget Allworthy's death but has concealed the fact. Allworthy reverses his judgment on Tom and instead banishes Blifil. The wounded man, in fact, recovers, and Tom is released. As Allworthy's heir, he is now quite acceptable to Squire Western, and the only problem Tom has left is to persuade Sophia to forgive him, which she does. The novel ends with their marriage.

It will be seen that there are strong similarities between *Tom Jones* and *Joseph Andrews*. Both have plots that include the dismissal of the hero from a place and his journey elsewhere in the company of an older man, encountering various adventures along the way. In both novels the hero heads toward marriage with his sweetheart, and in both cases obstacles to their union are removed by last-minute revelations about the hero's birth. Both novels are organized in a chain of episodes, like scenes in a play, where characters are displayed, themes explored, and moral points exemplified by what is said and done, with a linking commentary from the narrator. In each novel, along with a range of satirical attacks on venality, hypocrisy, and other human vices, Fielding attempts to explain and demonstrate the nature of virtue.

Although the idea of virtue is clear enough in *Tom Jones*, critics are divided over whether it is embodied by Mr. Allworthy or by Tom Jones himself. Allworthy's name seems to indicate that he is the personification of goodness, and his benevolence is frequently stressed. But for all his good nature and better intentions, he makes some near-disastrous mistakes in the course of the story, especially as a judge of character. This is particularly unfortunate given his position as an actual magistrate. He fails to see through his sister; her son, Blifil; the two tutors, Thwackum and Square; and sundry other cheats and liars, and, on the other hand, he wrongly condemns both Jenny Jones and Tom himself. Part of the problem seems to be that, except for a small circle of people, he rarely meets anyone outside the formal setting of a courtroom. Fielding almost seems to be saying that a benevolent man who bases his actions on the narrow sort of evidence used in court is doomed to misjudge people.

In contrast to Allworthy, Tom Jones has a wide circle of friends and acquaintances of all sorts and conditions, including poachers and horse dealers as well as his foster father's rich neighbors. He is also, of course, familiar with women. These relationships can lead him astray, and he too easily yields to temptations that he knows he should resist. Yet through these errors he learns to control his appetites more and discovers the consequences of giving way to impulse; in the end he appears to have a surer knowledge of the world than his uncle because he has been exposed to it more. Fielding may not exactly say that a rich man cannot know enough of human nature to succeed as a benefactor, but he does seem to imply that the insulation from the hardship and injustice of the world that riches bring can make it difficult to be sure what is best for other people. It also makes it difficult to learn and improve morally, which is surely what Tom does in the course of the novel.

What he learns seems summed up in the word "prudence," though this is a very debatable term in the novel. Many of the most hypocritical characters, including Blifil, are described as prudent, meaning that they habitually act with a calculating sense of their own interest. It is unlikely that Fielding meant Tom, or the reader, to learn how to be more like Blifil. Yet Tom's rash good intentions, especially in the early part of the novel, frequently get him into trouble; for example, in chapter 9 of book 3, it is discovered that Tom has sold his Bible, a present from Mr. Allworthy, to Blifil. It then emerges that he did so to give the money to a destitute family, and so Allworthy prevents Thwackum from punishing Tom, as Blifil had planned.

Tom's lack of foresight often seems to mean that his willingness to come to the aid of other people puts him, and them, in danger, especially from hidebound moralists like Thwackum and manipulators like Blifil. Fielding is revisiting the territory occupied by Parson Adams and his readiness to intervene on behalf of goodness, whatever the price. In *Joseph Andrews* Adams' status as a clergyman and his physical strength protect him from the risks of his muscular charity; in *Tom Jones*, Fielding takes the debate on a stage, to consider the case of active virtue without the benefit of religious authority. Tom's gradual entanglement in the consequences of his actions, so that he at length finds himself in a cell expecting to be hanged, suggests that Fielding, for all his good humor, is not very optimistic about the result of trying to be virtuous.

Why, then, try to be good? What, to express the question in Richardson's terms, are the rewards of virtue? Given his jaundiced picture of the worldly in his novels, ranging, in *Tom Jones*, from the amoral self-regard of Lady Bellaston to the insidious evil of Blifil, Fielding's answer is not likely to be a cheerful one, nor can it be anything like Pamela's acquisition of wealth and position. The key is in the description of Tom's behavior, his spontaneous sympathy with those in need and his readiness to help them. What these accounts bring out is the root of virtue in emotion. Fielding must be aligned with those of his contemporaries who were elaborating a theory of ethics based on what was called the moral sense, a faculty of mind that generated a response to moral dilemmas and situations not out of reason but out of feeling. Such feeling can be refined and made more effective, as *Tom Jones* shows, but it ought not to be rationalized. Alhough it may be nurtured, it cannot be simulated. The habitual possession of moral feelings makes for good nature, the virtuous character, which is a reward in itself, because the deepest pleasure in life is the feeling attendant on satisfying the desire to do good to others. The reward of virtue is emotional happiness.

There is a clear exemplification of this in book 13 of *Tom Jones*. In chapter 8 of that book Jones's landlady, Mrs. Miller, tells him of the desperate poverty of her cousin and his family. Tom immediately takes her aside and offers her all his money. She takes some of it and sends it to her cousin. Two chapters later the cousin himself comes to thank his benefactor. Mrs. Miller then says she has no doubt that Tom's goodness will meet a glorious reward, to which he replies that the pleasure of the act was reward enough and adds: "If there are men who cannot feel the delight of giving happiness to others, I sincerely pity them, as they are incapable of tasting what is, in my opinion, a greater honour, a higher interest, and a sweeter pleasure, than the ambitious, the avaricious, or the voluptuous man can ever obtain." Here the discussion of the reward for virtue, and Tom's definition of its essentially emotional nature, seems designed as an answer to *Pamela*.

Tom Jones therefore can be seen as Fielding's finest and fullest answer to Richardson's *Pamela*, bringing to its highest state the expression of his alternative view of morality and human nature. It also represents the culmination of his fictional technique. As in *Joseph Andrews*, the text is highly organized. *Tom Jones* is divided into eighteen books: the first six books deal with Tom's life up to the point when Allworthy sends him away, the next six describe his journey to London and other events during that time, and the last six cover all that happens to him in the capital. Each book begins with a chapter that is really an essay by Fielding on a topic more or less loosely related to the novel. Book 6 opens with an essay "Of Love," which is essential reading for understanding what *Tom Jones* is about; in it are found direct statements about the moral feeling discussed in the previous paragraphs.

But *Tom Jones* also is highly organized in terms of plot. Fielding shapes his story carefully so that scene after scene contributes to the continuing action; scenes are carefully linked; and the various revelations, especially at the end of the book, are fully prepared. The novel is almost like a detective story in the way it contains clues in its early chapters to the resolution of the plot at the end. Part of this skilful plotting consists in arranging the meetings and, often as important, the failure to meet of certain characters at crucial points. Unlike *Joseph Andrews,* in which many of the events in the middle of the novel are loosely strung together, in *Tom Jones* everything seems significant and planned, despite the great length of the novel. This led such critics as the Romantic poet Samuel Taylor Coleridge to praise the plot of *Tom Jones* as one of the greatest ever devised.

A major device for ordering the events of the novel is the narrator, again as in *Joseph Andrews* but with an important difference. In the earlier novel the narrator usually acts as a straightforward guide for the reader, but in *Tom Jones* the narrator is much less simple and reliable. He often refuses to draw conclusions or make inferences, leaving the reader to choose from a range of interpretations. Toward the end of the story he even sides with those who believe Tom was born to be hanged. In chapter 8 of book 12 the narrator refers to "the great, useful and uncommon doctrine, which it is the purpose of this whole work to inculcate" but immediately adds "we must not fill up our pages by frequently repeating" it, when, in fact, it is nowhere stated as such. The narrator therefore is not only a device for directing the plot of *Tom Jones* but also a means of encouraging the reader to engage with the story and speculate about its meaning. The reader must work at the novel to understand it.

Finally, it is worth noting the overall shape of the story. It begins with the birth of Tom, describes his childhood and upbringing, and then gives a detailed account of his first entry into the world and the few weeks up to his marriage to Sophia. The novel therefore implies a connection between Tom's early life and the way he begins adult existence. There is a focus on education both in the narrow sense of how and what Tom was taught (badly, by Thwackum and Square) and in the broader sense of how his character developed. *Tom Jones* is almost in this way a bildungsroman, or novel of the early development of its hero. It clearly influenced

the shape of many later novels, notably those of Charles Dickens, such as *Oliver Twist* (1837–1838) and *Great Expectations* (1860–1861).

AMELIA *AND* JONATHAN WILD

FIELDING'S last novel, *Amelia,* is the story of the married life of Captain Booth and his wife, Amelia. Booth is a weak man who, though he loves his wife, cannot resist the temptations of another woman, Miss Matthews. He also gambles away money that he cannot afford to lose, and when Amelia raises some cash by selling her jewelery, Booth wastes it in an attempt to bribe his way to preferment in the army. Booth is imprisoned more than once in the novel, though this is not always his fault. Part of Fielding's purpose is to attack the deficiencies of the legal system, but Booth seems unable to avoid being a victim, partly because he takes a rather despairing attitude to life, as though nothing really can be done to improve himself or his lot.

The Booths are surrounded by a circle of friends, mainly army officers, some of whom are more help to them than others. An attempt is made to seduce Amelia, but it is foiled by a soldier's wife, Mrs. Atkinson, who goes to a masked ball in her place. The Booth's best friend is another clergyman, Dr. Harrison, who offers advice that again seems to embody Fielding's morality. The narrator is far less ironic and humorous than in *Joseph Andrews* and *Tom Jones,* and the novel, which is set entirely in London, with no road scenes, lacks the comic exuberance of its predecessors.

Critics have suggested that *Amelia* is a continuation of *Tom Jones* in the sense that it shows what the marriage of an easygoing fellow like Tom to a faithful and intelligent woman like Sophia would be like. Booth, like Tom, means well but lacks foresight and too easily lets his desires get the better of him. Like Tom, he has to learn to value his relationship with the woman he loves above other things, and in the end he does so. But although Fielding provides a resolution of sorts to the central problem in the novel, he virtually abandons the larger social problem he reveals in his picture of the corrupt and corrupting London society that surrounds the Booths and makes it so hard for them to live in virtue and harmony. The novel ends with a sudden reversal of fortune that brings Amelia a legacy sufficient to allow her and her husband to go and live happily ever after in the country.

Amelia, in principle, ought to be a major novel. Fielding is writing of adults in an adult way, and his focus on a central couple and their circle and on daily life without the comic exaggeration of his earlier works should have made the novel a model of serious fiction. The moral concerns that many readers of *Joseph Andrews* and *Tom Jones* find obscured by the farcical action and bold satire are more soberly presented in *Amelia.* Probably this soberness is the first thing that disappoints readers, but it is perhaps also the case that Fielding lacks the psychological insight and vocabulary to create the kind of depth and interrelation of characters the situations of the novel require.

It is difficult to fit Fielding's other novel, *Jonathan Wild,* published in 1743, between *Joseph Andrews* and *Tom Jones,* into the pattern of his fiction. This short work is loosely based on a historical character, a notorious criminal who was hanged in 1725 after a career of robbery and swindling that made him legendary. Fielding does not try to write a serious biography but instead uses Wild as a type of absolute criminality, a man with no thought for anyone but himself and unable to imagine anything but illicit means for accomplishing his ends. The plot therefore consists of a series of episodes in which Wild cheats everybody he meets and glories in his triumph over those who are weak enough to trust him or treat him as a fellow human.

In a sense Wild is the complete reverse of Parson Adams or Squire Allworthy, a man who believes only the worst of himself and of other people and bases his actions solely on self-aggrandizement. Ironically, Fielding describes Wild throughout the novel as a great man; the word "great" is always printed in capitals to make it stand out, although it soon becomes clear that Wild's greatness is mere selfishness and in the end leaves him friendless and hated. The insistence on greatness as Wild's aim in life inevitably gives the book a political meaning, making Wild's criminal career a parallel to that of an ambitious leader or politician, the most obvious contemporary example being Sir Robert Walpole. *Jonathan Wild,* while it can be related to Fielding's other novels, has closer links to his political satire. Its relentless use of irony against its "great" hero is technically impressive but rather overwhelms the reader.

FIELDING'S REPUTATION

IN his lifetime Henry Fielding was known as a boisterous, witty man who enjoyed life and its pleasures, sometimes to excess, and expressed his opinions strongly. Many refused to take his claims to be a moral writer seriously because of his reputation for loose living. Though his skill as a writer was acknowledged and the success of *Tom Jones,* in particular, brought him undeniable fame, many critics virtually identified Fielding with his hero and condemned both as immoral. His fiction was regarded as vivid and realistic, but his refusal to condemn all the faults of his characters, especially those of Tom, led to accusations of moral laxity.

Nevertheless, he was regarded as a founding father of the English novel, but as time went on his work was seen as near the crude beginnings of the form. In the nineteenth century, there was a growing dislike of the technique of his novels as well as even more disquiet at his impropriety and dubious morals. Even the plot of *Tom Jones* could not defend it against the claim that Fielding's fiction was loose and episodic, like other eighteenth-century novels, and his prominent use of narrators began to seem artificial and intrusive. By the end of the nineteenth century, with the rise of the theory of fiction associated with Henry James and the idea that the author of a novel should not appear in it at all but instead allow the characters to speak and act for themselves, Fielding's methods were quite out of favor. The nadir was reached in F. R. Leavis' book *The Great Tradition: George Eliot, Henry James, Joseph Conrad,* in which Leavis writes, "There can't be subtlety of organization without richer matter to organize, and subtler interests, than Fielding has to offer" (p. 12).

Even before Leavis dismissed Fielding in this way, other scholars were beginning to explore the serious moral implications of his work. The book that established that there was more to Fielding than just the simple comedy Leavis scorned was Martin Battestin's *The Moral Basis of Fielding's Art,* a study of *Joseph Andrews* that showed the close links between that novel's ideas and those of a whole group of theologians and moralists of Fielding's day. This approach was taken further and extended to his masterpiece by Bernard Harrison in his book on *Tom Jones.*

Fielding's modern reputation was not established, however, by a book but by a film. In 1963 an adaptation of *Tom Jones,* directed by Tony Richardson and scripted by the playwright John Osborne, who both received Academy Awards, was a popular and critical success that brought Fielding and his greatest novel to the attention of millions. The film, with Albert Finney in the title role and Susannah Yorke as Sophia, brilliantly captures the humor and liveliness of the novel, but more significantly it also echoes something of its style. Defying cinematic convention, Richardson employs a number of devices, such as an unseen narrator, written captions, and a wide range of obvious camera tricks, to distance the audience from the action. The style of acting is broad and self-conscious, and at critical moments the characters turn to the camera and speak directly to it. The effect is like that of the narrator in the novel itself, forcing the audience to acknowledge the fictionality of what they are experiencing. That cinema audiences found this approach fresh and amusing made it clear that Fielding's own use of similar techniques also could succeed with readers and that criticism of the novel's artificiality was missing the point. In any case, since the success of the film version of *Tom Jones,* readers have come to Fielding expecting to be entertained. Few are disappointed. He himself no doubt would be amused that he owes his popularity so much to another Richardson.

SELECTED BIBLIOGRAPHY

I. COLLECTED WORKS. *The Works of Henry Fielding,* 11 vols. (London, 1902), ed. by James P. Browne; *The Wesleyan Edition of the Complete Works of Henry Fielding* (Oxford), comprising *Joseph Andrews* (1967), ed. by Martin C. Battestin; *Miscellanies,* 3 vols. (1972, 1993, 1997), ed. by Henry Knight Miller and Bertrand A. Goldgar; *The History of Tom Jones, a Foundling,* 2 vols. (1975), ed. by Martin C. Battestin; *The Jacobite's Journal and Related Writings* (1975), ed. by W. B. Coley; *Amelia* (1983), ed. by Martin C. Battestin; *The True Patriot and Related Writings* (1987), ed. by W. B. Coley; *The Covent Garden Journal and a Plan of the Universal Register-Office* (1988), ed. by Bertrand A. Goldgar; *An Enquiry into the Causes of the Late Increase of Robbers and Related Writings* (1988), ed. by Malvin R. Zirker.

II. PLAYS. *Love in Several Masques: A Comedy* (London, 1728); *The Temple Beau: A Comedy* (London, 1730); *The Author's Farce* (London, 1730); *Tom Thumb: A Tragedy* (London, 1730), rev. ed., with annotations, titled *The Tragedy of Tragedies; or, The Life and Death of Tom Thumb, the Great* (London, 1731); *Rape upon Rape; or, The Justice Caught in His Own Trap: A Comedy* (London, 1730); *The Welsh Opera; or, The Grey Mare the Better Horse* (rewritten and renamed *The Grub-Street Opera*) (London, 1731); *The Letter-Writers; or, A New Way to Keep a Wife at Home: A Farce* (London, 1731); *The Lottery: A Farce* (London, 1732); *The Modern Husband: A Comedy* (London, 1732); *The Covent-Garden Tragedy* (London, 1732); *The Old Debauchees: A Comedy* (London, 1732); *The Mock Doctor; or, The Dumb Lady Cur'd: A Comedy Done from Molière* (London, 1732).

The Miser: A Comedy, Taken from Plautus and Molière (London, 1733); *Deborah; or, A Wife for You All* (London, 1733); *The Intriguing Chambermaid: A Comedy* (London, 1734); *Don Quixote in England: A Comedy* (London, 1734); *An Old Man Taught Wisdom; or, A Virgen Unmask'd: A Farce* (London, 1735); *The Universal Gallant; or, The Different Husbands: A Comedy* (London, 1735); *Pasquin: A Dramatick Satire upon the Times* (London, 1736); *Tumble-Down Dick, or, Phaeton in the Suds: A Dramatick Entertainment* (London, 1736); *Eurydice: A Farce* (London, 1737); *The Historical Register for the Year 1736* (London, 1737); *Eurydice Hiss'd* (London, 1737); *Miss Lucy in Town: A Farce* (London, 1742); *The Wedding-Day: A Comedy* (London, 1743); *The Fathers; or, The Good-Natur'd Man: A Comedy* (London, 1778).

III. NOVELS. *An Apology for the Life of Mrs. Shamela Andrews* (London, 1741); *The History and Adventures of Joseph Andrews and of His Friend Mr. Abraham Adams,* 2 vols. (London, 1742); *The Life of Mr. Jonathan Wild the Great* (London, 1743); *The History of Tom Jones, a Foundling,* 6 vols. (London, 1749); *Amelia,* 4 vols. (London, 1751).

IV. OTHER WRITINGS. *A Journey from This World to the Next* (London, 1743); *Miscellanies,* 3 vols. (London, 1743), including *A Journey from This World to the Next* and *The Life of Mr. Jonathan Wild the Great; An Enquiry into the Causes of the Late Increase of Robbers* (London, 1751); *A Proposal for Making an Effectual Provision for the Poor* (London, 1753); *The Journal of a Voyage to Lisbon* (London, 1755).

V. MODERN EDITIONS. *Jonathan Wild* (Harmondsworth and New York, 1982), ed. by David Nokes; *Joseph Andrews with Shamela and Related Writings: Authoritative Texts, Backgrounds and Sources, Criticism* (New York and London, 1987), ed. by Homer Goldberg; *Tom Jones: The Authoritative Text, Contemporary Reactions, Criticism* (New York and London, 1995), ed. by Sheridan Baker; *Tom Jones* (Oxford, 1996), ed. by John Bender and Simon Stern; *A Journey from This World to the Next; and, The Journal of a Voyage to Lisbon* (Oxford, 1997), ed. and with an intro. and notes by Ian A. Bell and Andrew Varney; *The History and Adventures of Joseph Andrews And of his Friend Mr. Abraham Adams; and, An Apology for the Life of Mrs. Shamela Andrews* (Oxford, 1999), ed. by Thomas Keymer.

VI. BIBLIOGRAPHY. John A. Stoler and Richard S. Fulton, *Henry Fielding: An Annotated Bibliography* (New York, 1980).

VII. BIOGRAPHICAL STUDIES. Sir Walter Scott, "Henry Fielding," in his *Lives of the Novelists* (London, 1825); Pat Rogers, *Henry Fielding: A Biography* (London, 1979); Martin C. Battestin, with Ruthe R. Battestin, *Henry Fielding: A Life,* (London and New York, 1989).

VIII. CRITICAL STUDIES. Ian P. Watt, *The Rise of the Novel: Studies in Defoe, Richardson, and Fielding* (London, 1957); F. R. Leavis, *The Great Tradition: George Eliot,*

Henry James, Joseph Conrad (London, 1948); Martin C. Battestin, *The Moral Basis of Fielding's Art: A Study of* Joseph Andrews (Middletown, Conn., 1959; repr., 1964); Ronald Paulson, ed., *Fielding: A Collection of Critical Essays* (Englewood Cliffs, N.J., 1962); Sheldon Sacks, *Fiction and the Shape of Belief: A Study of Henry Fielding, with Glances at Swift, Johnson, and Richardson* (Chicago and London, 1964); Andrew Wright, *Henry Fielding: Mask and Feast* (London, 1965); Ronald Paulson and Thomas Lockwood, eds., *Henry Fielding: The Critical Heritage* (London and New York, 1969); Neil Compton, ed., *Henry Fielding, Tom Jones: A Casebook* (London, 1970); Claude Julien Rawson, *Henry Fielding and the Augustan Ideal Under Stress: "Nature's Dance of Death" and Other Studies* (London and Boston, 1972); Bernard Harrison, *Henry Fielding's Tom Jones: The Novelist as Moral Philosopher* (London, 1975).

Peter Jan de Voogd, *Henry Fielding and William Hogarth* (Amsterdam, 1981); Thomas R. Cleary, *Henry Fielding: Political Writer* (Waterloo, Ontario, 1984); K. G. Simpson, ed., *Henry Fielding: Justice Observed* (London and Totowa, N.J., 1985); Harold Bloom, ed., *Henry Fielding* (New York, 1987); Clive T. Probyn, *English Fiction of the Eighteenth Century, 1700–1789* (London and New York, 1987); Albert J. Rivero, *The Plays of Henry Fielding: A Critical Study of His Dramatic Career* (Charlottesville,Va., 1989); Angela J. Smallwood, *Fielding and the Woman Question: The Novels of Fielding and Feminist Debate, 1700–1750* (Hemel Hempstead, Hertfordshire, and New York, 1989); Simon Varey, Joseph Andrews: *A Satire of Modern Times* (Boston, 1990).

WILLIAM GOLDING

(1911–1993)

Peter Kemp

NO MODERN WRITER imprinted his view of life more indelibly upon the consciousness of the English-speaking world and beyond than Sir William Gerald Golding. Attracting an enormous readership, his fiction powerfully informed the way humanity saw itself in the later decades of the twentieth century.

What makes this achievement particularly remarkable is that Golding's imagination was itself most markedly shaped by the literature of the ancient world. He taught himself classical Greek in order to read Homer and the Athenian tragic dramatists (Aeschylus, Sophocles, Euripides) in the original. The literary work he most admired, he always said, was the *Odyssey*. (As if to show its persisting influence on him, at the end of his career he wrote his own epic trilogy about a hazardous voyage, reverberating with symbolic resonance).

What Golding found congenial about classical Greek literature was partly its lucidity and its tautness of structure but also the fact that "the Greek view of the psyche . . . was relatively simple" ("William Golding Talks to John Carey," in *William Golding: The Man and His Books*, p. 182). These qualities are all apparent in his own work, but interfused with other elements. Well before he was drawn to classical Greek literature, Golding became imaginatively enthralled by ancient Egypt. At the age of seven he began to learn hieroglyphics in an attempt to write a play set there (an ambition that later found fruition in a different genre with the title novella of his 1971 book *The Scorpion God*). Identifying closely with elements of ancient Egyptian culture—"I recognize in their relics, through the medium of archaeology and art, my own mournful staring into the darkness," he said in *The Hot Gates* (1965) (p. 81)—he wryly defined himself as "an Ancient Egyptian, with all their unreason, spiritual pragmatism and capacity for ambiguous belief" (p. 82). In his fiction, these Greek and Egyptian elements fruitfully interact.

Golding's initial aspiration was not to be a novelist but a poet. One of the essays in *The Hot Gates* speaks of his lifelong regret at his "inability to write poetry" (p. 26). Although he published a volume of predominantly late-Romantic lyric verse, *Poems*, in 1934, it made no impact and proved an abortive start to his real career as a writer, which only got under way twenty years later with *Lord of the Flies*. During that career Golding published eleven novels, a trio of novellas, two collections of essays, a travel journal, and a play. Two years after his death in 1993 his semi-completed final novel, *The Double Tongue*, saw publication.

Much of Golding's fiction is near-allegoric, making frequent use of symbol, myth, and pattern, and strives toward poetic compression and intensity. At its core is his belief that "man produces evil as a bee produces honey" (p. 87). Anatomizing what he calls "the terrible disease of being human" (p. 89), his novels seek to make man confront "the sad fact of his own cruelty and lust" (p. 87).

In its settings, Golding's fiction is exceptionally varied. "I have always felt that a writer's books should be as different from each other as possible," he said (*A Moving Target*, [1982] p. 198). True to this, his chronological range is strikingly wide, taking in Neanderthal victims of Homo sapiens at one extreme and human victims of nuclear war at the other. His fiction has surveyed the Egypt of the pharaohs, ancient Greece, imperial Rome, a medieval cathedral community, a ship en route to Australia at the start of the nineteenth century, and a provincial English town in the early twentieth century. Behind this diversity of time and place, though, is the fixed conviction that "Man is a fallen being. He is gripped by original sin, His nature is sinful and his state perilous" (*The Hot Gates*, p. 88).

As Golding was aware, this is an insight that could be regarded as "trite, obvious and familiar in theological terms." But, he contends, "what is trite is true, and a truism can become more than a truism when it is a belief passionately held" (p. 88). His fiction can be seen as an attempt to justify this claim. Sometimes what he calls his "savage grasp on life" (p. 81) looks like a rather heavy-handed clutching at standard religious props. More usually it takes imaginative hold and molds his material into memorably dramatic contours—never more so than in his first novel, *Lord of the Flies* (1954).

One of the twentieth century's most widely read and influential works of fiction, *Lord of the Flies* was rejected by twenty-one publishers before being accepted by Faber and Faber. Even before this, Golding's path toward authorship had not been straightforward.

EARLY LIFE

BORN on 19 September 1911 in St. Columb Minor, Cornwall, in the southwest of England, he was the younger son of Alec and Mildred Golding. His mother (with whom he felt he shared temperamental affinities as well as a taste for storytelling) was Cornish. His father, who came from a working-class Quaker family near Bristol, was a science teacher at Marlborough Grammar School. Golding and his brother, José, attended this school and grew up in Wiltshire (the county in which he was to spend most of his life until the attention generated by his winning the Nobel Prize for Literature in 1983 drove him to seek seclusion back in Cornwall, where he died, at Perranarworthal, on 19 June 1993). Strongly influenced by his father, he enrolled at Brasenose College, Oxford, to study natural science. But after two discontented years, eager to escape "the labs where the frogs twitched and the rabbits' guts swelled in the hot summer humidity" (*A Moving Target,* p. 152), he switched to English and became especially fascinated by Anglo-Saxon poetry.

On leaving Oxford, Golding worked for a time in the theater as a producer and actor. Then he began what would be a far more prolonged career as a schoolmaster, although, he said, "I wasn't teaching because I wanted to teach, I was teaching because it was a way of earning enough money to keep myself while I moved towards other things (*William Golding: The Man and His Books*, p. 178). In 1939 he married Ann Brookfield, with whom he would have two children, David and Judith. When World War II broke out he was teaching at Bishop Wordsworth's School, Salisbury. And it

was to this school that he returned—after serving in the Royal Navy during the war—to continue as an English teacher until 1961.

LORD OF THE FLIES *AND* THE INHERITORS

LORD of the Flies (1954), the novel with which Golding launched the literary career that would bring him a Nobel Prize, and a knighthood in 1988, draws its fierce energies from both his teaching and wartime experiences. Speaking about the novel's genesis in a lecture in 1976, he recalled that:

More than a quarter of a century ago I sat on one side of the fireplace and my wife on the other. We had just put the children to bed after reading to the elder some adventure story or other—Coral Island, Treasure Island, Coconut Island, Pirate Island, Magic Island, God knows what island. Islands have always and for good reason bulked large in the British consciousness. But I was tired of these islands with their paper-cutout goodies and baddies and everything for the best in the best of all possible worlds. I said to my wife, "Wouldn't it be a good idea if I wrote a story about boys on an island and let them behave the way they really would?" She replied at once, "That's a first class idea. You write it." So I sat down and wrote it.

(*A Moving Target*, pp. 162–163)

The result was a novel that hauntingly encapsulates mid-twentieth-century pessimism about human nature. But its sources were personal ones. Depicting preadolescent schoolboys lapsing into savagery on a tropical island, *Lord of the Flies* is evidently the work of someone long familiar with children of that age: "I have lived for many years with small boys," Golding once said, "and understand and know them with awful precision" (*The Hot Gates*, p. 88). Sections of the novel were in fact written in the staff room of Bishop Wordsworth's School, with the yells of schoolboys loud in the playground outside. Clamoring even more insistently inside Golding's consciousness were memories of atrocities he had witnessed during the war, a time when "we saw, little by little, what man could do to man" (*A Moving Target*, p. 163). "There were things done during that period from which I still have to avert my mind lest I be physically sick" he said (*The Hot Gates*, p. 87). "Years of wordless brooding" about it ("like lamenting the lost childhood of the world") went into *Lord of the Flies*, the theme of which is "grief, sheer grief, grief, grief, grief" (*A Moving Target*, p. 163).

The cause of this grief is intimated by the novel's title. "Lord of the Flies" is a translation of Beelzebub, one of the biblical names for the Devil. Evil, this reminds us, was once seen as a malign force external to humanity and personified as Beelzebub, Satan, or some such diabolic figure. But, Golding's novel insists, evil lurks not outside but inside us. His Lord of the Flies is a manifestation of human viciousness, not supernatural malevolence.

To demonstrate this he portrays what happens when a group of English schoolboys—refugees from nuclear war—land on a beautiful and fertile island in the tropics. Restored to an Eden, they quickly reduce it to a hell. Flames, agony, and terror devastate the former paradise as the book ends. In this twentieth-century version of the Fall, however, there is no Devil—although the boys attempt to create one. Troubled by a sense of menace from the start, they externalize their dread in scared talk about a "beast" roaming the island. These frightened rumors find something of substance to cluster around when a monstrous figure is sighted grotesquely swaying and lurching on the mountaintop where they maintain their signal fire. To placate this nightmarish creature, an offering is made to it of a pig's head on a stick. In a bizarre pun on the novel's title, flies buzz around this sacrifice. Golding effects further subliminal punning when the bravest of the boys climbs the mountain to confront the horror. What he encounters there isn't a "beast" but a very literal incarnation of human corruption: the rotting corpse of an airman who has been shot down during an aerial battle and is now held in place, swaying in gusts of wind, by the strings of his parachute.

Around this macabre emblem of mankind's corruption, Golding's grim, compelling fable sets decay of other kinds. Although the castaways at first cooperatively band together, things soon begin to degenerate. As this happens, the boys—jetsam from a nuclear war—re-enact in a speeded-up, microcosmic fashion the historical process that has brought them to this pass. Humanity's social evolution is charted as a grisly decline from fruit-eating, tranquil commune to totalitarian butchery.

In the course of this, characters acquire allegoric aspects. Fair-minded Ralph, the stubbornly decent boy who struggles to hold things together, comes to represent liberalism. It is he who introduces the use of a conch shell to achieve a rudimentary kind of democracy on the island: when blown into, it summons everyone to an assembly where ideas can be exchanged and argued over; when passed around in the assembly, it guarantees freedom of speech to its holder. In opposition to this, Jack, who is first seen leading a phalanx of black-clad choirboys marching in formation across the scorching beach, increasingly personifies fascism as he fights for power, hunts down scapegoats, and turns the island into a miniature police state. As a political fable *Lord of the Flies* focuses on the to-the-death antagonism between this contrasting pair.

As a religious parable it highlights two other boys: Piggy and Simon. Piggy, the most intelligent of the castaways, who acts as a kind of personal adviser to the slower-minded if right-thinking Ralph, exemplifies scientific rationalism. He provides technological aid in the form of his spectacles, which are used to ignite a fire. (This is, ironically, a scientific solecism on Golding's part, as various critics have pointed out, most interestingly John Sutherland with his essay "Piggy's Burning (?) Glasses" in *Where Was Rebecca Shot?: Curiosities, Puzzles, and Conundrums in Modern Fiction*, pp. 65–71). Piggy is more logical and sensible than the other boys and has inklings, though in purely secular terms, of the inherent instability in humanity that the book spotlights. But although he reaches correct conclusions, he does so, in Golding's eyes, by an erroneous route. As personified by Piggy, scientific rationalism lacks allure. He is encumbered with the obese physique that gives him his nickname, along with myopia, asthma, flat feet, and a timorous disposition. Unlike the other castaways he is lower-class, as his dropped *h*'s, vulgar accent, and bad grammar repeatedly proclaim.

In Golding's portrayal of Piggy, admiration for the boy's acumen coexists with an almost contemptuous insistence on his limitations. Whole-hearted authorial approval is reserved for his opposite, Simon, who acts as mystic to Piggy's materialist. Simon has a stammer that impedes him in everyday communication and is subject to fits. But these things take on charismatic significance with his emergence as the novel's saint and seer: he is, Golding has made explicit, "a Christ-figure . . . a visionary" (*The Hot Gates*, pp. 97–98). Not merely kind, sympathetic, and courageous, Simon is spiritually enlightened enough to perceive the nature of "mankind's essential illness" (*Lord of the Flies*, p. 111), the predisposition to evil with which this novel is so concerned. Venerating Simon's viewpoint, Golding places him in surroundings where flowers with candlelike buds open around him and depicts him after his death as "a silver shape beneath the steadfast constellations" (p. 190). Piggy's corpse, in unglamorous contrast, "twitched a bit, like a pig's after it has been killed" (p. 223).

Like other events on the island, the deaths that occur there signal an accelerating descent into barbarism. The first death, that of one of the youngest boys in a forest fire, is accidental, the result of dangerously slackening vigilance. The second, Simon's, is the consequence of mass hysteria, a deliberate fomenting of loss of control: dazed and excited by the frenzied chanting they have been indulging in around a fire, the other boys mistake him for the "beast" as he stumbles out of the shadows to tell them what he has discovered about the monster on the mountaintop. The third death, Piggy's, when he goes to demand the return of his stolen glasses from Jack and his henchmen because "what's right's right" (p. 211), is cold-blooded murder. Before the story ends an even more sadistic kind of killing is attempted when Jack and his followers hunt the fugitive but still defiant Ralph with a stick sharpened at both ends.

What saves Ralph is the timely arrival of a naval officer. But this turn of events isn't to be seen as unambiguously heartening. Irony surrounds the officer as deus ex machina. The revolver he carries, like the submachine gun held by one of his fellow-sailors, is merely a sophisticated version of the sticks and stones with which the boys have fought. His military uniform is just a more advanced variant on the paint marks and masks with which they have daubed themselves. His cruiser isn't simply a rescue vessel but part of the international war machine. Beyond the ravaged island, civilization is "in ruins" (p. 78). Salvation isn't to be found there or, Golding believes, anywhere on earth. As the story closes, far from exulting in his escape, Ralph (who has painfully learned what Simon mystically intuited) "wept for the end of innocence, the darkness of man's heart" (p. 248).

The eleventh-hour arrival of an adult rescuer is one of the ways in which *Lord of the Flies* deliberately resembles an earlier novel: Robert Michael Ballantyne's enormously popular nineteenth-century boy's story *The Coral Island: A Tale of the Pacific Ocean* (1858). The names of the trio shipwrecked on Ballantyne's desert island—Ralph, Jack, and Peterkin—are adopted by Golding, with Peterkin modified to Simon (called Peter in the Bible). Like Ballantyne's, Golding's characters are menaced by savagery. But in Golding's twentieth-century twist to the story, this doesn't come from outside in the shape of cannibals and pirates but from within in the form of aggressive and resentful instincts. Where Ballantyne's trio are presented as representatives of civilized progress, colonists in miniature, Golding's castaways regress in order to exhibit mankind's primal imperfection.

Serious parody of this kind—the inventive subverting of what Golding sees as a falsely optimistic text—also lies behind his next novel, *The Inheritors* (1955). This time the literary work that provokes Golding's imagination into creative life is H. G. Wells's short story "The Grisly Folk." In this virtuoso feat of anthropological speculation Wells peers back into the reaches of prehistory and envisages the kind of territorial battle that must have occurred between Neanderthals and early human beings on the windswept glacial steppes of western Europe. For Wells the Neanderthals are ungainly, solitary creatures, "snarling, bloodstained, and horrible" (*H. G. Wells's Selected Short Stories*, p. 294); ogrelike figures, they "thought the little children of men fair game and pleasant eating" (p. 296). Unlike these cannibalistic beings who "had not learnt even the rudest elements of cooperation" (p. 296), our ancestors, though "still savages, very prone to violence and convulsive in their lusts and desires" (p. 288), understand the benefits of teamwork and are further unified by a phenomenon unknown to the Neanderthals: laughter, which acts as "a social embrace" (p. 293).

Borrowing the basic pattern of Wells's narrative, Golding likewise depicts a deadly encounter between Neanderthals and Homo sapiens. As in Wells's story, it occurs when the Neanderthals are heading north from their winter quarters to their summer pastures. As in Wells, one group steals children from the other. But in Golding it is Homo sapiens that is the predatory species. His novel endows the Neanderthals with the sympathetic traits—humor, cooperation—Wells reserved for humans. Inverting Wells's vignette of evolutionary advance, Golding portrays the ousting of the Neanderthals by our ancestors as a step backwards, a regressive loss of innocence. Like *Lord of the Flies*, which it closely resembles in combining a masterly suspense narrative with a somber assessment of humanity's nature and prospects (both books end with a stress on the "darkness" of mankind), *The Inheritors* presents an acutely original version of the Fall.

Most of what happens is conveyed via the alert senses of an only partly comprehending Neanderthal called Lok. The situation he finds himself caught up in resolves itself (again as in *Lord of the Flies*) into a conflict between two tribal groups, one peaceful and one belligerent. The Neanderthals—who venerate the female principle in the form of their goddess, Oa—are gentle beings. Although physically agile, with movements that are "a miracle of sensitive ingenuity" (*The Inheritors*, p. 129), they do not hunt but largely subsist on berries, honey, and fungi. While willing to eat meat from animals already slaughtered by other creatures (which they do with feelings of guilt), they never kill. They have no weapons or aggressive urges and are virtually devoid of any sense of individuality. Warmly communal, they often intertwine together in "a lattice of protection and comfort" (p. 21); as one of their elders dies, they huddle consolingly around him "in a cradle of warm flesh" (p. 39). Their speech is rudimentary, and they find the formation of thoughts (which they call "pictures") difficult.

With an imaginative flexibility that is itself "a miracle of sensitive ingenuity," Golding registers the Neanderthals' keenly sensuous responses to the world around them, and the mixture of puzzlement, worshipful admiration, and slowly growing fear with which they react to the "new people" who have entered it. His story pits them—hopelessly—against these beings who (rather like the boys in *Lord of the Flies* with their imaginary "beast") see them as devils and are murderously frightened of them. Inexorably the brainier species—worshippers of male force represented by the totem of a rutting stag, fierce, inventive, and armed with poison-tipped arrows—exterminates them. But with this victory comes a kind of defeat. Admirable qualities are blotted out by uglier ones. Among the novel's early humans, cruelty and selfishness are rife. Murderous jealousy festers (just as Jack in *Lord of the Flies* sharpened his spear in the hope of impaling Ralph, so here a knife is whetted to kill a rival).

A magnificent feat of imaginative advocacy, Golding's realization of the Neanderthals' perception of the world—pristine, generous, unclouded by egotism, drenched in sensory richness—is so beguiling that it comes as a jolt when he ultimately lets the reader see Lok from the outside as an apelike, bow-legged creature matted with a russet pelt. This sudden, final, dramatic change of viewpoint at the last moment is a technique Golding much favors in his fiction. *Lord of the Flies* ends by lifting its camera angle up from the boys to an adult's perception of them. *The Inheritors* swivels, at its conclusion, from the consciousness of the Neanderthals to that of the humans who have ruinously dispossessed them. With the closing sentence of his next book, *Pincher Martin* (1956), Golding perpetrates a particularly startling change of perspective.

PINCHER MARTIN *AND* FREE FALL

AFTER the intense achievement of his first two novels, Golding's career lapsed into a phase of less assurance and accomplishment. Partly this was because he was attempting something different and less immediately congenial to him. Instead of using the activities of near-tribal groups to exhibit dark truths about human nature as *Lord of the Flies* and *The Inheritors* had done, his next four novels each focus on an individual (in two of them, *Free Fall* (1959) and *The Pyramid* (1967), the individual narrates the story; in the others, *Pincher Martin* and *The Spire* (1964), the individual's consciousness comprises most of the book). One of the things this new approach reveals is Golding's awkwardness, at this stage, in dealing with psychological and emotional complexities. (Only in the trilogy he wrote at the end of his career, *To the Ends of the Earth* (1991), does he come into his own in this sphere.)

Pincher Martin is a novel that idiosyncratically combines the extravagant and the banal. At first sight the situation it depicts appears straightforward and symbolic in a conventional way. Cast up on a rock in the Atlantic after a U-boat torpedoes the destroyer he was serving on, a naval lieutenant struggles to survive. As if epitomizing the urge to stay alive, he clings to the inhospitable rock rather like the limpets that encrust its sides. Around him stretches the vast expanse of the ocean like an emblem of oblivion, death, eternity.

Resembling a drastically contracted version of the island-castaway scenario in *Lord of the Flies*, the book seems to be a stark epic of endurance. With searing immediacy Golding records a man's efforts to turn even the harshest of environments into a life-support system. Or so it seems until the novel's final line, which abruptly reverses this interpretation. Inspecting Pincher Martin's washed-up corpse, a naval officer observes that the drowned man didn't even have time to kick off his boots; he died almost instantaneously. Portrayed with such graphic rawness, Martin's ordeal proves to have been a fantasy. What the book consists of, it now transpires, is a series of baroque conceits on the theme of the self's perverse reluctance to dissolve into eternity. As Golding eventually found himself called upon to explain in the face of considerable bafflement from readers and critics:

Christopher Hadley Martin had no belief in anything but the importance of his own life, no God. Because he was created in the image of God he had a freedom of choice which he used to centre the world on himself. He did not believe in purgatory and therefore when he died it was not presented to him in overtly theological terms. The greed for life which had been a mainspring of his nature forced him to refuse the selfless act of dying. He continued to exist separately in a world composed of his own murderous nature. His drowned body lies rolling in the Atlantic but the ravenous ego invents a rock for him to endure on. It is the memory of an aching tooth. Ostensibly and rationally he is a survivor from a torpedoed destroyer: but deep down he knows the truth. He is not fighting for bodily survival but for his continuing identity in face of what will smash it and sweep it away—the black lightning, the compassion of God. For Christopher, the Christ-bearer, has become Pincher Martin who is little but greed. Just to be Pincher is purgatory; to be Pincher for eternity is hell.

(Quoted in Kermode, *Modern Essays*, pp. 247–248)

Starting life with the virtuous potential suggested by "Christopher," Golding's protagonist ends it as the aggressively grasping creature suggested by "Pincher" (the traditional nickname for anyone called Martin in the British navy). With his ruthless clawings and clingings on to life, he exemplifies the unregenerate state that his friend, the theologically inclined Nat, says marks a person as unready for heaven: "Take us as we are now and heaven would be pure negation" (*Pincher Martin*, p. 70). Accordingly, when Martin drowns he enters into the only kind of paradise he can envisage: "The sort of heaven we invented for ourselves after death, if we aren't ready for the real one" (p. 183). Rigid with egotism, he is only able to conceive of an afterlife as personal survival—even at the cost of hanging on to this amid increasingly agonizing pain.

This weird postmortem phantasmagoria which gives the novel its central conceit (and which derives perhaps from theological notions about the soul lingering in the dead body for a time before entering eternity) is intercut with scenes from Martin's past life (proverbially said to flash across the mind of a drowning person). A motif prominent in both sections is eating. As Golding's gloss on the novel spells out, the hallucinatory rock derives from Martin's memories of an aching tooth. Episodes from his life are correspondingly fitted out with images of voracity. Spotlighting this particularly glaringly, Martin (like Golding, an actor before joining the navy) is at one point allocated the role of Greed in a morality play.

The blatancy of that symbolism accords with the generally simplistic quality of the episodes set up to demonstrate Martin's predatory nature when alive. Crudely posed moral tableaux displaying his sexual exploitativeness recur frequently. Rejected by the virtuous Mary Lovell, who prefers saintly Nat, he responds with stagily murderous jealousy such as might be expected from a villain in a melodrama.

Pincher Martin is a novel that seems lopsided. Audacious originality goes into its febrile fantasia about the rock, but its more naturalistic interludes tend to be trite and flat. While Golding's deployment of theological allegory can strike the reader as over-ingenious, his portrayal of people often looks under-imagined. Although writing of impressive power occurs in *Pincher Martin,* it is oddly directed. Paradoxically the episodes that feel most alive—those describing Martin's battle with the elements, his hunger, injury, and pain on the wave-lashed rock—turn out to be a dead man's delusions. In contrast, the scenes from his life lack vitality.

Sexual callousness is again silhouetted against momentous religious dimensions in *Free Fall*. Like Pincher Martin, its protagonist—Sammy Mountjoy, a celebrated artist—personifies selfish lust and heartlessness. Where Martin was spurned by the pure (and symbolically named) Mary Lovell, Sammy seduces, then abandons and thus drives into insanity, the pure (and symbolically named) Beatrice Ifor.

As the novel's title indicates, it is in part another of Golding's fables about the Fall: in it, innocence curdles into corruption, "the little boy, clear as spring water" becomes "the man like a stagnant pool" (*Free Fall*, p. 9). But it is also about being suspended between two worlds, the transcendental and the everyday.

As Sammy emerges from his slum upbringing as an illegitimate child, he encounters two teachers who represent these apparently opposing spheres. Nick Shales, a kindly and talented science master (who has marked affinities with Golding's father), expounds a rationalistic creed. Rowena Pringle, a spiteful religion teacher, outlines the message of the gospels. The novel contends that although Nick is by far the more decent person, it is Miss Pringle whose doctrine is the redemptive one.

Swaying between "the world of miracle" (p. 217) and Nick's "cool and reasonable" (p. 217) but "stunted" (p. 226) universe, Sammy as a painter (like Golding as a novelist) seeks to fuse the two. In the novel's climactic scene—where Sammy is released from solitary confinement in a pitch-dark room he has been locked in while a prisoner of war—he ecstatically achieves this. The huts in the camp, he now sees, "shone with the innocent light of their own created nature" (p. 186). Dust on the ground is "a universe of brilliant and fantastic crystals, that miracles instantly supported in their being"; mountains in the distance "were not only clear all through like purple glass, but living. They sang and were conjubilant" (p. 186). His fellow prisoners are likewise transfigured: "a lieutenant, his wonderful brain floating in its own sea" now appears a "marvel" and an "awesome" phenomenon (p. 187).

The high-flown prose straining here to convey the visionary nature of Sammy's experience is of a piece with other self-consciously elevated sections of the book. Its opening paragraph blazes with religious motifs—"hosanna," "the power and the glory," "miraculous and pentecostal" (p. 5). Referred to at one point as "the infant Samuel" (p. 77), Sammy shares attributes as well as a name with the biblical prophet. His surname, Mountjoy, gestures toward paradise. Reinforcing this, we learn that he lives on Paradise Hill.

The strengths of this rather meandering and heavily allegorical novel don't, however, reside in Sammy's visions as a mystic but in his vision as an artist. Under his vividly pictorial gaze, on a windy washing day in April, "The clothing on the lines was horizontal and shuddering, the sharp, carved clouds hurried, the sun spattered from the soap suds in the gutter, the warm bricks were bright with a dashing of rain" (p. 20). When he and another boy trespass by night in the grounds of a rich man's residence, "The high parapet of the house began to shine, a full moon lugged herself over the top and immediately the gardens were translated. There was a silver wink from a pool nearer the house, cypresses, tall and hugely still, turned one frosted side to her light" (p. 44). Prose of this lucid, accurate beauty throws into relief the overwrought uplift of the novel's would-be transcendental interludes and the diagrammatic stiffness that cramps its depiction of human behavior and motive.

Both *Pincher Martin* and *Free Fall* seem imperfectly achieved. Both fail to make their visionary and everyday dimensions cohere convincingly. Both feature a protagonist who exemplifies moral defects and theological concepts so crudely that he lacks human credibility. In both books, scenes of near-contemporary life do little to stir Golding's deepest imaginative powers. As if aware of these shortcomings, he sets out to overcome them in his next novel, *The Spire*. Here Golding creates a fable of acutely concentrated focus, at the center of which is a figure of harrowing credibility. By placing his story in a medieval cathedral community, he finds a milieu where religious belief is part of the everyday atmosphere and is able to give brilliant scope to the imaginative archaeology that is such a compelling aspect of his genius.

THE SPIRE *AND* THE PYRAMID

ISOLATION is a factor that always adds intensity to Golding's fiction. Moments of terror come from it (Ralph, the sole opponent of barbarism on the island, fleeing for his life; Lok, the lone survivor of the Neanderthal band, pining away; Pincher Martin scrabbling to hold on to his lonely rock; Sammy Mountjoy tormented by his dreads in solitary confinement). So do moments of insight, such as Simon confronting the "beast" and discovering the true nature of evil.

With *The Spire*, his most potently claustrophobic novel, Golding clenches these elements together. Virtually the whole story is enclosed within a consciousness that is cut off—terrifyingly and occasionally inspirationally—from the world around it. Chronicling the determination of Jocelin, a fourteenth-century ecclesiastic, to add a four-hundred-foot-high spire to the cathedral of which he is dean, the novel is a tale of obsession, its cost, and its almost accidental rewards. Driven by his vainglorious ambition to erect the great spire, Jocelin at first seems an exemplar of the blindness of spiritual pride. In a narrative whose viewpoint is presented with telling obliquity, we only gradually perceive all the things he has shut his eyes to.

Jocelin's grandiose plan, it becomes apparent, is almost suicidally foolhardy. The cathedral has no real foundations. Its pillars aren't solid, just thin layers of stone containing rubble. Spiritually his endeavor rests on an equally flimsy basis. He has gained his position as dean of the cathedral not through his merits but because of the patronage of his aunt, a mistress of the king; a postcoital whim launched his ecclesiastical career. Other corrupt factors fester at the root of his enterprise, in particular suppressed sexuality, manifest in his heated dreams of a young woman he has self-interestedly married off to the cathedral's crippled and impotent caretaker.

Trying to ignore his own impulsions, Jocelin likewise averts his gaze from the toll his building work is taking. As the spire precariously rises over it, the cathedral is desecrated and physically endangered. Brutish workmen bury the human victim of a pagan sacrifice in its foundations. (Stonehenge, we are reminded, isn't far from this Christian edifice.) To stop his head mason from defecting, Jocelin tacitly connives at an illicit love affair the man is guiltily caught up in. The body count of those destroyed by Jocelin's hubris mounts. Finally, he himself succumbs. The mysterious warm glow across his back which he has assured himself is a sign of the presence of a guardian angel turns out to be caused by consumption of the spine. Conceived as an emblem of spiritual uplift, the spire in fact rears up from murder, lust, pride, delusion, and disease. But despite all this, even on its shaky underpinnings it towers magnificently towards the heavens. As Golding explained:

The book is about the human cost of building the spire . . . the protagonist forces through the building of the spire against all odds, not counting the cost to himself or anyone else because he thinks he does God's will. He does not think of beauty—might never have heard of it. He only sees it part by part and when it is finished cannot bear to look at it because of the folly and wickedness the job forced on him. Only when he is dying does he see the spire in all its glory; and the sight reduces him to understanding that he had no understanding.

(*A Moving Target*, pp. 166–167)

What makes this diagrammatic plan expand and complicate into compelling fiction is the imaginative energy, stemming from very personal sources, that Golding channels into it. The novel's cathedral is, for instance, clearly modeled on the one that loomed over most of his adult life and was continually visible from Bishop Wordsworth's School: Salisbury, whose spire (the highest in England) is just a few feet taller than that in his book. In his essay "An Affection for Cathedrals," published a year after *The Spire*, Golding paid tribute to Salisbury cathedral and the "memories of inexpressible beauty" it had given him: "a floodlit cathedral, a magic cathedral under the full moon; a bonewhite spire against the smoke from burning Dunkirk, with the lightning conductors glittering like emeralds; a rose-coloured cathedral, yet washed from below with the reflected whiteness of a million open daisies" (*A Moving Target*, pp. 14–15). A similar enraptured responsiveness shimmers from the pages of *The Spire*, which are additionally and enthrallingly stocked with gritty practicalities about the logistical challenges presented by Jocelin's audacious venture. A lifelong sufferer from vertigo, Golding gives dizzying menace to scenes on the scaffolding around the spire. At ground level, too, things quiver with peril. Under the pressure piled upon them, the pillars emit an eerie sound. As the earth shifts, heaps of pebbles stir as though they were alive. Around all this Golding expertly packs a medieval community whose behavior and assumptions he seems almost uncannily familiar with.

The community under scrutiny in his next novel is one that makes fewer demands on his imagination. Taking its title from another upward-pointing structure, *The Pyramid* surveys an English provincial town between the 1930s and 1960s. Sammy in *Free Fall* spoke of "our social pyramid" (p. 193), and Golding has written angrily about "the dreadful English scheme of things" prevailing during his youth: "a scheme which so accepted social snobbery as to elevate it to an instinct" (*The Hot Gates*, p. 168). Portraying that snobbery, the novel uses the image of the pyramid to convey not just the notion of stratified layers narrowing towards a peak, but a pervading deathliness.

A rather slackly put-together book, *The Pyramid* consists of three sections (two of which had appeared previously in literary periodicals). The theme interlacing these sections is the devitalized and devitalizing nature of small-town English provincial life with its cruel class distinctions, mean-spirited repressiveness, hypocritical conventionality, and, worst of all, lack of love. The novel's epigraph, from an ancient Egyptian text, is "If thou be among people make for thyself love, the beginning and end of the heart." This is advice few characters in *The Pyramid* heed. In the first story, a gold cross with the inscription *Amor Vincit Omnia* (Love Conquers All) is lost. And love seems a lost cause in each of these three narratives.

Golding's familiar concern with heartless sexual exploitation surfaces almost immediately when Oliver, the novel's narrator, who is eighteen years old at this stage, coerces Evie Babbacombe into a sexual relationship she doesn't want. This is partly, we later learn, because she is being sexually abused by her father as well as being treated as easy game by other local menfolk, one of whom likes to whip her until she is covered with welts. Another continuing preoccupation in Golding's fiction—the misery caused by intolerance of homosexuality—features in the second section of the novel. Pressed into helping with the local operatic society's production of a piece of Ruritanian tosh called *The King of Hearts* during his college vacation, Oliver (to whom Golding gives something of his own considerable musical talents) is doted on by the effeminate Mr. Evelyn De Tracy, who has been brought in to produce the operetta. Like other homosexuals in Golding's pages—the platonically pederastic Father Watts-Watt who rescues Sammy from the slums in *Free Fall*, the sleazy but ultimately redeemed Mr. Pedigree in *Darkness Visible* (1979), the gawky, doomed Reverend Colley in *Rites of Passage* (1980)—De Tracy is portrayed with an ambivalent mixture of sympathy and grotesqueness. This mix is also apparent in the presentation of the final victim of lovelessness in this novel: Miss Dawlish, an unprepossessing spinster driven mad (like Beatrice in *Free Fall*) by being emotionally exploited.

Stilbourne, the setting for these casualties of callousness, is clearly a version of Marlborough, the Wiltshire town where Golding grew up and was educated, just as the setting for *The Spire* was based on Salisbury, where he taught for many years. Both Salisbury and Marlborough feature, fictionally transmuted, in Anthony Trollope's nineteenth-century sequence of novels about "Barsetshire." Allusions to those books are strewn throughout *The Pyramid*: Oliver gets a train to Barchester; there's mention of Bumstead Episcopi, a derisive reworking of Trollope's Plumstead Episcopi. But whereas in *Lord of the Flies* and *The*

Inheritors Golding's imagination was spurred into strikingly original creativity by Victorian fiction, no such process occurs here. *The Pyramid* is one of his weakest books in its rather lame reiteration of his well-worn themes and exudes the sense of a talent running out of momentum. After writing it Golding didn't publish another novel for twelve years. The only new book of his to appear during that period was *The Scorpion God* (1971), a collection of three novellas. One of these, "Envoy Extraordinary," had actually been written much earlier (it appeared in a 1957 anthology along with stories by John Wyndham and Mervyn Peake) and had been subsequently reshaped by Golding into a play, *The Brass Butterfly* (1958). Although interestingly varied in their settings—ancient Egypt, the Stone Age, imperial Rome—the stories revolve around habitual Golding concerns (especially the impasse between visionary and secular views of the world) in a rather slight and sometimes surprisingly waggish way. When Golding returned to writing novels with *Darkness Visible* in 1979 it was in a drastically different style.

DARKNESS VISIBLE *AND* THE PAPER MEN

DARKNESS Visible resembles *The Pyramid* in being divided into three sections. Apart from this, it might have been written to get as far away from its predecessor as possible. Where *The Pyramid* was naturalistic, *Darkness Visible* is mythic. Where *The Pyramid* verged on the pedestrian, *Darkness Visible* strives towards the apocalyptic. Far from peering at provincial snobberies, it spans two hemispheres in its overview of evil. Its title, a quotation from John Milton's *Paradise Lost*, refers to hell. And infernal scenes, populated with devilish creatures, glare out from its pages.

The novel opens with one of the most dramatic sequences Golding ever wrote. Returning to a constant preoccupation—the damage wreaked by the World War II—he plunges the reader into the midst of a band of exhausted and nerve-wracked firemen fighting a furnacelike conflagration raging in London's East End during the Blitz. Out of this scene of incandescent devastation walks, to their incredulous consternation, a small boy. From "the shuddering backdrop of the glare" (*Darkness Visible*, p. 13)—which is so fierce that it melts lead and distorts iron—this naked little figure, hideously burned down one side of his face, advances steadily. He is, the book soon starts to stress, a being of some portent. The fire from which he miraculously has emerged is repeatedly likened to the burning bush in the Old Testament. The name he is given in hospital—Matty—links him with the evangelist Matthew, and as the book progresses he is heaped with a further abundance of scriptural symbolism. At a school for foundlings, where he falls foul of a pederastic teacher, Mr. Pedigree, and brings about the death of another boy, he learns large amounts of the Old and New Testaments by heart. Eventually journeying out to Australia, accompanied by his Bible, which he continues to study and memorize, he undergoes a series of increasingly outlandish ordeals which culminate in his mock-crucifixion by an Aborigine.

Saturated with scriptural allusions and analogies, the first section of the novel establishes Matty as the most extravagantly symbolic of Golding's visionary misfits. Its second section swivels the focus toward evil, as personified by a beautiful but schizoid and sadistic dark-haired girl called Sophy and her ash-blond twin sister, the affectless and amoral Toni. Around them, in a narrative harsh with almost hysterical loathing of contemporary life in the 1960s and 1970s, Golding piles up instances of characters reveling in depravity and destructiveness. In the third section, amid a welter of terrorism, drugs, incest, kidnapping, and would-be killing, Matty (by now a figure of charismatic potency) and Sophy (seen by him as a contemporary avatar of the Apocalypse's malign Whore of Babylon) confront each other. An inferno triggered by a bomb explosion she has engineered rages out of control in a flaming reprise of the firestorm with which the book opened. Although Matty perishes in it, he is blazingly transfigured as a Christlike redemptive figure. Where he previously caused a boy's death, he now saves a boy's life. First seen as a horribly disfigured waif, he is last witnessed—in what is presented as a vision of salvation appearing to the tormented Pedigree—with a face "gold as the fire and stern and everywhere there was a sense of the peacock eyes of great feathers and the smile round the lips was loving and terrible" (p. 265).

Full of transcendental mysteriousness and riddled with complex scriptural allusions, *Darkness Visible* nevertheless makes a crude and simplistic impression. Although sometimes obscure in its procedures, it is lurid in its view of life. Exacerbat-

ed cameos of modern godlessness intersperse turbid visionary fantasies. Carrying Golding's preoccupation with original sin and redemption to a feverish extreme, it is a kind of novel he was never to attempt again.

Its view of the world as something grotesquely rebarbative does resurface, however, in his next-but-one novel, *The Paper Men* (1984). What is notable about this book is its disappointing willingness to indulge in contemptuous caricature. Sarcasm quivers through its pages. Essentially a bitter fable (in the form of a struggle between a writer and his would-be biographer) about the dangers of the literary life, it begins with Wilfred Barclay, a distinguished but alcoholic author in late middle age, discovering a young American academic, Rick L. Tucker from the University of Astrakhan, Nebraska, furtively rummaging in his dustbin. Initially mistaking the scavenging Tucker for a badger (and hence opening fire on him with an airgun), Barclay continues to regard him as less than human. So does Golding. One of the persisting weaknesses of this novel is its deployment of cartoonish derision. Rick's wife, Mary Lou, who has "majored in flower arranging and bibliography" (*The Paper Men*, p. 65), expresses herself in jinglelike vapidities such as "That would be fun, hon" (p. 73) or naive mouthfuls of jargon: "He said no one else was doing you as of this moment in time" (p. 64). A gross parody of unsavory biographical intrusiveness, Tucker is depicted as a kind of academic pimp, blatantly using his wife as sexual bait to entice Barclay into authorizing him as his biographer and thus boosting his tenure prospects.

Complicating this crude picture a little, though not adding any real depth to it, is the fact that Barclay himself is shoddy in many ways. Golding teasingly endows him with some of his own literary traits and something of his own physical appearance—"scraggy yellow-white beard, yellow-white thatch and broken-toothed grin" (p. 30)— then turns him into yet another demonstration model of the damage done, to the self and others, by male sexual selfishness. Other elements notable in previous books are recycled too. Barclay has a terrifying vision of human insignificance and divine power. There's a scary episode on the edge of a mountain that wouldn't have been out of place amid the vertiginous dreads of *The Spire*. But even high-intensity moments such as these are muffled by the prevailing atmosphere of exasperated loathing Golding conveys, venting all his irritation at being hounded by the publicity circus and the academic thesis industry after winning the prestigious Booker Prize for fiction in 1980 and the Nobel Prize for Literature in 1983. Barclay and Tucker, both "paper men," ultimately destroy each other. Long before this, though, Golding's detestation has shredded them.

Best understood as an indignant riposte to the harassments increased celebrity had subjected him to, *The Paper Men* is Golding's flimsiest work. The novel that preceded it, however, *Rites of Passage* (1980), and those that succeeded it, *Close Quarters* (1987) and *Fire Down Below* (1989), show his genius at its finest. With these late novels he triumphantly displays his persisting ability to surprise by striking out in new directions. Having begun his literary career with two masterpieces, Golding concluded it with three others.

RITES OF PASSAGE, CLOSE QUARTERS, *AND* FIRE DOWN BELOW

THE sea was a key element in Golding's life and in his fiction. Sailing was one of his keenest activities. Serving in the Royal Navy during World War II gave him experience of cruisers, destroyers, and minesweepers. He was one of the sailors who took part in the sinking of the *Bismarck*, and during the D-Day operation he commanded a rocket-launching craft. When he returned to Bishop Wordsworth's School after the war, a former pupil recalled, he introduced naval uniform and the study of knots, semaphore, and seamanship to the Combined Cadet Corps of which he took charge (*William Golding: The Man and His Books*, p. 27). In his boat the *Wild Rose* (a converted Whitstable oyster smack), he sailed the Dutch waterways and around the North Sea and the Baltic. A further plan to explore the canals of Europe was scuppered in July 1967 when his later boat, the *Tenace*, was run down and sunk in a collision with a tanker off the Isle of Wight in the English Channel. Ironically, in an essay, "The English Channel," written some years earlier, he had asked, "Is there any water that can be so vast and dangerous to sail in a small boat, yet seem so small and placid when you fly across it?" (*The Hot Gates*, p. 41).

Combining his passion for Egypt with his passion for sailing, Golding traveled up the Nile on two occasions. The second of them, when he was a passenger on an awesomely ramshackle hired cabin cruiser, provided him with his material for his wry travelogue of nautical disasters and discomforts, *An Egyptian Journal* (1985). Previously, of course, watery menace had made its presence powerfully felt in his fiction: the sea surrounding the island in *Lord of the Flies*, the rivers the Neanderthals are terrified of crossing in *The Inheritors*, the freezing Atlantic pounding at Pincher Martin on his rock.

With *Rites of Passage*, the first book of the trilogy, Golding launches one of English literature's great fictional voyages: at its start passengers embark on an antiquated ship of the line that has been converted to carry them across the dangerous seas of the Napoleonic era to Australia. By the time the next book, *Close Quarters*, begins, the decrepit old vessel is just south of the equator, laboring in the doldrums where its hull has become choked with weed. The finale, *Fire Down Below*, carries the crippled ship and its storm-tossed freight of humanity to landfall in Sydney Cove. (Golding subsequently revised the three novels into the one-volume edition *To the Ends of the Earth*, 1991).

As always in Golding's novels, the physical setting is pungently and ruggedly actual. Life on the Australia-bound sailing ship reeks of and resounds with authenticity. Its sand and gravel ballast stinks. The sweetish odor of laudanum hangs over its fetid sickbeds. Wind whistles in its rigging and thunders in its sails. On its planking is heard "the leathery slap of the seamen's naked feet" (*Fire Down Below*, p. 49).

But, again as usual, Golding is as keen to re-create his characters' inner worlds as he is to reconstruct their external milieu. For most of *Rites of Passage* the reader is confined within the narrow, snobbish mind of Edmund Talbot, a supercilious young man who is keeping a journal of the voyage to entertain and gratify the powerful lord back in England who is his godfather and patron. Bound for a government post in the upper colonial echelons of Australia, Talbot reports on the turbulent journey in sedulously blasé tones. Exuding condescension, reeling out classical allusions as shibboleths of class distinction, alternating between seigneurial disdain and sycophantic regard for rank, his journal lets the reader hear the last, jaded accents of Augustan civilization.

Golding's purpose, it becomes evident, isn't just to chronicle the hazards of an early-nineteenth-century voyage across the globe but to chart the eddies of a crucial watershed in British cultural history. In *Rites of Passage*, ebbing Neoclassicism and the first waves of Romanticism meet. For also onboard is a gawky, evangelical clergyman, Robert Colley. Viewed through Talbot's derisive gaze, he seems a clownish bumpkin, outlandish in manner and unmodish in dress. Then, after a murky incident below decks leads to Colley's collapse into catatonia and death, a journal he also has written comes into Talbot's possession. And, as it is unfolded to the reader, the narrative enters a new world.

The last and best of the figures of ungainly decency Golding often introduces into his fiction, Colley turns out to have been alive with Romantic susceptibility. His response to the journey glows with entranced appreciation of natural splendor. In contrast to Talbot's cynicism and smart knowingness, Colley's vision of their voyage is rapt and receptive to the Turneresque seascapes of mist and lightning, gleam and vapor.

But Colley's uncircumspect responsiveness finally destroys him. Gradually the novel discloses how, after he has been plied with drink, his suppressed homosexuality has been jeeringly made sport of by one of the young crewmen whose bronzed bodies he has innocently rhapsodized about in his journal. As Colley subsequently wills himself to death out of shame, Golding invests with fierce desolation a theme that always haunts his pages: the damage done by human cruelty.

Not that *Rites of Passage* is a cheerless book. Far from it. In this novel Golding's gifts of irony and humor are often deployed to hilarious effect. Talbot's callow satire, crowing over the absurdities of his fellow passengers, is itself satirized with mature finesse, tinged with a humane tolerance for his youth. Around him there are scenes of exuberant comedy. Mr. Prettiman, an irascible rationalist, stalks the afterdeck with a blunderbuss, hoping to bring down an albatross and thus explode the superstition he believes Coleridge's *Rime of the Ancient Mariner* has deplorably promoted. (The poem's relevance to the victimization of Colley taking place on the ship goes unnoticed by him and everyone else.) Talbot is entangled in a grotesque amour with a rouged belle, Zenobia Brocklehurst, and unnerved by a snappishly intelligent governess, Miss Granham, who seems disconcertingly indifferent to his assumptions of social superiority.

As characters literally tread the boards and the ship becomes increasingly bedecked with theatrical metaphor, all this seems like a brittle comedy of manners played out above an underlying physicality and brutality. Around this cabined-in tableau of humanity, Golding opens up, elatingly and chasteningly, vast dimensions of ocean and cosmos.

The collision between eighteenth-century rationality and nineteenth-century romanticism in *Rites of Passage* sometimes calls to mind the novels of Jane Austen. With *Close Quarters*, Golding steers his fiction even further into the atmosphere of her world. When the emigrants' ship is becalmed alongside another—so that, it is observed, the two vessels resemble adjoining streets in a country village—the voyagers enjoy a social life very like that in an Austen novel. As if responding to the complaint that her fiction parochially ignores the Napoleonic wars, Golding buoyantly suggests what it might have been like if it hadn't. Jubilant when they receive news of Boney's defeat, dashing young officers, a puffed-up aristocrat, his sentimental wife, and their spirited ward, who has captivated Talbot, exchange visits and notes, meet for a dinner party, and attend a ball. In the background, new and old attitudes clash as Benét, a lieutenant of Byronic disposition, devises a bold scheme—stubbornly opposed by the ship's cautious second-in-command, Summers—for scraping the weed from the hull.

In *Fire Down Below* the antagonism between Benét and Summers is brought to the fore. The ship's progress to Sydney Cove, already so dangerously prolonged as to threaten provisions, is now jeopardized by a new menace. The foremast has worked loose and is splitting the huge block of timber, "the shoe," at its base. With characteristic panache Benét proposes sealing the cracked shoe by inserting red-hot irons which, bolted to metal plates, will pull the wood together as they cool and contract. A horrified Summers contends that this will ignite the core of the timber. Overruled, he watches with chagrin as Benét's risky ploy apparently succeeds. Then, in one of the most blazingly exciting sequences Golding ever wrote, Summers is proved fatally right.

Fire down below isn't just a real hazard in this novel. It is also the main image running through it. Potentially calamitous heat smoldering in the depths of the personality is the book's subject. On the fraught ship, opposing factions gloweringly coalesce. Anger and banked-down sexuality flame out. Jealousy flares. Sparks fly between the flamboyant Benét and the staid Summers, and beneath the latter's dispassionate exterior, dangerous elements kindle: resentment, ambition, and suppressed homosexuality. Subtly, Golding makes it evident to the reader, though never to Talbot, that Summers is in love with him, tactfully contriving ways to help and protect him without embarrassing him. There are interludes of delicate tension where the two men, sharing the watch in the middle of the night, exchange quiet confidences, Summers' just perceptibly tinged with bitterness welling from his thwarted tenderness.

The atmospheric nature of these and other scenes is heightened by the transformation effected in Talbot's narrative style after he reads Colley's awed account of the voyage. Talbot's own Augustan prose—epigrammatic, neat, and witty—now often alight with visual responsiveness: in full moonlight, dazzlingly blanched sails hang above a ghost ship of silver and ivory; its wake bursts into "a splendour of diamonds" (p. 89); crenellated clouds tower up like ominous "castles of storm" (p. 122).

Brilliantly navigating a range of period styles, the novel has grotesque set pieces, such as a hideously incongruous wedding ceremony at sea, that recall Tobias Smollett, one of the eighteenth-century authors Talbot plumes himself on emulating. But most of all, as Talbot's pride and prejudice give way to sense and sensibility, similarities to Jane Austen flood into the book. Behind a glitter of witty, politely edged verbal skirmishing, faults of inexperience are rectified, education is achieved through admission of error, and moral growth begins with a recognition of limitations.

The journey to the other side of the globe overturns Talbot's preconceptions and widens his horizons. Once shallow and mocking, he now registers deeper dimensions as characters he thought farcical undergo a sea change before his eyes. Mr. Prettiman, for example, initially "our comic philosopher" (p. 17), swells, after incurring grave physical injury, into a painfully suffering fellow creature.

Talbot's maturing process includes a developing respect for Prettiman's utopian scheme of founding a model community, purged of privilege and superstition, in the pristine heart of Australia. This project adds a second connotation to the image of fire down below. Under the gleaming constellations of the Southern Hemisphere, Prettiman, a romantic rationalist, speaks of his Promethean ideal of people as visionaries: "we, a fire down below here—sparks of the Absolute—matching the fire up there" (p. 219). This is a height, Talbot ruefully recognizes, that he himself can never attain. His career will be more worldly. Indeed, for a time, it looks likely to be merely mundane. Upon arrival in the Antipodes his plans are overturned by the news that his influential godfather has expired of apoplexy brought on by overenthusiastic celebration of Britain's victory over "the Corsican Tyrant" (p. 273).

A sequence of brisk ups and downs, cunningly held in reserve to keep anticlimax at bay after the ship has docked at Sydney Cove, finally takes Talbot to a happy, Jane Austen-ish ending with an ironically commonsensical young woman. But around the edges of this prospect—in a book in which atmosphere is as ever-shifting as its seascapes—melancholy drifts in. The elderly Talbot penning these pages looks back with wondering wistfulness at the ability he once had to experience intense emotion. Regret at not being able to rise to the challenge of Prettiman's idealism still sometimes surfaces in his dreams.

Starting as an arrogant social figurehead, Talbot ends as a decently self-questioning human being. This interior journey is charted with psychological and emotional nuance, while the marathon sea voyage during which it occurs gives full leeway to Golding's skills at vigorous action writing. Throughout the book, idioms now dryly stranded in the English language—"taken aback," "pipe down," "sailing close to the wind"—are drenched in the immediacy of their maritime origins. In *Fire Down Below*, pouring oil on troubled waters isn't just something characters metaphorically attempt during stormy disputes but a literal maneuver desperately undertaken as cliff-high waves crash around the ship and miles of ocean seethe up under its precarious timbers.

Eighteenth- and early-nineteenth-century literary influences are richly present everywhere in *To the Ends of the Earth*. But a more distant and more long-standing creative stimulus is discernible too. With his sea trilogy Golding could be seen as offering his own version of an odyssey, a concluding homage to Homer's epic, which he described in *A Moving Target* as "a book as remarkable in its way as the Bible" (p. 91) and whose "ancient words" with their "familiar surge and thunder" (p. 93) had spoken to him for most of his life. Appropriately, after his sudden death in June 1993, he left behind in near-final draft form one last book that testified to his lifelong engagement with classical Greek literature.

THE DOUBLE TONGUE

THE *Double Tongue* (1995) is narrated by Arieka, an aged prophetess at the shrine to Apollo in Delphi. Like Golding when he wrote the book, she is in her eighties. Having spent most of her life as an oracle trying to look forward, she now looks back over her long years at Delphi and her childhood in the household of her father, a harsh provincial aristocrat. As she does so, Golding compellingly exhumes the Greece of the first century B.C. In Delphi, reputed to be the center of the earth, the sacred college of priests clings to the steep side of Mount Parnassus. Swathed in veils, the Pythian prophetess travels in an archaic carriage hauled by young men along the cobbled way to Greece's holiest shrine. There, in an underground vault, a bronze tripod holds half-moons of glowing charcoal onto which she sprinkles crushed laurel leaves before giving utterance among the fumes. Outside, jostling crowds testify to the veneration in which the shrine is still held. But within, stumps of metal, from which pillagers have wrenched away treasures such as a life-sized statue of the priestess in solid gold, serve as reminders of the dangerous decline the temple is now facing.

Always as keen an anthropologist as an archaeologist, Golding also vividly re-creates the mental milieu circumscribing Arieka. The early pages of her memoirs stress the restrictions placed on her as a young woman in her father's house—trained to sit in silence throughout social occasions and expected to submit to an arranged marriage. Her bid to escape the latter fate topples her into shameful farce. Attempting to flee, she is thrown from a donkey and found disheveled and half-naked on the ground. When her husband-to-be then rejects his claim on her, her enraged father hands his sallow, difficult, irregularly featured daughter over to the temple at Delphi.

As Arieka attains the status of First Prophetess there—becoming the mouthpiece for oracular messages to mankind—Golding moves into the mysterious region beyond rationality: psychic territory, the realm of heightened and hallucinatory states of mind, which his fiction always likes to explore. In interviews he often compared literary inspiration to possession by inexplicable forces. In keeping with this, Arieka's experiences sometimes weirdly parallel his own. Just as, he once recounted (*The Hot Gates*, p. 166), he was first stirred by a sense of awe and terror in the dark cellar beneath his parents' house, so she descends to a cellarlike grotto where eerie responses take her over.

In the case of the young Golding, receptivity to the uncanny kept encountering a contrasting, robustly canny mentality, as embodied by his scientific rationalist father who "inhabited a world of sanity and logic" (p. 168). From mystic Simon and pragmatic Piggy in *Lord of the Flies* onwards, opposites of this kind recur throughout Golding's fiction. *The Double Tongue* works a last variant on this interaction. At Delphi, Arieka's closest companion is the cynical high priest Ionides. Skeptical, politic, ever mindful of the need to placate the powerful, flatter benefactors, and keep the populace in a state of tractable credulity, he heightens the ambivalence Arieka already feels about her role by using his position as her interpreter to fix questions and rig answers (a state of affairs at the shrine that Golding had envisaged as far back as 1967 in an essay on Delphi subsequently collected in *A Moving Target*, p. 41).

When Ionides accompanies Arieka to a performance of Euripides's *Ion*, Golding makes explicit a homage implicit elsewhere in this book. Like Euripide drama about Delphi, Golding's novel adds a secular dimension to Apollo's temple, which is seen not merely as a sacred site but as a tourist attraction and a business enterprise dependent on sponsorship and patronage. Going further, Golding incorporates another aspect, presenting Delphi as a center of political dissension where Ionides plots the overthrow of Roman rule. The contemptuous quashing of this would-be revolt, and the crushing of Ionides self-respect by a casually brutal Roman governor, briefly tug the book toward the themes of cruelty and shame that pulsed through Golding's greatest novels, such as *Lord of the Flies*, *The Inheritors*, and *Rites of Passage*. Here, though, they are handled rather cursorily and mutedly, as is another of his lasting preoccupations: the desolation caused by lovelessness.

Arieka's emotionally bleak existence exhibits this plight, as well as enabling Golding to accomplish a notable feat of female, and feminist, characterization. But it is as a figure who allows him a last look at the ambivalences of inspiration that she seems most significant. Circling around her double-tongued communications, the novel keeps asking whether they derive from hysteria or seer-like prescience, craftiness or visionary uplift, and whether they constitute revelation or just cunning fiction. Fittingly the conclusion reached in this work riddled with ambiguity is an enigma. When Arieka unlocks the double doors of the shrine's innermost recess, she is confronted with a wall of sheer rock, elemental and impenetrable.

What this posthumous work does make unequivocally clear, though, is that until his death Golding never lost his imaginative versatility or his ability to occupy very different worlds with knowledgeable assurance. Nor was there any slackening in what is far from the least of his fictional skills: his masterly flair for narrative, or, as he once put it with characteristic literary unpretentiousness, "the journeyman's job of keeping the covers of a book apart by sticking a story between them" (*A Moving Target*, p. 154).

SELECTED BIBLIOGRAPHY

I. WORKS BY GOLDING. *Poems* (London, 1934); *Lord of the Flies* (London, 1954); *The Inheritors* (London, 1955; New York, 1962); *Pincher Martin* (London, 1956); *The Brass Butterfly* (London, 1958); *Free Fall* (London, 1959); *The Spire* (London and New York, 1964); *The Hot Gates* (London, 1965; New York, 1966); *The Pyramid* (London and New York, 1967); *The Scorpion God: Three Short Novels* (London, 1971; New York, 1972); *Darkness Visible* (London and New York, 1979); *Rites of Passage* (London and New York, 1980); *A Moving Target* (London and New York, 1982); *The Paper Men* (London and Boston, 1984); *An Egyptian Journal* (London and Boston, 1985); *Close Quarters* (London and New York, 1987); *Fire Down Below* (London and New York, 1989); *To The Ends of the Earth* (London, 1991); *The Double Tongue* (London and New York, 1995).

II. CRITICAL STUDIES. Samuel Hynes, *William Golding* (New York and London, 1964); Mark Kinkead-Weekes and Ian Gregor, *William Golding: A Critical Study* (London, 1967; New York, 1968); Bernard F. Dick, *William Golding* (New York, 1967); Leighton Hodson, *William Golding* (Edinburgh, 1969; New York, 1971); Howard S. Babb, *The Novels of William Golding* (Columbus, Ohio, 1970); Jack I. Biles, *Talk: Conversations with William Golding* (New York, 1970); Frank Kermode, *Modern Essays* (London, 1971); Virginia Tiger, *William Golding: The Dark Fields of Discovery* (London, 1974); Don Crompton, *A View from the Spire: William Golding's Later Novels*, ed. and completed by Julia Briggs (Oxford, 1985); Norman Page, ed., *William Golding: Novels 1954–67: A Selection of Literary Criticism* (London, 1985);. John Carey, ed., *William Golding: The Man and His Books* (London, 1986; New York, 1987); L. L. Dickinson, *The Modern Allegories of William Golding* (Tampa, Fla., 1990); John Sutherland, *Where Was Rebecca Shot?: Curiosities, Puzzles, and Conundrums in Modern Fiction* (London, 1998).

THOMAS HARDY

(1840–1928)

Barbara Hardy

THOMAS HARDY WAS born on 2 June 1840 in Higher Bockhampton, near Dorchester, in rural Dorset, and his birthplace still exists in not wholly transformed surroundings. His handsome, dashing father, Thomas Hardy, came from generations of stonemasons and builders; some of his strong-minded, ambitious mother's ancestors were small farmers, her father was a shepherd and gardener, she was a servant, and, like many of the family, she was poor enough to need parish relief. In later life Hardy sometimes suppressed details of his family's poverty and speculated about grander ancestors, but he was always loyal to his parents and siblings.

He once described himself, refuting the charge of philosophical pessimism, as temperamentally responsive to tragic events, and stories of his childhood have acquired apt symbolic or metonymic force: perhaps his parents married with reluctance, urged by Jemima Hand's pregnancy; his mother may have contemplated leaving her husband soon after the marriage to work as cook in a London club; Hardy was a weak baby declared dead by the doctor but revived by the midwife, living to be a precocious infant; he overheard his parents discussing his likely early death; he was found in his cradle curled up with a (harmless) snake; as a small boy he was a willing pet of the lady of the manor, Mrs. Julia Augusta Martin, meeting her in later life to be disillusioned by her advanced age; the poem "Childhood Among the Ferns" records an adolescent experience of lying on the ground and not wanting to grow up.

LIFE

HIS family life and environment were soil for creative roots—rich in nature, folklore, parish history, and ritual. The rhythm of the year is marked in his novels and poetry as it was, and as it was changing, in the rustic reality in which he grew up: seasonal work, midwinter bonfire at the solstice, Christmas carols and feast, mummers' play, maypole, whitsun walking, midsummer eve, harvest festival, the village culture of church, christening, wedding, funeral, dance, music, song, and story. Rural life had squalor, violence, and suffering as well as charm, and if Hardy memorialized and mourned the passing of traditions like the church band and the mummer's play, he deplored want, illiteracy, superstition, heavy drinking and promiscuity, in crucial scenes like the death of the Durbeyfield's horse, the mayor of Casterbridge's poverty, drunkenness, and wife-auction, the "randy" turned rough on the night of Tess's rape, and the skimmity-riding in *The Mayor of Casterbridge* (1886), in which Lucetta Farfrae and Michael Henchard are cruelly exposed in effigy.

Hardy's studiousness and intelligence were encouraged by his mother, herself a reader, who gave him Dryden's translation of Virgil and Samuel Johnson's *Rasselas* at an early age. He was educated until he was sixteen at the local National School, a school in Hatfield kept by a Congregationalist minister, the Dorchester British school, and an independent "academy." He started work in the congenial environment of the architect John Hicks's office, went on educating himself in a strict early-morning routine, and made friends in the office and outside who broadened his mind, knowledge, and religious opinion. Like his tragic hero Jude Fawley, he wanted to go to university, in his case Cambridge, and to go into the church, but his thwarted ambition developed more creatively and contentedly than Jude's. Less of a dreamer than Jude, he studied with practical purpose, contemplating various means of living a cultured, intellectual, and materially comfortable life. He continued classical studies with a view to taking orders; he thought of being an art historian so studied the philosophy and practice of painting and sculpture; attracted by literature, he read systematically in literary history and learned about genre, convention, and form. His interests were not narrow: he loved dancing, folk music, music hall, popular theater, and when he worked for the architect Arthur Blomfield in London, he haunted theaters, dance halls, and sleazy quarters of town, though as a shy and late-developing young man, his pleasures may have been largely those of spectator. His culture widened, his taste in the arts grew adventurous; he admired A. C. Swinburne and the late "mad" J. M. W. Turner, came to see the limits of realism in painting and literature, and in later life, at least read T. S. Eliot and Ezra Pound; he sketched, drew, and painted, illustrating his own *Wessex Poems* (1898). His grandfather was a good cellist, his father a violinist, and Hardy played the fiddle for village dances and weddings, was influenced as a poet by dance, folk song and ballad, imitated minuet and trio in "Lines to a Movement in Mozart's E-Flat Symphony," admired Tchaikovsky and late Wagner, and wrote one poem, "the Impercipient," an agnostic's defense, in the meter of a hymn tune.

Hardy was an apprentice then jobbing architect, working within the limits of his masters' projects and designs, and his fourteen years as a designer and church restorer, first in Dorchester, then London, then again in Dorchester, led him to contemplate architecture as a permanent career. He prudently overlapped professions, beginning to write while earning a living from architecture, not giving it up until the books began to succeed, just as later he overlapped two literary genres, publishing *Wessex Poems* while still writing novels.

His career as a published author did not begin until he had met and courted his first wife. His work as an architect introduced him to the lively, golden-haired, horse-riding Emma Lavinia Gifford and the romantic Cornish seascape, not far from Arthurian Tintagel, when he visited her brother-in-law, the rector of St. Juliot, to restore the parish church in a rage for Gothic improvement he came to regret.

Some of the couple's early scenes and feelings are fictionalized, especially in Hardy's third novel, *A Pair of Blue Eyes* (1873). Before Emma he had various fancies and loves, which are remembered in "Neutral Tones," "Lizbie Brown," "Louisa in the Lane," and poems about his cousins Rebecca, Martha, and Tryphena Sparks. Biographical speculation has indulged itself about his affection for Tryphena, to the extent of inventing a hypothetical illegitimate son (in *Providence and Mr. Hardy*, by Lois Deacon and Terry Coleman), a fiction demolished by scholars (for example, Robert Git-

tings' *The Young Thomas Hardy*, 1975). During courtship and the early years of marriage (which took place in 1867) Emma helped and encouraged Hardy in his writing, but she grew increasingly conventional and conservative in middle age, becoming obsessed by a fanatical narrow-minded protestantism. Not alone, but like many critics, churchmen, and friends, she detested his last novel, *Jude the Obscure* (1895), for its sexual candor, bitter critique of marriage, and subversive anti-Providence plot illustrating life without guiding God or consoling heaven. She also found it hard to accept love poems addressed to others, and Hardy's insistence on the "dramatic and personative" nature of his verse may have been a defense against her jealousy. The long-haired, dashing girl rider became middle-aged, more snobbish, heavy, and girlishly dressed, her scatter-brained chattiness and impulsive habits lost their charm, and Hardy's success introduced him to elegant, educated, and perhaps more talented women—admirers and literary aspirants like Florence Henniker, with whom he collaborated, and his second wife, Florence Dugdale, who came from a social background similar to his own and had an independent career as teacher and writer. Hardy's tendency to fall in and out of love, usually without return or commitment, provided Emma with a continued source of grievance. She formalized her harsh diary confidences under the heading "What I think of my husband," which he found and destroyed after her death. Some biographers (for instance, Michael Millgate) suggest that Emma's eccentricity and neurosis amounted to insanity; others (for instance, Gittings) see the story as a distortion promoted by Hardy's second wife. There is some evidence that Hardy feared for Emma's sanity, and two poems, "The Interloper" and "The Division," suggest this. Apart from the elegies for Emma, Hardy's writing is reticent about his love life, though reserve has stimulated biographical speculation.

His disillusionment in marriage is conspicuous because it became a subject of his impassioned art. The Cornish romance dwindled into sterile incompatibility and, at the end, a painful separation under one roof, but the pair were not always unhappy and shared many pleasures and tastes. Increasing prosperity and an upwardly mobile social life—the latter embarrassingly detailed in the memoir on which he and his wife Florence collaborated—entertained and flattered them both.

They shared the delights and trials of sightseeing in London and abroad, as Emma records in her journal and Hardy in his poetry and memoir. They went to church together, though with separate motives and responses, enjoyed making their home, garden, and pets' graveyard in Max Gate, the house Hardy designed and his brother Henry built, loved nature, like many childless couples lavished affection on dogs, and shared a humanitarian concern for animal rights, campaigning against vivisection, blood sports, and the use of horses in war.

Emma died in November 1912, of a fatally impacted gallbladder, after months of illness. Her suffering was apparently unnoticed or even ignored by Hardy, who is sometimes thought to have exaggerated the suddenness of her death, though biography cannot prove his deception, or self-deception, and her family, friends, and doctor also found the death unexpected. Whatever his guilt about her illness, his rational and irrational remorse about the painful estrangement inspired a powerful poetry of nostalgia and regret.

Soon after the death he summoned Florence Dugdale to Max Gate, servants gossiped, and there is a telling phrase in one of his letters: "once I get you here again won't I clutch you tight." Just over a year later, in February 1914, when she was thirty-five and he was seventy-three, they married. They had been friends for fourteen years, she had done research and secretarial work for him, had been introduced to his friends, was on good terms with Emma, who was not easy to please, and when she visited Max Gate some time after she and Hardy met, he wrote "After the Visit," in which he praised her "large luminous living eyes." She was less of a muse than her predecessor, and the second marriage, also childless, was difficult for the wife, though happier for Hardy since she was more supportive and generally more competent than Emma. In the end, she too was jealously tormented into erratic behavior. An aspiring writer, she published some children's stories, but her only successful writing is the ghosted memoir written and dictated by Hardy (with secretive systematic destruction of his handwritten notes and records as she typed). It was finished, edited, and published by her as *The Early Life of Thomas Hardy, 1840–91* (1928) and *The Later Years of Thomas Hardy, 1892–1928* (1930) and reedited by Michael Millgate as *The Life and Work of Thomas Hardy* (1984). The stiff, jerky, censored

memoir seems more personal and revealing for its fragmentary form and impersonal disguise.

The hostile reception of *Jude* and *Tess* contributed to Hardy's decision to stop writing novels. He observed in the ghosted autobiography that radical opinion is more acceptable in poetry than in novels; poets can get away with subversion, even of religion, as novelists cannot. The novel-reading public probably included and includes more uneducated and conventional tastes and opinions than poetry-reading circles, and the novel is fuller, more complete, plainer, and more explicit than poetry, which can be reticent, indirect, and allusive. Turning back to his first ambition, Hardy published "The Bride-Night Fire" and "Lines" in magazines and in 1898 his first collection *Wessex Poems*, with old and new poems. It provoked some obtuse reviews, especially from critics who misheard metrical subtlety as ignorant clumsiness, but overall was well received. It became clear that the reputation of the novelist assured a readership for the poet, and the first selection was followed by seven others, ending with *Winter Words*, which came out soon after Hardy died, on 11 January 1928. There were no more problems getting poems published, but they were too subtle and experimental to be popular. He was very touchy about criticism, incorrigibly remonstrating with reviewers, composing aggressive mock-epitaphs for George Moore and G. K. Chesterton, two of his literary enemies, the day before he died. His ashes are in Westminster Abbey, his heart in Stinston churchyard, buried with his "two bright-souled women," the compound epithet revising the original "thoughtful" in the inscription he composed for the grave he chose for all three.

THE NOVELS

PRIVATE life nourishes art. Novelists often begin with autobiography, but Hardy's first books, *Desperate Remedies* (1872), *A Pair of Blue Eyes* (1872), and the less personally centered *Under the Greenwood Tree* (1872), are only partly or slightly life-based. His passive young writer-architects Ambrose Graye and Edward Springrove in *Desperate Remedies*, Stephen Smith in *A Pair of Blue Eyes*, and George Somerset in *A Laodicean* (1881) resemble their author but are not exactly portraits of him as a young man. Jude draws on some aspects of Hardy but also on his clever alcoholic uncle John

Antell and his mentor, the self-destructive Horace Moule. Hardy's educated school-teaching heroines Fancy Day, Grace Melbury, and Sue Bridehead recall the experiences of his sister Mary and his cousin Tryphena but are distinct and particular. His mother inspired the plain speaking Mrs. Dewy, the tranter's wife, in *Under the Greenwood Tree*, Stephen Smith's blunt, strong mother in *A Pair of Blue Eyes*, and the tragically maternal Mrs. Yeobright in *The Return of the Native* (1878), but all these powerful, articulate mothers are individual in mind, personality, and history. Sources have been found for Tess, and much made of Hardy's way of speaking as if she existed, but she too is a fictional character. Tess and Jude are placed in circumstances reflecting Hardy's compassionate knowledge of rural poverty and squalor but reinvented as dramatic scene and organized plot. The place-name "Wessex" is drawn from real maps but re-imagined in Hardy's mind and language.

As a novelist he was markedly idealistic but commercially pragmatic. He wanted literature to change the world but was always alert to market forces, and he made radical changes to please editors, reviewers, and readers. He hated the reading public's Grundyism—the narrow-minded refusal to deal frankly with sex and religion—but made concessions to it. When he had the chance he reclaimed his former preferred text, and his publications show striking contrasts between censored versions for magazine serial, and revisions, or returns to an original, for final three-volume editions. Even close friends like Edmund Gosse criticized his "impropriety," the influential library Mudies protected its readers by not subscribing, and copies of *Jude* were burned by a bishop.

Hardy's first story, "The Poor Man and the Lady," self-described as a "socialist" story of class contrast, was never published. Hardy scrapped it, though its outline can be reconstructed from what he told friends. He mined it for *Under the Greenwood Tree* and the long story or novella "Indiscretions of an Heiress" and used parts of it in *Two on a Tower* (1882) and *A Laodicean*, where a wealthy heroine is loved by a poor hero; and in *Desperate Remedies* and *The Woodlanders* (1887), where titled rich ladies are prominent and the plots draw on memories of Hardy's patroness, Julia Augusta Martin, and deplore social injustice. He felt loyalty, pride, and shame about his origins, so a passionate sense of class inequality is often present, also a more general social compassion, sometimes

underestimated because of his conservative streak, which showed itself in his and in his novels.

"The Poor Man and the Lady" was rejected by Macmillan, then accepted by Chapman and Hall, but George Meredith, as publisher's reader, advised Hardy to rewrite it or try something less polemical, more artistic and highly plotted. The next prospective publisher, Tinsley, asked for a larger financial backing than Hardy could afford. Meanwhile, Hardy applied Meredith's advice in the over-plotted *Desperate Remedies* (1871), which is what Victorians called a sensation novel and we call a thriller. It features violence, complicated mystery, amateur detective work, and lubricious sex toned down for publication—a rape removed but a lesbian bed scene left. An unfavorable review correctly condemned the strained coincidental plot, implausible psychology, and melodrama. There is some reality of feeling in the heroine and rural characters, but the book generally is crude and superficial. Critics have analyzed its classical symbolism—two Cythereas (Venus) and an un-Virgilian Aeneas—but allusion scarcely redeems the sensationalism. It is not helped by abstract, wooden, ponderous language, Hardy's worst prose. There is some autobiographical and aesthetic interest in the use of architecture, music, and poetry. But the subject of art is not treated dramatically or assimilated into the action, and it is a pleasure to turn from the novel's overly ambitious elaboration and turgid prose to Hardy's flawless second novel.

Under the Greenwood Tree is an under-plotted domestic story of village life. Hardy simplifies action and language to write a love story of delicate pathos and humor. His first developed chorus of rustics, the Mellstock Quire, gave the book its original title, kept as subtitle. The novel is full of music: the choristers comment wisely and wittily on the neat, light, understated love dance, the hero sings, and the heroine plays the church organ. Encouraged by Macmillan's admiration of the country scenes in *The Poor Man and the Lady* and reviewers' praise of rural subjects in *Desperate Remedies*, Hardy wrote a unified, varied, and balanced short masterpiece. It drew, intuitively and artfully, on his parents' and grandparents' lives, in a landscape altered but still visible, and his native culture of music, work, church, family, and home.

It is also remarkable for its prominent placing of the natural world, which he knew and loved all his life, in that most social of forms, the novel. Its formal ordering is fine: aptly for a novel about music, it begins with sounds in a dark wood, brilliantly orchestrating the individual tree-voices as the choir listens and emerges to sing Christmas carols. Dick Dewy, one of the treble "set," falling in love as he sings. The novel ends as it began, symmetrically, with natural music. As Dick and Fancy drive off on their wedding journey, Hardy invents a daring hybrid language for his Shakespearean bird: "Tippiwit! swe-e-et! ki-ki-ki! Come hither, come hither, come hither!" (Conclusion, chap. 2). Not the romantic nightingale's melody of Keats and Coleridge, but a faintly mocking note. Hardy joins wordless bird-talk which tells no lies or secrets, with a tactful echo of *As You Like It,* where "Come hither, come hither" calls character and audiences, in danger of being enchanted by the pastoral, like Hardy's readers, to remember that "most friendship is feigning, most loving mere folly." Irony is gentle, the greenwood shadowed but not spoiled, the newly wedded lovers allowed their moment.

In this second novel, begun before *Desperate Remedies,* Hardy establishes the place, history, and community that are to grow into Wessex, that famous blend of geography, chronicle, and fantasy. He also introduces formal features that continue through all the novels: a blend of serious or pathetic emotion with comedy of character and language, lavish dramatized anecdote, and a chorus of clever, ordinary, and foolish rustics, solidly realized in work, history, and manners, given dialect and idiolect, and, to my mind, never patronized. (Not all critics have agreed with this judgment, including several of Hardy's contemporaries and a recent scholar, Paul Turner, in *The Life of Thomas Hardy,* 1998.) The ironic love story turns on psychological and social cross-purposes and is set in a vivid, sensuous, green world. The author relaxes into memory, but his idyll is strengthened by wide reading, experience of poetry, and also of painting, though the subtitle, *A Rural Painting of the Dutch School,* is slightly misleading in emphasizing interiors. The novel contains some excellent domestic descriptions, like the festive Dewy kitchen at Christmastime and the gamekeeper's cottage, where all the furniture is in duplicate, but it is strong on external nature too, as the title promises, not to mention its delicately drawn inner world of love, memory, and fantasy.

Hardy develops the melancholy, humor, fantasy, and historical consciousness of *Under the Greenwood Tree* as he ambitiously evolves a tragic, quasi-philosophical form of fiction. His tragic novels begin with *A Pair of Blue Eyes.* The moving and comic heroine Elfride, writer of a failed romance, reflects something of the character and situation of Emma Gifford, her low-life lover Stephen Smith resembles Hardy, and her third lover, Henry Knight, is partly modeled on Hardy's gifted neurotic friend Horace Moule; but the plot is invented, not autobiographical. It develops into a drama of a woman's tragic oppression by love, creating a world where the men promote ludicrously conservative ideas about love and marriage. It is not an openly feminist novel, its tragic end is huddled and unprepared, but the sparkling, lively heroine trapped, and destroyed, by convention looks ahead to Tess and Sue Bridehead. The comedy includes hilarious though ugly conversations, individual but representative, in which uneducated woman is intellectually bullied by cultivated man. Its drama rises to a wonderful epic crisis when Henry Knight hangs life-threatened on a sea-cliff, appraising human existence from the perspective of a trilobite, in a glimpse of fossil history. The highly effective geological imagery is reinforced by Tennysonian echoes from *In Memoriam.*

Far from the Madding Crowd (1874), which he was invited to contribute as a serial to Leslie Stephen's prestigious magazine *The Cornhill,* shows Hardy the writer had arrived. More complex and resonant in social history and psychology than its predecessors, it creates a love quartet, ironically and sympathetically: the courageous, susceptible farmer, Bathsheba; the failed sheep-farmer and deep-feeling countryman Gabriel Oak; the dashing, unfaithful, but surprising extrovert Sergeant Troy; and the victim of repression and obsession, Farmer Boldwood. A sensational plot of death, adultery, illegitimate baby, and failure is made moving and substantial in rural scene and detail—a novice sheepdog, a devastating storm, a shepherd's skills, a distracted lover's neglect of his farm, rustic superstition, song, and feasting, all play their part, dramatically or implicitly, in the pattern of cause, effect, and cross-purpose. Rural life and psychological tension keep changing places, as foreground and background; comedy is made integral to the tragic incidents and beautifully used to animate and particularize the love story. Bathsheba and Gabriel are rare among Hardy's couples in provoking amusement as well as sympathy, and she takes an individual place in Hardy's gallery of women who work. The novel includes grim destinies but bestows a happy ending on the hero and heroine, a working couple whose lives skirt but survive tragedy.

The Hand of Ethelberta (1876) is weaker, though its plot is original. A strong, ambitious, creative heroine of low birth, whose father is a butler, appraises the time and seizes her destiny, making a career as a public storyteller and overcoming class disadvantage. She is eventually thrown back on the marriage market. Ethelberta is interesting, but what happens to her unconvincing, the supporting cast is thin, and the themes of poetry, performance, and narrative, intrinsically fascinating, are undeveloped and undramatized. The interest is too abstract, and it is hard to care about the characters and their fate.

It is followed by a success, *The Return of the Native* (1878), where the strong, selfish Eustahia Vye, the idealistic Clym Yeobright and his magnificent mother are fully imagined and made imaginatively responsive to time and place. The natural world is grandly vitalized in Egdon Heath, often sentimentally and misleadingly described as a character, but Hardy's poetry never reduces inhuman nature to a symbol. Nature is felt in its power. It is the unplumbed dangerous environment which human beings try to civilize or use as workplace and playground. Occupations are solidly set in action, from the reddleman's craft to the making of a featherbed, accompanied by marvelously comic choruses. Hardy invents such narrators as the virile, dispassionate Timothy Fairway, man of many parts, whose life story is never told, and assistants gifted in praise, history, gossip, and boast, including the "hermaphrotight" fool Christian Cantle, born on a moonless night, and his father, an old soldier behaving like a young rake. The fate of star-crossed lovers is balanced by a happy marriage, and Clym Yeobright, as interesting an idealist as Jude, is the solitary returned native who survives tragic sufferings. His mother is a tragic figure, and her sense of filial ingratitude, her cruel exposure to blazing heat and a real serpent's tooth, revive and revise King Lear's heath, storm, and parental sorrow. Like *Under the Greenwood Tree*, the novel shows Hardy as a master of literary allusion.

The Trumpet-Major (1880) is tragicomedy flawed by heavy farce but as subtle a historical novel as Sir Walter Scott's *Rob Roy* or William Makepeace Thackeray's *Henry Esmond*, like them placing fictions in the context of history. George III makes a brief, effective appearance, and the creative John Loveday—one of Hardy's best good men—brings past and present startlingly together at the end, within one single sentence saying farewell on the "doorstone," and plunging "into the darkness . . . to blow his trumpet till silenced for ever upon one of the bloody battlefields of Spain" (chap. 41). The exit is a fine example of Hardy's lyrical narrative, powerful as it forms the flow of characters' and readers' feelings in such rhythmical shifts, or "dissolves" from present to future like this, more often from present to past or past to present, playing with the riddle of narrative time: the characters' present is the readers' past. This ironic and pathetic time-shift, found in Keats's "The Eve of St. Agnes" ("And they are gone, aye, vanished long ago / These lovers fled away into the storm"), is Hardy's structural contribution to the historical novel. He regularly punctuates dramatic immediacy with reminders that it ended long ago; all these brave, clever, silly, anxious, talking, desiring people are in their graves.

The next minor work, *A Laodicean*, shows Hardy's continued concern for the power and powerlessness of women, as his heroine, Paula Power, empowered by money and technology, becomes painfully dependent on men, for better or worse. Written under the strain of serious illness, it has its strengths: the villainies are mostly improbable, but the best villain, William Dare, is odd and sinister enough, and the architect, one of Hardy's passive young heroes, more psychically and physically alive than they usually are. There is a good image, erotic and aesthetic, when the hero guides the heroine's hand to feel the mason's crafty carving. Its theme of Laodiceanism (after St. Paul's image of the uncommitted) is assimilated and developed.

It is followed by one of the weakest novels, *Two on a Tower*, about a rich woman, her astronomer, and her very unlikely marriages. Hardy was still capable of the implausibility and complication that flaw *Desperate Remedies*, though the novel does create an original image, as the lovers explore extraterrestrial worlds through their state-of-the-art telescope. Hardy enjoyed incorporating instruments and machines in his fiction: Jude and Sue are always meeting and missing trains, and Paula Power has an electric telegraph in her old castle.

The Well-Beloved, written in 1892, revised, and published in 1897, after *Jude*, is an allegory, different from Hardy's other novels, resembling such poetic fables as "You on the Tower" and "The

Masked Face." *The Well-Beloved* is a fable of desire, in which Hardy flatters his tendency to shift love objects, by using a Platonic model and inventing a creative artist as hero. He called it "slight" and "fanciful" and emphasized its conspicuous geometrical structure but hoped some bits might claim "imaginative feeling." It concentrates on creativity, an implicit concern in all his novels and poems, but the subject is treated too abstractly, at times almost ludicrously. The sculptor Pierston, enamored of three generations of women, seems a grotesque, even silly, parody of Keats's chameleon poet. Proust, however, admired the story. J. Hillis Miller makes much of its alternative endings, though, as Rosemary Sumner points out, these are not read together, so the forked openness Miller sees is not truly a structural effect. Sumner, this novel's most careful and zealous critic, sees Hardy as an experimental novelist, compares *The Well-Beloved* to Virginia Woolf, and argues that it asserts geometry and uses parody to develop a modernist form, like D. H. Lawrence breaking down the old, stable ego (*A Route to Modernism: Hardy, Lawrence, Woolf*). She quotes a subtle passage where Hardy shows the diffuse, complex nature of consciousness as Pierston reads a letter about death at a party. Hardy is certainly like modern, even postmodern, artists in his marked creative self-consciousness, but I believe his strength is to use such reflexiveness within the genre of psychological realism.

This is certainly true of the last four tragedies. Michael Henchard, mayor of Casterbridge, is one of Hardy's simplest tragic characters, less sympathetic than Marty South, tragic woodlander, simpler-minded than Tess, Jude, and Sue, but like them made ethically and psychically subtle in imaginative enterprise. He suffers, as do all Hardy's heroic characters, but he is more faulty than any of them, a wife-seller, an alcoholic who loses control—yet he is articulate. Just before he auctions his wife, he delivers a message on behalf of trapped human nature, arguing that he "did for" himself by marrying: "if I were a free man again I'd be worth a thousand pound before I'd done o't. But a fellow never knows . . . till all chance of acting . . . is past" (chap. 1). "If I were a free man" has a deep meaning: he is aware of bonds, wanting to free himself from history, dying for the unconditional. He issues a dare, and his Fate, his God, his novelist, undoes the marriage, grants his wish, even gives him money, to illus-

trate the impossibility of freedom. Tess is the other character who imagines a might-have-been and escape from contingency, more poetically and less brutally, when she compares herself with "the poor Queen of Sheba who lived in the Bible" and as she looks out of the window of Bramshurst Manor, when she and Angel Clare are on the run, saying she is not going to look "outside of now" (chap. 58). Henchard is tragic in suffering, especially in his loss of his supposed daughter, Elizabeth-Jane, who survives tragedy to acknowledge happiness and to insist, in the final chapter, on the need to appreciate forms of "minute satisfaction." (Hardy, like another childless author, George Eliot in *Silas Marner*, movingly imagines parental love.) Henchard is given a curt, tragic poetry, especially in his will; the will, penciled on a scrap of paper, forbids "murners" and is delivered by a poor man who "can't read writing" (chap. 45).

The Woodlanders (1887) is not as grandly intense as the other late tragedies, lacking a center and perhaps too diffuse in comic anecdote. But it subtly combines comic and tragic tones, and the affective contrast at the end is equaled only by Shakespeare, perhaps Dickens. The poetic novel modulates from gossip and jokes to Marty, Hardy's only virgin-heroine, "always a lonely maid," Upjohn says. Bringing flowers to the grave, she praises Giles, planter of trees: "you was a good man, and did good things." Her elegy, like Hardy's, is romantic but truthfully human and individual: "you are mine, and only mine; for she has forgot 'ee at last" (chap. 48).

Hardy faced increased misunderstanding in the attack on his so-called philosophical pessimism, notoriously misread in his clearly allusive personification "the President of the Immortals, in Aeschlyean phrase, had ended his sport with Tess" (chap. 59). He repeated that he had no metaphysic, did not believe the universe was ruled by a malign supernatural power, but—perhaps a shade disingenuously—had a temperament made expressive by tragedy. He was an agnostic, and wrote novels in which the course of development was not providential, as it is in Daniel Defoe, Charlotte Brontë, and Charles Dickens. For Hardy, as for Thackeray and George Eliot, human beings are not beneficiaries of Providence but conditioned creatures. Like these more discreet literary predecessors, he raises and does not answer philosophical questions of power. How are Henchard's, Tess's, and Jude's tragedy shaped by biological, social, and economic causes? The question and a range of possible answers are implicit in the story's shifting emphasis on alcoholism, sexual desire, class, poverty, education, and labor conditions. Of course Hardy shows what Henry James calls the creature in his circumstances, but he also, compassionately shapes the plot to make it illustrate his sincere rejections of Providence.

Henchard, Marty, and Giles have moments of pleasure or joy. Even in *Tess* and *Jude,* those black, bitter novels, there are good moments. Indeed, the two most tragic novels contain most relief from tragedy: holidays, fine weather, exercise, the beauty of nature, music and art, jokes, work, companionship, even once or twice satisfied desire. The harsher the tragedy the more need to show light colors in the spectrum. Tess rallies and walks with spring in her blood, she and Angel wait for the milk-train and talk about life, she relates her out-of-body experience and her pleasure in Angel's music, and on the brief honeymoon in Bramshurst Manor she delights in the moment. Jude celebrates a sublime sunset and moonrise by quoting Horace, gets genuine, strong pleasure in expecting new knowledge and in his first thrilling sexual attraction, enjoys walking, talking, and sightseeing with Sue, loves hearing her play the piano and teasing her about roses, in their most sensual scene, at the agricultural show. Such recognitions and excursions prevent Hardy's novels from being simply formulaic in tragic destiny—with snakes and no ladders—and include, if transiently, the reality, release and relief of life outside tragedy.

Tess's is the most painful tragedy, because she is often forced to be passive, but her active imagination is revealed—as she describes visionary experience, as she articulates her own tragic waste, always in the fresh poetry of her imagination, her metaphorical energy controlled like her author's by the intelligent rhetoric of "seeming": "The trees have inquisitive eyes, haven't they?—that is, seem as if they have. And the river says,—'Why do ye trouble me with your looks?' And you seem to see numbers of tomorrows just all in a line . . . they all seem very fierce and cruel and as if they said, 'I'm coming! Beware of me!' " (chap. 19).

Jude imagines himself for a long time to be the hero of a Providence novel, in which events are shaped, teleologically and theologically, for his guidance, but he comes to share his author's bleak, subversive vision. On his deathbed he breaks down, his language fails, and all he can do

is quote Job, but a little earlier, though his mind is maddened, his weaknesses have been humiliatingly exploited, and his suffering is almost unbearable, there is an enlivening ability to generalize, comprehend, and articulate tragic waste and history. His mind is still "clear" enough to see this: "As for Sue and me when we were at our own best, long ago—when our minds were clear, and our love of truth fearless—the time was not ripe for us! Our ideas were fifty years too soon to be any good to us" (part 6, chap. 10). Hardy's tragic heroes and heroines, like Shakespeare's, are creative centers, and creative intelligence is there in negation and despair.

While writing novels, Hardy published short stories, in magazines and eventually in several collections. He draws on historical and antiquarian records and, very strongly, on oral history, conceiving of the short story as a special genre, an enlargement of anecdote which must be justified by memorable event and characterized by a storyteller's personal style. Some stories originated in the storytelling of his mother and the grandmother evoked in "One We Knew." His best stories turn on event but create characters, like the female smuggler in "The Distracted Preacher," an amusing story based on family memories of smuggling, the odd and individual "Melancholy Hussar," and the wild or weird people in the grim, morbid, sometimes horrific tales, the surprising "Three Strangers" and the dangerous, erotic "Fiddler of the Reels," in whom Hardy gleefully develops the idea of music's sensual abandon. His stories are as compressed and foreshortened as his short poems, freed to emphasize passion, leave gaps and mysteries, if necessary sidestep realism. Their fantastic, morbid, and grotesque material places them with some of the verse narratives, "The Workbox," "Her Second Husband Hears Her Story," "The Chapel Organist," "The Sailor's Mother" and "A Sunday Morning Tragedy," in the folk tradition that liberated Hardy, as psychological fiction did not, to indulge a taste for horror and hauntings. Tess is hanged but the execution, corpse, and gibbet are excluded, to be freely enjoyed in "The Withered Arm." Superstition is believed, discussed, even acted on, when Joan Durbeyfield refuses to keep a fortune-telling book in the house or Eustachia Vye is pricked with a needle by a woman who thinks she is a witch, but marginal to the novels, though horrors, like the hanging of the children by Little Father Time, are sometimes let in. Grim thrills are common and central in the stories; Hardy liked them. Many tales include or depend on what was unpalatable sexual detail, and like the novels Hardy submitted to magazines without gauging the response of publishers and readers they were censored. His excuse, after a shocked review of "Barbara of the House of Grebe," that a Chinese box form of story within story and a foregrounded narrator were distancing devices, shows a sophisticated sense of anecdotal structure but would not persuade Mrs. Grundy.

POETRY

TURNING to poetry after *Jude*, Hardy published early poems, revised in some detail but not extensively; he said too much revision spoiled the "freshness." From the 1890s until his death he rewrote old and wrote new poems in many genres and forms. Although put down and patronized by T. S. Eliot (in *After Strange Gods*), his combination of experiment and tradition, and his clear, plain language, excited innovators like W. H. Auden and conservatives like Philip Larkin; and we have learned to admire his deliberated awkwardness, Wordsworthian matter-of-factness, occasional prosaism, and inventive oddities of language. Criticism and skilful editing have enlarged the acceptable canon, and now it's hard to find a Hardy poem nobody loves. As in the novels, Hardy found language and forms in poetry to reimagine the past and respond to personal and topical public event: seasons, the weather, loves and deaths, the Boer War, World War I, all go into the poems.

One of his best-known early poems, "Neutral Tones," is a link with the novels. A little more melodramatic in style than the later poetry, it is as remarkable a Victorian poem as Meredith's *Modern Love*. It is plainly and naturally phrased, using indirection, white and gray colors, and bleached nature to suggest character and concentrate the passions, of bitterness, and, worse, lovelessness after love. It is like the bleak confrontations of Eustachia and Clym, Jude and Arabella, Jude and Sue, recognizably by Hardy the novelist: "Your eyes on me were as eyes that rove / Over tedious riddles of years ago; / And some words played between us to and fro / On which lost the more by our love." The natural diction and speech rhythm, the interplay of inner and outer life, and emotional intensity are marked in the elegies written after his wife's death, and for most of his life. The sec-

ond Mrs. Hardy dryly observed that he wrote his poetry of grief with great zest, and it is ironic that Emma was jealous of the love poems her husband wrote about other women. The poetry she inspired, and never saw, is in the great tradition of English elegy, with Milton's "Lycidas" and Shelley's "Adonais," though these poems mourn dead poets, and speak of poetry, while Hardy's are personal, domestic, and intimate. Emma's successor soon dropped the humorous tone, suffering in her turn from a husband's poetry as she supported him in bereavement. The elegies are grouped together in *Satires of Circumstance* (1914), as "Poems, 1912-13," with a Virgilian motto *"Veteris Vestigia Flammae"* ("remains of an old flame"). They are highly original but also traditional in their blend of memorial, encomium, and nature ritual, like other elegies remembering, even partaking of, funeral rites in which flowers and foliage sweeten decay and symbolize the life cycle, and earth and sea are graves.

Hardy sometimes makes elegy dialogic, inventing a voice for the dead woman and re-creating her in dramatic soliloquy and conversation poem. "The Haunter" is a monologue that shows both the imaginative effort to let her speak for herself and a gradual lapse of effort. First it startlingly imagines the dead's desire to "Hover and hover a few feet from him," not just floating ghost but alienated wife, "Just as I used to do," and implies (his) remorse, "Now that he goes and wants me with him," but gradually it slides into poetic self-indulgence as it puts hard feelings aside to recall the shared tender love of nature, "Where the shy hares print long paces"; it then softens even more, to end wish-fulfillingly (for him) with an offer of support and consolation: "Tell him a faithful one is doing / All that love can do."

He imagines less self-indulgently in "The Monument Maker," written about three years later, where a male mourner designs and sets up his beloved's tomb—as Hardy actually did. A woman's voice that puts him in his place rejects the monument ("It spells not me!") and the devotion ("you felt none, my dear!"), so deconstructing elegy, Hardy's monument.

Most of these poems are more sorrowing and nostalgic than the two just discussed, but each track of grief and nostalgia is individual and mobile, in story and affective trajectory. Many were written soon after the death, others in response to his sentimental journey to the old Cornish haunts in 1913, some much later. "The Going" is a response to sudden death, and uses excited and numb apostrophe, understatement, flat prosaism, and sharp image to mingle incredulous shock and loss: "Why did you give no hint?"; her "great going" has "altered all," leaving "yawning blankness" for "a dead man held on end." It moves at the end to loving praise and recall ("You were the swan-necked one who rode"), remorse, and the acceptance of remorse—"Why, then, latterly, did we not speak?" and "All's past amend."

"After a Journey" is a sensual poem of desire, which succeeds, as art or dream can, in reviving the dead. There is a movement of feeling: solemnity ("the unseen waters' ejaculations awe me"), affection, admiration and desire ("nut-coloured hair," "gray eyes, and rose-flush coming and going"), regret ("Summer gave us sweets, but autumn wrought division?"), fond teasing and excited erotic complicity ("I see what you are doing: you are leading me on"). All leads to an astonishing final assertion of live love in the present: "I am just the same as when / Our days were a joy."

"Beeny Cliff" moves from amorous nostalgic tribute ("the woman whom I loved so, and who loyally loved me") to a sense of nostalgia's futility, and the deadness of the past, and life ("The woman now is—elsewhere"). "At Castle Boterel" makes the strongest nostalgic claim ("was there ever / A time of such quality . . .?"), scrupulously qualified ("To one mind never"), absorbing philosophical irony ("Time's unflinching rigour" and "mindless rote"). The last striking image of sinking sand enlarges farewells—to the poem, the associations of this particular sentimental journey, the revived past, and his life.

Hardy writes other personal and poignant lyrics with similarly fluent feeling. They often rely on compression and implication, stressing emotion by cutting down narrative, making the reader work: "Overlooking the River Stour," "Before and After Summer," and "The Division" are understated, sad poems, remarkable compressions in which a flow of strong feeling is acted out, not described or named. In "After a Romantic Day," a short and taut lyric, a speaker recalls his day: "The railway bore him through / An earthen cutting out from a city / There was no scope for view / Though the frail light shed by a slim young moon / Fell like a friendly tune."

The poem is bare, like its setting, and Hardy dares to be more prosaically awkward in the sec-

ond stanza as he spreads a sentence around the line-end: "the blank lack of any charm / Of landscape did no harm." He restrains his feeling, and since his expressive scene is that blank cutting, the plain language works well, expressing in subtle understatement the personally felt excited memory, of what we are not told, though the slim young moon and its tune are suggestive. In its small compass it also touches on two artistic ideas, both large subjects, "the poetry of place" and, presented more implicitly, emotional reserve. The poem acts out its subjects, finds room to name a concept, and is a cunning love poem, hinting but hugging its secret.

Hardy said he had an unusual capacity for burying past emotion and "exhuming" its freshness, a process especially important and inspirational for him because of the gap between early life and his active poetic career. This exhumation, rather like William Wordsworth's formula "emotion recollected in tranquillity," but with less stress on tranquility, is evident in a number of lyrics about his family affections and childhood. For instance, times and feelings are layered in the wonderfully rapt "The Self-Unseeing," where the poet recalls a house's floor and door, already old in his childhood, details minimally shaping a scene for three characters, a woman "Smiling into the fire" a fiddler, and a child. The parallel clauses of the last stanza blend and contrast the feelings in, and the feelings for, the past: joyful love, caught in memory, pierced by an insight—Proust in four lines—that it can only be caught in memory, not in the present: "Childlike, I danced in a dream; / Blessings emblazoned that day; / Everything glowed with a gleam; / Yet we were looking away!"

We do not think of Hardy as a poet of joy, and his joys are seldom unmixed, but there are many poems retrieving warm memory, two about his dead sister Mary—"Molly Gone," where he rejoins her, in spirit or memory, companionably gazing at "a many-flamed star," and "Logs on the Hearth," a startlingly physical joining of life and death, where burning apple-wood regrows into a live tree, and his sister rises from a "chilly grave" to wave "a young brown hand" and climb with her brother. I know no other poet who can fuse past and present in quite this way: Hardy remembers his maternal grandmother's storytelling in "One We Knew," praising her way of telling "not as one who remembers, / But rather as one who sees" and this is what one feels about these memory-lyrics.

"Afterwards" is a poem about his own death, a modest and speculative self-elegy that looks ahead in order to remember. The repeated "such things" is joined by "such . . . creatures" to emphasize his attention to all non-human nature. The poem brims with love for the natural world, expressed in delicate, attentive particularizing images, sometimes similes ("glad green leaves like wings," a hawk's flight "like an eyelid's soundless blink," a night "mothy and warm," a bell's sound interrupted by "a passing breeze" that "cuts a pause in its outrollings"). The examples are related, generally or specifically, to images in the novels, and they are careful observations—full of caring for nature. The omission of Hardy the artist, in a poem about posthumous praise, makes the poem demonstrate empathy, by a modest boast.

A. E. Housman saw nature as a witless, heartless enchantress. Hardy agrees about indifference, but his nature is minutely and individually particularized, his birds, beasts, and flowers attentively re-created in poetry alive with sympathy. The nature poetry can be sentimental, as in one or two dog poems, but usually Hardy imagines animals—as far as humanly possible—as different, other, not human.

Each nature poem finds its own way of imagining and respecting difference and otherness. "Birds at Winter Nightfall" amusingly asserts the human artifice of an intricate musical form, triolet, as an odd but sensitive vehicle for non-human life: he allows starving birds their egocentric viewpoint, turning the tables on the usual anthropocentrism of poetry by reducing the poet to human provider, confirming this in the clever nonce compound "crumb-outcaster," amusingly rhymed with horticultural polysyllabic, "cotoneaster." In one of the best animal-rights poems since "The Ancient Mariner," "The Blinded Bird" calls for compassion by challenging Paul's epistle to the Corinthians: "Who hath charity? This bird," so claiming a famous Christian definition of love, according to which humanity fails, for its non-human, innocent, all-accepting victim. In the strange poem "The Fallow Deer at the Lonely House," a pronoun, "We," denotes people who do "not discern" the "One without." The deer is identified only in the title, and there is no point of view from which it is seen, making it mysteriously but aptly isolated and separate. In "Shelley's Skylark" he praises art but reimagines the skylark of whom Percy Shelley said, "Bird thou never wert," to insist on the creature's reality.

"The Darkling Thrush," Hardy's poem for the twentieth century, almost imagines optimism, through pessimism, as he particularizes an aged, frail, gaunt bird at the century's end. He insists on its individuality, seeming to approach anthropomorphic symbolism, but hesitantly, saying the ecstatic winter "caroling" seems so without "cause" "That I could think there trembled through / His happy goodnight air / Some blessed Hope, whereof he knew / And I was unaware." Even more strenuously resisting anthropocentric temptation, "An August Midnight" introduces four insects, and places them "on this scene," the speaker feeling the usual impulse to patronize them as "God's humblest," but revising projection to admit otherness: "They know Earth-secrets that know not I." An unsentimental poem alive with the affectionate humor that can temper this poet's gloom, it is about art as well as nature. It shows creative improvisation and openness in action, as he welcomes diversion, even collaboration, in a generous image of hospitality: "My guests besmear my new-penned line." This is Hardy's reflexive art, not self-consciously abstracted or analytic but insinuating, indirect, artfully artless.

The process is repeated in "On a Midsummer Eve," a magical poem set on the date when country superstition encouraged girls to see their future husband in a mirror, as Mrs. Penny the shoemaker's wife in *Under the Greenwood Tree* tactlessly relates in comic mode, and *The Woodlanders* shows more seriously. This rapt lyric recounts casual rites of nature and art: a parsley stalk whistled towards the moon summons a ghost's steps to shiver in tune, water scooped from a stream invokes a reflected figure, "rough rhymes of chance, not choice" call up a voice "that turned a tenderer verse for me"—more collaborations. It is a poem of ritual, memory, and love that quietly insists, as Yeats was to do more grandly, on the role of chance and choice in imagination. It is a theme usually left, as here, to be insinuated and demonstrated by the poem's action, but it is discussed in one of Hardy's poems about architecture, "The Abbey Mason," explicated by the invention of the English Perpendicular style.

"The Convergence of the Twain" is a fine example of public, occasional poetry, commemorating the *Titanic* by creating its convergence of personified disaster, the collision of machine and nature, and the critique of luxury: "Over the mirrors meant / To glass the opulent / The sea-worm crawls—grotesque, slimed, dumb, indifferent."

The poem is powerfully imagistic, ironic, even satirical, and unusual among Hardy's social poems in a certain abstraction and impersonality, perhaps the result of the absence of human characters. His social sympathies are implicit in many narrative ballads and dramatic monologues, though in some, like "The Burghers," the usual strong psychological interest is thrilling, sensational, and melodramatic rather than concerned to bring out the pity and irony of human life. But at his most imaginative, for instance in a poem he once said was his best, "A Trampwoman's Tragedy," he writes compassionate and sympathetic melodrama. This poem uses the music of ballad-form, its strong, regular rhythm, refrain, and repetition, with narrative curtness and compression. As in the tales, Hardy foregrounds the act of telling, and the nameless trampwoman tells compulsively and penitently, like the ancient mariner, her grim story of careless flirtation, jealousy, murder, and miscarriage, with individualized irony, control, remorse, and black humor. Her "fancy-man's" ghost is a character, passionately driven in haunting as in killing: "The ghost of him I'd die to kiss / Rose up and said: 'Ah, tell me this! / Was the child mine, or was it his?' "

This is followed by her plain narration of her simple reply, and a proper ghostly exit, all solemnized and varied by repetition and refrain:

> O doubt not that I told him then,
>   I told him then,
> That I had kept me from all men
>   Since we joined lips and swore.
> Whereat he smiled, and thinned away
> As the wind stirred to call up day

It is a good story, but more than that. Hardy never forgets that these are tramps, poor, rough-living men and women, walking miles in all weather, living on the edge of promiscuity and violence, and he uses poetry, unsentimentally but warmly, to imagine their working lives, companionship, passions, and habitat:

> From Wynyard's Gap the livelong day,
>   The livelong day,
> We beat afoot the northward way
>   We had travelled times before.
> The sun-blaze burning on our backs,
> Our shoulders sticking to our packs

Such compression of narrative and lyrical power marks many of his social narratives—the sad, strange anecdote at the heart of "The White-washed Wall"; the ambiguity and irony of "The Ruined Maid," a poem about a prostitute and an innocent country girl, less funny than is sometimes suggested; the bitter feminist aggression and self-destruction of "The Chapel Organist"; the erotic analysis of a voyeuristic clergyman in "The Collector Cleans His Picture." Hardy's neurotic characters are like Robert Browning's, revealed by implication. His repressed collector, hysterical mothers, and the wife in a grim comic marriage-monologue, "Her Second Husband Hears Her Story," who sews up her drunken husband to avoid his embrace, belong with the cruel connoisseur of Browning's "Last Duchess," his fake medium Sludge, and the bishop ordering his tomb. Hardy, like Browning, joins psychological portrait with social criticism, implicit or explicit, often of particular institutions—church, prostitution, workhouse, marriage, city, class, money. And war.

His best war poem, "Drummer Hodge," anticipates the sentiment of Rupert Brooke's "The Soldier," in which a foreign grave is imagined, less substantially and strangely. Drummer Hodge—"Hodge" was the stock nickname for a peasant—is thoroughly imagined, as the unknown soldier who joins the life cycle of unknown, foreign land and vegetation, in a story tenderly insisting on the ordinary soldier's passiveness:

> Yet portion of that unknown plain
>   Will Hodge for ever be;
> His homely Northern breast and brain
>   Grow to some Southern Tree,
> and strange-eyed constellations reign
>   His stars eternally.

Hardy could write simple war poetry, conventionally rousing, like "Men Who March Away," or romantically lyrical, like "In Time of 'The Breaking of Nations', " with its images of transcendent love and rural work, inspired by a horse harrowing a Cornish field during the Franco-Prussian War but not written till World War I, forty-four years later. "Drummer Hodge," "The Man I Killed," which anticipates Wilfred Owen, "The Pity of It," whose title quotes *Othello* to anticipate Owen again, and shows the poet's ear for language, recognizing the kinship of Dorset dialect and German, and "His Country," where an imaginary global tour puts nationalism in its place as the speaker finds his country is " worldwide," are strongly anti-war, internationalist, and pacifist. They are like many others, on miscellaneous subjects, which show Hardy's compassionate and caring imagination, and his talent for the minimalist moving sketch: "The Convict and the Fiddler," in which a child plays his fiddle to cheer a convict, who sings back; "To an Unborn Pauper Child," tenderly apostrophizing an unborn, ungendered scrap of humanity, and "Squire Hooper," a character study, and a plain tale about a stoical country gentleman.

Hardy wrote a number of poems about the life of Christ, for instance "The Wood Fire," about the cross, and "The Servants' Quarters," about Peter's denial of Christ, approaching gospel stories from an unusual angle, suspending and surprising our recognition of characters, events, and endings, domesticating and refreshing old, familiar stories, their narrative irony working with respect and sympathy. He also wrote theologically argumentative poems, like "God's Funeral" and "Aquae Sulis," that are ironic and hortatory, but one or two, like "The Voice of Things" and "The Impercipient," are subtle, quiet, and reserved. The latter poem's unironic, grave tones urgently claim reverence for true disbelief:

I am like a gazer who should mark
   An inland company
Standing upfingered, with, "Hark! hark!
   The glorious distant sea!"
And feel, "Alas, 'tis but yon dark
   And wind-swept pine to me!"

Its hymnlike meter and diction control emotion in poetic self-awareness, and the solemn rhythms and images present lack of faith as a possible failure of imagination, but try to persuade sincere belief to be more imaginative, to imagine sincere disbelief as this disbelief can try to imagine faith.

Any discussion of Hardy's public poetry must mention his lumbering epic *The Dynasts* (1903), not intended for performance, though once or twice performed. Its fragmentary, kaleidoscopic, mixed-genre narrative, with choruses and lyrics peopled by abstraction and type, shifts of viewpoint, world and space images, historical narrative, with language often lapsing into flat commentary, turgid generalization, and monotonous, predictable alliteration and rhyme unworthy of Hardy's sharp, subtle ear, do not make easy reading. It is a literary white elephant, a work driven by tremendous literary and philosophical ambi-

tion, reaching forward, ironically and compassionately, to imagine the life force, Immanent Will, or blind First Cause becoming conscious. The most original felt poetry in this immensely long piece, one of the "Choruses of the Years" in the much-anthologized section "The Road to Waterloo," is pacifist in imagination, conceiving the bloody battlefield from the viewpoint of minute life forms, moles, worms, snails, butterflies, green shoots, and buds. *The Dynasts* shows Hardy's stamina, his ambition to push beyond his two genres, and his common-sense perception that such art is not for the theater. Its conceptualism and mixed-genre structure look very like modernist experiment and adventure. Its fragmentation, visual shifts, and montage have led to comparisons with cinematic form: perhaps it is his *Star Wars*.

Hardy the Victorian novelist is also Hardy the twentieth-century poet, excelling like Emily Brontë and D. H. Lawrence in passionate, sensuous, self-aware, personal, and social prose and poetry. Crossing forms, styles, ideas, and emotions, he imagines imagination, negative, positive, candid, speculative, open, tentative. In his profound, oblique, deep reflexivity, Hardy anticipates later sophistications of art with rare creative energy, over a long lifetime.

SELECTED BIBLIOGRAPHY

I. Novels. *Desperate Remedies* (London, 1871); *Under the Greenwood Tree* (London, 1872); *A Pair of Blue Eyes* (London, 1873); *Far from the Madding Crowd* (London, 1874); *The Hand of Ethelberta* (London, 1876); *The Return of the Native* (London, 1878); *The Trumpet-Major* (London, 1880); *A Laodicean* (London, 1881); *Two on a Tower* (London, 1882); *The Mayor of Casterbridge* (London, 1886); *The Woodlanders* (London, 1887); *Tess of the Durbervilles* (London, 1891); *Jude the Obscure* (London, 1895); *The Well-Beloved* (London, 1897); *Our Exploits at West Poley* (Oxford, 1952).

II. Short Stories. *Wessex Tales* (London, 1888); *A Group of Noble Dames* (London, 1891); *Life's Little Ironies* (London, 1894); *A Changed Man and Other Tales* (London, 1913); *The Collected Short Stories*, New Wessex, ed. F. B. Pinion (London, 1988); *The Excluded and Collaborative Stories*, ed. Pamela Dalziel (Oxford, 1992).

III. Poems. *Wessex Poems* (London, 1898); *Poems of the Past and Present* (London, 1902); *The Dynasts: A Drama of the Napoleonic Wars, in Three Parts, Nineteen Acts, and One Hundred and Thirty Scenes* (New York and London, 1903; New York and London, 1905; London, 1908); *Time's Laughingstocks* (London, 1909); *Satires of Circum-*

stance (London, 1914); *Moments of Vision* (London, 1917); *Late Lyrics and Earlier* (London, 1922); *The Famous Tragedy of the Queen of Cornwall* (London, 1923); *Human Shows* (London, 1925); *Winter Words* (London, 1928); *The Complete Poems of Thomas Hardy,* ed. James Gibson (London, 1976); *The Variorum Edition of the Complete Poems of Thomas Hardy,* ed. James Gibson (London, 1979); *The Complete Poetical Works of Thomas Hardy,* 5 vols. (4 and 5 contain *The Queen of Cornwall* and *The Dynasts*), ed. Samuel Hynes (Oxford, 1982–1996).

III. Biography, Letters, Journals, Notebooks.

Florence Emily Hardy, *The Early Life of Thomas Hardy 1840–91* (London, 1928) and *The Later Years of Thomas Hardy 1892–1928* (London, 1930); Sir Arthur Blomfield, *Memoirs of an Architect* (London, 1932); Emma Hardy, *Some Recollections,* ed. Evelyn Hardy and Robert Gittings (London, 1961); Claude Beatty, *The Architectural Notebook of Thomas Hardy* (Dorchester, 1966); Lois Deacon and Terry Coleman, *Providence & Mr. Hardy* (London, 1968); Michael Millgate, *Thomas Hardy: His Career as a Novelist* (Oxford, 1971); Emma Hardy and F. B. Pinion, eds., *One Rare Fair Woman: Thomas Hardy's Letters to Florence Henniker* (London, 1972); Robert Gittings, *Young Thomas Hardy* (London, 1975); Robert Gittings, *The Older Hardy* (London, 1978); Thomas Hardy, *The Personal Notebooks of Thomas Hardy,* ed. Richard H. Taylor (London, 1978); Robert Gittings and Jo Manton, *The Second Mrs. Hardy* (London, 1979); Michael Millgate, *Thomas Hardy: A Biography* (Oxford, 1982); Thomas Hardy, *The Life and Work of Thomas Hardy,* ed. Michael Millgate (London, 1984), a reediting of Florence Emily Hardy's (and Thomas Hardy's) memoir above; Emma Hardy, *Emma Hardy Diaries,* ed. Richard H. Taylor (Ashington, Northumberland, 1985); Thomas Hardy, *The Literary Notebooks of Thomas Hardy,* ed. Lennart A. Björk (London, 1985); Simon Gatrell, *Hardy the Creator: A Textual Biography* (Oxford, 1988); Brenda Tunks, *Whatever Happened to the Other Hardys?* (Canford Heath, Poole, 1990); Timothy Hands, *A Hardy Chronology* (London, 1992); Martin Seymour-Smith, *Hardy* (London, 1994); James Gibson, *Hardy: A Literary Life* (London, 1996); Emma Hardy and Florence Hardy, *Letters of Emma and Florence Hardy,* ed. Michael Millgate (Oxford, 1996); Paul Turner, *The Life of Thomas Hardy* (Oxford, 1998).

IV. Critical Studies. D. H. Lawrence, "A Study of Thomas Hardy," in *Phoenix* (London, 1936).

T. S. Eliot, *Selected Prose,* ed. John Hayward (London, 1953); R. L. Pinion, *A Hardy Companion: A Guide to the Works of Thomas Hardy and Their Background* (Oxford, 1954); Albert J. Guerard, *Thomas Hardy: The Novels and Stories* (London, 1959).

Samuel Hynes, *The Pattern of Hardy's Poetry* (Chapel Hill, 1961); William R. Rutland, *Thomas Hardy: A Guide to His Writings and Their Background* (New York, 1962); Albert J. Guerard, ed., *Hardy: A Collection of Critical Essays* (Englewood Cliffs, N.J., 1963); Barbara Hardy, *The Appropriate Form* (London, 1964); J. Vera Mardon, *Thomas Hardy as a Musician* (Beaminster, 1964); W. F. Wright, *The Shaping of "The Dynasts"* (Lincoln, Nebr. 1967); Kenneth Marsden, *The Poems of Thomas Hardy: A Critical Introduction* (London, 1969).

J. O. Bailey, *The Poetry of Thomas Hardy: A Handbook and Commentary* (Chapel Hill, 1970); R. G. Cox, *Thomas Hardy: The Critical Heritage* (New York and London, 1970); J. Hillis Miller, *Thomas Hardy: Distance and Desire* (Cambridge, Mass., 1970); R. Jean Brooks, *Thomas Hardy: The Poetic Structure* (London, 1971); Barbara Hardy, *Tellers and Listeners* (London, 1971); F. R. Southerington, *Hardy's Vision of Man* (London, 1971); Joan Grundy, *Hardy and the Sister Arts* (London, 1972); Donald Davie, *Thomas Hardy and British Poetry* (London, 1973); Ian Gregor, *The Great Web: The Form of Hardy's Major Fiction* (London, 1974); James Richardson, *Thomas Hardy: The Poetry of Necessity* (Chicago and London, 1975); Tom Paulin, *The Poetry of Perception* (London, 1976); John Bayley, *An Essay on Hardy* (Cambridge, 1978); Peter Mudford, *The Art of Celebration* (London, 1979).

Rosemary Sumner, *Thomas Hardy: Psychological Novelist* (London, 1981); Penny Boumelha, *Thomas Hardy and Women: Sexual Ideology and Narrative Form* (Cambridge, 1982); John Goode, "Sue Bridehead and the New Woman," in Mary Jacobus, ed., *Women Writing and Writing About Women* (London, 1983); Mary Jacobus, ed., *Women Writing and Writing About Women* (London, 1983); Barbara Hardy, *Forms of Feeling in Victorian Fiction* (London, 1985); John Goode, *Thomas Hardy: The Offensive Truth* (Oxford, 1988); Dennis Taylor, *Hardy's Metres and Victorian Prosody* (Oxford, 1988); Patricia Ingham, *Thomas Hardy* (Brighton, 1989); J. Rabbetts, *Hardy to Faulkner* (London, 1989).

George Wing, " 'A Group of Noble Dames': Statuesque Dynasties of Delightful Wessex," in *Thomas Hardy Journal* 7, no. 2 (May 1991); Roger Ebbatson, *Hardy: The Margin of the Unexpressed* (Sheffield, 1994); Samuel Hynes, "Mr. Hardy's Monster: Reflections on *The Dynasts,*" in *Sewanee Review* 2 (spring 1994); Martin Ray, *Thomas Hardy: A Textual Study of the Short Stories* (Aldershot, 1997); John Sutherland, *Can Jane Eyre Be Happy?* (Oxford, 1997); Roger Ebbatson, "The Authorial Double: Hardy and Florence Henniker," in *English* 48, no. 191 (summer 1999).

Barbara Hardy, *Thomas Hardy: Imagining Imagination* (London, 2000); Rosemary Sumner, *A Route to Modernism: Hardy, Lawrence, Woolf* (New York and London, 2000).

V. Bibliographies. Richard L. Purdy, *Thomas Hardy. A Bibliographical Study* (Oxford, 1954; 1968); H. E. Gerber and W. E. Davis, *Thomas Hardy: An Annotated Bibliography of Writings About Him* (De Kalb, Ill., 1973); Ronald P. Draper and Martin S. Ray, *An Annotated Critical Bibliography of Thomas Hardy* (New York and London, 1989).

SEAMUS HEANEY

(1939–)

Henry Hart

FEW MODERN POETS have received the sort of critical and popular acclaim that Seamus Heaney has enjoyed. For his range of themes, his seriousness of purpose, and his expert craftsmanship he is generally acknowledged to be the Irish heir to William Butler Yeats. What W. H. Auden said of Yeats—"Mad Ireland hurt you into poetry"—also could be said of Heaney. Ireland's long history of bloody conflict is his creative wound. What distinguishes his poetry is its artistry, its expert way of getting "feeling into words," to borrow the title of one of his essays. Whether he writes about potato digging on his family farm near Belfast, Vikings pillaging Ireland during the Middle Ages, or the Irish Republican Army and Protestant paramilitary groups killing friends in Northern Ireland, he manages to universalize his subjects. In local doings and undoings, he sees a general rhythm. His international reputation testifies to his skill at imbuing personal and national experience with the appeal of myth.

If, as the poet Robert Graves once proclaimed, "there is one story and one story only" that each writer tells in many versions, Seamus Heaney's "one story" harks back to his childhood on his family farm, Mossbawn, in County Derry, Northern Ireland. Many of his early poems nostalgically recall the rural activities of his family and community: butter churning, house thatching, peat cutting, flax harvesting, cattle raising, blackberry picking, and horse plowing. In these poems Heaney consciously draws on one of the central stories in Western culture: the fall of an innocent person from a pastoral Eden into knowledge of the real world's labor and strife. Heaney's upbringing as a Catholic in a society dominated by Protestants made the story especially relevant. His first poems repeatedly dramatize his innocent childhood coming to an end when he learned of the centuries-old blood feud between Protestants and Catholics, English and Irish. It should come as no surprise that the poets Robert Frost and William Wordsworth were early models, since they also made use of the pastoral tradition, which stretches back to the Greek poet Theocritus and the Roman poet Virgil, to trace their own painful rites of passage from rural innocence to adult awareness of historical conflicts beyond the bucolic pastures.

Like most pastoral writers, Heaney incorporates great sophistication and complexity in what appear to be simple tales about country matters. Informing much of his poetry is a highly charged argument with himself, with his pastoral background, with sectarian Ireland, with his Anglo-Irish heritage, and with the Catholic nationalism that watermarked his personality as a child. Revising Yeats, who declared, "We make out of the quarrel with others, rhetoric, but of the quarrel with ourselves, poetry," Heaney makes poetry from a quarrel with all issues and all factions, including himself. His first poems are especially moving because of the tensions that drive them. Rather than sentimentalize his childhood farms as utopian, he acknowledges the many serpents that slithered through them. While he praises the fertile pastures, he laments the forces of decay and death that menace them. His poem "Blackberry-Picking," in *Death of a Naturalist* (1966), is typical in that it celebrates the harvesting and eating of berries in the countryside as an almost sacramental rite but then laments the natural cycle that destroys the fruit: "It wasn't fair / That all the lovely canfuls smelt of rot. / Each year I hoped they'd keep, knew they would not." The poem's traditional form—it is written in rhyming iambic pentameter couplets—accentuates the difference between the permanence of artifice and the impermanence of nature, the ideals of the imagination and the facts of the world.

Heaney's career follows a general pattern of descent and ascent reminiscent of Dante's journey in *The Divine Comedy,* sections of which Heaney has imitated, analyzed, and translated. Although his early characters resemble Adam tending Edenic pastures more than Christ descending

123

from the cross to harrow hell, the characters populating his middle poems are as grotesque and pitiful as any that inhabit Dante's *Inferno*. In the late 1960s and early 1970s, partly in response to the escalating violence in Northern Ireland, Heaney wrote some of his most memorable poems about dead bodies exhumed from Irish and Danish bogs. The bog is his inferno, and in it he searches for "symbols adequate to our predicament." The corpses preserved by chemicals in the bogs are not so much Dantesque sinners, however, as martyrs who, for one reason or another, sacrificed their blood to Mother Ireland. Heaney's short, staccato lines, which echo the alliterative sound effects of Anglo-Saxon verse, are incantatory. They are also rigorously self-reflexive. Chanting for the dead, he indicts himself and his poems for being perversely fascinated with the dead, for possibly abusing the dead as symbols, and for colluding in contemporary atrocities by not resisting them more forcefully through political activism. As in his pastoral poems, his quarrels in the historical elegies make them all the more dynamic.

Heaney once compared his early poetry to a tree rooted firmly in the ground, his later poetry to a tree uprooted with its bowl pointing toward heaven. He vows in "Digging," the first poem of his first book, *Death of a Naturalist,* to use his pen as a spade to dig for personal and cultural roots in the soil around him. After writing the bog poems in *North* (1975), he concentrated on present atrocities in a more contemporary way. The proselike poems at the end of *North* foreshadow his new style. In the next book, *Field Work* (1979), he cast aside the historical personae of the bog poems and imitated the sort of reportorial candor that Robert Lowell made famous in his *Life Studies* and *Notebook* periods. Like Lowell, Heaney wrote about friends, family members, and historical figures caught up in excruciating crises, and he did so in a style that was more colloquial than incantatory.

The volumes after *Field Work* move further from the gruesome underworld of the bogs and closer to the visionary realm of the supernatural. In these poems, Heaney shows a greater willingness to entertain signs of transcendence and to take imaginative flights. Somewhat like Dante on his purgatorial mountain, Heaney gazes toward Paradise while keeping earth and its infernos in his peripheral vision. In the volume *Station Island* (1984), he wrote his own *Purgatorio,* at times borrowing Dante's terza rima verse form and his way of communing with the dead. But Heaney locates himself firmly on Irish soil—in a place called St. Patrick's Purgatory (or Station Island) on Lough Derg in northwest Ireland. Here, in imitation of Saint Patrick (who supposedly fasted and prayed on the island), Heaney meditates on, converses with, and is rebuked by various familiar ghosts.

In the title poem of *Seeing Things* (1991), Heaney writes about another purgatorial journey to an Irish island and again stresses the bifocal nature of his vision:

All the time . . .
. . . . . .
It was as if I looked from another boat
Sailing through air, far up, and could see
How riskily we fared into the morning.

Like the medieval Irish bird-man Sweeney, who appears in many of the *Station Island* poems, Heaney flew over the nets of nation and religion that threatened to ensnare him, to see them more clearly. Assessing the evolution of his career in "Fosterling," he points to his early obsession with "lowlands of the mind. / Heaviness of being. And poetry / Sluggish in the doldrums of what happens," almost chastising himself for "waiting until I was nearly fifty / To credit marvels." He concludes that it is now "Time to be dazzled and the heart to lighten." Although he gazes more fixedly on a paradise full of marvels, he never loses sight of his troubled homeland. His contrary desires and principles keep him vacillating and also keep his redemptive journey moving forward.

Whether writing about corpses in the peat or boats floating through heaven, Heaney has remained remarkably consistent in his craft. After he was awarded the Nobel Prize for literature in 1995 and his selected poems, *Opened Ground*, was published three years later, the critic Michiko Kakutani, writing in the *New York Times*, spoke for many: "Seamus Heaney's extraordinarily rich and varied oeuvre . . . stay[s] 'true to the impact of external reality' while at the same time remaining 'sensitive to the inner laws of the poet's being.'" The poet's peaceful temperament often clashed with the violent realities mustered against it. But, as Blake proclaimed in "The Marriage of Heaven and Hell": "Without Contraries [there] is no progression." The Nobel Prize confirmed Heaney's triumph in the struggle that could easily have defeated him.

SEAMUS HEANEY

In his Nobel lecture, *Crediting Poetry* (1996), Heaney says that he never expected to visit Stockholm when, as a child during World War II, he first heard the name of the city on BBC radio broadcasts. Little in his background suggested that he would make a triumphant journey to Sweden in 1995. He was born the eldest of nine children on 13 April 1939, to parents who left secondary school around the age of fourteen and never attended college. His father, Patrick, was a cattle dealer who owned a forty-acre farm near Castledawson, County Derry. Raising nine children in three rooms of a thatched farmhouse was not easy. Debt was a constant worry. Although the young Heaney admired his father's farming skills, he came to resent his long silences. He felt closer to his mother, Margaret McCann, who was gregarious and fun-loving. If he inherited a quiet, down-to-earth practicality from his father, from his mother he inherited a joie de vivre and love of language.

Heaney has described his boyhood at Mossbawn as a kind of "hibernation" in a hinterland that was "ahistorical, pre-sexual, in suspension between the archaic and the modern." The family wireless that brought news of a world at war gave him an inkling of what lay beyond the farm. So did his education in the primary school at Anahorish from 1945 to 1951. Unlike most primary schools in Northern Ireland, this one included both Protestants and Catholics. Heaney received history lessons in sectarian animosities both inside and outside the classroom. Catholics on the playgrounds recited a rhyme that mocked King William of Orange, who, by defeating the Catholic King James in 1690 at the Battle of the Boyne, ensured Protestant domination of Ireland for centuries. "Up the long ladder and down the short rope / To hell with King Billy and God bless the Pope." the Catholics would say. Protestants would respond:

> Splitter splatter holy water
> Scatter the Papyshes every one
> If that won't do
> We'll cut them in two
> And give them a touch of the
> Red, white and blue.

Heaney later recalled the beginnings of his student years in "Anahorish," a poem collected in *Wintering Out* (1972); he paid homage to his most influential teacher there, the Latin master Bernard Murphy, in part 5 of "Station Island."

A beneficiary of the 1947 Northern Ireland Education Act, Heaney earned a scholarship to St. Columb's College, a boarding school in Derry, and began classes in 1951. There he met Seamus Deane, who would become a lifelong friend and prominent scholar of Irish literature. Although he was at first homesick, as "The Ministry of Fear" in *North* attests, he soon distinguished himself as one of the school's best students. He acted in plays, participated in the Gaelic Society, and cultivated a passion for William Wordsworth, John Keats, and Gerard Manley Hopkins. His academic successes, to a certain extent, alienated him from his family, which he makes clear in "Mid-Term Break," a poem about returning home to attend the funeral of his four-year-old brother (Christopher Heaney, who had been hit by a car near Mossbawn). Heaney continued to excel academically during his final years at St. Columb's, passing his senior certificate with some of the highest grades in his class and earning the equivalent of advanced-level grade A in English language and literature, Latin, Irish, French, and mathematics. He also won one of the twelve state bursaries to study at Queen's University in Belfast.

In October 1957 Heaney began his four-year course at Queen's, where the curriculum's emphasis on British literature at times irked him because it had so little to do with his Irish Catholic background. He recalled studying the tradition of courtly love; the ironies and niceties of Jane Austen's vicarages; Alfred, Lord Tennyson's loss of faith; D. H. Lawrence's phallic consciousness; and the rituals of British India's club life in E. M. Forster's novels while he was still driving his mother to church for evening devotions and participating in the university's Catholic Sodality. If his family found his learning strange, so did he: "Far from the melodies of courtly love, I was . . . trying to master a way of coaxing a training college student into the back of our Austin Sixteen. And far, far from Lawrence's phallic candour, [I was] finding myself subsequently confessing sins of immodest and immoderate embraces [in church]." Despite the exotic nature of much of the required reading at Queen's, Heaney found many British and American authors to admire, among them the anonymous Anglo-Saxon poets, the Elizabethan dramatists John Webster and Christopher Marlowe, Ernest Hemingway, and Robert Frost.

Heaney's wide reading revealed itself—often in undigested form—in his first poems, which began to appear in university literary journals such as *Q* and *Gorgon* in 1959. In these poems the styles of Wordsworth, Keats, Hopkins, Frost, and the Welsh poet Dylan Thomas tended to overwhelm his subjects. Heaney used a pen name, Incertus, to acknowledge the uncertainty about his efforts. "Nostalgia in the Afternoon" is characteristic in that it expresses as much nostalgia for Thomas' gorgeous music as for the farmlands of Derry:

> Times when the cuckoo curled lobes of smooth music
> Over sunny acres of hay coloured sound
> And larks were spilling light pebbles of all
> Sand falling, stumbling, tinkling,
> Sound torn ragged and open with a corn-crake's
> Jagged-edge noise . . .

Soon Heaney toned down these derivative sound effects and forced his subjects to stand more clearly on their own.

For his accomplishments in the classroom Heaney earned a first-class honors degree in 1961 as well as the McMullen Medal for academic achievement. The chairman of the English Department urged him to accept a scholarship to Oxford University. Keenly aware of his parents' financial sacrifices over the previous decade, he decided to get a job as a teacher in Northern Ireland and pay them back. To that end, he entered St. Joseph's College of Education in Belfast and later took a job at St. Thomas Intermediate School in Ballymurphy. There his career as a writer entered a new phase when the headmaster, the short-story writer Michael McLaverty, loaned him *A Soul for Sale*, by the poet Patrick Kavanagh. Like McLaverty himself, whom Heaney commemorated in his poem "Singing School," Kavanagh helped him write more confidently and realistically about the rural farming life he found so underrepresented in his courses at Queen's.

As the result of an essay Heaney wrote on Ulster literary magazines for his degree at St. Joseph's College, he soon met other Irish writers, such as W. R. Rodgers and John Hewitt. Their poems, as well as those by Austin Clarke, Richard Kell, Thomas Kinsella, John Montague, Richard Murphy, and Richard Weber, published in an anthology by Robin Skelton, bolstered Heaney's confidence in his Irish subject matter. Daniel Corkery's *Hidden Ireland: A Study of Gaelic Munster in the Eighteenth Century* (1925), which celebrated Gaelic traditions eclipsed by modernity, and James Joyce's *Portrait of the Artist as a Young Man* (1916) were also influential. Along with Heaney's growing sense of enabling precursors came a willingness to confront the injustices suffered by Catholics in jobs, housing, politics, and every other area of social life in Northern Ireland.

Among Heaney's non-Irish mentors, the English poet Ted Hughes played the dominant role. Heaney borrowed Hughes's book *Lupercal* from the Belfast Public Library in 1962 and immediately fell under the spell of its powerful depictions of predatory animals and elemental landscapes. Before long Heaney was dwelling on nature's savage beauties in similarly enchanting music.

Heaney's career took an unexpected turn when he met Marie Devlin at a party for a retiring chaplain at Queen's University in 1962. Like Heaney, she was from a large Catholic family, had a passion for poetry, and also entertained ambitions to be a teacher. Having recently finished a course in English, speech, and drama at St. Mary's Teacher Training College, she began spending time with Heaney. One of their meeting places was a literary workshop organized by Philip Hobsbaum, a new lecturer in English at Queen's University. These talented writers, critics, and translators, who would soon be known as the Belfast Group, gathered in Hobsbaum's house to scrutinize each other's work and to socialize. Heaney, who was one of the stars of the group, forged close friendships with fellow members, among them the poet Michael Longley. Under the critical aegis of Hobsbaum, from 1963 to 1965 Heaney produced many of the poems that went into his highly acclaimed volume *Death of a Naturalist*. Hobsbaum not only helped perfect Heaney's early poems, but he also gave him crucial advice about publishing them in England. The year 1965 proved to be a watershed for Heaney: he received a contract for his first book from the Faber and Faber editor Charles Monteith, married Marie Devlin, and published his first pamphlet, *Eleven Poems*.

DOORS INTO THE DARK

HEANEY'S first book-length collection, *Death of a Naturalist*, opens with a poem that adumbrates what will follow. In "Digging," he celebrates his connection to traditional Irish skills, his family, and familiar Irish territory while affirming his freedom from these things. He pays homage to his father and grandfather for their skills digging potatoes and peat, but—the pen being lighter than the spade—he chooses writing over farming. "Between my finger and my thumb / The squat pen rests. / I'll dig with it," he says at the end. His stance as a writer is Janus-like. He will strike out on his own as well as faithfully return to the family farm for poetic models and subject matter. He will become that alien creature, a poet, but in his poetry he will imitate his family's diggings by delving into the historical roots of Irish troubles. The style of the poem—its mix of iambic pentameter lines and shorter, irregularly metered lines—is another indication of Heaney's vacillation between traditionalism and nonconformity.

The title poem "Death of a Naturalist" also foreshadows the sort of ambivalence that would characterize his early work. Recalling his homeland and its indigenous industry of flax making, he shifts between a child's and an adult's perspective. As an adult, he finds the flax that "festered in the heart / Of the townland" beneath "huge sods" and "the punishing sun" an apt metaphor for the anger and frustration festering at the heart of oppressive Northern Ireland. But in the middle of the poem Heaney speaks for the innocent child, who finds the buried wounds of Ireland wrapped and sanitized by "a strong gauze" of idyllic sounds and sights. When he brings "frogspawn" from the flax dam to his primary school, his teacher discourses on the facts of life in childish talk about daddy frogs and mammy frogs. Heaney then shifts his perspective dramatically to focus on the frogspawn that has grown up into "angry frogs" that are "cocked" like guns and poised like "mud grenades." The innocent naturalist has died into a new knowledge of reality. Once a childish Adam wandering among pastoral fields and ponds, now he is a typical Irishman all too aware of the perpetual blood feuds that threaten to engulf him. The frogs have turned militant: "The great slime kings / Were gathered there for vengeance and I knew / That if I dipped my hand the spawn would clutch it." In his first poems, Heaney repeatedly deconstructs the traditional pastoral, using sophisticated poetic forms to expose the grim social realities lurking beneath idyllic fictions.

In the late 1960s Heaney lived at the epicenter of the Troubles with his family, which had grown to four after Michael was born in 1966 and Christo-

pher in 1967. The year Michael arrived, Heaney left St. Joseph's College of Education in Belfast, where he had taught for three years, and took a new job as a lecturer in English at Queen's University. While the civil rights movement for African Americans gathered momentum in the United States, a similar movement for Catholics, which borrowed some of its strategies and rhetoric from America's great civil rights leader Martin Luther King, Jr., gathered momentum in Northern Ireland. Both groups experienced vicious backlashes from police and citizens. In 1966, when Catholics took part in a banned march to protest injustices in employment, housing, and voting policies, the Royal Ulster Constabulary rallied against them. Seventy-two civilians and eleven policemen were hurt in the melee. Heaney wrote an article for the *Listener* expressing his anger over the confrontation and before long was taking part in the demonstrations himself.

Having applauded Heaney's first book, some critics were hesitant to deem his second, *Door into the Dark* (1969), an "advance on its predecessor." While *Door into the Dark* may not reveal a transformation in style or subject matter—Heaney still uses traditional forms to depict rustic activities, such as farming, fishing, and thatching—the poems do show a psychological advance. If he tended to shy away from "doors into the dark" in his first poems, now he actively seeks them out as part of the dialectic between dark and light, public speaking and private writing, forgetting and remembering, blindness and insight, destruction and creation, and repression and expression that defines his psyche. As in traditional Christian meditations, Heaney writes about striving for moments of illumination and communion in a "dark night of the soul" and how those moments alter his vision of the world.

Heaney's "door into the dark" also opens onto the nightmare of history. In "Requiem for the Croppies," he elegizes those Irishmen who cropped their hair to evince solidarity with fellow revolutionaries in eighteenth-century France. Most of these "croppies," unfortunately, ended up as crops. They were among the fifty thousand killed during the Irish Rebellion of 1798, and, because they had carried seeds in their pockets for food, "the barley grew up out of the grave" as if to memorialize their sacrifices. Heaney suggests at the end of his elegy that although the Irish farmers "shaking scythes at cannon" were no match for the imperial English, their deaths sowed the seeds of future uprisings, like those of the 1960s.

The poem "The Forge" encapsulates Heaney's tension between meditative withdrawal and political activism, writing and socializing. The gruff, anachronistic blacksmith who looks at the modern world of cars with disdain (he makes horseshoes, not tires) appears heroic and even holy as he "expends himself in shape and music" at his "altar." For Heaney he exemplifies the traditional artisan, like his father and grandfather. Although the blacksmith discountenances the sectarian strife beyond the walls of his forge, his devotion to his craft offers a model of creativity that rebuffs the destruction and decadence suggested by the "old axles and iron hoops rusting" outside. Although he is older and more down to earth than Stephen Dedalus in James Joyce's *A Portrait of the Artist as a Young Man*, like Dedalus in Joyce's novel he is "forging in the smithy of his soul the uncreated conscience of his race."

When *Wintering Out* appeared in 1972, it attracted some of the same quibbles as *Door into the Dark*. An anonymous reviewer in the *Times Literary Supplement* stated that the book was "slightly unsatisfactory" and "transitional" because it was "skirting round themes he is reluctant to tackle head on." The reviewer wanted Heaney to be more journalistic—to show the Catholics and Protestants hurling cobbles in the streets. The poems, in fact, are saturated with the painful knowledge of conflict; it is just that they approach the conflict obliquely. In "Servant Boy," for instance, Heaney never draws overt connections between the resentful, impenitent Catholic boy who is "wintering out / the back-end of a bad year" and the Catholics suffering various indignities in Northern Ireland in the 1960s, but the connections are clear. In some of the book's most striking poems, Heaney exposes the roots of contemporary clashes by delving into the etymological roots and different pronunciations of place names. In poems like "Anahorish" and "Broagh," he points to Irish-Gaelic origins that have been altered by English conquerors and the language that came with their empire. Just by saying the words, he can hear the din of ancient battles.

Heaney himself was "wintering out" the renewal of rioting, shooting, and bombing in Belfast as he wrote his book. Matters became so atrocious by 1969 that the British government sent soldiers to Derry and Belfast. Responding to what appeared to be another British invasion (the soldiers, in fact, were supposed to protect Catholics from marauding Protestants), the Provisional Army Council of the Irish Republican Army organized itself to combat the British. At about this time, Heaney read P. V. Glob's *The Bog People,* a book about the discovery in the bogs of Denmark of bodies that were more than two thousand years old. The book galvanized Heaney's imagination by providing emblems for the adversity he found around him. "The Tollund Man," which Heaney collected in *Wintering Out,* was the first in a series of poems that recalled in harrowing detail the preserved bodies exhumed from bogs in Jutland. The Tollund Man, according to Glob, was "an Iron Age man who, two millennia before, had been deposited in the bog as a sacrifice to the powers that ruled men's destinies." Some of the bodies, Glob speculated, were deposited in the bogs as gifts to a fertility goddess, Nerthus, to ensure the recrudescence of vegetation and crops in the spring. Heaney immediately saw parallels between these grisly victims and the Irish people who also sacrificed themselves to a demanding goddess—Mother Ireland. His bog poems approach contemporary affairs by way of ancient, and even foreign, precedents and personae, but they are all the more gripping for doing so.

As if to distance himself further from the atrocities of his homeland, Heaney left Queen's in 1970 for a sabbatical year at the University of California in Berkeley, a hotbed of political activism at the time. The poets Robert Bly and Gary Snyder, who in word and deed were protesting American injustices in the Vietnam War and elsewhere, convinced Heaney that poetry could be "a mode of power, certainly a mode of resistance." Along with William Carlos Williams, they encouraged Heaney to write in a more colloquial and confrontational way about the ills of his own country, which were growing worse. By the time Heaney returned to Belfast in September 1971, the government had initiated a policy of internment without trial. The smallest infractions aroused suspicion. Because his car tax was out of date, a policeman marched Heaney and his three-year-old son to the station for questioning. At about the same time, a bomb set off in an office block on University Road came close to hitting Heaney's wife with debris. The killings mounted. One of the worst incidents occurred on 30 January 1972, when British paratroopers killed thirteen unarmed civilians and wounded twelve others for participating in a march organized by the Civil Rights Association, an event that came to be known as Bloody Sunday. A government inquiry blamed Catholic protesters for shooting at the soldiers, but journalists on the scene contended that it was the British soldiers who fired first. Outraged and saddened, Heaney and some of his friends took part in another protest march in Newry, which also was deemed illegal by the government.

Heaney said that coming home was like "putting on an old dirty glove again." Before long fifteen hundred people had been jailed, and the British government had assumed direct rule to try to resolve the conflict. Partly as a response to the mayhem of the north, Heaney resigned from Queen's University and, in the summer of 1972, took his family to Glanmore Cottage in Ashford, County Wicklow, where the gatekeeper for the estate of the Irish dramatist John Synge once had lived. (He at first rented the cottage from Professor Anne Saddlemyer, the editor of Synge's letters, and then bought it.) In the isolation of Glanmore, he planned to earn his living as a freelance writer. Financially, he would benefit from the Republic's policy of not taxing authors. He also hoped that his children would enjoy a rural setting a safe distance from exploding car bombs and sniper fire and that he would have more time to write poetry. Protestant rabble-rousers egged on by the Protestant militant leader Ian Paisley cheered the departure of "the well-known papist propagandist," while Heaney's friends were saddened and at times even angry that he had left them in the strife-ridden north.

In his new home about twenty-five miles south of Dublin, Heaney experienced a new beginning: "What happened to us personally as a couple, as a family, was that we got married again in a different way. We started life again together." Domestic tranquility proved to be as beneficial for his poetry as his marriage. He wrote many of his most celebrated poems at Glanmore and soon collected them in *North*. He finished his sequence of prose poems, *Stations* (1975), which he had commenced while living in California. He began translating *Buile Suibhne*, a medieval Irish tale about the peregrinations of an Ulster king who was cursed, transformed into a bird, and sent into exile. This ultimately became *Sweeney Astray: A Version from the Irish* (1984). There were other beginnings as well. His wife gave birth to their third child,

Catherine Ann, in April 1973. Heaney studied Yeats and Osip Mandelstam, finding in both an exemplary commitment to poetry during times of extreme duress. He also got to know Robert Lowell after reviewing favorably for Radio Eirann the American poet's sequences of free-form sonnets in *History, For Lizzie and Harriet,* and *The Dolphin.* Lowell's visceral rhetoric and obsessions with historical savagery spurred the poems Heaney was writing for *North*.

As news of Northern Irish protests, killings, and government upheavals reached Heaney in the south, the mummified bog people in P. V. Glob's study exerted an inexorable appeal. His bog poems in *North* express contradictory feelings—his sorrow for all victims of violence, his conviction that an artist must withdraw from social turmoil to create, his guilt about not speaking or acting more forcefully to stop sectarian killings, and his awareness that working in "a room of one's own" amounts to a kind of collusion with the killers. Innocent bystanding is not innocent in Heaney's reflections on atrocities. And yet he remained faithful to his distancing devices, bearing witness to present Irish violence through the medium of ancient sacrifices in a foreign country. He admitted: "My emotions . . . quickened more when contemplating a victim, strangely, from 2,000 years ago than they did from contemplating a man at the end of a road being swept up into a plastic bag."

Many reviewers praised *North* for its incantatory rhythms and intelligent perspectives on Northern Ireland. Several Ulster critics, such as Ciaran Carson and Edna Longley, however, faulted Heaney for mystifying and mythologizing the Troubles or giving a one-sided, Catholic view of them. While his poems highlight connections between Irish blood feuds and mythical antecedents, they also strive to demystify the myths and reveal the gruesome realities from which the myths spring. In his title poem, "North," he refuses to submit to the mystiques of heroic warriors, whether they are from Viking histories, Norse sagas, or Irish legends. "I returned to a long strand, / the hammered shod of a bay," he says, "and found only the secular / powers of the Atlantic thundering." Heaney reduces Thor's hammer and thunder to waves on a beach and further dismantles the god's status by turning him into a kind of dim-witted Mafia godfather obsessed with turf wars, new markets, sleazy women, and revenge killings:

Thor's hammer swung
to geography and trade,
thick-witted couplings and revenges,
the hatreds and behindbacks.

Heaney admonishes himself to keep his "eye clear / as the bleb of the icicle" and to "trust the feel of what nubbed treasure / your hands have known." He refuses to be swept away by the hysteria of internecine warfare. Instead, he retires to his studio to witness the situation as coolly and clearly as he can with what he treasures—poetic language.

DOORS INTO THE LIGHT

THE cottage at Glanmore proved to be too cold in winter and too remote from good schools and stores, so in 1976, a year after *North* appeared, Heaney moved his family to a comfortable Edwardian house in Dublin's Sandymount area. He already had started to teach at Carysfort Teacher Training College in Dublin, where he served as chairman of the English Department from 1976 to 1981, and to work on the poems for his next collection, *Field Work*. In interviews Heaney observed that his books up to *North* represented one stage in his career, those including and following *Field Work* another stage. If, in his earlier volumes, he had compulsively opened doors into the dark, now he turned—sometimes tentatively, sometimes boldly—toward doors into the light. His new openness to the everyday world can be felt in his expanded lines. He tends to abandon the constricted "artesian wells" into history's bogs and to walk more confidently through the sunlit "field" of the present. But like Lowell in his poem "Crossing the Alps," Heaney leaves religion and politics behind only to confront them once again. History's gravity continues to pull him back from reveries of transcendent sensuality to the stubborn world of painful facts. His numerous poems about beasts—otters, skunks, dogs, badgers—dwell on the animal passions that keep him rooted to the earth.

Heaney elegizes numerous relatives, friends, and artists in *Field Work* so that they reflect his own conflicting responsibilities to marriage, society, and art. In his elegy for Lowell, Heaney depicts his new friend as an emperor (Lowell's nickname, Cal, drew attention to his Caligula-like traits) and humbled slave, a majestic clipper ship and riotous night ferry, a conquering seaman and

conquered islander, an ungovernable invader and well-governed native. Self-interrogatory, self-accusing, and self-punishing, Lowell becomes Heaney's alter ego. By similarly highlighting their contradictory loyalties, Heaney elegizes other artists, such as Sean O'Riada, a famous Irish composer who died in 1971, and Francis Ledgewidge, a writer who sympathized with Ireland's Sinn Féin, the Irish Republican political party in favor of Irish independence, but who fought and died for Britain in World War I. "Casualty" exemplifies his new style and subject matter. He writes almost conversationally, not about an ancient victim of a Danish vegetation ritual but about a drinking friend who was blown up in his father-in-law's pub in a reprisal bombing by the Irish Republican Army after Bloody Sunday. The ghost of his friend returns to haunt Heaney with questions about his complicity in the Irish Troubles.

In 1981 Heaney made another break with his homeland when he resigned from Carysfort College and agreed to teach for five years at Harvard. In 1984 his attachment to the United States became more secure when Harvard elected him to the Boylston Chair of Rhetoric and Oratory. Meanwhile, events in Northern Ireland continued to spin out of control. Hoping to "criminalize" the violent activists, the British government built new accommodations at the Maze Prison in Long Kesh. The prisoners protested their conditions by wearing only blankets, by smearing excrement on cell walls, and in 1980 by going on hunger strikes. Almost two dozen strikers, including their leader, Bobby Sands, died. In Heaney's next book, *Station Island*, he allows one of the hunger strikers—perhaps his friend Francis Hughes—to speak about the new round of Northern Irish horrors. As the critic Michael Parker points out: "The anguish and anger of his fellow Catholics in the North in the wake of the strikes must have had no little influence on Heaney's 'decision' in *Station Island* to embark on a rigorous reappraisal of his conduct and role as an artist." Once again he entered the force field between political activism and artistic withdrawal. One way he became more involved in Irish affairs was by joining Field Day, an organization dedicated to furthering art in Ireland.

The purgatorial nature of Heaney's "rigorous reappraisal" is most evident in his long title poem, "Station Island." Set on Lough Derg in County Donegal, the poem depicts rituals on Station Island, where Saint Patrick supposedly fasted in a cave, had a vision of the otherworld, and underwent the sufferings of purgatory. Later, one of his disciples established a retreat called Saint Patrick's Purgatory, where pilgrims prayed, fasted, and replicated Christ's stations of the cross. In Heaney's "Station Island," the place becomes a site for communions with "familiar ghosts." Among the ghosts are a tinker, Simon Sweeney; Heaney's Aunt Agnes; a priest, Terry Keenan; an Anahorish teacher, Barney Murphy; a football friend, William Strathearn; an archaeologist, Tom Delaney; a murdered cousin, Colum McCartney; William Carleton, who wrote about the island in *The Lough Derg Pilgrim* (1828); Patrick Kavanagh, who wrote *Lough Derg*; and James Joyce.

What is surprising about many of Heaney's ghosts is the way they rebuke him for his pious desire to go on a Catholic pilgrimage. Sweeney at the beginning and Joyce at the end advise him to stay clear of all such sanctimonious processions. Their stinging criticism becomes part of the purgatorial ritual. The Dantesque poem, some of which is written in Dante's terza rima, is more a journey through stations in Heaney's tortured psyche than an actual walk on a holy island. His feelings of guilt and various doubts about pilgrimages, paradoxically, make such journeys all the more necessary. His colloquy with Colum McCartney typifies his self-incriminations. In part 8 of "Station Island," McCartney scoffs at an elegy Heaney wrote in *Field Day* that "whitewashed ugliness, and drew / the lovely blinds of the *Purgatorio* / and saccharined my death with morning dew." McCartney echoes some of Heaney's critics who argued that he mystified or sentimentalized violence. In one of the most scathing recriminations, Heaney confesses: "I hate how quick I was to know my place. / I hate where I was born, hate everything / That made me biddable and unforthcoming." This is inspired by a hunger striker, possibly Frank Delaney, whose funeral occurred when Heaney was staying at All Souls in Oxford for a poetry reading.

In a 1991 interview with Blake Morrison, Heaney revealed: "The most important thing that has happened to me in the last ten years [has been attending] . . . two death beds." He was referring to the deaths of his mother and father. His grief over the passing of his parents changed his poetry in unexpected ways. He acknowledged that he was now prepared to "enjoy the whole truancy and sport of the lyric process," as if somehow his boyish impulses had been liberated from parental strictures. In the sonnet sequence "Clearances," which appeared in *The Haw Lantern* (1987), he memorializes his mother by recalling mundane chores they shared, like bed making and potato peeling. But, as he notes in the eighth sonnet, his overwhelming feeling is of being transported to empty space:

> I thought of walking round and round a space
> Utterly empty, utterly a source
> Where the decked chestnut tree had lost its place
> In our front hedge above the wallflowers.

The chestnut tree planted by his aunt the year he was born and cut down in his teens by the new owners of Mossbawn becomes a symbol for his lost mother. He also associates the vanished tree with a luminous void that acts as a "source" for his new writing. In his essay "The Placeless Heaven," he could be speaking of himself when he notes that Patrick Kavanagh grew out of a poetry imbued with "a strong physical presence" to write a poetry more concerned with "luminous spaces within his mind."

"As the earth loses for him the mass and gravity of familiar presences—parents and friends taken by death," the critic Helen Vendler wrote in a review of Heaney, "desiccation and weightlessness threaten the former fullness of the sensual life." Heaney's sense of weightlessness and desiccation after his parents' deaths did little to stymie his productivity. He published *The Haw Lantern* in 1987, a collection of essays titled *The Government of the Tongue* in 1988 (the year he also began his tenure as Oxford's Professor of Poetry), *New Selected Poems 1966–1987* in 1990, a version of Sophocles' *Philoctetes* titled *The Cure at Troy* in 1990, and *Seeing Things* in 1991. Once wary of Wallace Stevens' philosophical "mind of winter" and its tendency to view the world abstractly, now Heaney embraced it. His poems in *The Haw Lantern* dwell on such abstract matters as hierarchical differences between speech and writing and the Socratic tradition in Western philosophy that has demeaned writing as a faulty conduit for the truth. In "Alphabets," the poem that begins the book, he traces his autobiography in terms of the political connotations of different languages—Gaelic, Latin, English—so that the languages mirror his divided identity and divided allegiances. Other poems resemble allegories, parables, or fables by such Eastern European poets as Zbigniew Herbert and Czeslaw Milosz, whom he greatly admired.

Heaney continues his exploration of more abstract, "visionary" realms in *Seeing Things*. His ambivalence toward otherworldliness, however, is scored into the title. Worried that he might float off into a never-never land of ideas, into "The Republic of Conscience" or "The Land of the Unspoken"—to borrow from titles in *The Haw Lantern*—he seems to chide himself gently for being enchanted by illusory places and to remind himself to concentrate on real things. Heaney begins and ends *Seeing Things* with journeys to imaginary places (to the mythic underworlds of Virgil's *Aeneid* and *The Divine Comedy),* and he communes with imaginary people (such as the shades of the poet Philip Larkin, Richard Ellmann, and his father, Patrick Heaney). But he also gives many examples of "the forewarned journey back / Into the heartland of the ordinary." What distinguishes Heaney's book from previous ones is the way he combines the heavy, earthbound "plop and slap" music of his first books and the more subliminal, philosophical style of *Station Island* and *The Haw Lantern,* creating a "middle style" that seeks to balance the two.

The poem "Field of Vision" in *Seeing Things* demonstrates Heaney's new style and themes. The poem begins with a memory of an ordinary woman in a wheelchair looking out a window in her home at a rural scene composed of sycamore trees, a hawthorn bush, cows, a field of ragwort, and a mountain. The woman is stoical, stationary, crippled. From her, Heaney learns something about patiently contemplating the ordinary until it appears extraordinary. Looked at long enough, "the field behind the hedge / Grew more distinctly strange as you kept standing / Focused and drawn in by what barred the way." What separates the observer from the landscape—a wheelchair, barred gate, or, in Heaney's case, geographical distance from it—makes the landscape all the more significant and strange. *Seeing Things* obsessively investigates gates, thresholds, borders, limits, lines, doors, ceilings, roofs, circles, and squares as obstacles that bar the way but stimulate the mind to find new, transcendental ways of "seeing things." In a dialectical manner, he points to how physical limits make possible metaphysical sublimities. "Blessed be down-to-earth! Blessed be highs!" he says in the poem "Man and Boy," imitating one of Blake's parables from "The Marriage

of Heaven and Hell." In the seventh poem of his sonnet sequence "Glanmore Revisited," entitled "The Skylight," he recalls an argument with his wife about cutting a hole in their roof for a skylight. At first preferring their house "low and closed" like a claustrophobic nest, he eventually concedes that his wife was right and relishes the moment when "extravagent / Sky entered and held surprise wide open." Heaney's sequences of tercets, "Squarings," take up old concerns—his family, literary precursors, sectarian divisions in Northern Ireland—to confront his limits and find strategies to go beyond them.

The title of Heaney's next book, *The Spirit Level* (1996), alludes to a carpenter's tool used to make sure that a building's boards and bricks are level. Having won the Nobel Prize in 1995, Heaney found that life as a globetrotting bard made keeping on a level footing ever more difficult. In one poem, "A Brigid's Girdle," he writes about finally finding time to write in South Carolina. His poem is addressed to a friend in Ireland and is reminiscent of his earlier poem "The Harvest Bow." Here Heaney says: "I was glad of the early heat and the first quiet / I'd had for weeks." Among the magnolias and mockingbirds of the Deep South, he returns to Irish crafts to find balance and a sense of roots. Like his father weaving straw into a harvest bow, he plaits straw into another circle as "a rite of spring / . . . strange and lightsome and traditional." Appearing at the beginning of the book, the poem celebrates all traditional springlike makings. "The Rain Stick" also harks back to fertility rites and to his many other poems equating the fertility of the land with the productivity of the artist. Aware that he may be repeating himself, he stands up for his right to summon a familiar muse and declaim a familiar music. Unlike Prospero in Shakespeare's *The Tempest,* Heaney is not ready to break his artistic "staff." He shakes his "rain stick" (a hollow cactus stalk presumably used to bring rain) as if it were the pen he vowed to dig with in his first poem in *Death of a Naturalist:*

> What happens next
> Is undiminished for having happened once,
> Twice, ten, a thousand times before.
> Who cares if all the music that transpires
>
> Is the fall of grit or dry seeds through a cactus?
> You are like a rich man entering heaven

Through the ear of a raindrop. Listen now again.

In standing up for his right to repeat himself and others, Heaney also plays with and subverts traditional sayings. If it is more difficult for a rich man to enter heaven than for a camel to pass through the eye of a needle, as the Bible says, Heaney mischievously affirms that he is both rich man and camel passing into a heaven through an ear. He playfully recasts the traditional biblical parable and, in doing so, recasts traditional notions of poetic music. Sounds as ordinary as dropping rain or seeds, he suggests, are sufficient to transport him to heaven.

Wealth and fame have ruined many talents (the Nobel Prize, indeed, made Heaney a rich man), but Heaney in *The Spirit Level* shows few signs of flagging. In his poems about making pottery, laying bricks, folding paper into boats, or picking blackberries, he seems to be reminding himself once again, as he had done in "North," to

> Keep your eye clear
> as the bleb of the icicle,
> trust the feel of what nubbed treasure
> your hands have known.

The bleb of the icicle has metamorphosed into the bubble of the spirit level, an image that appears in a poem tracing Heaney's linguistic inventiveness and playfulness back to his father. "Keep level-headed and clear-sighted amid all the hoopla of your good fortune," Heaney seems to be telling himself. "Trust the style and subjects that have brought you so far."

In *The Spirit Level*, Heaney returns to familiar territory: to his childhood farms in Derry, to his parents, to rural artisans, to Tollund, to questions about the poet's political responsibilities, to California, to Wicklow. In "Mint" he demonstrates his devotion to the simple and often disregarded things of his childhood, claiming: "My last things will be first things slipping from me. / Yet let all things go free that have survived." Pondering his own approaching death and the death of loved ones, Heaney elevates memories as ordinary as a clump of mint into a private Elysium, but he also shows a willingness to accept the inevitable oblivion of all memories in death. Ruminating on first and last things, Heaney pays homage to Caedmon, the Anglo-Saxon herdsman who entered a monastery at Whitby in Yorkshire as an old man (sometime between A.D. 658 and 680) after receiving the power of song in a vision; he is considered the earliest English poet. In the monastery he versified passages from the Bible. Because of his combination of rural practicality and Christian spirituality, his love of ordinary things and susceptibility to extraordinary visions, Heaney claims him as a precursor.

If Heaney's early books were preoccupied with earthy realities and his middle books with a trust in heavenly marvels, his late books aim to reconcile the two. But he also emphasizes that the dialectic between reality and imagination was there from the start, pushing his career forward like an engine's pistons. In "A Sofa in the Forties," he finds in a childhood game of "train" played with siblings in a farmhouse an endearing symbol for the contraries and uncertainties that have always impelled his poetry. The magic sofa upon which the Heaney children make chugging and whistling noises is "Potentially heavenbound, earthbound for sure, / Among things that might add up or let you down." Despite the inevitable ups and downs of their imaginative enterprise, Heaney affirms: "Constancy was its own reward already / . . . Our only job to sit, eyes straight ahead, / And be transported and make engine noise." In a similar poem, "The Swing," he reaches the same conclusion that Robert Frost reached in "Birches"—that he will indulge the temptation to fly toward heaven only because he knows his swinging will bring him back to earth.

At times, however, Heaney expresses frustration with the ideal of constancy and equanimity. In "Weighing" he contemplates throwing off the attempt to "Balance the intolerable in others." Rather than "abide / Whatever we settled for and settled into / Against our better judgment," like the older Yeats entertaining thoughts of becoming a wild, wicked, violent old man, Heaney declares: "I held back when I should have drawn blood / . . . At this stage only foul play cleans the slate." A violent strike at those who perpetuate injustice would be a catharsis. Other poems contemplate similar risks. In "The Gravel Walks," recalling how wheelbarrows full of gravel once kept him slowly plodding over the ground, he admonishes himself: "So walk on air against your better judgment." He never wholly renounces the virtues of balance and judgment, but as an older man he is more willing to act with calculated wildness.

The same oscillation between probity and recklessness characterizes many of the poems in Heaney's book *Electric Light* (2001). In his "Sonnets from Hellas," he uses one of the most traditional forms—the sonnet sequence—to remember a trip to one of the most traditional places in Western culture, Greece. But the actions he highlights in the sonnets are often disorderly. In the first sonnet, "Into Arcadia," there is no Garden of Eden with apples ripening on the trees. Instead, Heaney records an accident in which a truck dumps hundreds of apples on the road. The noise of car tires popping and scrunching the apples fills him with boyish ecstasy: "We drove on, juiced up and fleshed and spattered, / Revelling in it." Having moved from an Apollonian respect for order, rules, and traditional forms to a Dionysian delight in anarchy, Heaney has "crossed the border / From Argos" in many senses. Many of the other poems reveal a similar need to trespass beyond borders and boundaries, whether poetic or social.

In the fifth sonnet, "Castalian Spring," Heaney seems to wear the mantle of a law-abiding Apollo at one moment and a law-breaking Dionysus the next. He commemorates the traditional ideas that continue to rule his poetry, from the Greek muses to iambic meters, but flouts Greek rules to do so. Alluding to the myth of Castalia, a nymph pursued by Apollo and metamorphosed into a spring on Mount Parnassus, Heaney plays the role of a rambunctious tourist whose poetic license allows him to defy the woman guarding the roped-off spring. He trespasses in order to drink from the sacred waters under "Apollo's giddy cliff." As for the guard and her orders, he bluntly declares: "To hell with that, / And to hell with all who'd stop me." Acting like criminals on a getaway, Heaney and his friends drive perilously fast (and drunkenly) down the winding road to the valley. He has come a long way from his decorous courting of his Irish muse in "Personal Helicon," a poem he collected a quarter-century earlier in *Death of a Naturalist*.

Many of the poems in *Electric Light* resurrect classical forms, such as the eclogue, epigram, and elegy, but in unconventional ways. In "Bann Valley Eclogue," which revisits Heaney's pastoral origins in Northern Ireland, he transforms Virgil into the master of an Irish hedge school and directs his poem to an unnamed "child that's due." He looks to the past in order to "sing / Better times for her and her / generation." Because of recent progress made in reconciling sectarian conflicts in Northern Ireland (a tentative cease-fire was declared in 1994), Heaney can hope the child will hear "A chug and slug going on in the / milking parlour"

rather than "gunfire / or explosions." The future might not portend a "paradise regained," but his poem suggests that there is a chance that the child of the twenty-first century will enjoy the kind of pastoral equanimity that the traditional eclogue consecrates and that Heaney elegized in many of his early poems.

Heaney bears witness to moments in his own past that shattered his sense of pastoral peace, but usually he stresses their pastness. In "The Border Campaign," he recalls when he heard the word "attack" at St. Columb's College in 1956, which was the year an Irish Republican Army splinter group began blowing up customs huts, telephone exchanges, bridges, Protestant paramilitary halls, and lough gates on the southern border of Northern Ireland. Rather than document military specifics of the insurrection, however, Heaney compares it to the monster Grendel's attack of Heorot, the hall of Hrothgar, king of the Danes, in *Beowulf*, a poem that he translated in the 1990s. (His version of *Beowulf* was an international bestseller in 2000.) In the first poem of the book, "Toombridge," he remembers a boy hanged at the site during the Irish Rebellion of 1798 and a more recent military checkpoint located there. Nevertheless, he expresses hope that Irish bloodshed has run its course like so much water "pouring over the weir out of Lough Neagh."

In the *New York Times Book Review*, Langdon Hammer pointed out that *Electric Light* is "the work of a world citizen aware of his cultural authority and the rights and responsibilities that come with it." Many of the new poems track Heaney's travels around the world to poetry festivals or to other places related to poetry in Greece, Macedonia, Belgrade, England, Spain, Finland, and Ireland. He elegizes numerous foreign poets—Ted Hughes, W. H. Auden, Joseph Brodsky, Robert Fitzgerald, and Zbigniew Herbert. He translates or imitates Virgil, Dante, Yeats, and the Russian poet Aleksandr Pushkin and pays homage to Thomas Hardy, the Scottish poet Hugh MacDiarmid, William Faulkner, Elizabeth Bishop, and many lesser-known writers. Confident of his mastery, but keenly aware of his career moving closer to its end, Heaney repeatedly pays his respects to the great dead as well as to teachers and friends who helped his career along the way. The last poem in the volume, "Electric Light," ends with another respectful glance back at beginnings. Heaney portrays himself as a frightened young boy visiting a relative, perhaps a grand-mother, and getting his first hint of the modern world through her electric light and radio. Like the Sybil at Cumae prophesying the future of world-famous Aeneas and giving him instructions for his journey to the underworld, the mysterious Irish woman initiates the young Heaney by letting him use the wireless to "roam . . . at will the sta-tions of the world." *Electric Light* movingly expresses gratitude to all those voices that made Heaney's astonishing career possible and that ensure its continuation.

SELECTED BIBLIOGRAPHY

I. COLLECTED WORKS. *Selected Poems, 1965–1975* (Lon-don and Boston, 1980), republished as *Poems 1965–1975* (New York, 1980); *The Rattle Bag: An Anthology of Poetry* (London, 1982), selected by Seamus Heaney with Ted Hughes; *New Selected Poems, 1966–1987* (London, Boston, and New York, 1990); *Opened Ground: Selected Poems, 1966–1996* (London and New York, 1998).

II. POETRY. *Eleven Poems* (Belfast, 1965); *Death of a Nat-uralist* (London and Boston, 1966; New York, 1969); *A Lough Neagh Sequence* (Manchester, England, 1969); *Door into the Dark* (London and New York, 1969); *Wintering Out* (London, 1972; New York, 1973); *Soundings '72* (Belfast, 1972); *Stations* (Belfast, 1975); *North* (London and Boston, 1975; New York, 1977); *Field Work* (London, Boston, and New York, 1979); *An Open Letter* (Derry, 1983); *Station Island* (London and Boston, 1984; New York, 1985); *Hailstones* (Dublin, 1984); *The Haw Lantern* (London, Boston, and New York, 1987); *Seeing Things* (London and New York, 1991); *The Spirit Level* (London and New York, 1996); *Electric Light* (London and New York, 2001).

III. PROSE. *Preoccupations: Selected Prose, 1968–1978* (London and New York, 1980); *The Government of the Tongue: Selected Prose, 1978–1987* (London and Boston, 1988; New York, 1989). *The Place of Writing* (Atlanta, Ga., 1989); *The Redress of Poetry* (London and New York, 1995); *Crediting Poetry: The Nobel Lecture* (London, 1996).

IV. TRANSLATED WORKS. *Sweeney Astray: A Version from the Irish* (London and New York, 1984); *The Cure at Troy: A Version of Sophocle's* Philoctetes (Derry and London, 1990; New York, 1991); *Beowulf: A New Verse Translation* (London and New York, 2000).

VI. CRITICAL STUDIES. Robert Buttel, *Seamus Heaney* (Lewisburg, Pa., 1975); Edward Broadbridge, ed., *Seamus Heaney* (Copenhagen, 1977); Blake Morrison, *Seamus Heaney* (London and New York, 1982); Harold Bloom, ed., *Seamus Heaney* (New York, 1986); Neil Corcoran, *Sea-mus Heaney* (London and Boston, 1986); Nicholas McGuinn, *Seamus Heaney: A Student's Guide to the Selected Poems, 1965–75* (Leeds, England, 1986); William Cookson and Peter Dale, eds., *Agenda: Seamus Heaney Birthday Issue* (London, 1989); Thomas C. Foster, *Seamus Heaney* (Dublin and Boston, 1989); Ronald Tamplin, *Seamus Heaney* (Milton Keynes, England, and Philadelphia, 1989); Sidney Burris, *The Poetry of Resistance: Seamus Heaney and the Pastoral Tradition* (Athens, Ohio, 1990); Elmer Andrews, *The Poetry of Seamus Heaney: All the Realms of Whisper* (London, 1992); Henry Hart, *Seamus Heaney: Poet of Contrary Progressions* (Syracuse, 1992); Michael Parker, *Seamus Heaney: The Making of the Poet* (Dublin and Iowa City, 1993); Tony Curtis, ed., *The Art of Seamus Heaney* (Bridgend, Ireland, 1994); Bernard O'Donoghue, *Seamus Heaney and the Language of Poetry* (New York, 1994); John Wilson Foster, *The Achievement of Seamus Heaney* (Dublin, 1995); Stratis Haviaras, ed., *Sea-mus Heaney: A Celebration* (Cambridge, Mass., 1996), a *Harvard Review* monograph; Andrew Murphy, *Seamus Heaney* (Plymouth, England, 1996); Michael Allen, ed., *Seamus Heaney* (London and New York, 1997); Helen Vendler, *Seamus Heaney* (Cambridge, Mass., 1998).

SAMUEL JOHNSON

(1709–1784)

Adam Potkay

SAMUEL JOHNSON WAS born in Lichfield, England, near the city of Birmingham, on 7 September 1709. He was the son of Michael Johnson, a fifty-two-year-old bookseller, and his forty-year-old wife, Sarah. The couple employed a younger woman as a wet nurse for the child, with disastrous results. From her, Samuel contracted scrofula, a tubercular infection of the lymph glands, which left him blind in the left eye, visually impaired in the right eye, and deaf in the left ear. Both the scrofula itself and a later operation on his lymph gland left him with permanent scars on the neck and face. In 1712, the Johnsons had one more child, Nathaniel; he died in 1737, perhaps a suicide.

Despite his untoward beginnings, Samuel proved to be a gifted scholar at the Lichfield and Stourbridge grammar schools and a voracious reader of all books that came his way, from the Greek and Roman classics to Petrarch to chivalric romances. In October 1728, at nineteen years old, he was sent to Pembroke College, Oxford, but a lack of funds forced him to leave without a degree thirteen months later. There followed several years of severe depression spent in Lichfield and Birmingham. In 1735, at the age of twenty-five, Johnson married Elizabeth ("Tetty") Porter, the forty-six-year-old widow of a Birmingham mercer and, with her money, set up as a schoolmaster in Edial, two miles west of Lichfield. The school was not a success; when it opened in late autumn, only three pupils showed up. One of them, however, was eighteen-year-old David Garrick, the man destined to be the greatest dramatic actor of the century. In 1737 Johnson left with Garrick for London, temporarily leaving Tetty behind (she would often live apart from Johnson during the remaining fifteen years of their marriage; she died in 1752). Johnson hoped to establish himself as a professional writer in the metropolis; he was motivated in part by the desire to repay Tetty the money his ill-starred school had cost her and to provide for her future support and in part by the thirst for fame as a scholar and man of letters in the Renaissance humanist tradition.

He soon found employment as a writer and editor for Edward Cave's *Gentleman's Magazine*. Johnson's productions for this popular magazine included biographical sketches of naval heroes and creative reconstructions of parliamentary debates (thinly veiled as *Debates in the Senate of Lilliput*). Aside from his work for Cave, Johnson published anonymously a 263-line poem, *London* (1738), which creatively updated the Roman poet Juvenal's *Third Satire*.[1] As Juvenal's speaker bids farewell to the corrupt city of Rome on his way to rural retirement, so Johnson's speaker takes his leave of London:

> Here malice, rapine, accident, conspire,
> And now a rabble rages, now a fire;
> Their ambush here relentless ruffians lay,
> And here the fell attorney prowls for prey;
> Here falling houses thunder on your head,
> And here a female atheist talks you dead.
> (*Poems*, p. 47, ll. 13–18)

Alexander Pope, the leading English poet of the day, read the anonymous *London* and inquired after its author. Upon discovering "only that his name was Johnson, and that he was some obscure man, Pope said, 'he will soon be *déterré'*"—that is, brought to light, made well-known (Chapman, 1980, p. 92).

By the middle of the 1750s, with the appearance of his *Rambler* moral essays and *A Dictionary of the English Language* (1755), Johnson had acquired literary fame. From his day through to our own, Samuel Johnson has been viewed as a literary colossus, towering over his contemporaries and casting a long shadow into the future. In an honor

---

[1] Whenever possible, quotations have been taken from *The Yale Edition of the Works of Samuel Johnson*. Titles of the individual volumes are given in parentheses. Occasionally, other works have been quoted, mainly George Birkbeck Hill's *Lives of the English Poets*, R. W. Chapman's *Letters of Samuel Johnson*, and Donald Greene's *Samuel Johnson: The Major Works*.

awarded no other English author—not even Shakespeare or John Milton—his name supplies the standard label for the time period during which he wrote: students of English literary history customarily refer to the second half of the eighteenth century as "the age of Johnson." It is not so much his achievement in any one literary genre or kind of writing that distinguishes Johnson from most other great writers of the past, but his unparalleled mastery of a broad range of genres and of literary and scholarly pursuits, all of which he infused with superb psychological insights and sui generis stylistic craftsmanship. We tend today to limit the designation "literature" to poems, plays, and prose fiction, but eighteenth-century writers used the term to refer as well to historiography, philosophy, political writing, travel writing, biography, periodical essays, sermons, translations, lexicography, and encyclopedia writing. According to this more capacious definition of literature, Samuel Johnson, along with David Hume of Scotland and Voltaire and Jean Jacques Rousseau in France, was one of eighteenth-century Europe's greatest men of letters.

JOHNSON ON LITERATURE: INSTRUCTION AND PLEASURE

"THE end of writing is to instruct; the end of poetry is to instruct by pleasing": so Johnson pronounced in the preface to his edition of *The Plays of William Shakespeare* (1765). For Johnson, poetry aims immediately at pleasure, but all writing must teach a lesson. Johnson found Shakespeare without an equal in his ability to teach how things actually work in the human world; he admired Shakespeare's plays as "the mirrour of manners and of life" (*Johnson on Shakespeare,* vol. 1, p. 62). From reading Shakespeare, he marveled, "a hermit may estimate the transactions of the world, and a confessor predict the progress of the passions" (*Johnson on Shakespeare,* vol. 1, p. 65). It is in relation to Shakespeare's model of excellence that Johnson enunciated most clearly his general principles of literary criticism:

Nothing can please many, and please long, but just representations of general [human] nature. Particular manners [i.e., modes of human behavior peculiar to specific times and places] can be known to few, and therefore few only can judge how nearly they are copied. The irregular combinations of fanciful invention may delight a-while, by that novelty of which the common

satiety of life sends us all in quest; but the pleasures of sudden wonder are soon exhausted, and the mind can only repose on the stability of truth.

Shakespeare is above all writers, at least above all modern writers, the poet of nature; the poet that holds up to his readers a faithful mirrour of manners and of life. His characters . . . are the genuine progeny of common humanity, such as the world will always supply, and observation will always find. His persons act and speak by the influence of those general passions and principles by which all minds are agitated, and the whole system of life is continued in motion. In the writings of other poets a character is too often an individual; in those of Shakespeare it is commonly a species.
(*Johnson on Shakespeare,* vol. 1, pp. 61–62)

Johnson's first requirement of poetry, then, is that it be mimetic, a just imitation of general human nature, as this alone affords audiences enduring pleasure. Ultimately, however, Johnson demands that poetry serve a moral purpose—it must, in effect, show the rewards of virtue and the punishment of vice. Shakespeare's main fault, in Johnson's eyes, is that he

is so much more careful to please than to instruct, that he seems to write without any moral purpose. . . . He makes no just distribution of good or evil, nor is always careful to shew in the virtuous a disapprobation of the wicked; he carries his persons indifferently through right and wrong, and at the close dismisses them without further care, and leaves their examples to operate by chance.
(*Johnson on Shakespeare,* vol. 1, p. 71)

Still, Johnson concludes his assessment of Shakespeare with an encomium to his sheer fecundity as an imitator of nature: "The composition of Shakespeare is a forest, in which oaks extend their branches, and pines tower in the air, interspersed sometimes with weeds and brambles, and sometimes giving shelter to myrtles and to roses; filling the eye with awful [awe-inspiring] pomp, and gratifying the mind with endless diversity" (*Johnson on Shakespeare,* vol. 1, p. 84).

Johnson, in his own extraordinarily diverse writings in verse and prose, sought both to please and, unerringly, to instruct. While working as a schoolmaster in Lichfield, Johnson began writing a play, *Irene: A Tragedy* (1749)—a blank-verse drama concerning the temptation of a Greek Christian slave by her Turkish Muslim master, which was eventually staged, with Garrick's support, in 1749. *Irene,* however, is not one of Johnson's happier performances, and he never again turned his hand to dramatic poetry. Literary characterization and realistic dialogue would not prove his forte. He succeeded far better at lyric poetry, both in English and in Latin, which he wrote throughout his life.

POETRY AND PROSE FICTION: VANITY OF HUMAN WISHES AND RASSELAS

AFTER *London* (1738), Johnson's second great poem is *The Vanity of Human Wishes* (1749), another "imitation," or free translation, of a Latin work by Juvenal. Juvenal's *Tenth Satire* might be descriptively titled "On false and worthwhile objectives." Humans, Juvenal has it, tend to pray for things that will only bring unhappiness: riches, power, beauty. Riches are accompanied by the fear of robbery and dispossession; the rise to political or military power merely sets the stage for a downfall; physical beauty invites lust and rape. At the end of his poem Juvenal recommends that we pray only for "a sound mind in a sound body" (*mens sana in corpore sano*), a valiant heart fearless of death, and the virtuous conduct that alone brings a life of peace. In *The Vanity of Human Wishes*, Johnson adapts Juvenal's poem into English closed couplets; updates his historical examples (for example, substituting Charles XII of Sweden for the Carthaginian general Hannibal as the type of the hubristic military conqueror); and, finally, Christianizes the poem's conclusion. For Johnson, the proper objects of prayer are the theological virtues of faith, patience, and love: "With these celestial wisdom calms the mind, / And makes the happiness she does not find" (*Poems*, p. 109, ll. 367–368).

In addition to freely adapting Latin poets, Johnson sometimes worked as a prose translator. His first book, *A Voyage to Abyssinia* (1735), translates into English a French version of a seventeenth-century Portuguese Jesuit's manuscript account of his travels to Abyssinia (Ethiopia). Later, Abyssinia and Egypt would provide the "oriental" setting for his great work of prose fiction, *The History of Rasselas, Prince of Abyssinia* (1759). *Rasselas* is a philosophical tale—critics hesitate to call it a novel because it lacks realism of character or of dialogue (all the characters tend to sound like Johnson and to speak in discursive essays). The tale, however, does have a cohesive plot. Prince Rasselas, with his sage guide, Imlac; his sister, Nekayah; and his sister's maid, Pekuah, leaves his home in the Edenic but sequestered "Happy Valley" to pursue in the broader world a "choice of life"—a profession, a place to live—that he hopes will bring a simple and enduring happiness, a life uncomplicated by hardship and suffering. The company enters Cairo and examines life among a wide variety of character types, including young wastrels (ironically called "young men of spirit and gaiety" in the title of chapter 17), a philosopher who preaches Stoic impassivity (chapter 18), shepherds (chapter 19), a rich man (chapter 20), and a hermit (chapter 21). Rasselas hopes to find happiness naturally attaching to some one state, condition, or locale of life, and his hopes are repeatedly frustrated: none of the men he meets turns out to be happy. Johnson's tale dramatizes inflated expectation and disappointment time and again. For example, the Stoic philosopher who preaches that happiness lies in the subjugation of all passions and affections is last seen in despair over the death of his beloved daughter. The hermit who has fled urban life is preparing, when Rasselas and company arrive in his cave, to return to the city, having concluded, "The life of a solitary man will be certainly miserable, but not certainly devout" (*Rasselas*, p. 83). Princess Nekayah concludes from her own study of domestic life that nothing is worse than being single: "To live without feeling or exciting sympathy, to be fortunate without adding to the felicity of others, or afflicted without tasting the balm of pity, is a state more gloomy than solitude: it is not retreat but exclusion from mankind. Marriage has many pains, but celibacy has no pleasures" (*Rasselas*, pp. 98–99).

In chapter 37, Rasselas and his company travel outside Cairo to visit the pyramids, which Imlac interprets as emblems of unbridled desire. The Great Wall of China serves a purpose, he explains:

But for the pyramids no reason has ever been given adequate to the cost and labour of the work. . . . It seems to have been erected only in compliance with that hunger of the imagination which preys incessantly upon life, and must be always appeased by some employment. Those who have already all that they can enjoy, must enlarge their desires. He that has built for use, till use is supplied, must begin to build for vanity, and extend his plan to the utmost power of human performance, that he may not be soon reduced to form another wish.

I consider this mighty structure as a monument of the insufficiency of human enjoyments. A king, whose power is unlimited, and whose treasures surmount all real and imaginary wants, is compelled to solace, by the erection of a pyramid, the satiety of dominion and tastelesness of pleasures, and to amuse the tediousness of declining life, by seeing thousands labouring without end, and one stone, for no purpose, laid upon another. Whoever thou art, that, not content with a moderate condition, imaginest happiness in royal magnificence, and dreamest that command or riches can feed the appetite of novelty with perpetual gratifications, survey the pyramids, and confess thy folly!

(Rasselas, pp. 118–119)

In the end the travelers return, sadder but wiser, to Abyssinia. Although they have been unable either to find a happy man or to limit their own desires (Rasselas, for one, imagines ruling over "a little kingdom"—but "was always adding to the number of his subjects"), they at least recognize the vanity of exorbitant wishes (chapter 49). The lapse from unreasonable hope to its disappointment—a lapse that sometimes leads to wisdom—was and would remain Johnson's great didactic theme. Happiness may be found in life, but it lies in the regulation rather than the (impossible) satisfaction of an ever-hungry imagination. It lies with the inner peace that a virtuous life affords and—as Imlac implies in his final speech (chapter 48)—with the Christian faith that looks beyond the natural evil of death to the immortality of the soul and a future state of just rewards and punishments.

THE RAMBLER *AND* A DICTIONARY OF THE ENGLISH LANGUAGE

"TIME, which puts an end to all human pleasures and sorrows, has likewise concluded the labours of the Rambler": so Johnson began his 208th and last installment of the *Rambler*, a series of essays he published as individual pamphlets, twice a week, between March 1750 and March 1752. The closest modern equivalent to the eighteenth-century periodical essay is the opinion and editorial column of a daily newspaper, but the concerns of the *Rambler* are less topical than those of most columnists today. Roughly half of the *Rambler* essays directly analyze the timeless features of human psychology, with an eye toward how to regulate the passions that, unbridled, lead to unhappiness: envy, anger, avarice, excessive ambition, cowardice, delusive hopes, and fears. In a related vein, thirty-six numbers of the *Rambler* draw gently satiric sketches of character types that Johnson implicitly cautions the reader against emulating: the fop, the legacy hunter, the spendthrift, the gambler, the lottery player, the aging mother jealous of her blos-

soming daughter, and so on. Thirty-one of the *Rambler* papers may be classified as literary criticism—on topics ranging from pastoral poetry to Milton's versification to the eighteenth-century novel—and five others address more general issues concerned with the life of writing. Johnson also included didactic allegories, oriental tales (some of which seem to be rough sketches for *Rasselas*), and contrived "letters" supposedly sent to "Mr. Rambler" from the periodical's readers.

The solemn and sesquipedalian voice of the *Rambler* chiefly distinguishes it from contemporary essay writing. For example, the fifth number of the *Rambler* begins:

Every man is sufficiently discontented with some circumstances of his present state, to suffer his imagination to range more or less in quest in future happiness, and to fix upon some point of time, in which, by the removal of the inconvenience which now perplexes him, or acquisition of the advantage which he at present wants, he shall find the condition of his life very much improved.

When this time, which is too often expected with great impatience, at last arrives, it generally comes without the blessing for which it was desired; but we solace ourselves with some new prospect, and press forward again with equal eagerness.

(Rambler, vol. 3, p. 25)

Although Johnson assumed a somewhat more familiar tone in his later ventures into periodical writing—in the *Adventurer* (to which Johnson contributed intermittently from 1753 to 1754) and the *Idler* (which Johnson wrote weekly from April 1758 to April 1760)—the polysyllabic, Latinate, and syntactically expansive "Rambler style" would ever after be associated with Johnson's name. Johnson structures his sentences here in short clauses, each of them animated by a verb or infinitive. In the first sentence alone, we find "is," "to suffer," "to range," "to fix," "perplexes," "wants," and "shall find." A great deal *happens* in this sentence. There is, however, not much specificity to the action. Johnson prefers generalizing, abstract nouns (often of Latin origin), such as "circumstances," "inconvenience," "advantage," and "condition." The sentence aims at universal applicability. Its analysis of deluded but sustaining hope—and, more generally, of the motives of our moiling *activity*—pertains to "every man," and all any particular individual needs to do is to fill in the blanks with his or her own particular wants or perplexities. Johnson's capacious terms contain them all.

The *Rambler's* extensive vocabulary seems unsurprising when we consider that while writing these essays Johnson proceeded apace on his great scholarly undertaking, *A Dictionary of the English Language*, which appeared in two volumes in 1755. Johnson's *Dictionary* would remain authoritative for a century and a half, until the appearance of the *Oxford English Dictionary*. Its greatest advance over earlier English dictionaries lies in Johnson's pioneering use of extensive literary quotations to illustrate the meanings of words. For each word in the *Dictionary*, Johnson supplies examples, chronologically arranged, of previous usage. Moreover, his definitions derive in large part from the illustrations he has arranged: Johnson's method is empirical. Take, for example, a word we saw Johnson himself use in *Rambler* no. 5—"perplex." Johnson's entry for this verb in his *Dictionary* begins with the etymology: the English word derives from the Latin *perplexus*. Next comes Johnson's definition of the primary sense of the word (other, less familiar senses will follow): "To disturb with doubtful notions; to entangle; to make anxious; to teaze with suspense or ambiguity; to distract; to embarrass; to puzzle." This definition is grounded in four quotations, from the King James version of the Bible (1611) through to John Locke's *Essay Concerning Human Understanding* (1690).

Johnson's work on the *Dictionary* led to the most innovative aspect of his prose style, especially the prose of the *Rambler*. As the great Johnson scholar William K. Wimsatt demonstrated fifty years ago, Johnson adapted many of the scientific terms he included in the *Dictionary* for the purposes of psychological analysis in the *Rambler*. "Frigorifick," for example, appears in the *Dictionary* with a lone illustration from John Quincy's *Lexicon Physico-Medicum* (4th ed., 1730) and the definition "causing cold. A word used in science." In the *Rambler*, however, Johnson ventures to use the term metaphorically, in the "frigorifick torpor" that presages death (no. 120), the "frigorifick power" of bashfulness (no. 159), and "the fatal influence of frigorifick wisdom" (no. 129). "Frigorifick" may not be the comeliest or most enduring of Johnson's metaphoric coinages, but Johnson also popularized the psychological use of terms that now sound more familiar: "acrimonious," "repulsion," "diffusion," "disruption," "dissipated," "effervescence," and "evanescence."

JOHNSON'S POLITICAL WRITINGS, INCLUDING LONDON AND THE LIFE OF MR. RICHARD SAVAGE

IN his *Dictionary*, Johnson self-deprecatingly defined "lexicographer" as "a harmless drudge"— but "Dictionary Johnson" was never a cloistered scholar. From early to late in his life, Johnson addressed topical political issues. In the London that Johnson entered in 1737, many writers (Pope among them) wrote in opposition to the policies of Sir Robert Walpole, George II's "prime minister" (the term began as a piece of opposition sarcasm and did not become an official title until 1905). Johnson embraced the ideals of the opposition. His pamphlet *Marmor Norfolciense* (1739) is a fictive account of an ancient "Norfolk Marble" that contains a gloomy prophecy of Walpole's England and that prophecy's ludicrous misinterpretation by a half-witted Walpole supporter. Johnson's satire includes the opposition themes of the day: attacks on standing armies as instruments of ministerial tyranny, on excise laws and commissioners, on bribing members of parliament with the lucrative public offices and pensions at the minister's disposal, and on ministerial extravagance and the government's consequent debt. The added spice of *Marmor Norfolciense* comes from its anti-Hanoverian sentiment—its satire on King George II as a foreigner who is heedless of England's present and future good.

Opposition themes may be found in other of Johnson's work from the 1730s and early 1740s, including another ironic-satiric pamphlet, *A Compleat Vindication of the Licensers of the Stage* of 1739 (Walpole, exasperated by theatrical attacks on his ministry, had ushered through parliament a statute allowing for the censorship or "licensing" of plays), and the poem *London*, whose embittered speaker explains why he must leave the metropolis:

Here let those reign, whom pensions can incite
To vote a patriot black, a courtier white;
Explain their country's dear-bought rights away,
And plead for pirates in the face of day;
With slavish tenets taint our poison'd youth,
And lend a lye [lie] the confidence of truth.
Let such raise palaces, and manors buy,
Collect a tax, or farm a lottery,
With warbling eunuchs fill a licens'd stage,
And lull to servitude a thoughtless age.
(Poems, pp. 50–51, ll. 51–60)

These lines allude to various forms of perceived political corruption. "Pleading for pirates" refers to Walpole's policy of allowing the Spanish to stop and search all ships trading with America, and "farming" a public lottery meant acquiring the very profitable right to run a lottery through paying a fixed amount to the government. The "warbling eunuchs" on Walpole's licensed stage were the castrati, Italian opera singers that (to opposition writers) represented the triumph of emasculated corruption over manly English virtue.

It was at this time of patriotic opposition fervor—and of living hand to mouth as a hack writer in London—that Johnson befriended the man who would become the subject of his biographical masterpiece, *An Account of the Life of Mr. Richard Savage* (1744). Savage, a talented but improvident poet, a denizen of London's colorful underworld, and a one-time murder suspect, was Johnson's friend when both men were struggling to get by in the late 1730s. Johnson later recalled one night, in particular, when, without money for lodging, he and Savage wandered about St. James's Square. As he put it, "not at all depressed by their situation; but in high spirits and brimful of patriotism, [they] traversed the square for several hours, inveighed against the minister, and 'resolved they would *stand by their country*'" (Chapman, 1980, p. 119). For all his claims to civic virtue, however, Savage was not above vicious behavior, including writing scandalous accounts of a noblewoman, the countess of Macclesfield, of whom he claimed to be the illegitimate, spurned, and persecuted son. Accepting this dubious claim is Johnson's one significant lapse from the impartial biographical stance he professes and, for the most part, practices in his *Life of Savage*. Yet Savage's anger at the noblewoman he supposes to be his mother translates into Johnson's broader indignation at social and judicial injustice during his years in opposition to Walpole.

After Walpole's resignation from office in 1742, the literature of opposition slowly but steadily lost steam, and with the accession in 1760 of George III, many who had disapproved of the earlier Georges warmed to the Hanoverian monarchy. Johnson joined his fellow Englishmen in celebrating George III as a potential "patriot king," committed to the common interest of all Britain and opposed to the narrow commercial interests of a wealthy Whig aristocracy. In 1762 Johnson accepted a government pension of three hundred pounds per annum, in honor of his literary achievements, despite having earlier defined a "pension" in his *Dictionary of the English Language* as "an allowance made to any one without an equivalent. In England it is generally understood to mean pay given to a state hireling for treason to his country." Johnson accepted his pension, however, because it was offered not for political services expected of him but for literary services already rendered.

Still, in the 1770s Lord North's ministry called upon Johnson to write several political pamphlets. *Thoughts on the Late Transactions Respecting Falkland's Islands* (1771) presents Johnson's defense of North's avoidance of war with Spain over conflicting claims to these South Atlantic islands. *The Patriot* (1774) defines its title figure as one "whose public conduct is regulated by one single motive, the love of his country; who, as an agent in Parliament, has for himself neither hope nor fear, neither kindness nor resentment, but refers every thing to the common interest" (*Political Writings*, p. 390). From this definition Johnson deduces:

He that wishes to see his country robbed of its rights, cannot be a Patriot.

That man therefore is no Patriot, who justifies the ridiculous claims of American usurpation; who endeavours to deprive the nation of its natural and lawful authority over its own colonies, which were settled under English protection; were constituted by an English charter; and have been defended by English arms.

(*Political Writings*, pp. 396–397)

His final reply to rebellious American colonists, *Taxation No Tyranny* (1775), is Johnson's most powerful piece of political writing; it also brought Johnson an honorific that later would come to be associated indelibly with his name. Johnson counters the resolutions of the American Continental Congress with carefully marshaled arguments. Taxation is not tyranny or enslavement, but a necessary governmental levy for the common welfare; Americans have benefited from the protection of the British government; and government does not derive its powers from the myth of representation (indeed, very few taxpayers in England were qualified to vote—Johnson himself was not). Johnson's most famous paragraph, however, comes near the end of the pamphlet: "We are told, that the subjection of Americans may tend to the diminution of our own liberties: an event, which none but very perspicacious politicians are able to foresee. If slavery be thus fatally contagious, how is it that we hear the loudest yelps for liberty among the drivers of negroes?" (*Political Writings,* p. 454). *Taxation No Tyranny* is, in all likelihood, what earned Johnson an honorary doctorate from Oxford University, of which Lord North was the chancellor, in March 1775. (Earlier, in 1765, Johnson had been awarded an honorary LL.D. from Trinity College, Dublin. Still, it was not until he was fifty-five years old that Johnson might be called—as he rarely was in his own lifetime but almost always has been since, thanks to James Boswell's *Life of Johnson*—"Dr. Johnson.")

Finally, we may classify among Johnson's political writings his account of a trip he made with James Boswell, *A Journey to the Western Islands of Scotland,* published in the same year as *Taxation No Tyranny* (1775). Historians and philosophers of the later eighteenth century were greatly interested in the evolution of civil society from hunting-gathering stages through pasturage and agriculture and finally to high urban or "commercial" civilization. At each stage of this development, they maintained, something was lost—virtue, self-sufficiency, and tribal ties—and something was gained—manners, politeness, and civic peace. In the popular imagination of the English and lowland Scots, the Scottish highlanders—especially those of the Hebridean islands Johnson and Boswell visited—embodied an earlier and in some ways more admirable stage of social evolution, figuring as patriarchic, cattle-driving Gaelic warriors and bards. Johnson debunked this popular, romantic image of the highlanders with a sobering portrait of a people uncomfortably suspended between two worlds, one dying—the patriarchal clan system with its pasturage economy—and one struggling to be born—the modern economic system of production and commerce.

JOHNSON'S GHOSTWRITING: LAW LECTURES AND SERMONS

JOHNSON often expressed regret that he had never entered the legal profession. He had studied law, and his mastery of theoretical jurisprudence was such that in the late 1760s he helped in writing the law lectures of his friend Robert Chambers, Vinerian Professor of English Law at Oxford. These lectures have been published in a modern edition, *A Course of Lectures on the English Law: Delivered at the University of Oxford 1767–1773 by Sir Robert Chambers . . . And Composed in Association with Samuel Johnson.*

At roughly the same time that he assisted Chambers with his law lectures, Johnson began ghostwriting sermons "for sundry beneficed clergymen that requested" them (*Sermons,* p. xxi). The Yale edition of Johnson's *Sermons* attributes twenty-eight to him, but this number may not represent the total number of sermons he wrote. Of those now attributed to Johnson, most were written for his friend John Taylor, a clergyman in Westminster. Johnson's sermons, in theme and style, belong to a great tradition of Anglican preaching extending back through John Tillotson and Richard Hooker to the Tudor Book of Homilies. As a homilist, Johnson's main topics include charity, the respective obligations of governors and the governed, the vanity of human wishes, the evil of intellectual pride, and the doctrine of Holy Communion.

A more intimate glimpse of Johnson's Christian life may be found in his diaries and private prayers. Although he burned most of his diaries before his death, the portions that remain may be found in the Yale edition of Johnson's *Diaries, Prayers, and Annals.* In the prayers he composed, Johnson exhorts himself to live better—to rise earlier, work harder, and use his God-given talents more assiduously. Remarkably, Johnson—one of the most productive authors of all time—privately thought of himself as a sensualist and idler and feared for his immortal soul.

CRITICISM AND BIOGRAPHY: THE LIVES OF THE ENGLISH POETS

JOHNSON'S final enterprise, late in life, consisted of writing biographical and critical prefaces for each of the fifty-two poets, from Abraham Cowley to George Lyttleton, contained in the sixty-eight-volume set *Works of the English Poets* (1779–1781). In 1781, Johnson's prefaces were published separately as a four-volume set, *The Lives of the Most Eminent English Poets*; the work is now commonly known as Johnson's *Lives of the Poets.* Along with his preface to *The Plays of William Shakespeare,* the best of the *Lives*—those of Cowley, Milton, John Dryden, Pope, and Thomas Gray—have earned Johnson a claim to being the greatest literary critic in English, a man whose general principles of literary merit derived from his expert responses to individual literary works.

In *Lives of the Poets,* Johnson qualifies his criterion of literary pleasure as, more specifically, the pleasure of the "common reader" (the phrase is Johnson's)—that is, the reader without great or exceptional erudition and without rarified or perverse taste (there is no accounting for oddballs, Johnson implies). Thus, Johnson writes of Abraham Cowley and the "metaphysical" school of seventeenth-century English poetry: "As the authors of this race [i.e., family, type] were perhaps more desirous of being admired than understood they sometimes drew their conceits [conceptions or metaphors] from recesses of learning not very much frequented by common readers of poetry" (*The Lives of the English Poets,* vol. 1, p. 23). (He goes on to chide poetical passages from Cowley that presume an arcane knowledge of "that right Porphyrian tree," "Meleager's fate," and "th' antiperistasis of age.") Johnson greatly preferred Thomas Gray's popular poem *Elegy Written in a Country Churchyard* (1751), especially the four stanzas on the rough-hewn tombstones of the village poor (ll. 76–92):

In the character of his *Elegy* I rejoice to concur with the common reader; for by the common sense of readers uncorrupted with literary prejudices, after all the refinements of subtlety and the dogmatism of learning, must be finally decided all claim to poetical honours. The *Church-yard* abounds with images which find a mirrour in every mind, and with sentiments to which every bosom returns an echo. The four stanzas beginning 'Yet even these bones' are to me original: I have never seen the notions in any other place; yet he that reads them here persuades himself that he has always felt them. Had Gray written often thus, it had been vain to blame, and useless to praise him.

(*Lives of the English Poets*, vol. 3, pp. 441–442)

We may note in passing the features of Johnson's late prose style, as displayed in this passage. It is a less commanding and more conversational style than that which is found in the *Rambler* or even in his preface to *The Plays of William Shakespeare*; it has been tailored, we may surmise, in some measure to Johnson's notion of the common reader. However, Johnson's sentences retain comprehensiveness— and thus authority—carefully crafted through antithesis ("I have never seen the notions . . . yet he that reads them . . . has always felt them"), balance ("images which find a mirrour . . . sentiments to which every bosom returns an echo"), and both ("vain to blame, and useless to praise him").

There is a greater proportion of criticism to biography in Johnson's later *Lives* than in his earlier *Life of Savage,* but the biographical element remains crucial. Each of Johnson's fifty-two *Lives* shares the same tripartite structure. First, there is a birth-to-death account of the poet's life (more or less extensive, depending on what Johnson knew or could gather about the poet); second comes an analysis and assessment of the poet's general character as a man and as a writer; and, third, there follows a critical essay that canvases the poet's works in chronological order. Within each *Life,* then, Johnson had ample room for biographical observation, and nowhere else in his vast writings are his insights into human psychology more subtle or acute—as a glance at Johnson's *Life of Pope* may suggest. Johnson describes Pope's teenage years:

He then returned [from studying French and Italian in London] to Binfield, and delighted himself with his own poetry. He tried all styles, and many subjects. He wrote a comedy, a tragedy, an epick poem, with panegyricks on all the princes of Europe; and, as he confesses, "thought himself the greatest genius that ever was." Self-confidence is the first requisite to great undertakings; he, indeed, who forms his opinion of himself in solitude, without knowing the powers of other men, is very liable to errour: but it was the felicity of Pope to rate himself at his real value. . . .

He that is pleased with himself easily imagines that he shall please others. Sir William Trumbal, who had been ambassador at Constantinople, and secretary of state, when he retired from business fixed his residence in the neighbourhood of Binfield. Pope, not yet sixteen, was introduced to the statesman of sixty, and so distinguished himself that their interviews ended in friendship and correspondence. Pope was through his whole life ambitious of splendid acquaintance, and he seems to have wanted [lacked] neither diligence nor success in attracting the notice of the great; for from his first entrance into the world, and his entrance was very early, he was admitted to familiarity with those whose rank or station made them most conspicuous.

(*Lives of the English Poets*, vol. 3, pp. 89–90)

In Johnson's telling, while Pope's boyish self-confidence never wanes, it does, in early maturity, run against the clock. Pope begins his great verse translation of Homer's *Iliad* in 1712, at the age of twenty-five, and finishes it in 1718, at thirty. This biographical fact occasions one of Johnson's general observations on human life:

The progress of Pope may seem to have been slow; but the distance is commonly very great between actual performances and speculative possibility. It is natural to suppose, that as much as has been done to-day may be done to-morrow; but on the morrow some difficulty emerges, or some external impediment obstructs. Indolence, interruption, business, and pleasure, all take their turns at retardation; and every long work is lengthened by a thousand causes that can, and ten thousand that cannot, be recounted. Perhaps no extensive and multifarious performance was ever effected within the term originally fixed in the undertaker's mind. He that runs against Time has an antagonist not subject to casualties.

(*Lives of the English Poets*, vol. 3, p. 117)

Time is ever the writer's antagonist; his chief anxiety, however, is typically the quality of his public reception and the uncertainty of his enduring fame. Johnson is at his satiric best in treating Pope's pique at the unfavorable reception of his poem *An Epistle to the Right Honourable Richard Earl of Burlington*:

Pope, in one of his letters, complaining of the treatment which his poem had found, "owns that such criticks can intimidate him, nay almost persuade him to write no more, which is a compliment this age deserves." The man who threatens the world is always ridiculous; for the world can easily go on without him, and in a short time will cease to miss him. . . . Pope had been flattered till he thought himself one of the moving powers in the system of life. When he talked of laying down his pen, those who sat around him intreated and implored, and self-love did not suffer him to suspect that they went away and laughed.

(*Lives of the English Poets*, vol. 3, pp. 153–154)

Johnson's lesson is that as self-love grows exorbitant, it grows ridiculous—even the self-love of a genius (so much the worse for the rest of us).

Johnson takes it upon himself in his *Lives* to instruct and—through the achievement of his prose—to instruct by pleasing. Biography for quite some time had seemed to him the perfect vehicle for doing so. In the *Rambler* no. 60, Johnson maintained, "No species of writing seems more worthy of cultivation than biography, since none can be more delightful or more useful" (*Rambler*, vol. 3, p. 319). In the *Idler* no. 84, Johnson revisits his praise of biography and speculates that a frank and candid *autobiography* might be more useful still, since "he that recounts the life of another, commonly dwells most upon conspicuous events, lessens the familiarity of his tale to increase its dignity, . . . and endeavours to hide the man that he may produce a hero" (*The Idler and the Adventurer*, p. 262). By an ironic twist of fate, in the nineteenth century Johnson's voluminous writings were largely superseded by his role in a new kind of biography, one that

incorporated autobiographical elements (such as private letters and prayers) and that clearly aimed at displaying a man as well as a hero. That biography was written not by but about Samuel Johnson.

BOSWELL AND THE LIFE OF JOHNSON

JOHNSON is the subject of the greatest biography ever written—James Boswell's monumental *Life of Samuel Johnson* (1791). Boswell (1740–1795) recognized that his biography was unprecedented. Writing to a friend in 1788 (in *Letters of James Boswell*, edited by Chauncy B. Tinker), he said:

I am absolutely certain that *my* mode of biography, which gives not only a *history* of Johnson's *visible* progress through the world, and of his publications, but a *view* of his mind, in his letters and conversations, is the most perfect that can be conceived, and will be *more* of a *Life* than any work that has ever yet appeared.

In addition to working from letters, documents, and whatever facts and anecdotes he could collect from Johnson's other acquaintances, Boswell—who spent approximately four hundred days in Johnson's presence between their meeting in 1763 and Johnson's death in 1784—learned to render Johnson's conversations more vividly than conversations had ever before been rendered. He kept a journal of his conversations with Johnson and fleshed out Johnson's voice with creative zest. He also employed dramatic techniques in the *Life*, animating many of his encounters with Johnson as theatrical scenes, complete with buildups and denouements and parenthetical cues that clarify the developing tone of a conversation, for example, "said he, with a stern look" or "laughing heartily as I spoke."

One of Boswell's great scenes dramatizes his own first meeting with Johnson in Mr. Davies's bookshop on 16 May 1763. The Scottish Boswell, then twenty-two years old, had been in London since the previous November, attempting without success to gain a commission in the Foot Guards. Johnson, then fifty-four, was the literary lion of London. In awe of his literary reputation, Boswell was also wary of his supposed prejudice against Scots (in his *Dictionary*, Johnson had puckishly defined "oats" as "a grain, which in England is generally given to horses, but in Scotland supports the people"). Boswell re-creates their meeting:

At last, on Monday the 16th of May, when I was sitting in Mr. Davies's back-parlour, after having drunk tea with him and Mrs. Davies, Johnson unexpectedly came into the shop; and Mr. Davies having perceived him through the glass-door in the room in which we were sitting, advancing towards us,—he announced his aweful approach to me, somewhat in the manner of an actor in the part of Horatio, when he addresses Hamlet on the appearance of his father's ghost, "Look, my Lord, it comes." . . . Mr. Davies mentioned my name, and respectfully introduced me to him. I was much agitated; and recollecting his prejudice against the Scotch, of which I had heard much, I said to Davies, "Don't tell him where I come from."—"From Scotland," cried Davies roguishly. "Mr. Johnson, (said I) I do indeed come from Scotland, but I cannot help it." I am willing to flatter myself that I meant this as a light pleasantry to sooth and conciliate him, and not as an humiliating abasement at the expence of my own country. But however that might be, this speech was somewhat unlucky; he seized the expression "come from Scotland," which I used in the sense of being of that country, and, as if I had said that I had come away from it, or left it, retorted, "That, Sir, I find, is what a very great many of your countrymen cannot help." This stroke stunned me a good deal; and when we had sat down, I felt myself not a little embarrassed, and apprehensive of what might come next. He then addressed himself to Davies: "What do you think of Garrick? He has refused me an order for the play for Miss Williams [one of the waifs who then comprised Johnson's household], because he knows the house will be full, and that an order would be worth three shillings." Eager to take any opening to get into conversation with him, I ventured to say, "O, Sir, I cannot think Mr. Garrick would grudge such a trifle to you." "Sir, (said he, with a stern look,) I have known David Garrick longer than you have done: and I know no right you have to talk to me on the subject." Perhaps I deserved this check, for it was rather presumptuous in me, an entire stranger, to express any doubt of the justice of his animadversion upon his old acquaintance and pupil. I now felt myself much mortified, and began to think that the hope which I had long indulged of obtaining his acquaintance was blasted. . . . Fortunately, however, I remained upon the field not wholly discomfited; and was soon rewarded by hearing some of his conversation.

(Chapman, 1980, pp. 276–278)

Among the ensuing gems of Johnson's conversation is this: "The notion of liberty amuses the people of England, and helps to keep off the *taedium vitae*. When a butcher tells you that *his heart bleeds for his country*, he has, in fact, no uneasy feeling" (Chapman, 1980, p. 279). Johnson sees through all cant, be it a butcher's stock expression of patriotism or Boswell's merely polite expres-

sion of belief in the deference owed by Garrick to his former schoolmaster. And lest we end the scene persuaded of Johnson's penetration, but despairing of his heart, Boswell concludes:

I had, for a part of the evening, been left alone with him, and had ventured to make an observation now and then, which he received very civilly; so that I was satisfied that though there was a roughness in his manner, there was no ill-nature in his disposition. Davies followed me to the door, and when I complained to him a little of the hard blows which the great man had given me, he kindly took it upon him to console me by saying, "Don't be uneasy. I can see he likes you very well."

(Chapman, 1980, p. 279)

It was, of course, the beginning of a famous friendship. Eight days after their initial meeting Boswell paid Johnson a visit at his home:

He received me very courteously; but, it must be confessed, that his apartment, and furniture, and morning dress, were sufficiently uncouth. His brown suit of cloaths looked very rusty; he had on a little old shriveled unpowdered wig, which was too small for his head; his shirt-neck and knees of his breeches were loose; his black worsted stockings ill drawn up; and he had a pair of unbuckled shoes by way of slippers. But all these slovenly particularities were forgotten the moment that he began to talk.

(Chapman, 1980, p. 280–281)

When Boswell eventually rises to leave, Johnson detains him: "Nay, don't go. . . . Sir, I am obliged to any man who visits me" (Chapman, 1980, p. 281).

Johnson's is a touching avowal, its genuineness underscored by the gruffness he had displayed earlier, at Davies' shop. Johnson, we now know, is not one to bandy empty civilities or to stand on ceremony. He can be bluff or pugnacious, but—it turns out—he is also quite vulnerable. By this point in his narrative, Boswell the biographer, as distinct from the young character who enters Johnson's life in 1763, has already allowed us glimpses of Johnson's "vile melancholy" (Chapman, 1980, p. 27) and unsettling obsessions. Writing early in his biography about Johnson's tics and convulsive movements, Boswell introduces the opinion of their friend Sir Joshua Reynolds:

Those motions or tricks of Dr. Johnson are improperly called convulsions. He could sit motionless, when he was told to do so, as well as any other man; my opinion is that it proceeded from a habit which he had indulged himself in, of accompanying his thoughts with certain untoward actions, and those actions always appeared to me as if they were meant to reprobate some part of his past conduct. Whenever he was not engaged in conversation, such thoughts were sure to rush into his mind; and, for this reason, any company, any employment whatever, he preferred to being alone. The great business of his life (he said) was to escape from himself; this disposition he considered as the disease of his mind, which nothing cured but company.

(Chapman, 1980, pp. 105–106)

Aside from past behavior painfully recollected (though why it brings pain we are never told), Johnson's thoughts gravitate toward death; he once confessed to Boswell, "The whole of life is but keeping away the thoughts of it" (Chapman, 1980, p. 416). To keep bad thoughts at bay, Johnson sought company—visitors, guests, taverns, clubs, the whole sociable metropolis brought to life in Boswell's pages. ("When a man is tired of London," Boswell records Johnson saying, "he is tired of life; for there is in London all that life can afford" [Chapman, 1980, p. 859]). He also acquired a large household of dependents, including the blind Miss Anna Williams; the mysterious Poll Carmichael, who was, in all likelihood, a prostitute Johnson had rescued from the streets; and Robert Levet, an unlicensed physician who worked among London's poor. (Johnson would immortalize Levet in a touching elegy, "On the Death of Dr. Robert Levet.") Boswell offers in his biography's concluding character sketch these thoughts about both Johnson's troubled mind and his charitable conduct:

The solemn text, "of him to whom much is given, much will be required" [Luke 12:48], seems to have been ever present in his mind, in a rigorous sense, and to have made him dissatisfied with his labours and acts of goodness, however comparatively great; so that the unavoidable consciousness of his superiority was, in that respect, a cause of disquiet. He suffered so much from this, and from the gloom which perpetually haunted him, and made solitude frightful, that it might be said of him, "If in this life only he had hope, he was of all men most miserable."

(Chapman, 1980, p. 1400)

In the *Life of Johnson*, Boswell proves his genius for delineating character and crafting dialogue. Boswell's Johnson is a vivid and unforgettable character, brought to life by his conversation—his seemingly endless supply of opinion, wit, and repartee—and by his tics, eccentricities, largely harmless prejudices, and very real pains. This Johnson—"*Dr.* Johnson," as Boswell has bequeathed him to us—is a blunt man who renders sure verdicts on all matters, a gruff old bear of a man who can barely conceal a heart of gold, and a sociable man who heroically holds at bay the inner demons that threaten to consume him. He is one of the greatest literary characters in English, along with those of Shakespeare, Charles Dickens, and George Eliot.

It is from Boswell's *Life of Johnson* that we get many of the best-known Johnson quips, those that are to be found in most dictionaries of quotations. "No man but a blockhead ever wrote, except for money" (p. 731). "No man will be a sailor who has contrivance enough to get himself into a jail; for being in a ship is being in a jail, with the chance of being drowned" (pp. 246–247). "Sir, a woman's preaching is like a dog's walking on his hinder legs. It is not done well; but you are surprised to find it done at all" (p. 327). "A gentleman who had been very unhappy in marriage, married immediately after his wife died: Johnson said, it was the triumph of hope over experience" (p. 444).

By a curious twist of literary history, in the nineteenth century Johnson the writer was to a large extent eclipsed by "Dr. Johnson," the literary character deftly sculpted by Boswell from Johnson's own personality. The decided preference for Boswell's Johnson to Johnson the writer can be dated back at least as far as William Hazlitt, writing in 1819 (found in his *Selected Writings*, edited by Ronald Blythe):

The most triumphant record of the talents and character of Johnson is to be found in Boswell's *Life* of him. The man was superior to the author. When he threw aside his pen . . . he became not only learned and thoughtful, but acute, witty, humorous, natural, honest; hearty and determined, "the king of good fellows and wale [best] of old men."

Hazlitt's sentiments were echoed and expanded upon by other great nineteenth-century men of letters, most notably Thomas Carlyle and Thomas Macaulay.

In the twentieth century, critics have done much to bolster Johnson's reputation as a writer, and scholars have made great progress toward ascertaining and editing the full body of his extensive writings (not always easy with a writer whose work was often anonymous or written for others).

Numerous biographies—by James Clifford, Walter Jackson Bate, Robert DeMaria, and others—have greatly increased our knowledge of Johnson the man and the writer. Developments in both Boswell and Johnson studies also have taught us to be skeptical of some of Boswell's claims about Johnson (for example, that he was from birth to death a Jacobite, or supporter of the deposed Stuart line of British monarchs). Some scholars, most notably Donald Greene, through research into Boswell's manuscripts have come to doubt the style and the substance of many of the quotations Boswell attributed to Johnson. Nevertheless, Boswell's *Life of Johnson* remains indispensable, a literary masterpiece that affords a rich view, however tinted, into Johnson and the literary London of his later years.

JOHNSON'S GREAT THEME: THE PURSUIT OF HAPPINESS

As a moralist—whether in his own writings or in the pages of Boswell—Johnson's chief theme is quite simply the pursuit of happiness. In 1739 Johnson writes of the notion of a "Ruling Passion": "I am conscious of none but the general desire of happiness" (annotations to Jean Pierre de Crousaz's *Commentary* on Pope's *Essay on Man*, in *Samuel Johnson: A Critical Edition of the Major Works*, p. 92). In a work published eighteen years later, his book review of Soame Jenyns' *Free Inquiry into the Nature and Origin of Evil* (*Literary Magazine*, 1757), Johnson approves of little in Jenyns save for his "opinion of the value and importance of happiness." He quotes it thus: "Happiness is the only thing of real value in existence" (*Major Works*, p. 530).

The question, then, becomes this: What did Johnson mean by the term "happiness"? Johnson used the term in two distinct and perhaps incompatible ways. First, there is what we might call Johnson's "phenomenological" use of "happiness" to refer to "persistently deferred satisfaction." Phenomenology, as I use the term here, aims at a description of things not as they are but as they appear to consciousness. For Johnson, happiness is phenomenologically distinctive, as that which does not appear to present consciousness—at least not unaltered consciousness. While the better part of Johnson's *Rasselas* could be read as concerning this sense of happiness, Johnson's most succinct illustration of it comes from a conversation with Boswell from 10 April 1775:

[Johnson] this day enlarged upon Pope's melancholy remark, "Man never *is*, but always *to be* blest." He asserted that *the present* is never a happy state to any human being; but that, as every part of life, of which we are conscious, was at some point a period yet to come, in which felicity was expected, there was some happiness produced by hope. Being pressed upon this subject, and asked if he really was of opinion, that though, in general, happiness was very rare in human life, a man was not sometimes happy in the moment that was present, he answered, "Never, but when he is drunk."

(Chapman, 1980, pp. 617–618)

Johnson's point here seems to be that as long as people retain their intellectual faculties—that is, as long as one is not completely drunk—the present moment cannot satisfy. A person will always seek "supplemental satisfactions" (a phrase that Johnson uses in *Rambler* no. 41) from the contemplation of the past and the future. This temporal condition is clarified in a later exchange with Boswell from 29 March 1776. [Boswell:] "'Sir, you observed one day at General Oglethorpe's, that a man is never happy for the present, but when he is drunk. Will you not add,—or when driving rapidly in a post-chaise?' JOHNSON. 'No, Sir, you are driving rapidly *from* something, or *to* something'" (Chapman, 1980, p. 720). There is, in Johnson's phenomenology of happiness, an apprehension of the vacuity of the present moment that derives ultimately from the voice of Ecclesiastes: "The eye is not satisfied with seeing, nor the ear filled with hearing" (1:8). Like Ecclesiastes, both *The Vanity of Human Wishes* and *Rasselas* concerns the unavailability of happiness—if happiness is understood as present satisfaction or contentment.

Yet Johnson often uses the term "happiness" in a second way, to denote something that is to a greater or lesser degree available. Thus Johnson pronounced to Boswell in February 1766: "Sir, that all who are happy, are equally happy, is not true. A peasant and a philosopher may be equally *satisfied*, but not equally *happy*. Happiness consists in the multiplicity of agreeable consciousness. A peasant has not capacity for having equal happiness with a philosopher" (Chapman, 1980, p. 357). Johnson here harks back in a general way to classical notions of the happy or flourishing life as the one form of life that is best for everyone, although it is not in everyone's power to attain. More specifically, Johnson appears to allude to Aristotle's argument against identifying happiness with pleasure or present satisfaction. Aristotle notes that one can be entirely satisfied with one's life and still fail to achieve what others would recognize as "happiness." In *Nichomachean Ethics,* he adduces the case of the mentally retarded adult: "No one would choose to live his entire life with the mentality of a child, even if he were to enjoy to the fullest possible extent what children can enjoy."

We might say that the childish adult, or Johnson's peasant, has not the same capacity for happiness as the philosopher because happiness involves a certain caliber of rational activity. Johnson clarifies this point in a conversation from April 1778, during one of the periodic intervals in which he abstained from wine: "BOSWELL. 'I think, sir, you once said to me, that not to drink wine was a great deduction from life.' JOHNSON. 'It is a diminution of pleasure, to be sure; but I do not say a diminution of happiness. There is more happiness in being rational'" (Chapman, 1980, p. 911).

For Aristotle, the objective good for a human being is a virtuous life guided by reason and graced by good fortune—this is human flourishing and also, secondarily, subjective happiness. Johnson's second notion of happiness is a neoclassical one; it is also the one that he shared with the better part of his literary contemporaries (it lies, for example, behind Thomas Jefferson's famous triad of "life, liberty, and the pursuit of happiness"). This rational happiness or flourishing that humans can attain, in either a qualified or an unqualified manner, is the happiness of which Johnson generally speaks in his periodical essays and sermons. Johnson's one change of heart concerning this ideal of happiness is that he begins his literary career believing, as Aristotle did, that political activity is central to it; this is the Johnson of the late 1730s, resolute against the evils of Walpole's ministry and "brimful of patriotism." Later in life, however, Johnson came to agree with the Hellenistic philosophers who succeeded Aristotle—especially those of the ancient Stoic and Epicurean schools—that human flourishing had little to do, fundamentally, with forms of government or political conditions. In the coda Johnson wrote for his friend Oliver Goldsmith's poem *The Traveller* (1764), which can be found in Goldsmith's *Collected Works,* edited by Arthur Friedman, we find:

> How small, of all that human hearts endure,
> That part which laws or kings can cause or cure.
> Still to ourselves in every place consign'd,
> Our own felicity we make or find . . .
> (ll. 429–432)

He confirmed in March of 1772, "I would not give half a guinea to live under one form of government rather than another. It is of no moment to the happiness of an individual" (Chapman, 1980, p. 477).

Johnson's stance on rational happiness may be summarized through the following *Rambler* citations. Although there is only in an afterlife with God "total happiness" (vol. 3, p. 151)—and hence only religious hope can appease "decaying man" (p. 367)—a "reasonable being" on this side of the deathbed nonetheless has in his power "a great part . . . of his present happiness" (p. 159). As Johnson maintained in one of the sermons he wrote for his friend John Taylor, "While it is in our power to be virtuous, it is in our power to be happy, at least to be happy to such a degree as may have little room for murmur and complaints" (*Sermons,* p. 55). Through nearly all of the many genres in which he worked—from poetry and prose fiction to political tracts and sermons and literary lives—it was Johnson's constant aim as a moralist to teach us the way to reasonable happiness. He made clear that the happiness of rational beings is not the same as present contentment or satisfaction but is rather attendance to the dictates of reason and conscience and, finally, of faith. This lesson, which draws upon classical and Christian traditions of virtue, continues to impress and challenge readers with its poignant humanity.

SELECTED BIBLIOGRAPHY

I. COLLECTED WORKS. *The Yale Edition of the Works of Samuel Johnson* (New Haven, 1958–), comprising *Diaries, Prayers, and Annals* (1959), ed. by E. L. McAdam, Jr., with Donald and Mary Hyde; The Idler *and* The Adventurer (1963), ed. by W. J. Bate, John M. Bullitt, and L. F. Powell; *Poems* (1964), ed. by E. L. McAdam, Jr., with George Milne; *Johnson on Shakespeare,* 2 vols. (1968), ed. by Arthur Sherbo; *The Rambler,* 3 vols. (1969), ed. by W. J. Bate and Albrecht Strauss; *A Journey to the Western Islands of Scotland* (1971), ed. by Mary Lascelles; *Political Writings* (1977), ed. by Donald J. Greene; *Sermons* (1978), ed. by Jean Hagstrum and James Gray; *A Voyage to Abyssinia* (1985), ed. by Joel J. Gold; *Rasselas and Other Tales* (1990), ed. by Gwin J. Kolb.

The Works, 13 vols. (London, 1787), ed. by Sir John Hawkins and J. Stockdale; *The Works,* 12 vols. (London, 1806), ed. by Alexander Chalmers; *The Lives of the English Poets,* 3 vols. (Oxford, 1905), ed. by George Birkbeck Hill; *Samuel Johnson's Prefaces and Dedications* (New Haven, 1937), ed. by Allen T. Hazen; *The Letters of Samuel Johnson, with Mrs. Thrale's Genuine Letters to Him,*

3 vols. (Oxford, 1952), ed. by R. W. Chapman; *Johnson's Dictionary: A Modern Selection* (New York, 1963), ed. by E. L. McAdam, Jr., and George Milne; *The Life of Savage* (Oxford, 1971), ed. by Clarence Tracy; *Samuel Johnson: Rasselas, Poems, and Selected Prose* (New York, 1971), ed. by Bertrand Harris Bronson; *Selected Poetry and Prose* (Berkeley, 1977), ed. by Frank Brady and W. K. Wimsatt; *Samuel Johnson: The Major Works* (Oxford, 1984), ed. by Donald Greene; *A Course of Lectures on the English Law: Delivered at the University of Oxford 1767–1773 by Sir Robert Chambers . . . and Composed in Association with Samuel Johnson*, 2 vols. (Madison, Wis., 1986), ed. by Thomas Curley; *The Letters of Samuel Johnson*, 5 vols. (Princeton, 1992–1994), ed. by Bruce Redford.

II. SEPARATE WORKS. *A Voyage to Abyssinia* (London, 1735), translation from the French version of the travelogue of a Portuguese Jesuit, Jeronimo Lobo; *London: A Poem* (London, 1738), a creative adaptation of Juvenal's *Third Satire*; *A Compleat Vindication of the Licensers of the Stage* (London, 1739), satiric pamphlet; *Marmor Norfolciense* (London, 1739), political pamphlet; *Life of Mr. Richard Savage* (London, 1744), biography; *Irene: A Tragedy* (London, 1749), a play; *The Vanity of Human Wishes* (London, 1749), a creative adaptation of Juvenal's *Tenth Satire*; *Rambler* (London, 1750–1752), essays; *A Dictionary of the English Language*, 2 vols. (London, 1755); *The History of Rasselas, Prince of Abyssinia*, 2 vols. (London, 1759), a philosophical tale; *The Plays of William Shakespeare*, 8 vols. (London, 1765; 10 vols., 1773), ed. by Samuel Johnson; *Thoughts on the Late Transactions Respecting Falkland's Islands* (London, 1771), political pamphlet; *The Patriot* (London, 1774), political writings; *Taxation No Tyranny* (London, 1775), political pamphlet; *A Journey to the Western Islands of Scotland* (London, 1775), political travelogue; *Prefaces to the Works of the English Poets*, 10 vols. (London, 1779–1781), reiss. as *The Lives of the English Poets*, 4 vols. (London, 1781), biographical and critical writings.

III. BIBLIOGRAPHY. J. D. Fleeman, *A Bibliography of the Works of Samuel Johnson, Treating His Published Works from the Beginnings to 1984*, 2 vols. (Oxford, 2000).

IV. BIOGRAPHICAL STUDIES. Hester Thrale Piozzi, *Anecdotes of the Late Samuel Johnson* (London, 1786); Sir John Hawkins, *Life of Samuel Johnson* (London, 1787); George Birkbeck Hill, ed., *Johnsonian Miscellanies*, 2 vols. (Oxford, 1897), includes Hester Thrale Piozzi's *Anecdotes of the Late Samuel Johnson* and Sir John Hawkins' *Life of Samuel Johnson*; John Boswell, *Life of Johnson*, ed. by George Birkbeck Hill and rev. by L. H. Powell (Oxford: 1934–1964), includes *Journal of a Tour to the Hebrides with Samuel Johnson*; James Lowry Clifford, *Young Sam Johnson* (New York, 1955).

Paul Fussell, *Samuel Johnson and the Life of Writing* (New York, 1971); O. M. Brack, Jr., and Robert E. Kelley, eds. *The Early Biographies of Samuel Johnson* (Iowa City, 1974); John Wain, *Samuel Johnson* (London, 1974); Walter Jackson Bate, *Samuel Johnson* (New York, 1977); James

Lowry Clifford, *Dictionary Johnson* (New York, 1979); *Life of Samuel Johnson*, ed. by R. W. Chapman with intro. by Pat Rogers (Oxford and New York, 1980), Boswell's biography; *Journey to the Western Islands of Scotland and* The Journal of a Tour to the Hebrides, ed. by Peter Levi (Harmondsworth, England, 1984); Thomas Kaminski, *The Early Career of Samuel Johnson* (New York, 1987); Robert DeMaria, Jr., *The Life of Samuel Johnson: A Critical Biography* (Oxford, England, and Cambridge, Mass., 1993); Lawrence Lipking, *Samuel Johnson: The Life of an Author* (Cambridge, Mass., 1998).

IV. CRITICAL STUDIES. William K. Wimsatt, *Philosophic Words: A Study of Style and Meaning in the* Rambler *and* Dictionary *of Samuel Johnson* (New Haven, 1948); Walter Jackson Bate, *The Achievement of Samuel Johnson* (New York, 1955); Jean H. Hagstrum, *Samuel Johnson's Literary Criticism* (Chicago, 1967); James Lowry Clifford and Donald Greene, *Samuel Johnson: A Survey and Bibliography of Critical Studies* (Minneapolis, 1970); T. S. Eliot, "Johnson as Critic and Poet," in his *On Poets and Poetry* (London, 1971); James Gray, *Johnson's Sermons: A Study* (Oxford, 1972); William Vesterman, *The Stylistic Life of Samuel Johnson* (New Brunswick, N.J., 1977); William C. Dowling, *The Boswellian Hero* (Athens, Ga., 1979).

Isobel Grundy, ed., *Samuel Johnson: New Critical Essays* (Totowa, N.J., 1984); Fredric V. Bogel, *Literature and Insubstantiality in Later Eighteenth-Century England* (Princeton, 1984); Donald Greene and John A. Vance, *A Bibliography of Johnsonian Studies, 1970–1985* (Victoria, British Columbia, 1987); Paul Korshin, ed., *The Age of Johnson* (New York, 1987–), scholarly annual; Nicholas Hudson, *Samuel Johnson and Eighteenth-Century Thought* (Oxford and New York, 1988); Edward Tomarken, *Johnson, Rasselas, and the Choice of Criticism* (Lexington, Ky., 1989); Leo Damrosch, *Fictions of Reality in the Age of Hume and Johnson* (Madison, 1989).

Allen Reddick, *The Making of Johnson's* Dictionary, *1746–1773* (Cambridge, England, and New York, 1990); Donald Greene, "The Logia of Samuel Johnson and the Quest for the Historical Johnson," in *The Age of Johnson: A Scholarly Annual* 3 (1990); Donald Greene, *The Politics of Samuel Johnson*, 2nd ed. (Athens, Ga., 1990); John Cannon, *Samuel Johnson and the Politics of Hanoverian England* (Oxford and New York, 1994); Greg Clingham, ed., *The Cambridge Companion to Samuel Johnson* (Cambridge, England, and New York, 1997); David F. Venturo, *Johnson the Poet: The Poetic Career of Samuel Johnson* (Newark, Del., and London, 1999); Jack Lynch, *A Bibliography of Johnsonian Studies 1986–1998* (New York, 2000); Adam Potkay, *The Passion for Happiness: Samuel Johnson and David Hume* (Ithaca, N.Y., 2000); Steven Scherwatzky, "Complicated Virtue: The Politics of Johnson's Life of Savage," in *Eighteenth-Century Life* 25 (Fall 2001).

VI. INTERNET RESOURCES. Jack Lynch maintains an updated bibliography of Johnson studies at http://andromeda.rutgers.edu/~jlynch/Johnson/.

BEN JONSON

(1572–1637)

Charles Robert Baker

THAT WE KNOW anything at all of Ben Jonson's childhood is something of a miracle. He was just one child of many born on an uncertain day in an uncertain place. Indeed, were it not for a remarkable piece of writing commonly known as "Ben Jonson's Conversations with William Drummond of Hawthornden" (cited in Herford et al., vol. 1, appendix I), virtually nothing would be known of Jonson's early years. The conversations took place in late December 1618 and early January 1619, when Jonson was the most celebrated literary figure in England. At forty-six, Jonson had decided to make a walking tour of the countryside between London and Edinburgh, following the King's Highway. He was received with great ceremony in the Scottish capital and was welcomed as a guest at Drummond's castle in Hawthornden, nine miles south of Edinburgh. The wealthy squire, and a poet in his own right, kept a record of Jonson's three-week stay. Jonson may not have been aware of Drummond's note taking, for much of the record is mere literary gossip and unflattering portraits of fellow writers. Jonson did speak briefly about his childhood and education, however. Centuries of biographical detective work have added much to Drummond's somewhat terse information, but without Drummond there would have been no reliable starting point.

ANCESTRY AND CHILDHOOD

IT appears that Jonson took pride in his Scottish ancestry. He related to Drummond that his grandfather "came from Carlisle, and he thought from Annandale to it, he served Henry VIII, and was a gentleman" (Herford et al., vol. 1, p. 139). From this one can gather that Jonson's grandfather switched monarchical allegiance during the border wars of the 1540s. Many Scots did this, preferring a new life under Henry VIII to the one they had had under the disgraced and despised Scottish king, James V. There was no dishonor or disloyalty attached to such a choice of action, and Jonson proudly took up

the family coat of arms. Jonson's father, according to Drummond's notes, "lost all his estates under Queen Mary, having been cast in prison and forfeited, at last turned minister: so he was a minister's son" (Herford et al., vol. 1, p. 139). Mary Tudor, "Bloody Mary" as she was known, ascended the throne in 1553, after the deaths of her father, Henry VIII, and her half-brother, Edward VI. She made it clear from the start that it was her intention to bring her Protestant subjects back to the Old Faith, the Roman Catholic Church, by whatever means necessary. During her five-year reign, those who held fast to their Reform beliefs suffered the consequences in a variety of ways, ranging from loss of property to public execution. What Jonson's father suffered in prison, or how long he was held there, is not known, but it was not enough to persuade him to recant. Other than the fact that he became a minister, the only other information Drummond provides concerning Jonson's father is that he died a month before his son was born.

Although no birth certificate has been discovered, there are a few clues left by Jonson himself that have helped scholars attach a date, if not a place, to his emergence into the world. The first clue is in the form of a direct declaration that Jonson made in his poem "An Epigram to My Muse, the Lady Digby, on Her Husband, Sir Kenelm Digby":

> His breast is a brave palace, a broad street,
> Where all heroic ample thoughts do meet;
> Where nature such a large survey hath ta'en,
> As other souls to his dwelt in a lane:
> Witness his action done at Scanderoon;
> Upon my birthday the eleventh of June.[1]

As to the year of his birth, the clues are not as forthright. In a sworn deposition dated 1610 (cited in Herford et al., vol. 1, p. 228), Jonson declared his

---

[1] For the sake of clarity, the language and spelling of the poetry and some other writings of Jonson and his contemporaries have been modernized by the author.

age to be "thirty-seven years or thereabouts." In another deposition, this one taken in 1623 (Herford, vol. 11, p. 582), he stated his age as "fifty years and upwards." Another piece of evidence appears in a poem dated 19 January 1619, "My Picture Left in Scotland," that Jonson sent to Drummond:

> Oh, but my conscious fears,
>   That fly my thoughts between,
>   Tell me that she hath seen
> My hundreds of grey hairs,
> Told seven and forty years.

Taken together, and with the application of simple mathematics, these clues would tend to support 1572 as the year of Jonson's birth. Since no conclusive evidence exists, however, scholarly disagreement continues. Perhaps the best argument in favor of the 11 June 1572 date can be found in the appendix to Rosalind Miles's *Ben Jonson: His Life and Work.*

The place of his birth is another puzzle, this one with even fewer clues. In his book *Worthies of Westminster* (1662), Thomas Fuller wrote, "Ben Jonson was born in this city. Though I cannot with all my industrious inquiry find him in his cradle, I can fetch him from his long coats. When a little child, he lived in Harts-horn-lane near Charing Cross, where his mother married a bricklayer for her second husband" (Herford et al., vol. 11, p. 508). Although Fuller firmly claims Westminster as Jonson's birthplace, he quickly confesses that his best efforts can do no more than place him there as "a little child." Where Jonson was born remains a mystery.

The identity of the bricklaying stepfather remained unknown for several centuries. Drummond does not mention him at all, and the only information Fuller offers is a mention of his profession. Even as late as 1953, in Marchette Chute's *Ben Jonson of Westminster,* the man was identified simply as "a bricklayer." In 1960 the *Times Literary Supplement* published an article by J. B. Bamborough, "The Early Life of Ben Jonson," in which the author claims to have found the name of the shadowy figure. Bamborough's thorough search of the parish records in St. Martin's-in-the-Fields, one of the two parishes that composed the town of Westminster, revealed that a man by the name of Robert Brett leased property in Hartshorn Lane in the 1580s. When Brett died in 1609, he was listed as a Master of the Tilers' and Bricklayers' Company. Modern biographers, such as David Riggs in

his *Ben Jonson: A Life* and Rosalind Miles, tend to accept Brett as Jonson's stepfather.

Although it was an ancient and necessary craft, bricklaying was considered an occupation requiring more brawn than brains. Sons of bricklayers in Jonson's time could expect little more from life than to follow in their father's profession, continuing a cycle of ignorance and poverty. (Drummond reports that Jonson was "brought up poorly" [Herford et al., vol. 1, p. 139]) Chances to rise above their station in life were rare. Jonson would have walked from his home a short distance to the small schoolhouse at St. Martin's Church to receive a rudimentary education with the understanding that as soon as his schooling was completed, he would be apprenticed to a master.

SCHOLAR, BRICKLAYER, SOLDIER

AN opportunity to escape his fate was presented to Jonson by an unknown benefactor. Someone supplied the funds that made it possible for the bricklayer's stepson to attend the great Westminster School. Although Westminster was a "free school," endowed by Queen Elizabeth I, who hoped it would one day rival Eton, there were incidental expenses. Books, quills, ink, parchment, candles, and other supplies were the student's responsibility. Even if Jonson had been inclined to do so, it would have been difficult, if not impossible, for him to bear the costs. Drummond states that Jonson was "put to school by a friend (his master Camden)" (Herford et al., vol. 1, p. 139). An additional clue comes from Jonson's epigram 14, "To William Camden":

> Camden, most reverend head, to whom I owe
> All that I am in arts, all that I know,
> (How nothing's that?) to whom my country owes
> The great renown, and name wherewith she goes.

It is unlikely, however, that Camden was the benefactor. During the years Jonson spent at Westminster School, 1579 being the first year he could have attended and 1590 the last, William Camden held the position of second master, earning less than eight pounds a year. There is a better chance that since Westminster was a church school, Jonson's mother, being the widow of a minister, had an ecclesiastical connection that made it possible for her son to attend. Since Jonson's mother proved herself, later in his life, to be a strong and determined woman when it came to his welfare, it is not outside the realm of possibility that she fought hard to get him the best education.

Although Camden may not have been responsible for getting Jonson in the door of Westminster School, he was responsible for the remarkable education Jonson acquired. Camden was recognized in his day as the foremost educator and antiquarian scholar in all of Tudor England. An amazingly industrious man, Camden wrote a Greek grammar that was the authoritative text for several generations and an enormously popular history of Roman Britain, *Britannia; or, A Chorographical Description of England, Scotland and Ireland* (1586). This is quite remarkable, considering the numerous duties he performed as second master of the school. As it was organized in Jonson's time, the Westminster School's entire student body, consisting of 120 boys ranging in age from seven to eighteen years, was taught by the headmaster Edward Grant and his second in command, Camden.

The student hierarchy consisted of four divisions: Queen's Scholars, Pensioners, Peregrines, and Oppidans. The Queen's Scholars were forty boarders who had earned scholarships after their first year and therefore had all their expenses paid by the Queen. The Pensioners also boarded at the school but had not yet passed the examinations for full scholarship. The Peregrines were boys from throughout England who boarded with relatives or friends in Westminster. The Oppidans were the sons of parents living in the immediate Westminster area. Whatever the living arrangements of the boys, they all entered the school as equals and were taught the standard Tudor curriculum: copying, translating, and memorizing vast amounts of the works of such Latin authors as Horace, Cato, Vergil, Plautus, and Ovid. Marchette Chute, in her biography of Jonson, wrote, "It might be said in general of the Tudor school system that its aim was to turn out little Roman-Christian gentlemen who could write exactly like Cicero" (p. 26).

Earning a scholarship and becoming a Queen's Scholar was of paramount importance to those boys who sought entrance into Oxford or Cambridge. Westminster School awarded six scholarships annually: three for Christ's Church, Oxford, and three for Trinity College, Cambridge. For whatever reason, Jonson did not rise to the ranks of Queen's Scholar and therefore was not eligible to compete for one of the coveted scholarships. As Drummond reported (Herford et al., vol. 1, p. 139), he was "taken from it and put to another craft (I

think it was to be a wright or bricklayer), which he could not endure," before he finished the school's course of study. His time at Westminster School, though cut short, was what made Ben Jonson.

In addition to the regular studies, the production of school plays was regarded as essential to a complete education. The boys of Westminster School were expected to perform three plays each year. These productions not only taught the boys all of the arts of stagecraft but also strengthened them in the self-confidence that comes from being able to speak well before an audience. The importance of mastering these talents was made clear by the fact that Queen Elizabeth often attended the school's productions. To what he learned of stagecraft and the writing of classical authors must be added another essential element that was passed on to Jonson by his teacher, mentor, and lifelong friend Camden, that is, the love of learning for its own sake.

The education he gained walking to and from school proved valuable as well. Jonson's schooldays began early; students were expected to arrive ready for class at seven in the morning during the fall and at six in the spring. The route he took from his home in Hartshorn Lane led through a labyrinth of disreputable alleyways known as the "Bermudas," an area where the lower end of society plied their trades: whores, pimps, cutthroats, and thieves. Once out of the Bermudas, Jonson walked down King's Street and through the grounds of Whitehall, the seat of government and the royal residence, replete with tilting yards, tennis courts, and magnificent gardens. The contrast produced by such a short walk could not have been greater.

The disappointment and anger the young scholar felt at being forced from the groves of academe surely must have been overwhelming. There exist contemporary reports from John Aubrey (quoted in Herford et al.) and Fuller that Jonson worked briefly in his stepfather's craft. He refused, however, to abandon his scholarly pursuits. Fuller wrote that "he helped in the building of the new structure of Lincoln's Inn, when, having a trowel in his hand, he had a book in his pocket" (Herford et al., vol. 11, p. 509). Jonson's situation in the late 1580s and the early 1590s bears a remarkable resemblance to that of the unfortunate hero of Thomas Hardy's *Jude the Obscure,* another frustrated scholar who built walls through which he could not enter.

Eventually, perhaps as early as 1591, Jonson found an outlet where he could honorably vent his building frustrations—soldiering. He left the craft "he could not endure" and joined Her Majesty's forces in the Netherlands. Catholic Spain ruled the Netherlands and violently suppressed the Dutch Protestants, who, under the leadership of William of Orange, demanded freedom of worship. Elizabeth I, as much a Protestant as Mary had been a Catholic, sent English troops to aid the besieged rebel's towns. In the arena of this campaign Jonson gave savage release to his pent-up furies. He challenged an enemy soldier to single combat. Drummond wrote, "In his service in the Low Countries, he had, in the face of both camps, killed an enemy and taken *opima spolia* from him" (Herford et al., vol. 1, p. 139). *Opima spolia* translates to mean "rich spoils." In other words, Jonson killed his enemy and stripped him of his armor and weaponry in true Homeric fashion.

Jonson returned to England soon after accomplishing this feat of arms. In the short time he spent among military men, he developed a profound respect for those men who risked all to fight for their country. He made a clear distinction, however, between the valiant men-at-arms and the inept posers who often led them. Epigram 108, "To True Soldiers," which is also an answer to those who found his portrayal of the cowardly soldier Captain Bobadill in his play *Every Man in His Humour* (1601) offensive, reads:

> Strength of my country, whilst I bring to view
> Such as are miscalled captains, and wrong you;
> And your high names: I do desire, that thence
> Be nor put on you, nor you take offence.
> I swear by your true friend, my muse, I love
> Your great profession; which I once did prove:
> And did not shame it in my actions, then,
> No more, than I dare now do, with my pen.
> He that not trusts me, having vowed this much
> But's angry for the captain, still: is such.

Additionally, in epigram 66, "To Sir Henry Cary," he wrote, "He's valiant'st, that dares fight and not for pay: / That virtuous is when the reward's away." His admiration of courage in war notwithstanding, he quickly returned to England after his heroic feat, never to enter the ranks of soldiers again.

THE ENGLISH THEATER IN THE LATE SIXTEENTH CENTURY

WHEN Jonson returned home from the war, there was little choice for him but to take up once again the unendurable trade of bricklaying. He did, however, continue his scholarly habits. Drummond reports, "Then returning soon he betook himself to his wonted studies" (Herford et al., vol. 1, p. 139). It is believed that sometime between 1592 and 1594, Jonson once again put the bricklayer's trowel aside and joined a company of traveling actors who toured the countryside while the London theaters were closed. The closure of all the playhouses in and around London was prompted by a riot that broke out in Southwark on 23 June 1592. Government and church authorities had long held the belief that playhouses, or theaters, were places of immorality and political subversion. Any excuse to shut down these seditious operations was acted upon swiftly.

The disturbance in Southwark, whose cause is unknown, was enough to close all London area theaters. Acting companies accepted these temporary setbacks as occupational hazards. Some companies would load their costumes, sets, and properties onto wagons and tour neighboring communities, setting up productions in town squares, farmyards, or country manor houses. Once the problems in London had settled down, they would return to their theaters. In August of 1592, however, a serious outbreak of plague swept through London, and, in an attempt to control the spread of the disease, its citizens were forbidden by proclamation to gather in crowded places. This order was in effect in London until June 1594. Any acting company that hoped to survive as such was forced to find an audience elsewhere. Jonson joined one of these traveling shows as an actor. From the writings of a rival playwright, Thomas Dekker, Jonson's biographers surmise that Jonson played the role of Hieronimo in Thomas Kyd's popular play, *The Spanish Tragedy*. This speculation leads to the possibility that Jonson toured with the Earl of Pembroke's Men, who had Kyd's play in their repertoire. Dekker wrote in the dedication to his play *Satiromastix* that Jonson "took mad Hieronimo's part, to get service among the mimics." He also reminded Jonson that "thou hast forgot how thou amblest in leather pilch by a playwagon, in the high way."

Jonson certainly possessed abilities that would lend themselves to a successful career as an actor: a good background in classical literature, an ability to memorize and declaim long passages of poetry, some instruction in stagecraft, and proven ability as a swordsman. It appears that the only ingredient lacking was talent. Jonson's acting career began and ended with his role as Hieronimo.

HUSBAND AND FATHER

ANOTHER role Jonson took on, and one that lasted a bit longer, was that of husband. An entry in the parish register of St. Magnus the Martyr in London, dated 14 November 1594, reads, "Beniamine Johnson and Anne Lewis married" (Herford et al., vol. 11, p. 574). It should be noted here that Jonson chose to drop the "h" in his last name in 1604, although most contemporary documents relating to him as well as the writings of his fellows include it. Jonson told Drummond little about his wife, other than that "he married a wife who was a shrew yet honest" (Herford et al., vol. 1, p. 139), and that he spent a great deal of time away from their home, as long as five years at one point. The couple did live together as husband and wife long enough to produce several children[2]; the first, named Benjamin for his father, was born sometime in the spring of 1596. Three more children followed: a second son, Joseph (1599–1603); a daughter, Mary (1601); and a third son, also named Benjamin (1608–1611). It was not uncommon for children not to survive their parents in Elizabethan England. Indeed, according to an article by Thomas R. Forbes, "Life and Death in Shakespeare's London," 50 percent of children did not live to the age of five, and less than 30 percent saw their fifteenth birthdays.

Epigrams 22 and 45, written to commemorate the deaths of his first two children, give some insight into Jonson's love and fatherly attachment. In an era when infant mortality was commonplace, Jonson's published grief is quite remarkable indeed, especially when one considers that Shakespeare wrote no such memorial on the death of his son, Hamnet, who died at the age of eleven in 1596. Mary, the first to die, is remembered in epigram 22, "On My First Daughter":

Here lies to each her parent's ruth,
Mary, the daughter of their youth:
Yet, all heaven's gifts, being heaven's due,

---

[2] There is considerable disagreement among scholars and biographers regarding the names, dates of birth and death, and in some cases even the existence of Jonson's children. In presenting this information the author has used the findings of David Riggs in his 1987 biography *Ben Jonson: A Life.*

It makes the father, less, to rue.
At six month's end, she parted hence
With safety of her innocence;
Whose soul heaven's queen, (whose name she bears)
In comfort of her mother's tears,
Hath placed amongst her virgin train:
Where, while that severed doth remain,
This grave partakes the fleshly birth.
Which cover lightly, gentle earth.

His first son, Benjamin, clearly lived long enough to have given his father some hope that he would not be lost as well, as is reflected in epigram 45, "On My First Son":

Farewell, thou child of my right hand, and joy;
My sin was too much hope of thee, loved boy,
Seven years thou wert lent to me, and I thee pay,
Exacted by thy fate, on the just day.
O, could I lose all father, now. For why
Will man lament the state he should envy?
To have so soon 'scaped world's and flesh's rage,
And, if no other misery, yet age?
Rest in soft peace, and, asked, say here doth lie
Ben Jonson his best piece of poetry.
For whose sake, henceforth, all his vows be such,
As what he loves may never like too much.

Why no epigrams exist commemorating the deaths of Jonson's other children may be explained by this note from Fuller, found in Chute's biography; "[Jonson] was not very happy in his children, and most happy in those who died first, though none lived to survive him" (pp. 286–287).

FIRST PLAYWRITING AND FIRST IMPRISONMENT

THE profession of playwright did not exist in England when Ben Jonson was born. Traveling companies of actors took their plays to their audiences and could therefore use the same material over and over, changing locations rather than scripts. As the population of London grew, these companies found that it was to their advantage to settle in an established theater and draw audiences to them. Jonson's company, the Earl of Pembroke's Men, for instance, found a home in a newly erected theater, the Swan. Establishing themselves in one location, however, required an expanded repertoire, and new material was in great demand. Some scripts were cobbled together by the actors themselves, and others were created by university-educated men, men who were destined for service in the government or church and who took up scriptwriting as a sideline or as a way of expressing their views uncensored.

One such "university man" was Thomas Nashe. Nashe was a caustic satirist and virulent anti-Puritan who courted controversy and notoriety. In 1597, Nashe was writing a comedy for Pembroke's Men when he suddenly had a change of heart. He abandoned the work and left London, spending the following year writing in seclusion in Yarmouth. The acting company turned the job of finishing the script over to Jonson. The play, *The Isle of Dogs*, has not survived. How much of it was Nashe's work and how much Jonson's is not known. What is known is that on 28 July 1597, the Queen's Privy Council moved swiftly to close the play and arrest all those associated with it. Orders were issued that no plays were to be presented in or around London for the remainder of the summer and that all playhouses were to be torn down. Pembroke's Men hurriedly left London and soon were performing in Bristol. Three of their number, however, were arrested and thrown into cells in Marshalsea Prison: Robert Shaw, Gabriel Spencer, and Ben Jonson.

The Privy Council, determined to discover who was responsible for the play and to uncover the whereabouts of the other members of the company, called upon the services of the Queen's master torturer, Richard Topcliffe. Three years earlier, Topcliffe had questioned Thomas Kyd, who had been arrested on charges of atheism, in such a gruesome manner that Kyd died shortly after his release. The forms the questioning of Jonson and his fellows took are unknown. Jonson, however, was proud to tell Drummond that the only answers he gave to his inquisitors were simply "Aye" and "No." Drummond (Herford et al., vol. 1, p. 139) adds that "they placed two damned villains to catch advantage of him," but the keeper of the Marshalsea had alerted Jonson to this ploy, and the spies got no information from him. Jonson remembered these nefarious fellows in epigram 59, "On Spies": "Spies, you are lights in state, but of base stuff, / Who, when you have burnt yourselves down to the snuff, / Stink, and are thrown away. End fair enough."

We may never know what the Queen and her Privy Council found offensive or seditious in *The Isle of Dogs*. Government agents apparently confiscated and destroyed all copies of the script. Her Majesty's outrage, however, did not last long. After a little more than two months in prison, Jon-

son, Shaw, and Spencer were released on 8 October 1597. The theaters were not torn down, but Queen and Privy Council established firm control over what was performed. The Queen's Master of the Revels was allowed to issue licenses to only two companies: the Lord Admiral's Men, who performed at the Rose, and the Lord Chamberlain's Men, who performed at the Curtain. The Earl of Pembroke's Men and the Swan were effectively put out of business.

One man who kept his wits about him during this time of theatrical turmoil, and who benefited from it, was Philip Henslowe. Henslowe, who came to London as an apprentice dyer, made his fortune by marrying the owner's daughter and thereby inheriting the business. He invested his money in other lucrative businesses, such as starch making, wood selling, and pawnbroking. Noticing the healthy profits made by James Burbage's theaters north of London—the Theatre, built in 1576, and the Curtain, built shortly after—Henslowe decided to enter the theatrical business. Henslowe and his partner, John Cholmley, leased a plot of land that had been a rose garden south of the Thames and built the Rose Theatre in 1587. Attracting a company to perform at the Rose was made easy by the fact that the leading actor of the day, Edward Alleyn, was Henslowe's son-in-law. Soon Alleyn and his fellow actors in the Lord Admiral's Men made the Rose their home.

A shrewd businessman, Henslowe read the temper of the Queen and her Privy Council correctly. During the months of uncertainty, Henslowe wisely secured the services of many displaced actors and scriptwriters. Indeed, on the very day the Privy Council issued its order closing the theaters, Henslowe's account book shows that he loaned Jonson the handsome sum of four pounds. Perhaps both men knew that Jonson would be arrested and arranged the loan to meet the needs of Jonson's family during his time of imprisonment. Jonson would have needed money for his own needs as well. The Marshalsea required all its prisoners to pay for their own food and other common necessities. When Jonson emerged from prison, he did so as a playwright for the Lord Admiral's Men and as a debtor to Henslowe.

What brought Jonson to Henslowe's attention could have been a popular play that was being performed in the first half of 1597 by the Children of the Chapel Royal, *The Case Is Alter'd* (1609). This is regarded as Jonson's first surviving full-length play. To create it, he borrowed heavily from the works of Titus Maccius Plautus, a Roman comic poet and playwright who lived from 254? to 184 B.C. Plautus' adaptations of Greek comedies were very popular among the masses in ancient Rome, and there is little doubt that Jonson read some of his twenty extant plays while at Westminster School. In the creation of *The Case Is Alter'd*, Jonson made liberal use of two of Plautus' plays: *Captivi* (The captives) and *Aulularia* (The pot of gold). Both of these Latin plays contain the usual assortment of stock characters (miserly fathers, irresponsible sons, twin siblings, lost children, boastful soldiers, scheming servants, villains, and courtesans) that became the mainstay of English comedy for several centuries.

The Case Is Alter'd, with its combination of sentiment and satire, appealed to the Children of the Chapel Royal's audience, and it remained a popular part of the company's repertoire for some time, but Jonson did not include it in the 1616 folio of his collected works. Perhaps he considered it too dependent upon Plautus to claim it as his own. The play's success resulted in Jonson's continued association with the company, but his main source of work in late 1597 was Henslowe.

However generous Henslowe was to Jonson, he was first and foremost a businessman intent on turning a profit. To survive, Elizabethan theater companies depended on a rapid production of new material. Henslowe employed several playwrights—Thomas Dekker, Henry Chettle, Henry Porter, Ben Jonson, and others—to keep his actors busy and his audiences entertained. Plays were a product of collaboration, and Henslowe's payment for a work, which averaged six pounds, was divided among the writers. An entry in Henslowe's account book dated 18 August 1598 recorded a payment of six pounds to Chettle, Porter, and Jonson for a script, now lost, entitled *Hot Anger Soon Cold*. Jonson's portion, two pounds, was certainly not enough to provide a decent living for Jonson alone, much less his wife and children. The economic realities of the time dictated that Jonson would have to produce three scripts, completely on his own, every year to equal the amount of money he would have earned as a bricklayer's apprentice. Even Shakespeare at the height of his artistic output averaged only two and a half plays a year. Shakespeare, however, was able to supplement his playwriting income with his acting skills and his share of the earnings

of the Lord Chamberlain's Men. Jonson could neither act nor gather together enough money to become a company shareholder. Actors, it would appear, were more valuable to their managers than writers. For example, an actor by the name of Robert Browne was in such a secure economic situation that he was able to lend Jonson the princely amount of ten pounds on 2 April 1598.

Despite the financial hardship, Jonson worked diligently for Henslowe, gaining experience and recognition. In addition to *Hot Anger Soon Cold*, Jonson wrote, *The Page of Plymouth* with Thomas Dekker and *Robert the Second, King of Scots* with Chettle and Dekker. The profession's demand for quantity rather than quality, however, ran counter to Jonson's high standards, standards that had been instilled at Westminster School and later were refined by Jonson's reading of Sir Philip Sidney's *An Apology for Poetry*, also known as *Defence of Poesie* (1595) and George Puttenham's *Art of English Poesy* (1589). Both works bemoaned the state of English poetry and were particularly harsh in their assessment of the player-poets, in other words, the playwrights. Sidney, in particular, had a profound effect on Jonson. *An Apology for Poetry* was the first of its kind, a systematic examination of English poetry. It sought to correct what Sidney perceived as the errors of the current fashion in writing and to remind poets of the high dignity and function of their calling. Jonson, the budding liberal humanist, seized upon Sidney's lofty ideals and began the laborious process of reinventing himself, of turning a skilled artisan who produced plays for general entertainment into a poet whose works would hold up folly to ridicule and thereby cleanse society of its corruption.

An early example of how completely Jonson absorbed Sidney's philosophy is found in Jonson's first play that is considered wholly his own, *Every Man in His Humour*. There were two versions of *Every Man in His Humour* published in Jonson's lifetime. In the first, a quarto published in 1601, the play is set in Italy, and the characters bear such names as Lorenzo, Thorello, and Giuliano. Sometime between 1604 and 1612, it was rewritten extensively, moving the action to London and its environs and giving the characters recognizable English names: Kno'well, Kitely, Down-right, and so on. Since the latter version is the one Jonson chose to include in the 1616 folio of his works, that is the one that is cited in this essay. Those interested in a complete comparison of the two versions are encouraged to seek a copy of *Every Man in His Humour: A Parallel Text Edition of the 1601 Quarto and the 1616 Folio.*

THE EARLY COMEDIES AND AN ACT OF MURDER

THERE is an intriguing story told by Nicholas Rowe in his 1709 edition of the works of Shakespeare, and quoted in Samuel Schoenbaum's *William Shakespeare: A Compact Documentary Life,* that tells of the twenty-six-year-old Ben Jonson presenting a script to the Lord Chamberlain's Men for consideration. Rowe relates that the actors were about to reject the play "with an ill-natur'd answer" (Schoenbaum, pp. 203–204) when Shakespeare, the company's leading playwright-actor, asked to read it, found merit in it, and persuaded the others to accept it for performance. Whether or not this romantic tale is factual, the play, *Every Man in His Humour,* premiered at the Curtain in 1598 and featured the best actors among the Lord Chamberlain's Men: Will Kemp, Richard Burbage, John Heminges, Henry Condell, and Shakespeare himself.

When Jonson revised this play for the folio edition, he added a prologue that made clear what the theatrical world could expect from him. He states that he will adhere to the principles of classical Greek and Roman comedy. In other words, Jonson's play will reflect the daily lives of familiar personality types realistically and show plainly the consequences of their moral choices and their treatment of others. The action will take place within a framework of time and space that is within the realm of probability, and it will have a moral purpose. He writes that he will not "make a child, now swaddled, to proceed / Man, and then shoot up, in one beard and weed, / Past threescore years." He hopes that his audience "will be pleased to see / One such, today, as other plays should be." There will be no sound effects to simulate nature, nor will there be anything shocking that might "make afeard / The gentlewomen." What he offers is this:

> deeds and language such as men do use,
> And persons such as Comedy would choose,
> When she would show an image of the times,
> And sport with human follies, not with crimes;
> Except we make 'em such, by loving still
> Our popular errors, when we know they're ill.
> I mean such errors, as you'll all confess,

> By laughing at them, they deserve no less;
> Which when you heartily do, there's hope left then,
> You, that so graced monsters, may like men.

All this flies in the face of what the Elizabethan audiences were accustomed to seeing on the stage. Shakespeare filled his plays with the theatrical gimmicks that Jonson disowns and enjoyed tremendous success. Nonetheless, Jonson, for the remainder of his life, held fast to the neoclassical belief that art's purpose was not merely to entertain but to draw minds away from wickedness and toward virtue.

In the play's first act, Kno'well, a country gentleman and father of Edward, a studious poet, intercepts a letter meant for his son. He reasons that since the name on the letter is the same as his own, there is no crime in reading it. He finds that the letter is from Edward's city friend, Well-bred, who is writing to invite Edward to join him in London for some harmless merrymaking. Kno'well is dismayed by the insolent tone of the message and is puzzled by an unkind reference to himself. He decides to follow Edward secretly to London and persuade him to turn away from vain foolishness. When Edward reads the letter, he is delighted at the prospect of amusing himself at the expense of the two buffoons (William, a poetaster, and Captain Bobadill, a boastful yet cowardly soldier) Well-bred has to show him. Indeed, he brings along another, his foolish country cousin, Stephen, to provide more sport.

Beginning with this thread, Jonson wove a complicated plot and subplot of mischievous deceptions and comic misunderstandings that was to become his trademark. This play and the three that followed—*The Comicall Satyre of Every Man out of His Humour* (1600), *The Fountain of Self-love; or, Cynthia's Revels* (1601), and *Poetaster; or, His Arraignment* (1602)—often are referred to as "humors" plays. Around 400 B.C. Greek physicians had identified the four physical humors as black bile, phlegm, choler (yellow bile), and blood. They contended that a perfect balance of these liquids was necessary for good health. Any imbalance in these humors would result in illness or unusual behavior. When the humor invaded an organ, the organ either would absorb it (causing the organ to expand and burst) or would expel it and return the body to a state of equilibrium. By Jonson's time, it was the popular fashion to refer to anyone acting in an eccentric or obsessive manner as being "in a humor."

In *Every Man in His Humour,* Stephen's melancholy, Matthew's lovesickness, Bobadill's cowardice, Down-right's violent anger, the jealousy that controls Kitely and his wife as well as Tib and Cob, and Kno'well's suspicions are examples of invading humors. By the play's end, it falls to Justice Clement—to whose home all the characters have been drawn through the machinations of Kno'well's manservant, Brain-worm—to expel the unwholesomeness. This he accomplishes in two ways: those who are foolish beyond hope (Matthew, Stephen, and Bobadill) he physically removes to jail, while those who have been only temporarily foolish (Down-right, Kno'well, and the Kitelys) are shown the error of their ways and given remedies. Edward and Well-bred emerge as the epitomes of well-balanced gentlemen.

The play was well received. The title page of the 1601 quarto edition claims that it was "sundry times publicly acted." At this point, however, there began a cycle of professional triumph followed quickly by personal tragedy that was to hound Jonson for the remainder of his life. Soon after the premier of *Every Man in His Humour,* and less than a year after his release from Marshalsea Prison, Jonson was arrested for the murder of a fellow actor, Gabriel Spencer. There were many possible reasons for the quarrel that led to Spencer's death; perhaps he held a grudge against Jonson for his part in the *Isle of Dogs* scandal that destroyed the acting company of which Spencer was a leading actor and shareholder and which landed Spencer in prison. Whatever the reason, the two men drew swords on each other on 22 September 1598 in a field near the Curtain theater, and Spencer died instantly as the result of a stab wound in his right side. Although Spencer was a violent man who had committed a murder in 1596, a jury found that Jonson was the aggressor, and he was imprisoned at Newgate.

While awaiting arraignment, and certainly in the shadow of the hangman's noose, Jonson took the extraordinarily dangerous step of converting to Catholicism. A priest of that outlawed religion had visited Jonson in Newgate Prison at the risk of his own life. As Drummond tells it, Jonson "then took his religion by trust of a priest who visited him in prison" (Herford et al., vol. 1, p. 139). At his arraignment, Jonson pleaded guilty to the crime of manslaughter and asked for "benefit of clergy." Since the Middle Ages, this curious loophole in the law allowed a first-time offender to translate aloud a passage from the Latin Bible. If the offender read his "neck verse" correctly, he was set free. Thanks to his education at Westminster and his subsequent studies, Jonson escaped the gallows, but all his goods were confiscated, and a capital *T* was branded at the base of his left thumb. The brand identified him as one who had avoided execution at Tyburn and therefore was not entitled to claim benefit of clergy a second time.

CITIZEN OF LONDON AND WARRIOR POET

JONSON was released from Newgate on 6 October 1598, a branded murderer, stripped of all his property, and in debt. His most pressing need was money. Henslowe was an unlikely source, since he had lost one of his best actors to Jonson's rapier. It appears that Jonson returned to bricklaying for a few months, long enough to serve out his apprenticeship. Whatever difficulties he faced as a result of leaving the trade twice before were resolved, and he was made a Citizen of London and a member of the Tilers' and Bricklayers' Company. This entitled him to set up his own business as a master bricklayer, but he lacked the funds to do so. Indeed, Jonson found himself back in Marshalsea Prison in late January 1599 because he could not discharge the debt he owed to Robert Browne. It is unknown who came to his aide this time; it may have been Henslowe, since Jonson was back in his employ by August 1599.

Hackwork for Henslowe was a good source of quick money, and it did not prevent Jonson from working on his next "humors" play, *Every Man out of His Humour.* This play was one of the first performed in the new theater of the Lord Chamberlain's Men, the Globe, in late 1599 or early 1600. Theatergoers who may have expected a sequel to his previous play were surprised to find something quite different. *Every Man out of His Humour* is essentially a plotless parade of various characters, each possessed by a particular humor. The audience is aided in their understanding of the action by two "observers"—Cordatus, a friend of the play's author, Asper (Jonson), and Mitis—who stand to the side and comment on the brilliance of the proceedings. The frequent references to Greek and Roman literature were aimed directly at the sort of audience Jonson was hoping to cultivate: those who were rich, educated, and intelligent enough to recognize his genius. The young gentlemen of the Inns of Court fit the description perfectly. "Inns of Court" is the collective name of the four schools of law in London: Lincoln's Inn, Gray's Inn, the Inner Temple, and the Middle Temple. Jonson refers to them in his dedication as "the noblest nurseries of humanity and liberty in the kingdom." He goes on to say, "When I wrote this poem, I had friendship with divers in your societies, who, as they were great names in learning, so they were no less examples of living." In a bold attempt to project his doctrines further and, it was hoped, attract a patron, Jonson had this play printed in a quarto edition. The bookseller Jonson chose to sell this work was William Holme, whose shop was located conveniently in Fleet Street, near the Inns of Court. The book sold well and quickly, nearly fifteen hundred copies in nine months. Jonson was determined to raise his scripts to the level of literature and to present himself as a man of letters.

Not all the attention Jonson gained was favorable. Indeed, in addition to satirizing most aspects of contemporary life in England, it seems he was courting confrontations with members of his theatrical circle. Jonson imagined that he was unflatteringly portrayed as the character Chrisogamus in John Marston's play *Histriomastix* (1599), and Marston took offense at a character in *Every Man out of His Humour,* the foolish dandy Clove, whose vocabulary and speech parodied Marston's. Thus began the so-called War of the Theaters, the theaters being the Children of the Chapel Royal at Blackfriars, who performed Jonson's plays, and St. Paul's Boys, who presented the works of Marston and Thomas Dekker. Marston shot back with a savage portrait of Jonson in the character of Brabant the elder in *Jack Drum's Entertainment* (1600). Jonson retaliated with *Cynthia's Revels,* in which he attacked both Marston as Hedon, "a light voluptuous reveler," and Dekker as Anaides, "a strange arrogating puff." There followed Marston's *What You Will* (1600), in which Jonson is lampooned as Lampatho Doria. Somehow Jonson got word of Marston and Dekker's plot for their next attack and beat them to the stage with *Poetaster,* in which Jonson as the poet Horace ridicules the pretensions of Marston/Demetrius and Dekker/Crispinus. It took Jonson only fifteen weeks to write *Poetaster.* In it he unleashed all his venom and spite, not only attacking Marston and Dekker but also offending many others: military men, actors, and practitioners of law. Marston and Dekker countered with *Satiromastix* (The satirist

whipped) (1601), in which they portray Jonson/Horace as a fake and a fraud who demands praise from everyone and a vile vainglorious oaf who is nothing like the true Horace. The "war" did not confine itself to the stage; Drummond reports that at one point "he [Jonson] beat Marston and took his pistol from him" (Herford et al., vol. 1, p. 140).

The "war" was getting out of hand. Legal authorities, infuriated by Jonson's satiric portrayal in *Poetaster,* sought to muzzle him. It was only through the efforts of his friend, the lawyer Richard Martin, that he avoided another serious encounter with the law. In spite of the tremendous amount of work he had produced, Jonson was barely making ends meet. In addition, his daughter, Mary, and his friend and fellow dramatist Richard Nashe had died. Jonson was nearing thirty, and he felt that it was time to withdraw. He wrote in his postscript to *Poetaster,*

> Since the comic muse
> Hath proved so ominous to me, I will try
> If Tragedy have a more kind aspect.
> Her favours in my next I will pursue.
> He concluded this farewell to the "war" with these
>   words:
> There's something come into my thought,
> That must, and shall be sung, high, and aloof,
> Safe from the wolves black jaw, and the dull asses
>   hoof.
>   (Herford et al., vol. 4, p. 324)

PATRONAGE AND TRAGEDY

THE leisure to pursue tragedy's favors was provided by the first of Jonson's many patrons, Sir Robert Townshend. By 1602, Jonson had removed himself from all professional and personal obligations. After Townshend's hospitality, Jonson enjoyed the patronage of Esme Stuart, Seigneur D'Aubigny, a cousin of the new king, James I. This was the beginning of a five-year separation from his wife.

Just before Queen Elizabeth's death in March 1603, the plague again erupted in London. More than thirty-eight thousand people died in the city during the twelve-month period that began in late December 1602. The theaters were closed once more, and those Londoners who could do so fled to the countryside. Jonson and his former teacher, Camden, were guests at the country estate of Sir Robert Cotton when Jonson experienced a horrifying dream. In the dream he saw an image of his son, on whose forehead was cut a bloody cross. This proved prophetic, for he soon received word that the boy had died of plague in London.

Jonson's grief was assuaged somewhat by a commission he received to produce an entertainment for Queen Anne and the heir apparent, Prince Henry. The royal party, which was traveling separately from James and his entourage, stayed for several nights at the home of Sir Robert Spencer at Althorp. One of Jonson's many contributions to the extravaganza held there was an interactive piece entitled "Entertainment of the Queen and Prince at Althorpe." It featured such non-Jonsonian elements as elves, nymphs, fairies, and a controlled deer hunt on the grounds of the estate. Whatever reluctance Jonson may have felt about participating in such artistically questionable merriment was outweighed by the practical gain he hoped to achieve. Court entertainments were a lucrative source of income, paying as much as forty pounds for just a few hundred words.

Despite this attractive diversion, Jonson devoted most of 1603 to the creation of his first tragedy, *Sejanus His Fall* (1605). If Jonson intended to remove himself from the ranks of comic satirists, he could not have chosen a more appropriate subject. The story of Sejanus is brutally violent and without hope of heroic action or happy outcome. It presents the rise to power of an obscure man who becomes the favorite of the Emperor Tiberius. Through cunning manipulations, Sejanus encourages Tiberius' private depravities and acts as his henchman in dealing with those who would stand in the way of his desires. Sejanus is free to destroy anyone who might pose a threat to the emperor including Tiberius' son, Drusus. Yet when Sejanus asks for permission to marry Drusus' widow, Livia, Tiberius realizes the extent of his favorite's ambition. From his pleasure palace on Capri, Tiberius sends letters to the Senate in Rome suggesting that Sejanus is a traitor. Stirred up by Tiberius' new favorite, Macro, the Senate quickly condemns Sejanus, and he is beheaded. The frenzied crowd of Roman citizens then proceeds to tear his body limb from limb. Sejanus' young daughter and son are disposed of gruesomely as well.

This is the stuff of great classical tragedy, but Jonson's play was a failure when it was performed in late December 1603. Not even the great acting abilities of the King's Men (formerly the Lord Chamberlain's Men), with Richard Burbage as Sejanus and Shakespeare as Tiberius, or the collaborative assistance of the gifted playwright George Chapman could rescue this play from a fate similar to that of its title character. Jonson wrote in his dedicatory epistle to Lord D'Aubigny, "If ever any ruin were so great, as to survive; I think this be one I send you: The Fall of Sejanus. It is a poem that (if I well remember) in your lordship's sight, suffered no less violence from our people here, that the subject of it did from the rage of the people of Rome." It was eight years before Jonson staged another tragedy, *Catiline His Conspiracy* (1611). It, too, was regarded as a failure, a work of much scholarship but little poetry.

ROYAL MASQUE-MAKER

ANOTHER opportunity to make a favorable impression on the royal family was offered to Jonson in early 1604. The plague had abated, and the long-delayed coronation celebrations of James I finally could take place. Jonson was the chief designer, director, and writer of the civic festivities that welcomed King James to London. The success of this project, known as the Magnificent Entertainment, brought Jonson closer to James's court and the nobility, who could advance his career. His greatest advancement came from the hands of Queen Anne, who commissioned him to write a masque for performance on Twelfth Night (6 January) 1605.

The Jacobean masque was an extravagant form of theater involving elaborate sets and costumes, music, songs, poetry, and dance. Ideally, courtiers and members of the royal family made up the cast, but Jonson employed professional actors as well for the more demanding roles. The king, however, was the center of attention and the principal audience. This was a perfect vehicle for Jonson; it allowed him to entertain and flatter the court and simultaneously to give the king moral instruction in the proper behavior of a monarch (without risking his head).

His first masque, *The Masque of Blackness*, performed in 1605, featured, at her request, Queen Anne and several of her ladies-in-waiting in blackface. (It was published in 1608 with *The Masque of Beauty* in *The Characters of Two Royall Masques, the One of Blackness, the Other of Beautie*). These "African" ladies, on the advice of the moon goddess, Aethiopia, seek the "greater light" (James), who has the power to change their dark complexions (bad reputations) and cleanse them (restore them to his court). The queen was well pleased, and Jonson began a long career of providing entertainments for the court. Between 1603 and 1634, Jonson created thirty-six productions, thirteen of them with the remarkable set designer and architect Inigo Jones. In the preface to this second masque, *Hymenaei* (1606), Jonson put forth his theory of the masque. He states that it is made up of two parts: the body, or visual aspect of the production, and the soul, which is the story and its moral instruction. Jonson and Jones quarreled often over whose works should take precedence, the poet's or the designer's.

A Jonsonian innovation to the masque was the anti-masque. Its purpose was to provide a sense of conflict and contrast to the masque itself. A good example of its effect is found in *The Masque of Queens* (1609). The opening scene, created by Jones, presents Hell in all its foulness. A coven of twelve witches representing such evils as ignorance, suspicion, malice, and mischief are instructed by their chief to disrupt the serenity of the night. As they set about to do so, there is suddenly heard a loud blast of music, at which Hell and the witches vanish. In their place appear the House of Fame and the person of Heroic Virtue, who denounces the witches' efforts and extols the virtues of true fame. She introduces the witches' opposites, twelve queens from history and myth. Foremost among them is Queen Anne herself, in the role of Bel-anna.

As so often happened in the life of Ben Jonson, public disgrace and personal endangerment followed artistic success. Soon after achieving the enviable position of masque-maker for the queen, Jonson collaborated on a comedy with Chapman and Marston. The play, *Eastward Ho* (1605) was performed in the early spring by the Queen's acting company, the Children of the Chapel Royal. It contained many irreverent jokes aimed at the king and the favorites he had brought with him from Scotland. One of the favorites, Sir James Murray, complained so loudly about the libelous offenses he found in the work that Jonson and Chapman were imprisoned. (It appears that Marston fled to avoid arrest.) Facing the rumored punishment of having their ears and noses mutilated, Jonson and Chapman set about writing letters to those in power who might prevail upon the king on their behalf. Jonson was indeed fortunate that his patron, D'Aubigny, was one of King James's favorites from Scotland and that the earl of Suf-

folk, the king's right-hand man, had done favors for Jonson in the past. The king's wrath soon subsided, and Jonson and Chapman were released unharmed. To celebrate his deliverance, Jonson held a banquet for all his friends. In their company was Jonson's mother, who regaled all present with her confession that she had prepared a poison that she intended to smuggle into the prison for her son to take should the sentence be put into effect. She also boasted that she would have taken the first drink. This is the last we hear of this remarkable woman, who appears to have loved her sometimes troublesome son very much.

GUNPOWDER, COMMUNION, AND VOLPONE

AN opportunity for Jonson to prove his love and loyalty to King James occurred in early November 1605. On the night of 4 November, a Catholic named Guy Fawkes was discovered in the basement of Parliament House with thirty-six barrels of gunpowder. It was his intention to blow up the building and all in it when King James opened a session of Lords and Commons the next day. Jonson, a known Catholic, was called before the Privy Council, and he cooperated fully with their request for help in unraveling the assassination plot. He tried diligently to uncover information but was disappointed in his endeavor by his fellow Catholics' refusal to come forward in their country's time of need.

On 10 January 1606, Jonson and his wife, to whom he had returned after a five-year absence, were summoned by church officials to answer the charge that they had refused to take Anglican Communion in accordance with the law. Jonson also was charged with leading others to the Catholic religion, an act of high treason. At the full hearing on 26 April, Jonson acknowledged that he and his wife had attended his parish church regularly for the previous six months. He further testified that although his wife had taken communion, he had not, because of religious scruples. As to the more serious charge, Jonson denied it and demanded that his accusers produce witnesses to his supposed treason. None came forward, and the charge was dropped. Jonson, however, was ordered to receive religious instruction twice a week to resolve his doubts about receiving communion from the Church of England. Jonson readily agreed, but it would be another four years before he fully embraced the Anglican Church.

In the midst of this political and religious turmoil, Jonson was writing what may be his masterpiece, *Volpone; or, The Foxe* (1607). Jonson, who was considered a slow writer by his contemporaries, finished *Volpone* in only five weeks for a performance by the King's Men at the Globe in February 1606. Within the year the same troupe presented the comedy at both Oxford and Cambridge. *Volpone* opens with a prologue in which Jonson answers his critics and assures his audience that this work will follow the rules of comedy established by the classical authors. Additionally, he promises that he will amuse the audience as well as show them something about themselves.

The main plot tells the story of a rich Venetian, Volpone, who delights in discovering unusual means of increasing his wealth. With the help of his cunning servant, Mosca (the fly), Volpone (the fox), who has no family, devises a scheme. Three men—Voltore (the vulture), Corbaccio (the raven), and Corvino (the crow)—are each led to believe that he might be named Volpone's sole heir, if his gifts find favor. True to their names, these three hover over the seemingly ill fox and await his demise. Volpone pretends to be near death, and the three men, goaded by Mosca and their own greed, scramble to do whatever it will take to ensure being named sole heir. Their greed is so overwhelming that Corbaccio is persuaded to disinherit his son and Corvino agrees to give up his wife, Celia, to Volpone's lusts.

Volpone decides to further irritate his victims by feigning death and leaving all his wealth to Mosca. This plan backfires, however, when Mosca betrays Volpone. Rather than allow Mosca to get away with his betrayal, Volpone reveals his misdeeds to the authorities, the four magistrates who make up the "Avocatori." Volpone and Mosca are punished severely. Mosca is to be whipped and made a galley slave, and Volpone is to be bound in irons in prison for life. Voltore is banished, Corbaccio is confined in a monastery, and Corvino is to be oared through the canals of Venice wearing donkey's ears and then pilloried and pelted with garbage. Corbaccio's son is rewarded with all of his father's property, and Corvino's wife is sent home to her father with her dowry tripled. In act 5, scene 7, the primary Avocatore sends everyone away with these words: "Let all, that see these vices thus rewarded, / Take heart, and love to study 'em. Mischiefs feed / Like beasts, till they be fat, and then they bleed." What helps classify this grim tale of avarice and attempted rape as a comedy is a subplot that Jonson weaves through the play. The misadventures of a trio of English travelers, Peregrine and Sir Politic Would-be and his wife, do much to lighten the darkness.

A TUTOR ABROAD

IN 1607, at the age of thirty-five, Jonson entered into a routine of production that continued for most of the rest of his life. He followed the success of *Volpone* with two other plays that were equally well received: *Epicoene; or, The Silent Woman* and *The Alchemist* (1612). His popularity at court is evidenced by the numerous entertainments and masques he was called upon to provide. In 1611, however, his luster faded a bit with the failure of his tragedy *Catiline*. A welcome opportunity to get away from the London literary circle was offered to Jonson by Sir Walter Raleigh. Raleigh had fallen out of favor with King James in 1603 and had been confined to the Tower of London ever since. He was still free to conduct his professional and private affairs from within the Tower's walls. In 1612, Raleigh decided to expand his son's education by sending him abroad, with Jonson employed as the boy's tutor. It seems that Jonson's love of wine was matched equally by young Raleigh's love of pranks. Once when Jonson was dead drunk, the boy had him loaded into a basket and hauled through the streets of Paris, stopping occasionally to show off his "governor."

The England to which Jonson and young Raleigh returned in the early summer of 1613 was beginning to show signs of decline. The court of King James was rife with scandal and low on money. To make matters worse, the heir to the throne, Prince Henry, had died at the age of eighteen on 6 November 1612. The London theater had undergone changes as well: Shakespeare had retired to his home in Stratford; debt-ridden Thomas Dekker had been sentenced to six years imprisonment; and, on 29 June, Jonson witnessed the fiery destruction of the great Globe. He described the conflagration in his poem "An Execration Upon Vulcan."

There was a change in Jonson's domestic life as well. After 1606, nothing more is known of Jonson's wife, Anne. It appears, however, that their life together had ended by the time of his return from Europe. It was then that Jonson hired a young man, Richard Brome, to take care of his household needs. Brome came from a background much like Jonson's and had no chance of a university education. Under Jonson's tutelage, however, he grew to gain some recognition as an actor, poet, and playwright.

In the midst of all this change and loss, Jonson's star was ascending. *Volpone* and even the ill-received *Sejanus* were riding a crest of public popularity. Jonson, still smarting from the failure of *Catiline,* once again risked the favor of his all too fickle audience by presenting his first new play in three years, *Bartholomew Fair: A Comedie* (1631). The comedy, staged by Henslowe's new acting company, Lady Elizabeth's Men, in their new theater, the Hope, was very well received. There is a tradition that a member of the audience stood at the play's end and shouted, "O rare Ben Jonson!"

JONSON'S ANNUS MIRABILIS—1616

JONSON'S long service to the court of King James was rewarded in a manner that must have been as pleasing to Jonson as it was galling to his critics. On 1 February 1616, King James granted Jonson a lifetime pension of one hundred marks a year. Although the office did not exist at that time, Jonson generally is considered to be England's first poet laureate. As if to prove his worthiness, Jonson published his collected works. This was a bold and revolutionary act on his part, since he chose to include nine of his plays. Scripts for the stage were not considered serious literature, and several of his contemporaries jeered him for attempting to raise a "play" to the respected level of a "work." Indeed, his critics regarded his magnum opus as an arrogant act of self-promotion.

Jonson oversaw every aspect of printing the more than one thousand pages that made up his book, working closely with William Stansby, the printer, and William Hole, the engraver. The elaborate title page bears a slightly altered quotation from Horace's *Satires* (book 1, satire 10, lines 73–74) that echoes Jonson's philosophy: "I do not work so that the crowd may admire me: I am content with a few readers." Jonson was forever protecting the validity of his plays by stating in prologues and introductions that only a select few, the highly intelligent, would understand his work.

In addition to the plays, masques, and entertainments, Jonson included two collections of his poetry: *Epigrams* and *The Forest*. An epigram is best defined as a short poem, usually twenty lines or fewer, that makes its point with conciseness and wit. Jonson, as much a social commentator in his poems as in his plays, uses the epigram as a vehicle for praise and blame. The true value of these 133 epigrams, however, lies in their ability to transport us to Jonson's London. Through him we meet the great—King James (epigrams 4 and 51), William Camden (epigram 14), the Countess of Bedford (epigrams 76, 84, and 94)—as well as the infamous—Sir Luckless Woo-All (epigram 46), Groom Idiot (epigram 58), and Captain Hazard the Cheater (epigram 87). We are invited to supper at Jonson's home (epigram 101), to visit a new whorehouse (epigram 7), and to listen to Jonson rail at his bookseller (epigram 3). *The Forest* is a collection of fifteen poems in various forms: epistles, lyrics, and odes. Seven of the poems concern love, and one, in particular, "Song. To Celia" (no. 9), is perhaps Jonson's most beautiful evocation of desire and rejection:

> Drink to me, only, with thine eyes,
> And I will pledge with mine;
> Or leave a kiss but in the cup,
> And I'll not look for wine.
> The thirst, that from the soul doth rise,
> Doth ask a drink divine:
> But might I of Jove's nectar sup,
> I would not change for thine.
> I sent thee, late, a rosy wreath,
> Not so much honouring thee,
> As giving it a hope, that there
> It could not withered be.
> But thou thereon didst only breathe,
> And sent'st it back to me:
> Since when it grows, and smells, I swear,
> Not of itself, but thee.

Of particular interest in this collection is "To Penshurst." Rather than addressing an individual, the poem commends an individual's country estate. Penshurst, the home of Sir Robert Sidney and his family, is presented and praised as the exemplar of the ideal society.

The 1616 folio firmly established Jonson as the preeminent man of letters in England. He attracted a group of admirers who called themselves the Sons of Ben, or the Tribe of Ben. Jonson held forth at gatherings of his followers at various London taverns, but the wine and wit flowed most often in the Apollo Room of the Devil's Tavern. A visitor to these meetings would be greeted by a welcome, composed by Jonson, painted over the door in gold and black lettering: "Welcome all who lead or follow / To the oracle of Apollo" (Riggs, pp. 285–286). Once inside, the visitor would see a list of twenty-four rules of behavior, again composed by Jonson, engraved in Latin over the fireplace.

In the fall of 1616, Jonson risked plunging from the pinnacle of his popularity by producing *The Devil Is an Ass: A Comedie* (1631). This harshly satirical play about fraudulent moneymaking schemes was all too obviously based on similar practices that were being conducted by the king and many others in his court. Jonson was called to appear before King James, who persuaded him to rewrite portions of the script. The year ended well, however, with the presentation of the delightful, almost Dickensian *Christmas His Masque,* and King James's exotic guest from Virginia, the Princess Pocahontas, enjoyed the Twelfth Night masque *The Vision of Delight.*

DECLINE AND DEPARTURE

IN 1618 Jonson made his famous and somewhat inexplicable journey to Scotland by foot. There he was welcomed and honored in a manner befitting his literary stature. An additional honor was granted Jonson soon after his return to London. At the behest of the Earl of Pembroke, Oxford University conferred upon Jonson the degree of master of arts in a ceremony held on 19 July 1619. The recognition by Oxford may have resulted in Jonson's being asked to join Gresham College as a lecturer or deputy to the Professor of Rhetoric. This possibility is indicated in a document concerning legal proceedings in which Jonson was called to testify on 20 October 1623. The document declares him to be "Benjamin Jonson of Gresham College of London, gent." This intriguing description is well investigated by Rosalind Miles in her biography *Ben Jonson: His Life and Work* (pp. 221–224.)

It seems that Jonson was settled into an academic life when tragedy struck again. A fire swept through his lodgings in November 1623, destroying all his books and papers. In his 216-line poem on the event, "An Execration Upon Vulcan," Jonson asks:

And why to me this, thou lame lord of fire,
What had I done that might call on thine ire?
Or urge thy greedy flame, thus to devour
So many my years' labours in an hour?

Jonson goes on to list the works in progress that were consumed and to recommend to Vulcan contemporaries who were better deserving of his fiery visit.

November 1623 also saw the publication of Shakespeare's first folio, to which Jonson contributed two poems. The first was an introductory poem, "To the Reader," printed opposite Martin Droeshout's engraving of Shakespeare on the title page: "This figure, that thou seest put, / It was for gentle Shakespeare cut." The other contribution was an elegy, "To the Memory of My Beloved, the Author Mr William Shakespeare: And What He Hath Left Us." (Both appear in Jonson's *Complete Poems* under "Miscellaneous Poems," numbers 14 and 15.) The publication of the folio did much to bolster Jonson's long-held belief that plays were worthy of the respect given to other forms of literature.

On 9 January 1625, Jonson's Twelfth Night masque (which had been postponed for three days for political reasons) was performed with the new heir to the throne, Prince Charles, as the chief masquer. *The Fortunate Isles, and Their Union* (1624) was the last masque Jonson wrote for the court of King James. The fifty-seven-year-old monarch died on 27 March 1625. Curiously, his death ushered in the worst outbreak of plague that London had seen since his accession to the throne twenty-two years earlier. This event, of course, closed the theaters, but that was not of any consequence to Jonson, who had not written anything for the stage in the previous nine years. What was of deep concern to Jonson's future at court was the character of King Charles. Charles inherited a court that was deeply in debt. In imposing a strict economy, he did away with the costly Twelfth Night masques. This had been a major source of income for Jonson, and its loss forced him to return to the stage. Jonson's final plays, *The Staple of News* (1631), *The New Inne; or, The Light Heart* (1631), *The Magnetick Lady,* and *A Tale of a Tub* (both first published in the 1640 folio) never rose to the artistic level of his earlier work. Indeed, *The New Inn* was booed off the stage before it reached the end of the first act. Jonson's friend and fellow poet Michael Drayton dismissed these later works as Jonson's "dotages."

Failing artistically and plagued by ill health and debt, Jonson suffered a paralytic stroke in 1628. Although King Charles had increased his pension by 30 percent and added an annual bonus of a tierce of Canary wine (forty-two gallons of sherry), the payments were irregular. When Jonson died on 6 August 1637, his estate, valued at just over eight pounds, was awarded to one of his many creditors.

Realizing that death was near, Jonson made arrangements through his friend, John Williams, Dean of Westminster, to be buried in the abbey. He is said to have told Williams that he could not afford the traditional burial plot measuring six feet long by two feet wide and asked to be buried standing upright. On 9 August 1637, his wish was carried out. Amid the more ornate monuments, a small blue marble square that is easy to overlook marks his final resting place in the north nave of the abbey. Engraved on the marker are the words he may have heard shouted by a member of the audience at the conclusion of *Bartholomew Fair*:

O RARE BEN JONSON

Through the centuries Jonson has gone in and out of favor. Soon after Jonson's death, his friend and literary executor, Sir Kenelm Digby, collected thirty-three elegies on the death of Jonson written by his friends and "sons." The collection was published under the editorship of Bryan Duppa, Bishop of Chichester, and entitled *Jonsonus Virbius; or, The Memory of Ben Jonson Revived by the Friends of the Muses* (1638). Digby furthered Jonson's reputation by seeing to the publication of a handsome two-volume folio of his works in 1640. The first volume is a reproduction of the 1616 folio, and the second contains Jonson's later plays, masques, and entertainments plus two fragments, *The Sad Shepherd* and *Mortimer His Fall*. The second volume also contains a collection of poems, *Underwood*; a translation of Horace's *Ars Poetica*; the unfinished *English Grammar*; and Jonson's commonplace book, *Timber; or, Discoveries*. Jonson's plays enjoyed a great resurgence of popularity during the Restoration and again in the Victorian era. Charles Dickens toured England with his troupe of amateur actors performing *Every Man in His Humour*, with Dickens playing the role of Captain Bobadill. Jonson, however, remains a poet who is known but seldom read. In *The Sacred Wood: Essays on Poetry and Criticism*, T. S. Eliot wrote,

The reputation of Jonson has been of the most deadly kind that can be compelled upon the memory of a great poet. To be universally accepted; to be damned by the praise that quenches all desire to read the book; to be afflicted by the imputation of the virtues which excite the least pleasure; and to be read only by historians and antiquaries—this is the most perfect conspiracy of approval.

(p. 104)

Indeed, the admonition Jonson gave in his introductory poem printed in Shakespeare's first folio would serve Jonson equally well: " Reader, look / Not on his picture, but his book."

SELECTED BIBLIOGRAPHY

I. COLLECTED WORKS. *The Workes of Benjamin Jonson* (London, 1616), first folio; *The Workes of Benjamin Jonson*, 2 vols. (London, 1640–1641), second folio: vol. 1 ed. by Richard Bishop and vol. 2 ed. by Richard Meighen and Thomas Walkley; *Poems* (London, 1640); *Ben Jonson*, 11 vols. (Oxford, 1925–1952), ed. by C. H. Herford, Percy Simpson, and Evelyn Mary Simpson, including John Aubrey's notes on Jonson and official documents of the times, *Conversations with Drummond*, and *Worthies of Westminster*; *The Complete Masques* (New Haven, 1969), ed. by Stephen Orgel; *Ben Jonson and the Cavalier Poets* (New York, 1974), ed. by Hugh MacLean; *The Complete Plays of Ben Jonson*, 4 vols. (Oxford, 1981), ed. by George Wilkes; *The Complete Poems* (New York, 1988), ed. by George A. Parfitt; *Volpone and Other Early Plays* (London and New York, 1999), ed., with an introduction and notes, by Lorna Hutson, including *Every Man in His Humour*, *Sejanus, His Fall*, *Volpone; or, The Foxe*, and *Epicene; or, The Silent Woman*; *Ben Jonson: Five Plays* (Oxford and New York, 1999), ed. by G. A. Wilkes, including *Every Man in His Humour*, *Sejanus*, *Volpone; or, The Fox*, *The Alchemist*, and *Bartholomew Fair*; *Ben Jonson's Plays and Masques*, 2d ed. (New York, 2000), ed. by Richard Harp, including *Volpone, Epicoene, The Alchemist, Mercury Vindicated from the Alchemists at Court, Pleasure Reconciled to Virtue*, and *The Masque of Blackness*.

II. PLAYS AND MASQUES. *The Comicall Satyre of Every Man out of His Humour* (London, 1600); *Every Man in His Humour* (London, 1601); *The Fountain of Self-love; or, Cynthia's Revels* (London, 1601); *Poetaster; or, His Arraignment* (London, 1602); *Part of King James His Royal and Magnificent Entertainment . . . Also, a Brief Panegyre of His Majesties Entrance to Parliament . . . [together with] the Entertainment of the Queene and Prince to Althorpe* (London, 1604); *Sejanus His Fall* (London, 1605); *Eastward Ho* (London, 1605), with John Marston and George Chapman; *Hymenaei* (London, 1606); *Volpone; or, The Foxe* (London, 1607); *The Characters of Two Royall Masques, the One of Blackness, the Other of Beautie* (London, 1608); *The Description of the Masque . . . Celebrating the Happy Marriage of . . . Viscount Haddington* (London, 1609); *The Case Is Alter'd* (London, 1609); *The Masque of Queens* (London, 1609); *Catiline His Conspiracy* (London, 1611); *The*

Alchemist (London, 1612); *Lovers Made Man* (London, 1617); *The Masque of Augures* (London, 1622); *Time Vindicated* (London, 1623); *The Fortunate Isles, and Their Union* (London, 1624); *Neptunes Triumph* (London, 1624); *Loves Triumph Through Callipolis* (London, 1630); *Bartholomew Fair: A Comedie* (London, 1631); *Chloridia* (London, 1631); *The Devil Is an Ass: A Comedie* (London, 1631); *The New Inne; or, The Light Heart* (London, 1631).

III. MODERN EDITIONS. *The Sad Shepherd: The Unfinished Pastoral Comedy of Ben Jonson* (New York, 1944), completed by Alan Porter; with a foreword; *Volpone* (New York, 1970), ed., with an introduction, by Louis B. Wright and Virginia A LaMar; *Every Man in His Humour: A Parallel-Text Edition of the 1601 Quarto and the 1616 Folio*, ed. by J. W. Lever (Lincoln, Nebr., 1971); *Catiline* (Lincoln, Nebr., 1973), ed. by W. F. Bolton and Jane F. Gardner; *Epicoene; or, The Silent Woman* (New York, 1979), ed. by R. V. Holdsworth; *The New Inn* (Manchester, N.H., 1984), ed. by Michael Hattaway;

The Staple of News (Manchester, England, and Wolfeboro, N.H., 1988), ed. by Anthony Parr; *Sejanus His Fall* (Manchester, England, 1990), ed. by Philip J. Ayers; *The Devil Is an Ass* (Manchester, England, and New York, 1994), ed. by Peter Happe; *Poetaster* (Manchester, England, and New York, 1995), ed. by T. G. S. Cain; *The Alchemist* (Cambridge, England, 1996), ed. by Brian Woolland; *Every Man in His Humour* (New York, 1998), ed. by Robert N. Watson; *The Magnetic Lady* (Manchester, England, 2000), ed. by Peter Happe; *Bartholomew Fair* (Manchester, England, 2001), ed. by Suzanne Gossett; *Every Man out of His Humour* (New York, 2001), ed. by Helen Osotvich.

IV. BIBLIOGRAPHIES. Samuel Aaron Tannenbaum, *Ben Jonson: A Concise Bibliography* (New York, 1938; suppl., 1947); D. Heyward Brock and James M. Welsh, *Ben Jonson: A Quadricentennial Bibliography, 1947–1972* (Metuchen, N. J., 1974).

V. BIOGRAPHICAL STUDIES. Marchette Gaylord Chute, *Ben Jonson of Westminster* (New York, 1953); J. B. Bamborough, "The Early Life of Ben Jonson," in *Times Literary Supplement* (8 April 1960); J. B. Bamborough, *Ben Jonson* (London, 1970); George Parfitt, *Ben Jonson: Public Poet and Private Man* (New York, 1977); Samuel Schoenbaum, *William Shakespeare: A Compact Documentary Life* (New York, 1987); Richard Dutton, *Ben Jonson: To the First Folio* (Cambridge, England, 1983); Rosalind Miles, *Ben Jonson: His Life and Work* (London and New York, 1986); David Riggs, *Ben Jonson: A Life* (Cambridge, Mass., 1987); Park Honan, *Shakespeare: A Life* (Oxford, 1998);

VI. CRITICAL STUDIES. Bryan Duppa, ed., *Jonsonus Virbius; or, The Memory of Ben Jonson Revived by the Friends of the Muses* (London, 1638), reprinted in Herford et al., vol. 11; Algernon Charles Swinburne, *A Study of Ben Jonson* (London, 1889; New York, 1969); T. S. Eliot, *The Sacred Wood: Essays on Poetry and Criticism* (London, 1920; rev. ed. 1964); Robert E. Knoll, *Ben Jonson's Plays: An Introduction* (Lincoln, Nebr., 1964); Thomas R. Forbes, "Life and Death in Shakespeare's London," in *American Scientist* 58, no. 5 (1970), pp. 511–520; D. Heyward Brock, *A Ben Jonson Companion* (Bloomington, Ind., 1983); Robert N. Watson, ed., *Critical Essays on Ben Jonson* (New York, 1997); Ted-Larry Pebworth and Claude J. Summers, *Ben Jonson Revised* (New York, 1999); Richard Harp and Stanley Stewart, *The Cambridge Companion to Ben Jonson* (Cambridge, England, and New York, 2000).

JAMES JOYCE

(1882–1941)

James A. W. Heffernan

"WELCOME, O LIFE! I go to encounter for the millionth time the reality of experience and to forge in the smithy of my soul the uncreated conscience of my race."

So says Stephen Dedalus to his diary at the end of *A Portrait of the Artist as a Young Man* (1916), the autobiographical novel in which James Joyce takes his fictional self from infancy to early manhood. If ever a man was destined to re-create in language the conscience of his race, to capture in words the life and soul of Ireland and, above all, the life and spirit of Dublin, its capital and his birthplace, it was James Joyce. Though he spent nearly all of his adult life in Europe, he carried Dublin within him wherever he went. He made it the setting of his best-known novel, *Ulysses* (1922), as well as of its dauntingly dense successor, *Finnegans Wake* (1939). In the process, he also contrived to make Dublin represent the whole world and the entire history of humankind—even while re-creating ancient epic in modern terms and fundamentally reshaping the form of the novel. If it is not quite accurate to say that all of Western literature went into the making of Joyce, we do know that out of him came what T. S. Eliot, writing in the *Dial*, called "the most important expression" of the early twentieth century (p. 480). Now that we have seen our way to the end of the twentieth century and beyond, we can safely say that *Ulysses* remains one of its greatest literary achievements—perhaps the greatest of all.

EARLY LIFE

JAMES Augustine Aloysius Joyce was born on 2 February 1882 in Rathgar, a south Dublin suburb, the first surviving son of John Stanislaus Joyce and Mary Jane (May) Murray Joyce. Although John drew a comfortable salary from his work in the office of Dublin's Collector of Rates (taxes)—and though he also had inherited properties in his native Cork that brought in more than £300 a year—he had already started mortgaging his properties when James was born. By the time the boy was twelve years old, his father had sold them all. In the meantime, John and May had nine more children, moved several times, and finally settled in Dublin in 1893—all the while sinking inexorably into poverty and debt. They nonetheless managed to give young James a few years of private schooling. At six he was enrolled in a boarding school called Clongowes Wood College, about twenty miles west of Dublin. Run by an order of Roman Catholic priests called Jesuits because they belonged to the Society of Jesus, Clongowes exposed him for the first time to their spirit of moral and intellectual discipline. Joyce was taught largely by Jesuits for the rest of his years in school, and they influenced him profoundly. Even though he renounced his faith in the Catholic Church at about the age of twenty and refused to pray for his mother when she lay dying of cancer in 1903, he called himself a Jesuit and treasured the fruits of his Jesuit education. From it, Joyce said, he "learnt to arrange things in such a way that they become easy to survey and to judge" (quoted in Ellmann, 1982, p. 27).

Joyce's first experience of Jesuit training lasted just three years. In 1891, when he was nine, he had to leave Clongowes because his father had lost his job as tax collector. Nonetheless, he wrote his first known poem this year, "Et Tu, Healy." Prompted by the death of Charles Stewart Parnell, a champion of home rule for Ireland who was politically destroyed by the revelation of his affair with a married woman named Kitty O'Shea, this poem, no longer extant, anticipates Joyce's lifelong fascination with the figure of Parnell as well as with the theme of betrayal. Yet if Joyce himself felt betrayed by his forced departure from the Jesuits of Clongowes and his consignment to the much coarser tutelage of the Christian Brothers' school in Dublin, which he briefly attended in early 1893, he did not have to wait long for recompense.

Through the intervention of Father John Conmee, who had known Joyce at Clongowes when he was rector there, Joyce and his brothers were admitted free of tuition in April 1893 to the Jesuit-run day school called Belevedere College. There Joyce won a series of scholarships and honors by the time he graduated in 1898 and then progressed to yet another Jesuit-run institution—Dublin's University College.

At University College Joyce began to display the originality, intellectual independence, and fearless commitment to the renewal of literature that would stamp the rest of his life. In 1899 he refused to join his fellow students in a formal protest against William Butler Yeats's play *The Countess Cathleen* (1892), which they thought slandered Irish peasants. In a paper called "Drama and Life," which he read before the Literary and Historical Society of University College in January 1900, when he was not quite eighteen, he vehemently argued that drama must "put life—real life—on the stage" (*The Critical Writings of James Joyce*, p. 44). Shortly afterward, he published an essay extolling the "New Drama" of Henrik Ibsen and especially his final play, *When We Dead Awaken* (1899), where "Ibsen," Joyce wrote, "has striven to let the drama have perfectly free action" (*Critical Writings*, p. 67). In the summer of 1900 Joyce first tried his hand at drama with an Ibsenian play of his own, "A Brilliant Career," which he brashly dedicated to "My own Soul." Though the play was never performed (William Archer called it "wildly impossible" for the stage [Ellmann, 1982, p. 79]) and has not survived, we know enough about it to see that it begins to develop Joycean themes within an Ibsenian framework. Its young protagonist not only recalls Dr. Stockmann in *An Enemy of the People* (1882) but also exemplifies the price to be paid for betrayal. Having deserted the woman he loves for the sake of professional advancement, he comes to see that his "brilliant" career as a doctor and mayor cannot recompense him for what he has lost.

Joyce himself denounced betrayal wherever he found it. In an article called "The Day of the Rabblement," which Joyce dashed off one morning in October 1901 and published at his own expense in pamphlet form, he attacked the Irish Literary Theatre for pandering to the vulgar, insular, nationalistic tastes of the "rabblement" even though it had "proclaimed war against commercialism and vulgarity" (*Critical Writings*, p. 70). In Joyce's eyes, the Irish Literary Theatre had betrayed the mission of art—the lonely, uncompromising, heroic mission that he would shortly undertake for himself. "Until," Joyce wrote, "he has freed himself from the mean influences about him—sodden enthusiasm and clever insinuation and every flattering influence of vanity and low ambition—no man is an artist at all" (*Critical Writings*, pp. 71B72).

In February 1902, during his final year at University College, Joyce delivered to the Literary and Historical Society a paper on an early-eighteenth-century Irish poet named James Clarence Mangan. Its eloquent conclusion anticipates the aesthetic theory that fully emerged in the later chapters of *A Portrait of the Artist as a Young Man*: "Beauty, the splendour of truth, is a gracious presence when the imagination contemplates intensely the truth of its own being or the visible world, and the spirit which proceeds out of truth and beauty is the holy spirit of joy" (*Critical Writings*, p. 83).

Shortly before Joyce graduated from University College in June 1902 with a degree in modern languages, his paper on Mangan appeared in *St. Stephen's*, the college magazine. He then resolved to make himself known in Dublin's literary circles. One night, early in August of 1902, he called on George Russell (known as "A.E."), a poet devoted to mysticism and a leader of the Irish Literary Revival. After talking with Joyce and hearing him read his poems, Russell urged Yeats to meet Joyce during Yeats's visit to Dublin in October. When they met, the well-established poet told Joyce why he had turned for inspiration to Irish folklore: "The folk life, the country life," said Yeats, "is nature with her abundance, but the art life, the town life, is the spirit which is sterile when it is not married to nature. The whole ugliness of the modern world has come from the spread of the towns and their ways of thought" (quoted in Ellmann, 1982, p. 107). In making this grand pronouncement, Yeats could hardly foresee that his young auditor would go on to write the supreme novel of town life. Joyce said simply that Yeats's generalizations were of "no use," and when he learned Yeats's age, which was then thirty-seven, the twenty-year-old Joyce declared, "I have met you too late. You are too old" (quoted in Ellmann, 1982, p. 108).

CHAMBER MUSIC

BY the time Joyce met Yeats in October 1902, he had written most of the thirty-six lyric poems that would appear in 1907 as *Chamber Music,* published by Elkin Mathews in London. (He had begun writing them in 1900, when he was just eighteen. Starting in 1904, several of them had appeared in such magazines as the *Saturday Review.*) Although they were ignored by many of the leading magazines and dismissively treated by one of them, the book won favorable notice from more than ten periodicals and special praise from Arthur Symons, the well-known critic who had helped Joyce publish his poems after meeting him through Yeats. Writing in the *Nation,* Symons called the poems "firm and delicate and yet . . . full of music and suggestion," evoking "not only roses in mid-winter but the very dew on the roses" and displaying a Jacobean blend of sharpness and sweetness (*Chamber Music,* p. 18). Likewise laudatory was Thomas Kettle's review in the *Freeman's Journal* of Dublin, which indirectly exposed the sharp difference between Joyce and Yeats: "The inspiration of the book," wrote Kettle, "is almost entirely literate. There is no trace of the folk-lore, the folk dialect, or even the National feeling that have coloured the work of practically every writer in contemporary Ireland" (*Chamber Music,* p. 20).

Despite his refusal to share Yeats's admiration for Irish folklore, Joyce greatly admired Yeats's poetry, especially *The Wind Among the Reeds* (1899), which he called "in aim and form . . . poetry of the highest order" (*Critical Writings,* p. 71). More than Ernest Dowson or A. E. Housman or any other poet of the 1890s whose work may have touched Joyce, Yeats's poetry strongly influenced *Chamber Music* and would be echoed repeatedly in Joyce's later work. But William York Tindall also has found in *Chamber Music* evocations of earlier poets: Romantics such as Paul Verlaine, Percy Bysshe Shelley, and William Blake, and Elizabethans such as Ben Jonson and Shakespeare. In poem 13, for instance, the words "courteously" and "Epithalamium" lend an Elizabethan air to the simple diction around them, "and by that discord serve to complicate the harmony" (*Chamber Music,* p. 198). Joyce particularly cherished Elizabethan songs, for he had a fine tenor voice and set to music Yeats's poem "Who Goes with Fergus?" (from *The Countess Cathleen*), which Stephen Dedalus remembers singing to his dying mother in the first chapter of *Ulysses.*

The poems of *Chamber Music* were arranged by Joyce's brother Stanislaus rather than by Joyce himself, who sent the manuscript of them to his brother with instructions "to do what [he] liked with it" (*Chamber Music,* p. 44). By this time, in October 1906, Joyce was living in Rome with Nora Barnacle, a barely educated young woman from Galway who had been working at a Dublin hotel when he met her in June 1904 and who had left with him for Italy four months later. (Though not married until 1931, they had two children: a son named Giorgio, born in 1905, and a daughter named Lucia, born in 1908.) Since Joyce had begun his "voluntary exile" in 1904, Stanislaus meant "the poems to be read as a connected sequence, representing the closed chapter of that intensely lived life in Dublin, or more broadly, representing the withering of the Adonis garden of youth and pleasure" (*Chamber Music,* p. 44). Consequently, says Tindall, "the thirty-six poems tell a story of young love and failure. At the beginning the lover is alone. He meets a girl and their love, after suitable fooling, is almost successful. Then a rival intrudes. The hero's devotion gives way to irony and, at last, despair. Alone again at the end, the lover goes off into exile" (*Chamber Music,* p. 41).

DUBLINERS

DUBLINERS (1914) is a collection of short stories about lower-middle-class characters drawn with "exacting, diagnostic realism" (*Dubliners,* 1993, p. xv). By the time Joyce wrote the first of these stories ("The Sisters") at the suggestion of George Russell, and promptly saw it published in the August 1904 issue of the *Irish Homestead,* he already had started work on his autobiographical novel, *A Portrait of the Artist as a Young Man.* He also had spent a little more than four months in Paris, where he earned a bare subsistence by writing book reviews for the *Daily Express* until he was summoned home in April 1903 by news of his mother's imminent death. After she died in August, he dabbled with thoughts of a singing career, taking a few lessons to cultivate his fine tenor voice and even winning a bronze medal in the Feis Ceoil (Festival of Music) in May 1904. He also taught briefly at a private school for boys in the village of Dalkey, which gave him material for chapter 2 of *Ulysses.* As soon as he wrote "The Sisters" in July 1904, he began to see it as the first of a series of what he called "epicliti"—a misspelling of a term found in both Latin and Greek that is used to designate a moment in the Mass of the Eastern Orthodox Church when the priest invokes the Holy Ghost to turn the host and wine into the body and blood of Christ. Joyce used the term to designate the sense of revelation or "epiphany" that he hoped to generate from ordinary figures and events. Like a priest at Mass, he sought to convert "the bread of everyday life into something that has a permanent artistic life of its own" (Ellmann, 1982, p. 163). But the everyday life he set out to catch in these stories was grim, frustrating, and bleak—a life of stagnation. "I call the series *Dubliners*," he wrote, "to betray the soul of that hemoplegia or paralysis which many consider a city" (Ellmann, 1982, p. 163). By the beginning of the twentieth century, the decline of manufacturing in Dublin and of activity in its port had left many unemployed and packed into slum tenements on the north side of the river Liffey in central Dublin, the same quarter to which Joyce's debt-ridden family had moved in 1893, when he was eleven years old.

"The Sisters" exemplifies Joyce's vision of Dublin. It tells the story of a just-dead priest whose paralysis has been "identified with that general paralysis of the insane which characterizes the terminal stage of syphilitic infection" (*Dubliners*, 1993, p. xxxi). The story ends on a note of mysterious joy, however, when one of the sisters recalls the night on which the old priest was found alone in the chapel, "sitting up by himself in the dark in his confession-box, wide-awake and laughing-like softly to himself" (*Dubliners*, 1993, p. 10). Furthermore, since the story is told by a boy who is based on Joyce's own boyhood self, it may be linked to the autobiographical story that Joyce had begun to write. But *Dubliners* is not so much autobiography as "moral history," in Joyce's phrase. "I have tried to present [Dublin] . . . ," Joyce wrote, "under four of its aspects: childhood, adolescence, maturity and public life. The stories are arranged in this order" (*Letters of James Joyce*, vol. 2, p. 134).

The stories, in fact, trace an arc of development from the child narrators of the first three tales through the young men and women of such stories as "Eveline" and "The Boarding House" to the middle-aged Gabriel Conroy of the final story, "The Dead." While reflecting the ages of humanity in a modern city, the stories repeatedly sound a note of frustration mingled with the light of bitter revelation. At the end of "Araby," the speaker, a boy who has dreamed eagerly of attending a Middle Eastern bazaar and buying something there for the girl who has taken his fancy, fails to reach the place until the stalls are nearly all closed and the lights are extinguished: "Gazing up into the darkness I saw myself as a creature driven and derided by vanity; and my eyes burned with anguish and anger" (*Dubliners*, 1993, p. 28). At the end of "Eveline," a young woman suddenly refuses to sail off with her lover because she cannot bear to defy her father, who disapproves of him. As Frank desperately calls her to follow him onto the ship, "she set her white face to him, passive, like a helpless animal. Her eyes gave him no sign of love or farewell or recognition" (*Dubliners*, 1993, p. 34). At the end of "A Painful Case," a mature bachelor who has rejected the overtures of an unhappily married woman learns that she evidently has killed herself. Even while self-righteously justifying his rejection of her, he sees the price he has paid for it: "He gnawed the rectitude of his life; he felt that he had been outcast from life's feast. One human being had seemed to love him and he had denied her life and happiness: he had sentenced her to ignominy, a death of shame" (*Dubliners*, 1993, p. 113).

The pain of love lost or denied haunts these stories to the very end—above all in the almost unbearably poignant ending of "The Dead." As Gabriel Conroy prepares for bed in a hotel room with his wife, Gretta, after they have spent the evening at the Misses Morkan's annual dance, he learns that one of the songs they heard that night has awakened her memory of a young man whom she knew and loved in Galway and who used to sing it for her. He died at seventeen—heartbroken by her departure for a convent school in Dublin. Knowing that he has never loved any woman as Michael Furey once loved Gretta, Gabriel lies down carefully beside his wife under the sheets as if he were slipping into his grave. "Better pass boldly into that other world, in the full glory of some passion," he thinks, "than fade and wither dismally with age" (*Dubliners*, 1993, p. 224). As the story ends, snow begins to patter at the window, and Gabriel knows that it is falling all over Ireland, on plains and hills and graveyards, "faintly falling, like the descent of their last end, upon all the living and the dead" (*Dubliners*, 1993, p. 225).

As "a realist's study of his native city . . . conducted with unflinching Ibsenite moral rigor" (*Dubliners*, 1993, pp. xv-xvi), *Dubliners* did not easily find its way into print. Though it was first submitted to an English publisher named Grant Richards in 1905, and though Joyce wrote the final story in 1907, the book did not appear in print until 1914, when the timid and vacillating Richards finally screwed up the courage to publish it. In the meantime, Joyce had finished his first novel.

A PORTRAIT OF THE ARTIST AS A YOUNG MAN

A PORTRAIT of the Artist as a Young Man began as an autobiographical story dashed off in a single day—7 January 1904—and called, at the suggestion of Stanislaus, "A Portrait of the Artist." When this story was rejected by the editors of *Dana,* a new intellectual journal, Joyce began to rewrite it as a novel called *Stephen Hero.* By the summer of 1906, when Joyce moved from Trieste to Rome with Nora and their newborn son, Giorgio, he had drafted a very long work of twenty-five chapters, but he also had found himself unable to proceed further—partly because he was struggling to get *Dubliners* into print. In September 1907, after returning to Trieste, seeing *Chamber Music* into print, and writing "The Dead," he began to compress and remake *Stephen Hero* as a novel of five chapters, completing the first three by April 1907. Again the road to publication was an obstacle course. Finally, in 1915, after almost seven years and a near disaster (Joyce at one point threw the manuscript into the fire, whence it was rescued by his sister Eileen), most of the work was serialized in the (London) *Egoist.* The following year it was published in book form by B. W. Huebsch in New York.

A Portrait of the Artist as a Young Man tells in fictional form the story of Joyce's life from infancy to the age of nearly twenty, when, in December 1902, he left Dublin for Paris shortly after graduating from University College. Against the background of his family's decline from prosperity to privation and the series of moves provoked by this decline, Stephen Dedalus—Joyce's fictional self—progresses from grammar school at Clongowes Wood College (chapter 1) to adolescence at Belvedere College (chapters 2–4) and then to University College, Dublin (chapter 5). Stephen's early life closely resembles Joyce's. Like Stephen, the young Joyce failed to do his lessons one day, after another boy broke his glasses. Accused by the prefect of studies of deliberately breaking them to avoid work, he was beaten on the palm with a ferule. He successfully protested to the rector of the school, Father Conmee, who appears under his own name in *A Portrait of the Artist as a Young Man* and who briefly reappears in chapter 10 of *Ulysses.*

When the sixteen-year-old Stephen gives himself to a prostitute at the end of chapter 2, he reenacts what Joyce did at age fourteen—a little more sexually precocious, in fact, than he made himself in fiction. And we know, too, that like Stephen, Joyce broke away from Roman Catholicism in his late teens. He "probably did not take communion after his burst of piety at Easter in 1897" (Ellmann, 1982, p. 65), when he was fifteen, and in the spring of 1903, when his dying mother begged him to make his Easter duty by confessing his sins and taking Communion, he resolutely refused.

If Joyce renounced Roman Catholicism, he nonetheless remained steeped in its history and traditions. Stephen Dedalus takes his name from Saint Stephen, the first Christian martyr, and Dedalus, the ancient artificer who not only built the labyrinth of Crete but also fashioned wings with which he and his son, Icarus, escaped from it. This combination of Christian and pagan names aptly expresses Joyce's conception of his younger self: a frail and sensitive boy victimized by others but also an artist destined to take flight, to free his soul from the claims of friendship and from all the nets that Irish nationalism, Roman Catholic dogma, and the cult of Irish language study might fling upon it.

To represent himself in this way, Joyce takes some revealing liberties with the facts of his life. While Joyce himself at Clongowes was a spunky athlete who, just after turning seven, was punished for using "vulgar language" (Ellmann, 1982, p. 30), little Stephen Dedalus is a small, weak boy who tries to avoid the "rude feet" of the football players during a scrimmage and who is distressed to hear other boys using such indelicate words as "rump" (*Portrait of the Artist as a Young Man*, pp. 8–9; page numbers of quotes from this text refer to the 1964 edition throughout). The order of this novel—the story that Joyce constructs from the raw material of his life—requires a boyhood of sensitive, vulnerable innocence that is martyred by a tyrannical priest, saved by a kindly rector, stained by a fall into sexual experience, redeemed by a hellfire sermon that leads him back to the Communion rail, stultified by the regimen of piety, thrilled by a vision of aesthetic beauty, and finally moved to declare his intellectual independence. Hence Stephen becomes a young man who finally stands alone, uncompromised by family ties or friendship or allegiance to anything other than his own commitment to artistic self-expression.

While Stanislaus was a devoted and intelligent admirer who served his brother in many ways, he makes only a fleeting appearance as Maurice in chapter 2 of *Portrait of the Artist as a Young Man.* And while Cranly in chapter 5 is based on John Francis Byrne, Joyce's closest friend at University College, he comes across in the novel as a rival for the affections of Stephen's girlfriend "E.C." (identified in *Stephen Hero* as Emma Clery) and a conventionally minded spokesman for Roman Catholic doctrine and the claims of mother love. Cranly emerges as one more false friend, like Heron in chapter 2 of *Portrait of the Artist as a Young Man,* who beats Stephen when he will not admit that "Byron was no good" (p. 82), or like the simpleminded Davin, who frets over Stephen's refusal to sign a petition for universal peace and urges him to study the Irish language, to identify himself with Irish nationalism. All three would betray Stephen by forcing him to surrender, to submit, to compromise. "If friendship exists," writes Ellmann, "it impugns the quality of exile and of lonely heroism. . . . Joyce allows his hero to savor friendship before discovering its flaws, and then with the theme of broken friendship represents Stephen's broken ties with Ireland and the world" (1982, p. 116).

Stephen's sense of betrayal is reinforced by the story of Parnell, whose name provokes a bitter argument at the Christmas dinner table in chapter 1. When the pious Dante (Mrs. Riordan) calls Parnell "a traitor to his country . . . an adulterer" and defends the priests for abandoning him, little Stephen is "thrilled" to hear Mr. Casey—his father's friend—denounce the bishops and priests of Ireland for betraying their own country to the English (p. 38). In chapter 5, when Davin urges Stephen to join the Irish nationalists, Stephen recycles Mr. Casey's words: "No honourable and sincere man," he says, "has given up to you his life and his youth and his affections from the days of Tone to those of Parnell but you sold him to the enemy or failed him in need or reviled him and left him for another. . . . Do you know what Ireland is? . . . Ireland is the old sow that eats her farrow" (p. 203). If Parnell is Ireland's uncrowned king, as he was sometimes called (Mr. Dedalus

sobbingly calls him "my dead king," p. 39), Stephen becomes Ireland's uncanonized conscience. For in denouncing Ireland's betrayal of its own champions, he echoes Saint Stephen's denunciation of the Jewish elders for persecuting and betraying their own prophets—right up to and including Christ (Acts of the Apostles 7:51-53).

A Portrait of the Artist as a Young Man, however, is not just the political story of how Stephen wrests his independence from all of those who threaten to stifle it. It is also the story of how he discovers the power of language, beginning with the words of the children's story read to him by his father on the very first page. From the beginning, language and literature are essential parts of the reality Stephen experiences; for him there is no absolute difference between literature and life. The first thing he remembers doing is using language or, more precisely, singing about "wild rose blossoms / On the little green place." But in lisping his own version of the song, "O, the green wothe botheth," he also is beginning to compose by transforming, changing the color of the roses and thereby creating a world of his own (p. 7).

Stephen soon discovers that language by turns can be menacing, repulsive, mystifying, and illuminating. He is frightened by such words as "apologise," which come with threats of dire punishment, such as eagles plucking out his eyes. He is repelled by the word *Foetus* carved into a desk at his father's medical school. He is mystified by the phrases applied to the Blessed Virgin Mary—such as *Tower of Gold* and *House of Ivory.* But when he notices that Eileen, the girl who lives nearby, has "cool white hands" like ivory and that her fair hair streams out "like gold in the sun" as she runs, he discovers what the phrases mean. "By thinking of things," he says to himself, "you could understand them" (pp. 42B43).

Pure and virginal though she is, Eileen introduces Stephen to sex. By putting "her hand into his pocket where his hand was" (p. 43)—a potentially erotic move—she unwittingly initiates the process whereby Stephen's veneration of the Virgin Mary turns into his fascination with the whore, with the violation of purity, with lecherous transgression. The prospect of sexual experience stirs in Stephen a paradoxical combination of feelings. At the end of chapter 2, he is aroused by lust and yet also envisions the moment of sex as a sacred rite of initiation, a "holy encounter . . . at which weakness and timidity and inexperience were to fall from him" (p. 99). In the encounter itself, however, Stephen surrenders himself to a prostitute like a child nestling in the arms of his mother, "conscious of nothing in the world but the dark pressure of her softly parting lips" (p. 101).

This falling into the "swoon of sin" (p. 101) is followed by Stephen's experience of a spiritual "retreat" in chapter 3, with its hair-raising sermons on the punishments of hell and the torments of the damned. Since chapter 3 ends with Stephen renouncing the bestiality of lust and receiving Communion, the first three chapters seem to reenact a familiar evangelical progression: innocence, fall into sin, return to virtue and God. In some ways, Stephen's story reenacts the *Confessions* (397–401) of Saint Augustine, who recalls his own teenage wallowing in the fleshpots of Carthage before telling how he came to Christianity. But in the final chapter of *A Portrait of the Artist as a Young Man*, Stephen dramatically swerves from this precedent by rejecting the church to which he has returned. Having unleashed the full force of Jesuit eloquence in a series of sermons calculated to terrify anyone who hears them, he then calmly declares—in the words of Satan—"I will not serve" the church (p. 239). For by this time Stephen has discovered a religion of his own, the religion of art.

The discovery comes at the end of chapter 4, when Stephen sees a girl wading in the sea. While her physical attractiveness might precipitate another fall into sexual desire such as we find at the end of chapter 2, Stephen sees her through a veil of metaphor as "a strange and beautiful seabird" whose "ivory" thighs and "slateblue skirts" (p. 171) compose a "mortal" version of the Virgin Mary and thus complete the circle initiated by the movement of Eileen's "ivory" hand. For Stephen, this idealized figure is an object not of lust but of enraptured contemplation; she provokes in him what he later calls an "esthetic" or "static" emotion, wherein "the mind is arrested and raised above desire and loathing" (p. 205).

Just before seeing her in this way, Stephen hears his own name shouted at him by a crowd of his schoolmates swimming naked in the sea. The name of Dedalus conjures up before him a vision of "the fabulous artificer" flying above the waves and raises a potent question: "Was it . . . a prophecy of the end he had been born to serve . . . , a symbol of the artist forging anew in his workshop out of the sluggish matter of the earth a new soaring

impalpable imperishable being?" (p. 169). In the final words of the novel, this question is decisively answered *yes*. From the vantage point of its conclusion, *A Portrait of the Artist as a Young Man* tells the story of how Stephen moves from one father to another. From the biological father who reads to him in infancy he turns to the religious fathers who educate and discipline him and then to the mythical father who at last inspires him. With a final salute to Dedalus, Stephen goes "to encounter for the millionth time the reality of experience and to forge in the smithy of my soul the uncreated conscience of my race" (pp. 252–253).

EXILES *AND* ULYSSES

IN 1914, Joyce started writing an Ibsenian play called *Exiles*, which was finished in 1915, published in 1918, and first staged in Munich the following year. In Ibsen's *When We Dead Awaken* (which Joyce had saluted warmly and described extensively in an essay he wrote at the age of eighteen), a middle-aged, spiritually dead sculptor named Rubek leaves his petulant wife to the seductive charms of a hard-drinking hunter while he returns to Irene, once the model for the central figure in his masterpiece "The Resurrection Day." Realizing that she once gave him not only all her "naked loveliness" but also her "young living soul" (*Critical Writings*, p. 55), and thus had emptied herself for him, Rubek suddenly decides to climb with her to a snow-capped peak—in the face of certain death from an avalanche—so that they might "live life to its uttermost, before [they] go down to [their] graves again" (*Critical Writings*, p. 62).

In *Exiles*, the counterpart of Ibsen's Rubek is an Irish writer named Richard Rowan, a character loosely based on Joyce himself. Having run off to Rome nine years earlier with Bertha, his "bride in exile" (p. 111; page numbers refer to the 1961 edition of *Exiles*)—an act for which his now dead mother never forgave him—he recently has returned to Dublin with her and their eight-year-old son, Archie. Though Richard enjoys the unwavering fidelity of Bertha, he knows from her own lips that she is being pursued ardently by his best friend and disciple, Robert Hand, a journalist who has known her as long as Richard has. But the familiar theme of betrayal gets a startling new twist. To justify a move that might destroy the friendship between the two men, Robert quotes Richard's own words to Richard himself: "The blinding instant of passion alone—passion, free, unashamed, irresistible—that is the only gate by which we can escape from the misery of what slaves call life" (p. 71). But this "language of [his] youth"—which sounds remarkably like the language of the middle-aged, briefly resurrected Rubek—fails to move Richard, because he has become a man of almost Olympian detachment. Knowing that Bertha's body "was always [his] loyal slave" and that he has "many times" betrayed her with other women, he says that he felt guilty for not allowing her "to give to another what was hers and not mine to give" and also that he resented her innocence. Consequently, he says to Robert, "In the very core of my ignoble heart I longed to be betrayed by you and by her—in the dark, in the night—secretly, meanly, craftily" (p. 70). Yet even though Richard now gives Bertha perfect freedom to meet Robert alone in his own cottage, she declines to gratify his passion. Having once again failed to win Bertha from Richard, Robert promptly writes an editorial hailing him as a "spiritual exile" who left Ireland "to seek in other lands that food of the spirit by which a nation of human beings is sustained in life" and has now returned (p. 99). Richard thus seems assured that Bertha and Robert both love him, but he hears their voices telling him "to despair" (p. 109). Although he will not despair and will remain in Ireland, he tells Bertha at the end that he feels "a deep deep wound of doubt in [his] soul"—a wound "which can never be healed" (p. 112).

While Joyce was writing *Exiles,* he also was writing the opening chapters of *Ulysses,* which he started in Trieste, Italy, in 1914 and finished in Paris in 1921—just in time for the novel to be published by Sylvia Beach's Shakespeare and Company on his fortieth birthday on 2 February 1922. *Ulysses* first presents itself as a sequel to *A Portrait of the Artist as a Young Man,* since it takes up the story of Joyce's life in June 1904, a little more than a year after news of his mother's imminent death brought him home from Paris. But Stephen Dedalus now plays only a supporting role. For *Ulysses* tells the story of what is done, felt, thought, and dreamed on a single day, Bloomsday—16 June 1904—by Leopold Bloom. Bloom is a thirty-eight-year-old advertising canvasser of Hungarian Jewish extraction who leaves home in the morning, wanders around Dublin, agonizes over his wife's affair with a flashy promoter named Blazes Boylan (betrayal again), and finally returns to his home and his bed in the early hours of the next day. Improbable as it seems at first, Bloom is the reincarnation of Ulysses, the Latin name for the ancient Greek hero of Homer's *Odyssey.* In the course of a single day, Bloom reenacts the ten-year-long adventures of the homeward-bound voyager returning from the conquest of Troy.

In the eighteen chapters of *Ulysses,* Joyce re-creates Homer's epic within the Dublin of his own time. On the one hand, he sets out "to give a picture of Dublin so complete that if the city one day suddenly disappeared from the earth it could be reconstructed out of [his] book" (Budgen, pp. 67–68). On the other hand, he makes the life of a particular Dubliner both Homeric and heroic. As T. S. Eliot observed in the *Dial,* Joyce uses ancient myth as "a way of controlling, of ordering, of giving a shape and a significance to the immense panorama of futility and anarchy which is contemporary history" (p. 483).

The *Odyssey* opens on the island of Ithaca, where the wife and son of Ulysses—Penelope and Telemachus—have spent twenty years awaiting his return and enduring the insolence of suitors who have usurped his palace to devour his livestock, abuse his serving women, and seek the hand of his wife. Since the first part of the *Odyssey* treats Telemachus and his efforts to get news of his long-absent father, this section of the *Odyssey* is called the *Telemachiad.* Correspondingly, the first three chapters of *Ulysses* treat Stephen Dedalus, who has no wish to see anything more of his biological father but who nonetheless is destined to meet a father figure in the wandering Bloom. Like Telemachus, he also must contend with usurpers: a hard-drinking, irrepressibly playful medical student named Buck Mulligan and a supercilious Englishman named Haines. In September 1904 Joyce himself spent five days living in Martello Tower on the south shore of Dublin Bay with two young men like these. As Stephen breakfasts in the tower with Mulligan and Haines, he feels doubly usurped: Haines embodies the English usurpation of Ireland, including its language, and Mulligan—life of the party—takes center stage and threatens to appropriate Stephen's whole life, turning him from an aspiring writer into a hopeless lush. In a complicated way, the black-coated Stephen recalls the inky-suited Hamlet as well as Telemachus, a fact that anticipates Stephen's long discourse on Shakespeare in chapter 9. In the same way that Hamlet is haunted by the ghost of his father, Stephen is haunted by the ghost of his newly dead mother. But instead of being asked to kill her murderer, he is made to feel like a murderer himself—guilty of killing her by refusing to kneel down and pray at her bedside.

Stephen spends the morning teaching a class at a boys' school, talking with its dim-witted headmaster (who paradoxically recalls the wise old Nestor visited by Homer's Telemachus), and ruminating on the Protean theme of metamorphosis while walking the sands of Sandymount Strand. While Stephen's morning is presented thus in chapters 1–3, chapters 4–6 introduce us to Leopold Bloom by treating his adventures of the morning: He makes breakfast for his wife, Molly, who stands in for Penelope and yet whose power to captivate Bloom recalls the nymph Calypso's seven-year detainment of Ulysses. He visits a drugstore, thinks of narcotics, and, in this way, reenacts Ulysses' visit to the land of the Lotus-Eaters. And, in attending the funeral of Paddy Dignam, he reenacts Ulysses' visit to the realm of Hades, the world of the dead. Chapters 4–6 thus initiate the long middle section of the novel, which corresponds to the wanderings of Ulysses and culminates in the "Circe" episode of chapter 15, where Homer's island of the enchantress becomes the brothel of Bella Cohen in Dublin's red-light district—Nighttown.

In saving Stephen from arrest at the end of the episode and escorting him to the cabman's shelter, Bloom finally gets to play a paternal role. His meeting with Stephen leads to something like Ulysses' reunion with Telemachus: a conversation in Bloom's own house. Though Stephen declines Bloom's invitation to stay, the last three chapters carry Bloom decisively homeward, which is why they are collectively called *Nostos*, the homecoming phase. And just as Ulysses ends up in bed with his wife, Penelope, Bloom finally gets into bed with Molly, who closes the novel by taking a mental journey of her own, in what is perhaps the most extraordinary monologue ever written.

Despite parallels like these, Joyce repeatedly exposes the gaps between his major characters and Homer's. While Ulysses was a warrior king as well as a heroic voyager, Bloom sells advertising space in a Dublin newspaper. He has spent his whole life in Dublin, and, so far as we can tell, his nautical experience includes nothing more than a boat tour of Dublin Bay and a few hours of rowing with his wife and daughter during which his totally inept management of the oars nearly swamps the boat. Ulysses gets himself shipwrecked, of course, but he always manages to land on his feet and to find his way into the beds of some lovely ladies—notably Circe and Calypso—while slowly making his way back to the bed of Penelope. Bloom's sex life falls far short of this success. On Bloomsday itself, he conducts a mildly erotic correspondence with a ditzy, half-literate typist whom he has never met; he furtively masturbates while rapturously gazing at the underclothes of a young woman sitting on a beach; and, while he sleeps with Molly every night, including Bloomsday night, he has had no complete intercourse with her for more than ten years.

Furthermore, this would-be counterpart of Homer's indefatigable warrior—the man who would not leave Troy until the Greeks sacked it—is a fervent pacifist who is opposed to violence of any kind. He knows from early morning on Bloomsday that Boylan is coming to see Molly at four o'clock that day, and when he finally joins her in bed after midnight, he finds incontestable evidence that Boylan has been there. But while Ulysses slaughters the suitors for daring even to tempt the fidelity of his wife, Bloom takes no revenge on his rival, and after struggling with his own feelings of envy and jealousy, he accepts Molly's adultery "with equanimity" (p. 602; page numbers refer to the 1986 edition of *Ulysses*). Finally, Molly's own adulterous behavior makes her seem wholly disqualified for the role of the supremely faithful Penelope.

It is not easy to reconcile these discrepancies with the claim that Leopold Bloom reenacts the adventures of Ulysses, but two episodes can help us see the qualities and characteristics these two figures share. The first is Bloom's return to his home in chapter 4 after he has gone out to buy a pork kidney for his breakfast. When he opens the front door of his own house, "two letters and a card lay on the hallfloor. He stooped and gathered them. Mrs. Marion Bloom. His quickened heart slowed at once. Bold hand, Mrs. Marion" (p. 50). The reference to "Mrs. Marion Bloom" should remind us that the very first sentence of the chapter begins with the phrase "Mr. Leopold Bloom" (p. 45). "Leopold" means "the people's prince" (Gifford, 1988, p. 70), and the title of Mister indicates that he is the man of the house and presumably the master of it as well. In the days when a married woman took the name of her husband, the only proper way to address her would be by that name: Mrs. Leopold Bloom. But the bold hand on the envelope thrusts the husband aside and goes straight for the name of the wife. The bold hand is that of Blazes Boylan, who is arranging a concert tour for Molly's soprano voice and who writes to say that he is coming in the afternoon to bring the program of her songs. Yet Bloom knows full well what kind of music he plans to make with her and what his bold hand will be doing with her that afternoon. At the very moment when he reenters his house, therefore, he finds that his place has been usurped by another. It is the first unmistakably Ulyssean moment in the novel.

Another telling example comes later in the day, when Bloom encounters a figure known only as the "citizen." The citizen corresponds to Homer's Polyphemus, the one-eyed giant who lives in a cave, despises strangers, and tramples on the rules of hospitality by eating his visitors. When Ulysses and his men become trapped in the cave of Polyphemus, Ulysses escapes with his men by getting Polyphemus drunk, blinding him with the burning point of an olivewood stake, and then tricking him into rolling away the huge stone that blocks the entrance. Caught in a pub with the drunken, xenophobic, rabidly anti-Semitic citizen, Bloom likewise uses his brain against the citizen's brawn, denouncing the persecution of Jews and the blindness of a militant nationalism—"force, hatred, history, all that"—in favor of love (p. 273). Bloom fits no stereotypical categories. As a man genuinely bent on helping others, such as the family of the late Paddy Dignam, he is neither the miserly, grasping Jew of anti-Semitic legend nor a militant Zionist. He is a pacifist, and if we wonder how a pacifist can possibly reenact the life of Ulysses, we should remember that Homer's polytropic hero—a man of many turns—did not even want to fight the Trojan War to begin with. If we remember also that Joyce wrote this novel between 1914 and 1921, during the greatest and bloodiest war ever fought, we can see why his Ulyssean hero could not be just another warrior. Instead, he had to be brave enough to do battle with war itself, "with force, hatred, history, all that."

Bloom also takes deadly aim at anti-Semitism. Just as the departing Ulysses boldly throws his identity at Polyphemos, telling him exactly who this would-be "nobody" is, the departing Bloom—riding off in an open car—defiantly proclaims his Jewishness and thereby his kinship with Christ. "Your God," he tells the citizen, "was a jew. Christ was a jew like me" (p. 280). In thus identifying himself and his Jewishness with Christ, Bloom drives the citizen into a truly Polyphemic rage. Like the blinded Polyphemus, who vainly threw a boulder at Ulysses' departing ship, the drunken, flabby, onetime shot-putter tries to hit the departing Bloom with a cracker box. He fails because he cannot see straight in any sense, and unlike Polyphemus, who calls down on Odysseus the wrath of Poseidon (god of the sea), all the citizen can do is to send racing after Bloom his mongrel dog Garryowen.

Throughout *Ulysses*, Joyce replays Homer's ancient song in an unmistakably modern rhythm and key. Homer's epic never becomes a procrustean bed that contemporary Dublin is cut or stretched to fit, and even as the major characters—Bloom, Stephen, and Molly—unwittingly reenact the lives of Ulysses, Telemachus, and Penelope, respectively, they remain as free, indeterminate, and idiosyncratic as any three fictional characters can be. Stephen yearns to make his name as a writer but so far has written almost nothing, and when he declines Bloom's invitation to spend the night or even take up residence in the Bloom household, he leaves with no idea where he is headed. Bloom returns to a house and a bed where his wife has committed adultery and where she eagerly anticipates her lover's next visit, but he takes no action against either of them. In the end, he and Molly lie in the same bed but positioned head to foot, still sexually estranged. Yet for all the wanderings of Molly's monologue and for all her ruminations on other men, especially Blazes Boylan, her thoughts and desires finally come home to Bloom.

They make their way to him through a maze of contradictions. Although she often is construed as an earth mother, Molly seems relieved to learn, from her menstruation, that Boylan has not made her pregnant. Even though she is known around Dublin as a "gamey mare" (p. 193), her fling with Boylan is her first experience of complete sexual intercourse in more than ten years. And, though she desperately yearns to see Boylan again, she finds him boorish and vulgar: "no thats no way for him has he no manners nor no refinement nor no nothing in his nature slapping us behind like that on my bottom because I didn't call him Hugh the ignoramus that doesnt know poetry from a cabbage" (p. 638).

Whereas her final word for Boylan is emphatically "no," her final word for the refined and sensitive Bloom is "yes." Launching the final "sentence" of the chapter, the hammer beats of "no" here anticipate by contrast the resounding repetition of "yes" at the end, where Molly remembers passionately affirming her desire for Bloom on the day he proposed and they first made love:

then I asked him with my eyes to ask again yes and then he asked me would I yes to say yes my mountain flower and first I put my arms around him yes and drew him down to me so he could feel my breasts all perfume yes and his heart was going like mad and yes I said yes I will Yes.

(*Ulysses* p. 644)

In Molly's final, resounding *yes* we can hear what the novel as a whole offers us: a resounding, uncompromising, uninhibited affirmation of life.

FINNEGANS WAKE

ULYSSES seems an impossible act for any novelist to follow, but in 1923, just the year after it first appeared, Joyce started work on a book even more daring and daunting. Aside from letters and an occasional poem, such as "A Prayer" (May 1924), which appeared in his *Pomes Penyeach* (1927), he wrote almost nothing else in the last nineteen years of his life, all the while struggling to see through failing eyes that required one operation after another but that somehow kept on working until he died. From 1924 to 1937 the new book was called simply "Work in Progress," and it was published in fragments, chiefly in the Paris magazine *transition*. Joyce refused to give the title to his publisher until just before the book was to be bound. He kept even close friends wondering until 2 August 1938, when—having offered a thousand francs to the first correct guesser of the magic words—he was startled to hear them spoken at dinner by Eugene Jolas, cofounder of *transition*, who promptly was sworn to secrecy. In 1939, two years before Joyce died, the whole book was published as *Finnegans Wake* by Faber and Faber in London and by Viking Press in New York.

Finnegans Wake takes its title from a ballad about a hod carrier named Tim Finnegan who fell to his death from a ladder but was revived at his wake when a scuffle among the mourners scattered a noggin of whiskey over his corpse. The ballad itself shows how the Irish can turn a funeral into a party, or what Joyce called in his book a "funferal" (1958, p. 120)—a perfect example of the punning deformation and reformation of the English language that relentlessly permeates *Finnegans Wake*. Since the ballad gives an irresistibly Irish twist to the doctrine of the Resurrection, it furnished the seed of a novel about sleep and wakening, death and regeneration. Joyce told a friend that he conceived the book as the dream of a legendary wise man named Finn MacCumhal. Lying in bed beside the river Liffey, Finn sees the history of Ireland and the whole world flowing through his mind. *Finnegans Wake* thus follows the course that *Ulysses* initiated. If Bloom can relive the wanderings of an ancient Greek hero, the soul of the human being is timeless, and history repeats itself in an endless series of cycles, as Joyce learned from an eighteenth-century Italian philosopher named Giambattista Vico.

As a book of the night written to follow the novel of a day, *Finnegans Wake* recycles the material of *Ulysses* in something like the way that a dream recycles the events of a day. Leopold Bloom—the paterfamilias of *Ulysses*—now becomes a middle-aged pub keeper named Humphrey Chimpden Earwicker (HCE), an Irish Protestant of Scandinavian extraction who lives and works in Chapelizod, a village spanning the river Liffey about three miles west of the center of Dublin. Molly, whose nocturnal monologue prefigures the night vision of *Finnegans Wake*, becomes Humphrey's wife, Anna Livia Plurabelle, whose middle name evokes the endlessly renewed flowing of the Liffey and whose initials (ALP) suggest her mountain majesty. Milly, Bloom's daughter, who captivates him with her sexual vitality and thereby excites Molly's jealousy, becomes Earwicker's daughter, Isabel, who in his dream arouses his incestuous desires and thus burdens him with guilt. (Seen apparently exhibiting himself in Phoenix Park to two Irish girls, who together signify Isobel, Earwicker is accused, tried, imprisoned, and eventually buried.) In the course of HCE's dream, his particular guilt becomes the collective guilt of humankind embedded in the cycles of history. Like Adam from Paradise, like Humpty Dumpty from his wall, like Napoleon at Waterloo, like Parnell tripped by scandal, like Ibsen's Master

Builder from his tower, like Finnegan from his ladder, the human being falls and then rises and falls again—till the end of time.

Anthony Burgess notes that Joyce "make[s] his hero re-live the whole of history in a night's sleep" (*A Shorter* Finnegans Wake, p. xii), but Earwicker sees history through fallen eyes. As Margot Norris writes:

The Wakean vision of a universe ever hurtling toward chaos is based on the theme of the fallen father. He is named rather than namer. He is uncertain of name and identity, unlocatable rather than a center that fixes, defines, and gives meaning to his cosmos. He is a lawbreaker rather than lawgiver. As head of the family, he is incestuous rather than the source of order in the relations of his lineage.

(*The Decentered Universe of* Finnegans Wake, p. 61)

Although Earwicker has no more knowledge of Giambattista Vico than Bloom has of Homer, his dream is made to reenact a Viconian cycle just as the wanderings of Bloom reenact the wanderings of Ulysses. In something like the way that each chapter of *Ulysses* recalls an episode in the *Odyssey*, each of the four sections of *Finnegans Wake* evokes a phase in one complete cycle of history as Vico defined it, with each phase marked by a distinctive type of government. Section 1, comprising the unnumbered chapters 1–8, evokes the theocratic stage, when gods create language and law by means of thunderous pronouncements, such as the hundred-letter word that first appears in parentheses on the first page of the book; they also speak to humankind through patriarchs and prophets. In the aristocratic, or heroic, second stage of section 2 (chapters 9–12), great men become fathers of their people and make laws of their own without feeling obliged to have them divinely ratified. In the democratic third phase of section 3 (chapters 13–16), demagogues vulgarize the process of governing and lead the way to chaos and anarchy. This condition necessitates what Vico calls a *ricorso*, or return, manifest in section 4, the final section (chapter 17). The gods speak again in thunder: "A hand from the cloud emerges, holding a chart expanded" (*Finnegans Wake*, 1959, p. 593)—and humankind must worship them once again, so the theocratic stage begins anew and the cycle is complete. The cyclic energy of the novel first emerges in its very first word, "riverrun." Since this word comes in the middle of a sentence that begins at the very end of

the novel, the whole book is written to exemplify the process of returning and recycling. The twin sons of the Earwickers, Shem and Shaun, can be traced to James Joyce and his brother John Stanislaus, just as their father—according to Richard Ellman—was "the chief model for Earwicker" (Ellmann, 1982, p. 22). The twins are normally Shem the Penman and Shaun the Post, respectively the author of the Word and the man who delivers it—often deforming it in the process. As Ellmann notes, however, Shem and Shaun also stand for "every possible pair of brothers or opponents" (Ellmann, 1982, p. 545) beginning with old Nick and Saint Mick, otherwise known as Satan and the archangel Michael, and including such figures as Cain and Abel, which means that their parents may likewise stand for Adam and Eve. Yet this vision of universal history keeps its eyes on Dublin, as the very opening lines reveal: "Riverrun, past Eve and Adam's, from swerve of shore to bend of bay, brings us by a commodius vicus of recirculation back to Howth Castle and Environs" (*Finnegans Wake*, 1958, p. 3).

Vicus means "street" in Latin, but it also evokes the wisdom of Vico, whose cyclic theory of history runs like a river through all that follows. By inversion, "Eve and Adam's" designates a church called Adam and Eve's that stands on the south bank of the Liffey and turns up several times in *Ulysses*. Of course, it also refers to our first parents, primordial versions of Leopold and Molly, Humphrey and Anna Livia, and Ulysses and Penelope. Howth Castle stands on Howth Head, the northern promontory of Dublin Bay, where Bloom and Molly first consummated their love, a place to which each of them rapturously returns in memory. The castle and the river tell an ageless story. With the castle signifying "the city-building resourcefulness of mankind," as Harry Levin says, the river manifests "the vital fertility of womankind" (*The Portable James Joyce*, p. 149). Together they make up a city whose rivers flow to the sea, to the mighty mother blessed by Buck Mulligan on the very first page of *Ulysses*.

Since cycling and recycling permeate the dream of HCE, the characters play a profusion of parts. As Burgess writes:

What HCE does in his sleep is to turn his family into a kind of amateur dramatic society which, with help from customers, the cleaning-woman, the pub handyman and a few others, is prepared to impersonate, however unhandily, a whole corpus of beings from myth and literature (including popular magazines, barnstorming melodramas and doubtful street-ballads) as well as from history-books.

(*A Shorter* Finnegans Wake, p. xiv)

And the cast itself is formidable. Besides the Earwicker family and Kate the cleaning woman, it includes four old men who play the four evangelists, the four provinces of Ireland, and the four posts of the bed; twelve customers at the bar who serve by turns as apostles and jurymen; and twenty-eight girls from the academy of St. Bride's who—with the help of Isabel—evoke Joyce's birth month of February, a month of twenty-eight and sometimes twenty-nine days. *Finnegans Wake* thus offers us a vast and inexhaustibly complex network of associations woven together to represent the dream state. As Margot Norris observes, the notorious complexities of its language "show the work of the dreamer as he constructs and observes the incredible artifact of his dream" (*Decentered Universe*, p. 117).

While writing much of *Ulysses*, Joyce lived in Zurich, the capital of neutral Switzerland, for the duration of World War I. By a cruel irony, World War II broke out just a few months after the last great work of this ardent pacifist was published. In December 1940, Joyce and his family were forced to leave France, which had been occupied by German troops. They returned to Zurich, where Joyce died of a perforated ulcer on 13 January 1941 and where he is buried. In death he remains an exile from his native land but an exile who, like Richard Rowan, sought "in other lands that food of the spirit by which a nation of human beings is sustained in life" (*Exiles*, 1961, p. 99). If Ireland were suddenly annihilated, its spirit would nonetheless live on in the works of Joyce, who not only forged the conscience of his race but also re-created in Dublin the history of the human race.

SELECTED BIBLIOGRAPHY

I. COLLECTED WORKS. *The Critical Writings of James Joyce* (New York and London, 1966; repr. Ithaca, N.Y., 1989), ed. by Ellsworth Mason and Richard Ellmann; *The Portable James Joyce*, rev. ed. (New York, 1978), ed. and with an intro. and notes by Harry Levin; *Poems and Shorter Writings* (New York and London, 1991), ed. by Richard Ellmann and A. Walton Litz with the assistance of John Whittier-Ferguson.

II. SEPARATE WORKS. *Chamber Music* (London, 1907), poems; *Dubliners* (London, 1914), short stories; *A Portrait of the Artist as a Young Man* (New York, 1916), novel; *Exiles* (London and New York, 1918), play; *Ulysses* (Paris, 1922), novel; *Poems Penyeach* (Paris, 1927), poems; *Finnegans Wake* (New York, 1939; repr. 1971), with the author's corrections incorporated into the text, novel; *Exiles: A Play in Three Acts* (New York, 1951; London, 1952), with unpublished notes by the author and an intro. by Padraic Colum; *Chamber Music* (New York, 1954; repr. 1982), ed. by William York Tindall; *Finnegans Wake* (New York, 1959; repr. 1971), with the author's corrections incorporated into the text; *Stephen Hero* (Norfolk, Conn., 1963; London, 1969), ed. and with an intro. by Theodore Spencer and rev. by John J. Slocum and Herbert Cahoon; *A Portrait of the Artist as a Young Man: Text, Criticism, and Notes* (New York and London, 1964; repr., New York, 1968), ed. by Chester G. Anderson; *A Shorter* Finnegans Wake (New York, 1967), ed. by Anthony Burgess; *Giacomo Joyce* (New York and London, 1968), posthumously published notebook ed. and with an intro. and notes by Richard Ellmann; *Dubliners* (New York, 1969), ed. by Robert Scholes and A. Walton Litz; *Ulysses: The Corrected Text* (New York and London, 1986), ed. by Hans Walter Gabler with Wolfhard Steppe and Claus Melchior; *Dubliners* (New York, 1993), ed. by Terence Brown.

III. LETTERS. Richard Ellmann and Stuart Gilbert, eds., *Letters of James Joyce*, 3 vols. (New York, 1966); Richard Ellmann, *Selected Letters of James Joyce* (New York, 1975).

IV. MANUSCRIPT INDEX AND BIBLIOGRAPHY. Michael Groden, comp., *James Joyce's Manuscripts: An Index* (New York, 1980); Thomas F. Staley, *An Annotated Critical Bibliography of James Joyce* (New York, 1989).

V. BIOGRAPHICAL STUDIES. Stanislaus Joyce, *My Brother's Keeper: James Joyce's Early Years* (New York and London, 1958), ed. by Richard Ellmann; Stanislaus Joyce, *The Complete Dublin Diary of Stanislaus Joyce* (Ithaca, N.Y., 1971), ed. by George H. Healey; Frank Budgen, *James Joyce and the Making of* Ulysses *and Other Writings* (London, 1972; repr. New York, 1989); Richard Ellmann, *James Joyce*, rev. ed. (New York, 1982); Brenda Maddox, *Nora: The Real Life of Molly Bloom* (Boston, 1988).

VI. CRITICAL STUDIES. T. S. Eliot, "Ulysses, Order, and Myth," in *Dial* 75 (November 1923); Stuart Gilbert, *James Joyce's* Ulysses: *A Study*, 2d rev. ed. (New York, 1952); S. L. Goldberg, *The Classical Temper: A Study of James Joyce's* Ulysses (New York, 1961); Anthony Burgess, *Re Joyce* (New York, 1965), published in England as *Here Comes Everybody: An Introduction to James Joyce for the Ordinary Reader* (London, 1965). Darcy O'Brien, *The Conscience of James Joyce* (Princeton, 1968); Weldon Thornton, *Allusions in* Ulysses: *An Annotated List* (Chapel Hill, N.C., 1968); Clive Hart, ed. *James Joyce's* Dubliners: *Critical Essays* (London and New York, 1969); Robert H. Deming, *James Joyce: The Critical Heritage*, 2 vols. (London, 1970); Samuel Beckett, Marcel

Brion, Frank Budgen, et al., *Our Exagmination Round His Factification for Incamination of Work in Progress* (Paris, 1929; repr. London and New York, 1972); Zack R. Bowen, *Musical Allusions in the Works of James Joyce: Early Poetry Through Ulysses* (Albany, N.Y., 1974); Clive Hart and David Hayman, eds., *James Joyce's* Ulysses: *Critical Essays* (Berkeley, 1974); Mark Shechner, *Joyce in Nighttown: A Psychoanalytic Inquiry into* Ulysses (Berkeley, 1974); Margot Norris, *The Decentered Universe of* Finnegans Wake: *A Structuralist Analysis* (Baltimore, 1976); Michael Seidel, *Epic Geography: James Joyce's* Ulysses (Princeton, 1976); Richard Ellmann, *The Consciousness of James Joyce* (Toronto, 1977); James H. Maddox, *Joyce's* Ulysses *and the Assault upon Character* (New Brunswick, N.J., 1978); Richard Ellmann, *Ulysses on the Liffey* (London, 1972).

Shari and Bernard Benstock, *Who's He When He's at Home: A James Joyce Directory* (Urbana, Ill., 1980); Dominic Mangianello, *Joyce's Politics* (London and Boston, 1980); Roland McHugh, *Annotations to* Finnegans Wake, rev. ed. (Baltimore, 1991); Karen Lawrence, *The Odyssey of Style in* Ulysses (Princeton, 1981); Don Gifford, *Joyce Annotated: Notes for* Dubliners *and* A Portrait of the Artist as a Young Man, 2d ed., rev. and enlarged (Berkeley, 1982); Seamus Deane, *A Short History of Irish Literature* (London and Notre Dame, Ind., 1986); Hugh Kenner, *Ulysses*, rev. ed. (Baltimore, 1987); Don Gifford and Robert J. Seidman, *Ulysses Annotated: Notes for James Joyce's* Ulysses, 2d ed., rev. and expanded (Berkeley, 1988); Vicki Mahaffey, *Reauthorizing Joyce* (New York, 1988); Umberto Eco, *The Aesthetics of Chaosmos: The Middle Ages of James Joyce,* trans. by Ellen Esrock and David Robey (Tulsa, Okla., 1982; repr. Cambridge, Mass.,1989).

Derek Attridge, ed., *The Cambridge Companion to James Joyce* (Cambridge, 1990); Suzette A. Henke, *James Joyce and the Politics of Desire* (New York, 1990); James Fairhall, *James Joyce and the Question of History* (New York, 1993); Richard Pearce, *Molly Blooms: A Polylogue on "Penelope" and Cultural Studies* (Madison, Wis., 1994); Vincent John Cheng, *Joyce, Race, and Empire* (Cambridge, England, 1995); Morris Beja and David Norris, eds., *Joyce in the Hibernian Metropolis: Essays* (Columbus, Ohio, 1996); Harry Blamires, *The New Bloomsday Book: A Guide Through* Ulysses, 3d ed. (New York, 1996); Maria Tymoczko, *The Irish Ulysses* (Berkeley, 1997); Margot Norris, ed., *A Companion to James Joyce's* Ulysses: *Biography and Historical Contexts, Critical History, and Essays from Five Contemporary Critical Perspectives* (New York, 1998); Paul Schwaber, *The Cast of Characters: A Reading of* Ulysses (New Haven, Conn., 1999).

JOHN KEATS

(1795–1821)

Brian Henry

NO ENGLISH POET has developed as quickly and as impressively as John Keats. Of humble origin and initially modest promise, Keats became, in the space of four years, one of the greatest poets in the English language. His death at age twenty-five cut off a genius only recently becoming manifest, yet the few poems he left behind—especially "Lamia," "The Eve of St. Agnes," the sonnets "On first looking into Chapman's Homer" and "When I have fears that I may cease to be," and the odes "Ode to a Nightingale," "Ode on a Grecian Urn," "Ode on Melancholy," and "To Autumn"—have secured his place in history. Keats is an exquisite model of artistic development, and his best poems rival those of any poet in English, including William Shakespeare, John Milton, and John Donne.

LIFE AND CAREER

JOHN Keats was born on 31 October 1795, the first child of Thomas Keats and Frances Jennings Keats, at his grandfather's livery stable. He was eight years old when his father died in a riding accident, and his mother's hasty second marriage ended disastrously. (Because of the laws at the time, she lost her property to her second husband.) John had two younger brothers, George and Tom, and a younger sister, Fanny; another brother, Edward, died in infancy. Their mother died of tuberculosis when John was fourteen years old, and the children's finances fell under the control of Richard Abbey, a parsimonious and conservative businessman. Abbey removed John from the liberal Enfield School, which he had attended since the age of eight, the year after his mother's death, and apprenticed him for five years to a surgeon. Cutting short his apprenticeship, Keats also worked at Guy's Hospital, where he attended lectures and operations. Although certified as an apothecary in 1816, he decided to try to earn a living by writing poetry. This decision, along with Abbey's consistent refusals to

give him money, placed a tremendous financial strain on the poet and adversely affected the quality of his life.

Throughout his childhood, which is "refreshingly remote from precocity" (Bate, 1963, p. 36), Keats possessed "an appealing combination of qualities rarely found together—courage, sensitivity, and generosity" (p. 17). Popular and always willing to fight to defend his friends, Keats frequently displayed a bravery and desire for justice that would assist him when he started writing and publishing poetry. He sometimes overcompensated for his small stature with a fierce courage, but this courage enabled him to maintain his confidence in his art when potentially harmful forces—illness, criticism, doubt—later discouraged him.

At Enfield School, Keats was friendly with Charles Cowden Clarke, the headmaster's son, and learned about poetry from Clarke, who first introduced him to Edmund Spenser's *Faerie Queene*, which inspired Keats to try to write poetry himself. While in school Keats voluntarily translated Virgil's *Aeneid* from Latin and was especially drawn to the Greek myths, which figure prominently in his poetry. Clarke also introduced Keats to Leigh Hunt, whose friendship would prove vital to Keats and whose own sentimental and undisciplined poetry served as an example, mainly harmful, for the young poet. Nevertheless, Hunt recognized Keats's potential and introduced him to many artists who would become his close friends.

Hunt also edited the liberal periodical the *Examiner* and was jailed for two years for libeling the prince regent. His liberal politics harmed the critical reception of Keats's first volume of poetry, *Poems*, which appeared in 1817 and carried a dedicatory sonnet to Hunt. The book, immature and unrealized, was a financial and critical failure, and Keats's publisher dropped him. Refusing to be discouraged, he remained determined to outgrow the faults of his early poems. He achieved this growth mainly by reading Shakespeare intensely and constantly. He also read Wordsworth and Milton. He admired Wordsworth and studied his poetry carefully, but Wordsworth's subjectivity eventually came to dissatisfy him. Likewise, Milton's *Paradise Lost* deeply interested him until he decided Milton, like Wordsworth, also had faults. "I have but lately stood on my guard against Milton," he wrote in a letter to his brother George and sister-in-law Georgiana, because *Paradise Lost*, "though so fine in itself is a curruption of our Language—it should be kept as it is unique—a curiosity" (Rollins, vol. 2, p. 212).

Keats's determination to become a better poet lay partly in his belief that great poets must write long poems. Accordingly, his second volume, the 4,050-line *Endymion*, appeared in May 1818, the same year that Keats's brother George emigrated to America with Georgiana. Unlike *Poems*, which stirred little interest in literary circles outside Keats's own, *Endymion* was savaged by critics, and Keats's hopes of supporting himself by writing poetry were shattered. In a letter dated 22 December 1818 to the artist Benjamin Robert Haydon, he writes, "I never expect to get any thing by my Books: and morever I wish to avoid publishing—I admire Human Nature but I do not like *Men*—I should like to compose things honourable to Man—but not fingerable over by *Men*" (Rollins, vol. 1, p. 415). Although shaken by the response to his book, Keats persevered with his poetry and maintained his faith in both his abilities and human nature.

During a walking tour of Scotland with Charles Brown in the summer of 1818, Keats's health deteriorated. He undertook the tour to experience more of the world, but the cold, wet environment and the exertion of so much walking brought about a chronic sore throat and compelled Keats to return to London by ship while Brown continued the tour alone. Keats was then faced with the severe illness of his brother Tom, who died of tuberculosis in December. Despite his own poor health, Keats tended to Tom during his final months.

The beginning of 1819 was remarkably productive for Keats. He wrote "The Eve of St. Agnes," "The Eve of St. Mark," "La Belle Dame sans Merci," and most of his great odes while working on the epic "Hyperion." During this time, Keats also fell in love with Frances ("Fanny") Brawne. Because of his poor health and precarious finances, they never married, but they remained unofficially engaged until his death. Toward the end of his life Keats expressed jealousy about Fanny's socializing and frustration about his own misfortunes. Some of his letters, written after the tuberculosis had begun to ravage his body and mind, show a demanding, bitter, and insecure side of the poet.

Even while healthy Keats had a complex personality, by turns joyous and despondent. On 11 May 1817, he wrote to Haydon, "I have a horrid Morbidity of Temperament which has shown itself at intervals—it is I have no doubt the greatest Enemy and stumbling block I have to fear" (Rollins, vol. 1, p. 142). In a later letter to Haydon dated 22 December 1818, Keats writes, "I feel in myself all the vices of a Poet, irritability, love of effect and admiration" (Rollins, vol. 1, p. 414). But Keats's large capacity for eliciting loyalty and affection from others overcame the effects of whatever vices he had.

In February 1820 Keats became too ill to write, and he spent the next year in sickness and despair despite the publication of his third book, *Lamia, Isabella, The Eve of St. Agnes, and Other Poems*, in July (1820). The book, which included the verse narratives "The Eve of St. Agnes," "Isabella," and "Lamia" as well as "Hyperion" and the odes "Ode to a Nightingale," "Ode on a Grecian Urn," "Ode to Psyche," "To Autumn," and "Ode on Melancholy," was generally well received by critics. Ernest de Sélincourt has remarked that "no poet at the age of twenty-four has produced work comparable in maturity of thought, in richness of imagery, in easy mastery of execution, with the contents of the 1820 volume" (p. xix). Unfortunately, Keats's departure for Rome with his friend the artist Joseph Severn in September 1820 and his death from tuberculosis on 23 February 1821, at the age of twenty-five, kept him from seeing his poetry attain the acclaim it had earned. Before his death he had asked that his tombstone bear the phrase "Here lies one whose name was writ in water" instead of his name. His seemingly simple wish, expressed in the 1817 "Sleep and Poetry"—"O for ten years, that I may overwhelm / Myself in poesy" (96–97)—sadly did not come true.

THE LETTERS

KEATS'S letters to his friends and brothers exhibit his most penetrating and original thoughts on life, poetry, and philosophy. Despite his lack of a formal literary education, Keats became an astute reader of poetry as well as a brilliant theorist. His letters are among the best—the most useful, lively, and revealing—commentary on his poetry available. T. S. Eliot has commented on "the general brilliance and profundity of the observations" (p. 101) in the letters and calls them "certainly the most notable and the most important ever written by any English poet" (p. 100). In Lionel Trilling's view, "even among the great artists Keats is perhaps the only one whose letters have an interest which is virtually equal to that of their writer's canon of created work" (p. 3). And Robert Gittings refers to the letters as "handbooks of poetical thought and practice" (1968, p. 436).

Upon finding some of Keats's letters in 1836, the publisher James Freeman Clarke commented that "they are of a higher order of composition than his poems" and praised the letters for "a depth and grasp of thought; a logical accuracy of expression; a fulness of intellectual power, and an earnest struggling after truth" (quoted in Rollins, vol. 1, p. 3). Richard Monckton Milnes published about eighty of the letters in his 1848 biography of the poet; and in 1878 Harry Buxton Forman published the controversial *Letters of John Keats to Fanny Brawne*, which was attacked by most of the people writing about the book in the nineteenth century, including Matthew Arnold and Algernon Charles Swinburne. Offended by Keats's sensuousness, critics claimed that the publication of the letters performed a disservice to his reputation as a poet. But by the twentieth century, most readers of Keats had come to value his letters highly for their biographical details, emotional candor, philosophical explorations, and poetic ideas.

KEATS'S POETIC DEVELOPMENT AND REPUTATION

LIKE Coleridge, Wordsworth, and Shelley, Keats honors the single human consciousness and its capacity for invention. Rather than rely on external accounts of the world, he relies on his own mind—his intellect, imagination, and emotions—to understand the world. Keats's poetry emphasizes the importance of human imagination, the sacredness of the individual, and the centrality of nature and natural change, combining the visionary and the elemental as essential aspects of life and demonstrating a belief in the potential of the human imagination to transcend the material world around it. Throughout his poetry, Keats explores the imagination, reality, mortality, and art with uncommon insight and an unparalleled sincerity and compassion.

The speed of Keats's poetic development is without parallel in English poetry. In *The Stylistic Development of Keats*, Walter Jackson Bate writes, "during the four or five years of his active writing career, Keats attained a mature and penetrating insight into the workings of his art which few poets have possessed, while at the same time he developed from a gifted but awkward apprentice to a poet of the most dexterous craftsmanship" (p. 1). Many scholars have observed in Keats's childhood the absence of any signs of precocity or literary talent. He started writing poetry at eighteen, became serious about being a poet at twenty, and stopped writing because of tuberculosis at twenty-three. If Wordsworth, Shelley, or Byron had died at twenty-five, their work would not be read today. Furthermore, Shakespeare had hardly begun to write at twenty-five, Spenser had not published, and Milton had written only short minor poems.

Yet at the time of his death Keats was not considered a major poet; his reputation was nowhere near that of Coleridge, Wordsworth, Byron, or Shelley. In the twentieth century, however, critics placed Keats's poetry on par with or above that of his Romantic counterparts, and numerous critics have compared Keats at his best to Shakespeare. Indeed, Bate considers Keats "the most Shakespearean in character of all poets since Shakespeare himself" (1963; p. vii). So it is surprising that critical accounts of Keats's poetry were for many years inadequate. Remarking on the scant amount of useful Keats criticism in the fifty years following the poet's death, G. M. Matthews writes, "It had been agreed by friend and foe alike that Keats had died before his promise had been fulfilled; obviously, therefore, it would not be fair to apply the rigours of criticism to a body of work unfit to be criticized. To the extent that its many faults allowed, Keats's poetry could be enjoyed and wondered at, but not analysed or judged" (pp. 2–3). The criticism following Keats's death, then, fell into predictably hostile or friendly camps, depending on the writer's politics and relationship to Keats or Hunt.

R. M. Milnes's *Life, Letters and Literary Remains of John Keats* (1848) announced a shift in the general critical attitude toward Keats in that the book validated Keats's poetry as a topic of criticism and provided a biography of Keats's life as well as the text of some of his letters. Nevertheless, Milnes did not consider the poetry worthy of the most rigorous of criticism because it was the work of a poet cut off before his prime: Discussions of Keats's anti-intellectualism and sensuality continued for several more decades, and Keats's poetry did not receive real critical attention until 1880, when Matthew Arnold published a seminal essay on his work. Since then Keats's poetry has been interpreted by critics employing strategies of New Criticism, Freudian psychoanalysis, Jungian criticism, Marxism, feminist criticism, new historicism, revisionism, structuralism, poststructuralism, reader-response criticism, negative dialecticism, and dialogism, among other approaches, and critics as highly regarded as Arnold, Eliot, Cleanth Brooks, F. R. Leavis, Lionel Trilling, Northrop Frye, Paul De Man, Harold Bloom, Helen Vendler, and Jerome McGann have written in depth about Keats's poetry. The longevity of his poetry has more than confirmed Keats's prediction in an 1818 letter to George and Georgiana: "I think I shall be among the English Poets after my death" (Rollins, vol. 1, p. 394).

Why have so many critics from so many schools of thought written about Keats's poetry? What is in the poems that produces such an array of responses? Jack Stillinger has commented on the "Keatsian inexhaustibility" (1999; p. viii) that enables readers to return to Keats's poems and glean new and different meaning from them over time. And he points to the "internal complexity" of Keats, who embodies an "unresolved imaginative dividedness between the serious and the humorous, the straight and the ironic, the fanciful and the real, the high-flying and the down-to-earth, the sentimental and the satiric, the puffed up and the deflated" (1999, p. 102).

Perhaps predictably with such a complex poet, each entry in the succession of the great biographies of Keats offers distinct views of the poet's life and work, and the composite view of Keats offered by these books is rich indeed. Bate's *John Keats* (1963) is widely considered a masterpiece of New Critical biography, whereas Aileen Ward psychoanalyzes Keats and his poems in *John Keats: The Making of a Poet* (1963). Robert Gittings' *John Keats* (1968) benefits from newly discovered information about Keats, correcting many of the factual errors of previous biographies. And most

recently, Andrew Motion, in *Keats* (1997), seeks both to dispel the commonly held notion that Keats was generally apolitical and "to show that his efforts to crystallise moments of 'Truth' combine a political purpose with a poetic ambition, a social search with an aesthetic ideal" (p. xviii). Motion treats Keats primarily as a political creature: uneasily poised between the working class and the lower middle class, Keats could not afford *not* to be political; his future in many ways depended on political decisions.

While some critics see more political motivation in Keats's poems than others do, very few think Keats wrote in a vacuum. In truth, Keats is both a political poet and an aesthete, a pure poet and a theorist, a borrower and a creator, an ascetic and a sensualist, a philosopher and a dreamer. He, like Shakespeare before him and Walt Whitman after him, "contains multitudes."

KEATS'S POETICS

KEATS'S complexity stems in large part from his poetics, articulated most forcefully in several letters and embodied most clearly in his later poems, especially the odes. For Keats a central problem of poetry was subjectivity, which can mar "the poetical Character." In describing that poetical character to his friend Richard Woodhouse in a letter dated 27 October 1818 he writes that it

has no self—it is every thing and nothing—It has no character—it enjoys light and shade; it lives in gusto, be it foul or fair, high or low, rich or poor, mean or elevated. . . . What shocks the virtuous philosopher, delights the camelion Poet. . . . A Poet is the most unpoetical of any thing in existence; because he has no Identity—he is continually in for—and filling some other Body—The Sun, the Moon, the Sea and Men and Women who are creatures of impulse are poetical and have about them an unchangeable attribute—the poet has none; no identity.
(Rollins, vol. 1, p.387)

This description of the poet, genuinely negative in that it requires an absence of identity, forms the foundation of Keats's mature poetics. To Keats, the personality of the poet must be mutable, unintrusive, and all-embracing.

This notion of selflessness informs his most famous poetic theory, that of negative capability. He first outlined this theory in a letter to his brothers on 21 December 1817: negative capability is made possible "when a man is capable of being in uncertainties, Mysteries, doubts, without any irritable reaching after fact & reason" (Rollins, vol. 1, p.193). According to Keats, this ability to dwell in "uncertainties, Mysteries, doubts" is most evident in the work of Shakespeare, whose personality never overwhelms his writing and whose imagination is so capacious it seems infinitely sympathetic. Keats's own sympathetic imagination allows him to enter into objects and describe what it feels like to be those objects. This ability to reproduce the experience of other objects is a hallmark of Keats's poetic genius: his humility allows him to subordinate his own personality to that of his subject matter, and this sloughing of egotism is what makes his poetry so universal. As Richard Church has asserted, Keats's selflessness "gave him the cloak of invisibility, and so equipped him with a completely detached habit of observation" (p. xiii); like Shakespeare's, Keats's poetry displays "that special intuition or consciousness by which an artist becomes capable of total recognition of all experience as it comes into his life, either directly or through his imagination" (p. xiii). Shakespeare and Keats are "all and nothing, pervasive yet elusive. They are the constant paradox" (p. xiii).

In its embrace of paradox, Keats's negative capability presents his approach to bringing together reason and intuition, thought and emotion. He does not want his poetry to reconcile paradoxes or employ systematized thinking. In a letter to John H. Reynolds dated 3 February 1818 he writes: "We hate poetry that has a palpable design upon us.... Poetry should be great & unobtrusive, a thing which enters into one's soul, and does not startle it or amaze it with itself but with its subject" (Rollins, vol. 1, p.224). And in a letter to George and Georgiana he claims: "The only means of strengthening one's intellect is to make up ones mind about nothing—to let the mind be a thoroughfare for all thoughts" (Rollins, vol. 2, p. 213). For Keats, a single perspective limited the possibilities for knowledge. This desire to be free of doctrines enabled him to become a complete personality. As Trilling has noted, Keats viewed negative capability as "an element of intellectual power" (p. 29), and "only the self that is certain of its existence, of its identity, can do without the armor of systematic certainties" (p. 33).

In the same letter in which he defined negative capability, Keats also writes, "with a great poet the sense of Beauty overcomes every other consideration, or rather obliterates all consideration" (Rollins, vol. 1, p. 194), thus providing a key to the sensuousness of his poetry. Keats believed an intense sensuosity of response to the world was necessary to produce imaginative transcendence of that world. Because Keats ties beauty so inextricably to truth—in a letter to Benjamin Bailey on 22 November 1817 he writes "What the imagination seizes as Beauty must be truth" (Rollins, vol. 1, p. 184)—he cannot be justly accused of decadence or evasion. Church has described Keats's pursuit of beauty as "the private aspect of truth" (p. xvi) that infuses his best poems with individuality, and Trilling believes that "Beauty was not for Keats, as it is for many, an inert thing, or a thing whose value lay in having no relevance to ordinary life; it was not a word by which he evaded, but a word by which he confronted, issues" (p. 32).

THE EARLY POEMS

A READER would be justified in seeing little promise in Keats's early poems. Even a critic as sympathetic as Bate has remarked, "most of Keats's earlier poetry is interesting as poetry only to the specialist in the psychology of styles . . . or to the fellow writer, healthfully reassured that an imaginative and mental endowment so impressive should itself have begun . . . haltingly" (1963, p. viii). But what Keats lacked in ability he more than compensated with enthusiasm, and the poems collected in his first volume, *Poems* (1817), are indeed marked by youthful exuberance. The poems evince debts to the poetry of Spenser and, more problematically, Hunt, to whom the book is dedicated. The first poem Keats wrote, "Imitation of Spenser," reflects his intense admiration for the author of the *Faerie Queene*. Early on, Keats's attraction to poetry stemmed from its surfaces—the delights of melody and imagery—rather than its depths. Therefore, many of the poems in his first book succumb to the "vapid sentimentalism" (p. xxviii) of the day and possess "the vulgar and mawkish sentiment and . . . indefiniteness of the abstract style of Hunt" (p. xxix), according to de Sélincourt.

The subjects of Keats's early poems are romantic love, nature, and the relationship between poetry and nature. When experience failed to provide subject matter, he wrote about wanting to be a poet. In addition to several overt imitations of Spenser, the book includes "To Hope," "Woman! When I behold thee flippant, vain," three verse epistles (to his friends George Felton Mathews and Charles Cowden Clarke and his brother George), seventeen sonnets, and "Sleep and Poetry," at 404 lines the longest poem in the volume. Except for his sonnets, most of the poems are narrative or epistolary.

Poems is marred by a general lack of control—of line, of rhythm, of image, of metaphor. Throughout the book Keats reveals an undisciplined fondness for catalog and metaphor, and rhyming couplets predominate. His couplets are not closed, as in the neoclassical tradition of Alexander Pope, but frequently run into each other. By renouncing the closed couplet, Keats is rejecting the rigidity of the heroic couplet of Pope and other neoclassicists. This raised the ire of conservative critics, who linked Keats's open couplets to those of Hunt. Of course, Keats's jibe at the style of neoclassical poets in "Sleep and Poetry"—"with a puling infant's force / They sway'd about upon a rocking horse, / And thought it Pegasus" (185–187)—earned him no friends from that group.

Soon after *Poems* appeared Keats began to realize Hunt's flaws as a poet and to criticize him in letters to friends. He turned to Wordsworth and Milton as models, and in an April 1818 letter to his publisher, John Taylor, he writes:

I find that I can have no enjoyment in the World but continual drinking of Knowledge—I find there is no worthy pursuit but the idea of doing some good for the world—some do it with their society—some with their wit—some with their benevolence—some with a sort of power of conferring pleasure and good humour on all they meet and in a thousand ways all equally dutiful to the command of Great Nature—there is but one way for me—the road lies through application study and thought.

(Rollins, vol. 1, p. 271)

This determination in Keats led to a deep study of English poetry, particularly Shakespeare, which enabled Keats to outgrow the faults of his early work.

Despite its many faults, *Poems* is not without merits. The book's most successful poem, "On first looking into Chapman's Homer," recounts how Chapman's translation of Homer's *Iliad* made Keats feel "like some watcher of the skies / When a new planet swims into his ken" (9–10) or "like stout Cortez when with eagle eyes / He stared at the Pacific" (11–12). Keats mistakes Cortez for Balboa, a crippling error in a poem about discovering a touchstone of Western culture. Nonetheless, the sonnet is the strongest in the book, and John Mid-

dleton Murry considers it Keats's first poem that is "masterly throughout" (p. 14). The poem's emotion is palpable yet controlled, the lines flow naturally yet contain a well-modulated music, and the poem balances enjambed lines and end-stopped lines. For Keats, discovering the *Iliad* is not only a literary pleasure but a pleasure on par with that of astronomers or the great explorers.

In another of the book's more accomplished poems, "To Hope," Keats attempts to enlist Hope in the battle against "Despondency," "Disappointment," sorrow, "unhappy love," and "the base purple of a court oppress'd" (39). The poem begins:

When by my solitary hearth I sit,
   And hateful thoughts enwrap my soul in gloom;
When no fair dreams before my 'mind's eye' flit,
   And the bare heath of life presents no bloom;
      Sweet Hope, ethereal balm upon me shed

Keats's social conscience also emerges in the poem, thus expressing a desire for a poetry that benefits others: "Let me not see our country's honour fade: / O let me see our land retain her soul, / Her pride, her freedom; and not freedom's shade" (32–34). This humaneness also emerges in the camaraderie of his verse epistles—"To Charles Cowden Clarke," for example, in which Keats acknowledges Clarke as his first guide to poetry:

   you first taught me all the sweets of song:
The grand, the sweet, the terse, the free, the fine;
What swell'd with pathos, and what right divine:
Spenserian vowels that elope with ease

                (53–56)

Keats's question "Ah! had I never seen, / Or known your kindness, what might I have been?" (72–73) gives Clarke much credit in the onset of Keats's poetic career.

One of the more compelling issues presented by *Poems* is Keats's attitude toward women. Women in these poems are two-dimensional, never given any depth of intellect or emotion. "Woman! When I behold thee flippant, vain," composed of three unnumbered Spenserian sonnets, demonstrates Keats's ambivalence:

Woman! When I behold thee flippant, vain,
   Inconstant, childish, proud, and full of fancies;
   Without that modest softening that enhances
The downcast eye, repentant of the pain
That its mild light creates to heal again:

E'en then, elate, my spirit leaps, and prances,
E'en then my soul with exultation dances

(1–7)

The poem expresses chivalric aims: "when I see thee meek, and kind, and tender, / Heavens! how desperately do I adore / Thy winning graces;—to be thy defender / I hotly burn" (9–12). Yet the woman in the poem never attains the fullness of humanity; she remains a symbol for Keats's womanly ideal: "she is like a milk-white lamb that bleats / For man's protection" (31–32).

Despite his own ambivalence toward women—in his life, letters, and poetry—Keats's poems have generally appealed to women, including feminist critics. Part of this response is due to Keats's sympathetic imagination, which many critics consider more female than male. Yet Keats occasionally criticizes women in his letters. For example, in a July 1818 letter to his friend Benjamin Bailey, he admits, "I am certain I have not a right feeling towards Women—at this moment I am striving to be just to them but I cannot—Is it because they fall so far beneath my Boyish imagination? . . . I have no right to expect more than their reality. I thought them etherial above Men" (Rollins, vol. 1, p. 341). And he continues, "When I am among Women I have evil thoughts, malice spleen . . . I am full of Suspicions and therefore listen to no thing—I am in a hurry to be gone" (Rollins, vol. 1, p. 341). Keats's feelings toward women stem partly from his frustration at being unable to marry because of his financial situation, partly from his distrust of people in general, and perhaps partly from male bravado.

But more interesting than his prevailing attitude toward women is Keats's reluctant reliance on them. As he points out in a letter to Charles Brown, "One of the causes . . . of the unpopularity of this new book, and the others also, is the offence the ladies take at me. On thinking that matter over, I am certain that I have said nothing in a spirit to displease any woman I would care to please: but still there is a tendency to class women in my books with roses and sweetmeats,—they never see themselves dominant" (Rollins, vol. 2, p. 327). This perspicacious comment demonstrates a real awareness in Keats of his relationship to women. As Margaret Homans notes:

Keats understood a major part of his problem with the public as a failure to attract a female audience. He also understands that power can be given and withheld through figuration, and that a woman who has been made a sweetmeat cannot also be dominant . . . . implicitly the passage is about his fear of women's real dominance, for he attributes to women readers, rightly or wrongly, the power to make him succeed or fail in the marketplace.

(p. 346)

Attracted to women, scornful of them, and dependent upon them, Keats unfortunately did not live long enough to explore these tensions in his poetry.

ENDYMION: *A POETIC ROMANCE*

KEATS published *Endymion* with a preface apologizing for the book's imperfections, predicting that the reader "must soon perceive great inexperience, immaturity, and every error denoting a feverish attempt, rather than a deed accomplished." His modesty, however, did not prevent critics from focusing on its faults—primarily its idiomatic expressions, vague sense of story, forced or arbitrary rhymes, intermingling of archaic and colloquial dictions, and sentimentality—as well as its overt sensuality, which offended many readers. Critics also attacked the book's author because of his affiliation with Hunt, his politics, and his humble background. The anonymous review published in the Scottish *Blackwood's Magazine* in August 1818 focused on Keats's lack of formal education, his ignorance of Greek, and his "prurient and vulgar lines" depicting female beauty. The end of the review is particularly caustic, and unfair: "It is a better and a wiser thing to be a starved apothecary than a starved poet; so back to the shop Mr John, back to 'plasters, pills, and ointment boxes,' &c. But, for Heaven's sake, . . . be a little more sparing of extenuatives and soporifics in your practice than you have been in your poetry" (quoted in Briggs, p. 485). *Endymion* was also denounced by John Wilson Croker in the *Quarterly Review*, who confessed to not having read the book but managed to despise it anyway.

These devastating and influential reviews were followed by less visible defenses by Keats's friend John Hamilton Reynolds and an anonymous writer, probably a friend of Keats. Writing belatedly in August 1820, Francis Jeffrey asserts that *Endymion* is "at least as full of genius as of absurdity"; furthermore, Jeffrey claims, "he who does not find a great deal in it to admire and to give delight, cannot . . . find any great pleasure in some of the finest creations of Milton and Shakespeare" (Briggs, p. 503). But the initial assaults on the book and its author sealed its fate, and the book sold poorly. In a letter to Keats, Shelley remarked on the "treasures poured forth with indistinct profusion" (Rollins, vol. 2, p. 311) in *Endymion*, reflecting the general attitude toward the poem at the time. In many ways the poem's chief characteristic—excess—was its chief cause of failure.

Keats himself was critical of *Endymion*, and expressed a dislike for it in a letter to his publisher, John Taylor: "My Ideas with respect to it I assure you are very low—and I would write the subject thoroughly again, but I am tired of it" (Rollins, vol. 1, p. 168). But in a letter to Taylor's partner James Hessey on 9 October 1818 he justifies the poem as a step in his poetic development and foresees greater works to come: "Had I been nervous about its being a perfect piece, & with that view asked advice, & trembled over every page, it would not have been written; for it is not in my nature to fumble—I will write independently.—I have written independently *without Judgment*. I may write independently, & *with Judgment* hereafter" (Rollins, vol. 1, p. 374). Elsewhere in the same letter he writes, "That which is creative must create itself. In Endymion, I leaped headlong into the Sea, and thereby have become better acquainted with the Soundings, the quicksands, & the rocks, than if I had stayed upon the green shore, and piped a silly pipe, and took tea & comfortable advice.—I was never afraid of failure; for I would sooner fail than not be among the greatest" (Rollins, vol. 1, p. 374).

Despite his low opinion of *Endymion*, Keats blamed the public for the book's failure. Unendowed with wealth or nobility, as opposed to Shelley and Byron, Keats's decision to support himself by writing meant his livelihood depended on the reading public. He could not afford to ignore his potential readers or his critics, yet his high-mindedness and confidence in his abilities compelled him to view them with scorn or indifference. In a letter to John Hamilton Reynolds, dated 9 April 1818 he refers to "the Public" as "a thing I cannot help looking upon as an Enemy, and which I cannot address without feelings of Hostility" (Rollins, vol. 1, p. 266–267). And in the same letter he claims, somewhat disingenuously, "I never wrote one single Line of Poetry with the least Shadow of public thought" (Rollins, vol. 1, p.

267). In a later letter to James Hessey, on 8 October 1818 he writes, "Praise or blame has but a momentary effect on the man whose love of beauty in the abstract makes him a severe critic on his own Works. . . . when I feel I am right, no external praise can give me such a glow as my own solitary reperception & ratification of what is fine" (Rollins, vol. 1, pp. 373–374). While Keats did not allow outside criticism or praise to alter his poetics, the opinions of others had a palpable effect on his finances.

Critics and readers reciprocated Keats's ill feelings, viewing him, as Marjorie Levinson has pointed out, as "a marginally middle-class, professionally unequipped, nineteenth-century male adolescent" (p. 76). According to Levinson, "To those early readers, 'Keats' was the allegory of a man belonging to a certain class, and aspiring . . . to another: a man with particular but typical ambitions and with particular but typical ways of realizing them" (p. 5). Thus, Keats's hostility toward his critics and the public is in part a manifestation of the class conflict prevalent in England in the early 1800s. Unlike his contemporaries, Keats received his poetic education almost entirely from English poets. He could not read Greek, and his knowledge of Latin was respectable but rudimentary, such that he did not absorb much literature in Latin. The mythology he used in his poetry was found in Chapman's translation of Homer's *Iliad* or in the works of other English poets. Because of Keats's low standing in society, some critics tried to bar him from the literary establishment he so strongly desired to enter. That he sought to enter this establishment by bending its rules did not make his task any easier.

Though written in heroic couplets, *Endymion* demonstrates Keats's determination to reject the rigidity of the neoclassical couplet, which is characteristically closed. Keats's handling of the couplet—he frequently enjambs lines and couplets—and his use of colloquial language in particular infuriated critics, who attributed those aspects of Keats's style to ignorance. In retrospect, the consistency with which Keats avoids end-stopped lines and closed couplets seems an impressive achievement considering both the strong attraction of poetic conventions and the care and energy such convention-breaking requires. Keats's ability to break from the strictures of the heroic couplet shows at least as much technical skill as adhering to those strictures does.

While writing *Endymion*, Keats refers to the poem in a letter as "a test, a trial of my Powers of Imagination and chiefly of my invention which is a rare thing indeed—by which I must make 4000 Lines of one bare circumstance and fill them with Poetry. . . ." He explains that he is drawn to the long poem because it is "a test of Invention, which I take to be the Polar Star of Poetry, as Fancy is the Sails, and Imagination the Rudder" (Rollins, vol. 1, pp. 169–170). Yet his imagination is not ready for such an undertaking, as he later realizes and explains in his preface: "The imagination of a boy is healthy, and the mature imagination of a man is healthy; but there is a space of life between, in which the soul is in a ferment, the character undecided, the way of life uncertain, the ambition thick-sighted." Written at age twenty-two and with great speed (Keats averaged forty lines per day and wrote the poem between May and November 1817), the poem bridges his adolescent efforts and his mature work, succumbing to most of the weaknesses of the former and hinting at the glories of the latter.

The ultimate meaning of *Endymion* is unclear, and most critics have expressed frustration at its obscurity, vague structure, and length. However, the digressions, though seemingly arbitrary or intrusive, usually contribute to the poem's movement, mood, or theme, if not to its primary narrative; and the poem does have a simple structure—that of a vision seen and, after many trials, realized. It is the sheer amount of invention in the poem, the digressions and inundation of images, that obscures its overall structure. But a poem occupying "the mazy world / Of silvery enchantment" (1.460–461) probably cannot avoid some measure of obscurity.

Book 1 of Endymion begins by praising beauty and justifying the poem's conception:

A thing of beauty is a joy for ever:
Its loveliness increases; it will never
Pass into nothingness; but still will keep
A bower quiet for us, and a sleep
Full of sweet dreams, and health, and quiet
    breathing.

(1.1–5)

Although beauty is eternal, it changes, gaining magnificence with time. Keats then introduces the poem's protagonist, the shepherd prince Endymion. Melancholy, he leaves a festival honor-

ing Pan with his sister Peona and tells her of his three visionary meetings with a goddess. He has fallen in love with this goddess and is dejected because of her unattainability, explaining to Peona, "Wherein lies happiness? In that which becks / Our ready minds to fellowship divine, / A fellowship with essence; till we shine" (1.777–779). He first sees the goddess in the sky then later sees her face in a pool of water and hears her voice in a cave. These three visions foreshadow, in reverse order, Endymion's actions in books 2, 3, and 4, which occur underground, in the ocean, and in the air, respectively.

Book 2 begins with Keats's meditation on history, in which the feelings of the individual lover "are things to brood on with more ardency / Than the death-day of empires" (2.33–34). His belief in the importance of the individual is reinforced by Endymion's quest, which takes him away from the real world and begins when he enters a subterranean realm. After walking "to and fro, to acquaint / Himself with every mystery, and awe" (2.269–270), he happens upon Adonis' chamber, where Venus tells Endymion, "one day thou wilt be blessed" (2.573). After further wanderings, Endymion finds a "jasmine bower, all bestrown / With golden moss" (2.670–671), where he falls asleep "to dream deliciously" (2.708) of an embrace from Cynthia. Having fallen asleep within his dream, he cannot hear Cynthia admit, "I love thee, youth, more than I can conceive; / And so long absence from thee doth bereave / My soul of any rest" (2.774–776). Book 2 ends with Endymion witnessing the attempted seduction of the nymph Arethusa by the river god Alpheus, which is unsuccessful because Arethusa has pledged herself to Diana and, therefore, to chastity. The torment of the would-be lovers causes Endymion to weep and pray for "these lovers' pains" to be assuaged (2.1016), thus indicating a growing sympathy in him.

Book 3 opens with an extended encomium to the moon and, because the moon is often a physical representation of her in the poem, to Cynthia. On the ocean floor Endymion meets an ancient man, Glaucus, the sight of whom fills him with pity. Glaucus was a young fisherman in love with Scylla, a nymph, who fled from him. Jealous of Glaucus's love for Scylla, the "cruel enchantress" (3.413) Circe seduced him, and he was "condemn'd" (3.457) to a life of sex and sleep. Glaucus eventually fled Circe, who sentenced him to an old age a thousand years long at the bottom of the ocean. Circe also killed Scylla.

Glaucus' existence was one of unremitting anguish until he found a book that seemed to describe his own life and promised that

> If he utterly
> Scans all the depths of magic, and expounds
> The meanings of all motions, shapes, and sounds;
> If he explores all forms and substances
> Straight homeward to their symbol-essences;
> He shall not die.
>
> (3.696–701)

The book further stipulated that *"he must pursue this task . . . / Most piously"* (3.702–703) and prophesied that after he fulfills these tasks, *"a youth, by heavenly power lov'd and led"* (3.708) will appear and help Glaucus. These tasks, then, resemble Endymion's as well as the poet's, since life, love, and art can be found only through intense concentration and feeling. After Endymion follows his instructions, Glaucus' youth and Scylla's life are restored, as are the lives of the thousands of lovers who have died in the ocean. At a celebration, Endymion again sees Venus, who reiterates her promise that he will be united with his beloved. He falls unconscious and in his sleep hears Cynthia tell him they will soon be together in "endless heaven" (3.1027), thus foreshadowing the events of book 4.

In the fourth and final book, Endymion meets the Indian Maid. He falls in love with her and swears to Cynthia, "Goddess! I love thee not the less" (4.92). Endymion's love for both Cynthia and the Indian Maid is "so immense," he feels his "heart is cut for them in twain" (4.96, 97). Immediately after he pledges himself to the Indian Maid, Mercury appears and strikes the ground with his wand, producing two horses that carry Endymion and the Indian Maid into the air, where the horses and the lovers fall asleep. Endymion dreams of walking with the gods and awakes to see the gods watching him; the moon "bends towards him crescented" (4.438), and Endymion is torn between her and the woman sleeping at his side. He vacillates between his two loves and feels he has "no self-passion or identity" (4.477).

Later that night, the Indian Maid vanishes from Endymion's embrace. After being returned to the earth, he exclaims, "I have clung / To nothing, lov'd a nothing, nothing seen / Or felt but a great dream!" (4.636–638), and swears not to be enchanted by "cloudy phantasms" (4.651) or "airy voices" (4.654) again. The Indian Maid returns to tell Endymion she is forbidden to be his love, and he plans to retire, alone, to a cave for the rest of his life. Having pledged himself to solitude and thought, like Glaucus, Endymion is finally "spiritualiz'd" (4.993), and the conflict between the imaginative and real worlds is resolved when the Indian Maid is revealed to be Cynthia in disguise. Ultimately Endymion's quest represents a search for ideal love, which must involve earthly love. For Keats, true love encompasses both the ideal and the earthly, and Endymion cannot find ideal love until he accepts the earthly.

LAMIA, ISABELLA, THE EVE OF ST. AGNES, AND OTHER POEMS

KEATS'S third and final book, *Lamia, Isabella, The Eve of St. Agnes, and Other Poems*, was well received by critics at the time, and most of the poems in the book were highly praised by critics throughout the twentieth century. The poems' achievements, which include formal dexterity and variety, masterful handling of imagery, and imaginative sympathy, have been explored in depth; and Keats's theories of poetry attain their finest articulation in these poems.

Critics regard "Lamia," the first poem in the book, as one of Keats's strongest narrative poems. He preferred it to all the other narrative poems in the volume, and his opinion was corroborated by critics in the twentieth century. Composed in heroic couplets, "Lamia" is technically superior to any of Keats's previous poems in couplets, and the action emerges from the characters themselves, overcoming the problems of characterization that mar *Endymion*.

In "Lamia," Hermes desires a nymph but cannot find her. Lamia, a snake with a woman's mouth and voice, knows where the nymph is and tells Hermes "by my power is her beauty veil'd / To keep it unaffronted, unassail'd" (1.100–101). He promises to provide "whatever bliss thou canst devise" (1.85) if Lamia reveals the nymph's location; when she shows Hermes where the nymph is hiding, he grants her wish—to be given a human form and be transported to Corinth, so she can find the man she loves. Lamia's metamorphosis from a snake into a woman is violent and sensational, but it results in her becoming "a lady bright, / A full-born beauty new and exquisite" (1.171–172).

Though a serious student of philosophy, Lycius is easily seduced by Lamia, who removes him from Corinth to a sumptuous palace. After a period of intense passion, Lycius remembers the world outside the palace and insists on inviting his friends for a wedding banquet. He prevails despite Lamia's protests, though she succeeds in making him promise not to invite his teacher, the philosopher Apollonius. Keats's critique of philosophy, in an authorial intrusion, emphasizes philosophy's illusion-dispelling aspects:

> Do not all charms fly
> At the mere touch of cold philosophy?
> There was an awful rainbow once in heaven:
> We know her woof, her texture; she is given
> In the dull catalogue of common things.
> Philosophy will clip an Angel's wings,
> Conquer all mysteries by rule and line
>   (2.229–235)

Keats here criticizes the dispelling of the beautiful illusion of the rainbow and, implicitly, the illusion of love itself in the relationship between Lamia and Lycius. This attack on philosophy, while understandable for a Romantic poet, seems paradoxical in this poem, since Lamia's illusion serves evil purposes. Keats is neither embracing nor condemning illusion per se, as the value of an illusion depends on its effects. Thus, in "Lamia" he attempts to do justice to the world's complexity, composed as it is of both good and harmful illusions. Lamia's illusion, based on deception, is evil. When Apollonius appears uninvited at the banquet, he recognizes Lamia's true form; his gaze "like a sharp spear, went through her utterly" (2.300), and Lamia vanishes "with a frightful scream" (2.306). Lycius, caught between false beauty and moral beauty, cannot endure the tension and dies. The poem dramatizes the dangers of seduction and enchantment by juxtaposing them against reality.

The divide between illusion and reality also figures prominently in "The Eve of St. Agnes." Composed in Spenserian stanzas, the poem is rich in detail, solid in structure, and somber in atmosphere. One of Keats's most visually vivid poems, "The Eve of St. Agnes" occurs on a freezing winter's night at a medieval castle, where a family is occupied with revelry. The daughter of the family, Madeline, believes that she can see her future husband in a dream if she follows the proper rites, so she plans to leave the festivities and prepare for bed. Meanwhile, Porphyro, the son of Madeline's

family's most hated enemy, has secretly entered the castle and convinced Madeline's nurse to allow him to hide in Madeline's room so he can observe her undressing. He conceals himself and watches Madeline prepare for bed; after she has fallen asleep, he prepares a sumptuous feast for her and plays her lute until she is half-awake—sufficiently awake to see Porphyro but not so awake as to realize he is there in the flesh. She admits to her love for him and, after consummating their love, they flee the castle.

Because a snowstorm has developed during the night and Keats does not describe their actions after they leave the castle, the reader does not know if the lovers survive. This irresolution points to the negative capability Keats employs in the poem, and the different levels of interpretation available point to its complexity. Stillinger summarizes fifty-nine interpretations of "The Eve of St. Agnes," which he says are a "token array of possibilities" (1999, p. 76), thus conveying the difficulties and complexities of interpretation. These possible interpretations include readings of "The Eve of St. Agnes" as a celebration of romantic love, a celebration of sexual love, a "narrative of desire," a "fantasy of wish-fulfillment," a rape poem, an allegory of creativity, an attempt at a Gothic tale, a parody of a Gothic tale, and a "successful merging of romance and reality, or of beauty and truth" (1999, p. 55). And Porphyro has been interpreted as a poet figure, a devout Christian, a peeping Tom, and a vampire, among other things.

In the book's other major narrative poem, "Isabella; or, The Pot of Basil," Keats attempts to write in the simpler style of Shakespeare and Chaucer. Composed in ottava rima and based on Boccaccio's *Decameron*, the poem fluctuates between strained simplicity and genuine simplicity and therefore is not as consistently powerful as "Lamia" is. In the poem, Isabella has fallen in love with Lorenzo, who works for her brothers. Enraged by Lorenzo's low social standing, Isabella's brothers murder him and bury his corpse in a forest. After Lorenzo appears to Isabella in a vision and explains what happened to him, Isabella finds his body in the forest, cuts off his head, and plants it in a pot of basil. She hardly leaves the pot of basil, watering the plant with her tears until her brothers, suspicious of her grief, steal the pot. When they discover Lorenzo's head, they flee Florence, "never to return again." The loss of the pot of basil causes Isabella to lose her mind, and she soon dies. "Isabella" was the most praised poem in the book throughout the nineteenth century. Keats originally wanted to exclude the poem from the book but his publishers convinced him to include it. Dissatisfied with the romance genre itself, Keats felt that "disinterestedness" could not be achieved through tales of romance.

However, Keats accomplishes disinterestedness in "Hyperion," a fragment of an epic projected to be the same length as *Endymion*. Keats's most respected poem during the first half of the nineteenth century, "Hyperion" was written under the influence of Milton's *Paradise Lost* and in a blank verse at least as fluid and flexible as Milton's. An exploration of the intersections of myth and history, the poem begins after the Titanomachia, in which the Olympian gods, led by Jove, have overthrown Saturn and his Titans. All of the Titans except Hyperion have fallen, and he remains responsible for the sun's movements until Apollo replaces him.

Book 1 of "Hyperion" is composed primarily of Keats's description of the defeated, confused, and grieving Titans. In Book 2, the Titans try to understand their new condition, and Saturn asks Oceanus, previously the god of the sea, for advice. The philosophical Oceanus explains, "We fall by course of Nature's law, not force / Of thunder, or of Jove" (2.181–182), pointing out, "as thou wast not the first of powers, / So art thou not the last" (2.188–189). Furthermore, "on our heels a fresh perfection treads, / A power more strong in beauty, born of us / And fated to excel us" (2.212–214). Book 3 introduces Apollo, yet to achieve godliness. Apollo attains immortality by staring into Mnemosyne's face, which teaches him "a wondrous lesson" (3.112):

Knowledge enormous makes a God of me.
Names, deeds, gray legends, dire events, rebellions,
Majesties, sovran voices, agonies,
Creations and destroyings, all at once
Pour into the wide hollows of my brain,
And deify me

(3.113–118)

The fragment of "Hyperion" ends with Apollo's transformation into a god, which resembles a death because of the pain involved:

Soon wild commotions shook him, and made flush
All the immortal fairness of his limbs;
Most like the struggle at the gate of death;
Or liker still to one who should take leave
Of pale immortal death, and with a pang
As hot as death's is chill, with fierce convulse
Die into life

(3.124–130)

This birth/death represents Apollo's birth into self-knowledge, or tragic consciousness, which is what makes the Olympian gods so powerful: by understanding mortal suffering, they become truly divine. Keats strongly identifies with Apollo, god of poetry and medicine as well as the sun, and links Apollo's own "knowledge enormous" to the knowledge required for the creation of art.

Keats intended "Hyperion" to be written in "a more naked and grecian Manner" than *Endymion* and for its "march of passion and endeavour" to be "undeviating" (Rollins, vol. 1, 207). But he gave up the poem, most likely because of his dissatisfaction with its governing philosophy, which he considered too optimistic, and because, as he noted to Reynolds, "there are too many Miltonic inversions" (Rollins, vol. 2, p. 167). Keats abandoned "Hyperion" in April 1819, and his letters from that time evince a belief that suffering is inevitable and that beauty and happiness are to be found not in art but in the real world. Thus, Keats wanted his poetry to embrace the real world and seek beauty and happiness there rather than escaping to ancient Greece for its themes.

However, Keats returned to "Hyperion" from July to December 1819, attempting to revise the poem to fit his new beliefs. He retitled it "The Fall of Hyperion" and switched from third- to first-person narration, giving the poem more immediacy and humanity by contrasting more starkly the human and the divine. He also replaced Milton with Dante as his model, switching from the "book" to the "canto" and following Dante's own descent into the underworld. The poet himself emulates Apollo's fall into knowledge, perhaps in an effort to become divine himself. In "The Fall of Hyperion" the condition for immortality is not "knowledge enormous," but sympathy and imagination. "Those to whom the miseries of the world / Are misery" (1.148–149) become immortal, but only if they are "vision'ries" (1.161); only through imagination can the poet achieve the sympathy necessary for redemption. This change allows Keats to imbue the poem with poignancy because the revision of "Hyperion" is one of his last poetic efforts; this revised view of immortality gives the dying poet hope that his poetry will outlive him.

THE ODES

KEATS certainly achieves immortality in his odes, which have been the most consistently praised of his poems for the past century. Helen Vendler considers the odes among "that group of works in which the English language finds an ultimate embodiment" (p. 3), and de Sélincourt claims that Keats "stands without a rival as the poet of the richly meditative Ode. . . . [In the odes] all the different elements that moulded or inspired his genius are completely harmonised in the imaginative expression of his present mood" (p. lx). Indeed, the odes reveal Keats at his most mature, as they thrive on oppositions and superbly embody his notion of negative capability. As Levinson has observed, Keats's "style . . . contains, idealizes, and exists by contradiction" (p. 85).

The form of most of the odes (those except "Ode to Psyche" and "To Autumn") emerged from Keats's dissatisfaction with his previous work and from a desire to create a new stanzaic structure. Attempting to revise the sonnet, he created the form for his odes, which are composed primarily of a Shakespearean quatrain (*abab*) and a Petrarchan sestet *cdecde*). This new formal pattern gives the odes a formal integrity and ingenuity that surpasses the styles of his earlier work.

Written mostly in April and May 1819, the odes demonstrate Keats's concern with reconciling reality and poetry. The overarching question the odes attempt to answer is how to bring together art—or beauty—and life. For Keats, imagination is the key, because it is the most profound vehicle to knowledge, more effective and powerful than reason. But because Keats never attempts to systematize his thought, each ode approaches this problem differently.

In "Ode to a Nightingale" and "Ode on a Grecian Urn," Keats is unsuccessful in his attempt to reconcile beauty and permanence; yet his failures produce beautiful, lasting poetry. "Ode to a Nightingale" contrasts the poet's suffering with the eternal beauty of the nightingale's song, dispelling the illusion that imagination—and therefore art—allow for transcendence. The poem opens with stasis:

> My heart aches, and a drowsy numbness pains
> My sense, as though of hemlock I had drunk,
> Or emptied some dull opiate to the drains
> One minute past, and Lethe-wards had sunk
>
> (1.1–4)

The poet wishes to "fade away" with the bird "into the forest dim" (2.10) in order to "quite forget" (3.1) what the bird, being inhuman, has never experienced–"the weariness, the fever, and the fret, / Here, where men sit and hear each other groan" (3.3–4). "Here" is the human world—less a specific place than any place "where youth grows pale, and spectre-thin, and dies" (3.6). In this human world, "to think is to be full of sorrow" (3.7), so Keats proposes to fly to the bird "on the viewless wings of Poesy" (4.3), which is contrasted with numbness and with thinking, namely philosophy.

In the poem's sixth stanza, Keats expresses a desire for self-extinction, for a release from self and from life:

> for many a time
> I have been half in love with easeful Death,
> Call'd him soft names in many a mused rhyme,
> To take into the air my quiet breath;
> Now more than ever seems it rich to die,
> To cease upon the midnight with no pain,
> While thou art pouring forth thy soul abroad
> In such an ecstasy!
>
> (6.1–8)

Because death for Keats allows for an escape from the self, it is perhaps the ultimate form of negative capability. But the seventh stanza presents a contrast to the sixth, emphasizing the importance of enduring: "Thou wast not born for death, immortal bird!" (6.1). Although the bird itself is not immortal—as a creature of nature, it must die—its song, like art, is immortal.

In the poem's final stanza, the poet is jolted out of his reverie, and the bird's "plaintive anthem fades" (8.5), leaving the poet to ask, "Was it a vision, or a waking dream? / Fled is that music:—Do I wake or sleep?" (8.9–10). Here the poem explicitly becomes an exploration of reality as a dream state and a state of the imagination, and the boundaries between these areas have dissolved. By declaring the nightingale unable to assuage his "drowsy numbness," Keats questions art's ability to transcend the material nature of human life. What begins with certainty—the poet's feelings of lethargy—ends in mystery and doubt.

Like "Ode to a Nightingale," "Ode on a Grecian Urn" is a meditation on mortality and art. Since "Ode on a Grecian Urn" immediately follows "Ode to a Nightingale" in the book, the poems are placed in dialogue with each other. With its emphasis on song, the beginning of the second stanza—"Heard melodies are sweet, but those unheard / Are sweeter" (2.1–2)—recalls "Ode to a Nightingale," but this poem arrives at a different conclusion. In his meditation on the urn, Keats contrasts human mortality with the immortality of beauty and art. The urn, being immortal, serves as a counterpoint to the mortal poet.

The urn portrays a dance which is also an amorous pursuit. The figures on the urn are both vibrant and static—both alive and dead—but because they are depicted in art, they are immortal. This immortality has its price:

> Fair youth, beneath the trees, thou canst not leave
> Thy song, nor ever can those trees be bare;
> Bold Lover, never, never canst thou kiss,
> Though winning near the goal—yet, do not grieve;
> She cannot fade, though thou has not thy bliss,
> For ever wilt thou love, and she be fair!
>
> (2.5–10)

Because they cannot move, the figures in the urn will never achieve what they desire; but what they desire will remain forever desirable. The poem's ending seems to give voice to the urn:

> When old age shall this generation waste
> Thou shalt remain, in midst of other woe,
> Than ours, a friend to man, to whom thou say'st,
> "Beauty is truth, truth beauty," that is all
> Ye know on earth, and all ye need to know.
>
> (5.6–10)

Critics have been unable to agree on the voice of the final two lines of the poem, though the majority of critics concur that the urn says, at the least, "'Beauty is truth, truth beauty'" (5.9). Whether the urn or the poet says "that is all / Ye know on earth, and all ye need to know" (5.9–10) is a question that has not been settled. Nevertheless, by asserting "Beauty is truth, truth beauty," the poem reiterates the central tenet of Keats's poetics. This poetics, able to find such memorable and powerful articulation in such a brief career, deserves all the attention and admiration it has received.

SELECTED BIBLIOGRAPHY

I. COLLECTED WORKS. H. Buxton Forman, ed., *The Complete Works of John Keats*, 5 vols. (Glasgow, 1900–1901); Ernest de Sélincourt, ed., *The Poems of John Keats* (London, 1905); H. Buxton Forman, *The Poetical Works and Other Writings of John Keats*, Hampstead edition, 8 vols. (New York, 1938); Richard Church, ed., *John Keats: An Introduction and a Selection* (London, 1948); Harold Edgar Briggs, ed., *The Complete Poetry and Selected Letters of John Keats* (New York: Modern Library, 1951); H. W. Garrod, ed., *The Poetical Works of John Keats*, 2d edition (Oxford, 1958); Miriam Allott, ed., *The Poems of John Keats* (London, 1970); Jack Stillinger, ed., *John Keats: Complete Poems* (Cambridge, Mass., 1978); Stephen T. Steinhoff, ed., *Keats's Endymion: A Critical Edition* (Troy, N.Y, 1987); *The Complete Poems of John Keats* (New York: Modern Library, 1994); Elizabeth Cook, ed., *John Keats: Selected Poetry* (Oxford, 1996); *Complete Poems and Selected Letters of John Keats*, intro. by Edward Hirsch (New York: Modern Library, 2001).

II. FIRST EDITIONS. *Poems* (London, 1817); *Endymion: A Poetic Romance* (London, 1818); *Lamia, Isabella, The Eve of St. Agnes, and Other Poems* (London, 1820).

III. LETTERS. Richard Monckton Milnes, *Life, Letters, and Literary Remains of John Keats*, 2 vols. (Philadelphia, 1848); Harry Buxton Forman, *Letters of John Keats to Fanny Brawne* (New York, 1878); Sidney Colvin, *Letters of John Keats to His Family and Friends* (London, 1891); Maurice Buxton Forman, ed., *The Letters of John Keats* (Oxford, 1931); Hyder Edward Rollins, ed., *The Letters of John Keats, 1814–1821*, 2 vols. (Cambridge, Mass., 1958); Robert Gittings, ed., *Letters of John Keats: A New Selection* (Oxford, 1970).

IV. BIOGRAPHIES. Richard Monckton Milnes, *Life, Letters, and Literary Remains of John Keats*, 2 vols. (Philadelphia, 1848); Sidney Colvin, *John Keats: His Life and Poetry, His Friends, Critics, and After-Fame* (London, 1917); Amy Lowell, *John Keats*, 2 vols. (Boston, 1925); Walter Jackson Bate, *John Keats* (Cambridge, Mass., 1963); Aileen Ward, *John Keats: The Making of a Poet* (New York, 1963); Robert Gittings, *John Keats* (Boston, 1968); Andrew Motion, *Keats* (London, 1997).

V. BIBLIOGRAPHIES. J. R. MacGillivray, *Keats: A Bibliography and Reference Guide* (Toronto, 1949); David Bonnell Green and Edwin Graves Wilson, eds., *Keats, Shelley, Byron, Hunt, and Their Circles: A Bibliography, July 1, 1950 to June 30, 1962* (Lincoln, Neb., 1964); Robert A. Hartley, ed., *Keats, Shelley, Byron, Hunt, and Their Circles: A Bibliography, July 1, 1962 to December 31, 1974* (Lincoln, Neb., 1978); Ronald B. Hearn, *Keats Criticism Since 1954: A Bibliography* (Salzburg, 1981); Jack Wright Rhodes, *Keats's Major Odes: An Annotated Bibliography* (Westport, Conn., 1984).

VI. CRITICAL STUDIES. John Middleton Murry, *Keats and Shakespeare* (London, 1926); Clarence Dewitt Thorpe, *The Mind of John Keats* (Oxford and New York, 1926); John Middleton Murry, *Studies in Keats* (Oxford, 1930); T. S. Eliot, "Shelley and Keats," in his *The Use of Poetry* (London, 1933); M. R. Ridley, *Keats' Craftmanship: A Study in Poetic Development* (Oxford, 1933); Claude Lee Finney, *The Evolution of Keats's Poetry*, 2 vols. (Cambridge, Mass., 1936); Walter Jackson Bate, *Negative Capability: The Intuitive Approach in Keats* (Cambridge, Mass., 1939); Heathcote William Garrod, *Keats*, 2d ed. (Oxford, 1939).

Walter Jackson Bate, *The Stylistic Development of Keats* (New York, 1945); Cleanth Brooks, "Keats's Sylvan Historian," in his *The Well Wrought Urn* (New York, 1947); Richard Harter Fogle, *The Imagery of Keats and Shelley: A Comparative Study* (Chapel Hill, N.C., 1949); Newell Ford, *The Prefigurative Imagination of John Keats* (Stanford, Calif., 1951); Earl R. Wasserman, *The Finer Tone: Keats' Major Poems* (Baltimore, 1953); Lionel Trilling, "The Poet as Hero: Keats in His Letters," in his *The Opposing Self: Nine Essays in Criticism* (New York, 1955); Bernice Slote, *Keats and the Dramatic Principle* (Lincoln, Neb., 1958).

Harold Bloom, ed., *The Visionary Company: A Reading of English Romantic Poetry* (Garden City, N.Y., 1961); Walter H. Evert, *Aesthetic and Myth in the Poetry of Keats* (Princeton, N.J., 1965); Robert Gittings, *The Mask of Keats: A Study of Problems* (London, 1965); Lawrence John Zillman, *John Keats and the Sonnet Tradition: A Critical and Comparative Study* (New York, 1966); Ian Jack, *Keats and the Mirror of Art* (Oxford, 1967); Northrop Frye, "*Endymion*: The Romantic Ephiphanic," in his *A Study of English Romanticism* (New York, 1968); Robin Mayhead, *John Keats* (Cambridge, 1967); Judith O'Neill, comp., *Critics on Keats* (Coral Gables, Fla., 1968); Jack Stillinger, ed., *Twentieth Century Interpretations of Keats's Odes: A Collection of Critical Essays* (Englewood Cliffs, N.J., 1968); John Jones, *John Keats's Dream of Truth* (New York, 1969).

Charles Ivey Patterson, *The Daemonic in the Poetry of John Keats* (Urbana, Ill., 1970); Allan Danzig, ed., *Twentieth Century Interpretations of "The Eve of St. Agnes": A Collection of Critical Essays* (Englewood Cliffs, N.J., 1971); Morris Dickstein, *Keats and His Poetry: A Study in Development* (Chicago, 1971); G. M. Matthews, ed., *Keats: The Critical Heritage* (New York, 1971); Jack Stillinger, *The Hoodwinking of Madeline, and Other Essays on Keats's Poems* (Urbana, Ill., 1971); Stuart M. Sperry, *Keats the Poet* (Princeton, N.J., 1973); Christopher Ricks, *Keats and Embarrassment* (Oxford, 1974); Geoffrey Hartman, "Poem and Ideology: A Study of Keats's 'To Autumn,' " and "Spectral Symbolism and Authorial Self in Keats's 'Hyperion,' " in his *The Fate of Reading and Other Essays* (Chicago, 1975); Judy Little, *Keats as a Narrative Poet: A Test of Invention* (Lincoln, Neb., 1975); Stuart A. Ende, *Keats and the Sublime* (New Haven, Conn., 1976); Robert M. Ryan, *Keats: The Religious Sense* (Princeton, N.J., 1976); Aileen Ward, " 'That Last Infirmity of Noble Mind': Keats and the Idea of Fame," in Donald Reiman, Michael C. Jaye, and Betty J. Bennett, eds., *The Evidence of the Imagination* (New York, 1978); Jerome J. McGann, "Keats and the Historical Method in Literary Criticism," in *Modern Language Notes 94* (December 1979), repr. in his *The Beauty of Inflections: Literary Investigations in Historical Method and Theory* (Oxford and New York, 1985); Ronald A. Sharp, *Keats, Skepticism, and the Religion of Beauty* (Athens, Ga., 1979).

Barry Gradman, *Metamorphosis in Keats* (New York, 1980); Nancy M. Goslee, "Phidian Lore: Sculpture and Personification in Keats's Odes," in *Studies in Romanti-cism* 21 (spring 1982); Richard E. Brantley, "Keats's Method," in *Studies in Romanticism* 22 (fall 1983); Helen Vendler, *The Odes of John Keats* (Cambridge, Mass., 1983); Philip Fisher, "A Museum with One Work Inside: Keats and the Finality of Art," *Keats-Shelley Journal* 33 (1984); Donald C. Goellnicht, *The Poet-Physician: Keats and Medical Science* (Pittsburgh, 1984); David Pollard, *The Poetry of Keats: Language and Experience* (New York, 1984); Martin Aske, *Keats and Hellenism* (Cambridge, 1985); Leon Waldoff, *Keats and the Silent Work of Imagination* (Urbana, Ill., 1985); Jeffrey Baker, *John Keats and Symbolism* (New York, 1986); Cynthia Chase, " 'Viewless Wings': Keats's 'Ode to a Nightingale,' " in her *Decomposing Figures: Rhetorical Readings in the Romantic Tradition* (Baltimore, 1986); Susan Wolfson, *The Questioning Presence: Wordsworth, Keats, and the Interrogative Mode in Romantic Poetry* (Ithaca, N.Y., 1986); David Bromwich, "Keats's Radicalism," in *Studies in Romanticism* 25 (summer 1986); William Keach, "Cockney Couplets: Keats and the Politics of Style," in *Studies in Romanticism* 25 (summer 1986); Evan Radcliffe, "Keats, Ideals, and 'Isabella,' " in *Modern Language Quarterly* 17 (September 1986); John Barnard, *John Keats* (Cambridge, 1987); Harold Bloom, ed., *The Odes of Keats* (New York, 1987); Mark Edmundson, "Keats's Mortal Stance," in *Studies in Romanticism* 26 (spring 1987); Kurt Heinzelman, "Self-Interest and the Politics of Composition in Keats's 'Isabella,' " in *English Literary History* 55 (spring 1988); Marjorie Levinson, *Keats's Life of Allegory: The Origins of a Style* (New York, 1988); Daniel P. Watkins, *Keats's Poetry and the Politics of the Imagination* (Rutherford, N.J., 1989).

Margaret Homans, "Keats Reading Women, Women Reading Keats," in *Studies in Romanticism* 29 (fall 1990); Marc Wortman, "Shattering the Urn," in *Yale Alumni Magazine* 54 (December 1990); Beth Lau, *Keats's Reading of the Romantic Poets* (Ann Arbor, Mich., 1991); John A. Minahan, *Word Like a Bell: John Keats, Music, and the Romantic Poet* (Kent, Ohio, 1992); Karla Alwes, *Imagination Transformed: The Evolution of the Female Character in Keats's Poetry* (Carbondale, Ill., 1993); Geraldine Friedman, "The Erotics of Interpretation in Keats's 'Ode on a Grecian Urn': Pursuing the Feminine," in *Studies in Romanticism* 32 (summer 1993); Andrew Bennett, *Keats, Narrative, and Audience: The Posthumous Life of Writing* (Cambridge and New York, 1994); Nicholas Roe, ed., *Keats and History* (Cambridge and New York, 1995); Thomas H. Schmid, "Silence and Celebration: Pastoral and Dialogism in Keats's 'Ode on a Grecian Urn,' " in *Keats-Shelley Journal* 44 (1995); James L. O'Rourke, *Keats's Odes and Contemporary Criticism* (Gainesville, Fla., 1998); Robert M. Ryan and Ronald A Sharp, eds., *The Persistence of Poetry: Bicentennial Essays on Keats* (Amherst, Mass., 1998); Jack Stillinger, *Reading "The Eve of St. Agnes": The Multiples of Complex Literary Transaction* (Oxford and New York, 1999).

CHRISTOPHER MARLOWE

(1564–1593)

Daniel G. Brayton

ON 30 MAY 1593 a young man by the name of Christopher Marlowe was killed in a barroom brawl in Deptford, a suburb of London, stabbed through the eye with a dagger. Marlowe had already been in trouble on several occasions before his death. Two weeks earlier, he had been summoned before the Privy Council to answer to the charge of atheism, a grave crime in Elizabethan England, which had no separation of Church and State. Some five years before that, he had been imprisoned for taking part in a street brawl. There is considerable evidence that Marlowe had been engaged in secret service for the government, and these clandestine activities almost certainly played a part in his death. Marlowe's name was associated with many of the forces and activities considered dangerous in Elizabethan England: atheism, Catholicism, conspiracy, and writing plays.

LIFE AND CAREER

THE son of a Canterbury shoemaker, Marlowe was born early in 1564 and baptized on 26 February of that year. He won a scholarship to King's School, Canterbury, at age fifteen, and later attended Corpus Christi College of the University of Cambridge, where he received his BA in 1584 and continued studying for the Master of Arts degree. Before finishing he encountered difficulties. The heads of the university were reticent to grant the latter degree because of his frequent absences and rumors of his doubtful morality. It was rumored that he had secret connections to Catholics on the Continent—at the time, a dangerous charge. Yet, in 1587 the powerful Privy Council intervened with the Cambridge officials, defending Marlowe on the grounds that he had been pursuing "matters touching the benefit of his country" and claiming that he had been "defamed by those that are ignorant in the affairs he went about." These tantalizing words suggest a great deal about Marlowe's secret life and help to separate legend from historical evidence. Whatever his affinities may have been, Marlowe had done noteworthy service for England.

In an era when any and all clandestine activities were considered suspect, Marlowe was linked to "The School of Night," a group of intellectual freethinkers, and associated with such forward-looking men as the scientist Thomas Harriot, who was suspected of atheism. Accused of being a sodomite and an atheist, he lived on the edge of respectability, with actors for friends and radicals for associates. It was among such associates that Marlowe was killed. The four men who met at the widow Eleanor Bull's tavern that day worked as secret agents. The primary activity of such spies was to keep watch on English Catholics studying at Reims in France. Marlowe was almost certainly one of them. Documentary evidence from the inquest on Marlowe's death fortunately remains, and we know that Marlowe's last hours were spent in the company of men who were known to be spies and dangerous men. One of these, Ingram Frizer, stabbed Marlowe in the eye during a debate over who would pay the bill for the tavern.

For all the controversy and mystery surrounding Marlowe, the most remarkable facts about him are not his sensational life and the dramatic manner of his death, but his stunning contributions to the English stage. Although he only wrote seven plays, a handful of lyric poems, and one unfinished narrative poem, Marlowe's career as a writer was spectacularly successful. For a brief period, Marlowe was the preeminent playwright in Elizabethan London. In creating extravagant plays about legendary strivers who resemble no one more than himself, Marlowe gave Londoners what they wanted, bringing audiences in crowds to the public theaters between 1588 and 1593.

The irreverence and recklessness of his life characterize Marlowe's plays as well. No Elizabethan playwright save Shakespeare rivals Marlowe for the brilliance or the popularity of his creations. Marlowe more than any other writer established the public playing house as perhaps the preeminent source of entertainment for Londoners in the late Elizabethan period. It was Marlowe who first transformed English Renaissance drama from something highly conventional and overly academic into the supple and subtle art form that it would become in the late years of Queen Elizabeth's reign. In fact, the few plays that Marlowe lived to create are so spectacular that conspiracy theorists have often claimed that he secretly lived on after 1593 and wrote the plays attributed to Shakespeare. As unfounded as such claims undoubtedly are, they attest to Marlowe's greatness as a dramatist and poet. Marlowe remains so popular that he is one of only a handful of writers whose names have become adjectives. The word "Marlovian" signifies the qualities of grandeur and ambition that characterizes both the life and the works of the playwright.

MARLOWE'S MIGHTY LINE

TODAY a memorial to Marlowe exists at Canterbury, and another at St. Nicholas's Church in Deptford is marked by a brass plate inscribed "To the Immortal Memory of Christopher Marlowe, M.A., The Founder of Grandiloquent Blank Verse." A stylistic innovation that contributed greatly to Marlowe's success and enduring legacy, blank verse is unrhymed iambic pentameter (not to be confused with Free Verse, a much more modern innovation, which does away with formal features altogether). Although blank verse does not rhyme, it requires a level of dexterity with meter which, at its best, can make carefully crafted lines sound much like spontaneous speech. Marlowe's greatest achievement with verse form was to write plays in blank verse that sounded both spontaneous and elevated at the same time. The following passage from *The Tragedy of Dr. Faustus* exemplifies Marlowe's use of blank verse in lines that are at once intensely expressive and carefully crafted:

> Was this the face that launched a thousand ships
> And burnt the topless towers of Ilium?
> Sweet Helen, make me immortal with a kiss.
>   [They kiss.]
> Her lips suck forth my soul. See where it flies!
> Come, Helen, come, give me my soul again.
>   [They kiss again.]

> Here will I dwell, for heaven is in these lips,
> And all is dross that is not Helena.
> I will be Paris, and for love of thee
> Instead of Troy shall Wittenberg be sacked,
> And I will combat with weak Menelaus,
> And wear thy colours on my plumed crest.
> Yea, I will wound Achilles in the heel
> And then return to Helen for a kiss.

> O, thou art fairer than the evening's air,
> Clad in the beauty of a thousand stars.
> Brighter art thou than flaming Jupiter
> When he appeared to hapless Semele,
> More lovely than the monarch of the sky
> In wanton Arethusa's azure arms;
> And none but thou shalt be my paramour.
> (*Doctor Faustus and Other Plays*, 5.2.,
> lines 93–112, pp. 238–239)

Faustus has called upon the occult forces to resurrect Helen of Troy for his own pleasure. The language seems driven to exalt its subject: Troy is represented in terms of "topless towers," and the beauty of Helen rivals the impact of the gods on mortal sight. The comparatives piled upon one another, "fairer," "brighter," and "more lovely" add a breathless intensity to the classical subject matter—the "theft" of Helen by Paris and the subsequent burning of Troy.

When Faustus asks of Helen, "is this the face that launched a thousand ships," he does so in a strict verse form that sounds remarkably like regular speech while remaining within formal parameters. This is blank verse. The metaphors are also quite striking. In one of the most beautiful of them, Helen is compared with "the evening's air, / Clad in the beauty of a thousand stars," which has the effect of making her seem both a force of nature and an eternal standard of beauty. The personification of Faustus' magic and of Marlowe's stagecraft, Helen embodies an art that defies the boundaries of time and space and the conventions of religion and morality. Marlowe's great theme is the transgression of boundaries, and his verse seems to soar above the conventional limits of poetic expression as well.

PLAYWRIGHTING IN ELIZABETHAN LONDON

IT should come as no surprise that such a risk-taker should have chosen to write for the stage, for the careers of playwright and spy were, in Elizabethan England, similarly perilous endeavors. Both were dangerous and socially marginal ways to earn a living; both depended on the patronage of powerful political figures; both were potentially rewarding; both involved the risk of imprisonment, infamy, even death. Actors had the same social status as prostitutes and beggars, and were often accused of being both. Playing itself was subject to the repeated criticism of the Puritans, reformers who were quite often wealthy, powerful, and connected with the political leaders of the City of London. Financial success was by no means certain. The playing houses were continually being shut down by outbreaks of the plague, and they were under the scrutiny of state-appointed censors. A playwright could very well find himself in prison, accused of blasphemy, heresy, or treason.

Writing for a public audience in Renaissance England was seen by many as a distasteful activity, but the risks of writing for the theater went beyond the social stigma attached to it. Playwrights in Elizabethan England were not authors in the modern sense of the term. They wrote plays not to be read but to be acted, and they wrote them for particular playing companies that would then use the scripts as they saw fit. In this context, there was none of the respect or reverence that we have today for playwrights like Shakespeare and Marlowe. In fact, writing plays was a far less respectable activity than writing other kinds of literature—an epic poem, for example, or a collection of sonnets, or even a translation from Latin or Greek (Marlowe tried his hand at translating Lucan's *Pharsalia* and Ovid's *Amores*). Playwrights wrote for a profit, although they did not always make one, and they wrote for a popular commercial venue. To be a playwright, then, one had to be willing to risk one's reputation for the sake of selling plays to playing companies that were not always successful or lucrative.

Part of the reason for the risky status of the stage was its youthfulness as an institution. The commercial stage was a relatively new phenomenon in London at the time Marlowe began to write for it in the late 1580s. The first public, open-air playhouses had been built in London only about a decade earlier, and stagecraft was primarily something practiced in schools, in churches, and by nonprofessionals on holidays. Changes in the laws governing financial credit and loans made it possible in the 1570s for entrepreneurs to invest in the building of large, open-air theaters in London dedicated to putting on spectacles for commercial purposes. These theaters were built in areas of London known as "Liberties," which were free of the legal restrictions of the City of London, with its rather puritanical government and laws. The largest of these, which formed something of a Renaissance red-light district, was Southwark, just across the Thames from London itself. Here were found houses of prostitution ("bawdy houses"), bearbaiting and bullbaiting theaters, and several of the most popular playing houses.

Not only were playing houses suspect because of their location and their association with other public forms of entertainment, acting itself was thought by many to be an inherently dishonest occupation. The job of an actor is to feign, mimic, or (in the early modern idiom) to "personate" persons and events. Impersonating someone or something else means feigning or misrepresenting one's own social identity, if only for a brief moment on the stage, and religious reformers in England, often called "Puritans," were deeply concerned about what they conceived to be the immorality of such impersonation. Playing itself was seen as a form of transgression that could lead all too readily to other kinds of crime

Suspicion towards playing was in part due to the relatively rigid social structure of Elizabethan society. English society at the time was hierarchical, divided according to "rank" or social standing, and those who enforced the social hierarchy worried about those who pretended to be of higher standing than they actually were. Even people's daily dress was regulated: "sumptuary laws" dictated what people could and could not wear according to their "rank," or social standing. In this setting Marlowe was a threateningly ambiguous and mercurial presence: As a university-educated gentleman, Marlowe belonged to a higher social class than many of his contemporaries in the theater (including Shakespeare). As a playwright and spy, he knew something about disguise.

THE TRANSVESTITE THEATER

ISSUES of social status and transgression permeate Marlowe's plays. For instance, the importance of clothing as an indication of social rank can be seen in the following lines spoken by Mortimer, in Marlowe's play *Edward II*, in criticism of the king and the king's favorite, Gaveston:

Uncle, his wanton humour grieves not me,
But this I scorn, that one so basely born

Should by his sovereign's favour grow so pert
And riot it with the treasure of the realm.
While soldiers mutiny for want of pay
He wears a lord's revenue on his back,
And Midas-like he jets it in the court
With base outlandish cullions at his heels,
Whose proud fantastic liveries make such show
As if that Proteus, god of shapes, appeared.
I have not seen a dapper jack so brisk.
He wears a short Italian cloak,
Larded with pearl, and in his Tuscan cap
A jewel of more value than the crown.
Whiles other walk below, the king and he
From out a window laugh at such as we,
And flout our train, and jest at our attire.
Uncle, 'tis this that makes me impatient.
(*Doctor Faustus and Other Plays*, 1.4.,
lines 402–419, p. 344)

Gaveston, who is "basely born," wears the most expensive clothes he possibly can: "a short Italian cloak / Larded with pearl" and a cap from Italy with a huge jewel in it. These are the "proud fantastic liveries" that anger Mortimer—gaudy clothes that cost a fortune and seem inappropriate attire for someone not born to wear them. By invoking Proteus, the playwright here gestures towards his own craft, for actors, too, change their shapes to "make [a] show."

Another reason for Mortimer's dislike of Gaveston is implied by the word "favour." Edward favors Gaveston not simply as a friend but because the two have an erotic relationship: *Edward II* is a play that depicts a notoriously weak king of England as what we would today call a homosexual. Marlowe put his finger on a sore spot for the Puritan critics of theater: the possibility of same-sex desire. For the Elizabethan stage was a transvestite theater in which all female roles were played by cross-dressed boys. Women were not allowed to act on the public stage until after the Restoration of the monarchy in 1660, nearly a century after Marlowe was born and many decades after his death. Women certainly formed part of the audience at any given play, but they were not allowed upon the stage.

The erotic implications of a transvestite theater were not lost on playwrights or critics, and a good deal of meta-theatrical humor in Elizabethan drama is derived from references to cross-dressing (Shakespeare's comedies, for instance, are full of gender-bending). Thus when Faustus addresses Helen in the lines I have quoted above ("Was this

the face that launched a thousand ships?"), we can readily imagine the laughter of an audience that was perfectly aware that the face in question belonged to a boy-actor dressed up as the legendary Helen. "This" face was certainly *not* the face that led to the Trojan War, a fact that no member of the audience would have been likely to forget.

Such is the case in *Edward II*, when the Queen refers to herself in terms of "chang[ing] my shape":

O, miserable and distressed queen!
Would when I left sweet France and was embarked,
That charming Circe, walking on the waves,
Had changed my shape, or at the marriage day
The cup of Hymen had been full of poison,
Or with those arms that twined about my neck
I had been stifled and not lived to see
The king my lord thus to abandon me.
Like frantic Juno will I fill the earth
With ghastly murmur of my signs and cries,
For never doted Jove on Ganymede
So much as he on cursed Gaveston.
But that will more exasperate his wrath.
I must entreat him, I must speak him fair,
And be a means to call home Gaveston;
And yet he'll ever dote on Gaveston,
And so am I forever miserable.
(*Doctor Faustus and Other Plays*, 1.4.,
lines 170–186, p. 338)

The unhappy queen compares herself to the classical goddess Juno (or Hera), frantic at the loss of her husband's love to the young—and male—Ganymede. The comparison is apt and charged. The term "ganymede" was widely used in Tudor England to mean a lovely boy; to use it in describing Gaveston's relationship to Edward II was to reference same-sex desire quite directly. Once again, it is not likely that an Elizabethan audience would have overlooked the fact that the actor playing Queen Isabella was himself a ganymede—a cross-dressed boy. To overlook the meta-theatrical humor in the Queen's speech is to miss an important dimension of Marlowe's stagecraft.

Acknowledging the theatrical context of Elizabethan London is crucial to understanding Marlowe's achievement as a dramatist. It was Marlowe's ability to put sensational political and social issues to theatrical use that, in part, makes his plays so startling and so entertaining. And yet, within a volatile theatrical context Marlowe made an impact as much for the kind of character he created as for his stagecraft. Each of his plays is dominated by a single character who resembles no one so much as the playwright himself. Whether set in Persia, Malta, or Germany, Marlowe's plays tell us a great deal about the imaginary life, ambitions, anxieties, and desires of a man who was very much of his time.

INFLUENCES AND WORKS

THE playwright Thomas Kyd once mentioned Marlowe's "rashness in attempting sudden privy injuries to men," and it seems clear that the latter had a particular affinity for danger and violence. The roles that Marlowe played in life were dangerous and disreputable ones, and his heroes tend to be reckless and wild. They all end up dying spectacular deaths much like their creator's. Even though they hail from different parts of the globe, all are recognizably Renaissance types, primarily men whose aspirations and ambitions vastly exceed the bounds of safety and security as well as the limits of tolerance of those around them. They all want too much, and they all transgress the social and moral standards of the worlds they inhabit. Marlowe preferred tragedy to comedy, and as a tragedian he depicted the careers of spectacularly doomed heroes: Tamburlaine the Great, a ruler who conquered much of Asia; Edward II, an English king put to death by his own subjects; Doctor Faustus, who made a pact with the devil in order to learn and experience all that was possible; and Barabas the Jew, gleefully wreaking havoc in Malta while revenging himself upon his enemies.

While Marlowe's characters closely resemble their creator in the violence of their passions and the fatality of their ambitions, they also resemble the people with whom Marlowe was associated. Preeminent among these was Sir Walter Ralegh, the great Elizabethan courtier, poet, explorer, and striver who would eventually be executed by Queen Elizabeth's successor, James I. It is not known if Marlowe knew Ralegh personally or not, but the latter would certainly have appealed to a man who wrote about characters with unbounded ambitions, and Ralegh's reputation as a poet, historian, and original thinker was well established by the time of Marlowe's own rise to fame. Richard Chomley, a onetime friend of Marlowe's, once claimed "Marlowe told him that he had read the atheist lecture to Sir Walter Ralegh and others." There is a good deal of Ralegh in Marlowe's character Dr. Faustus, whose desire for unlimited knowledge, travel, and

experience leads him to catastrophe. Both Ralegh and Marlowe were poets, and the former even wrote a reply to Marlowe's popular poem, "The passionate Sheepheard to his love."

Not all playwrights were successful poets as well. Poems generally circulated in manuscript form before being printed—if they ever saw print at all (not one of Marlowe's works was published in his own lifetime). Like Shakespeare, however, Marlowe's talents brought his poetry to the attention of some of the most accomplished members of Elizabethan society. The sole lyric poem of Marlowe's that remains, "The Passionate Shepherd," is a charming pastoral song of love spoken in the voice of a shepherd. The original version of the poem appeared posthumously in a collection called *England's Helicon*, but the poem was highly popular and appeared in many different versions. While the sentiments that it voices are conventional pastoral ones, the freshness and sensuality of the language are striking. Within a relatively simple structure of quatrains (four-line stanzas) rhyming aa-bb, Marlowe paints a sensual picture of pastoral love:

Come live with me and be my love,
And we will all the pleasures prove,
That Vallies, groves, hills and fieldes,
Woods, or steepie mountaine yields.

And wee will sit upon the Rocks,
Seeing the Sheepheards feede theyr flocks
By shallow Rivers, to whose falls
Melodious birds sing Medrigalls.

And I will make thee beds of Roses,
And a thousand fragrant poesies,
A cap of flowers, and a kirtle,
Imbrydred, all with leaves of Mirtle.
(*English Sixteenth-Century Verse*, p. 497)

In this, the first half of the poem, we can see that the speaker's object is seduction: the shepherd wishes to test or "prove" the romantic and sexual pleasures conventionally associated with pastoral life. The landscape reflects the speaker's mood; all is in harmony and all the objects are symbolic of love. This is a wholly poetic landscape in which birds sing artfully constructed songs to the accompaniment of waterfalls.

The speaker promises to make "a thousand fragrant Poesies" for his lover, which has an interesting and important ambiguity. On the one hand, a "posy" or "poesy" meant a flower or group of flowers; on the other hand, it referred to a poem or to poetry in general. The poem itself is just such a po[e]sy, a performance in verse that implies an identity between the shepherd and the poet. It ends with a festive pastoral vision of social harmony characteristic of the arcadian pleasures idealized by generations of Renaissance poets: "The Sheepheards Swaines shall daunce and sing / For thy delight each May-morning. / If these delights thy minde may move, / Then live with me, and be my love." The last line of the poem, then, repeats the first almost exactly, providing a cadence in which the speaker's desire for union with his loved one is repeated not simply as a plea but as a promise of pleasure.

Ralegh's reply is nearly as well known. Ralegh puts his own poem in the voice of the female love object, the shepherdess, who responds to the Marlovian shepherd's entreaties with an elaborate rejection based upon the futility and transitory nature of human desires, promises, and pleasures. "The Nimphs reply to the Sheepheard," thus, refuses the offer of love contained in Marlowe's poem, and in doing so voices a conventional response to poems of seduction. This poetic exchange suggests that the two writers either knew each other or, at the very least, took a serious interest in each other's work.

Although Ralegh was such an important figure in Elizabethan court life and letters that he could hardly have failed to make an impact on Marlowe's writing, we need not limit our understanding of Marlowe's characters to contemporary English models of self-fashioning. His characters also owe a great debt to continental figures, in particular to their author's knowledge of the works of Niccolo Machiavelli, a political theorist of the late fifteenth and early sixteenth centuries whose career in Florence quickly became associated with that city's violent politics. Machiavelli's most influential works, *The Prince* (1512) and the *Discourses* (1513–1517), dealt with the proper—or most efficacious—activities of political leaders in autocratic states, and his writings quickly became associated with intrigue, scheming, and the notion that "the ends justify the means."

To the English, Machiavelli became associated with everything immoral, with atheism, and with the devil himself. Unlike most ignorant Englishmen who had never read Machiavelli, however, Marlowe most certainly had done so at Cambridge. Realpolitik—politics as they happen not ideally but really—was a subject of persistent importance in Marlowe's life. Under torture for suspicion of writing libels, Thomas Kyd led authorities to Marlowe in their search for the author of papers described as "vile and heretical conceits denying the deity of Jesus Christ." Subsequent writings by Kyd and others add weight to the suspicion that Marlowe was a heretic and a blasphemer. In his "Theatre of God's Judgements" of 1597, the Puritan Thomas Beard represents Marlowe's death as divine punishment:

Marlin [Marlowe], by profession a scholar, brought up from his youth in the University of Cambridge but by practice a playmaker and a poet of scurrility who, by giving too large a swinge to his own wit and suffering his lust to have the full reins, fell, not without just desert, to that outrage and extremity that he denied God and his son Christ, and not only in word against it, affirming our Saviour to be but a deceiver, and Moses to be but a conjurer and seducer of the people, and the Holy Bible to be but vain and idle stories, and all religion but a device of policy.

(*Doctor Faustus and Other Plays*, p. viii)

"Policy" is the pivotal word in this harangue, for it was as a spy working on behalf of his queen's foreign policy that Marlowe first fell under religious suspicion. Moreover, it is for the sake of policy, or strategic self-representation for the sake of acquiring power, that Marlowe's characters speak their mighty lines. As the eponymous Barabas says in *The Jew of Malta*, "in extremity / We ought to make bar of no policy" (1., lines 507–508). As we might put the point today, when the going gets tough, anything goes.

TAMBURLAINE THE GREAT, PART I

MARLOWE'S first play, and the one that established him as a smashing success with London audiences, was *Tamburlaine the Great, Part I* (1590). This play examines the relationship of sheer force to political legitimacy in some depth. Tamburlaine himself, a Scythian (Asian) shepherd who rose to great power, eventually conquering much of what is now the Middle East, illustrates the principle of "might makes right." The embodiment of ambition and martial prowess, Tamburlaine is an enormously charismatic and powerful leader who holds himself and others to the highest standards of physical courage while remaining unconcerned with moral issues such as mercy and compassion. While in most of Renaissance drama such a character would inevitably find his downfall within five acts, Marlowe's Tamburlaine endures through two plays.

As many readers and audiences have noted, Tamburlaine is a monster of force and will, a demigod or robot who stalks across the stage wreaking havoc at every step, inexorable and without remorse. Characterized by his utter disdain for conventional human motivations such as the fear of pain, pity, or remorse, Tamburlaine becomes the scourge of societies that would limit his mobility and circumscribe his power. Tamburlaine responds to one of his victims' when the latter accuses him of cruelty:

> Nature, that framed us of four elements
> Warring within our breasts for regiment,
> Doth teach us all to have aspiring minds;
> Our souls, whose faculties can comprehend
> The wondrous architecture of the world
> And measure every planet's wandering course,
> Still climbing after knowledge infinite,
> And always moving as the restless spheres,
> Wills us to wear ourselves and never rest
> Until we reach the ripest fruit of all,
> That perfect bliss and sole felicity,
> The sweet fruition of an earthly crown.
> (*Doctor Faustus and Other Plays*, 2.7.,
> lines 18–29, p. 28)

The language itself moves relentlessly forward: Tamburlaine describes his own nature as "aspiring" and "climbing," as if the goal of such a life were to go as high as possible. The course of his life reflects "every planet's wandering course."

This upward movement is associated with the acquisition of knowledge as well, for Tamburlaine understands his own primary goal—and the goal of those like him—as seeking to "comprehend / The wondrous architecture of the world." The ruthless warrior claims, remarkably, that knowledge, not merely conquest, is the proper goal of men like him. "Aspiring minds" like his not only strive to attain power, "an earthly crown," but "knowledge infinite" as well. This sentiment is a something of a constant in Marlowe's plays, and it will appear again in *Dr. Faustus*. Faustus, like Tamburlaine, aspires to know as much as he can, even to the point of transgressing all limits. While both plays are about long-dead characters, the sentiments they voice are very much those of "Renaissance men," like Ralegh and Marlowe, whose aspirations in several fields were as limitless as their own imaginations.

Tamburlaine's restless quest to rule over all other rulers gives this play a striking sense of movement. Marlowe makes dramatic use of the boom in sixteenth century cartography and geographical knowledge to give grandeur to the scope of Tamburlaine's ambitions and conquests. In the following passage, for instance, the Scythian warlord refers to the medieval European cartographic convention of representing the world as a "T" surrounded by an "O," with the three continents of Europe, Asia, and Africa forming the distinct regions of the world separated by the Mediterranean ("terrene") Sea and the Red Sea:

> I will confute those blind geographers
> That make a triple region of the world,
> Excluding regions which I mean to trace,
> And with this pen reduce them to a map,
> Calling the provinces, cities, and towns
> After my name and thine, Zenocrate.
> Here at Damascus I will make the point
> That shall begin the perpendicular.
> (*Doctor Faustus and Other Plays*, 4.4.,
> lines 78–85, p. 52)

Tamburlaine claims that he will set about redrawing the map of the world with a different kind of "pen," his sword. Moreover, his wish to "confute those blind geographers / That make a triple region of the world" would have reverberated with a Renaissance audience, for Renaissance cartographers were busy doing just that—confuting medieval "T and O" world maps by including newly discovered lands on their maps of the world.

Later in the play, Tamburlaine proclaims:

> when holy Fates
> Shall 'stablish me in strong Egyptia,
> We mean to travel to th'Antarctic Pole,
> Conquering the people underneath our feet,
> And be renowned as never emperors were.
> (*Doctor Faustus and Other Plays*, 4.4.,
> lines 138–142, p. 53)

Again Marlowe depicts his character's limitless ambition by appealing to the arts of the geographer, which gives Tamburlaine a larger-than-life rhetorical effect. Tamburlaine maps out in word a world in which he is both cartographer and explorer. By the end of the play, the former shepherd achieves his "earthly crown" and is able to crown his friends and his queen as well. He is also responsible for the downfall of numerous other characters who wear crowns less effectively than he, as well as for one character's dashing out his own brains while being held captive in a cage. This is a play in which crowns can tumble, break, and be seized by the mighty.

TAMBURLAINE THE GREAT, PART II

BECAUSE of its great popularity with London audiences, *Tamburlaine* was quickly followed by a sequel, *Tamburlaine the Great, Part II* (1590). The first play ends with its hero at the height of his fortunes, conquering much of the known world and appointing his friends as kings. The sequel picks up at this point and then proceeds to depict his decline and fall. In this play, the career of the great Scythian warrior runs its course, as we are told by the Prologue before the action even begins:

> The general welcome Tamburlaine received
> When he arrived last upon our stage
> Hath made our poet pen his second part,
> Where death cuts off the progress of his pomp
> And murd'rous Fates throws all his triumphs down.
> But what became of fair Zenocrate,
> And with how many cities' sacrifice
> He celebrated her sad funeral,
> Himself in presence shall unfold at large.
> *(Doctor Faustus and Other Plays*, p. 71)

Prologues generally provided broad overviews of the plays they preceded, and this one is no exception. In referring to the first *Tamburlaine,* the Prologue advertises the kind of spectacle that the audience can expect. We should keep in mind that these plays were produced for paying audiences and that playwrights and actors did all they could to draw in as many people as possible to the playhouse. In this Marlowe succeeded like no playwright before him.

Although the Prologue forewarns us of the ultimate end of Tamburlaine, for five acts we are treated to the Scythian warlord's incomparable pomp and bombast. Once again his language pushes at the barrier between the human and the divine, as in the following lines:

> Villain, I say,
> Should I but touch the rusty gates of hell,
> The triple-headed Cerberus would howl
> And wake black Jove to crouch and kneel to me;
> But I have sent volleys of shot to you,
> Yet could not enter till the breach was made.
> *(Doctor Faustus and Other Plays*, 5.1.,
> lines 95–100, p. 124)

Here the protagonist demonstrates even more hubris than we have come to expect from the first play; clearly, his author is setting him up for a fall. This moral sensibility appears more evidently in this play than in the first, to the point where the forces of Christendom, represented by a Hungarian king, are defeated by the Turks in punishment for having broken an oath.

The second *Tamburlaine* displays the geographical scope that also characterizes its predecessor. From North Africa to Persia, Turkey, and Hungary, the action of the play takes place at the border between Christian Europe and the Islamic Empire. Indeed, much of the known world receives mention, and the playwright seems eager to display his geographical and historical knowledge of the Islamic Empire that dominated the Mediterranean for centuries. In the fifth act, the Scythian warlord calls for a map to be brought to him. In the ensuing lines, we have an example of onstage map reading that will be repeated by Shakespeare in *Henry IV, Part I* and in *King Lear:*

> Here I began to march towards Persia,
> Along Armenia and the Caspian Sea,
> And thence unto Bythinia, where I took
> The Turk and his great empress prisoners;
> Then marched I into Egypt and Arabia,
> And here, not far from Alexandria,
> Whereas the Terrene and the Red Sea meet,
> Being distant less than full a hundred leagues,
> I meant to cut a channel to them both,
> That men might quickly sail to India.
> From thence to Nubia, near Borno lake,
> And so along the Ethiopian sea,
> Cutting the tropic line of Capricorn,
> I conquered all as far as Zanzibar.
> Then by the northern part of Africa
> I came at last to Graecia, and from thence
> To Asia where I stay against my will,
> Which is from Scythia, where I first began
> Backwards and forwards, near five hundred
>   thousand leagues.
> Look here, my boys see what a world of ground
> Lies westward from the midst of Cancer's line
> Unto the rising of this earthly globe,
> Whereas the sun, declining from our sight,
> Begins the day with our Antipodes;
> And shall I die, and this unconquered?
> *(Doctor Faustus and Other Plays*, 5.3.,
> lines 126–150, p. 133)

Here Tamburlaine describes the map of the world that he is holding in his hand, lamenting the fact that he will never have the opportunity to conquer all the lands that it depicts. In mentioning the tropics of Cancer and of Capricorn and lands such as the Antipodes that were relatively recent discoveries in the late sixteenth century, this passage describes not Tamburlaine's world but Marlowe's own. Tamburlaine anachronistically holds a European world map, a *mappa mundi*, and proudly catalogues some of the most recent geographical discoveries in the sixteenth century. In these lines and in numerous others like them, we can detect a strong note of intellectual longing that accompanies Tamburlaine's thirst for conquest. Once again, we should note, in the character of Tamburlaine, Marlowe paints the portrait of a Renaissance European sensibility.

DOCTOR FAUSTUS

THE *Tragedy of Doctor Faustus* (1604/1616), a magnificent play that has haunted readers and audiences for centuries, concerns the exploits of the German scholar Faustus and his pact with the devil (a subject that later writers, including Goethe and Thomas Mann, would later revisit). While the Faust myth is based on legends told about a real historical personage associated with Gutenberg, Marlowe's play has almost nothing to do with actual historical events. Instead it depicts the ambition and drive that characterized Elizabethans—like Ralegh and Marlowe himself—of his own day whose desire for knowledge and experience placed them outside the bounds of the normal and the "godly." Much like Tamburlaine, Faustus personifies the most powerful and extreme drives of Renaissance European society: the desire for power, knowledge, and limitless freedom. Faustus defies the status quo by signing a pact with the devil, mocking the pope, abusing powerful political figures, and contriving by magic to conjure up Helen of Troy to satiate his desire for the most beautiful woman in the world. Like Tamburlaine, Faustus is relentlessly ambitious and unwilling to stop his own meteoric career; like the Scythian warrior, too, he is doomed to a horrific death. Unlike Tamburlaine, however, Faustus does not achieve his ends as a warrior or a politician; his arena is the life of the mind.

While Marlowe's most popular works in his own day were the two *Tamburlaines, Dr. Faustus* has become Marlowe's most appreciated play in modern times. One of the reasons for its ongoing success is its spectacular use of the occult onstage. The play begins with a sensational premise. After a lifetime of study and dedication to his books, Faustus begins a new and reckless career when he takes up a book of magic and decides that there should be no limitations on his own access to knowledge, power, and experience. He thus conjures up the demon Mephistopheles from hell and commands the latter to aid him in his new endeavors. "I charge thee wait upon me whilst I live, / To do whatever Faustus shall command, / Be it to make the moon drop from her sphere, / Or the ocean to overwhelm the world" (1.3., lines 33–36). Magic has a particular affinity with theatrical illusion, and most of the spectacular scenes in *Dr. Faustus* involve the encounter between the mortal and the magical. As we have seen above, Faustus also causes Helen of Troy to be brought from hell to his chamber.

Interrogating Mephistopheles, Faustus learns that the former is "a servant to great Lucipher"; when Faustus asks his new servant how it happens that a demon can leave Hell, Mephistopheles famously replies:

> Why this is hell, nor am I out of it.
> Think'st thou that I, that saw the face of God
> And tasted the eternal joys of heaven
> Am not tormented with ten thousand hells
> In being deprived of everlasting bliss? .
> O Faustus, leave these frivolous demands
> Which strikes a terror to my fainting soul.
> (*Doctor Faustus and Other Plays*, 1.3.,
> lines 74–80, p. 143)

Thus, Mephistopheles initially attempts to dissuade Faustus from choosing an evil way of life but ends up aiding and abetting Faustus in the pursuit of ungodly experience. The demon is an instrument of the deity, and it is Faustus' repeated decision to persist in evil, even when given the opportunity to repent, that ensures his damnation.

Striving after the infinite, Faustus—like Tamburlaine before him—speaks in powerful blank verse permeated with geographical, astronomical, and astrological imagery. Faustus is a necromancer, one who deals in magic, but he is intimately concerned with this world. Faustus agrees to sign a written compact with the Prince of Darkness. The pact is written in the blood of Faustus himself, a spectacular theatrical moment of particular intensity when we consider its historical context. Marlowe's audiences lived in a world saturated with lore about the forces of darkness, witches, and demons. By putting a demon on the stage—and in several scenes—Marlowe appealed to the widespread belief in the supernatural and exploited that belief for spectacular theatrical effects. Moreover, Faustus renounces the Christian God in full view of a Christian audience. He is literally playing with fire.

Throughout the play, Marlowe puts the supernatural to good use, exploiting magic for theatrical effect. At one point Faustus has been transported to the Vatican, where he observes a conference between the pope and some cardinals. Making himself invisible, Faustus wreaks havoc and causes the churchmen to think that demonic forces are at play among them. Because Marlowe's London audience would have been almost exclusively Protestant, insulting the pope and committing symbolic violence on his impersonator was a way to appeal to anti-Catholic sentiment. *Dr. Faustus* has been compared to a medieval morality play, and it certainly owes a great deal to that dramatic tradition. A good angel and a bad one compete to win his soul—a stage device borrowed from medieval tradition. The character Mephistopheles, too, owes a good deal to the Vice, a stock character who tempts the Christian protagonist in medieval morality plays.

Both versions of the play, the so-called A-text and B-text, end with the moralizing statements of a Chorus that warns against striving after forbidden knowledge as Faustus does:

> Faustus is gone. Regard his hellish fall.
> Whose fiendful fortune may exhort the wise
> Only to wonder at unlawful things,
> Whose deepness doth entice such forward wits
> To practice more than heavenly power permits.
> (*Doctor Faustus and Other Plays*, lines 4–8, p. 183)

These closing lines from the Epilogue make an example of Faustus, a spectacle of sin that acts as a warning against Faustian transgression. As with Mozart's *Don Giovanni*, however, we are also invited to choose whether to accept such sentiments and regard the hero's horrible end as just punishment for his sins, or to see it as the angry intervention of a jealous God. In Goethe's *Faust*, written over two centuries later, the hero is redeemed. We cannot help thinking that for Marlowe, too, Faustus was never merely a negative example for the pious, but a hero of ambition and self-assertion.

THE JEW OF MALTA

THE JEW OF MALTA (first performed 1594; pub. 1633) is Marlowe's contribution to the revenge tragedy, a popular form among Elizabethan and Jacobean playwrights and audiences that owes a debt to Thomas Kyd, Marlowe's onetime roommate. Kyd wrote several very popular revenge tragedies, including *The Spanish Tragedy,* which greatly influenced Shakespeare's writing of *Hamlet*—also a revenge tragedy—some years later. Revenge tragedies are notable for their combination of inventive violence and dark humor; they tend to have gruesome scenes of violent crime and retribution with numerous morbidly funny lines. First produced in 1589–1591, *The Jew of Malta* is exuberantly dark and disturbingly comical. Barabas himself is a character who, in true Marlovian fashion, dominates the stage with charisma and with energetic poetry. First played by the leading actor of Marlowe's playing company, Edward Alleyn (who also played Tamburlaine and Faustus), the role of Barabas confronts audiences and readers with the dilemma of a likable, murderous, sinned-against and sinning hero/villain.

To understand the complexities of Barabas and of the play, we must be aware that the status of Jews in Christian Europe in the Middle Ages and Renaissance was a vexed one. There were very few Jews in Marlowe's London, due to the fact that they had been expelled centuries earlier. Barabas is a Jew who lives in Malta, a Christian island in the Mediterranean. In the course of the play, his fortunes wax and wane in a manner not unlike those of Marlowe's other protagonists. He is a wealthy merchant who concocts elaborate ways of taking revenge on the inhabitants of the island after his wealth is taken from him by the Maltese to pay a tribute to the Turks. Barabas can be understood as a cultural fantasy of the outcast. This is something that Marlowe represents physically, for Barabas is at one point quite literally thrown from the city walls of Malta.

The Jew of Malta examines a political world in which anything goes in the quest for power and vengeance. Barabas is perhaps Marlowe's most Machiavellian character, if we remember that from the Renaissance English perspective Machiavelli was the icon of ruthless political machination and power-driven immorality. In creating "Machiavels" such as Barabas for the English stage, Marlowe catered to the taste and expectations of his London audience. What is immediately striking about *The Jew of Malta,* however, is not simply that Barabas practices Machiavellian policy, but that Marlowe makes "Machiavel" a role to be played on the stage. "Old Nick," as he was popularly known, is himself the first character to take the stage, and serves as the play's Prologue. Following the stage direction, "enter Machiavel," the Prologue offers a version of what most Elizabethan Londoners would have taken to be the genuine Machiavellian political philosophy:

> Albeit the world think Machiavel is dead,
> Yet was his soul but flown beyond the Alps,
> And, now the Guise is dead, is come from France
> To view this land and frolic with his friends.
> To some perhaps my name is odious,
> But such as love me guard me from their tongues,
> And let them know that I am Machiavel,
> And weigh not men, and therefore not men's words.
> Admired I am of those that hate me most.
> Though some speak openly against my books,
> Yet will they read me and thereby attain
> To Peter's chair, and, when they cast me off,
> Are poisoned by my climbing followers.
> I count religion but a childish toy
> And hold there is no sin but ignorance.
> Birds of the air will tell of murders past!
> I am ashamed to hear such fooleries.
> Many will talk of title to a crown;
> What right had Caesar to the empery?
> Might first made kings, and laws were then most sure
> When, like the Draco's, they were writ in blood.
> Hence comes it that a strong-built citadel
> Commands much more than letters can import—
> Which maxime had Phalaris observed,
> He'd never bellowed in a brazen bull
> Of great ones' envy. O' th' poor petty wits
> Let me be envied and not pitied!
> But whither am I bound? I come not, I,
> To read a lecture here in Brittany,
> But to present the tragedy of a Jew,
> Who smiles to see how full his bags are crammed,
> Which money was not got without my means.
> I crave but this: grace him as he deserves,
> And let him not be entertained the worse
> Because he favors me.
> (*Doctor Faustus and Other Plays,* pp. 251–252)

Whether the audience is to view the spectacle with moral censure or approval, there can be no doubt that Marlowe's Machiavel articulates a radical political principle in these lines. If it is true that "might first made kings," then what right has any figure of authority to wield power? "Might

makes right" is not a political doctrine calculated to inspire confidence in one's rulers—especially in an era when the legitimacy of kings was understood in terms of a "Divine Right" to the throne.

"Machiavel" the Prologue tells us, then, that we are about to witness the actions of a character that operates by "my means," or scheming and double-dealing. Barabas does indeed proceed to commit heinous crimes for the next five acts of the play, periodically voicing his own reasons for doing so in terms that echo the Prologue. But his energy and the exuberance with which he extracts revenge from those who cross him threaten to steal the show. In the end, as with *Dr. Faustus,* we are left wondering whether the sheer force of will represented by the hero/villain does not redeem him from his morally exemplary end.

EDWARD II

MARLOWE also wrote a history play, *Edward II* (1594). While his other plays are set in exotic places such as Asia Minor and Malta, this one is set in England several centuries before Marlowe's own day. Nevertheless, this play resembles the others in its thoroughly negative depiction of politics and political leaders. The characters in *Edward II* are every bit as vicious as Barabas and Tamburlaine, even if they are English. They are also utterly self-interested. Both King Edward and his favorite, Gaveston, threaten the stability of the kingdom by their unconcern for others. It is characteristic of Marlowe that he makes a weak king and his lover/friend seem as rapaciously self-serving as Tamburlaine and Faustus.

The play opens with Gaveston reading a letter from the king and explaining himself to the audience:

> GAVESTON: [reads] "My father is deceased; come, Gaveston,
> And share the kingdom with thy dearest friend."
> Ah, words that make me surfeit with delight!
> What greater bliss can hap to Gaveston
> Than live and be the favourite of a king?
> Sweet prince, I come; these thy amorous lines
> Might have enforced me to have swum from France
> And like Leander gasped upon the sand,
> So thou wouldst smile and take me in thy arms.
> The sight of London to my exiled eyes
> Is as Elysium to a new-come soul—
> Not that I love the city or the men,
> But that it harbours him I hold so dear,

The king, upon whose bosom let me die
And with the world still be at enmity.
What need the arctic people love starlight,
To whom the sun shines both by day and night?
Farewell, base stooping to the lordly peers;
My knee shall bow to none but to the king.
                    (*Doctor Faustus and Other Plays*, 1.1.,
                                        lines 1–19, p. 325)

Gaveston's relationship to the king is frankly erotic: the reference to "these thy amorous lines" and to "him I hold so dear" give a sexual charge to the words "upon whose bosom let me die." To "die," in the early modern English of Marlowe's day, meant both to expire in the modern sense and, more importantly here, to reach sexual climax. Moreover, the reference to the popular story of Hero and Leander—the subject of Marlowe's long, unfinished poem—squarely frames the relationship between the king and Gaveston as a sexual one.

The opening lines of *Edward II*, thus, introduce an erotic relationship between the king and his "dearest friend." They also introduce the cause of Gaveston's unpopularity in court. When he bids farewell to "base stooping to the lordly peers," Gaveston in effect claims that from this point on he will be second in rank only to the king himself. He is quite self-consciously a social climber. When Mortimer refers to him as "one so basely born," he voices the scorn of the aristocrat for a courtier whose prestige in court rests solely on his being the king's favorite. Like Tamburlaine and Faustus, then, Gaveston represents a form of transgressive ambition, a political being hungry for power who must operate in hostile and dangerous surroundings.

Gaveston's social climbing as much as his flamboyantly amorous relationship with the king galls his enemies at court. But it is not clear that they are meant to gall audiences as well. Should we recoil in horror at Gaveston, or cheer him on? Much the same dilemma faces readers of Marlowe's other plays as well. Does Marlowe identify with Barabas and portray him sympathetically, or simply depict him as a bloodthirsty villain? Is there something noble in the curiosity and striving of Faustus, or is he merely a transgressor? Marlowe's complex characters entertain and vex; clearly, the playwright invests a great deal of his own vigor and zest for transgression in them.

The depiction of Gaveston demands a sophisticated interpretation that attends to the social history of same-sex desire at the same time that it acknowledges Gaveston's frankly manipulative intentions. The following passage, in which Gaveston dismisses three poor men from his presence, is a case in point:

These are not the men for me
I must have wanton poets, pleasant wits,
Musicians that with touching of a string
May draw the pliant king which way I please.
Music and poetry is his delight;
Therefore I'll have Italian masques by night,
Sweet speeches, comedies, and pleasing shows;
And in the day, when he shall walk abroad,
Like sylvan nymphs my pages shall be clad;
My men, like satyrs grazing on the lawns,
Shall with their goat feet dance an antic hay.
Sometime a lovely boy in Dian's shape,
With hair that gilds the water as it glides,
Crownets of pearl about his naked arms,
And in his sportful hands an olive tree
To hide those parts which men delight to see,
Shall bathe him in a spring, and there hard by
One like Actaeon peeping through a grove
Shall by the angry goddess be transformed,
And running in the likeness of an hart
By yelping hounds pulled down and seem to die.
                    (*Doctor Faustus and Other Plays*, 1.1.,
                                        lines 49–69, p. 326)

Gaveston describes a court in which the world of classical mythology, especially as recounted by Ovid, has been transformed to an all-male, crossdressed set piece. The nymphs of Gaveston's landscape would be male, not female, as would the virgin goddess of the hunt, Diana herself. The agony of Actaeon, torn to pieces by his own dogs, becomes transformed into a peep show at a boyish Diana pretending to hide "those parts which men delight to see" as other courtiers look on. "Masques" and "shows" were Renaissance terms for kinds of theater, and the entire passage describes a court transformed into a series of scenes taken from classical mythology. We should recall, too, that Gaveston shares the stage more than once with an actor playing his rival for the king's love, Queen Isabella, a boy dressed up to play a woman. The horrifying and symbolic offstage murder of the king is one of the most shocking moments in all of Tudor and Stuart drama, and it continues to prompt scholars and critics to investigate the status of gender roles and sexuality in Elizabethan England.

Edward II is a more mature and masterful work than Marlowe's prior plays; its poetry is subtler and its characterization more developed. Less static and bombastic than the *Tamburlaines* or *Faustus*,

Marlowe's history play deftly examines the nature of court politics, kingship, friendship, and the effects of unlicensed desire. We can only imagine what the dramatist might have written as his skills developed further, but this play gives us some sense of what we are missing.

HERO AND LEANDER

MARLOWE'S greatest accomplishment off the stage was his incomplete narrative poem *Hero and Leander* (1593; the poet George Chapman wrote an ending after Marlowe's death). The poem follows Ovid's treatment of a classic love story told by a prior poet, Musaeus. Most likely written in the last months of Marlowe's life (when the London playhouses were closed), *Hero and Leander* reveals a maturity of style that rivals Shakespeare's *Venus and Adonis*, a similarly classical narrative poem written at about the same time. Both are erotic narrative poems on classical themes, and both showcase the talents of the poet-playwrights who wrote them.

Marlowe's debt to Ovid is evident in the sensual language and erotic subject matter, as well as in the asides, which contain cynical remarks about women. Written in heroic couplets (rhyming pairs of lines of iambic pentameter), the poem tells the story of a brief affair between two lovers who live on either side of the banks of the Hellespont (a narrow body of water flowing from the Black Sea into the Mediterranean which separates Europe from Asia): "On Hellespont, guilty of true-loves blood, / In view and opposite, two cities stood, / Sea-borderers, disjoined by Neptune's might; / The one Abydos, the other Sestos hight" (ll., lines 1–4). Hero, paradoxically, is a chaste nun devoted to Venus, while Leander is a sexually innocent seducer.

The poem is in no hurry to tell the story of their passion, and it lingers in sensual descriptions of the two lovers' bodies, desires, and protestations, and on allusions to the activities of the gods of the classical pantheon. The mixture of humor and philosophical argument reveals Marlowe at his best, as in the following passage, where Leander argues against virginity:

> This idoll which you terme Virginitie,
> Is neither essence subject to the eie,
> No, nor to any one exterior sence,
> Nor hath it any place of residence,
> Nor is't of earth or mold celestiall,
> Or capable of any forme at all.

> Of that which hath no being doe not boast,
> Things that are not at all are never lost.
> (*English Sixteenth-Century Verse*, ll.,
> lines 269–276, pp. 507–508)

In a sense, the entire work is a poem in praise of form and beauty, the expression of a thoroughly Renaissance artistic sensibility that we might associate with a Michaelangelo or a Caravaggio. Marlowe's poem contains no trace of the moral lesson—that illicit sexual desire will be punished by the gods—contained in Chapman's later additions.

OTHER WORKS

MARLOWE also wrote two plays, *Dido, Queen of Carthage* (1594) and *The Massacre at Paris* (c.1593), which are not commonly read today. An early work, *Dido, Queen of Carthage*, attests to Marlowe's interest in classical lore and reveals flashes of the poetic imagination that would later create the great plays for which he is remembered. The plot, in which Aeneas comes to the court of the widow Dido in Carthage after the fall of Troy, comes from Virgil's *Aeneid* and Ovid's *Metamorphoses*. In fact, several passages come directly from the second and fourth books of the *Aeneid*. The play seems to have been composed at different times of Marlowe's life, and it contains some memorable lines—one of them, "heele make me immortall with a kisse," that the playwright liked enough to use again in *Dr. Faustus*. While this is not one of Marlowe's most dynamic plays, it was good enough for Shakespeare to note it in *Hamlet* as "an excellent play, well digested in the scenes, set down with as much modesty as cunning."

The Massacre at Paris is a play about the infamous St. Bartholomew's Day Massacre in which thousands of French Protestants were butchered in 1588. While the character of the Guise, a schemer in true Marlovian fashion, has some memorable lines, this is not a great play. Although its shortness and the poor quality of the text raise many questions about the play's authorship, there is a general consensus among scholars that it was written by Marlowe. Certainly its subject matter, the machinations of Catholics in France to combat the Protestant cause, lay close to the heart of Marlowe's work as a spy.

CONCLUSION

ONE of the leading scholars of English Renaissance literature, Stephen Greenblatt, has noted, "from his first play to his last, Marlowe is drawn to the idea of physical movement, to the problem of its representation within the narrow confines of the theater" (*Renaissance Self-Fashioning*, p. 194). Tamburlaine's restless marching across Asia and the stage, the evocation of the spirit of Machiavelli soaring over the Alps and across the English Channel, Faustus' magically soaring across impossible distances of time and space, and Gaveston's courtly social climbing all exemplify Marlowe's interest in depicting ambition and power in terms of physical mobility. Marlowe had an encompassing and a geographical imagination, and his characters personify the restlessness of his era. His characters embody different versions of the very idea of mobility. In each case, this mobility is temporarily upward; eventually, however, the trajectory of all of Marlowe's characters tends downward, and we cannot help seeing something of their author in them.

SELECTED BIBLIOGRAPHY

I. Collected Works. *Works of Christopher Marlowe*, ed. by C. F. Tucker Brooke (Oxford, 1929); *The Poems: Christopher Marlowe*, ed. by Millar MacLure (London, 1968); *The Complete Plays*, ed. by J. B. Steane (Harmondsworth, U.K., 1969); *The Complete Poems and Translations*, ed. by Stephen Orgel (Harmondsworth, U.K., 1971); *The Complete Works of Christopher Marlowe*, ed. by Fredson Bowers (Cambridge, 1981); *English 16th-Century Verse: An Anthology*, ed. by Richard S. Sylvester (New York and London, 1984); *The Complete Works of Christopher Marlowe*, ed. by Roma Gill (Oxford, 1987); *Doctor Faustus and Other Plays*, ed. by David Bevington and Eric Rasmussen (Oxford and New York, 1995).

II. Plays. *Dido, Queen of Carthage.* Although not entered in The Stationers' Register, "The Tragedie of Dido Queene of Carthage:" Played by the Children of Her Maiesties Chappell. Written by Christopher Marlowe, and Thomas Nash. Gent. Was printed by the Wido Orwin for Thomas Woodcock in 1594. The only three extant copies of the 1594 copy are in the Bodleian, Folger, and Huntington Libraries. The next edition did not appear until 1825. Editions include H. J. Oliver, ed., The Revels Plays edition (Cambridge, Mass., and London, 1968).

Tamburlaine. Both parts of *Tamburlaine* were entered in The Stationer's Register by Richard Jones in 1590, as "The twooe commicall discourses of Tomberlein the Cithian shepparde. They were each published in octavo form the same year. Editions include David Bevington and Eric Rasmussen, eds., *Doctor Faustus and Other Plays* (Oxford and New York, 1995). Further Reading: Mark Thornton Burnett, "*Tamburlaine* and the Body," in *Criticism* 33 (1991); Nancy T. Leslie, "*Tamburlaine* in the Theatre: Tartar, Grand Guignol, or Janus?" in *Renaissance Drama* 4 (1971); David Thurn, "Sights of Power in *Tamburlaine*," in *English Literary Renaissance* 19 (1989).

Dr. Faustus. This plays exists in two distinctly different versions, the A-text of 160- and the B-text of 160-. The A-text contains some thirty-six lines not found in the B-text, while the latter contains 676 lines not found in the former, and many changes. It is quite possible that the extra episodes of the B-text were added later by other playwrights, since in 1602 the owner of the Rose theater, Philip Henslowe, recorded that he paid four pounds to William Birde and Samuel Rowley "for ther adicyones in docter fostes." W. W. Greg insisted that the A-text was a "bad quarto," or memorially reconstructed text. Most modern editors disagree. Editions include W. W. Greg, *The Tragical History of the Life and Death of Doctor Faustus by Christopher Marlowe. A Conjectural Reconstruction* (Oxford, 1950); David Bevington and Eric Rasmussen, eds., *Doctor Faustus and Other Plays* (Oxford and New York, 1995). Further Reading: W. W. Greg, ed., *Marlowe's "Doctor Faustus" 1604–1616: Parallel Texts* (Oxford, 1950); John Philip Brockbank, *Marlowe: Dr. Faustus* (New York and London, 1962); Fredson T. Bowers, "Marlowe's *Doctor Faustus*: The 1602 Additions," in *Studies in Bibliography* 26 (1973); Michael H. Keefer, "Right Hand and Left Heel: Ideological Origins of the Faustus Legend," in *Mosaic* 22 (1989); Constance Brown Kuriyama, "*Dr. Greg and Doctor Faustus*: The Supposed Originality of the 1616 Text," in *English Literary Renaissance* 5 (1975); Michael J. Warren, "*Doctor Faustus*: The Old Man and the Text," in *English Literary Renaissance* 11 (1981).

The Jew of Malta. Although Nicholas Ling and Thomas Millington entered "the famous tragedie of the Riche Jewe of malta" in the Stationers' Register in May of 1594, no copy of their edition exists. The 1633 quarto printed by John Beale is the earliest extant edition; it contains a dedication to the playwright Thomas Heywood. Editions include Richard W. Van Fossen, ed., *Regents Renaissance Drama* (1964); N. W. Bawcutt, ed., *The Revels Plays* (London, 1978); David Bevington and Eric Rasmussen, eds., *Doctor Faustus and Other Plays* (Oxford and New York, 1995). Further Reading: J. C. Maxwell, "How Bad is the Text of *The Jew of Malta*?" in *Modern Language Review* 48 (1953); J. L. Simmons, "Elizabethan Stage Practice and Marlowe's *Jew of Malta*," in *Renaissance Drama* 4 (1971).

The Massacre at Paris. There is no date on the entry in the Stationers' Register of "The Massacre at Paris: With the Death of the Duke of Guise. As Is was plaide by the right honourable the Lord high Admiral his Seruants. Written by Christopher Marlow," printed by Edward Allde for Edward White in octavo form. The entry is undated. The first known production was by Lord Strange's Men at the Rose theater in 1593. Nor is much known about the date of the play's composition. Since, however, it contains the death of Henri III of France, it must postdate August 2, 1589, when that king in fact died. Marlowe died in 1593, which gives a four-year window for its composition. Because of its shortness and numerous textual errors, it seems extremely likely that the quarto is a stolen, memorially reconstructed text—a so-called "Bad Quarto." Editions include The Revels Plays edition, ed. by H. J. Oliver (London, 1968). Further Reading: J. H. M. Salmon, *The French Religious Wars in English Political Thought* (Oxford, 1959).

Edward II. The octavo edition of 1594, printed by William Jones, is the earliest extant edition; editions include W. W. Greg, ed., *Edward II* (London, 1925); W. Moelwyn Merchant, ed., *Edward II* (New York, 1967). Further Reading: Claude J. Summers, "Isabella's Plea for Gaveston in Marlowe's *Edward II*," in *Philological Quarterly* 52 (1973); Kathleen Anderson, A 'Stab, As Occasion Serves': The Real Isabella in Marlowe's *Edward II*," in *Renaissance Papers* (1992).

Hero and Leander. The poem was entered in the Stationers' Register in 1593, four months after the death of Marlowe. Chapman's rendition divided the poem into "Sestiads" (after Sestos, home of Hero), complete with summaries in verse. The best modern edition, which prunes the poem of Chapman's influence, is *Hero and Leander by Christopher Marlowe: A Facsimile of the First Edition London 1598*, ed. by Louis L. Martz (Washington, 1972). Further Reading: Marion Campbell, " 'Desunt Nunnulla': The Construction of Marlowe's *Hero and Leander* as an Unfinished Poem," in *ELH* 51 (1984); W. L. Godshalk, "*Hero and Leander:* The Sense of An Ending," in Kenneth Fridenreich, Roma Gill, and Constance B. Kuriyama, eds., *"A Poet & a Filthy Play-maker": New Essays on Christopher Marlowe* (New York, 1988); Joanne Altieri, "*Hero and Leander:* Sensible Myth and Lyric Subjectivity," in *John Donne Journal* 8 (1989); M. Morgan Holmes, "Identity and the Dissidence It Makes: Homoerotic Nonsense in Kit Marlowe's *Hero and Leander,*" in *English Studies in Canada* 21(1995).

III. BIOGRAPHIES. John Edwin Bakeless, *The Tragicall History of Christopher Marlowe*, 2 vols. (Cambridge, Mass., 1942); William Urry, *Christopher Marlowe and Canterbury* (London, 1988); Roger Sales, *Christopher Marlowe* (Basingstoke, U.K., 1991); Charles Nicholl, *The Reckoning: The Murder of Christopher Marlowe* (London, 1992); Lisa Hopkins, *Christopher Marlowe: A Literary Life* (New York, 2000).

IV. CRITICAL STUDIES. Una Ellis-Fermor, *Christopher Marlowe* (London, 1927); Harry Levin, *Christopher Marlowe: The Overreacher* (Cambridge, Mass., London, and New York, 1952).

David M. Bevington, *From "Mankind" to Marlowe: Growth of Structure in the Popular Drama of Tudor England* (Cambridge, Mass., and London, 1962); Eugene M. Waith, *The Herculean Hero in Marlowe, Chapman, Shakespeare, and Dryden* (New York, 1962); Clifford Leech, *Marlowe: Collection of Critical Essays* (Englewood Cliffs, N.J., 1964); Irving Ribner, "Marlowe and the Critics," in *Tulane Drama Review* vol. 8, no. 4 (1964); Norman Rabkin, ed., *Reinterpretations of Elizabethan Drama* (London and New York, 1969).

Constance Brown Kuriyama, *Hammer or Anvil: Psychological Patterns in Christopher Marlowe's Plays* (New Brunswick, N.J., 1980); Jonathan Dollimore, *Radical Tragedy: Religion, Ideology, and Power in the Drama of Shakespeare and His Contemporaries* (Brighton, 1984); Marjorie Garber, " 'Here's Nothing Writ': Scribe, Script, and Circumscription in Marlowe's Plays," in *Theatre Journal* 36 (1984); Catherine Belsey, *The Subject of Tragedy: Identity and Difference in Renaissance Drama* (London and New York, 1985); Simon Shepherd, *Marlowe and the Politics of Elizabethan Theatre* (Brighton, 1986); Jan Kott, *The Bottom Translation: Marlowe and Shakespeare and the Carnival Tradition* (Evanston, Ill., 1987); C. L. Barber, *Creating Elizabethan Tragedy: The Theatre of Marlowe and Kyd*, ed. by Richard P. Wheeler (Chicago and London, 1988).

Gregory W. Bredbeck, *Sodomy and Interpretation: Marlowe to Milton* (Ithaca, N.Y., 1991); Thomas Cartelli, *Marlowe, Shakespeare, and the Economy of Theatrical Experience* (Philadelphia, 1991); Thomas Dabbs, *Reforming Marlowe: The Nineteenth-Century Canonization of a Renaissance Dramatist* (Lewisburg, London, and Toronto, 1991); Emily Bartels, *Spectacles of Strangeness: Imperialism, Alienation, and Marlowe* (Philadelphia, 1993); Darryll Grantley and Peter Roberts, eds., *Christopher Marlowe and English Renaissance Culture* (Aldershot, U.K., 1996).

V. FURTHER READING: THEATER HISTORY. E. K. Chambers, *The Elizabethan Stage* (Oxford, 1923); Ernest K. Rhodes, *Henslowe's Rose, the Stage and Staging* (Lexington, Ky., 1977); C. C. Rutter, *Documents of the Rose Playhouse* (Manchester, 1984); Andrew Gurr, *Playgoing in Shakespeare's London* (Cambridge, 1997); Julian Bowsher, *The Rose Theatre: An Archaeological Discovery* (London, 1998); Scott McMillin, "Playwrighting in Shakespeare's London," in David Scott Kastan, ed., *A Companion to Shakespeare* (Oxford, 1999).

VI. FURTHER READING: RENAISSANCE ENGLAND. R. A. Foakes and R. T. Rickert, eds., *Henslowe's Diary* (Cambridge, 1961); Michael Hattaway, *Elizabethan Popular Theatre* (London and Boston, 1982); Stephen Greenblatt, *Renaissance Self-Fashioning: From More to Shakespeare* (Chicago, 1986); Peter Stallybrass and Allon White, *The Politics and Poetics of Transgression* (Ithaca, N.Y., 1986); Jean Howard, "Crossdressing, the Theatre, and Gender Struggle in Early Modern England," in *Shakespeare Quarterly* 39 (1988); Bruce R. Smith, *Homosexual Desire in Shakespeare's England, a Cultural Poetics* (Chicago, 1991); Jonathan Goldberg, *Sodometries: Renaissance Texts, Modern Sexualities* (Stanford, 1992); Claude J. Summers, ed., *Homosexuality in Renaissance and Enlightenment England: Literary Representations in Historical Context* (New York, 1992); Kate Chedgzoy, *Shakespeare's Queer Children: Sexual Politics and Contemporary Culture* (Manchester and New York, 1995); Stephen Orgel, *Impersonations: The Performance of Gender in Shakespeare's England* (Cambridge, 1996).

HAROLD PINTER

(1930–)

Melissa Knox

ON ONE OF the many occasions when he was asked what his plays were about, Harold Pinter replied that they "are what the titles are about," a true and characteristically unrevealing response, mirroring the uneasy reality of his works (Packard, p. 18). Commenting on this remark, Ruby Cohn observed that

> Pinter's titles are direction-pointers into the heart of his polyvalence. *The Room,* a theme as well as a place, is a diminished version of Kafka's *Castle.The Dumb Waiter,* a character as well as a prop, is a curtailed version of Beckett's waiters for Godot. *The Birthday Party* climaxes in a festivity of sorts, which proves to be a wake of sorts. The would be [sic] caretaker [of *The Caretaker*], doubly expelled from the room, has finally to take care of himself. . . . With Ruth [of *The Homecoming*] a home may be coming, in a double entendre that plays on the Janus-head of mother and whore. . . . The lack of an article in [the title] *Betrayal* generalizes behavior, as each character betrays the other two.
>
> (Cohn, 1990, p. 15)

Pinter's titles, in other words, are both precise and murky. As essential as they remain to the meaning of his plays, they resist complete elucidation.

All of his work seriously questions the traditional subject matter and purposes of drama. His characters do not explain where they come from or the source of their often surprising attitudes and beliefs. Their social and political backgrounds are only sketched in by passing remarks, ambiguities, and hints. An ominous sense of progressive discovery drives the plays forward. Violence that is hinted at by emotional manipulations occurring during entrances and exits often dominates the conclusion of the play. Pinter's victims usually helplessly dissolve into inarticulate sounds or mutterings or go blind or become mute.

He once quipped that he wrote about "the weasel under the cocktail cabinet" (*Plays: Four,* p. ix), a situation indeed suggesting the unseen and therefore mysterious menace so typical of his plays, but he apparently made the remark only to frustrate inquiry into their meaning. In a speech made in Hamburg, Germany, upon being awarded the 1970 German Shakespeare Prize, he mentioned the weasel remark, reiterating that it had meant "precisely nothing. Such are the dangers of speaking in public" (*Plays: Four,* p. ix). He returned to the remark again in the same address, suggesting that in spite of himself, it did hold some meaning for him. Many of Pinter's remarks have an almost uncanny quality of seeming entirely believable and patently false at the same time, for example:

> I don't write with any audience in mind. I just write. I take a chance on the audience. . . . First and finally, and all along the line, you write because there's something you want to write, have to write. For yourself.
>
> I'm convinced that what happens in my plays could happen anywhere, at any time in any place, although the events may seem unfamiliar at first glance. If you press me for a definition, I'd say that what goes on in my plays is realistic, but what I'm doing is not realism.
>
> (*Plays: Two,* pp. 10–11)

Pinter recognizes this mercurial sense of truth and reality in his plays, remarking:

> The desire for verification on the part of all of us, with regard to our own experience and the experience of others, is understandable but cannot always be satisfied. I suggest there can be no hard distinctions between what is real and what is unreal, nor between what is true and what is false. A thing is not necessarily either true or false; it can be both true and false. A character on the stage who can present no convincing argument or information as to his past experience, his present behavior or his aspirations, nor give a comprehensive analysis of his motives is as legitimate and worthy of attention as one who, alarmingly, can do all these things. The more acute the experience the less articulate its expression.
>
> (*Plays: One,* p. 11)

An exchange between a frustrated theatergoer and Pinter is revealing, however. The theatergoer wrote,

Dear Sir, I would be obliged if you would kindly explain to me the meaning of your play *The Birthday Party*. These are the points which I do not understand: 1. Who are the two men? 2. Where did Stanley come from? 3. Were they all supposed to be normal? You will appreciate that without the answer to my questions I cannot fully understand your play.

Pinter replied:

Dear Madam, I would be obliged if you would kindly explain to me the meaning of your letter. These are the points which I do not understand. 1. Who are you? 2. Where do you come from? 3. Are you supposed to be normal? You will appreciate that without the answers to my questions I cannot fully understand your letter.

(Esslin, 1984, pp. 37–38)

The razor-sharp wit so evident in this reply veers, in most of his plays, into existential dread and back again to laughter with dizzying speed, unpredictability, and force.

PINTER AND THE PINTERESQUE

THE earmark of virtually every Pinter play is an eerie surprise that holds all the shock of a supernatural event, occurring, as it inevitably does, in a setting that at first impresses viewers as ordinary, even pedestrian. In *The Basement* (1967), for instance, a man opens the door on a dark and stormy night to find on his doorstep an old friend, one whom he had expected never to see again and whom he is glad to see. Inviting his friend in, the man makes him comfortable, and the two are sitting by a warm fire and sipping drinks when the visitor suddenly announces that he has "a friend" waiting outside, adding, "Can she come in?" (*Plays: Three*, p. 154). The flabbergasted host entreats him to bring in the friend, a young woman, who proceeds to undress and get into bed naked, followed by the other visitor, who also is now naked. Listening to "a gasp" and a "long sigh" emanating from the distaff side of the bed, the host sits reading *The Persian Manual of Love* (*Plays: Three*, pp. 156–157). And this is only the beginning.

Typically, the situation in a Pinter play involves an intruder whose presence alters everything in a room. Describing how he arrived at certain dramatic situations, Pinter remarked:

The germ of my plays? I'll be as accurate as I can about that. I went into a room and saw one person standing up and one person sitting down, and a few weeks later I wrote *The Room*. I went into another room and saw two people sitting down, and a few years later I wrote *The Birthday Party*. I looked through a door into a third room and saw two people standing up and I wrote *The Caretaker*.

(*Plays: Two*, p. 10)

A critic might well ask who the persons were in the various rooms. It has been discovered, for example, that the seated person who inspired Pinter's play *The Room* (1957) was the famous sexual outsider Quentin Crisp, who called himself the "stately homo of England" (*Salon.com*) and was immortalized in his own book, *The Naked Civil Servant* (1968).

Pinter's most comprehensive biographer, Michael Billington, begins his critically acclaimed study *The Life and Work of Harold Pinter* with the confession "I am at the start of an attempt to crack the Pinter code. Who is he? What makes him tick? Why do his plays have such tenacity?" (Billington, p. 1). Pinter, he implies, baffles as much as he bedazzles, and his name is now the proverbial household word: "'Pinteresque' is now included in *The New Shorter Oxford English Dictionary*" (Billington, p. 1). Ronald Hayman remarks that "no adjectives have been derived from the names of Osborne, Beckett, Whiting, or Arden, but the words 'Pinterish' or 'Pinteresque' are already familiar, which must mean his style is the most distinctive, or at least the most easily recognizable" (p. 1). The London *Financial Times* defined "Pinteresque" as "full of dark hints and pregnant suggestions, with the audience left uncertain as to what to conclude" (Cusac). Billington goes on to ask: "Who is this mysterious figure who has spawned his own adjective?" (p. 1). His answers head in a different direction from those of earlier critics; he suggests that Pinter's works are indeed solidly grounded in his life experiences and that a knowledge of these experiences sheds light on the conundrum and heightens the appreciation of his plays.

Pinter's brilliance lies at least in part in his ability to induce audiences to accept, indeed to embrace, his intentional multiplicity and indefinability. He confessed to the theater critic Mel Gussow that his favorite of all his lines is "Stan, don't let them tell you what to do" from his play *The Birthday Party* (1958), because "I've lived that line all my damn life" (1979, sec. 2, p. 7). Woe betide the critic who tells Pinter what his plays are really about. At various times grouped with writers of the Theatre of the Absurd, especially Samuel Beckett and Eugene Ionesco, and with the so-called "angry young men" of the 1950s, Pinter defies any easy categorization. Neither comic nor tragic and yet both, seemingly, at once, Pinter's plays have drawn large audiences since the 1960s. In 1957, Irving Wardle referred to Pinter's works as "comedies of menace" (Esslin, 1984, p. 55), a term apparently derived from the genre known as the "comedy of manners," which portrays the mostly amorous intrigues of witty, sophisticated members of an aristocratic society contrasted with the ineptitude of those members of the lower orders excluded from it. "Comedy of menace" indeed captures the constantly shifting emotion of a Pinter play, in which moments of hilarity easily dissolve into terror or degradation and vice versa.

In 1958, Harold Hobson, the theater critic for the *Sunday Times* (London), hailed the twenty-eight-year-old Harold Pinter as "the most original, disturbing, and arresting talent in theatrical London" (Gale, 1977, p. 4), a view not widely held at that time. Hobson prefaced his praise with a defiance worthy of one of Pinter's characters: "I am willing to risk whatever reputation I have as a judge of plays by saying that *The Birthday Party* is not a Fourth, not even a Second, but a First" (Esslin, 1984, p. 20)). The well-known critic John Lahr, among many others, declared Pinter to be "the finest playwright to emerge in our technological society" (Lahr and Lahr, 1974, p. xi). J. L. Styan called him one of the "two most exciting playwrights in England" (Gale, 1977, p. 3). In 1994, after the September 1993 production of *Moonlight*, Mel Gussow called Pinter "England's foremost living dramatist," adding, "Only Tom Stoppard and Alan Ayckbourn are close contenders" (Gussow, *American Theatre*, p. 1).

Pinter's status as Britain's "best living playwright" is continually confirmed by writers whose work seems diametrically opposed to his own. In 1965, early in Pinter's career and before his works were being widely praised, Sir Noël Coward, the distinguished British playwright, actor, composer. and director known for his wit and world-weary sentimentality, wrote:

Pinter is a very curious, strange element. He uses language marvellously well. He is what I would call a genuine original. Some of his plays are a little obscure, a little difficult, but he is a superb craftsman, creating atmosphere with words that sometimes are violently unexpected.

(Esslin, 1970, p. 24)

Raymond Carver, one of the important originators of the minimalist genre of the short story, and Samuel Beckett, the Irish existential playwright, greatly admired Pinter's work. David Lodge, famous for his shrewd, witty portraits of academic life in a series of best-selling novels, among them *Changing Places*, *Small World*, and *Nice Work*, produced in his other life as a university professor a literary analysis of Pinter. In his study, Lodge concentrates on one of Pinter's brief revue sketches, "Last to Go," finding that it "presents in a condensed form the central paradox of his work" (p. 61). Lodge then asks, "How is it that dialogue superficially so banal, repetitive and full of silences, and a narrative so ambiguous and exiguous can interest and entertain an audience or reader?" (p. 61). He makes the point that he takes for granted that Pinter's work succeeds in doing so. Lodge arrives at an answer using structuralist poetics as well as linguistic analysis. One of the features of this brief, approximately sixty-two-line play is its use of what the anthropologist Bronislaw Malinowski termed "phatic communion," that is, speech whose main function is to keep contact between the two speakers rather than to convey information (Lodge, p. 62). In this play, Lodge concludes, one of the functions of this phatic communion is the attempt of the speakers to ward off the fear of death; the title "Last to Go" suggests this final journey that people fear to take.

Fear of death; uncertainty about or loss of identity, which is itself a form of death; and isolation find their way into all Pinter's plays. According to his biographer Michael Billington, they spring from Pinter's experiences growing up with his lively, unpredictable, and, in some ways, deeply disturbed family. They also spring from his terror and displacement as a child who was evacuated during the bombings of London and as a Jew growing up at the time of the Nazi Holocaust. "The more I discovered about the plays, however," Billington writes, "the more they seemed to be connected to Pinter's recollections of his own experience" (p. ix). Some of Pinter's remarks appear to confirm this. He described his first play, *The Room*, as one in which

this old woman is living in a room which, she is convinced, is the best in the house, and she refuses to know anything about the basement downstairs. She says it's damp and nasty, and the world outside is cold and icy, and that in her warm and comfortable room her security is complete. But, of course, it isn't; an intruder comes to upset the balance of everything, in other words points to the delusion on which she is basing her life. I think the same thing applies in *The Birthday Party*. Again this man is hidden away at a seaside boarding house . . . then two people arrive out of nowhere, and I don't consider this an unnatural happening. I don't think it is all that surrealistic and curious because surely *this thing, of people arriving at the door, has been happening in Europe in the last twenty years. Not only the last twenty years, the last two to three hundred.*

(Esslin, 1970, pp. 35-36)

This certainly can be understood as a reference to pogroms as well as to the Nazi persecution of the Jews. Indeed, Michael Billington records numerous instances of Pinter feeling persecuted as a Jew. To take one of many: Pinter was in a bar in the 1950s when he overheard a man say that Hitler had not gone far enough. He challenged the man, who called him a "filthy Yid," provoking Pinter to hit him so hard that "there was blood spurting out of his cheek" (Billington, p. 81). The violence of the victim-turned-aggressor, even the identification with the aggressor, underlies many of Pinter's plays.

Clearly the Nazi past and the persecution of the Jews have deeply influenced Pinter's thinking about violence and the abuse of power in his writ-

ing. In a 1966 interview for the *Paris Review*, he remarked:

The violence is really only an expression of the question of dominance and subservience, which is possibly a repeated theme in my plays. I wrote a short story a long time ago called "The Examination," and my ideas of violence carried on from there. That short story dealt very explicitly with two people in one room having a battle of an unspecified nature, in which the question was one of who was dominant at what point and how they were going to be dominant and what tools they would use to achieve dominance and how they would try to undermine the other person's dominance. A threat is constantly there: it's got to do with this question of being in the uppermost position, or attempting to be.

(Benskey, p. 30)

Some threat lies at the heart of every Pinter play, lurking unnoticed like the unsuspected culprit of a mystery novel before jolting the characters into a recognition that alters their lives irrevocably.

The critic Martin Esslin, who headed BBC radio for many years (on which many of Pinter's plays were produced), suggests that Pinter's plays are existential, in the sense that "coming to terms with one's own being . . . precedes, and necessarily determines, one's attitude to society, politics, and general ideas" (1970, pp. 34–35). Comparing Pinter to Beckett and Kafka, Esslin suggests that Pinter's attitude "is that of an existentialist: the mode of a man's *being* determines his *thinking*" (p. 35). Therefore, he says, Pinter attempts to catch his characters at points in their lives "when they are confronted with the crisis of adjustment to themselves" (p. 35). Esslin adds that Pinter probably was not influenced by the great German existential philosopher Martin Heidegger. Thus, it is all "the more significant that Pinter, like Heidegger, takes as his starting point . . . that fundamental anxiety which is nothing less than a living being's basic awareness of the threat of . . . annihilation" (p. 35). This threat in Pinter's plays is never "just a philosophical abstraction" (p. 35), Esslin remarks, but is based on the experience of a Jewish boy growing up in London in the shadow of Hitler's Europe.

Existential dread is evident in a confession Pinter made to an interviewer in 1967:

Sometimes, I don't know who I'm looking at in the mirror. There's no explanation for that face. The question: "Who am I?" is intimately linked with the question of motivation. Only if we know exactly who a character is, what his antecedents are, his tastes, his speed of reaction, his vocabulary, his personal values, can we predict with any accuracy how he will act in the future.

(Esslin, 1970, p. 38)

Curiously and perhaps revealingly, Pinter goes on to suggest in this interview that the "explicit" form taken by twentieth-century drama, that is, the playwright's assumption that we know a great deal about all the characters, is a form of "cheating," because the characters are "most of the time" only "conforming to the author's ideology" (Esslin, 1970, p. 38). The remark is an interesting one to ponder. Pinter described himself as a cheat in a story about his prowess as an athlete when he was at school, recounting an incident that perhaps throws light on his later tastes and strengths as a dramatist:

At school, I was . . . a fairly good soccer-player . . . Centre-forward. . . . I was on occasion a bit of a cheat. On one immortal occasion in a house-match . . . I never forgot it . . . I cried out in agony and collapsed. The whole game stopped . . . and I got up and continued and scored a goal. . . . It was disgraceful.

(Billington, p. 14)

This show-stopping instinct foreshadows a recurring theme in his later theatrical efforts. Suddenly a person cries out or simply collapses silently for no apparent reason. This is "a bit of a cheat," in the sense that the audience may feel deprived of any rhyme or reason for the event in a Pinter play. Early critics of Pinter not infrequently saw him as a cheat, in the sense of being a mere imitator of Samuel Beckett, but this is now very far from the prevailing view.

Nonetheless, Pinter's depiction of the traditional theatrical assumption that the author knows the characters as "cheats" remains arresting. A Freudian or a Romantic poet might take the point of view that it would be impossible for an author not to know his characters, reasoning that what we call knowledge of other people and situations is always a projection of our own wishes, fears, tastes, talents, and education. Explaining his methods, Pinter remarked at one point that he did not know his characters: "My characters tell me so much and no more" (Esslin, 1970, p. 44). (This is meant to justify the mystery and menace of "real

life" in his plays.) From the Freudian and Romantic points of view, we all invent some reason, or rather a reason appears to force itself upon us, when we see a fight or some other activity about which, in reality, we can know nothing. The interpretations we bring to these situations may be fantasy, but they are very real in the sense that we never perceive reality without them. They are largely unconscious. They are not ideologies, in the sense that an ideology is a conscious set of beliefs, even though its underpinnings may not be. Pinter's idea that he can represent reality without his own thoughts, wishes, tastes, dreams, coloring, and interpretation of it would be false from this point of view. In fact, his private sense of terror, displacement, loss, or lack of identity—or his constant changing of identity—informs all of his dramatic situations.

Martin Esslin originated the catchphrase "mystery and menace" to describe Pinter, and it does evoke the peculiar power of Pinter's work. Discovering the sources of that power remains an elusive pursuit. Esslin himself suggested as early as 1969 the value of a psychoanalytic approach in trying to illuminate the subject matter of Pinter's plays, adding:

This is not done to give a psychoanalysis of Harold Pinter or to probe his subconscious motivations, but merely to explain the *impact* and *effect* on audiences who obviously respond to the subconscious content of much that would otherwise remain enigmatic and inexplicable. To say that *Hamlet* derives some of its impact from the presence of an Oedipal theme does not amount to a psychoanalysis of Shakespeare, does not even postulate that Shakespeare must have had a mother complex (which would be a valueless discovery, as most normal men go through such a phase in their life, hence it would merely be a statement of the obvious) but it explains why a play which, on the surface has many unsatisfactory features of plot and characterization, has, through the centuries, retained such a deep fascination over audiences.

(Esslin, 1970, p. 8)

The idea of using psychoanalysis to explore the response of an audience is a novel one, and Esslin's point that Pinter's power arises from his ability to unleash unconscious forces on stage is well taken.

Pinter might be seen as a Picasso of the theater by virtue of his originality as well as his perhaps surprisingly traditional beginnings: anyone coming across Picasso's juvenilia cannot help but be struck by their exquisitely representational style. As a young man, Pinter won acting awards for classical roles such as Macbeth and Romeo, and over the years he has written screenplays (*The French Lieutenant's Woman,The Pumpkin Eater*, and *The Go-Between*, among them) that might be characterized as having a style that is primarily representational. Pinter and Picasso turned to their different nonrepresentational, nonrealistic style because it suited them, because they loved it. Pinter insists, however, that he has "never started a play from any kind of abstract idea or theory and never envisaged my own characters as messengers of death, doom, heaven or the milky way or, in other words, as allegorical representations of any particular force" (*Plays: One*, p. 11). He complains that when audiences and critics remain unable to define a character "comfortably . . . in terms of the familiar" they tend to "put him on a symbolic shelf, out of harm's way" (*Plays: One*, p. 11). Then the character becomes nonthreatening, defeating the playwright's purpose: "In this way, it is easy to put up a pretty efficient smoke screen, on the part of the critics or the audience, against recognition, against an active and willing participation" (*Plays: One*, p. 11).

EARLY LIFE AND WRITINGS

HAROLD Pinter was born 10 October 1930 in Hackney, an economically depressed borough of London just beyond the borders of the traditional East End. In an unpublished autobiographical memoir written in his early twenties, he described Hackney as a place that was, in his youth, brimming over with "milk bars, Italian cafés, Fifty Shilling tailors and barber shops" (Billington, p. 2). It was a lively, noisy area, with a large immigrant Jewish community that had arrived in the East End around 1900. Many were refugees from the Russian pogroms of 1905, but refugees from World War I and from Hitler's Germany arrived later. Harold's father, Jack Pinter, was a ladies' tailor whose twelve-hour workdays enabled him to open his own firm in Stoke Newington. His mother, Frances Moskowitz, came from a secular, skeptical Jewish family, while Jack Pinter's family was Orthodox Jewish. Although many Pinter sources suggest that his name is Sephardic Jewish of Spanish or Portuguese origin and was changed from Pinto, da Pinto, or Pinta, there seems "no evidence

for this whatsoever" (Billington, p. 2). In fact, as Pinter's second wife, the historical biographer and mystery novelist Lady Antonia Fraser, discovered when she sat down with his parents, three of Pinter's grandparents come from Poland and one from ssa, making them Askenazic rather than Sephardic Jews.

Pinter's father's family was characterized by intelligence and artistic leanings, and several committed suicide. His mother's family, outwardly more gregarious, also included several relations who killed themselves. Among the most tragic figures was Harold's mother's younger brother, Ben, who killed his infant daughter and himself after his wife's death from cancer. The young Harold, who loved the baby, was traumatized by this event, one of the first in a life filled with unusual shocks. Among such shocks, an uncle, Judah, who was a boxer, disappeared without warning one day, moving out of his room in a house around the corner from Pinter's parents' home. When Pinter's mother and grandmother saw him by chance seven or eight months later, hanging off the back of a moving garbage truck, he raised two fingers at them—the British equivalent of the American raised middle finger that is understood as an obscene gesture. The surprising and never explained exit of Uncle Judah, like the sudden loss of Pinter's infant niece and his uncle Ben, must have had their impact on the similarly suddenly shocked characters in Pinter's plays.

An only child, Pinter grew increasingly isolated, and he has mentioned his loneliness as a spur for the development of his skills as a dramatist:

I don't know . . . how it would have changed my life if I'd had brothers and sisters, but I can say one thing. I created a small body of imaginary friends in the back garden when I was about eight or nine. We had a lilac tree with an arch and beyond that arch was an untended piece of garden. I made that my home where I met these invisible friends who certainly weren't brothers and sisters but were definitely all boys. I had this total fantasy life in which we talked aloud and held conversations beyond the lilac tree. There was also—still is apparently—a laundry at the back of the garden so I was having this fantasy life with the laundry roaring away.

(Billington, p. 5)

Growing up during World War II, Pinter was, like many British schoolchildren, evacuated to the countryside to protect him from the bombings of London. For most of the war, including the worst part of the Blitz, he remained in London's East End, which saw the most destruction. At age nine, however, he was removed for a year with twenty-four other children from his elementary school to a mock-gothic castle on the Cornish coast. He felt completely uprooted and described the boys as cruel in their distress: "I think we were all a bunch of horrid little boys because of the loss of security" (Billington, pp. 6–7). To top it off, a friend, Maurice, learned of the sudden death of his parents back in London in an air raid. Pinter's parents visited whenever they could, although it was very difficult for them to do so, and these brief visits were marked by extreme emotion. Michael Billington points out that the Cornish landscape appears in much of Pinter's later work, especially *A Slight Ache* (1961), *Landscape* (1969), *Old Times* (1971), and *Moonlight*, and that as an adult Pinter returned obsessively to Cornwall, even on his first honeymoon.

Pinter attended Hackney Downs Grammar School from 1944 to 1948, during his formative years from fourteen to eighteen, and the experience was on the whole a positive one, enabling him to discover his talents for writing and theater. He read voraciously and starred as Macbeth in a student production of Shakespeare's tragedy, a production that was reviewed by a prominent theater critic, Alan Dent. Dent wrote that "Harold Pinter made a more eloquent, more obviously nerve-wracked Macbeth than one or two professional grown-ups I have seen in the part of late years" (Billington, p. 14). Meeting Pinter in a television studio in the mid-1960s, Dent apparently nervously regretted the cool reception he had given to Pinter's early plays, but Pinter put him at ease: "Don't you worry about that, Mr. Dent. You gave me the most treasured notice I ever had as an actor and I still keep it at home tucked away in my Shakespeare" (Billington, p. 14). The young Pinter was by no means a one-sided intellectual, however; he also excelled at cricket, soccer, and sprinting.

In addition to a number of poems, Harold Pinter's first two published works are nominally short stories, but a closer look reveals that they are dramatic monologues in disguise, perhaps unbeknownst to the young author. These stories, "The Black and White," and "The Examination," were written in 1954–1955 and 1955, respectively; in 1964, the BBC performed "The Black and White." In the early 1950s Pinter and some friends frequented the Black and White Milk Bar on Fleet Street, which provided much of the atmosphere for his early sketch. The story concerns two old women who seem to spend their evenings in milk bars watching all-night buses go by. They eat soup and bread, talk about transit schedules, reminisce about their youth, and look out the window. Their lives appear to have no purpose but are continuing according to a monotonous pattern. "The Examination" concerns a man, Kullus, who also appears in early poems written by Pinter. This story depicts a struggle in which the narrator is defeated by his opponent, Kullus. But power shifts continually between the two, so that the story could be written from Kullus' point of view as well. Kullus and the narrator are, perhaps, representatives of a struggle in Pinter between the desire to gain control and the desire to lose it.

In 1948–1949, Pinter attended the Royal Academy of Dramatic Art sporadically but did not obtain a degree. In 1956, he married the actress Vivien Merchant, who was to play major roles in a number of his plays. In 1958, a son, Daniel, was born. In 1980, Pinter's marriage to Merchant—which had for years been in a state of crisis—ended, and he was married to Lady Antonia Fraser, with whom he had begun a highly publicized affair in 1975. She had six children by her former husband. Together she and Pinter had no children.

THE ROOM

IN 1957, Pinter wrote his first play, a one-act, *The Room*, in four days for a friend at the University of Bristol. It is important because, as the first play, it establishes themes that have developed throughout Pinter's career, among them an intruder entering a room and the sudden deterioration of one character who has been intruded upon. In a 1968 interview with Joan Bakewell for the *Listener*, Pinter recollects that he went

into a room which I'd never been into before . . . and saw two people in this room. It was rather an odd image: a little man cutting bread and making bacon and eggs for a very big man who was sitting at the table quite silent, reading a comic. The big man never spoke—I was there about half an hour—the little man had a lot to say and he was in the meantime cutting this bread and butter.

(Almansi and Henderson, p. 35)

The "little man" turns out to have been, as mentioned, Quentin Crisp.

The characters growing out of this incident, Rose Hudd and her husband, Bert, seem initially like an ordinary old married couple: the husband sits at the table reading, and the wife fusses over him, cooks his bacon and eggs, and serves breakfast. As he begins to eat, she butters the bread and brings it over, encouraging him to eat. She keeps up a running monologue about the cold and about how she would not like to live in the basement of the house. She wonders who lives there. A knock is heard at the door, and Mr. Kidd, the landlord, enters and talks about the pipes; at this point the conversation becomes more unusual. Bert remains silent throughout, Rose answering all questions directed to him. Rose asks how many floors he has in the house (*Plays: One*, p 108), and he responds that he used to count them but lost track after his sister died. She "took after my mum. Yes, I think she took after my old mum. . . . I think my mum was a Jewess. Yes, I wouldn't be surprised to learn that she was a Jewess. She didn't have many babies" (*Plays: One*, p. 109). These remarks are quintessential Pinter non sequiturs, but they have referents that may be guessed: Pinter's mother, a Jewess, had one child, and he feels isolated and unsure of his identity.

At this point, Rose's husband and Mr. Kidd leave, and Rose tidies up and opens the door. A couple, Mr. and Mrs. Sands, are there, and it develops that they have been told that they can rent Rose's room. When Mr. Kidd, apparently the landlord, returns, he answers none of Rose's questions. Instead he responds with answers like "You've got to see him" (*Plays: One*, p. 119). Mr. Kidd goes out, and "a blind Negro" comes in. It is here that echoes of classical drama enter: Riley, the blind man, is a sort of Tiresias, the blind prophet who knows Oedipus' history and is reluctant to tell it. Riley seems to know Rose well or to be her father. Her father wants her home, he says, calling her "Sal," which she begs him not to do. She touches his eyes and at that moment apparently goes blind. Bert returns, chatting in sexualized language about a delivery he made with his truck: "I caned her along. She was good" (*Plays: One*, p. 126). He hits Riley, calling him "Lice!" The play closes with Rose protesting that she cannot see.

Elements of the Oedipus story are evident. An unbearable secret is being disclosed, one to which Rose must blind herself. What is it? Is it that her husband no longer finds her attractive? That her safe room and her safe life are anything but safe?

These questions burn into the audience but are never answered.

THE DUMB WAITER

LIKE *The Room,The Dumb Waiter*, another one-act play written in 1957 (and published in 1960), begins with characters in a room surrounded by a mysterious and threatening world outside. Two hit men, Ben and Gus, await orders to kill someone. The men loll on beds in this room, which is located in a derelict, uninhabited house. Tension builds, since the audience and the characters know that information about whom to kill will arrive via a knock at the door. The more the characters focus on the door, the less the audience remembers the dumb waiter situated in the wall between the two beds—a "door" of another kind that suddenly begins working, constantly delivering notes requesting increasingly extravagant and gourmet meals. Uneasy hilarity arises as the two hired guns try to cope with culinary requests far beyond their ken. Finally, using the dumb waiter, Gus exits to go upstairs to find the kitchen. He arrives downstairs without his gun and is pushed through the door: apparently he is the victim that Ben is supposed to kill. Will Ben kill him? Curtain! We are not told. *The Dumb Waiter* premiered in Germany as *Der Stumme Diener* in Frankfurt-am-Main in February 1959. Germany was initially far more receptive than England to Pinter and his work—as it had been to the Irish playwright Oscar Wilde.

A SLIGHT ACHE

FIRST aired on BBC Third Programme radio on 29 July 1959, *A Slight Ache* concerns a husband, a wife, and a progressive, disturbing loss of identity. Set in a large country house with a garden, the play opens with an elderly couple, Edward and Flora, eating breakfast as a wasp flies around the table. They disagree about which flowers exist and are in bloom in their garden, and Edward traps the wasp in the marmalade jar. The bickering couple offers hints of what is to come. Flora wonders why Edward is "clenching . . . blinking" his eyes, and he answers that he has "a slight ache" in them (*Plays: One*, p. 172). This is an ominous comment in a Pinter play, since his plays often end in the blinding or silencing or isolation of a character, that is, in some form of a symbolic death. Edward is happy to think that he has blinded the wasp and then squashes it on a plate—a figuring of his own fate.

Edward soon notices an old match seller standing at the back gate, where, Flora points out, he has been standing "for weeks" (*Plays: One,* p. 175). Flora brings the old man into the house, asking if he would like a cup of tea. The match seller, who never speaks a line, appears to become a catalyst for the dissolution of the marriage, the deterioration of Edward, and the rejuvenation of Flora. Edward speaks to him at length, questioning him and discussing essays that he is writing or wants to write. Finally, Edward backs the watch seller into a corner and weakly asks Flora to take him into the garden. Flora does so and then returns to the immobile match seller, confiding to him that he reminds her of an encounter with a poacher she once had when she was a young woman, a "ghastly rape" (p. 191). She wonders if the match seller thinks about women, begins to undress him for a bath, asks him to speak to her of love, and tells him that she will call him Barnabas. Edward returns from the garden and tells Flora that she is a lying slut and should get back to her trough (p. 193). But the match seller seems to have reverted miraculously to his youth, and Edward meanwhile has devolved into a weak and inarticulate old man. Flora then tells Barnabas that she will show him the garden, and, as a final touch, hands his match tray to the now-silent Edward and goes off with Barnabas.

A NIGHT OUT

THIS mother-son drama first aired on BBC Third Programme radio on 1 March 1960. A twenty-eight-year-old man, Albert Stokes, lives with his widowed mother and is getting ready to go out to a party. His mother harangues him, wanting him to stay home, change a light bulb, and have dinner, which she has ready for him. Protesting that he has told her a number of times that he planned to go out, he finally—over her many attempts to prevent him—heads for the door, whereupon she traps him with the question "Are you leading a clean life?" (*Plays: One,* p. 207). This question clearly unnerves him. She nearly snares him into a shepherd's pie dinner with her, but he manages to leave. Meanwhile, in an intervening scene, his friends discuss Albert and his mother: "He always gets a bit niggly when she's mentioned, doesn't he? A bit touchy" (p. 214). When he meets up with them later, he has

lost heart and appears inclined to return home to his mother, especially when his friends regale him with the names of women who will attend the party and who are "raring to go" (p. 215).

Clearly filled with conflict, Albert attends the party but resolutely is a wallflower, resisting the seductive attempts of a girl, Eileen, who several minutes later is aggressively groped and turns on Albert, accusing him of touching her. The real culprit, Mr. Ryan, smiles at the audience to indicate his role. Albert hits one of the other accusers, who tells him he is a "mother's boy." He rushes home to his mother, who asks him if he has been "mucking about with girls" and eventually provokes him to raise a clock violently over his head as if he were going to throw it at her. In the next scene he is approached by a prostitute, goes home with her, and becomes violent as soon as she asks him not to throw his cigarette on her floor. He grabs a clock from her mantel and threatens her with it, but eventually drops it, leaves, and returns to his mother. The play closes with Albert's mother stroking his hand, saying that they will go away together, and both telling him that he is a good boy and asking him whether he is one (p. 247).

THE LOVER

ORIGINALLY a television play aired on 28 March 1963, *The Lover* has been deemed "one of the most brilliant plays in the English Language since the [second world] war" (Hinchliffe, p. 118) and has been criticized as "not such a good play" (Hayman, p. 55). The play won the Italia prize for television plays in 1963. Like any work of art dealing with sexuality and raw emotion, this drama probably offended some critics. It describes an unusual arrangement between a husband and wife. Every day, the husband, Richard, preparing to go to work, casually asks the wife, Sarah, whether her lover is coming to visit her that day, wondering what time they plan to part, just so the husband can arrange to be home after the lover's departure. In the evenings, Richard comes home and talks about work and his commute.

At one point, Richard casually says, "Oh, by the way . . . I rather wanted to ask you something." Sarah asks what he wants to know. "Does it ever occur to you," he replies, "that while you're spending the afternoon being unfaithful to me I'm sitting at a desk going through balance sheets and graphs?" The wife merely comments, "What a funny question" (*Plays: Two*, p. 165), and we soon see why this is her reaction. The next time she opens the door to her lover, saying, "Hallo, Max," it is her husband, Richard, who walks in, dressed in a different style from his usual one. It becomes clear that for quite some time this wife and husband have been pretending that he is her lover, and they have been meeting to play this game most afternoons. As if they really were lovers, they discuss their spouses. Max asks Sarah why her husband has put up with her affair for so many years and then claims that he cannot go on deceiving his wife. Sarah protests that his wife must know everything anyway, and he insists that she does not, that she thinks he only knows a whore, not a "woman of grace, elegance, wit, imagination" (p. 182). They argue, and "Max" leaves. Richard returns, asking Sarah how her day went, and Sarah reacts as though Richard really were an entirely different man from Max. Richard harangues Sarah about her affair, insisting that it stop. The two of them end up kneeling and embracing, with Richard murmuring, "You lovely whore" (p. 196).

THE BIRTHDAY PARTY

PINTER'S first full-length play initially was panned and is now one of his most famous. Written in 1957, the same year as *The Room* and *The Dumb Waiter*, it concerns the same basic situation. An apparently safe room is threatened by an intrusion. Meg, the elderly proprietress of a run-down boardinghouse by the sea, has a favorite lodger—apparently the only lodger—Stanley, a young man whom she regards as a son but apparently also as a lover. Meg's husband, Petey, remains almost as silent as Bert in *The Room* but seems friendlier. A young woman, Lulu, expresses interest in the passive, seemingly depressed and inert Stanley. The strangely reclusive Stanley lets himself be overwhelmed by the motherly Meg. He seems to have come to this seaside resort as a pianist with a concert party that appeared at the pier and was thwarted or rejected when he attempted to give another concert: "They carved me up.... It was all arranged, it was all worked out" (*Plays: One*, p. 33). When Meg tells him that more boarders, two men, soon will arrive, Stanley becomes hostile and threatening.

The men, Goldberg, who is Jewish, and McCann, an Irishman, arrive, and Meg tells them that it is Stanley's birthday. A party is arranged,

but the birthday boy remains unenthusiastic, saying that he will not attend. Meg gives him a drum, and Stanley bangs on it, at first rhythmically and then with wild urgency. In the course of the birthday party, Stanley is controlled and degraded by Goldberg and McCann, who, during a game of blindman's buff, break his glasses. Stanley, however, also tries to rape Lulu and strangle Meg. By the end of the play he is either mute or has had his tongue ripped out. Straining to speak, he can only say, "Uh-gug . . . uh-gug . . . eeehhh-gag . . . Caahh . . . caahh . . ." (*Plays: One*, p. 94).

The play has autobiographical resonance: Pinter did once stay at a run-down boardinghouse with a Stanley-like character. In a 1988 public conversation with the theater critic Mel Gussow, Pinter confessed, "Between you and me, the play showed how the bastards . . . how religious forces ruin our lives" (Billington, p. 79). Goldberg and McCann, who behave like terrorists, therefore stand for Judaism and Catholicism, respectively. Stanley has a recognizably Jewish surname—Webber—and appears to symbolize the persecuted Jew. Pinter had abandoned Judaism at age thirteen, a significant age, since a religious Jew undergoes the ritual of bar mitzvah at that age, signifying that he has become a man. Pinter's love affair at about age twenty with an Irish Catholic woman, Pauline Flanagan, may well have ended because his mother objected to his marrying a non-Jew.

THE CARETAKER

WHEN Pinter's second three-act play opened, reviews were mixed and filled with comments like these from Patrick Gibbs in the *Daily Telegraph*: "Had *Waiting for Godot* never been written this piece would be judged to be masterly. As it is it appeared to be excessively derivative almost to the point of parody" (Esslin, 1970, p. 23). *The Caretaker* (1960), however, finally bestowed on Pinter an international renown and has been performed in every theatrical capital in the world. In 1961, *The Caretaker* won Pinter the Evening Standard drama award, and the following year it won him the Newspaper Guild of New York award.

First produced on 27 April 1960, it tells the story of two brothers living in a junk-filled room. Mick, the younger one, has an unnamed business, while the reclusive Aston seems unable to work and one day invites home an old tramp, Davies, who has nowhere to go. Davies soon confesses to Aston that his real name is Jenkins. He is almost a caricature of the British workingman: resenting any aspect of a job that appears to be beneath his station in life ("My job's cleaning the floor, clearing up the tables, doing a bit of washing-up, nothing to do with taking out buckets!") (*Plays: Two*, p. 18). He expresses race hatred for "Poles, Greeks, Blacks, the lot of them, all them aliens" (p. 17).

Aston is solicitous, almost maternal, in his care of Davies, finding him shoes and clothes. Mick returns when Aston is out, alternately terrorizing and politely questioning Davies until Aston returns. Separately, Aston and Mick offer Davies the position of caretaker, Mick asking for references. Davies senses that Mick is stronger and soon hears Aston's story of being in a mental hospital and being treated with electroshock therapy. Davies believes that he should ally himself with Mick and criticizes Aston to him. This proves fatal: the brothers unite against him, telling him to leave. The play ends with Davies—now almost a type of despair and isolation—begging the brothers to be allowed to stay as Aston stands with his back to him. A curious fact surrounding the play is that although it gave Pinter and his first wife, Vivien Merchant, much-needed financial security, she hated it on the ground that Pinter had, in her view, "betrayed" an eccentric man they knew, Austin, the model for Aston. He had dipped into his and other lives for the material out of which the play was made.

THE HOMECOMING

FIRST produced on 3 June 1965 in London, *The Homecoming* (1965) bewildered the British press, but in America it became a sensational success, establishing Pinter on Broadway. In 1965 and 1971, Pinter won the British Film Academy Award for this work. In 1966, it won him the title of Commander of the Order of the British Empire, and in 1967 it won a New York Drama Critics Circle award, a Whitbread Anglo-American Theater award, and an Antoinette Perry ("Tony") award. The play opens with a gathering of men: Max; his sons, Lenny and Joey; and his brother Sam live in a run-down house in north London, close to the neighborhood of Pinter's youth. Max often talks about his dead wife, Jessie, and hints are made that she may have slept with numerous other men; this remains, however, only an insinuation. All are working-class men—a butcher, a chauffeur, and a boxer.

That night, after the men are all asleep, without warning, another son of Max, Teddy, suddenly appears with his wife, Ruth, for a visit. He is a philosophy professor in America, and they are on their way home to their three children after a trip to Italy. After Teddy goes to bed, his brother Lenny, who has greeted him with no sense of shock, surprise, or interest after his six-year absence, happens to meet Ruth. He chats with her, having no idea that she is his brother's wife and saying at one point, "You must be connected with my brother in some way. The one who's been abroad." When she answers that she is his brother's wife, Lenny changes the subject to his insomnia, apparently not having heard her. He asks to hold Ruth's hand, talking at length about a woman who propositioned him and whom he beat up. Ruth is more and more drawn into conversation with him. When he gives her a glass of water and then says that she has had enough, requesting the glass back, she declines to give it back. When he says that he will take it, she answers, "If you take the glass . . . I'll take you" (*Plays: Three*, p. 50). By the end of the play, Ruth is entertaining the idea of living with the brothers, sleeping with them, and contributing to the household as a prostitute with Lenny as her pimp.

At first reading, Teddy appears to be the victim; he loses his wife when she decides to remain with his brothers. But the director Peter Hall interprets him quite differently:

> The problem . . . is that the biggest bastard in a house full of bastards is actually the man who at first sight appears to be the victim—that is, Teddy. He is actually locked in a battle of wills with his father and with his brothers, and of course with his wife, during which, in some sense, he destroys his wife, and his family, and his father, and himself, rather than give in. Now, it's very easy for an actor to fall into the "martyred" role in that part, because Teddy says so little—just sits there while all the other characters are speculating about his wife's qualities in bed. But this is the point—it's a tremendous act of will on his part to take it.
>
> (Page, p. 31)

In an interview with Anne-Marie Cusac in March 2001 in the *Progressive*, Pinter remarked that he was "happy to say" that Ruth "turns the tables on all of them . . . the whole damn bunch of them. . . . Ruth at the end of the play is a really free woman, and nobody knows what to do about her. They're all blown over. I truly believe it's a feminist play." Confirming this, the director Peter Hall observed that "in 1965 there was some slight sense that Ruth was a victim. In the second [1995] version there was no question that the men had been destroyed and rightly so" (Billington, p. 325).

MOONLIGHT

MOONLIGHT, a one-act play consisting of seventeen unnumbered segments, opened in September 1993 at the Almeida Theatre in Islington, London. One critic, Raymond Armstrong, asserts that this is "arguably the most self-referential of all its author's plays. . . . [It] reverberates with a seemingly infinite number of verbal, visual and thematic echoes of many of his other works" (p. 120). Andy, the hero, is a foul-mouthed, angry civil servant who is dying. Separation and loss are prominent in this play, as in many other Pinter plays, but his biographer Michael Billington suggests there "is something new . . . a total emotional openness" (p. 339). Bridget, Andy's daughter, speaks first in an otherworldly way; she may, in fact, be dead. She may be a spirit. Speaking of her parents, she praises them for giving their lives for her brothers and her and asserts that they need to sleep in peace and wake up rested.

Andy and his wife, Bel, are then seen together: he lies in bed, and she sits beside him working on her embroidery. This apparently tranquil image is shattered by Andy's first utterance. Angrily, he demands to know where the boys are. The scene then shifts to the two sons, who are both preoccupied by and estranged from their father. Fred, who remains in bed, and Jake, keep up a humorous, scatological dialogue that always returns to their father—or rather to their ideas about what kind of a father they would have liked to have had. The characters continually yearn to connect and cannot do so. At one point Bel phones her sons, and they pretend to be a Chinese laundry. A powerful sense of longing pervades this scene, but none of the characters ever dares to admit love. David Leveaux, who has directed two Pinter plays, suggested that Pinter was trying to "put on stage something that is almost unspeakable which is the experience of death" (Billington, p. 344).

PINTER'S SCREENPLAYS

ALTHOUGH Pinter has written twenty-three film scripts and increasingly has focused most of his energy on screenwriting, his film work did not receive much critical attention until the end of the twentieth century. An important new study published in May 2001, *The Films of Harold Pinter,* a collection of ten original essays by various writers, begins to rectify this omission in the vast canon of Pinter scholarship.

Pinter's most fruitful collaboration in film was with Joseph Losey, the American expatriate director who left the United States after becoming a target of the House Committee on Un-American Activities in 1951. The blacklisted director continued his film career in England, his primary interest being the use and abuse of power in personal relationships as well as institutions and social classes. These interests naturally allied him with Pinter, whose work invariably portrays the violent disruptions possible within human relationships and the impossibility of understanding arising between any one person and another. Together, the two collaborated on three films: *The Servant, Accident,* and *The Go-Between.*

The Servant, a novella of sixty-eight pages written by Robin Maugham, contains a theme bound to attract both Pinter and Losey: the subtle, absolute control of a master by his servant. The novella differs significantly from the screenplay by showing an explicit battle for a man's soul between the obviously evil servant and the master's would-be rescuer friends. Pinter's screenplay instead reveals an internal, psychological situation in which the servant and his master are drawn together in a homoerotic attraction that is all the more powerful in that it remains unconscious. Pinter is doubtless aware of the men's feelings for each other in a way that they are not, and perhaps Maugham was not either. The film, released in 1963, made Dirk Bogarde a star. Pinter acted in it too, in a minor role.

Pinter's *Accident,* written in 1965, was presented in 1967. It is an adaptation of a novel by Nicholas Mosely concerning the complications of various erotic relationships during an Oxford summer. Pinter's version of the story changes the novel by eliminating the first-person narration of the main character, with whom the reader sympathizes. In the film, this character, played by Dirk Bogarde, becomes, in Billington's view, "an archetypally Pinterish example of male insecurity. As a philosopher, he asks questions rather than provides answers" (Billington, p. 185). The film's story begins with a car crash, in which William, a man on his way to see Stephen, is killed. The driver, a beautiful Austrian princess, is rescued and seduced by Stephen, who conceals from the police that she was even in the car. The film then reveals the previous disastrous erotic entanglements of Anna with all the main male characters in the film and finally returns to the present, in which Anna deserts Stephen and also Charley, the man who is secretly her fiancé.

The Go-Between, starring Julie Christie and Alan Bates, was released in 1971 in the United States and a year earlier in Britain. Based on the story by L. P. Hartley, it tells of a twelve-year-old boy, Leo, who carries love letters between a farmer, Ted Burgess, and the beautiful aristocrat Marion Maudsley, who is engaged to marry a man of her own class. She is determined to marry the man to whom she is engaged, even though she does not love him. She shows a determination to do what is socially expected and proper, and her father as well as her fiancé tolerate her affair with the farmer, confident that she will conform in the end, as she does. The young boy apparently is traumatized by her capitulation to custom, although she is not.

The film shows Leo, now grown old, visiting Marion and returning in memory to the pastoral summer of 1900, during which his younger self witnesses the growth and ultimately the total destructiveness of a passionate love triangle. One of the messages of the film seems to be that Leo's experience as a young boy has destroyed his capacity for love. He has never married; in fact, he seems never to have had a love relationship, except perhaps with Marion in his dreams.

SUMMARY

IN 1975, Austin E. Quigley wrote in *The Pinter Problem* (p. xvii) that

Certainly Pinter's plays deal with problems of identity, illusion, menace, and verification, but so do many other plays. What is needed is a further set of generalizations to establish the characteristic kinds of concern that govern the ways in which these problems function in a Pinter play. As yet, this further level of generalization has not been achieved.

The situation has not changed. Pinter's power over his audience stems from more than mystery, menace, flashes of humor, and bursts of shocking surprises. It comes, perhaps, from a sense of his ability to assault an audience in a way that it finds acceptable, even intriguing—yet the way in which this paradoxically welcomed assault is achieved resists definition, and this resistance is itself perhaps a sign of Pinter's dramatic power. Michael Billington, attempting to draw conclusions about Pinter's life and work after an exhaustive study of it, admits that

I began this book by saying I hoped to unlock the mysteries surrounding Pinter's life and work, but in a sense the more you learn, the more these mysteries deepen. Pinter is a man of infinite complexity and abundant contradiction, but the first thing to say is that whatever the areas of sadness in his private life such as the failure of his first marriage and his recent estrangement from his son, and whatever his political discontent, the bedrock of his existence since 1975 has been his totally reciprocated love for Antonia Fraser.

(p. 384)

An intriguing sign of the continuing influence of his marital happiness on Harold Pinter's life and literary imagination is a poem, "It Is Here," written in 1990 (and quoted in Billington, p. 388). It is perhaps unique in his entire repertoire for its immediate comprehensibility and its faith in the power of words to communicate:

What sound was that?

I turn away, into the shaking room.

What was that sound that came in on the dark?
What is this maze of light it leaves us in?
What is this stance we take,
To turn away and then turn back?
What did we hear?
It was the breath we took when we first met.

Listen. It is here.

SELECTED BIBLIOGRAPHY

I. COLLECTED WORKS. *Plays: One* (London, 1991), including the introduction "Writing for the Theatre: A Speech Made by Harold Pinter at the National Student Drama Festival in Bristol in 1962," *The Birthday Party, The Room, The Dumb Waiter, A Slight Ache, The Hothouse, A Night Out, The Black and White,* and *The Examination; Plays: Two* (London, 1991), including the introduction "Writing for Myself: Based on a Conversation with Richard Findlater Published in the Twentieth Century, February 1961," *The Caretaker, The Dwarfs, The Collection, The Lover, Night School, Trouble in the Works, The Black and White, Request Stop, Last to Go,* and *Special Offer; Plays: Three* (London,

1991), including "Mac," *The Homecoming, Tea Party, The Basement,Landscape, Silence, Night, That's Your Trouble; That's All, Applicant, Interview, Dialogue for Three,* and the short story "Tea Party"; *Plays: Four,* rev. ed. (London, 1993), including "Speech at Hamburg," *Old Times,No Man's Land, Betrayal, Monologue, Family Voices, A Kind of Alaska, Victoria Station, Precisely, One for the Road, Mountain Language,* and *The New World Order; Collected Poems and Prose* (London, 1991, and New York, 1996).

II. PLAYS. *The Homecoming* (London and New York, 1965); *The Heat of the Day* (London and Boston, 1989); *Party Time* (London, 1991); *Moonlight* (London, 1993); *Ashes to Ashes* (London, 1997); Celebration *and* The Room (New York, 1999, and London, 2000).

III. SCREENPLAYS. *Five Screenplays* (London, 1971, and New York, 1973), including *The Servant, The Pumpkin Eater, The Quiller Memorandum, Accident,* and *The Go-Between; The Proust Screenplay:* A la Recherche du Temps Perdu (London, 1978); The French Lieutenant's Woman *and Other Screenplays* (London, 1982), including *Langrishe, Go Down* and *The Last Tycoon;* The Comfort of Strangers *and Other Screenplays* (London, 1990), including *Reunion,* Turtle Diary, and *Victory; The Trial* (London, 1993), adapted from Kafka.

IV. OTHER WORKS. *The Dwarfs* (London, 1990), a novel; "American Football," in *Pinter Review* 5 (1991); *Ten Early Poems* (London, 1992).

VI. CRITICAL STUDIES. Lawrence Benskey, "The Art of Theatre III: Harold Pinter, an Interview," in *Paris Review,* no. 39 (1966); William Packard, "An Interview with Harold Pinter," in *First Stage* 6 (summer 1967); Arlene Sykes, *Harold Pinter* (New York, 1970); Martin Esslin, *The Peopled Wound: The Plays of Harold Pinter* (London, 1970); Katherine H. Burkman, *The Dramatic World of Harold Pinter: Its Basis in Ritual* (Columbus, Ohio, 1971); John Lahr and Anthea Lahr, eds., *A Casebook on Harold Pinter's* The Homecoming (London, 1974); Arthur F. Ganz, *Pinter: A Collection of Critical Essays* (Englewood Cliffs, N.J., 1972); William Baker and Stephen Ely Tabachnick, *Harold Pinter* (Edinburgh and New York, 1973); Simon Trussler, *The Plays of Harold Pinter: An Assessment* (London, 1973); Austin E. Quigley, *The Pinter Problem* (Princeton, N.J., 1975); Bernard Frank Dukore, *Where Laughter Stops: Pinter's Tragicomedy* (Columbia, Mo., 1976); Martin Esslin, *Pinter: A Study of His Plays,* 3rd expanded ed. (London, 1977); Steven H.

Gale, *Butter's Going Up: A Critical Analysis of Harold Pinter's Work* (Durham, N.C., 1977); Mel Gussow, "The Prime of Harold Pinter," in the *New York Times* (30 December 1979).

Ronald Hayman, *Harold Pinter,* 4th ed. (London, 1980); Arnold P. Hinchliffe, *Harold Pinter* (New York, 1981); Bernard Frank Dukore, *Harold Pinter* (London and New York, 1982); Guido Almansi and Simon Henderson, *Harold Pinter* (London, 1983); Alan Norman Bold, ed., *Harold Pinter:You Never Heard Such Silence* (London, 1984, and Totowa, N.J., 1985); Martin Esslin, *Pinter: The Playwright,* 4th ed., rev. and expanded (London: Methuen, 1984); David T. Thompson, *Pinter: The Player's Playwright* (London, 1985); Elizabeth Sakellaridou, *Pinter's Female Portraits: A Study of the Female Characters in the Plays of Harold Pinter* (London, 1988); Volker Strunk, *Harold Pinter: Towards a Poetics of His Plays* (New York, 1989).

Enoch Brater and Ruby Cohn, eds., *Around the Absurd: Essays in Modern and Postmodern Drama* (Ann Arbor, 1990); Ruby Cohn, "The Economy of Betrayal," in *Harold Pinter: A Casebook* (New York, 1990), ed. by Lois Gordon; David Lodge, "Last to Go: A Structuralist Reading," in *Harold Pinter: A Casebook* (New York, 1990), ed. by Lois Gordon; Ruby Cohn, *Retreats from Realism in Recent English Drama* (New York, 1991); Malcolm Page, compiler, *File on Pinter* (London, 1993); Victor L. Cahn, *Gender and Power in the Plays of Harold Pinter* (New York, 1993, and London, 1994); Mel Gussow, *Conversations with Pinter* (London, 1994); Mel Gussow, "The Prime of Harold Pinter," in *American Theatre* 11, no 3 (1994); Ruby Cohn, *Anglo-American Interplay in Recent Drama* (New York, 1995); Martin S. Regal, *Harold Pinter: A Question of Timing* (Basingstoke, U.K., and New York, 1995); Michael Billington, *The Life and Work of Harold Pinter* (London, 1996); Raymond Armstrong, *Kafka and Pinter: Shadow-Boxing* (London and New York, 1999).

Penelope Prentice, *The Pinter Ethic: The Erotic Aesthetic* (New York, 2000); Gordon Rogoff, *Vanishing Acts: Theater Since the Sixties* (New Haven, Conn., 2000); Steven H. Gale, ed., *The Films of Harold Pinter* (Albany, N.Y., 2001).

VII. INTERNET RESOURCES. Jody Rosen, "People: Quentin Crisp," in *Salon.com* (3 December 1999) http://www.salon.com/people/obit/1999/12/03/crisp/; Anne-Marie Cusac, "Harold Pinter: The *Progressive* Interview," in *Progressive* (March 2001) http://www.progressive.org/intv0301.html.

ALEXANDER POPE

(1688–1744)

David Womersley

IN THE *EPISTLE to Dr. Arbuthnot* (1735), when the importunity of the dunces and false poets by whom he is besieged in that poem has reached its height, Pope, shaken by their clamor, reflects on how he has come to be exposed to such pertness:

> Why did I write? what sin to me unknown
> Dipt me in Ink, my Parents', or my own?
> As yet a Child, nor yet a Fool to Fame,
> I lisp'd in Numbers, for the Numbers came.
> I left no Calling for this idle trade,
> No Duty broke, no Father dis-obey'd.
> The Muse but serv'd to ease some Friend, not Wife,
> To help me thro' this long Disease, my Life,
> To second, ARBUTHNOT! thy Art and Care,
> And teach, the Being you preserv'd, to bear.
> (ll. 125–134)

For Maynard Mack, in his *Alexander Pope: A Life*, Pope is being playful here: "Why did I write? Because, answers the author of one of the most artful poetries in English (doubtless with a grin), it was all so effortless" (p. 641). However, to recognize that Pope's poetry is artful should not make us necessarily suspicious of the phrase "I lisp'd in Numbers." Rather, it should sharpen our interest in this unexpected moment of self-presentation.

POPE AND POETHOOD

ON one level, Pope's depiction of himself as originally and always a poet, dipped in ink and babbling metrically, is calculated to contrast him with the would-be poets of the first part of the poem, the mere "[men] of rhyme" (l. 13) who are always something else before being a poet, and who consequently have, unlike Pope, left a "Calling" to take up poetry: either "a Parson, much bemus'd in Beer" (l. 15), or a "ryming Peer" (l. 16), or "a Clerk, foredoom'd his Father's soul to cross" (l. 17), or the student of law

> who high in *Drury-lane*
> Lull'd by soft Zephyrs thro' the broken Pane,

> Rymes e're he wakes, and prints before *Term* ends,
> Oblig'd by hunger and Request of friends
> (ll. 41–44)

Pope proudly separates himself from these failed, imperfect poets through the assertion that he, by contrast, has never been anything other than a poet.

However, that defiance has buried within it the seeds of a more elusive anxiety. The assertion that Pope was always a poet does not seem to have been entirely hyperbolical. This is not to say (as is reported of the infant Keats) that his first words rhymed with the words that had just been addressed to him. But in 1743 Pope told Joseph Spence, "I began writing verses of my own invention farther back than I can remember" (Spence, *Observations*, no. 32, i.15). This intuited sense of his own poethood is a source of pride and consolation to Pope. It sustained him in what, in the Preface to the 1717 edition of his *Works*, he called the "warfare upon earth" that was his literary career. But its worrying corollary—and here the apparent factuality of what Pope says concerning his immemorial poethood is so vital—is that, because of the very completeness of his sense of being a poet, Pope is denied the possibility of inspecting the origins and inception of his character as a poet. Since, in his inner life, he has always been a poet, he cannot abstract his poethood from the other aspects of his existence, and consider it in and for itself. So fully is Pope a poet that, paradoxically, poethood cannot for him be an object of knowledge. It is, rather, a condition of experience. As Pope himself wrote of Newton in *An Essay on Man* (1733–1734), when seeking to mortify human pride by pointing out the blindness of even this most far-seeing philosopher:

> Superior beings, when of late they saw
> A mortal Man unfold all Nature's law,
> Admir'd such wisdom in an earthly shape,
> And shew'd a NEWTON as we shew an Ape.

> Could he, whose rules the rapid Comet bind,

Describe or fix one movement of his Mind?
Who saw its fires here rise, and there descend,
Explain his own beginning, or his end?

(ii. 31–38)

Such is exactly Pope's own predicament. Phenomena, things external to ourselves, we can comment on. But to ourselves we are all, finally and initially, a closed book.

Why does this matter? Why is this inability of Pope's to know fully the most important element of his individuality of significance? After all, as we have seen, in *An Essay on Man* he indicated that this was an original amnesia afflicting all men, even that cultural hero of the eighteenth century, Isaac Newton. As Milton has Adam say to Raphael: "For man to tell how human life began / Is hard; for who himself beginning knew?" (*Paradise Lost*, viii. 250–251). If this original unknowingness is common to all men, why make so much of it in the case of Pope?

There are, I think, four good reasons for doing so. In the first place, the question of identity is for Pope of great and unusual importance. As we shall see when we consider his *Imitations of Horace* (1733–1738), during the 1730s Pope aspired to write a poetry in which the various impulses and constituents of the self were harmonized into what Horace called "aequalitas" (which we might translate as "equability"). Pope's sense of himself is vitally important to the public success of those poems, because it is on the grounds of his own superior harmony of self that Pope will attempt to convince us of the centrality of the values on behalf of which he speaks. One of the rocks on which the whole project of the *Imitations* founders is Pope's growing awareness of the intractability—the obscurity, and possibly even the unmeaning contradiction—of his own identity. It is this sense of his own final strangeness to himself that shapes these lines from his imitation of the *Second Epistle of the Second Book*: "Years foll'wing Years, steal something ev'ry day, / At last they steal us from our selves away . . ." (Ep. II.ii, ll. 72–73).

What is intriguing here is the distinction between "us" and "our selves"; it surely carries the strange implication that something remains when "we" are taken from "our selves," that somehow we can notice that loss. This odd thought is vivid to Pope because the imperfection of his identity means that he has always been, if not exactly stolen *from* himself, then at least not always wholly present *to* himself.

Secondly, the occlusion of Pope's origins as a poet disturbs him because of English poets only Milton (whose *Paradise Lost* is the great poem of beginnings) and Wordsworth are more concerned with origins. In this Pope seems to have been typical of his age; for example, John Locke investigated the nature of human understanding by narrating the history of our intellectual life using what he called "this historical, plain method" (*Essay Concerning Human Understanding*, I.i.2). In Epistle 3 of *An Essay on Man*, Pope aspires to understand the nature of government by narrating the natural history of political forms. It is only through a knowledge of origins that one can acquire what Pope, in *An Essay on Criticism* (1711), called "the solid Pow'r of *Understanding*" (l. 57). As he put it in the Design of *An Essay on Man*: "to prove any moral duty, to enforce any moral precept, or to examine the perfection or imperfection of any creature whatsoever, it is necessary first to know what *condition* and *relation* it is placed in, and what is the proper *end* and *purpose* of its *being*."

Thirdly, Pope's inability to attain a full, conscious knowledge of his own poethood is disquieting because of the steadily greater importance with which Pope invests poetry, both in his own scale of values and in the scale of values he recommends for public adoption. In the Preface to the 1717 edition of his *Works*, Pope affects a patrician condescension toward poetry, and poses as one convinced of poetry's cultural and social marginality:

Poetry and Criticism being by no means the universal concern of the world, but only the affair of idle men who write in their closets, and of idle men who read there.

One may be ashamed to consume half one's days in bringing sense and rhyme together; and what Critic can be so unreasonable as not to leave a man time enough for any more serious employment, or more agreeable amusement [than poetry]?

Pope here casts himself as one of those who, perhaps in his youth, he wished he was; one of those he later styled "The Mob of Gentlemen who wrote with Ease" ("To Augustus," l. 108). Aristocratic, indolent, complaisant, the Pope of 1717 proposes nothing more exacting than his own amusement, and that of a few of his friends. But in the 1730s Pope bestows on poetry far greater social and cultural significance than could ever be justified by any mere idle diversion. The very poem from which the tautological phrase "Mob of

Gentlemen" is taken, the epistle "To Augustus," contends that a country which neglects its literature is sick—a notion that receives its fullest elaboration, of course, in the climactic poem of Pope's life, *The Dunciad* (1728–1743).

The fourth reason is close to the third. Not only is poetry in itself valuable to Pope, it also comes ever more strongly to be a means for him to define and generate values, the canvas on which he paints a morally polarized portrait of his cultural milieu. Pope repeatedly depicted the shape of his literary career as a movement from innocence to experience, from a naïve and innocuous art to an art that is committed, engaged and moral: he "stoop'd to Truth, and moraliz'd his song" (*Epistle to Dr. Arbuthnot*, l. 341), and "turn'd the tuneful art / From sounds to things, from fancy to the heart" (*Epilogue to the Satires*, II, l. 207). That moral turn is evident in the revisions Pope made to two important early poems, *Windsor-Forest* (1713) and *The Rape of the Lock* (1712 and 1714). There is not space here to consider those revisions in the detail they deserve, but in both cases we can see that Pope "moralized" the original poem by re-orienting it towards public affairs—that is, away from private life.

For these reasons, then, Pope's inability consciously to grasp the essence of the poethood he nevertheless experiences so intensely is profoundly disturbing. When he talks about poetry as a malaise or disease (as he does, for instance, when he comments in a letter to Henry Cromwell of 1709, "I had I know not what extraordinary Flux of Rhyme upon me for three days together," or when he speaks of catching the "itch of poetry" from Homer: *Correspondence*, i. 56 and 297) we should not quickly assume that he is speaking lightly. There is a literal sense in which poetry, the ruling passion that both defined and confined what Pope called "this long Disease, my Life" (*Epistle to Dr. Arbuthnot*, l. 132) both sustained and undermined him:

> As Man, perhaps, the moment of his breath,
> Receives the lurking principle of death;
> The young disease, that must subdue at length,
> Grows with his growth, and strengthens with his
>   strength:
> So, cast and mingled with his very frame,
> The Mind's disease, its ruling Passion came;
> Each vital humour which should feed the whole,
> Soon flows to this, in body and in soul.
>   (*An Essay on Man*, ii.133–140)

Poetry was Pope's ailment and his nourishment. It both supported and unnerved him. It is also the clue that will guide us as we survey his life and work.

EARLY LIFE AND WRITINGS

POPE was born in 1688, the son of a Roman Catholic linendraper. The family religion, to which Pope cleaved throughout his life, had the most far-reaching consequences for him, whether viewed materially (Roman Catholics were discriminated against under the tax system of eighteenth-century England) or educationally (he was unable to attend university, since all students had to subscribe to the Thirty-Nine articles of the Church of England before they could matriculate). His parents pursued a sequestered life at Binfield, just to the west of London, and Pope himself was for the most part self-educated. When he was twelve, he contracted tuberculosis of the spine, a serious disease that arrested his growth and undermined his constitution.

The central element in Pope's self-education was an immersion in English poetry. He composed his "Pastorals" when he was only sixteen, and by striking up a friendship with William Wycherley (1641–1715) gained imaginative access to the world of Restoration literature. He also inaugurated his literary career by composing a series of *Imitations of English Poets*, in which he followed the advice he would later give in *An Essay on Criticism*, namely that it is a good practice to "trace the Muses *upward* to their Spring" (l. 127). As we have seen, Pope's literariness was shaped by, on the one hand, his intensely felt identity as a poet, and on the other his inability to convert his poethood from an experience to an object of conscious knowledge. The *Imitations* give us an illustration of just this complexity in Pope's relation to the literary.

The *Imitations* are the fruit of Pope's dipping of himself in the ink of English poetry. Just as, when he tackled the Greek and Latin poets, he "did not follow the grammar, but rather hunted the authors for a syntax of [his] own" (Spence, *Observations*, no. 22, i.11), when it came to poetry Pope dispensed with principle and glutted himself with practice. The *Imitations* were written during the period 1701–1708, when (according to his sister, Mrs. Racket) Pope did "nothing but write and read." Spence says of the period: "Those five or six years, from about thirteen to twenty, were all poetical; he was then diverting himself wholly in wandering through the poets and the better sort of critics who showed and set off the beauties in the former" (*Observations*, no. 27, i.13, and no. 42, i.19).

Other anecdotes endorse this insight into the way Pope at this time seems to have *inhabited* the literary: for instance, his hanging of portraits of poets in his bedroom, or the story of his taking Walter Harte to the garret in Fleet Street in which Joseph Addison (1672–1719) was supposed to have written *The Campaign* (1705), the panegyric on the Duke of Marlborough that launched Addison on his twin literary and political careers (*Correspondence*, i. 120; Mack, *Alexander Pope: A Life*, p. 279). As a young man, Pope thrilled to the sensation of treading on classic poetic ground.

The poems that comprise the *Imitations*, in which Pope acquired and displayed "a thorough taste of [the] manner of writing" of Chaucer, Spenser, and the major English poets of the seventeenth century, also sprang from that desire to pass where others had gone before (Spence, *Observations*, no. 514, i.218). What is remarkable, however—especially when one considers the sophistication with which Pope will develop the form of the imitation in the 1730s—is the naiveté of these works and the simplicity of the literary hedonism that seems to have produced them. Just as Pope, we are told, learned to write "by copying printed books," and thereby acquired a hand virtually indistinguishable from type, there is an extraordinary subjugation of evident individuality in these poems, as Pope's own commentary on them suggests: "My first taking to imitating was not out of vanity, but humility. I saw how defective my own things were, and endeavored to mend my manner by copying good strokes from others" (Spence, *Observations*, no. 14, i.8–9). Yet, at the same time, Pope was indulging the bent of his nature, unreflectively and unmisgivingly following the promptings of his innocent reading: "In these rambles of mine through the poets, when I met with a passage or story that pleased me more than ordinary, I used to endeavor to imitate it . . . and this was the cause of my Imitations published so long after" (Spence, *Observations*, no. 45, i.20). There could be no more convincing evidence of the strength and simplicity—the *naturalness*—of Pope's sense of his own poethood. Poetry is his element.

A passage from a letter of 1706 addressed to William Walsh (1663–1708), Pope's chief literary mentor in his youth and the man he praises at the end of *An Essay on Criticism* as "the Muse's Judge and Friend" (l. 729), testifies to the exuberance of the young Pope's sense of poetic fellowship and betrays that exuberance is not the whole story:

Writers in the case of borrowing from others, are like Trees which of themselves wou'd produce only one sort of Fruit, but by being grafted upon others, may yield variety. A mutual commerce makes Poetry flourish; but then Poets like Merchants, shou'd repay with something of their own what they take from others; not like Pyrates, make prize of all they meet.

(*Correspondence*, i.19–20)

The profusion of metaphors—horticultural, commercial, criminal—suggests not only Pope's excitement at being free to ramble in the domain of poetry and his intoxication at the prospect of his own poetic increase, but also the difficulty of bringing this central feature of his poetic education clearly into view. The letter continues: "I desire you to tell me sincerely, if I have not stretch'd this Licence too far in these Pastorals?" (*Correspondence*, i.20). In other words, am I a poet or only a poetaster, an honest merchant in poetry or a pirate, a true admirer or a dull copier? Pope's intense experience of his own poethood still does not amount to the abstract, principled knowledge that, according to Pope's own theory of knowledge, is necessary for certainty.

The anxiety Pope betrays in that letter to Walsh goes some way toward explaining the remarkable manipulation his mature poetry performs upon the literary world of early eighteenth-century England, dichotomizing it into, on the one hand, Pope and his friends and, on the other, those he called the dunces. We shall consider this more fully when we come to examine *The Dunciad*. For the moment, let me suggest only that one reason for the vigor with which Pope endeavors to enforce that division, and to convince his readers of its substantial reality, is that he himself is troubled by his inability to make the distinction more secure than a question of sentiment—that is to say, of a conviction he feels very strongly. Surely Pope came sincerely to believe that there was a real distinction between himself and the dunces. But he was nevertheless troubled by the nagging possibility that that distinction might be nothing more than a chimera, a trick of imagination or passion. Two of the poems in *Imitations of English Poets* strongly support this view.

ALEXANDER POPE

The first is Pope's rewriting of Rochester's "Upon Nothing" as his own "On Silence." "Silence," Pope tells us, was "coeval with Eternity . . . e'er Nature's self began to be" (ll. 1–2): surely a significant characterization, given what we have observed about Pope's inability to speak about his own poetic origins. Significant, too, is the depiction of silence as the home of both wit and dullness. On the one hand, "Rebel Wit deserts thee oft in vain / Lost in the Maze of Words, he turns again, / And seeks a surer State, and courts thy gentle Reign" (ll. 13–15). But at the same time, "With thee in private modest *Dulness* lies, / And in thy Bosom lurks in *Thought's* Disguise; / Thou Varnisher of *Fools*, and Cheat of all the *Wise*" (ll. 19–21).

This notion of a point where wit and dullness meet, and where a distinction so crucial to Pope's sense of himself is confounded, recurs in the second poem, "To the Author of a Poem, intitled, Successio." This neglected poem attacking Elkanah Settle (1648–1724), who had composed *Eusebia Triumphans* (1702), a poem in praise of the Hanoverians, is nevertheless an important work for two reasons. It was the first of the series of poems Pope wrote on the subject of dullness in which he deployed the distinctive imagery he was to elaborate so strikingly in the various versions of *The Dunciad*, and it was the first poem in which Pope sought to make connections between literary value and political health. Here, too, we find poised expressions of the troubling thought that the bad is both an inversion of the good and yet also intimately attached to it: "Wit, past thro' thee, no longer is the same, / As Meat digested takes a diff'rent Name" (ll. 11–12). Wit and dullness, Pope and the dunces: these are as separate—and as close—as food and feces.

THE SCRIBLERIAN MAN OF LETTERS, 1711–1728

THE 1710s were the years in which Pope established himself as a leading literary figure. *An Essay on Criticism* (1711) and *The Rape of the Lock* (1712; enlarged and revised, 1714) demonstrated both his poetic versatility and his command of a poised and insinuating poetic style. Pope's versatility is evident in the contrasting forms of the two poems: *An Essay on Criticism* is a loosely Horatian verse epistle (although not strictly speaking an imitation), while *The Rape of the Lock* represents Pope's first venture into mock epic. What both poems have in common, however, is an ability to

keep in play and steer between apparently incompatible attitudes. In the case of *The Rape of the Lock*, Pope picks his way adroitly between affection for, and criticism of, polite English society in the reign of Queen Anne, showing delight at its polished surfaces and paradoxical intimacies while at the same time teasing out and touching delicately upon the more disturbing moral confusions that lay buried in its foundations. In *An Essay on Criticism*, the balance is present as a trade-off between the content of the poem's Horatian form, which highlights informality—"*Horace* still charms with graceful Negligence, / And without Method *talks* us into Sense, / Will like a *Friend* familiarly convey / The *truest Notions* in the *easiest* way" (ll. 653–656)—and the core of the poem's doctrine, which aspires to reinvigorate an attitude of reverence toward the achievements embodied in classical poetry, and to repress or curb what Pope was coming already to deplore as a shallow and ungrounded confidence in the intellectual culture of his own day:

> Still green with Bays each *ancient* Altar stands,
> Above the reach of *Sacrilegious* Hands,
> Secure from *Flames*, from *Envy's* fiercer Rage,
> Destructive *War*, and all-involving *Age*.
> See, from *each Clime* the Learn'd their Incense bring;
> Hear, in *all Tongues* consenting *Paeans* ring!
> In Praise so just, let ev'ry voice be join'd,
> And fill the *Gen'ral Chorus* of *Mankind*!
> Hail *Bards Triumphant*! born in *happier* Days;
> *Immortal* Heirs of *Universal* Praise!
> Whose Honours with Increase of Ages *grow*,
> As Streams roll down, *enlarging* as they flow!
> Nations *unborn* your mighty Names shall sound,
> And worlds applaud that must not yet be *found*!
> (ll. 181–200)

In the prefatory note to *The Temple of Fame*, an allegorical poem drafted by 1710 but not published until 1715, Pope remarked, "we find an uncommon charm in Truth, when it is convey'd by this Side-way [that is, allegory] to our Understanding." His other poems of this period reveal him to be already a connoisseur of a growing range of strategies of obliquity and indirection.

Pope's interest in such "side-ways" for the conveyance of truth was the expression of what was then his clement attitude toward the cultural conflicts of his time; these conflicts, so Pope's artful poise suggested, could be rendered harmless by good humor, wit, and a reasoned tolerance. Yet that mildness was coming under pressure, as we can see if we examine the social aspect of literature in the London of the 1710s. We find the Scriblerus Club (which had Pope as a central member) and the circle of writers that gathered around Addison at Button's coffee house in Covent Garden and the Kit-Cat Club; the latter group had as its mouthpiece *The Spectator* (1711–1712).

In 1728, when the *Memoirs of Scriblerus* were finally published, Pope told Joseph Spence about the origin and purpose of the Scriblerus Club, whose members had collaborated in composing these parodic works:

The design of the *Memoirs of Scriblerus* was to have ridiculed all the false tastes in learning, under the character of a man of capacity enough that had dipped in every art and science, but injudiciously in each. It was begun by a club of some of the greatest wits of the age: Lord Bolingbroke, Lord Oxford, the Bishop of Rochester, Mr. Pope, Congreve, Arbuthnot, Swift, and others.

(*Observations*, no. 135, i.56).

The date of the beginning of the club is unclear. Its founding purpose was announced by Pope in a letter to (interestingly enough) *The Spectator* of 14 August 1712, and we may therefore assume that those who were later to form the club had met informally in the preceding months. By January 1714 the club was meeting fairly regularly on Saturdays, though the fall of the Tory ministry later in that year robbed it of at least one and possibly two of its most eminent members (there is some doubt as to whether Bolingbroke actually did attend any meetings: Mack, *Alexander Pope: A Life*, p. 235). In his letter to *The Spectator*, Pope explained the project as follows:

I need not tell you, Sir, that there are several Authors in *France*, *Germany* and *Holland*, as well as in our own Country, that Publish every Month, what they call *An Account of the Works of the Learned*, in which they give us an Abstract of all such books as are Printed in any part of *Europe*. Now, Sir, it is my Design to Publish every Month, *An Account of the Works of the Unlearned*. Several late Productions of my own Country-men, who many of them make a very Eminent Figure in the Illiterate World, Encourage me in this Undertaking.

(*Spectator*, 14 August 1712)

The Works of the Unlearned, then (which later became the *Memoirs of Scriblerus*), were intended as a mocking response to what Pope perceived as a decline in contemporary English intellectual culture. We can see why Pope and his friends thought this if we consider one of the club's writings, *The Origine of Sciences*, which was drafted in 1714, and published in 1732 in the Pope-Swift *Miscellanies*.

The Origine of Sciences is an attack on Dr. John Woodward, professor of Physick at Gresham College, and a man who combined scientific research with a curious kind of speculative anthropology. In 1695 he published *An Essay Toward a Natural History of the Earth*, and he had also written a number of revisionist studies on the learning of the Egyptians, whom he wished to dislodge from their traditional position as the founders of human civilization. Hence the argument that Pope and his collaborators advance in *The Origine of Sciences*, that all human learning is derived from monkeys. This is clearly intended as a mocking expansion of Woodward's revisionism. The strategy, then, was to expose through exaggeration what the Scriblerians saw as the inhuman tendencies of the new, scientific revisionism, as exemplified by Woodward—in their eyes its wanton abandonment of traditional beliefs and pursuit of paradox and innovation. Martinus Scriblerus, the apparent author of the essay, comments on some of the great cultural collapses recorded by history:

Empires as great have been swallow'd up in the wreck of Time, and such sudden periods have been put to them as occasion a total ignorance of their story. And if I should conjecture that the like happen'd to this nation [the Pygmaeans], from a general extirpation of the people by those flocks of monstrous birds [cranes], wherewith Antiquity agrees they were continually infested; it ought not to seem more incredible, than that one of the Baleares was wasted by rabbits, Smynthe by mice, and of late Bermudas almost depopulated by rats.

(Pope, *Prose Works, Volume II*, p. 287)

In one sense this account of the laying low of the mighty by the minute is part of the burlesque of the essay. Yet it also has a serious dimension, in that according to the Scriblerians, early eighteenth-century England was itself faced with just such a threat. For Pope and his friends, the literary scene of the early 1700s was characterized by a mass of pamphleteers and littérateurs, individually contemptible but in a mass formidable, impertinently gnawing in a spirit of bumptious nationalism at an inherited culture that was classical and European in character.

The Spectator embodied some of the tendencies against which the Scriblerians were reacting. The flavor of the literary orientation of Addison's periodical can be swiftly suggested if we note three of its most characteristic innovations: firstly, the elevation of imagination as a literary faculty; secondly, its championing of the value of early English literature, such as the ballad *Chevy Chase*; and finally, its extended discussion of *Paradise Lost*. It is possible to see in all these projects an attempt to strengthen an indigenous, English literary culture, and thus to duplicate in the sphere of literature what the Glorious Revolution of 1688 had brought about in the realm of practical politics: namely, the English nation entering into its destiny under the guidance of providence. Whatever one might think of this, Pope responded to it negatively. The 1710s saw a growing estrangement between himself and Addison, whose society he increasingly shunned. It was at this time that Pope composed the shrewdly hostile character of Addison, which was published piratically in 1723, and which eventually became the character of "Atticus" in *An Epistle to Dr. Arbuthnot* (ll. 193–214). At the same time, his literary life moved towards translation and editing. A version of the *Iliad* was published in 1715–1720, followed in 1725–1726 by a translation of the *Odyssey* and an edition of Shakespeare: in terms of bulk, these works dwarfed his own *Works*, which were published in 1717. The translations of Homer were so successful that they provided Pope with financial independence for the rest of his life. At the same time, they can be seen as attempts by Pope to inoculate English literary culture with the important values he saw as increasingly under threat.

"TO VIRTUE ONLY AND HER FRIENDS A FRIEND"—PUBLIC POETRY IN THE 1730S

POPE'S edition of Shakespeare led him into controversy when its shortcomings were attacked by Lewis Theobald in *Shakespeare Restored* (1726). Pope's riposte was to install Theobald as the hero of his *Dunciad*, the first version of which appeared anonymously in 1728. However, under the influence of the charismatic Henry St. John, first viscount Bolingbroke (1678–1751), Pope also began to compose poetry in which satire was interwoven with a more positive moral vision. These were *An Essay on Man* (1733–1734) and the four *Moral Essays* (1731–1735), as well as the group of poems

on which we shall particularly focus, the *Imitations of Horace* (1733–1738), in which Pope rewrote certain of the poems of the celebrated Latin poet of the Augustan period, Quintus Horatius Flaccus (65–8 B.C.).

What was suggested by the label "Horatian" in the 1730s? Three main aspects of Horace's character are relevant to Pope. In the first place, there is Horace the plain, honest spokesman on issues usually clouded with pretension and cant. Secondly, there is Horace the poet of the balanced, harmonized self, which, by placing itself at a certain distance from the shocks of public life, and by willingly embracing a degree of modesty, or even mediocrity, achieves an inner stability that it can oppose to those shocks. Finally, there is Horace the sly insinuator, the poet who can censure the powerful without yet giving offense A striking feature of the *Imitations* is the way in which Pope will sometimes weave all these different strands of the "Horatian" together (as in the "First Satire of the Second Book," which we shall consider presently), while at others keeping them separate. "Sober Advice from Horace" is dominated by Horace the "plain man, whose Maxim is profest, / 'The Thing at hand is of all Things the *best'* " (ll. 153–154). "To Augustus" shows us primarily Horace the sly ironist, and the "Second Satire of the Second Book" emphasizes the balanced and virtuous Horace who is content with little: "What, and how great, the Virtue and the Art / To live on little with a cheerful heart" (ll. 1–2).

Yet here, for Pope, is the rub. In these *Imitations*, Pope brings his own personality into the foreground of the poetry. He hopes to recommend the values of these poems to their readers on the grounds that, like the character of the man who wrote them, they are balanced and central, possessing a gravity and authority superior to the narrowly interested, the merely *personal*, views of those against whom he is writing. However, as we have seen, Pope's sense of himself is, in at least one crucial respect, imperfect and occluded. And as we examine the *Imitations*, we shall see that Pope is steadily less able to present the variety of his own personality as balanced heterogeneity, less able to distinguish it persuasively from meaningless incoherence.

Pope's *Imitations* cannot be understood except in the context of their opposition to the administration of the then prime minister, Sir Robert Walpole (1676–1745). Walpole is alluded to in the first of the *Imitations*, and it seems likely that pressure from Walpole brought this series of poems to an end—Warburton reports that Pope's plan to round off the sequence with a poem particularly "severe and sublime" was frustrated by the threat of prosecution (Mack, *Alexander Pope: A Life*, p. 735). Walpole had come to prominence in the aftermath of the financial scandal of the South Sea Bubble, in 1720. Walpole was put in charge of the parliamentary inquiry into the affairs of the South Sea Company, and managed to disguise the profitable involvement of the royal family and of major politicians in the scandal. Thereafter he swiftly rose to dominate the House of Commons, which he managed with great adroitness (and occasional bribery) in pursuit of a pacific foreign policy and financial reform at home.

It was in the spirit of such reform that Walpole in 1732 introduced an Excise Bill, which would have extended the excise duties he had already established for tea, coffee, and chocolate to tobacco and wine. But the bill proved to be extremely unpopular, because of the enlarged powers it would have conferred on officials of the Crown. The Excise Bill thus came to be denigrated by Walpole's enemies (such as Bolingbroke and Pulteney) as an invasion of the hereditary, immutable, and sacred liberties of Englishmen. Ludicrous as the allegation was, it struck a chord: the Corporation of London threatened unconstitutional action if the bill were passed, and even Walpole's power base, the court, began to be infected with resentment against the measure. Realizing that, in his famous phrase, "this Bill will not run," Walpole swiftly changed tack, withdrew the bill, flattered those among the Whigs whom he judged essential to his continued authority, and sacked the rest. He survived, but the political landscape had changed. Before 1733 opposition to Walpole's administration had been brilliant but patchy. Since 1726 Bolingbroke's journal *The Craftsman* had seized on the central pillars of Walpole's policy—peace abroad, financial innovation at home—to paint a picture of a nation once proud and free, now corrupted by a depraved first minister into pusillanimity. But it had not proved possible to translate that propaganda offensive into effective parliamentary opposition when the only troops available in the House of Commons were a few hard-core Jacobites, a handful of Hanoverian Tories, and a small group of disaffected Whigs under Pulteney. But after 1733 the ranks of the opposition were swelled by the powerful Whig magnates whom Walpole had removed from office in the aftermath of the Excise Bill fiasco—men of political substance such as Chesterfield, Bolton, and Cobham. Suddenly the opposition was transformed from a miscellaneous troop of political untouchables to a possible alternative ministry. It was no accident that Pope's first *Imitation of Horace* was published in 1733.

The immediate occasion of this was a quarrel between Pope, Lady Mary Wortley Montagu, and Lord Hervey. This was the "case" to which Bolingbroke was referring, as Pope related the anecdote to Joseph Spence:

When I had a fever one winter in town that confined me to my room for five or six days, lord Bolingbroke came to see me, happened to take up a Horace that lay on the table, and in turning it over dipped on the First Satire of the Second Book. He observed how well that would hit my case, if I were to imitate it in English. After he was gone, I read it over, translated it in a morning or two, and sent it to the press in a week or fortnight after. And this was the occasion of my imitating some other of the Satires and Epistles afterwards.

(Spence, *Observations*, no. 321a, i.143)

But this poem, written at the explicit instigation of the intellectual leader of the opposition to Walpole, extends far beyond Pope's personal animosities, and engages with the wider political situation.

"The First Satire of the Second Book of Horace Imitated" takes the form of a dialogue between Pope himself and William Fortescue, his own friend and legal adviser, but at the same time the man who had been personal secretary to Walpole. The main theme of the poem—the scope and nature of satire—is announced in the poem's opening lines:

P. There are (I scarce can think it, but am told)
There are to whom my Satire seems too bold,
Scarce to wise *Peter* complaisant enough,
And something said of *Chartres* much too rough.
The lines are weak, another's pleas'd to say,
Lord *Fanny* spins a thousand such a Day.
Tim'rous by Nature, of the Rich in awe,
I come to Council learned in the Law.

(ll. 1–8)

That council is Fortescue, and as the poem develops a good deal of incidental comedy arises as the supposedly "tim'rous" Pope is contrasted with his cautious, worldly friend, who urges him either to abandon poetry for family life or to take sleeping draughts or (if he must write) to compose panegyrics on those in power. When Pope complains that "Fools rush into my Head, and so I write," Fortescue replies:

> F. You could not do a worse thing for your Life.
> Why, if the Nights seem tedious—take a Wife;
> Or rather truly, if your Point be Rest,
> Lettuce and Cowslip Wine; *Probatum est.*
> But talk with *Celsus, Celsus* will advise
> Hartshorn, or something that shall close your Eyes.
> Or if you needs must write, write CAESAR's Praise:
> You'll gain at least a *Knighthood*, or the *Bays.*
>
> (ll. 14–22)

However, out of this context of precise contemporary reference, and against the backdrop of his embarrassed, wriggling friend, Pope develops the notion of a satire that is not the vehicle of merely personal animosity but rather an impartial mirror rendered undistorting by the satirist's own balanced character:

> P. Each Mortal has his Pleasure: None deny
> *Scarsdale* his bottle, *Darty* his Ham-Pye;
> *Ridotta* sips and dances, till she see
> The doubling Lustres dance as fast as she;
> *F*[ox] loves the Senate, *Hockley-Hole* his Brother
> Like in all else, as one Egg to another.
>
> (ll. 45–50)

But Pope stands apart from this mere idiosyncrasy:

> I love to pour out all myself, as plain
> As downright *Shippen*, or as old *Montagne.*
> In them, as certain to be lov'd as seen,
> The Soul stood forth, nor kept a Thought within;
> In me what Spots (for Spots I have) appear,
> Will prove at least the Medium must be clear.
> In this impartial Glass, my Muse intends
> Fair to expose myself, my Foes, my Friends;
> Publish the present Age, . . .
>
> (ll. 51–59)

When the self is harmonized and balanced, satire becomes a truly moral poetry, not an opportunistic indulgence of hatred. Indeed, it marks an escape from personality into a central area of enduring human values:

> My Head and Heart thus flowing thro' my Quill
> Verse-man or Prose-man, term me which you will,
> Papist or Protestant, or both between,

> Like good *Erasmus* in an honest Mean,
> In Moderation placing all my Glory,
> While Tories call me Whig, and Whigs a Tory.
>
> (ll. 63–68)

It is because he stands in a moral tradition alongside which the temporal emergencies of England in the 1730s cannot but seem insignificant that Pope is able, without seeming pompous, suddenly to inflect the tone of the poem from conversationally playful to heroically defiant. Fortescue anxiously wrings his hands at the risks Pope is running, to which Pope replies:

> P. What? arm'd for *Virtue* when I point the Pen,
> Brand the bold Front of shameless, guilty men,
> Dash the proud Gamester in his gilded Car,
> Bare the mean Heart that lurks beneath a Star; . . .
> Hear this and tremble! you, who 'scape the Laws.
> Yes, while I live, nor rich or noble knave
> Shall walk the World, in credit, to his grave.
> To VIRTUE ONLY and HER FRIENDS, A FRIEND
> The World beside my murmur, or commend.
>
> (ll. 105–122)

When Fortescue takes fright at this, and reminds Pope of the dangers of offending the great, Pope, in one of those abrupt switches of mood that mark the Horatian harmony of character, makes a joke balancing moral heroism with knowing slyness, and at the same time glances at the cause of the malaise that calls his satire into existence. To Fortescue's fear of "*Libels, Satires,*" Pope responds with an arch horror:

> P. *Libels* and *Satires!* lawless Things indeed!
> But grave *Epistles*, bringing Vice to light,
> Such as a *King* might read, a *Bishop* write,
> Such as Sir *Robert* would approve—

At which Fortescue, vastly relieved, interjects:

> F. Indeed?
> The Case is alter'd—you may then proceed.
> In such a Cause the Plaintiff will be hiss'd,
> My Lords the Judges laugh, and you're dismiss'd.
>
> (ll. 149–156)

In other words, the laws have been reduced to the private pleasure of "Sir Robert." With Horatian slyness, Pope ends his poem by pointing obliquely at the corruption of public morals and public institutions that both requires and endangers his satire. Yet the two other strands of the Horatian we identified earlier—the plain speaker and the poet of inner balance—have also played their part in this imitation. They have been woven together by Pope to create a text that indicts Walpole as the source of debilitating corruption.

Although Pope uses his Horatian persona in this instrumental fashion, the *Imitations* seem also to have been at times genuinely introspective and properly self-analytical. Pope has turned the art of formal imitation into a process of self-definition and moral discrimination, thereby clarifying his role as Opposition satirist and affirming where he stood and what he stood for. But he also found his personality to be, on inspection, too turbulent and contradictory to play the role demanded by his public allegiances. The Horatian identity Pope had created for himself petered out, destroyed from within by its own internal tensions, rendered unavailing from without by political defeat. The opposition to Walpole formed in the wake of the Excise Bill had come to nothing. Despite their efforts, Walpole obtained a majority of fifty in the general election of 1734. And when he finally fell, in 1742, it was because of the desertion of his previously loyal associates, Newcastle and Hardwicke. That practical failure is duplicated within Pope's *Imitations* by the poet's inability to retain and give convincing expression to the Horatian balance of personality without which the ethical side of his poetry falls to the ground. The later imitations show Pope in troubled contemplation of the unmeaning contradictions of his personality. The "First Epistle of the First Book" was written in 1737, and contains this rueful portrait of the motley poet, where a comic diversity of dress develops with alarming speed into a more profound psychological confusion:

> You laugh, half Beau half Sloven if I stand,
> My Wig all powder, and all snuff my Band;
> You laugh, if Coat and Breeches strangely vary,
> White gloves, and Linnen worthy Lady Mary!
> But when no Prelate's Lawn with Hair-shirt lin'd,
> Is half so incoherent as my Mind,
> When (each Opinion with the next at strife,
> One ebb and flow of follies all my Life)
> I plant, root up, I build, and then confound,
> Turn round to square, and square again to round;
> You never change one muscle of your face,
> You think this Madness but a common case,
> Nor once to Chanc'ry, nor to Hales apply;
> Yet hang your lip, to see a Seam awry!
>
> (ll. 161–174)

Not only does Pope's variety amount to a kind of insanity, so does the response it evokes in even so generally admirable a man as Bolingbroke. What Pope confronts in these lines is the dejecting possibility that the distinction between the men of virtue and the rogues, for which he has argued with such passion, is simply the result of perspective. It was an anxiety whose turbulent energies fueled also the great poem of the final phase of Pope's career: *The Dunciad.*

"THE SMITHFIELD MUSES"— THE DUNCIAD *AND THE END OF THINGS*

As we have briefly noted above, in May 1728 Pope published a three-book version of *The Dunciad*, with Lewis Theobald (who in 1726 had attacked Pope's edition of Shakespeare) installed as the poem's hero. In April 1729 Pope followed this up with *The Dunciad Variorum*, in which for the first time the poem appeared encrusted with all the excrement of the text—the notes, the appendices, the introductory essays—which now seem so characteristic of it. There the poem rested until March 1742, when Pope published what we now know as Book IV under the title *The New Dunciad*. Finally, and only seven months before Pope's death, there appeared *The Dunciad* in four books, with Colley Cibber (1671–1757), the poet laureate since 1730, having taken the place of Theobald at the center of the poem.

Why did Pope in the early 1740s extend and revise a poem originally composed some twelve years earlier, and why in particular did he equip the poem with a new hero? One motive, I think, is to be found in the eventual failure and frustration of the Horatian poetry to which Pope had dedicated himself during the 1730s. If he was to continue to write public poetry, he had to find a new form. Thus he turned away from the Horatian epistle, and revived instead an impersonal, narrative poetry. He exchanged Horace for Virgil (whose *Georgics* and *Aeneid* are the major classical presences in *The Dunciad*). And he modulated his intention in the *Imitations of Horace* to "publish the present Age," preferring now to write a poem where contemporary England was but one layer in a historical palimpsest in which essentially the same cultural battle was being everywhere and at all times lost. In Books XI and XII of *Paradise Lost*, Michael instructs Adam that the events of the Fall form a pattern of human experience to be repeated until the apocalypse, when this loop of time will be forever broken:

> . . . so shall the world go on,
> To good malignant, to bad men benign,
> Under her own weight groaning till the day
> Appear of respiration to the just,
> And vengeance to the wicked, at return
> Of him so lately promised to thy aid
> The woman's seed, obscurely then foretold,
> Now amplier known thy saviour and thy Lord,
> Last in the clouds from heaven to be revealed
> In glory of the Father, to dissolve
> Satan with his perverted world, then raise
> From the conflagrant mass, purged and refined,
> New heavens, new earth, ages of endless date
> Founded in righteousness and peace and love
> To bring forth fruits joy and eternal bliss.
> (*Paradise Lost*, xii.538–551)

When Pope rewrote this in *The Dunciad*, he had the ghost of the poet Elkanah Settle (1648–1724) showing Cibber, not the future, but the past—a series of anticipations of the final triumph of dullness. Hence the overrunning of the Roman Empire by the barbarians foreshadowed the swarming dunces of Pope's own day:

> Lo! where Maeotis sleeps, and hardly flows
> The freezing Tanais thro' a waste of snows,
> The North by myriads pours her mighty sons,
> Great nurse of Goths, of Alans, and of Huns!
> See Alaric's stern port! the martial frame
> Of Genseric! and Attila's dread name!
> See the bold Ostrogoths on Latium fall;
> See the fierce Visigoths on Spain and Gaul!
> (iii. 87–94)

The historical parallel is not, so Pope insists, exaggerated. Dullness is not trivial, as he made clear in an important note added to Book I in 1743:

. . . Dulness here is not to be taken contractedly for mere Stupidity, but in the enlarged sense of the word, for all Slowness of Apprehension, Shortness of Sight, or imperfect Sense of things. It includes (as we see by the Poet's own words) Labour, Industry, and some degree of Activity and Boldness: a ruling principle not inert, but turning topsy-turvy the Understanding, and inducing an Anarchy or confused State of Mind. This remark ought to be carried along with the reader throughout the work; and without this caution he will be apt to mistake the Importance of many of the Characters, as well as of the Design of the Poet. Hence it is that some have complained he chuses too mean a subject, and imagined

he employs himself, like Domitian, in killing flies; whereas those who have the true key will find he sports with nobler quarry, and embraces a larger compass; . . .

(note to i.15)

That "larger compass" and "nobler quarry" make *The Dunciad* Pope's most ambitious poem—a work that takes for its subject nothing less than the collapse of Western civilization.

But, considered from another standpoint, one can also see the expansion in the scope of *The Dunciad* as it moved from 1729 to 1743, from three books to four, from Theobald (Pope's personal antagonist) to Cibber (the poet laureate, and thus a convenient embodiment of the notorious Hanoverian indifference to literature), as evidence of uncertainty; as the search for a wider compass that will provide a more secure grounding for his judgments, and in particular the all-important distinction he wishes to enforce between himself and the dunces. If we look now in more detail at the circumstances surrounding the writing of the first *Dunciad* in the late 1720s, we shall see that a challenge to the clarity of that distinction—so crucial to Pope's sense of his own poethood—is at their heart. We will then be in a position to appreciate how the broader scope of the final, four-book *Dunciad* of 1743 can be read as an attempt to give greater force to that distinction by assembling more "evidence," and yet at the same time as a despairing and courageous imaginative acknowledgment of his own succumbing to the incorporating compulsion of dullness.

The origin of the first *Dunciad*—the three-book poem of 1728 and 1729 that has as its hero Lewis Theobald, is to be found in Pope's edition of Shakespeare, and the hostile reaction it provoked in Theobald. The distinction between Pope and the dunces is so emphatically present in our minds that it is sometimes hard for us to recapture the actual intermingledness of eighteenth-century English literary life before that distinction (so flattering to Pope) attained general currency. For Theobald was, in unexpected ways, close to Pope. Setting aside the mere coincidence that they were both born in the same year (1688), it is nevertheless the case that Theobald had contracts with the bookseller Bernard Lintot (1675–1736), who also occasionally published Pope's work, for translation projects concerning classical authors with whom Pope was also involved through translation or imitation—namely, Homer and Horace.

Moreover, the editorial methods of the two men were not as dissimilar as their antipathy might suggest. When tackling the text of Shakespeare they both largely ignored the history of the text and the question of transmission, and instead proposed emendations on the basis of intuitive eclecticism. And this closeness of method rendered all the more irritating Theobald's accurate pointing out of Pope's errors. If Pope is so perfectly the poet, so intimate with Shakespeare that he can give the last correction to his work, why was he not alert to these errors? Why (to choose only one of the blunders Theobald discovered) did Pope follow Rowe's edition, and print a passage with a vital line omitted, notwithstanding his claim to have collated all the early editions?

The squabble with Theobald was not merely wounding to Pope's vanity, a brush with a literary insect who can irritate but not seriously harm. The episode confronts Pope with the unwelcome possibility that there is not an absolute division between the poet and the man of rhymes, between those who have a proper reverence for poetry, and the hacks and dunces who lay sacrilegious hands on it. In response, Pope writes the three-book *Dunciad* of 1728 and 1729, in which he narrates a myth—the myth of the duncical succession, which he takes over from John Dryden's *MacFlecknoe* (1682)—in which the division between poets and dunces is so far put beyond doubt that it is the meaning of the myth. It is in this connection that the parodic allusions to *Paradise Lost* that so plentifully stud *The Dunciad* are of such use to Pope. On the one hand these allusions are part of the mock-epic machinery of the poem, which dwarfs the dunces in the heroic language to which they impudently and illegitimately lay claim. On the other hand, to invoke *Paradise Lost*, with its unflinching separation of fallen and unfallen, redeemed and damned, heavenly and hellish is rhetorically convenient for Pope in the similarly absolute distinction he wishes to enforce between himself and the dunces.

However, as we have seen, the practical failure of Pope's *Imitations of Horace* in the 1730s, no matter how brilliant the individual poems, raised once more the nagging question of how secure was the distinction of his own poethood, upon which so much depended. In response, Pope returned to *The Dunciad* and, with the addition of Book IV, made the indictment of dullness more coherent and more weighty—in 1743 we are confronted with a much more explicit evocation of

complete cultural collapse than we were before. At the same time, however, he also acknowledged his own susceptibility to the power of dullness, including himself in the catalogue of those who have succumbed:

> Signs following signs lead on the mighty year!
> See! the dull stars roll round and re-appear.
> See, see, our own true Phœbus wears the bays!
> Our Midas sits Lord Chancellor of Plays!
> On Poets' Tombs see Benson's titles writ!
> Lo! Ambrose Philips is prefer'd for Wit!
> See under Ripley rise a new White-hall,
> While Jones' and Boyle's united labours fall:
> While Wren with sorrow to the grave descends,
> Gay dies unpension'd with a hundred friends,
> Hibernian Politics, O Swift! thy fate;
> And Pope's, ten years to comment and translate.
> (iii.321–332)

The point is also encapsulated in a detail of revision. In 1729, Pope had announced the advent of dullness—as yet only a dream, of course, and one Pope will dismiss through the ivory gate of delusions—in these lines: "She comes! the Cloud-compelling Pow'r, behold! / With Night Primaeval, and with Chaos old" (iii.337–338). This was a parodic rewriting of a poem composed by Pope in 1712, the apocalyptic *Messiah*, in which the Second Coming was heralded in these words:

> The SAVIOR comes! by ancient Bards foretold:
>
> Hear him ye Deaf, and all ye Blind behold!
> He from thick films shall purge the visual Ray,
> And on the sightless Eye-ball pour the Day.
> (ll. 37–40)

We can see in the allusion a self-aggressive act of repudiation of an earlier blitheness and faith. In 1743, when the false dream of the triumph of dullness has become a dreadful, imminent reality, Pope altered the phrasing:

> In vain, in vain—the all-composing Hour
> Resistless falls: The Muse obeys the Pow'r.
> She comes! she comes! the sable Throne behold
> Of Night Primaeval, and of Chaos old!
> (iv.627–630)

There is much here that would repay analysis, but the detail on which I wish to dwell is the revision of "She comes!" in 1729 to "She comes! she comes!" in 1743. In making that change, Pope extended the allusiveness of his poem, and also its aggression, beyond simply his own writing. In 1730 the first complete edition of *The Seasons* by James Thomson (1700–1748) had appeared. In "Autumn," which was published for the first time in that edition, Thomson had written: "He comes! he comes! in every Breeze the POWER / Of PHILOSOPHIC MELANCHOLY comes!" (ll. 1004–1005) "Philosophic Melancholy," as described by Thomson, has some of the qualities of Dulness as described by Pope. It:

Inflames Imagination; thro' the Breast
Infuses every Tenderness; and far
Beyond dim Earth exalts the swelling Thought.
The thousand thousand fleet Ideas, such
As never mingled with the vulgar Dream,
Crowd fast into the Mind's creative Eye.
(ll. 1011–1016)

This is akin to the hectic multiplicity and inflammation that Pope ascribes, among other things, to dullness. But the deeper significance of this alignment of Thomson with the dunces is that it testifies to Pope's isolation. After all, Thomson too—albeit from a different, Whiggish, standpoint—had played a part in the struggle against Walpole, and *The Seasons* itself can convincingly be read as an anti-Walpolean work. Yet in this allusion Pope proudly separated himself from Thomson, and from everything to which he was unsympathetic in the other man's poetic and political stance.

It was a proud but precarious gesture, and in making it Pope fell prey to the individualism of the dunces. His defiance is also his undoing, and so the Muse indeed obeys the power. Enmeshed in dullness so that even his efforts to extricate himself only entangle him more securely, Pope glimpses that the universal darkness that ends his last poem, his poetical career, and almost his life is not only the collapse of literary culture under the Hanoverians but also a monstrous extrapolation of that radical darkness, that original uncertainty as to his own poethood, which has enabled and unnerved him throughout his writing life, from his earliest imitations to his poetic valediction.

SELECTED BIBLIOGRAPHY

I. COLLECTED WORKS. *The Works of Mr. Alexander Pope* (1717); *Epistles of Horace Imitated* (1738); *The Works of Mr. Alexander Pope, in Prose* (1737); *The Works of Alexander Pope*, 4 vols. (1736); *The Works, with his Last Corrections, Additions and Improvements*, ed. William Warburton, 9 vols. (1751).

Modern Collected Editions: *The Works*, ed. W. Elwin and W. J. Courthope, 10 vols. (1871–1889); *The Prose Works of Alexander Pope*. Vol. 1, ed. N. Ault (1936), Vol. 2, ed. R. Cowler (1986); *The Twickenham Edition of the Poems*, ed. J. Butt et al., 10 vols. (1943–1967).

II. MAJOR INDIVIDUAL WORKS. *An Essay on Criticism* (1711); *Windsor-Forest* (1713); *The Rape of the Lock* (1714); *The Temple of Fame* (1715); *A Key to the Lock* (1715); *The Iliad of Homer* (1715, 1716, 1717, 1718, 1720); *The Works of Shakespeare* (1725); *The Odyssey of Homer* (1725, 1726); *Miscellanies in Prose and Verse* (1727, 1732); *The Dunciad* (1728); *The Dunciad Variorum* (1729); *An Epistle to Burlington* (1731); *An Epistle to Bathurst* (1732); *An Epistle to Cobham* (1733); *An Essay on Man* (1733–1734); *An Epistle to Dr. Arbuthnot* (1734); *Imitations of Horace* (1733–1738); *Of the Characters of Women* (1735); *The New Dunciad* (1742); *The Dunciad in Four Books* (1743).

III. LETTERS. *Letters of Mr. Pope and Several Eminent Persons* (1735); *Correspondence*, ed. G. Sherburn, 5 vols. (1956).

IV. BIBLIOGRAPHIES. R. H. Griffith, *Pope: A Bibliography* (1922–1927 and 1962); J. E. Tobin, *Pope: A List of Critical Studies* (1945).

V. BIOGRAPHICAL STUDIES. Joseph Warton, *An Essay on the Genius and Writings of Pope* (1756–1782); Joseph Spence, *Observations, Anecdotes, and Characters of Books and Men*, ed. J. Osborn (1966); M. Mack, *Alexander Pope: A Life* (1985).

VI. CRITICAL STUDIES. A. Warren, *Alexander Pope as Critic and Humanist* (1929); E. Sitwell, *Alexander Pope* (1930); R. H. Griffith, "The Dunciad," in *PQ* 24 (1945); G. Tillotson, *On the Poetry of Pope* (1938, 1950); W. Empson, "Wit in the Essay on Criticism," in *Hudson Review* 2 (1950); B. Dobrée, *Alexander Pope* (1951); I. Jack, *Augustan Satire* (1952); A. L. Williams, *Pope's Dunciad: A Study of Its Meaning* (1955); R. Brower, *Pope: the Poetry of Allusion* (1959); E. R. Wasserman, *The Subtler Language* (1959).

R. L. Brett, *Reason and Imagination* (1960); J. S. Cunningham, *Pope: The Rape of the Lock* (1961); B. A. Goldgar, "Pope's Theory of the Passions," in *PQ* 41 (1962); T. R. Edwards, *This Dark Estate: A Reading of Pope* (1963); M. Mack, ed., *Essential Articles for the Study of Pope* (1964, 1968); T. E. Maresca, *Pope's Horatian Poems* (1966); Emrys Jones, *Pope and Dulness* (1968).

M. Mack, *The Garden and the City: Retirement and Politics in the Later Poetry of Pope 1731–43* (1970); H. Erskine-Hill, *Pope: The Dunciad* (1972); H. Erskine-Hill, *The Social Milieu of Alexander Pope* (1975); D. H. Griffin, *Alexander Pope: The Poet in the Poems* (1978).

H. Erskine-Hill, H. and A. Smith, eds., *The Art of Alexander Pope* (1979); H. Erskine-Hill, *The Augustan Idea in English Literature* (1983); D. Brooks-Davies, *Pope's Dunciad and the Queen of the Night* (1985); L. Brown, *Alexander Pope* (1985); F. Stack, *Pope and Horace* (1985); G. Rousseau and P. Rogers, eds., *The Enduring Legacy:*

Alexander Pope Tercentenary Essays (1988); D. Foxon, *Pope and the Early Eighteenth-Century Book Trade* (1991).

D. Todd, *Imagining Monsters: Miscreations of the Self in Eighteenth-Century England* (1995); H. Erskine-Hill, *Alexander Pope: World and Word* (1998).

PERCY BYSSHE SHELLEY

(1792–1822)

Susan Balée

The most unfailing herald, companion, and follower of the awakening of a great people to work a beneficial change in opinion or institution, is Poetry. At such periods there is an accumulation of the power of communicating and receiving intense and impassioned conceptions respecting man and nature. . . . Poets are . . . the mirrors of the gigantic shadows which futurity casts upon the present. . . . Poets are the unacknowledged legislators of the World.

Percy Bysshe Shelley, *A Defence of Poetry*, 1821

In his own lifetime, Percy Bysshe Shelley's poetry and prose languished in the shadow of his personal reputation as an atheist and an adulterer. However, like a mirror, he reflected in his verse, his essays, and his political pamphlets, the best (most prominent and cogently argued) of the radical theories of the reformers of his day. Although he died long before the working classes had adequate representation or rights, and long before divorce and adultery lost their intense social stigma, his work indicated the future path of labor unions and equality between the sexes.

Shelley endured both social and literary exile during his own era, with many of his best works not published until long after his death. The futurity he imagined, however, finally arrived in the twentieth century. Percy Shelley's poems and essays routinely appear in anthologies devoted to nineteenth-century literature, and his name is recognizable to any student of English literature as one of the greatest of the Romantic poets.

EARLY LIFE

PERCY Bysshe Shelley was born on 4 August 1792 at Field Place, in Sussex, the son of Timothy Shelley, a member of Parliament, and the grandson of Bysshe Shelley, a wealthy landowner who was made a baronet in 1806. Shelley grew up in a respectable family of minor aristocracy, the first child and doted-upon elder brother of several little sisters. Verbally precocious, young Shelley delighted in telling stories of ghosts and devils and other supernatural horrors to his awestruck young listeners. Almost as soon as he could read, Shelley developed a taste for Gothic fiction—tales of ruined castles with ghosts and secret chambers, terrified maidens, and dark, gloomy heroes—a genre of literature that had become increasingly popular since the French Revolution of 1789.

In fact, in many ways Percy Shelley embodied the contradictions of the era into which he was born. His childhood corresponded with the Reign of Terror—both politically in France, and imaginatively in literature—and he also enjoyed the fruits of the eighteenth-century Enlightenment with its scientific advances in numerous fields, including those that Shelley soon found most intriguing: electricity, gases, and combustion. In fact, it was young Shelley's love of setting fires that determined his father to send him away to school to learn not only Greek and Latin, but also self-discipline. Thus, at age ten, the sensitive, proud boy, much attached to his mother and young sisters, left home to enter the all-male realm of Syon House, a prep school outside London.

Most of Shelley's major biographers agree that Shelley's experiences at the hands of his brutal schoolboy companions profoundly affected the course of his later life, and not in a way that Timothy Shelley could have desired. A country boy, pale and delicate of face and frame, with long curling hair and an effeminate voice, Percy Shelley was soon the object of daily torture from the school's bullies. When provoked beyond his breaking point, Shelley responded with fits of uncontrollable and ineffective rage, to the delight of his tormentors. At age twelve Shelley left Syon House for Eton, but he fared no better among his peers there. He refused to serve as a valet (or "fag") for the older students—a tradition of English boys' schools—and thus had no protection from the elder boys against the cruelties of his peers. Again, his more brutal companions sought him out for special punishment, tormenting him until he cried and screamed in impotent rage, earning him the nickname "Mad Shelley." Ever after, he remembered his school days with anguish and loathing. His only release from the emotional and physical pain of his life at Syon and Eton came from his own imagination and from books.

Shelley's early life, then, contained all the elements that would later produce his best writing. He felt oppressed by tyrants—his teachers, his fellow students, and later his father; he felt betrayed—by his father and mother, for sending him away to school; he was tormented for being different and yet refused to change—he would not "fag," no matter how much abuse he suffered for refusing to serve the older boys. The pattern of Shelley's life as a rebel was early established, as was his thirst for justice and his kindness to those who were powerless and oppressed.

His love of lurid, Gothic literature continued, as did his pleasure in being the adored (and occasionally feared) mentor of younger females. His experiments with electricity, fire, and explosives continued, and his knowledge of Greek and Latin prospered apace. A product of the Enlightenment as well as the governmental oppression that produced the American and French revolutions, Shelley laid the groundwork of his future notoriety during his sophomore year at Oxford when he published his first explosive work of literature, *The Necessity of Atheism.*

LIBERTY AND FREE LOVE

SHELLEY'S *Necessity of Atheism* made him infamous at Oxford. Indeed, the authorities there were so outraged by the principles outlined in it that Shelley, with his friend and collaborator, Thomas Jefferson Hogg, were expelled. Before the notorious pamphlet appeared, however, Shelley had already published several works of Gothic fiction and verse. Notable among these was *Zastrozzi*, a rather derivative romance based on his copious readings in the Gothic fiction of M. G. "Monk" Lewis and Ann Radcliffe, which appeared in 1810, when Shelley was a mere eighteen years old.

The Oxford University experience struck Shelley as suffocatingly clerical (daily attendance at chapel was mandatory for students), although at least the scion of Field Place did not have to endure the bullying of his peers. Instead he made his first really close male friend there in the person of Hogg, another freshman. Hogg turned Shelley's mind from Gothic fiction to political doctrine. Together they began to read and discuss the best—and most radical—works of eighteenth-century political philosophers, including Thomas Paine, David Hume, William Godwin, John Locke, Benjamin Franklin, and Jean-Jacques Rousseau. They burned to revolutionize English society, particularly the claustrophobic corridors of Oxford, and they felt inspired by the French Revolution, despite its long and bloody aftermath of anarchy.

Reacting to what they saw as the religious tyranny of Christianity—its wars and inquisitions, its insistence on "unnatural" institutions, such as marriage—they set out to prove that no evidence of the senses, reasoning, or personal testimony supported the existence of a supreme deity, and that, instead, such a belief is a "passion of the mind," full of prejudice and without proof. The pamphlet had its intended effect of shocking the Oxford authorities, and Shelley and Hogg were promptly expelled. Timothy Shelley was horrified by his son's "impious" pamphlet and tried to get him to recant his heretical views, which he would not do. At this point a rift began to open between father and son, and Shelley, no longer on speaking terms with Timothy, lived in a kind of exile in London, trying to decide what to do with his life.

During these months Shelley slept badly, troubled by nightmares about the existence of a "double self" (a very Gothic concept that recurred throughout his life in his dreams, his waking hallucinations, and ultimately his writings); he had also become a sleepwalker, sometimes waking in strange places outdoors. Idle, bored, and lonely, he began to visit the Westbrooks, a London family he knew slightly through his younger sisters. John Westbrook, the paterfamilias, owned a coffeehouse, and the family lived comfortably. His youngest daughter, Harriet, was a sixteen-year-old beauty. Within four months Shelley had worked his charm on her, culminating in their elopement to Scotland. (Although he did not believe in marriage, Harriet Westbrook emphatically did and would not run away with him otherwise.)

When Timothy Shelley discovered the elopement, and his aristocratic son's mésalliance with a shopkeeper's daughter, he cut off Percy's allowance. After Percy responded with several enraged and demanding letters, berating his father as a tyrant and a bigot, Timothy cut off all relations with his son. When Percy Shelley turned nineteen on 4 August 1811, he had been expelled from Oxford, alienated from his family, and married to a sixteen-year-old girl who depended on him for financial, intellectual, and emotional support. At this point his life took on a nomadic quality, as desperate finances and his reputation as a troublemaker forced him to move residences with regularity. The one ideal of this period that remained constant for the rest of his life was his desire to found a commune of like-minded spirits, whose members could live, love, and work together, equal in everything.

RADICAL POLITICS

NOW drawn to politics as much as he had once been drawn to Gothic fiction, Shelley began to read the works of William Godwin, in particular Godwin's *Enquiry Concerning Political Justice* (first published in 1793), which advocated the rights of the working classes. In January 1812 he wrote Godwin his first fan letter, and a correspondence began between the young atheist and the aging political philosopher.

During this time Shelley's writing was completely given over to political poems and pamphlets. The best poem of this era is his "A Tale of Society As It Is," based on the true story of a poor woman whose only son is pressed into the army, leaving her to provide for herself as best she can:

> For seven years did this poor woman live
> In unparticipated solitude.
> Thou might have seen her in the desert rude
> Picking the scattered remnants of its wood.
> If human, thou might'st there have learned to grieve.

In 1812 Harriet and Shelley went to Ireland, where Shelley hoped to inspire a revolution among the downtrodden peasants there, having written a political pamphlet, *An Address to the Irish People*, for precisely this purpose. Godwin, with whom he continued to correspond, worried about the incendiary nature of the pamphlet Shelley was distributing in Dublin. Godwin urged him to tone down his rhetoric or he would incite the mob to violence, causing them to "rise up like . . . seed of dragon's teeth, and their first act will be to destroy each other" (14 March 1812, *Letters*, vol. 1, p. 269).

Shelley responded that Godwin's was a sort of armchair radicalism and that *Political Justice*'s emphasis on gradual change through "fireside discussions" and congenial intercourse among those of different political persuasions had effected little change in the conditions of the working poor in twenty years. Shelley wanted to see real change occur, not just talk of its future possibility. In such a spirit Shelley addressed the Catholic Committee in Dublin but soon realized that the liberal wing of Irish politics was severely disorganized. More importantly he saw the real horrors of poverty and famine in the streets of Dublin, which he described to Godwin in a letter as the "depth of human misery," and the poor people themselves as "one mass of animated filth" (*Letters,* vol. 1, p. 268). He attempted to help the most miserable of those he encountered, but frequently his interference in their lives did little or no good at all. Shelley's idealism about an Irish revolution began to falter in the face of such abject poverty. He and Harriet determined to leave Ireland, and the one real change that Shelley took with him was a new system of diet: he had become a vegetarian.

QUEEN MAB

AFTER leaving Ireland, Shelley and Harriet lived in successive places in Wales and England, with a variety of people—Harriet's elder sister Eliza, Shelley's schoolmarm correspondent, Miss Hitchener, Shelley's Oxford friend, T. J. Hogg—as Shelley attempted to put into action his idea of a radical commune. During this period of his life he continued to read voraciously on a variety of subjects and began composition of his first long political poem, *Queen Mab*.

In the summer of 1813 Shelley's London publishers brought forth *Queen Mab*, and Harriet Shelley gave birth to their first child, Eliza Ianthe Shelley. The targets of *Queen Mab,* a poetic polemic, are organized religion, political tyranny, the destructiveness of war, and the perversion of love caused by marriage and prostitution. The poem advocates free love, atheism, vegetarianism, and democracy. *Queen Mab* was a radical poem by a radical and prodigiously intelligent young man. It survived until well into the nineteenth century as a text beloved by radical reformers and Marxists.

The poem itself, though immature in some ways (Shelley was only twenty years old when it appeared), exudes an angry eloquence.

> Power, like a desolating pestilence,
> Pollutes whate'er it touches; and obedience

Bane of all genius, virtue, freedom, truth,
Makes slaves of men, and of the human frame,
A mechanized automaton.

(3.177–180)

Like other Romantic poets, Shelley responded harshly to the Industrial Revolution and the demoralizing effect of factory life on the working classes. Another theme underscored in *Queen Mab*, particularly in light of Shelley's personal life, is his insistence that the "very essence of love is liberty" and that "any law which would bind [lovers] to cohabitation for one moment after the decay of their affection would be a most intolerable tyranny." (*Shelley's Prose*, pp. 115–117)

Shelley turned twenty-one in August, but the inheritance he and Harriet hoped he would come into did not materialize. Timothy Shelley, through his lawyers, obstructed the money, and Shelley and Harriet were forced to continue life in relative penury, with the addition of a new baby to their responsibilities. Shelley's only recourse was to negotiate with moneylenders for loans at ruinous interest rates (one as much as 300 percent a year), to be paid on the death of his grandfather or father, at which point he would certainly inherit a significant amount of money. During this period of uncertainty Shelley became even closer to William Godwin, whom he had now met several times in person, a relationship that would lead, in less than a year, to a surprising and rather shocking consequence. Also during this period, Shelley's diary records his first serious unhappiness with Harriet. She had become physically repugnant to him, and he began to regret that he had ever married her.

MARY WOLLSTONECRAFT GODWIN

MANY biographers have noted that the moment when Percy Shelley met Mary W. Godwin was a turning point in the course of his life. Certainly it was for Mary, whose mother, Mary Wollstonecraft, had written *Vindication of the Rights of Woman* (1792), a very early and much celebrated feminist text, and whose father, Godwin, was the revered author of *Political Justice*. Mary's mother had died shortly after giving birth to her, but she had endowed her daughter with a luminous intellect. Mary Godwin at age sixteen glowed with intellectual brilliance and physical beauty. Shelley, who was also intensely cerebral, well read, and

physically "beautiful" (a description that Godwin and many others used to describe him), recognized instantly that he had met his match in Mary. Her feelings, if anything, were even stronger. She knew that Shelley was a married man and a father, but her sense of connection to him was immediate and electric. At his first introduction to Mary in June 1814, he also met Jane (later "Claire") Clairmont, Mary's younger stepsister, the woman who would form the third angle of the triangular relationship that the three would share for the rest of Shelley's life.

Within a matter of weeks Mary and Shelley had declared their love for each other, and Shelley announced it to Godwin, surprised that Mary's father should be so appalled by this instance of true and "free" love. Godwin, who believed in many types of equality, didn't believe that his daughter should cast her lot with a married man and bring a scandal upon the family. He tried everything to dissuade the two, even bringing Harriet Shelley to London to remind Percy of his vows to her. For his part, Shelley calmly told Harriet that he felt for her a brother's love for a sister, but that his romantic passion burned for one woman only: Mary Godwin. Harriet's announcement that she was pregnant with their second child did not dissuade him.

Meanwhile, Godwin barred Mary and Claire from leaving the house, in a vain attempt to keep them from Shelley. In the end, all precautions were useless: Shelley carried away both Mary and Claire on 28 July 1814, spiriting the girls to Dover by carriage, then by boat to France.

FABLES AND ROMANCES: 1814–1816

SHELLEY and the girls' first impressions of France reflected the landscape's desolation—the country had been ravaged by years of the Napoleonic Wars. They passed through village after village that had been sacked and burned, their inhabitants famished and wretched. The Shelleys decided to press fast through this ruined landscape for Switzerland.

By the time they reached the Alps, Shelley was writing a romance about a sect of primitive Christians who had escaped the destruction of Jerusalem by the Romans and fled into a fertile valley of Lebanon to live in peace. This sect, and Shelley's romance, was called *The Assassins*. As Richard Holmes observes, the work's main theme of flight followed by a happy and productive community reflects the issues in Shelley's own life as he fled London with the girls and sought a new community of existence with them in Europe.

The Assassins is an unfinished work of approximately four chapters, but it was preparation for Shelley's long poem of the next year, *Alastor*, seven hundred lines of blank verse depicting, as Shelley explained, "one of the most interesting situations of the human mind." The poem is loosely based on the myth of Narcissus and Echo; the Narcissus character is a poet in search of an ideal vision of beauty. He dreams of such a woman, but as a product of his imagination, she cannot be possessed. He ignores an Arab girl who actually falls in love with him; instead he embarks on a perilous river journey, searching for the woman of his dreams. In the course of the journey he grows ill and old and ultimately finds himself in a grotesque landscape, staring at his own image in a pond, "as the human heart, / Gazing in dreams over the gloomy grave, / Sees its own treacherous likeness there" (472–474). All of the landscapes described, Shelley emphasized, were interior ones—mental landscapes that corresponded to emotional states he wanted to explore.

The poem's full title is *Alastor; or, The Spirit of Solitude*, and it is this spirit that Shelley tries hard to evoke. Mental solitude, Shelley emphasizes, ultimately brings despair to the individual. Humans are meant to live and love in communities, not alone. The poem appeared in 1816 and most of its reviewers found it obscure and difficult, though possessed of some striking imagery. The reception accorded *Alastor* would be echoed throughout Shelley's career. During his lifetime Shelley never enjoyed a regular readership of congenial minds.

Insofar as Bysshe Shelley, Percy's grandfather, had died in January 1815, Shelley returned with his ménage to England. His first wife, Harriet, gave birth to his son, Charles, in November 1814, but Shelley would have nothing to do with either Harriet or his two children by her. In January 1816 Mary gave birth to their first surviving child, William. Of all his children, this son was the one to whom Shelley was most attached.

Complications of old Sir Bysshe's will prevented the Shelleys from leaving London while they waited for a resolution to their financial problems. During this time Claire Clairmont set her cap at the most famous poet of the age, George Gordon, Lord Byron. Her pursuit of Byron introduced him to the Shelleys and linked them all for one memorable and intensely literary summer.

BYRON AND SHELLEY: SWITZERLAND 1816

BY THE END of April, Shelley had found out from the courts that he would not inherit anything yet from his grandfather's estates. Claire Clairmont had begun an affair with Lord Byron, who had succumbed to her persistent charms shortly before leaving London for the Continent (Byron, too, had had business with the courts—attaining a legal separation from his wife—and, also like Shelley, had a bad reputation in England as a sexual libertine). In late May the Shelleys connected with Byron in Geneva, Switzerland.

During the course of this summer the Shelleys and Byron became close friends and companions. They discussed the latest advances in science, philosophy, and literature. Regarding literature, they often discussed German Gothic fiction, of which all were fond. Byron found a collection of German horror tales and, after avidly reading and discussing these tales, Shelley suggested that all of them should try their hands at writing a ghost story. The most accomplished of the stories from that summer is still famous today: Mary Shelley's *Frankenstein: or, The Modern Prometheus*. Mary's story is similar to Shelley's long poem *Alastor* in that both show the way that humans who endure isolation for long periods ultimately succumb to despair. The significant difference between the two works is that Frankenstein's monster is forced by his creator into a life of spiritual and physical exile, whereas the young protagonist of *Alastor* chooses his solitary life. (Dr. Frankenstein, obsessed by his desire for knowledge about the sources of life and death, more closely resembles the youth, and by the time he tries to reconnect to his friends, family, and the woman he loves, it is too late.)

During this summer Shelley and Byron frequently sailed together on Lake Leman. Shelley, it turned out, could not swim, but he refused Byron's offer to teach him. Also during this summer, Shelley traveled with Claire and Mary through the Alps. The striking scenery provided Mary with a backdrop for the confrontation scene between Dr. Frankenstein and his monster on the Mer de Glace ("sea of ice"). Shelley, like virtually every other English visitor before him, felt overwhelmed by the cruel majesty of the Alps. Both fascinated and fearful, he felt the human mind to be a puny thing indeed in comparison with the brute force of nature represented by the Alpine landscape. Shelley's poem, "Mont Blanc," is the poet's attempt to understand the effect that viewing the huge mountain had on his mental landscape.

In the first section of "Mont Blanc," Shelley analyzes the way the mind amasses information through sensory experience: "The everlasting universe of things / flows through the mind" (1–2). The mind serves as a filter for experience, but it also adds something to the data it takes in, because "from secret springs / The source of human thought its tribute brings" (4–5). In section 2 of the poem, Shelley establishes the mind as a ravine through which a river of sensory perceptions flows. His fascination with his own (admittedly brilliant) mind is evident:

Dizzy ravine! . . . when I gaze on thee
I seem as in a trance sublime and strange
To muse on my own separate fantasy,
My own, my own human mind.
(34–37)

In section 3 the poet finally looks up at Mont Blanc and wonders: "Has some unknown Omnipotence unfurled / The veil of life and death?" (52–53). The sight of the massive peak does not merely inspire awe in the poet, it terrifies him: "For the very spirit fails, / Driven like a homeless cloud from steep to steep / That vanishes among the viewless gales!" (56–59). The poet goes on to muse that when humans contemplate the wilderness (Nature in its wildest, most inhuman landscapes), the contemplation inevitably provokes one of two conclusions: belief or disbelief in a supreme being.

Section 4 describes the ineluctable power of a moving glacier, the "flood of ruin" (107) that it causes, not just to rocks and trees but also to humans who attempt to live in its shadow. The glacier moves, but "Mont Blanc yet gleams on high," immune to the catastrophes below it, indifferent witness to scenes of both life and death. Section 5 provides the poem's finale, a difficult meditation on Nature and the human mind:

And what were thou, and earth, and stars, and sea,
If to the human mind's imaginings
Silence and solitude were vacancy?
(142–144)

Some critics suggest that Shelley implies that Nature has no meaning other than that assigned to it by the individual human mind. The fact that shortly after his visit to Mont Blanc he began signing "Atheist" in the hotel registers that asked for his occupation (a prank that got back to England and further inflamed popular sentiment against him) seems to support the notion that the sublime scenery of the Alps did not produce faith in Shelley, but only increased his doubt in the existence of a deity that cared about the fate of humankind.

LEIGH HUNT AND LONDON'S YOUNG POETS

BY the end of summer financial affairs prompted Shelley with Mary and Claire (now three months pregnant with Byron's child) to return to London. The autumn of 1816 saw a renewed interest in labor reform and poor relief in England. Shelley was a passionate advocate of these causes, as was Leigh Hunt, the editor of an important liberal journal, the *Examiner*. In the 1 December issue of his journal Hunt had listed Shelley with John Keats as rising English poets. Shelley, thrilled to finally receive a positive review, wrote Hunt a passionate and revealing letter. He identified himself as a reformer, one with "powers deeply to interest, or substantially to improve, mankind." Unfortunately he also felt like Frankenstein's monster, or the youth of *Alastor*, for he added, "I am an outcast from human society; my name is execrated by all who understand its entire import,—by those very beings whose happiness I ardently desire" (8 December 1816, *Letters*, vol. 1, p. 517). Hunt, he felt, understood him—and their friendship, as well as their professional connection, prospered.

Meanwhile, during the autumn of 1816 it was really Shelley's first wife, Harriet Westbrook, who felt like an outcast from human society. She had left her two children by Shelley with her parents and taken lodgings in Chelsea under an assumed name. Pregnant, presumably with the child of an officer stationed at the barracks in Chelsea, Harriet committed suicide on 9 November. She jumped into the Serpentine River, and her body was not found for over a month.

Harriet left a suicide note asking Shelley to raise their son, Charles, but to let her elder sister keep their daughter, Ianthe. Shelley refused and ultimately lost custody of both children. Meanwhile, Mary pressured him to marry her since Harriet's death had freed him, and he did so on 30 December 1816. Then, for several weeks beginning in late January, Mary and Shelley stayed with the Leigh Hunts. Although he did not reveal how deeply he was affected by Harriet's suicide at the time (presumably to spare Mary), Shelley later wrote to Byron that her death gave him a shock that he barely survived.

At the Hunts', Shelley got to know the other leading English poets and writers of the day, including John Keats and William Hazlitt. Keats remarked in his journals that he did not like Shelley's antireligious fanaticism, and Hazlitt found him full of book learning but with little real experience in the world. Hazlitt wrote, "Curiosity is the only proper category of his mind, and though a man in knowledge, he is a child in feeling. . . ." (A R. Walles and Arnold Glover, eds., *The Collected Works of William Hazlitt*, vol. 6., pp. 48–49). The Hunts, however, loved Shelley and gave much comfort to him and Mary.

MARLOW: 1817–1818

IN February the Shelleys moved to their own house in Marlow, outside London. Claire left her young daughter by Byron with the Hunts and moved back in with Percy and Mary. At the house in Marlow, Shelley wrote his long political poem *Laon and Cythna*, published in 1818 as *The Revolt of Islam*. In this poem Shelley tried to capture the primary event of his epoch, the one that influenced every writer of his time: the French Revolution. In his preface to the poem Shelley writes: "Can he who was the day before a trampled slave suddenly become liberal-minded, forbearing, and independent? . . . Such is the lesson which experience teaches us now. But, on the first reverses of hope in the progress of French liberty, the sanguine eagerness for good overleaped the solution of these questions. . . ." (*Poetical Works*, p. 33).

In early September, Mary gave birth to Clara, who joined big brother William in the Shelley household. During the fall Shelley wrote more political pamphlets about the wretched state of the working classes in Europe. His health was bad—he suffered from pains in his side that were later diagnosed as kidney stones—and he felt depressed.

In January *The Revolt of Islam* appeared to mixed reviews, at least one of which savaged the author personally. The poem's protagonists are Laon and Cythna, a man and woman (brother and sister in the original poem, which was why Shelley had to amend and retitle the work to get it published) who together battle the forces of oppression through their leadership of a revolutionary army. The Tyrant's army engages with the freedom fighters and the poem includes some gruesome battle scenes: "their eyes started with cracking stare / And impotent their tongues lolled in the air / Flaccid and foamy like a mad dog's hanging . . . (stanzas 16–17). Laon and Cythna, after capture and torture, regain their freedom, become lovers, and lead their revolutionaries back into the Tyrant's city, which they liberate. Laon looks to the future with hope in an impassioned speech.

"The seeds are sleeping in the soil: meanwhile
The Tyrant peoples dungeons with his prey,
Pale victims on the guarded scaffold smile
   Because they cannot speak; and day by day,
   The moon of wasting Science wanes away
Among her stars, and in that darkness vast
   The sons of earth to their foul idols pray. . . .

This is the winter of the world. . . .
Behold! Spring comes. . . .
   The future, a broad sunrise; thus arrayed
As with the plumes of overshadowing wings'
From its dark gulf of chains, Earth like an eagle
   springs."
                    (stanzas 24–25)

The poem is clearly a dark one, reflecting Shelley's feelings about the current state of politics in Europe. Only after much present despair and suffering can the future, the spring of the world, give hope to the downtrodden.

During the period he was composing *The Revolt of Islam*, Shelley was also visiting the British Museum and studying the many Egyptian artifacts, including the Rosetta stone, recently brought back to England by archaeologists who had explored Ramses' tomb. Shelley decided to write a sonnet about some of these fragments and produced one of his most famous poems, "Ozymandias." This poem describes a statue discovered in the desert by a traveler. The statue's trunk is missing and its head lies in the sand, "a shattered visage" whose "sneer of cold command / Tell that its sculptor well those passions read." The pedestal of the statue declares that its subject is Ozymandias, "King of Kings / Look on my works, ye Mighty, and despair!" However, what the desert traveler looks on beside the statue is nothing: "boundless and bare / The lone and level sands stretch far away."

By March 1818, Shelley realized that he could no longer stay in England. He didn't have the financial resources and the social stigma attached to his name was painful. Once again, he chose the exile's route and he, with Mary and Claire and their children, left for Europe. This time, they settled in Italy.

ITALY AND GREEK TRAGEDY

AFTER moving from inn to inn for several months, unable to get a lease on a house they liked, the Shelleys finally settled in the Mediterranean port of Livorno. Shelley began to read the Greek dramatists Euripides and Sophocles in the original. He was commencing the work that would later lead to his excellent translations of several major Greek, Latin, and Spanish works into English. Moreover, he discovered that the act of translating classic texts served to jumpstart his own ideas about particular myths. A poem he wrote in 1819, *Prometheus Unbound*, is such a refashioning of a classic myth to meet a present need.

As a fine practitioner of the art himself, Shelley, in his best-known work of prose, *A Defence of Poetry*, comments on translation. He acknowledges that the translator has a tricky task that he will never fulfill completely because he can never completely "transfuse from one language into another the creations of a poet." On the other hand, the masterpieces of literature possess a transcendent power. They continue to generate significance for readers far beyond their original time and culture.

All high poetry is infinite; it is as the first acorn, which contained all oaks potentially . . . after one person and one age has exhausted all of its divine effluence which their peculiar relations enable them to share, another and yet another succeeds, and new relations are ever developed, the source of an unforeseen and unconceived delight.

(*Shelley's Prose*, p. 291)

However, in 1818 Shelley's *Defence* had not yet been written and his reading among the classic authors primarily served to distract him from his inability to write anything original of his own.

When he began to jot down the translations it was simply to put some words in his otherwise blank notebooks. In this frame of mind he spent his early days in Italy outside, in the woods or fields and always near streams, alternately reading and bathing in the cool waters.

In April of that year Lord Byron demanded that Claire deliver their child, Allegra, to him so that he could have her educated. Claire did so, reluctantly, but by August was anxious to see her daughter, particularly as she had had no word of Allegra by post despite repeated requests. Shelley agreed to go to Venice, where Byron was now living in a palace on the Grand Canal, to check on Allegra. Claire traveled with him, though they did not tell Byron this because he had developed a strong aversion to his former mistress. She was to wait, in hiding nearby, for Shelley's report.

Shelley and Byron once again hit it off famously, and Byron offered the Shelleys the use of his country home, Este, in the Euganean Hills southwest of Venice. Shelley agreed, then promptly wrote to Mary that she should come immediately with the children from Livorno to Este and meet him, Claire, and Allegra there. Mary did so, though Clara was ill during the trip. To make matters worse, as soon as they arrived, Shelley insisted they all go to Venice to see Byron. Clara worsened and, when they reached Venice, she died in her mother's arms. After her funeral they returned to Este, where Mary fell into a deep and enduring depression and Shelley, sad as well as terribly guilty, wrote one of his best poems, "Lines Written Among the Euganean Hills."

This poem begins with one of Shelley's favorite images—a sea voyage, one in which the sailor's bark is freighted with human grief.

Many a green isle needs must be
In the deep wide sea of Misery,
Or the mariner, worn and wan,
Never thus could voyage on—

Reaching the green isle, however, the despairing mariner has a moment of clarity when he can enjoy the beauty around him and contemplate his surroundings free from the shroud of unhappiness that has enveloped him. Noon comes with "a soft and purple mist / like a Vaporous amethyst" (287–288), and the poet mariner sees flowers glimmering at his feet, with the distant line of "the olive-sandalled Apennine" to the south and the Alps,

whose snows are spread
High between the clouds and sun;
And of living things each one;
And my spirit which so long
Darkened this swift stream of song,—
Interpenetrated lie
By the glory of the sky:
Be it love, light, harmony,
Odour, or the soul of all
Which from heaven like dew doth fall,
Or the mind which feeds this verse
Peopling the lone universe.

(308–319)

Whether it comes from heaven, or simply from the narrator's own mind—imagination—the glory of the sky briefly lightens the speaker's darkened spirit. He longs for a place, an island of calm in the storm of life, where he can build a bower for those he loves, "far from passion, pain, and guilt" with "the light and smell divine / Of all flowers that breathe and shine / We may live so happy there" (350–353).

SHELLEY AND BYRON IN VENICE ("JULIAN" AND "MADDALO")

SHELLEY'S wish for a happy bower that he could share with his loved ones—with Mary, Claire, and their children—was a long time coming. But while Mary dealt with her grief in silence, Shelley wrote. They returned to Venice, and Shelley's stimulating relationship with Lord Byron resumed. They took leisurely gondola rides, rode horses on the Lido at twilight, and spent most of every night discussing politics, philosophy, and literature. The relationship invigorated Shelley and he captured their differences in a dialogic poem, *Julian and Maddalo.* Shelley is thinly disguised here as Julian, an optimist who believes that society can be improved and individuals can control their own fates. Byron is Count Maddalo, a cynic who believes that men are sheep, prey to their own desires as well as the caprices of fate and circumstance. Shelley describes the differences in the temperaments of his protagonists in a prose preface, then begins the poem with a detailed description of the marshland outside of Venice where Julian, the narrator, "rode one evening with Count Maddalo." Julian delights in the barren scenery: "I love all waste / And solitary places; where we taste / The pleasure of believing what we see / Is boundless, as we wish our souls to be. . . ." Maddalo points out a lunatic asylum in the distance, a place they will visit later in the poem.

The next day Julian visits Maddalo and they continue the debate they've begun the day before about whether humans have free will. Julian believes that men can choose their course in life: "We know / That we have power over ourselves to do / And suffer—what, we know not till we try / But something nobler than to live and die" (184–187). " 'My dear friend,' " Maddalo tells him, " 'my judgement will not bend to your opinion' " (191–192). He then adds, " 'I knew one like you / Who to this city came some months ago / With whom I argued in this sort, and he / Is now gone mad,—and so he answered me—' " (195–198). Maddalo suggests they go and visit the madman " 'and his wild talk will show / How vain are such aspiring theories' " (200–201).

They take another gondola ride out to the island where the asylum stands, enduring the shrieks and cries of its inhabitants as they climb its "oozy stairs" to where the Maniac sits in an upper chamber. The Maniac, once a brilliant and wealthy man, lost his mind when the woman he loved deserted him. He delivers a linguistically shimmering, though disconnected, monologue, and Maddalo observes that, based merely on the quality of his language and his metaphors, "the colours of his mind seemed yet unworn." He adds, " 'Most wretched men / Are cradled into poetry by wrong / They learn in suffering what they teach in song.' " Julian is virtually silenced, and the comment on poets being urged to their art by suffering is one that could be aptly applied to Shelley himself.

Shelley sent *Julian and Maddalo* to Hunt for publication, but it never saw print in his lifetime. Nevertheless, it is a psychologically acute poem that shows Shelley had reached a new level of maturity and self-awareness.

PROMETHEUS UNBOUND

BY the spring of 1819 Shelley and his ménage had settled into a house in Rome. Like millions of other tourists to the famous Italian city, they toured the ruins and the galleries with avidity. Shelley, in particular, was struck by the quality of the ancient architecture; the Arch of Titus and the Arch of Constantine located in the Forum drew his concentrated attention. Classically carved reliefs of chariots and Victory with her angel wings struck him as particularly important symbols. These were offset for him by the luxuriant growths of foliage over many of the Roman ruins—the power and imperialism of ancient Rome had been destroyed, but Nature had reassumed its primacy.

In this atmosphere Shelley took up the myth of Prometheus, the one who liberated humankind with his gift of fire, and began giving it his particular spin. (Mary had already given the myth her treatment in *Frankenstein*.) Shelley's model came from Aeschylus, whose drama he had read in Greek, but with more modern references to recent advances in science and medicine. (Shelley also read avidly in these fields.) And, of course, Prometheus resembles Shelley: both are extreme nonconformists; both have suffered for their "gifts" to humankind.

In Aeschylus' drama, whose outlines Shelley followed, Jupiter, the leader of the gods, has chained Prometheus to a rock where he is daily tortured by an eagle that gnaws upon his liver. Shelley had felt himself persecuted first by his father, and later by various branches of the British government, because of his avowal of atheism and his pursuit of free love. He suffered expulsion from Oxford and the loss of the bulk of his inheritance, but he would not recant his views. Similarly Prometheus in his poem will not recant, and fiends come to show him visions of war and famine, of all the evil deeds that the humans he tried to help have committed since his gift.

Some of these visions are the events of Shelley's era, such as the French Revolution's aftermath of bloody despotism, and the cruel fate of the poor caught in the wretched conditions of urban factories. Like Wordsworth and other Romantic poets who deplored what the Industrial Revolution had done both to the landscape and the working poor, he presents a grim view of a modern city:

> Look! Where round the wide horizon
> Many a million-peopled city
> Vomits smoke in the bright air.
> Hark that outcry of despair!
> (550–553)

In Shelley's poem, Prometheus (and by extension, humanity) can only be saved by love. Personified by the character Asia, love can make Prometheus whole again. He is a personality divided from Jupiter, his polar opposite and other half. Shelley is here playing with a concept that absorbed the writers of his era: the idea of the doppelgänger, or double. The study of mental processes that would even-

tually become the discipline called psychology had just begun to explore the idea that all humans possess a "second self," a part of the mind that lies hidden from the waking consciousness. Nowadays, thanks to Freud, we would call this second self the unconscious or subconscious mind, but in Shelley's era, doctors had only just begun to recognize that insanity was not the same as demonic possession, that individuals could be motivated by inner impulses they were unaware of in their normal states. Romantic writers, already fascinated with the idea of the individual self, were drawn to the concept of the double—thus, stories and poems featuring a doppelgänger occur frequently in literature of the early nineteenth century. (Indeed, Dr. Frankenstein's monster is clearly *his* double, a being he has created from his own mind.)

Asia travels to the volcanic center of the earth (Shelley had recently visited Vesuvius) to speak to the ruler there, Demogorgon, and plead for Prometheus' liberation. Demogorgon's realm is the past—history, memory, the world at its beginning. Asia asks him, "Who is the master of the slave?" (115). She wants to know who created evil in the universe and whether it is the same person who created good. Is it, she wonders, Jupiter, and if so, is he the master or the slave of his own creation? Demogorgon evades a direct answer, but he shows Asia the course of history bursting out of the center of the earth like lava from a volcano. Historic moments spark from the earth in the shape of hurtling chariots (like the ones Shelley had studied on the arches at the Forum).

> The rocks are cloven, and through the purple night
> I see cars drawn by rainbow-winged steeds
> Which trample the dim winds: in each there stands
> A wild-eyed charioteer urging their flight
> (2.4.129–32)

Demogorgon himself rides in the final chariot; he comes out of the center of the earth to restore Prometheus to freedom by ending Jupiter's reign over the earth.

Unfortunately, two acts follow this climactic event, and most critics agree that the poem weakens in its final sections. Shelley abandons his Aeschylus model at this point, and political rhetoric about dethroning tyrants is not enough to power the poem to a satisfying conclusion.

In May 1819, recovering from the intensity of writing *Prometheus Unbound*, Shelley resumed his tourist visits. This time, instead of focusing on classical Rome, he studied the Renaissance history and monuments of the city. This study brought him to the Palazzo Cenci, on the banks of the Tiber. This sinister old building contained the residue of a Renaissance tragedy: Count Cenci's murder of his two eldest sons and the rape of his eldest daughter, Beatrice. Shelley decided to rework the tale of the tragedy as a play and imagined it as a popular melodrama for the English stage.

Unfortunately, another tragedy was soon to befall Shelley's circle in Rome. His beloved son, four-year-old William, fell ill in late May and died on 7 June. Shelley wrote to a friend in England, "it seems to me as if, hunted by calamity as I have been, that I should never recover any cheerfulness again" (letter to Peacock, 10 June 1819, from *The Letters of Percy Bysshe Shelley*).

ANARCHY IN THE WIND

IN early September news reached the depressed Shelley household from England that served to stir Percy, at least, from the torpor caused by Will's death. The news was political and it was grim. On 16 August at St. Peter's Field on the outskirts of Manchester, some sixty thousand working men and women had gathered to discuss labor reform in the factories. Armed and mounted militia, sent by the government to break up the meeting, instead turned the field into the site of a massacre. Many of the unarmed workers, including women and children, were slaughtered that day on St. Peter's Field, and the event went down in history as "Peterloo."

Shelley was both horrified and immediately inspired to write a poem of political protest about the event. In twelve concentrated days of writing he produced *The Mask of Anarchy*. The poem begins with a scene depicting the English ministers arriving at St. Peter's Field riding the horses that will eventually trample the crowd. They bring murder, fraud, hypocrisy, and destruction with them, in a political echo of the four horses of the Apocalypse from the Bible. Anarchy rides the last horse, a white horse "splashed with blood":

> With a pace stately and fast
> Over the English land he passed,
> Trampling to a mire of blood
> The adoring multitude.
>
> (38–42)

A woman then lies beneath the horse's hooves—at Peterloo, a mother and her child fell before one of the horsemen and the child was trampled to death—and, in Shelley's poem, Anarchy halts. The woman, a "maniac maid" named Hope, tells the crowd that her father's name is Time and he is weak with waiting for a better day. " 'He has had child after child / And the dust of death is piled /Over every one but me— / Misery, oh, Misery!' " (94–97). She and the rest of the crowd expect Anarchy to trample her at this point, but instead a vengeful Shape rises out of the mist and strikes Anarchy from his horse, killing him. Hope is delivered, and she rises to issue a call for the English working classes to demonstrate for reform and to claim their political rights.

She asks everyone who suffers to assemble: "'From the workhouse and the prison / Where pale as corpses newly risen / Women, children, young and old / Groan for pain, and weep for cold. . . .' " (275–279). She begs them to stand calm if the Tyrant's militia attacks them, to cross their arms "like a forest close and mute" (320), and to wait for the laws of England to arbitrate for them and to set them free.

Shelley is advocating passive resistance and mass demonstrations as the instruments of political change—a far different solution from the one he had advocated years before in Ireland. Shelley's political philosophy had matured with experience, though his call for the people to seek justice was as eloquent as it had ever been. The final stanza of the poem exhorts them:

> "Rise like Lions after slumber
> In unvanquishable number—
> Shake your chains to earth like dew
> Which in sleep had fallen on you—
> Ye are many—they are few."
>
> (368–372)

As soon as he completed *The Mask of Anarchy*, Shelley sent it to Leigh Hunt in London for publication in *The Examiner*. If Hunt had published it, as Shelley wished, the poem would certainly have provoked an explosive reaction in England. Shelley might have finally reached the broad readership he sought; he might finally have found an audience that sympathized with him.

Instead, Hunt chose not to publish the poem. The reason had to do with English law at the time. Publishers of any material deemed seditious—

and anything demanding reform and addressed to the working classes was considered such—could be sued for libel, fined heavily, and even imprisoned. This had already happened on numerous occasions, and 1819 witnessed the worst of the English government's attack on the free press: there were more than seventy-five prosecutions for libel during that year. Hunt chose not to risk publication, and *The Mask of Anarchy* became another of Shelley's works that did not appear in print until long after his death.

In October the Shelleys moved to Florence; Mary was expecting a baby in November and they wanted to be near Dr. Bell, a famous surgeon residing there. Shelley spent his first weeks in Florence roaming the city, with many excursions to the Uffizi Gallery and its fine sculptures. In late October he walked alone along the banks of the Arno, the wind blowing in hard from the west. This experience prompted him to write the poem that remains one of his best known today, "Ode to the West Wind."

The poem begins with the wind itself bringing autumn: "O wild West Wind, thou breath of Autumn's being / Thou, from whose unseen presence the leaves dead / Are driven, like ghosts from an enchanter fleeing. . . ." The wind knocks the leaves and the seeds of trees to the earth, where they eventually rest like corpses underground. However, far from being the harbinger of death, the west wind provokes the seasonal change that culminates in spring, when the seeds germinate and push their buds up "with living hues and odours." The speaker wishes the west wind could take him up too like a leaf because "I fall upon the thorns of life! I bleed! / A heavy weight of hours has chained and bowed / One too like thee: tameless, and swift, and proud."

Shelley wishes the wind could scatter his "words among mankind," like the trumpet of a prophecy. No doubt Shelley wished some instrument could be the means of distributing his *Mask of Anarchy* to an audience in England. His urge to help the working classes was great, but exiled in Italy and blocked by his publishers in England, he felt powerless to reach them. Nevertheless, the poem ends on one of his characteristic moments of hope: "O Wind, / If Winter comes, can Spring be far behind?"

CITY OF GHOSTS

In January 1820 the Shelleys moved to Pisa, where the weather was warmer than Florence,

though the city itself was past its glory. Once a thriving port city, Pisa had since been enclosed by marshes; ruined medieval palaces marked its heyday. Shelley's thoughts, however, were on current politics, and in that frame of mind he added more to a prose work he was composing, *A Philosophical View of Reform*, as well as a poem on a similar theme, his "Ode to Liberty." In the prose work Shelley's aim was to trace the development of political thought and revolution from the emergence of human liberty in ancient times to the struggle for reform in his own. Shelley believed that liberty in human thought and action was a social "law" and that all societies moved toward it in the course of their development. Shelley also believed that periods of great social upheaval prompted the production of great literature.

Unfortunately, like so many of Shelley's political writings, these works did not appear during Shelley's life—indeed, *A Philosophical View of Reform* was not published until a century after his death. What did appear was an edition of his melodramatic play, *The Cenci*. This play, though considered shocking and gruesome by some critics, sold very well and garnered mostly positive reviews.

In the late summer of 1820 Claire left the Shelleys to take a position as governess in Florence. Mary Shelley had long resented Claire's presence in their household, so it was a relief to her, though a sad parting for Shelley. He worked, however, on other poems, such as "The Witch of Atlas," a fantasy about a witch who creates a hermaphrodite for a companion, and on translations from Homer and Dante.

Lonely without Claire, and needing a third woman to complete his idea of female companionship, Shelley went through a brief infatuation with a beautiful Italian girl, Emilia Viviani, whose parents had confined her in a convent while they found a suitable husband for her. Shelley, himself imprisoned that fall by ill health and depression, wrote her many a woeful poem. In January 1821 Shelley composed his *Epipsychidion* (meaning the "soul out of my soul," or "the beloved"), a poem that is as close as he ever came to autobiography in his writings. The poem is dedicated to Emilia, rather than to Mary, and many stanzas underscore Shelley's feelings of unrequited love for her.

I never thought before my death to see
Youth's vision thus made perfect. Emily,

I love thee; though the world by no thin name
Will hide that love from its unvalued shame.
(41–44)

The poem depicts a man in crisis; a man who has searched all his life for love but not been satisfied with the "mortal forms" of love he's found. Eventually an emotional crisis finds him "at bay, wounded and weak and panting" (273–274), at which point he is rescued by the being who seems to be his true love, a woman characterized as "the moon." Unfortunately, he ultimately discovers that his moon goddess is "cold" and he "lay . . . nor alive nor dead." It is clear from Shelley's manuscripts, and Mary Shelley's later comments on them, that she was the moon. She rescued him from his unhappy marriage to Harriet Westbrook, but ultimately she turned cold toward Shelley (prompted, perhaps, by the deaths of Clara and "Willmouse" in Italy). A vision then comes and rescues the poet once again, and this vision is the pure, lovely Emilia Viviani.

Epipsychidion is nothing if not sad. It reveals Shelley's constant search for a woman who will love him completely and his consistent failure to find her. Emilia Viviani, as it happens, was soon married to someone else, ending Shelley's courtly wooing of her with poetry and letters.

DEATHS AND POEMS

THE young poet John Keats died in 1821, and Shelley wrote *Adonais*, an elegy for him. Shelley told Claire of the poem, noting that writing poetry offered him his only mental relief from "the stormy mist of sensations." Storms were much on Shelley's mind, and they make their way into *Adonais*, a poem that owes much to Milton's *Lycidas*.

The breath whose might I have invoked in song
Descends on me; my spirit's bark is driven,
Far from the shore, far from the trembling throng
Whose sails were never to the tempest given;
The massy earth and sphered skies are riven!
I am borne darkly, fearfully, afar;
Whilst, burning through the inmost veil of Heaven,
The soul of Adonais, like a star,
Beacons from the abode where the Eternal are.
(487–495)

In the fall of 1821 the Greek war for independence was heating up, and Shelley was inspired to write *Hellas*, a long poem that mingles the current war

with an ancient one depicted in Aeschylus' *The Persians*. Shelley hoped the rapid publication of *Hellas* would help the Greeks in their struggle for independence, and when a small edition appeared in February 1822 it turned out to be the last of Shelley's works that he would ever see in print.

In 1822 Byron had once again joined the Shelleys in Pisa, and the two men resumed their camaraderie. It was hard, however, for Shelley to work in the shadow of the greatest living poet of his time. (Byron's *Don Juan* and *Cain* were thought by most critics, including Shelley, as two of the best poems ever written.) As usual when unable to spur his own creative work, Shelley turned to translation. During this period he translated Goethe's *Faust*. He also felt miserably alienated from Mary, as is evident from one of the poems he gave their friends Edward and Jane Williams. One stanza reads:

When I return to my cold home, you ask
Why I am not as I have lately been?
You spoil me for the task
Of acting a forced part in life's dull scene.
Of wearing on my brow the idle mask
Of author, great or mean,
In the world's carnival. I sought
Peace thus, & but in you I found it not.

Soon Shelley had developed a new infatuation with Jane Williams, to whom most of his final poems were dedicated.

THE BAY OF SPEZIA

IN April 1822 Claire Clairmont's worst fears about Allegra, her daughter being raised by Byron, were realized: Allegra died of typhus fever at the convent school where Byron had placed her. Shelley immediately decided to move his ménage from Pisa to Lerici, a fishing village on the Bay of Spezia, for the summer. Claire nearly went mad with grief, but at least their surroundings in Lerici were physically beautiful. Shelley wrote to Byron, "Nature is here as vivid as we are dismal, and we have built, as Faust says, 'our little world in the great world of all' " (*The Letters of Percy Bysshe Shelley*, p. 423).

Edward and Jane Williams lived with the Shelleys at their rented house on the shores of the Bay of Spezia, and Shelley, still an avid boater, acquired a swift twenty-four-foot schooner, the *Don Juan*. Shelley spent the summer sailing with the Edwards; his own creative force had been quenched by the presence of Byron; as he wrote to a friend in France, "I do not write—I have lived too long near Lord Byron & the sun has extinguished the glow worm. . . ." (letter to Horace Smith from *The Letters of Percy Bysshe Shelley*, p. 423). Nevertheless, in late May, Shelley began to compose the last poem he would ever write, "The Triumph of Life."

This poem, the title of which connotes a happy victory for modern readers, was anything but. Instead, it comes from a Roman concept that Shelley found on the arches of Constantine and Titus. The Roman triumph was a cruel moment of victory over conquered peoples, and Shelley's poem depicts the conquest of life over human happiness. Life brings physical aging, grief, guilt, intellectual failure, and remorse.

The poem follows the structure of Dante's *Inferno*, including the terza rima, or triple rhyme scheme of *aba, bcb, cdc,* and so on, with the middle rhyme of each tercet, or group of three, becoming the first and third rhyme of the following group. Further, in an echo of Dante's being guided through hell by Virgil, the poet-narrator of Shelley's poem is guided through "the pageant of life" by Rousseau—the spirit of Shelley's age, who believed in free love and social justice. The poem is grim: Life is depicted as a chariot that rolls over humanity with deadly force. Humans dance stupidly toward their inevitable death in a macabre image reminiscent of medieval paintings of the Black Plague.

In the historical evolution of personages and events that Shelley loved elaborating, Rousseau describes to the poet the successive ages of man and the fall of every empire, the death of every leader. Nevertheless, there is still one note of hope in the long dirge of death and remorse, and that note is still, for Shelley, love: "In words of hate and awe, the wondrous story / How all things are transfigured, except Love."

The last complete stanza of the poem that Shelley wrote begins: "Then, what is Life?" But he was never able to answer it, because the *Don Juan* sank under full sail, in the Bay of Spezia, on 8 July 1822. Shelley was on board, with Edward Williams and a boat boy, when a summer squall overtook their craft. The captain of a nearby boat looked away from the struggling schooner for a moment and when he looked back, the *Don Juan* had disappeared beneath the waves.

Shelley's body washed onto the beach ten days later. In the presence of Lord Byron, Leigh Hunt, and several local fisherman, his body was burned on the beach. Later, his ashes were placed in a Protestant cemetery in Rome. Mary Shelley returned to England to raise their one surviving child, Percy Florence Shelley, who later inherited the family fortune.

SELECTED BIBLIOGRAPHY

I. COLLECTED WORKS. *The Complete Poetical Works of Shelley*, edited by Thomas Hutchinson (Oxford, 1904), corrected in a new edition by G. M. Mathews (London, 1970); *Shelley's Prose: or, The Trumpet of a Prophecy*, edited by David L. Clark (Albuquerque, N.M., 1966); *The Complete Poetical Works of Percy Bysshe Shelley*, edited by Neville Rogers; two of four proposed volumes published to date (Oxford, 1972–); *The Lyrics of Shelley*, edited by Judith Chernaik (Cleveland, 1972); *Shelley's Poetry and Prose,* edited by Donald Reiman and Sharon B. Powers (New York and London, 1977).

II. FIRST EDITIONS OF INDIVIDUAL WORKS. *Zastrozzi; a Romance* (London, 1810); *Queen Mab; A Philosophical Poem, with Notes* (London, self-published anonymously, 1813); *Alastor; or, the Spirit of Solitude: and Other Poems* (London, 1816); *History of a Six Weeks' Tour Through a Part of France, Switzerland, Germany, and Holland* (written with Mary, published as "anonymous" by Hookham & Ollier, London, 1817, this volume contains the first edition of "Mont Blanc"); *Laon and Cythna,* suppressed and reissued as *The Revolt of Islam* (London, 1818); *Rosalind and Helen, A Modern Eclogue, with Other Poems* (London, 1819); *The Cenci: A Tragedy in Five Acts* (London, 1819).

Prometheus Unbound: A Lyrical Drama in Four Acts, with Other Poems (London, 1820); *Oedipus Tyrannus: or, Swellfoot the Tyrant. A Tragedy in Two Acts* (London, self-published anonymously, 1820); *Epipsychidion: Verses Addressed to the Noble and Unfortunate Lady Emilia V— Now Imprisoned in the Convent of—*(by Anonymous, London, 1821); *Adonais: An Elegy on the Death of John Keats, Author of Endymion, Hyperion, etc.* (Pisa, 1821); *Hellas: A Lyrical Drama* (London, 1822); *Posthumous Poems of Percy Bysshe Shelley*, edited by Mary Shelley (London, 1824); *The Mask of Anarchy. A Poem.* (London, 1832); *Essays, Letters from Abroad, Translations and Fragments*, ed., Mary Shelley (London, 1840); *A Philosophical View of Reform* (London, 1920).

III. LETTERS AND JOURNALS. *The Letters of Percy Bysshe Shelley*, edited by Frederick L. Jones, 2 vols. (Oxford, 1965); *The Journals of Claire Clairmont*, edited by Marion Kingston Stocking (Cambridge, Mass., 1968); *The Letters of Mary Wollstonecraft Shelley*, edited by Betty T. Bennett, 3 vols. (Baltimore and London, 1980–1988); *The Journals of Mary Shelley, 1814–44*, edited by Paula R. Feldman and Diana Scott-Kilvert (Oxford, 1987).

IV. BIOGRAPHIES. Thomas Jefferson Hogg, *The Life of Percy Bysshe Shelley*, 2 vols. (1858; reprinted London, 1933); Newman Ivey White, *Shelley*, 2 vols. (London, 1947); Kenneth Neill Cameron, *The Young Shelley: Genesis of a Radical* (London, 1950); Richard Holmes, *Shelley: The Pursuit* (London, 1975); Michael O'Neill, *Percy Bysshe Shelley: A Literary Life* (London, 1989; New York, 1990).

V. CRITICAL EDITIONS AND TEXTUAL STUDIES. Harold Bloom, *Shelley's Mythmaking* (New Haven, 1959); Kenneth Neill Cameron and Donald H. Reiman, eds., *Shelley and His Circle: 1773–1822* (Cambridge, Mass., 1961–1986; this is a catalog edition of extensively annotated manuscripts in the Carl H. Pforzheimer Library that includes mss. by the Shelleys, Byron, Mary Wollstonecraft, William Godwin, Leigh Hunt, and others); Donald H. Reiman, *Shelley's "The Triumph of Life": A Critical Study, Based on a Text Newly Edited from the Bodleian Manuscript* (Urbana, Ill., 1965); Earl R. Wasserman, *Shelley: A Critical Reading* (London and Baltimore, 1971); Timothy Webb, *The Violet in the Crucible: Shelley and Translation* (Oxford, 1976).

William Keach, *Shelley's Style* (London and New York, 1984); Angela Leighton, *Shelley and the Sublime: An Interpretation of the Major Poems* (Cambridge, 1984); Timothy Clark, *Embodying Revolution: The Figure of the Poet in Shelley* (Oxford, 1989); Alan M. Weinberg, *Shelley's Italian Experience* (London, 1991); Kelvin Everest, ed., *Percy Bysshe Shelley, Bicentenary Essays* (Bury St. Edmunds, U.K., 1992). Barbara Charlesworth Gelpi, *Shelley's Goddess: Maternity, Language, Subjectivity* (New York, 1992); Betty T. Bennett and Stuart Curran, eds., *Shelley: Poet and Legislator of the World* (London and Baltimore, 1996); Timothy Clark and Jerrold E. Hogle, eds., *Evaluating Shelley* (Edinburgh, 1996).

ROBERT LOUIS STEVENSON

(1850–1894)

Claire Harman

IN THE TWENTY years immediately following his early death in 1894, Robert Louis Stevenson enjoyed cult status as a sentimental hero. His bohemianism and chronic illness linked him in the popular imagination with the short-lived Romantic poets, while his travels and residence in the South Seas appealed to the Victorian taste for exoticism at a safe remove. As in the case of Robert Browning, Stevenson died at a time when his popularity was rising sharply; subsequently, he became admired as much for his life (particularly his stoic endurance of ill health) as for his many works, which were placed virtually beyond criticism. When the first biography of Stevenson appeared in 1901, written with the full backing of the Stevenson estate by his cousin, Graham Balfour, his former friend W. E. Henley was disgusted by the portrait that emerged of "this Seraph in Chocolate, this barley-sugar effigy of a real man" (*Pall Mall* 25, December 1901).

Henley's outburst was more than justified. The overpraise of Robert Louis Stevenson's eloquence and "literary tact"—to borrow a phrase from Stevenson's own essay on Walt Whitman (*Familiar Studies of Men and Books*, 1882)—and his categorization as a writer for children has obscured his real excellences, as a storyteller, descriptive writer, and acute analyst of character and motivation. Stevenson was the least "Victorian" of all Victorian writers, much more immediately appealing to modern audiences than the mannered fin-de-siécle school that postdates him. He was an ironist and iconoclast, an admirer of Herbert Spencer, Darwin, Thoreau, and Whitman: his essays addressed the urgent scientific, moral and aesthetic questions of the day, and his novels and stories dramatized them. As a young man, he longed to emulate the style and substance of Victorian multi-volume novels, but in fact became part of the movement that supplanted the model, a modern man of letters. His interest in psychology anticipated the concerns of the next century, his confessional tone was tuned to it, even the forms he liked best—those of short story and novella—have been more popular in our own day than his.

Reaction to the hagiographical view of Stevenson was sharp when it set in. The publication of Frank Swinnerton's 1914 biography, *R. L. Stevenson: A Critical Study*, started a process of debunking by which Stevenson was simultaneously stripped of his "seraph" status and excluded from serious consideration as a literary artist, not deemed fit for study in the new academic discipline of English Literature. J. L. Furnas's 1952 biography, *Voyage to Windward*, was the first to treat the subject unsentimentally and with objectivity; many further critical studies of Stevenson have appeared since then, and latterly Stevenson's work has enjoyed a surge of attention from scholars of colonialism, anthropology, gender, and literary theory.

EARLY LIFE

ROBERT Lewis Balfour Stevenson was born in Edinburgh, Scotland, on 13 November 1850. He came from a distinguished family of engineers and inventors; his grandfather Robert built the Bell Rock lighthouse and designed bridges, harbors and prisons, his father, Thomas Stevenson, made the first wave dynamometer, and his uncle Alan was another lighthouse builder, responsible for Skerryvore and Dhu Heartach, off the coast of Fife. "Whenever I smell salt water, I know that I am not far from one of the works of my ancestors," Stevenson wrote with pride in 1880. Within two generations the family had risen to the top of the Edinburgh professional class, the epitome of all that was respectable, hardworking, and God-fearing.

Stevenson's mother, Margaret, was the youngest daughter of the Reverend Lewis Balfour of Colinton, a family of impeccable Scots pedigree and piety. She was thin and frail: the birth of her son almost killed her, and she had no more children. The boy was weak in the chest and spent an unusually large part of his childhood in the sick room, a fact that had a marked effect on his personality, philosophy and writing. He was tended by his doting parents and "second mother," the nurse Alison Cunningham, a strict Calvinist, devoted to hellfire. Under her care, as Stevenson wrote later, "I continued to have my mind defiled with a whole crowd of dismal and morbid devotees. . . . I was sentimental, snivelling, goody, morbidly religious" (quoted in Nicholas Rankin, *Dead Man's Chest*, p. 19).

As a child, Stevenson was a daydreamer, fantasist, and voracious reader. He invented elaborate stories to while away the long days in bed, a dreamy state famously evoked in his poem for children "The Land of Counterpane" (from *A Child's Garden of Verses*, 1885). He had very little formal schooling. His closest companion was his cousin Bob (R. A. M. Stevenson, later a well-known art historian), with whom he drew maps of imaginary countries where they waged war with toy soldiers. Stevenson said once that he would have liked to have been a soldier better than anything else, had his health allowed. He maintained a romanticized view of military adventure and a consuming interest in games of war (and real wars) all his life.

Stevenson's career as a writer can be said to have begun even before he could write. At a very early age he dictated two works to his mother (a "History of Moses" and "The Book of Joseph") and composed plays for his toy theater. When he was only fifteen, he wrote a short history of a seventeenth-century religious dispute called *The Pentland Rising*, and by the time he reached maturity he had a string of half-made novels and plays in progress. "Men are born with various manias," he wrote in his essay "My First Book" (*My First Book*, ed. Jerome K. Jerome, 1894), "from my earliest childhood it was mine to make a plaything of imaginary series of events."

Stevenson intended to join the distinguished family firm of engineers, but after three years' apprenticeship gave up engineering in favor of the law, a compromise to placate his parents. Privately, he had formed "a determination to be an author" and gave up law in turn as soon as he had qualified. He found the low life of Edinburgh seductive; with his fellow law student and lifelong friend Charles Baxter, Stevenson became an habitué of the town's dives and gas-lit back streets. In pubs he was known as "Velvet Coat"

because of his bohemian clothes, and he considered himself "a dead hand with a harridan." He drank heavily and took opium (a habit he continued for at least ten years). The sense of Stevenson leading an experimental double life at this time is powerful; Edinburgh was a city of lawyers and doctors, drinkers and prostitutes, the city of Burke and Hare and, obliquely, of Jekyll and Hyde.

Thomas Stevenson had encouraged independence in his son, but when at the age of twenty-two "Louis" (as he had adapted his given name) declared himself to be an atheist, both parents were horrified. Stevenson's revolt against his strict religious upbringing was traumatic, and the tense and oppressive atmosphere that ruled in the household for months afterwards led to the first of Stevenson's many long visits away, the start of years of travel. One of his retreats was his cousin's house in Sussex, where he met and fell in love with Frances Sitwell, an unhappily married woman thirteen years his senior who was attractive, intelligent, and emancipated. His letters to her (published in their entirety for the first time in the 1994–1995 Yale edition of Stevenson's *Letters*) dramatize the difficulties Stevenson was having in defining this relationship with his "Madonna," who fell halfway between mother and wife.

EARLY PUBLICATIONS, ESSAYS, AND TRAVEL BOOKS

FRANCES Sitwell did not actively encourage her young admirer's suit but did nurture his literary ambitions. Through her Stevenson made the friendships and connections—with Sidney Colvin, Lesley Stephen, Edmund Gosse, and W. E. Henley—that were to sustain him as a writer in a life of self-imposed exile. Lesley Stephen was then editor of *Cornhill*, which published many of Stevenson's essays from 1874 onward; Colvin was an art critic and later the director of the Fitzwilliam Museum in Cambridge (he became Stevenson's literary executor); Henley was a poet whose triumph over invalidism and disability impressed Stevenson profoundly and with whom he collaborated on several plays, including *Deacon Brodie: or The Double Life* (1880), the true story of an Edinburgh cabinetmaker and thief who was eventually hanged on a gibbet of his own design. Stevenson in his turn inspired deep affection in his new friends; he was by all accounts a brilliant talker and keen to live up to the literary world's expectations of him.

During these years, Stevenson experimented with a wide variety of poetry and prose styles in a self-consciously regulated apprenticeship. "I practised to acquire [proficiency] as men learn to whittle, in a wager with myself," he wrote in an essay called "A College Magazine" (*Memories and Portraits*, 1887):

I was unsuccessful, and I knew it; and tried again and was again unsuccessful and always unsuccessful; but at least in these vain bouts, I got some practice in rhythm, in harmony, in construction and the co-ordination of parts. I have thus played the sedulous ape to Hazlitt, to Lamb, to Wordsworth, to Sir Thomas Browne, to Defoe, to Hawthorne, to Montaigne, to Baudelaire and to Obermann. . . . That, like it or not, is the way to learn to write.

The influence of these favorite writers, particularly that of Charles Lamb and William Hazlitt (of whom he wanted to write a biography), hangs over Stevenson's early essays. The market for such material was booming, and by the time of his first book in 1878, Stevenson was already well known as a contributor of short stories and quirky, amusing essays to the many literary magazines and periodicals of the day.

The year that he met Frances Sitwell, 1873, Stevenson had his first lung hemorrhage and was diagnosed as possibly tubercular, necessitating a long rest cure in the south of France. He was miserable there, "idle among spiritless idlers; not perhaps dying, yet hardly living either," but used the experience as the basis of his most famous early essay, "Ordered South" (included in his first collection *Virginibus Puerisque*, 1881). Awareness of his mortality was, from this time on, prominent in his thoughts and a sharp spur to his literary ambitions.

"Ordered South" contains the famous apothegm "To travel hopefully is better than to arrive," a stylized version of his statement in *Travels with a Donkey* that he wanted "not to go anywhere but to go." Stevenson had always been restless, and his illness made him even more so. In a deliberate attempt to generate material for a book, he set off in the autumn of 1876 on a canoe trip from Antwerp to Pointoise in northeast France with an old Edinburgh friend, Walter Simpson. His light-hearted account of the journey, *An Inland Voyage*, is constructed mostly from the logbook he kept, interspersed with descriptive and contemplative passages. Not surprisingly, in such an artificially conceived book, the tone seems rather uneven and the author uncertain whether to make his experiences over into purely comic material or not.

In a sense *An Inland Voyage* was also hijacked by events, because between making the trip (which he and Simpson cut short out of boredom) and composing the book the following year, Stevenson's objectives altered. He had gone straight from Pointoise to join his cousin Bob and a circle of expatriate artists living in Grez-sur-Loing, near Fontainebleau, and there met the formidable woman he would later marry.

Fanny Osbourne was ten years older than Stevenson, born in Indianapolis. At seventeen she had married charming but feckless Sam Osbourne, then secretary to the governor of Indiana, later a captain in a local regiment fighting for the Union in the Civil War. Sam set out on the prospecting trail to Nevada in the 1860s, where his wife and infant daughter Belle soon joined him, traveling perilously via the Panama Canal (the railroad was not finished by this date). When Sam Osbourne moved on to Montana in search of silver, Fanny went to live in San Francisco. Despite the births of two more children, it became clear that the marriage was a failure, and Fanny made the bold decision to move to Europe, ostensibly to study art with her teenaged daughter. Her youngest child died in Paris soon after, and the family was still recovering from this blow when they met the Stevenson cousins.

Over the next two summers, spent in Grez, and at intervals in Paris and London, Fanny and Louis became lovers, though she had to return to California at her husband's insistence in 1878. During these years, Stevenson's career started to take shape. He had written and published *An Inland Voyage* (1878) and a sardonic portrait of his hometown, *Edinburgh: Picturesque Notes*, the following year. His little travel book about canoeing (prefiguring the style and substance of Jerome K. Jerome's *Three Men in a Boat* and other Victorian "leisure" literature) had become, in the writing, a veiled message to Fanny, ending with the reflection "You may paddle all day long; but it is when you come back at nightfall and look in at the familiar room that you find Love or Death awaiting you beside the stove; and the most beautiful adventures are not those we go out to seek."

Trying to distract himself from Fanny's possibly permanent return to California, Stevenson made another trip, this time on his own: a twelve-day walking tour from Monastier to St. Jean de Gard, which he wrote up as *Travels with a Donkey in the*

Cévennes (1879). The book is admired for its atmospheric descriptions of the highlands, rivers, and lush valleys of the Ardêche and Cevennes, and for its acute and amusing character sketches (not least of which being the depiction of the relationship between the writer and his intransigent companion, Modestine the donkey), but what distinguished *Travels with a Donkey* from other travel memoirs was the autobiographical subtext suggested through its air of unspecified melancholy. Like *An Inland Voyage,Travels with a Donkey* is really a series of veiled declarations to his lover: "I blessed God that I was free to wander, free to hope, and free to love." This simultaneous suggesting and withholding of information is essentially a novelist's technique; Stevenson's use of it was highly influential in the development of "travel writing" in the twentieth century.

In July 1879 Fanny Osbourne summoned Stevenson by telegram to meet her in California. The journey was arduous and perilous for Stevenson, but he had reached an emotional watershed: embarking for America and his subsequent marriage to Fanny were the decisive acts of his life. He spoke of his journey as "a test," and the two books he wrote about his trans-American voyage, *The Emigrant Ship* and *The Emigrant Train,* were as much about psychological trial (as in the romance tradition of the lover's quest) as physical endurance. The descriptions of life in steerage and on road and rail across America were rawly sensual: "To descend on an empty stomach into Steerage No. 1, was an adventure that required some nerve, the stench was atrocious; each respiration tasted in the throat like some horrible kind of cheese: and the squalid aspect of the place was aggravated by so many people worming themselves into their clothes in the twilight of the bunks."

The books shocked Stevenson's father, who thought them "unworthy." To placate the family, they remained unpublished in Stevenson's lifetime (appearing eventually as *The Amateur Emigrant,* 1895) but indicate the kind of powerfully realistic turn Stevenson's writing might have taken this early in his career, prefiguring the kind of subject and style he adopted when writing of the South Seas in the 1890s.

1880–1884: *CALIFORNIA, SCOTLAND AND* TREASURE ISLAND

FANNY Osbourne's divorce came through in January 1880, and the following May she and Louis were married. The prospects were not good: they had little money and now complete responsibility for Fanny's children, Isobel and Lloyd Osbourne. They spent their honeymoon squatting in a deserted mining shack in the Napa Valley, ostensibly because it cost very little (though from the account Stevenson wrote of these months, in *The Silverado Squatters,* one can also detect a strong desire both to get "back to nature" in the manner of his admired Thoreau and to *épater les bourgeois* with details of the squalor he chose to live in). The short book, published in 1883, contains a memorable chapter on "The Scot Abroad," an unsentimental reflection on national loyalties and the enchantment lent by distance, mixed feelings that underpin all Stevenson's writings about his homeland.

Later that year, the couple made the long journey back to Scotland to present Fanny to Louis's parents. They were easier to please than Stevenson's London friends, who privately criticized Fanny's Americanness, her unconventional dress, forthright manner, and graying hair. An antipathy arose between her and Colvin and Henley in particular, that quickly helped alienate Louis from his former life and affected his later decision to move abroad permanently.

Stevenson published two collections of essays in 1881 and 1882, *Virginibus Puerisque* and *Familiar Studies of Men and Books,* both consisting of pieces he had contributed to periodicals since 1876. The first was the more reflective of the two, Stevenson self-consciously setting out a system of belief that was essentially kind ("violently kind" at times, to use his own description of love), humane, rational, and optimistic. His aim, as expressed in the dedication of the book to W. E. Henley, was to be an advocate of youth (the title means "from young men and maids"): "to state temperately the beliefs of youth as opposed to the contentions of age," which he did by assuming a rather tongue-in-cheek, heavily aphoristic style, loaded with facetious cynicism. The title pieces, four long meditations on love, marriage and faithfulness, are particularly full of this sermonizing tone (including Stevenson's famous definitions of marriage as "a field of battle, not a bed of roses" and "a sort of friendship recognized by the police").

Familiar Studies of Men and Books takes a more formal approach to its nine subjects (all literary, except for the Japanese social reformer Yoshida-Torajiro). Some of the pieces had a long history: "Walt Whitman" had been composed and recomposed over a period of more than five years and reflects Stevenson's deep admiration for the poet and his philosophy (both still treated with derision by a large part of the reading public at this date): "It is the duty of the poet to induce . . . moments of clear sight. He is the declared enemy of all living by reflex action, of all that is done betwixt sleep and waking, of all the pleasureless pleasurings and imaginary duties in which we coin away our hearts and fritter invaluable years."

It was this sympathy with Whitman's (and Thoreau's) anti-conventionality that caused the critic William Archer (in the first substantial review of Stevenson's work to date in *Time*, November 1885) to call Stevenson "an aggressive optimist, than whom, to some of us, there can scarcely be a more bewildering phenomenon." Stevenson replied to him in a series of lengthy letters defending his point of view: "not only do I believe that literature should give joy, but I see a universe, I suppose, eternally different from yours: a solemn, a terrible but a very joyous and noble universe; where . . . any brave man may make out a life that shall be happy for himself and, by so being, beneficent to those about him" (*Letters*, ed. Booth and Mehew, vol. 5). But Stevenson's claim, in the same letter to Archer, that illness did not "colour my view of life" was disingenuous. Expectation of death shaped and refined his stock-in-trade stoicism, and he was to a great extent at the mercy of circumstance.

Stevenson did not pursue the critical monograph style of *Familiar Studies of Men and Books*, but it indicates his virtuosity. Amply motivated by the need to make a living and naturally gifted with a facility to "play the sedulous ape," he seemed in the first ten years of his career to be trying his hand at every sort of writing. In 1882 his first collection of short stories, *New Arabian Nights*, was published in two volumes. They included "The Pavilion on the Links," an atmospheric melodrama set on the East Lothian coast, and the ingenious "The Suicide Club," a story based around the dark secrets of supposedly respectable people, prefiguring Stevenson's own "The Strange Case of Dr. Jekyll and Mr. Hyde" and the Sherlock Holmes stories of Stevenson's younger admirer and fellow-Scot, Arthur Conan Doyle.

Stevenson's enormous output of writing continued the following year with the children's adventure story for which he is probably now best known, *Treasure Island* (1883). It was Stevenson's first full-length fiction, begun casually on vacation in Braemar in the summer of 1880 to entertain his stepson Lloyd Osbourne, who was then twelve. Stevenson sold the unfinished story to *Young Folks*, a children's paper, which began publishing it almost immediately. "It had to be a story for boys. No need of psychology or fine writing," he wrote in an autobiographical essay, "My First Book" (*Essays and Poems*), but *Treasure Island* soon developed into something much more sophisticated than he had anticipated.

The plot is pure romance: a boy, Jim Hawkins, gains possession of a valuable treasure map when a disreputable old sailor named Billy Bones dies at the inn run by Jim's widowed mother. Bones, who has been followed by his ex-shipmate Blind Pew, turns out to have been one of a notorious band of pirates, led by the late Captain Flint. It is Flint's map that Jim and his mother find among Bones's things and hide from the gang when they storm the house. Jim shows the map to the local squire and doctor, who understand its significance and decide to mount an expedition to the Caribbean in search of Flint's gold.

The naiveté of the treasure-seeking party is immediately obvious. When Squire Trelawney goes to Bristol to rent and fit out a boat, the *Hispaniola*, his purpose is easily discovered and several of Flint's former comrades insinuate themselves onto the crew. The most flamboyant of these is Long John Silver, a one-legged sea cook whose friendliness and spirit attract Jim Hawkins' admiration; the two become close friends. Once they are at sea, however, Jim is appalled to overhear a conversation in which Silver makes clear his intention to mutiny and steal the map; from this point on he and his friends are constantly on the alert. When they reach Treasure Island, the mutiny takes place and Jim is separated from the squire's party, who take refuge in Flint's old stockade. Jim has his own adventures; he meets another of Flint's old cronies, Ben Gunn, who has been marooned on the island for years and has gone slightly mad; using Gunn's coracle, Jim rows out to the *Hispaniola* and rescues the ship from the pirates single-handedly (killing Israel Hands in an intensely dramatic scene on the rigging). Returning to the stockade, where there has been a bloody fight over possession of the treasure map, Jim is captured by Silver and his men. But the mutineers soon turn on their own leader, Silver, when the map leads them to an empty site (Ben Gunn had found the gold on his own years before) and they are only just prevented from killing both Silver and Jim by the timely reappearance of Squire Trelawney and the doctor. The story ends with departure from the island and Silver temporarily spared punishment (which he avoids altogether by jumping ship in South America).

The enduring appeal of the book resides as much in its psychological realism as in the gripping plot. The development of Jim Hawkins from gullible child to resourceful and active young man (who goes through a shocking rite of passage when forced to kill Israel Hands) gives the story weight and significance. There is no romanticization of the adult world Jim is about to join. Greed and self-interest rule everyone (with the exception perhaps of Dr. Livesey), and the former crimes of the pirates, though never made explicit, show in their brutal manners and powerful fear of each other. Even Silver's parrot, which as survivor of generations of buccaneer owners can be seen as a sort of record-keeper, uses language "passing belief for wickedness,"; as Silver remarks, "you can't touch pitch and not be mucked."

The creation of Long John Silver is in itself one of Stevenson's finest achievements. He was based deliberately on Stevenson's friend W. E. Henley, both in his physical disability (Henley had had his left leg amputated after a long and painful tuberculous disease) and in his charismatic personality. Silver can be brutal and cruel but presents a benign, even charming exterior most of the time. His abrupt changes of demeanor from willing servant to bloodthirsty gang leader (reflecting Stevenson's interest in duality) provide a constantly shifting background against which Jim Hawkins has to learn to evaluate character. The proof of Jim's maturing judgment, as well as of Silver's core qualities of courage and geniality, is that the two retain a grudging but genuine admiration for each other at the end of the book, despite discovering how little they actually have in common.

Overlapping with the composition of *Treasure Island* was Stevenson's other children's classic, *A Child's Garden of Verses*, finished under extraordinary circumstances while Stevenson was dangerously ill in Hyères in the South of France. Bedridden in a darkened room (because of an attack of ophthalmia), one hand bound close, and hemorrhaging from his lungs, Stevenson wrote laboriously on paper pinned to a board. The bright, poignant poems of childish pastimes and daydreams that he produced, including "My Shadow," "The Land of Counterpane," "The Lamp-lighter," "The Land of Nod" and "From a Railway Carriage," are remarkable for their replication of a child's point of view and are among the best-known and best-loved poems for children ever written:

> Faster than fairies, faster than witches,
> Bridges and houses, hedges and ditches;
> All charging along like troops in a battle,
> All through the meadows the horses and cattle:
> All of the sights of the hill and the plain
> Fly as thick as driving rain;
> And ever again, in the wink of an eye,
> Painted stations whistle by.
> ("From a Railway Carriage")

1884–1886: BOURNEMOUTH, KIDNAPPED, AND JEKYLL AND HYDE

IN 1884, Stevenson and his wife moved from Hyères to Bournemouth to be nearer to his ailing father in Edinburgh. Here he composed his two other classics, *Kidnapped* (1886) and *The Strange Case of Dr. Jekyll and Mr. Hyde* (1886), the latter one of the most influential psychological fables in literature, arising out of the same early scientific studies of schizophrenia and male hysteria that consumed Sigmund Freud at the same time. The way in which the story was composed was an almost too neat demonstration of the ideas contained in it. Stevenson was woken up by his wife while dreaming two short scenes, including the transformation of Hyde in front of his pursuers. In "A Chapter on Dreams" he attributes this initial spurt of inspiration to the "Brownies," the forces of his subconscious that have no moral sense, but "are somewhat fantastic, like their stories hot and hot, full of passion and the picturesque, alive with animating incident" (*Essays and Poems*). He wrote the story rapidly as a conventional "crawler," but argued with his wife over it and destroyed his work, later rewriting the whole thing in a matter of days. After a slow start, sales of the slim "shilling shocker" rose to forty thousand copies in the first six months, assuring Stevenson fame on both sides of the Atlantic.

The theme of duality had occupied Stevenson for years and appears in many of his works, from his early collaborative play with Henley (*Deacon Brodie, or The Double Life*) through his vision of

Edinburgh (in *Picturesque Notes*) as a city that leads "a double existence" to stories that feature an actual "fetch" or doppleganger, as in "Markheim" and "The Tale of Tod Lapraik." Doubleness is central to his very theory of composition, as set out in his essay "A Chapter on Dreams," where Stevenson claims that the inventive side of his writing was beyond his conscious control. In *Dr. Jekyll and Mr. Hyde* his concern is less with moral opposites (Hyde is pure evil, but Jekyll is a mixture of good and bad) than with moral ambivalence and the difficulty of controlling the self, or even knowing what "the self" means.

Much of the power of this great psychological thriller comes from its compactness and claustrophobic urban setting in the smog-filled streets of mid-Victorian London (which appears here strangely like Edinburgh at its most Gothic). The book is peopled entirely with male characters: bachelors, lawyers, and doctors, London Scotsmen "about as emotional as a bagpipe," who provide a skeptical audience for the action of the story. One of their number, Dr. Jekyll, is a mature, respected, and affluent man who seems to have everything he might desire (except a wife, though this is not mentioned as an issue). Jekyll is religious and an active philanthropist. His vices, which remain unspecified, are not criminal—"many a man would have blazoned such irregularities as I was guilty of"—but a morbid sense of shame leads him to believe that he has two natures. If he could only separate them, Jekyll believes that "life would be relieved of all that is unbearable" and with this benign motive he attempts to discover a drug that will "shake the very fortress of identity." However, the potion he invents does not discriminate between moral states but simply allows whichever is uppermost to predominate. As Jekyll's ambition and self-interest are in the ascendant when he first experiments with the drug, his wicked alter ego Edward Hyde appears.

The description of the first transformation is justly famous; after "racking pangs" and "grinding in the bones," Hyde feels "something indescribably new, and, from its novelty, incredibly sweet":

I felt younger, lighter, happier in body; within I was conscious of a heady recklessness, a current of disordered sensual images running like a mill race in my fancy, a solution of the bonds of obligation, an unknown but not an innocent freedom of the soul. I knew myself, at the first breath of this new life, to be more wicked, tenfold more wicked, sold a slave to my original evil; and the thought, in that moment, braced and delighted me like wine.

(1979 edition, pp. 83–84)

It is only because he is now Hyde that this birth into a life of license and immorality can be described so rapturously. Hyde is also aware that he is physically smaller than Jekyll, as well as thinner and younger, being the underdeveloped side of the man. People take him for Jekyll's young protégé (with an undeniable suggestion that they are interpreting the relationship as a sexual one); Utterson the lawyer addresses him as "Master Hyde," and smaller clothes have to be found to fit him.

Hyde experiences "a leap of welcome" when he sees himself in the mirror for the first time, but his effect on other people is very different. Though the only crime he commits in the novella is the murder of Sir Danvers Carew, Hyde incites hatred in onlookers even over the early incident of knocking down a little girl in the street. The crowd almost lynches him for this, so strong is the sense of pure evil he exudes. Enfield, narrator of this part of the story, finds he cannot describe Hyde physically: "he gives a strong feeling of deformity, although I couldn't specify the point." Utterson calls him "something troglodytic, shall we say?"—an inference which that has given rise to all the subsequent representations of Hyde on film and on stage as a kind of degenerate ape man.

Another misleading interpretation is that Jekyll and Hyde represent exclusive moral states, a point that proves crucial to the plot, as it is Jekyll's own assumption. Hyde is completely evil, but Jekyll is a mixture of good and bad; the moral weighting is therefore strongly towards the bad, making it difficult for Jekyll to retain the upper hand. In the end, Jekyll does not commit suicide but simply runs out of the powder necessary to make his transforming potion. The person who commits suicide is Hyde, in fear of the gallows and now unable to take refuge in Jekyll. The way in which Stevenson carries the characterization through to the very end is masterly, with the coup de theatre of the final section written by Jekyll as he sits in his cabinet with no more of the saving potion, waiting to be deposed forever by Hyde.

The issues raised in the story continued to interest Stevenson profoundly and recur in his writing.

In the 1890s, he was in correspondence with the folklorist Andrew Lang and F. W. H. Myers, founder of the Society for Psychical Research (of which Stevenson became a member), and he was performing psychological experiments on himself to prove that he was, in many ordinary instances, "two people,"; he referred to the two as *"myself"* and *"the other fellow."* The realization that parts of his own subconscious were continually in conflict with each other informed much of his writing and is at the root of his creative consciousness.

Contemporary critics have generally interpreted the "doubleness" in the story as a psychosexual allegory. According to Karl Miller, in *Doubles: Studies in Literary History,* "If there can be no certainty about Stevenson's sexual uncertainty or ambivalence, it is certain that this was the time for such a thing. . . . The Nineties School of Duality framed a dialect, and a dialectic, for the love that dared not speak its name" (p. 216). Elaine Showalter, in her chapter "Dr. Jekyll and Mr. Hyde" in *Sexual Anarchy,* has called the story "a fable of fin-de-siécle homosexual panic" (p. 107), while Wayne Koestenbaum (in *Double Talk: The Erotics of Male Literary Collaboration*) links Stevenson's repeated use of the word "queer" in the story to similar patterns in *The Ebb-Tide* and *The Wrecker* (both written in collaboration with his stepson, Lloyd Osbourne); Koestenbaum goes as far as to say that Stevenson "introduced homosexual desire under the guise of boyish escapism" into his adventure stories (p. 144). The accessibility of Stevenson's work to this kind of interpretation may be all the greater because it was so close in date to—but not yet inhibited by—the beginnings of "sexology." Richard von Krafft-Ebing's *Psychopathia Sexualis* was published in 1889, establishing definitions and borderlines to sexuality, the pathologizing influence of which Stevenson had escaped altogether.

Kidnapped was published the same year as *Dr. Jekyll and Mr. Hyde,* but was a very different kind of book; not quite a "story for boys" in the *Treasure Island* mode but something darker and more ambitious. It has had lasting appeal among adult audiences. Set in the Highlands of Scotland in 1751 (still recovering from the 1745 Jacobite rebellion), it follows the adventures of a priggish Lowland youth named David Balfour, who at the beginning of the story is attempting to claim his inheritance from his duplicitous Uncle Ebenezer. The uncle pays to have the boy kidnapped and put on a boat bound for America, but David escapes, with a new acquaintance, Alan Breck Stewart, after defeating villainous Captain Hoseason and his crew in a dramatic fight in the boat's roundhouse.

Alan Breck, rendered into a memorably charismatic, conceited, and voluble character by Stevenson, is one of several real figures from history incorporated into the book (others include Cluny Macpherson, the Jacobite chieftain,; Robin Oig, son of Rob Roy; and James Stewart, "James of the Glen," Alan's kinsman and former guardian). A committed Jacobite after the Battle of Prestonpans, Alan Breck fled Scotland for France, where he enlisted in one of Louis XIV's battalions and made sporadic sorties back home to enlist Highlanders in the Stewart cause. His involvement in the so-called "Appin Murder" of the pro-government Captain Colin Campbell of Glenure, or "Red Fox" as he was sometimes known, is made into the turning point of Stevenson's novel. The incident strains David's grudging loyalty to breaking point and sends him and Alan into a headlong flight from justice ("justice" itself being a target of satire all through this book and its sequel, *Catriona,* 1893).

Stevenson seemed particularly at home with a Scottish historical subject. He had a lifelong interest in the writing of history (although he never completed a conventional historical work, apart from his short account of the Pentland Rising of Scots Covenanters, written when he was fifteen) and had at one point seriously considered himself a candidate for the chair of History at Edinburgh University. *Kidnapped* shows complete confidence with factual material (Stevenson had written about the Appin Murder in an unpublished essay in 1881) while remaining highly imaginative in its organization. The treatment and writing bear comparison with Dickens, Thackeray, or Scott, for example in the following passage recording David's first impressions of the man who turns out to be his uncle:

He was a mean, stooping, narrow-shouldered, clay-faced creature; and his age might have been anything between fifty and seventy. His nightcap was of flannel, and so was the nightgown that he wore, instead of coat and waistcoat, over his ragged shirt. . . . What he was, whether by trade or birth, was more than I could fathom; but he seemed most like an old, unprofitable serving-man, who should have been left in charge of that big house upon board wages.

(1999 edition, pp. 24–25)

The composition of *Kidnapped* was brought to an abrupt conclusion when Stevenson grew ill suddenly in 1886, and it ends rather flatly with the restitution of David's property from Uncle Ebenezer through the offices of the lawyer Rankeillor. Up to that point, however, there is a remarkable narrative flow and a succession of vivid scenes: the bleak and sinister House of Shaws, where David's uncle tries to murder the boy by sending him up a staircase leading to a steep drop; the lonely island of Earraid, upon which David is marooned at high tide; Cluny Macpherson's hideout in the mountains; and the flight across the heathery moorlands with Alan Breck, all done with sharp attention to detail, especially physical discomfort:

I would be aroused in the gloaming, to sit up in the same puddle where I had slept, and sup cold drammach; the rain driving sharp in my face or running down my back in icy trickles; the mist enfolding us like as in a gloomy chamber—or perhaps if the wind blew, falling suddenly apart and showing us the gulf of some dark valley where the streams were crying aloud.

(1999 edition, p. 216)

The relationship between Alan and David replicates in part the tensions between Jim Hawkins and his equally charismatic companion Long John Silver in *Treasure Island*, but David is an older, more cautious, and withheld character than Jim and an unwilling accomplice in most of Alan's adventures. Their politics and temperaments are mutually incompatible, and David—who narrates the story—remains unconvinced by any of his volatile friend's arguments, however much he is affected by Alan's glamour and charm. Stevenson returned to the story of David Balfour six years later in *Catriona*, a less successful adventure story than its predecessor. *Catriona* allowed the author to continue a theme that interested him intensely, the friction between Lowland and Highland sensibilities. It is another example of troubled duality, reflected in both the matter and language of an internal narrative in *Catriona* known as "The Tale of Tod Lapraik," the story of a malign "fetch." This and "Thrawn Janet" (collected in *The Merry Men and Other Fables*, 1887) were the only Stevenson stories to be written entirely in Scots dialect, and he once said that had he achieved nothing else but these two, he would have been a writer. Both have the power of compact and controlled narrative, a skill essential to the oral tradition they clearly imitate, and, in this form, problems of good and evil are worked out in bold strokes: the "bogle," or demon, appears as a separate creature that can be chased away or reappear.

In "Thrawn Janet," the devil appears as a black figure and is at its most horrific when animating Janet's corpse, as in the ghastly scene where the minister, Mr. Soulis, hears it groping its way along the corridor in the dark.

Stevenson uses Scots again, in fine balance with English, in one of his most haunting stories, "The Merry Men" (*The Merry Men and Other Tales and Fables*). He called it "a fantasia or vision of the sea" (*Letters*, vol. 5, p. 365) and in it he drew on his knowledge and love of the Scottish coast, developed in his years as an apprentice engineer building harbors and lighthouses with his father and uncle. The story deals with the struggle between good and evil played out on an epic, elemental scale, with evil embodied in the shipwrecking squalls known as "The Merry Men," which "sing" during storms and seem to leap around in a sort of black joy and lust for death. Gordon Darnaway, the narrator's crazy uncle, is infected by their malign spirit and enjoys watching them bring ships to ruin. He dies being chased into the sea by a vengeful black man, a nameless, dehumanized figure oddly akin to the running black devil in "Thrawn Janet" and the "fetch" in "The Tale of Tod Lapraik."

The other great story in this collection (which includes a weird and suggestive tale of love thwarted by heredity, "Olalla") is "Markheim," a gripping vignette about a man who has just commited murder. When a devil-like figure appears, bearings "a likeness to himself," Markheim realizes that far from being changed by his crime, he feels as virtuous and self-justified as he did before. There is no "type" of the sinner; virtues and vices are equally likely to lead to evil deeds. This bleak but liberating anagnorisis prevents him from covering up the murder by committing another one, and he sees the "devil" transfigured by a "wonderful and lovely change" before he gives himself up to justice. Written earlier in the same year as *Dr. Jekyll and Mr. Hyde*, "Markheim" shares many of its preoccupations but treats the theme mystically and mysteriously.

The year after *Kidnapped* and the sensational debut of *Dr. Jekyll and Mr. Hyde*, Stevenson published his first book of adult poems, *Underwoods*

(1887), a collection split into two very different sections, one containing highly personal poems addressed to friends, the other made up of lyrics and narrative verses all written in the form of Scottish Lowlands dialect known as Lallans. In a prefatory note, Stevenson lamented the fact that Scots was a dying language and that no one would notice if he had made any mistakes in it: "if it be not pure, alas! what matters it?"

Underwoods contains all Stevenson's most famous verses, including "The Celestial Surgeon," "The tropics vanish . . . ," "The Last Sight" (a poem about his dying father), and "Requiem," which was used as Stevenson's own grave inscription:

> Under the wide and starry sky,
>   Dig the grave and let me lie.
> Glad did I live and gladly die,
>   And I laid me down with a will.
>
> This be the verse you grave for me:
>   *Here he lies where he longed to be;*
>   *Home is the sailor, home from sea,*
>   *And the hunter home from the hill.*

1887–1888: SARANAC LAKE AND THE MASTER OF BALLANTRAE

WHEN Stevenson's father died in the spring of 1887, there seemed little reason for him and his wife to stay in Britain. On the advice of doctors, he decided to try a new tuberculosis clinic in the Adirondacks, and soon the extended family group, now including his widowed mother, Margaret Stevenson, was on the move again.

It was at Saranac that Stevenson had the idea for and wrote much of *The Master of Ballantrae* (1889), another story on the theme of duality. Set in 1745, the year of the Jacobite rebellion, a tragic framework is established early on when the Duries of Durisdeer decide to split their loyalties between the Jacobites and the king's party in an attempt to save their ancient property from both. At the toss of a coin, the elder brother, James, rides off to join Prince Charlie while the younger, Henry, stays at home. When news comes that James has died at the Battle of Culloden, Henry inherits the right to the family property and marries his brother's fiancée, Alison Graeme. But James's malign influence seems to hang over their lives, blighting the marriage and souring Henry's good name.

When James turns up some years later to reclaim his place at Durisdeer, having been adventuring abroad, a bitter struggle breaks out between the brothers. In a dramatic scene, they duel by candlelight and James appears to have been mortally wounded (another of his many false deaths in the novel). Henry is branded as a fratricide, yet James is not dead: his second reappearance is a shock Henry cannot recover from, and he flees with his wife and children. The final scenes take place in America, first in New York and then in the Adirondacks, where the brothers chase each other across the wilderness, one in search of buried money, the other bent on revenge.

James is the "Master" of the title, a glamorously wicked character, explicitly compared at one stage in the book to Milton's Satan and expressing "all I know of the devil," as Stevenson wrote to Colvin. The Master's "fraternal enemy," his younger brother Henry, is not a correspondingly clear-cut model of virtue; he is said to be "neither very bad nor very able" and is motivated for the most part by jealousy. Neither of these characters can rightly assume the role of hero; Henry's sufferance of his brother is the nearest thing to goodness, but even this is insubstantial; as soon as his patience has worn away, Henry becomes crazed with revenge, spiritually and physically corrupt as the "devil" he thinks his brother is: "there was something very daunting in his look; something to my eyes not rightly human."

The uncertain moral framework of the book is reflected in its unusual structure, a pastiche of Sir Walter Scott's technique in the *Tales of My Landlord* novels. There are several narrators, the main one of which, the Durie family steward, Ephraim Mackellar, is ostensibly trying to set the record straight about the tragedy of Durisdeer, citing letters and eyewitness accounts to fill the gaps in his own knowledge. This archive is then entrusted to the family lawyer, with instructions that it must not be opened for a hundred years; through the lawyer's successors it falls into the hands of Johnstone Thomson (a cameo portrait of Charles Baxter), who shows it to his writer friend (Stevenson), who "edits" it for publication. This elaborate joke, set up in the preface and extended through footnotes in the text, sits rather uneasily with the essentially tragic and at times melodramatic narrative but shows Stevenson toying with an awareness of his place as the only contemporary heir to and developer of the Scott tradition.

The ending of the book, when the body of the Master of Ballantrae is exhumed on a moonlit plateau in the Adirondacks and resuscitated by his faithful servant, Secundra Dass (causing the instant death from shock of his brother), has been criticized for being contrived and farfetched but was actually based on a true story of a fakir being buried alive, told to Stevenson by his uncle. Its exoticism was part of Stevenson's plan to make this book "world-wide enough," setting scenes in the French Indies, the Atlantic Ocean, and India and including grittily realistic depictions of Native American warfare and behavior on board the pirate ship the *Sarah* (a far cry from the *Hispaniola* of *Treasure Island*). Stevenson was trying to differentiate between his adventures for boys and his adult novels, but what impressed one reviewer as providing "meat for men" struck another as "grimy." Critics generally preferred Stevenson in lighter mode.

Stevenson thrived in the intense cold of the Adirondack winter, but the rest of his family found Saranac Lake merely uncomfortable, and the following year the whole household moved on to San Francisco, where Fanny had hired a luxury yacht for an extended voyage around the Pacific. The novel was finished at sea on the *Casco,* on the brink of another of Stevenson's dramatic life changes.

1888–1894: SAMOA, IN THE SOUTH SEAS, AND THE LAST NOVELS

STEVENSON was thirty-eight years old when he set off on his first voyage to the Marquesas, Tahiti, and Hawaii, a cruise lasting eighteen months. Despite encountering "every sort of minor misfortune . . . contrary winds and seas, pertinacious rains, declining stores," he saw a dramatic improvement in his health and spirits. In Hawaii, where they were visiting Fanny's daughter Isobel, who had married a painter named Joe Strong, Stevenson was drawn into the sovereignty disputes that dominated island politics at the time and which became a sort of mission or crusade for him in the following years. Stevenson, the first influential westerner to take an interest in the cause of Polynesian independence, became a friend and ally of the king and was fired with the idea to write "*the* book about the South Seas." He was also attracted to the congenial climate of the Pacific and rather unexpectedly decided to set up home there in 1891, buying an overgrown 400-acre estate on Upolu.

The five years in Samoa saw Stevenson develop from a chronic invalid to the active and energetic head of a large and demanding estate, the respected "chief" of a strange clan of servants, family, and hangers-on. "Since Byron was in Greece," Edmund Gosse wrote to Stevenson, "nothing has appealed to the ordinary literary man as so picturesque as that you should be in the South Seas."

But Samoa was no paradise; despite the improvement in Stevenson's vitality, these were chaotic years full of backbreaking physical work and the necessity to turn out books as fast as possible to meet the expenses of his many dependents. It was imperative that Stevenson continued to write commercially viable novels such as the frothy romance *St. Ives* (a story set mostly in and around Edinburgh during the Revolutionary Wars and left unfinished at his death) and *Catriona*, the sequel to *Kidnapped.* But he was also experimenting with subjects suggested by his new surroundings, stories about the "white trash" of the Pacific (in *The Wrecker*, 1892, "The Beach of Falesá," and *The Ebb-Tide*, 1894), which he intuited that the "great hulking, bullering whale, the public" would probably reject on the very grounds of their novelty. The first of these, a collaboration with Lloyd Osbourne, was the nearest Stevenson came to writing a mystery story, with the opening chapters, set in Paris and San Fransisco, contributing less to the plot than to the establishment of character and atmosphere.

The physical and intellectual isolation of Stevenson's years in Samoa had many effects, from the obsessional interest he began to take in politics (writing a series of long essay-letters about the Polynesian wars to *The Times*) to the systematic questioning of his own methods and achievement. There was an aggressive new realism in his work, possibly fueled by the difficulty he had in "explaining" Samoa to his distant audience. In consequence, his nonfiction took on a tone very different from that of the charming, lighthearted essays and travel books with which he had first made his name in the 1870s. His essays on the South Seas and *A Footnote to History* have never yet caught the public imagination but were groundbreaking books, showing Stevenson to have been far ahead of his time in his awareness of depopulation in Polynesia and the kind of enervation and crises of racial identity it brought in its wake. The parallels he saw constantly between the South Sea islanders and the plight of Scottish Highlanders after the "clearances" of the eighteenth and early nineteenth centuries are illuminating as social history and also as a gloss on his own writing, obsessed as it always had been with the nature of Scottishness. In the South Seas, he became a native "makar," both of Polynesia (his long poem "Ticonderoga" was written for the king of Hawaii, and his story "The Bottle Imp" was the first western fiction to be translated into a Polynesian language) and of Scotland, writing some of his most Scots books in the tropics: *Weir of Hermiston, Catriona,* and his homage to his lighthouse-building forebears, *Records of a Family of Engineers.*

Stevenson was ready to broach the problem of how to deal with sex in his fiction, a subject he had veered away from for years. His almost exclusively all-male novels have often provoked the criticism that Stevenson lacked some vital ingredient from his imagination, but his letters show that this reticence was more to do with knowing that anything true he wanted to say about sex would sound vulgar. "I am a realist and a prosaist," he wrote to Colvin, "and a most fanatical lover of plain physical sensations plainly and expressly rendered; hence my perils. To do love in the same spirit as I did (for instance) D. Balfour's fatigue in the heather [in *Kidnapped*]; my dear sir, there were some grossness ready made!" When his story "The Beach of Falesá" was published (it deals with the tricking of a native girl into a sham marriage by a white trader), it was condemned as immoral, as Stevenson had feared. "I feel despair weigh upon my wrists," he wrote to Colvin. "Think how beautiful it would be not to have to mind the critics, and not even the darkest of the crowd. I should probably amuse myself with works that would make your hair curl."

On 3 December 1894 Stevenson died suddenly of a stroke (not the tuberculosis he had gone in fear of so long) at age forty-four and was buried, with great ceremony, on the top of Vâea mountain on Upolu. Up to the morning of his death, he had been working enthusiastically on a novel that stood at some 45,000 words. The story, published in 1896 as *Weir of Hermiston,* acquired a special sentimental status as Stevenson's "unfinished masterpiece" and has been valued as an indicator of how the author's talent might have developed. The story is set in the second decade of the nineteenth century and centers on the troubled relationship between the Lord Justice-Clerk, Adam Weir, and his son Archie. Weir is a "hanging-judge" on the Scottish bench and a speaker of pure Scots. He is natural, almost repulsively so, and finds a recon-

dite pleasure in his work (mostly condemning criminals to death) because it involves the exercise of a skill. His refined son Archie, a young law student, is repelled by Weir's relish for his vocation, interpreting it as sadism, but Stevenson makes it clear that Weir is not so much devoid of finer feelings as impotent to express them. His stoicism about this is depicted as bleakly admirable: "If he failed to gain his son's friendship, or even his son's toleration, on he went up the great, bare staircase of his duty, uncheered and undepressed."

The emotional stalemate between father and son is broken when Archie openly criticizes Weir's views on capital punishment and, after a traumatic confrontation, is banished to the family's country estate in Hermiston. There he meets and falls in love with Christina Elliott, the niece of the Weirs' servant Kirstie, but Archie's reticence and scrupulousness mean the romance proceeds only slowly. In the meantime, his dashing friend Frank Innes makes plans to seduce Christina, and at the point where the manuscript ends, is about to put them into action. Stevenson's plan for the book—as told to his amanuensis, Isobel Strong—included Archie's murder of Frank and subsequent trial by the "hanging-judge," his own father. This would have been a highly theatrical climax to the Oedipal conflict at the heart of the story.

The use of both Scots and English in *Weir of Hermiston* (far more integrated than in *Catriona,* for example) was ambitious, and Stevenson seemed at last to be prepared to make women characters central to the plot. Kirstie Elliott is a remarkable creation, a border-country earth goddess, emotional yet unsentimental, who, in an interestingly ambiguous passage, identifies herself with both lovers. Her niece, the younger Kirstie, is a fine portrait of youthful self-consciousness and egotism, "in love with herself" and the sexual power at her disposal. There is some evidence that Stevenson was drawing on an adolescent romance of his own in the depiction of the love story; certainly the ambivalent relationship between Weir and his son reflects that of Stevenson and his father, just as the landscape of the novel—Edinburgh and the Pentland Hills—had a powerful autobiographical significance for the author too.

CONCLUSION

STEVENSON'S most famous books—*Dr. Jekyll and Mr. Hyde, Kidnapped, Treasure Island,* and *A Child's*

Garden of Verses—have never been out of print since their first publications and are now established classics, more famous than the author could have imagined possible, yet few readers would necessarily connect them to the same source. Stevenson's extremely prolific and wide-ranging career, which has made him so hard to pigeonhole, has also diffused his reputation, which exists in separate pockets: children's writer, romance writer, Scottish writer, travel writer, writer on the supernatural and the darker side of human nature. Gifted with facility and spurred on by the powerful motivators of necessity and ill health, he wrote quickly and often with apparent lack of direction—something that can be identified in his work even when the overall result (*Treasure Island,* for example) is preeminently successful.

Various things draw together the diverse productions of this erratic but inspired writer. One is his eloquence, dazzling at times, another his frequent return to certain relationships (the protégé/mentor, father/son motifs in all the major novels) and certain themes, especially the theme of duality. This last is so integral to his work and his methods of composition (split narratives, collaboration with other writers, and the use of dreams as sources) that Elaine Showalter has described Stevenson as "the fin-de-siecle laureate of the double life" (*Sexual Anarchy,* p. 106). His preference is always for ambiguity over certainty, changeability over continuity, and he is almost obsessively concerned with the contradictions in character that problematize all theories of identity. These are traits that have made his work extremely useful and interesting to students of Victorian sexual and social constructs.

Of course the character who fascinated Stevenson most was himself, and there is a sense in which all his works are a form of autobiography. In his 1985 book *Footsteps,* Richard Holmes wrote: "Stevenson existed very largely in, and through, his contact with other people: his books are written for his public; his letters for his friends; even his private journal is a way of giving social expression—externalising—his otherwise inarticulate thoughts" (p. 68). Stevenson made himself his subject, not simply in the autobiographical essays and travel books (or through the manufacture of incidents to feed into such works) but in the constant investigation and exposure of his own motivations and creative processes. His *Letters,* available in their entirety only since 1994–1995, show this bet-

ter than anywhere else. In them, Stevenson's prevarications, false starts, misplaced enthusiasms, and creative anxieties are fully open to view. He emerges as someone who is at once deeply anxious about his own creative difficulties and at the same time fascinated by the process of composition.

Stevenson's stoic endurance of illness—amply documented in his early essays—undoubtedly placed him in a relation to his readers that was sympathetic to the point of indulgence. This continued and mushroomed after his death so that, for years, Stevenson was spoken about more in terms of his "potential" as a lost great figure of English (rather than Scots) literature than for what he had actually achieved. With hindsight, we can see that his potential was more than fulfilled during his lifetime, and if his complete oeuvre, so full of half-written novels, half-planned stories, and half-baked schemes for plays and histories, lacks the neatness and deliberation of a carefully ordered career, it is all the more interesting and instructive because of it.

SELECTED BIBLIOGRAPHY

I. COLLECTED WORKS. *Edinburgh Edition of the Works of Robert Louis Stevenson* (1894–1898); *Thistle Edition* (New York, 1895–1912); *Pentland Edition* (London, 1906–1907); *Biographical Edition* (New York, 1908–1912); *Swanston Edition* (London, 1911); *Vailima Edition* (London, 1922); *Tusitala Edition* (London, 1924); *Skerryvore Edition* (London, 1924–1926); *South Seas Edition* (New York, 1925); *Collected Poems of Robert Louis Stevenson,* ed. J. A. Smith (London, 1950; 2nd ed. 1971); *Robert Louis Stevenson: The Collected Shorter Fiction,* ed. Peter Stoneley (London, 1991); *Robert Louis Stevenson, The Complete Short Stories,* ed. Ian Bell (Edinburgh, 1993); *Robert Louis Stevenson, Shorter Scottish Fiction,* ed. Roderick Watson (Edinburgh, 1995); *Centenary Edition* (3 vols. to date; Edinburgh, 1995–).

II. NOVELS. *Treasure Island* (London, Paris, and New York, 1883); *Prince Otto* (London, 1885); *Kidnapped* (London, 1886); *The Black Arrow* (London and New York, 1888); *The Wrong Box* (London, 1889), with Lloyd Osbourne; *The Master of Ballantrae* (London and New York, 1889); *The Wrecker* (London, 1892), with Lloyd Osbourne; *Catriona* (London, Paris, and Melbourne, 1893); *The Ebb-Tide* (London, 1894), with Lloyd Osbourne; *Weir of Hermiston* (London, 1896), posthumously published; *St Ives* (London, 1897), posthumously published.

III. SHORT STORIES. *New Arabian Nights* (London, 1882); *More New Arabian Nights: The Dynamiter* (London, 1885), with Fanny Van de Grift Stevenson; *The Strange Case of*

Dr Jekyll and Mr Hyde (London, 1886); *The Merry Men and Other Stories* (London, 1887); *Island Nights' Entertainments* (London, 1893); *Fables* (New York, 1896), posthumously published.

IV. POETRY. *A Child's Garden of Verses* (London, 1885); *Underwoods* (London, 1887); *Ballads* (London, 1890); *Songs of Travel* (London, 1896), posthumously published.

V. PLAYS. (All in collaboration with W. E. Henley.) *Deacon Brodie, or The Double Life: A Melodrama* (London, 1880); *Admiral Guinea* (Edinburgh, 1884); *Beau Austin* (Edinburgh, 1884); *Macaire* (Edinburgh, 1885).

VI. NONFICTION. *An Inland Voyage* (London, 1878); *Edinburgh: Picturesque Notes* (London, 1879); *Travels with a Donkey in the Cévennes* (London, 1879); *Virginibus Puerisque* (London, 1881); *Familiar Studies of Men and Books* (London, 1882); *The Silverado Squatters* (London, 1883); *Memories and Portraits* (London, 1887); *Memoir of Fleeming Jenkin* (New York, 1887); *Across the Plains and Other Essays* (London, 1892); *A Footnote to History* (London, 1892).

Posthumously published: *The Amateur Emigrant* (Chicago, 1895); *Vailima Letters* (London, 1895); *In the South Seas* (New York, 1896); *Letters to His Family and Friends*, ed. Sidney Colvin (London, 1899); *Lay Morals and Other Papers* (London, 1911).

VII. LETTERS. *R. L. S.: Stevenson's Letters to Charles Baxter*, ed. Delancey Ferguson and Marshall Waingrow (London and New Haven, 1956); *The Letters of Robert Louis Stevenson*, ed. Bradford A. Booth and Ernest Mehew, 8 vols., (New Haven and London, 1984–1985); *Selected Letters of Robert Louis Stevenson*, ed. Ernest Mehew (New Haven and London, 1997).

VIII. SELECTED MODERN EDITIONS. *Dr Jekyll and Mr Hyde and Other Stories*, ed. Jenni Calder (London, 1979); *The Master of Ballantrae*, ed. Emma Letley (London, 1983); *Travels with a Donkey/An Inland Voyage/The Silverado Squatters*, intr. Trevor Royle (London, 1984); *The Lantern-Bearers and Other Essays,* ed. Jeremy Treglowan (London, 1988); *Essays and Poems*, ed. Claire Harman (London, 1992); *The Ebb-Tide*, ed. David Daiches (London, 1994); *The Wrong Box*, intr. David Pascoe (Oxford, 1995); *The Dynamiter*, ed. Neil Singard (Stroud, 1997); *In the South Seas*, ed. Neil Rennie (London, 1998); *Kidnapped; or The Lad with the Silver Button*, ed. Barry Menikoff (San Merino, 1999); *The Strange Case of Dr Jekyll and Mr Hyde,* ed. John MacRae (London, 2000).

IX. CRITICAL AND BIOGRAPHICAL STUDIES. William Archer, "Robert Louis Stevenson: His Style and Thought," in *Time 2* (London, November 1885); Graham Balfour, *The Life of Robert Louis Stevenson* (London, 1901); J. A. Hammerton, *Stevensoniana* (new ed., Edinburgh, 1907); Frank Swinnerton, *R. L. Stevenson: A Critical Study* (London, 1914); David Daiches, *Robert Louis Stevenson, A Revaluation* (London, 1946); Malcolm Elwin: *The Strange Case of Robert Louis Stevenson* (London, 1950); J. L. Furnas, *Voyage to Windward: The Life of Robert Louis Stevenson* (London, 1952); E. M. Eigner, *Robert Louis Stevenson and Romantic Tradition* (1967); Jenni Calder, *RLS: A Life Study* (London, 1980); Roger G. Swearingen, *The Prose Writings of Robert Louis Stevenson* (London, 1980); Paul Maixner, ed., *Robert Louis Stevenson: The Critical Heritage* (London, 1981); J. R. Hammond, *A Robert Louis Stevenson Companion* (London, 1984); Richard Holmes, *Footsteps: Adventures of a Romantic Biographer* (London, 1985); Karl Miller, *Doubles: Studies in Literary History* (Oxford, 1985); Wayne Koestenbaum, *Double Talk: The Erotics of Male Literary Collaboration* (New York and London, 1989); Elaine Showalter, *Sexual Anarchy: Gender and Culture at the Fin de Siècle* (New York, 1990; London, 1991); Ian Hamilton, *Keepers of the Flame: Literary Estates and the Rise of Biography* (London, 1992).

JONATHAN SWIFT

(1667–1745)

Fred Bilson

JONATHAN SWIFT WAS born 30 November 1667 in Dublin. His father had died shortly before Swift's birth, leaving his mother, Abigail Erick Swift, virtually penniless. Swift was therefore educated by his father's brothers, who sent him in turn to Kilkenny College, the leading school in Ireland at the time, and to Trinity College, Dublin, then Ireland's only University. Swift was an undisciplined student, resentful of authority, but was allowed to graduate Bachelor of Arts in February 1686. He was thus ready for a career in Ireland, either as a lawyer or as a minister of the Anglican (Protestant Episcopalian) Church.

Swift left Ireland in 1688, during King James's invasion, and eventually lived as a member of Sir William Temple's household at Moor Park, Surrey. Temple had been an acquaintance of Swift's Uncle Godwin. A former diplomat, he had by then retired to the seclusion of his estate in the country to indulge a taste for philosophy and criticism that showed a conservative set of mind. At Moor Park, Swift spent his time reading voraciously and began a career in public life, acting as a commissioner from Temple to King William III. In this household, he met Esther Johnson, the daughter of Temple's housekeeper, who is known to Swift and his readers as Stella (the Latin for "star," which is the meaning of the Hebrew name Esther). She was then eight years old, and the relationship between them was the closest either ever enjoyed. In 1745, Swift would be buried next to her.

At this time too Swift began to show signs of the illness that never left him. Ménière's syndrome is a defect of the inner ear that causes three symptoms that can occur either together or separately—tinnitus with vertigo, deafness, and vomiting. The treatment available at that time would have conspired to make the disease worse and Swift actually returned to Ireland because it was suggested that breathing his native air might improve him. He felt himself a prisoner there, and went back to England.

Some months of 1692 were spent in Oxford, where Swift graduated Master of Arts. This was an astute political move—it opened the possibility, if Swift decided to be a clergyman, of making a career in the much richer Church of England rather than in Ireland. This was also the period of his early poems.

Swift was ordained in Ireland and presented with a living near Belfast, where he met and proposed to Jane Waring ("Varina") in terms that forced her to refuse. He returned to Moor Park, where Temple died in 1699.

Soon Swift was back in Ireland as chaplain to Berkeley, the Lord Justice of Ireland. A thin living at Laracor and a post at St. Patrick's Cathedral, Dublin came his way, and Trinity College awarded him the degree of Doctor of Divinity in 1702.

Stella and her chaperone Rebecca Dingley were installed in Dublin in 1701 and lived as close friends of Swift.

In 1704 he published *A Tale of a Tub*, which acquired a scandalous reputation that was to interfere with his efforts between 1707 and 1714 to make an effective career in English politics. During these years he moved between Ireland and England. His overt mission was to persuade Queen Anne to relieve the Church in Ireland of part of its tax burden; his covert mission was to seek promotion, to become a bishop or dean in England. At first, Swift looked to the Whigs for support—Temple had been a Whig. The Whigs represented the most powerful members of society—large landowners and an emerging class of financiers. He made friends with Joseph Addison and Sir Richard Steele and in 1709 contributed to Steele's journal, *The Tatler*.

1710 was a year of crisis for the Whigs; by August their leader Sidney Godolphin had been forced out of office and replaced by a Tory ministry under Harley and Bolingbroke. Swift changed sides and began producing journalism for the Tories, particularly the journal *The Examiner*, from November 1710 to June 1711, and the pamphlet *The Conduct of the Allies* in November 1711. Swift remained at the center of the Tory Party and in 1713 was appointed Dean of St. Patrick's, Dublin. Friendships with Alexander Pope and John Arbuthnot took the place of those with Addison and Steele. Much of this is reported in Swift's letters to Stella, known as the *Journal to Stella* (1710–1713).

In August 1714, Queen Anne died and the Tories seemed for a moment to be temporizing with the supporters of the exiled Stuarts. They lost power, never to regain it in Swift's lifetime. Disappointed of promotion in England, Swift returned to live permanently in Ireland. At about this time a woman he had known in London, Esther Vanhomrigh (pronounced "VAN um ree"), also settled in Ireland.

Swift was to live another thirty years, outliving almost all his friends, including Esther Johnson and Esther Vanhomrigh. These thirty years were the years of Swift's greatest achievement. His works included *Gulliver's Travels,* his most mature poetry, and pamphlets on the condition of Ireland that are of substantial historical and literary importance. Two years before his death he lost his reason, and he died in October 1745.

REPUTATION

SWIFT wrote a considerable amount, both in prose and verse, but very little of it, apart from the political pamphlets, was meant for wide public distribution. He was only paid for one of his works (two hundred pounds for *Gulliver's Travels*). This means that his work is often aimed at a small circle of friends (sometimes a single individual) and is full of private references and shared knowledge, even including language code, like the baby-talk in *Journal to Stella,* or the regular knowing references to coffee-drinking in the correspondence with Vanessa. However, at least three of Swift's works were enormous successes within his own lifetime. *Gulliver's Travels* (1726, rev. 1735) was probably the most popular book written in the century. *The Conduct of the Allies* (1711), according to Samuel Johnson, was the founding document of Toryism (political Conservatism) and defined its ideology. *The Drapiers Letters* (1724) embodied the first stirrings of an Irish nationalist consciousness. Again according to Johnson, it demonstrated that a good cause, strongly argued, could succeed even where its

advocates had no political power. Swift himself was perhaps clearer-sighted, writing "all government without the consent of the governed is the very definition of slavery. But in fact eleven men well armed will certainly subdue one man in his shirt." (*A Letter to the Whole People of Ireland [Drapier's Letter IV]* in Ross and Woolley (1984), p. 442)

As a result, there were many books that attempted to explicate his work by revealing details of his life. Swift himself wrote *The Family of Swift,* which contains the story of his being kidnapped by his nurse as a baby. It also has the story of losing a catch while fishing as a boy; this was "the type of all my future disappointments." In fact, though he may have hoped for promotion, he cannot have expected it. Queen Anne was unlikely to make him a bishop; he was unmarried, he had no reputation as a preacher, he had put himself on the wrong side of intellectual debate in *The Battle of the Books* (1704), and he had appeared to write mockingly of religion in *A Tale of a Tub.*

On the other hand, his best autobiographical writing is probably in *Verses on the Death of Dr Swift* (1731). Here he claims to have been the advocate of the rights of the Irish, despite the risk of impeachment for treason; in this he had enjoyed the support of the people:

> Fair LIBERTY was all his cry;
> For her he stood prepared to die . . .
> Two kingdoms, just as faction led
> Had set a price upon his head;
> But not a traitor could be found
> To sell him for six hundred pound.

Not that he is blind to the faults of the Irish. He left his money to build a hospital for the insane—"He gave the little wealth he had / To build a house for fools and mad / And showed by one satiric touch / No nation wanted it so much." (p. 498)

Other writers who left memoirs included Deane Swift (Godwin Swift's grandson), Thomas Sheridan, and Laetitia Pilkington, who wrote as one of Swift's women acquaintances.

Johnson had fixed Swift's literary reputation in the *Lives of the English Poets.* He stressed Swift's originality: "perhaps no writer can easily be found that has borrowed so little, or that in all his excellencies and all his defects has so well maintained his claim to be considered as original" (Everyman, 1925, vol. 2, p. 274).

However there is also the question of his lack of taste, most strikingly in Book IV of *Gulliver's Travels*. "The greatest difficulty is to discover by what depravity of intellect he took delight in revolving ideas, from which almost every other mind shrinks with disgust. . . . He that formed these images [of the Yahoos] had nothing filthy to learn" (vol. 2, p. 272).

Above all, it was misanthropy of which Swift stood accused, a general hatred of the human race. Johnson, who had been snubbed by Swift, supports this by selected anecdotes from Swift's life. Swift's contemporaries tended to project his final decline back into his earlier life and see in what displeased them the effects of a developing madness. Swift's work then constituted a puzzle, whose solution was to be found in biographical detail.

The reevaluation of Swift has been led by work on *Gulliver's Travels*; first, studies of literary analogs and historical background have given deeper, if not richer, readings of Books I and III in particular. Above all, there has emerged a distinction suggested by James L. Clifford between "hard" and "soft" readings of Swift's work. Hard readings emphasize the difficulty and bleakness of, for example, Book IV of *Gulliver's Travels*, which is seen as a tragic work. Soft readings find Gulliver (who is carefully distinguished from Swift by such critics) a comic figure in his gullibility, and stress the role of the Portuguese captain de Mendez as a healer.

Modern critics who moved away from the biographical approach include Carole Fabricant, whose work locates Swift within the Irish context of his day. Norman O. Brown has drawn attention to the "excremental vision" in Swift, and called for the use of models drawn from psychoanalysis. The purpose is not to judge Swift sane or insane (a task to be "turned over to the psychoanalysts" in Brown's words), but to explicate his writing, to judge his insight into our collective neurosis. This approach has been particularly useful in placing Swift's writings on women. Though subjectively an anti-imperialist and anticolonialist, objectively he reflects the urge in his society to reduce the role of women, to transform them to mothers and potential mothers, and in effect to colonize their bodies.

PROSE WORKS

SWIFT is a leading writer of transactional prose—prose of advocacy in particular. For example, the *Conduct of the Allies* is very much in control of its material—the reasons for accepting the treaty that would bring to an end Queen Anne's War. First it manages the flow of long structured sentences ("periods") that build up an argument. Here Swift is arguing that classically states have one or more of five motives for war: "to check the power of some ambitious neighbor; to recover what has been unjustly taken from them; to revenge some injury they have received (which all political casuists allow); to assist some ally in a just quarrel or lastly to defend themselves when they are invaded" (*Conduct of the Allies* in Ross and Woolley (1984), p. 281).

His rhetoric displays marked parallelism. Five clauses each begin with an infinitive—"to check . . . to recover . . . to revenge . . . to assist . . . to defend." The rhythmic flow is broken by a full parenthetic clause ("which all political casuists allow") that cuts off the last two motives, which Swift wishes to address particularly. He also manages the faster mocking denunciation of England's enemies (the duke of Marlborough in particular). Here they are humiliating the queen by giving her no privacy: "Her Majesty was pursued through all her retreats, particularly at Windsor, where after the enemy possessed themselves of every inch of ground they at last attacked and stormed the castle forcing the Queen to fly to an adjoining cottage. . . . [I]t is a wonder how Her Majesty . . . was able to extricate herself" (p. 311). The general is mocked through a series of metaphors derived from strategy.

However, it is the allegorical prose of *The Battle of the Books*, *A Tale of a Tub* and *Gulliver's Travels* that is perhaps most creative—prose capable of being read at several levels.

THE ALLEGORICAL PROSE: PARODY, PASTICHE, AND POLEMICS

MIKHAIL Bakhtin has drawn attention to a particular mode of writing common in medieval times. Authors would take the dialectic they used for understanding texts and turn it loose on the most central and holy of the texts they studied. They produced a variety of songs, sermons, and other work, rereading and even mocking texts from the bible and the liturgy. Because the license such writers gave themselves was like the license people took when they dedicated themselves to misrule before Lent, Bakhtin called this mode Carnival. The archetypal writer in this tradition is François

Rabelais and he is clearly a major influence on this group of books. They may be seen as Carnival, exuberant and exhibitionistic, rich in parody and pastiche, where normal rules are suspended.

A parody is a rewriting of another text that lies below the surface. For example, Swift writes at one point in *The Battle of the Books*, "[Homer] slew Denham a stout modern who from his father's side derived his lineage from Apollo, but his mother was of mortal race"(Ross and Woolley, 1984, p. 15).

Here Swift has taken a characteristic Homeric formula, found throughout the *Iliad*, removed a classical name and replaced it with the modern Denham. He has removed part of that first text (the process is called erasure in critical theory) and substituted it. Swift's footnote tells us that Denham's poems were "unequal, extremely good and very indifferent" (Swift's footnote); this inconsistency can be comically assigned by the substitution to Denham's mixed parentage—part god, part mortal. Pastiche pays less regard to the particular wording of an original text, and is instead a sustained imitation of its general style.

Swift's writing is usually polemical, arguing one side of a question—not necessarily the right side; the viewpoint of *The Battle of the Books* is obscurantist. All three books are constructed with a first-person narrator, who is not identical with the author; irony maintains a distance between the two, as the author allows the reader access to knowledge or responses hidden from the narrator. Occasionally that irony collapses. There is a famous passage in a later pamphlet, *A Short View of the State of Ireland* (1728), where this happens in front of the reader's eyes. Swift has been ironically suggesting that Commissioners should come from England to see the wealth of Ireland: "What glorious reports would they make when they went back to England?" Then he switches perspective: "But my heart is too heavy to continue this irony longer for it is manifest that [such a] stranger would . . think himself . . . In Lapland or Iceland [seeing] . . . The miserable dress and diet and dwelling of the people . . . The families of farmers who pay great rents living in filth and nastiness upon butter-milk and potatoes. . . ."(Greenberg and Piper, 1973, p. 500).

Even the sentence structure breaks down. The question of whether the ironic control is lost is critical for a reading of *Gulliver's Travels*.

There is a strong element of game playing designed almost to baffle the dull reader, but representing some fact about reading/writing. Editions of classical texts regularly print "lacunas," gaps in the text to show where part of the original is lost. Both *The Battle of the Books* and *A Tale of a Tub* contain false lacunas, where the author simply leaves lines of asterisks to indicate breaks in the action or items too complicated to explain. This is clearly in breach of normal contracts between author and reader.

Another technique common to all three books is to wrapper the central core text with preliminary matter—advertisements, introductions, or letters. These reflect the knowledge we bring to books; we know something about them, even if we have never read them. Books "have their own fates" as objects separate from the texts they represent. In the case of *Gulliver's Travels*, the new, revised edition of 1735 has two sets of interventions between reader and text. This edition opens with a letter from Captain Gulliver to his cousin Sympson. Itself a fake in that it is dated 1727, immediately after the first publication, though it was written later, it makes claims that subvert the text of *Gulliver's Travels*. Gulliver himself had not wanted publication; the text is inaccurate; the book is a failure because it has led to no change in the behavior of the Yahoos who surround Gulliver. But Gulliver washes his hands of the situation. The manuscript of *Gulliver's Travels* is now destroyed; there is no appeal from the book the reader holds to any more original state of the text. To find Richard Sympson's original introduction to the 1726 edition after this letter is disorientating, as though Gulliver was being ignored, in a metaphor of the disregard of which he complains.

A Tale of a Tub opens with a list of other volumes the writer plans to publish that develop out of the text. *Gulliver's Travels* has a frontispiece that refers to this as Book Three of the works of Lemuel Gulliver. Where are the other books? Is our reading of *Gulliver's Travels* conditional on the fact that someone may one day choose to write Volume I or Volume II, as Defoe had done with *Robinson Crusoe*? Facing the title page is a curious portrait of Gulliver in which the line of the brow, nose, lips, and chin strongly suggests Swift himself. This has a Latin motto, *"splendide mendax"* ("a liar on a splendid scale").

In fact, this title page is itself a parody. Nigel Wood (1999) reproduces this item and also the title page of one of the volumes of the simultaneously published collected works, *The Works of J. S., D.D, D.S.P.D*, which have a conventional portrait of Swift. *Gulliver's Travels* is, in fact, Book III of this edition. The portrait of Gulliver is Swift wearing his own hair and dressed in seaman's slops. A final game is that, although nominally anonymous, *Gulliver's Travels* is signed. Book III, chapter 6 reports on the skill of police spies in reading people's letters. Correcting "hath" to "has" the passage reads: "if I should say in a letter to a friend "Our brother Tom [has] just got the piles" a man of skill in this art would discover how the same letters [could be rearranged] to the words 'Resist—a plot is brought home—The Tour'."

In fact, the original letters rearrange to "Resist— a plot is brought home. The Tour. J. S." Fox, 1995, p. 181; spelling and punctuation normalized).

THE BATTLE OF THE BOOKS

SWIFT wrote this book in support of Sir William Temple, who had entered literary controversy by advocating the merits of two classical works— Aesop's *Fables* and the *Letters* of Phalaris. The leading critic and scholar of his day, Richard Bentley, had published a negative reaction; Temple had mistaken the dates of these works and his recommendation was based on faulty scholarship. Temple and Bentley were on opposing sides in the major literary controversy of the day, the opposition between the Ancients (of which Temple and Swift were advocates) and the Moderns. As Temple and Swift saw it, the reader of taste and discrimination was superior to the critic with his arid scholarship and the work of classical authors in Latin and Greek was superior to anything contemporary.

The Battle of the Books opens with a sustained pastiche of modern histories of warfare. The first paragraph begins by advancing great theories— that invasions come from the North, because people are hungrier there—and ends with an ethnology of dogfights in the street (a satirical reference to Thomas Hobbes's model of politics). Then comes a brief history of the quarrels between Ancient and Modern authors visualized as two groups of hill dwellers on Mount Parnassus. Finally there is a sustained description of the battle of the books in the King's Library (where Bentley was the librarian); the books contain the spirits of the authors and participate in their quarrels.

Central to the book is the incident of the spider and the bee. The books watch a bee extricate himself from a spider's web that he has destroyed. The quarrel of the spider and the bee encapsulates the quarrel of the Ancients and the Moderns in its tone. Further, the two are emblematic of two approaches to reading and learning—the a priori attitude of the spider, who waits for the flies to come to him, representing the critic, and the proactive bee representing both the reader of taste and discrimination, and the pragmatic approach to life.

Aesop (who had been slighted by Bentley) draws attention to the "sweetness and light" of the bee and the infuriated modern's attack. The story continues in a pastiche of Homer's *Iliad*. This Greek poem is incomplete in the sense that it is set before the final victory of the Greeks in the Trojan War, though every reader has that victory in mind. Nor does Swift award victory to either side; in *The Battle of the Books* as in the *Iliad*, the struggle continues, suspended only by truce.

A TALE OF A TUB

A TALE of a tub is a story with no point. Swift, through the persona of the Hack—a writer who will write anything for money—moves from the title phrase itself through a series of metonyms, or words that stand for other things with which they have become associated. First he recalls an old tale about how whalers will throw a barrel off their ship so that the whale attacks it and is distracted from the whaleboat. *A Tale of a Tub* will be designed to distract the dull reader (Bentley and his sort) from the main drive of the work. The whale by a second metonymy represents Hobbes, whose book *Leviathan* (which means "the whale") was an attack on the Christian religion, because it suggests all law is made by man. The whale in turn must be distracted from its attack. Finally, there is a metonymic rereading of the tub itself. What are the three wooden structures where an ambitious man can place himself above the crowd (above the critics especially) so that those below him take in his words (literally drink in his breath)? They are the gallows, the pulpit, and the fit-up stage of the mountebank (the snake-oil man); an early illustration to the work shows a preacher in a pulpit shaped like a barrel.

The central core of *A Tale of a Tub* is a parable that probably represents the reworking of a tale from Giovanni Boccaccio's *Decameron* (Day 1, Tale

3), in which Melchisedech, a Jew, defends himself against Saladin who demands he say which is the true religion—Judaism, Christianity, or Islam. Melchisedech tells of a man who has an antique ring that is his greatest treasure. He announces that, when he dies, whichever of his sons is found to possess the ring will be his heir. For some generations this custom continues in the family, but eventually comes a father with three sons he loves equally. He has two exact copies of the ring made, so he can give a ring to each son. Now the old man is dead, explains Melchisedech, the dispute about who is the heir continues. Again, as with the *Iliad* in *The Battle of the Books*, *A Tale of a Tub* uses an analog with no resolution.

The rewritten parable has an old man with three sons, who are left not a ring, but a coat each. There is no doubt that each coat is genuine, so the focus shifts to the use the sons make of their coats. Their father's will gives rules for wearing the coats (will is, of course, a synonym of Testament). Just as in Boccaccio's tale, at first all works well. Then the brothers begin decorating their coats in accordance with the fashions they find in the world. One of the brothers, Peter, becomes arrogant both in the sense that he seeks power and wealth, and in the sense that he claims to be entitled to reinterpret the rules for wearing the coats on the basis of oral tradition, rather than the text of the will. In the end, he turns his brothers out of doors. They begin to try to restore their coats. Martin works carefully, but Jack rips his coat to shreds and eventually goes mad.

There is little difficulty interpreting this parable, but the text contains many footnotes pointing out the interpretation to the dull. Peter is the Roman Catholic Church, Jack is Calvinism, and Martin is the central tradition of the Protestant Reformation—Lutheranism or Anglicanism. Only Martin's way will prevail against Hobbes.

Interspersed in the narrative of the three coats is a series of what the author calls "digressions," which certainly arise out of the narrative but constitute a cohesive element. They deal partly with what is meant by "authorship"—making texts—and the nature of reading and inspiration. The first digression deals with critics. The old types of critic, who discriminated good writing from bad, or who established texts from manuscripts have given way to the (ironically named) TRUE CRITIC, a discoverer and collector of writer's faults, who strikes terror into writers as the sound of asses braying terrified the Scythian army. The second and third digression accuse critics of distilling books, seeking their essence, making anthologies rather than reading deeply. They know books by their indexes, "by which the whole book is governed and turned, like fishes by the tail."

A digression on Eolism discusses inspiration. Eolus was appointed by Zeus to keep the winds in a cave and control when they could go out. The Hack wishes to say that just as Peter relied on oral tradition to set aside the strict terms of the father's written will, so Jack relies on Inspiration to do the same. The syllogism, or deliberately specious argument, is: "Words are but wind; Learning is nothing but words [therefore] Learning is nothing but wind." The Hack describes how the leaders of the Eolists, such as Jack, fill themselves with wind and belch it out in their followers' faces. The description is extremely aggressive, and the aggression is directed both inwards and outwards, emphasizing the punitive nature of the process.

A digression on Madness claims that madness is essential to all advances in statecraft, in politics, and in religion, for no one but a madman could put himself forward as having superior understanding to the common sense of generally agreed-upon standards. So valuable is madness that Bedlam (the great hospital for the insane) should be emptied and its patients sent to contribute to government, commerce, and the Law.

The final section of the fable considers Jack's madness, satirizing the strange behavior of the extreme Protestants. It is comedy of stereotype and, as in all such cases, the comedy quickly evaporates, leaving only the stereotype.

Swift suffered for this book; the centrality of divine inspiration is one of the teachings of his own church, and his notion that all words are but wind is blasphemous to Christians who believe in the creating Word as a type of God. Why did he write the book? Possibly he wished to give form to two of his preoccupations. He was always disturbed by the way in which the instability of language can threaten meaning; he comes back to this theme in *Gulliver's Travels*. Swift longed for some way to stabilize and purify language, and part of the urge behind *A Tale of a Tub* is to convey the flux and fluidity that threatens it. Secondly, the book's disintegration of language is meant to convey the exhaustion of the professional preacher, teacher, or writer constantly filling his mind by reading and emptying it by writing.

JONATHAN SWIFT

GULLIVER'S TRAVELS

SINCE 1726 *Gulliver's Travels* (especially books 1 and 2) has been read and reread by millions of readers, and reworked by writers and other artists. These facts give a clue to the particular pleasure reading it offers—it is a dense text; its meanings are interlinked and complex and are not all seen at once. It is at one level a political allegory whose relevance is not restricted to the Britain of Swift's day; many readers see parallels between the corruption and timeserving of Queen Anne's court satirized in book 1 and those that surround them in their own context.

It is also an early work of science fiction/fantasy. Swift's telling of Gulliver's shipwreck in Lilliput originates an important technique of the form, giving the small detail that foretells the terror to come; Gulliver notices before he falls asleep in Lilliput that the grass was "very short and soft." Swift also has a knack for selecting narrative detail which draws obliquely on the scientific knowledge of his time.. He tells us, for example, that the Emperor of Lilliput was "past his prime, being twenty eight years and three quarters old" (book 1 chapter 2); the Lilliputian life span is shorter than the European, and the reader is left with the task of working out why.(Fox, p. 49)

The reason is, of course, that the Lilliputian metabolism is faster. One consequence of this is that Lilliputians will need to eat more, and, again without comment, Swift has them overfeed Gulliver as a result. He gets each day a pound of beef, a pound of mutton or lamb, "other victuals" (including turkey, geese, and other birds) and a "proportionable quantity of bread and wine" (book 1, chapter 2).

Sometimes the meaning of the text can be construed through a process akin to translating a foreign text, phrase by phrase. The episode of the Big-Endians and Little-Endians can be read in this way (Fox, p 64). The present king's grandfather (who equals Queen Anne's grandfather, Charles I) decreed that henceforth everyone should open boiled eggs at the big end rather than the little end, as had been the custom (which equals Charles I's attempts to change the constitution of England and the practices of the Church of England). As a result, there have been many wars (read the First and Second Civil Wars, Monmouth's Rebellion, William III's invasion of England, James II's invasion of Ireland) in which one Emperor lost his life (that is, Charles I) and another lost his throne (that is, James II). The Big-Endians are in exile in Blefuscu, where they plot war against Lilliput (substitute the Jacobites exiled in France who plot against England). You can recognize a Big-Endian by the way he eats his eggs at breakfast (just as you can recognize a Jacobite by the way he drinks his wine at dinner: when he drinks the toast "The King," he passes his wine glass across a glass of water to show he drinks to the King over the water—James III, not George II).

Translating these encoded equivalencies, however, leaves things no clearer. Swift avoids implication here as elsewhere. Are we to think that the Jacobites should be reconciled with the Hanoverians because the differences between them are so trivial? Or, more dangerously, that it would make little difference if James III replaced George II tomorrow? In fact, Swift does not interpret at all. His ironic conclusion is that in politics, as in science, you can have a great deal of knowledge without being in any way empowered by that knowledge. To understand the conflict between Hanover and Stuart is not to control that conflict.

There are strong structural parallels between the four parts of *Gulliver's Travels*. Each begins with a sea voyage during which Gulliver is separated from his companions and has to face the experience of a new society alone. The experience represents a change of perspective or scale that alienates Gulliver increasingly from the values of England. Each experience in turn reveals the new society to be dystopic—a society in which Gulliver cannot live, even if he finds it potentially ideal, and from which he must be driven out or escape. Each part ends with Gulliver returning to Europe on a ship where he is a supercargo. Neither a passenger, nor a member of the crew, he is dependent on the goodwill of the captain. There is also an element of Carnival in the American sense; one way Gulliver distances himself from his new societies is by accepting and playing up to his position as freak ("Come and see the Man Mountain, the Freak of Nature, The Man in Clothes"). The exception is the floating island of Laputa, where the scientists are the freaks, and Gulliver is in the crowd with the servants and wives.

Book 1 and book 2 are traditionally available to children, to whom they often appeal strongly. The elements of the excremental vision are usually expurgated for them, but the infantile element remains. In Lilliput, Gulliver is the Empowered Child; in Brobdignag the Threatened Child.

In Lilliput, he is suddenly the largest person in the world. Two men are appointed to take away his feces each day. His urine is magic—when he first empties his bladder in front of his captors "the people . . . opened to the right and left . . . to avoid the torrent which fell with such noise and violence" (Fox, p. 45). The other direct mention of his magic urine occurs when he extinguishes the fire in the queen's apartments, but throughout his size is his power—often an aggressive power; he pretends to want to eat some recalcitrant Lilliputians, as a Brobdignagian baby will later want to eat him.

In Brobdignag, on the other hand, he crawls away and relieves himself under a sorrel leaf—the magic of his feces and urine is gone. He is in the care of a nine-year-old girl whom he calls Glumdalclitch—Little Nurse, who is able to take care of him because she can already "dress her baby" (her doll). He is the plaything of the adolescent maids of honor in a parody of an infantile sexual initiation.

Gulliver's viewpoint emphasizes the smallness and triviality of the Lilliputians. There is some obvious satire at the expense of the courts of Queen Anne and King George I. Gulliver ingratiates himself by capturing the fleet of Lilliput's enemy Blefuscu, but his success is turned against him by enemies at court and he has to escape, first from Lilliput to Blefuscu, then by boat to the open sea. In Brobdignag he must undergo the reverse experience. He is a tiny thing from a tiny society. The philosopher king inspects Gulliver's description of England and finds it as trivial as Lilliput—worse, corrupt.

From the first, Gulliver is the great event in Lilliputian life, the Man Mountain. At first they want him to be a slave—building walls, delivering mail (or mailmen); next they make him a duke and finally they want to kill him, strip his bones, and leave them on show. He moves from slave to show.

In Brobdignag Gulliver moves from show to slave. The pattern is anticipated at the end of book 1. Gulliver takes home some Blefuscan cattle—one is eaten by rats on the journey, the rest are put on show, and make Gulliver's fortune. One of his first encounters in Brobdignag is with two rats; he has to fight for his life and survives to be put on show, and make his master's fortune.

Throughout the Brobdignag experience Gulliver is at the mercy of small animals—wasps, dogs, a frog, and a monkey all threaten his life, to the amusement of his hosts. His response is to clown (the defense of many children faced with aggression) and he ends up half drowned in cream, force-fed by the monkey, stuck in a marrow-bone by the dwarf, stunned by crab apples—always the victim of other people's magic manipulation of these fecal substitutes.

Finally, the king decides to capture a European ship, find Gulliver a wife, and breed a race of slaves who will be a sideshow forever. The final life-threatening encounter with the eagle saves Gulliver from this.

The narrative technique of all four books imposes almost complete silence on all but Gulliver. In particular, none of the women ever speaks directly, and so none ever achieves subjectivity, becoming an interesting character in her own right. We have passages of courteous description, where Gulliver tells us for example that the queen of Brobdignag and Glumdalclitch always smelled clean, unlike the maids of honor, but we also see the queen, mirroring Gulliver himself in Lilliput, as a gross feeder, "which was to me a very nauseous sight. She would crunch the wings of a lark . . . though it were nine times as large as that of a full-grown turkey" (Fox, p.110). We are told that Glumdalclitch was negligent and used to curry favor with the queen by telling her if Gulliver did something more than usually stupid.

There are only four places that report the actual words of anyone involved in the action, and three of them mark either Gulliver's arrival or his departure from one of his societies, and emphasize his alienation. In Lilliput, Gulliver gives the words the Lilliputians shout in chorus when he is pinioned (*Tolgo phonac,* for example); their collective malevolence breaks through his inability to hear them clearly. In part 2 when Gulliver's box is opened, a sailor shouts in English "If there be anybody beneath, let them speak"—the first English words Gulliver has heard in two years, and all the more disorientating for that. In part 4 the sorrel nag calls out repeatedly "Take care of thyself, gentle Yahoo" as Gulliver sails away.

The only other directly quoted words are those of the king of Brobdignag in chapter 6 of Book 2, who:

taking me into his hands, and stroking me gently, delivered himself in these words[:] . . . "My little friend Grildrig . . . for yourself (who have spent the greatest part of your life in travelling), I am well disposed to hope you may hitherto have escaped many vices of your country. But . . . I cannot but conclude the bulk of your natives to be the most pernicious race of odious little vermin that Nature ever suffered to crawl upon the surface of the earth."

(Fox, p. 132)

Swift is careful to remind us that this is not an encounter between two equal humans. That strange detail about the king stroking Gulliver creates a background impression of a man stroking, say, a cat; Gulliver is reduced from human to pet. He resolves to restore himself to favor with the king and decides to impart the secret of gunpowder. The king forbids him to mention the subject again on pain of death, and Gulliver writes "A strange effect of narrow principles and short views!" (Fox, p. 134). Gulliver clearly lacks the sense of irony that is made available to the reader.

What disappears in books 3 and 4 is the distance between the voice of the narrator, and the voice of the character Gulliver, who is no longer kept at a distance by irony, and is no longer the ingenious and clever clown who survives by his wits.

In book 3 all Gulliver's pragmatist beliefs are destroyed by his encounters with the scientists of Laputa, the projectors of Lagado, the ghosts of Glubbdubdrib, and the Struldbrugs of Luggnag. Many readers find this progressive demolition of all modern thinking alienating, and in this way they relive Gulliver's experience. Science brings fear—the mathematicians of Laputa live in daily, even hourly, expectation of a comet that will destroy the earth. Empirical technology brings chaos; in Lagado, Gulliver meets an old-fashioned landowner (Lord Munodi—one of the few characters whose name we hear in *Gulliver's Travels*). His estate is still fruitful, but he fears he may soon have to switch to modern methods that will bring ruin and hunger—as in both Britain and Ireland, where corn-growing is giving way to sheep-raising, and the peasantry go hungry.

The ghosts reveal to Gulliver that history is a chronicle of decline and decadence, from the old Roman Senate of dignified patriots to the modern Parliament of rogues.

Finally, in the Struldbrugs he sees that immortality would not make life better, that death is to be welcomed. From all this madness Gulliver returns home from Japan, then the most exotic society known to Europeans, but a haven of normality to Gulliver. The bleakness at the end is unrelieved, as Gulliver, protected by the Japanese against the Dutch, tramps with his soldier escort along the coast road (passing through a town called Hiroshima, though he does not know it) to board his ship at Nagasaki.

Book 4 is even bleaker. It seems impossible to reconcile the hard and soft readings of this book. Soft readers see it as novel-like: Gulliver, the sorrel nag, and de Mendez are characters; behind them lurks the ghost of an author. For these readers, textual problems can be resolved by appealing to "facts" about the author. Swift was a Protestant clergyman and therefore the book "must" be about a man who tries to live without God, goes mad as a result, and is gradually reconciled to the human race by de Mendez and his own family. Hard readings tend to see the book as pure text, with nothing to be read in from outside that text.

In either case, this is a picture of man not as reasonable animal but only capable of reason. On an island, a race of reasonable creatures, the "Perfection of Nature" (Houyhnhnms), live without passion, but with heroism and social structure; other than poetry, they practice few arts and they live on a simple diet. They share the island with a depraved and corrupt race, the Yahoo, who revel in the power given them by their own filth. One of them, a female about the same age as Glumdalclitch would now be, tries to rape Gulliver. Gulliver realizes with horror that the nearest beings in Europe to the Houyhnhnms are horses and the nearest things to Yahoos are humans. His schizoid response on his return will be to treat horses as Houyhnhnms (though he knows they are not Houyhnhnms) and humans as Yahoos (he is less sure of the distance here). On the island, all his energy goes into concealing the fact that he is a sort of Yahoo, but in the end, his master is compelled by the general will of the Houyhnhnms to send him into exile, for fear he will stir the "other" Yahoos up.

The only political question for the Houyhnhnms is whether the Yahoos should all be killed off. Catching their view of Yahoos, Gulliver makes a boat of Yahoo skin, caulked with Yahoo tallow with which to make his escape. It is a filthy object, but whether it is the Yahoo material or the human use of that material that makes it filthy is part of the dichotomy. Gulliver hides from the Portuguese who would rescue him, and we see this madman, who wears boots he has made from the skins of young Yahoos, refusing Western clothes that he thinks smell of Yahoo. It is a black view of the human condition. Women come off worse as a result. Mary Burton Gulliver, who has kept the family estate together for sixteen years, is excluded from her own dining table because the memory of the young female Yahoo works on Gulliver's shame, as he wonders how he could ever have taken a Yahoo wife and had Yahoo children.

If book 4 is a document of madness, and schizoid madness at that, we must remember a truism of schizoid conditions; the madness may not be in here but out there. Life for many Irish people in the eighteenth century was one meal away from the condition of the Yahoos. There were powerful voices, claiming to be rational, that said the population of Ireland must be reduced if the country was to be economically viable and this implied forced emigration or starvation. And this was the fate that lay in wait for Ireland one hundred years in the future.

SWIFT'S POETRY

AN ongoing project among some Swift critics is to relocate him—that is to assess his creativity as a poet with a particular vision, living in the Ireland, and particularly the Dublin, of the eighteenth century. For Carole Fabricant, Swift, like the Lilliputians, sees "with great exactness but at no great distance" and this is reflected in his antipathy to the local landscape. Where others see the country round Dublin as an idyllic scene, with the Big House set among green fields surrounded by whitewashed cottages, Swift sees the Big House as the center of a system that takes the greatest share of Ireland's wealth and spends it on luxuries from England. The fields are green because landlords refuse to let tenants plow and grow corn, and insist on preserving sheep pasture; the cottages are hovels, in which people live in appalling misery—he never sentimentalizes cottage life, as Oliver Goldsmith does later in the century. An icon of Swift's life in Ireland is Naboth's Vineyard. St. Patrick's Cathedral is situated in the Liberties, one of the worst slums in Europe. In a walled space that he calls Naboth's Vineyard, Swift tries to make a garden, his efforts mocked as a local stream regularly overflows and floods it with filth.

Swift is by inclination a satirist, a poet for whom a primary impulse of poetry is moral and social judgment, even where the work is comic in tone. Particularly influential texts for him are the works of the major Latin satirical poets Horace (Quintus Horatius Flaccus, 65–8 B.C.) and Juvenal (Decius Junius Juvenalis, 60–130 A.D.), who represent two modes of feeling; both approaches can be found in Swift's work. Both are moralists; for them the function of satire is to reinforce the commonly agreed-upon conventions of their age.

For Horace, the method is "to combine the entertaining and the useful"; moral observations are the useful element of such poetry. The language of his poems often reflects the spoken language of every day, and it celebrates cheerfully the pleasures of social occasions among friends content to live within modest bounds.

Juvenal is more magisterial; he has a more generalized view and when he looks at his Rome he sees corruption. Like Swift, he had been disappointed in his hopes of promotion in the imperial service, and finds himself in a city whose noise and filth he can barely tolerate. Juvenal describes his stance in a word that was to be enormously potent to Swift, *indignatio*, an obsessive feeling of having been treated unfairly.

A DESCRIPTION OF THE MORNING

FIRST published in *The Tatler* to popular acclaim in 1709, the poem begins:

> Now hardly here and there a hackney coach
> Appearing, showed the ruddy morn's approach.
> Now Betty from her master's bed has flown,
> And softly stole to discompose her own.

There is an obvious disjunction here between the form (ten-syllable lines in heroic couplets—rimed iambic pentameters with a caesura in the second line), which is appropriate to descriptions of country pastoral, and the content, which represents a town scene. The first couplet is a parodic rewriting of some such stock couplet as "Now hardly here and there the faintest ray / Appearing, showed th' approach of ruddy day." Swift does not intend to mock or destroy the heroic couplet, but to extend it and create a town pastoral, rather than a country pastoral. The hackney coach (always a comic object to Swift) is a stroke of genius—we know that morning has come in the town because there are cabs about again, both because the drivers are starting work and because people are coming home after late nights. It accurately catches the feeling of life in the city (London in this case).

In the next couplet, a servant leaves her master's bed and returns to her own. Typically for this form, the couplet works through its verbs. The contrastive movements suggested by "flown" (getting out of the bedroom fast) and "stole" (getting quietly up the stairs) lead to the "difficult" "discompose." The meaning of this last verb is not apparent at first—Betty will ruffle the bed (and at the same time try to "compose" herself). The strong caesura (break in the rhythm) after "stole" emphasizes this. (Read it "And softly stole [pause, speed up slightly] to discompose her own"). The movement is helped by the alliteration s-t-l s-t-l in "softly stole" in the first half of the line.

A Description of the Morning is closer to the spirit of Juvenal than to that of Horace. Juvenal tended to respond to the sheer noise of Rome, as Swift does in "And Brickdust Moll had screamed through half a street." Juvenalian satire is more generalized, viewing conduct within the group or crowd, and recording the sordidness of life—the idle, undisciplined servants, the prisoners let out of jail to "steal for fees," the knots of bailiffs waiting to serve writs. One of Juvenal's most potent themes is the influence of this corruption upon innocent children, and Swift's poem ends with the picture of schoolboys observing what passes. As they "lag" they pick up the watchfulness of the bailiffs from the previous line "The watchful bailiffs take their silent stands / And schoolboys lag with satchels in their hands" (p. 108).

MRS HARRIS'S PETITION

THIS poem (probably written earlier than *A Description of the Morning* but printed about the same time) may be taken as an example of a Horatian satire based on the ordinary speech of the people that surrounded Swift, and on a simple domestic incident. Rogers calls this poem "famous and much-anthologized," it is popular and easy to access. The action is placed in the household of the earl of Berkeley, Lord Chief Justice of Ireland. Swift is chaplain in the household and Mrs. Harris a companion to Lady Berkeley. Mrs. Harris tells the tale of how she has lost her purse and the pleasure of the poem arises from Swift's exuberance in telling this tale in the cadences and rhythms of Mrs. Harris' speech, setting it off against a mock

legalistic jargon at the same time. Told through one voice, yet managing to suggest several other voices in conversation, it has obvious dramatic strengths in the best sense. The poem concludes with the petition itself. Mrs. Harris (who has been refused Swift's help in using astrology to find the money and who has ambitions to be a parson's wife) asks the earl for "a share in next Sunday's collection; and over and above . . . an order for the chaplain aforesaid; or instead of him, a better." So Swift comes off the worse and in this last phrase is repaid for his refusal to help. (p. 85)

CADENUS AND VANESSA *AND OTHER POEMS OF MEN AND WOMEN*

SUCH was the lack of autonomy experienced by women in Swift's time that most women passed from dependency on their fathers to dependency on their husbands and then to dependency on their sons. Few men believed in the value of education for women—Swift was an exception. The Utopian chapter 6 of book 1 of *Gulliver's Travels* illustrates this concern, but even then women's claim to education was to be restricted by their class. All classes for Swift were best off living in the conditions of their fathers; women were thus doubly oppressed. The critical question is whether Swift's writing creates discourses of the oppression of women.

Swift's poem *Cadenus and Vanessa* (1712–1713) was probably written early in the relationship between Swift and Esther Vanhomrigh. Vanessa is his nickname for her, derived from her name; Cadenus is an anagram of Decanus, the Latin for the Dean. It was a private poem, not published till after her death. The poem is written in iambic tetrameters (eight-syllable lines) rimed in couplets and tending strongly to be stopped at the end of the couplet, or even at the end of the line. Though often a meter for the broadest comic poems, poets from Andrew Marvell to A. E. Housman have used it seriously, probably because it fits well to the rhythm of spoken English, tending to give two phrases to the line and matching the two-phrase sentence that is very common in normal speech. For Swift it is a favorite meter for Horatian satire.

The poem is puzzling in the way much of the prose is puzzling; its narrative line is unresolved and it is difficult to place its ultimate moral vision. Venus, the goddess of Love, is called on to adjudicate between the shepherds and the nymphs; the nymphs claim that men no longer are capable of love: "Now love is dwindled to intrigue / And marriage grown a money-league" (p. 130). The shepherds for their part claim women have lost the art of spiritual love: "And only know the gross desire . . . / A dog, a parrot, or an ape . . . / Engross the fancies of the fair" (p. 131).

On consideration, Venus creates a maiden, Vanessa, with every virtue; Pallas, goddess of Wisdom, thinking her to be a boy, "Then sows within her tender mind / Seeds long unknown to womankind / The seeds of knowledge, judgement, wit." More, knowing "Bare virtue could not lie on praise," she endows Vanessa with just the amount of money that would support her without rendering her neglectful of her studies "'Twould come to just five thousand pound"—Vanessa's actual inheritance from her father (p. 135–6).

Venus hopes that this perfect woman would be universally imitated by other women and would restore her reign, but Pallas has undone her work. Vanessa will not take part in the love-commerce of the day; her intelligence forbids her to. She has no time for gossip; she talks of ancient virtue and modern instances. Society concludes: "She may be handsome, young and rich / But none will burn her for a witch" (p 139).

Repulsed by society, she has few intimates except those of taste and modesty. These include some of the clergy; "But this [her love] was for Cadenus' sake / A gownsman of a different make / Whom Pallas once Vanessa's tutor / Had fixed on for her coadjutor (p. 142)." Cupid, to vindicate his mother, Venus, has Vanessa fall in love with Cadenus, her new tutor. "Vanessa, not in years a score / Dreams of a gown of forty-four . . . / She fancies music in his tongue / No further looks but thinks him young" (p 143). No longer able to concentrate ("She wished her tutor were her lover . . . / The nymph would gently press his hand" (p. 144). She grows inattentive. Thinking he has bored her, he comes to take his leave. She confesses her feelings. He is at a loss. She tells him:

"Your lessons found the weakest part,
Aimed at the head, but reached the heart."

Cadenus felt within him rise
Shame, disappointment, guile, surprise . . .
And yet her words were so expressed
He could not hope she spoke in jest

(p. 146)

And he is unable to face what the world would say. "How should his innocence be clear . . . / The world must think him in the wrong . . . / Five thousand guineas in her purse: / The doctor might have fancied worse" (p. 146–147).

Vanessa's passion is intellectual. Cadenus to her is like a great book, which comprises "All that was witty, learned and wise." And if you came across such a book, you would seek out the author and make him your friend: "Cadenus answers every end / The book, the author and the friend" (p. 148). In turn, Cadenus is flattered by her intellectual success: "In learning let a nymph delight / The pedant gets a mistress from it." Yet Cadenus cannot love: "But friendship in its greatest height / A constant, rational delight . . . / Which gently warms but cannot burn / He gladly offers in return" (p. 150).

So Vanessa vows to change roles, to teach Cadenus how to love.

Here the narrative of Vanessa and Cadenus breaks off. We are not to know what the result was. Venus returns to heaven sadder and wiser. Her experiment is a failure. All love is now to be decided by the random flight of Cupid's arrows.

The description of Vanessa comes near apotheosis—she is almost a goddess, heaven-born and heaven-blessed, but the higher the praise is heaped, the more other women are demeaned, and there is the insulting suggestion that Vanessa is a perfect woman insofar as she is like a man. The early setting at the court of Venus and the description of Vanessa's encounters with the other women of her day belittle women. Further, she is the victim of love; underlying the poem is the story of Cupid and Psyche from Apuleius' *Golden Ass*; Cupid loves Psyche, but remains invisible when he visits her. One night he falls asleep; she holds a candle over him to see him as he is, wakes him (he is burned by hot wax) and loses him. Similarly, Vanessa can see in Cadenus the qualities of a lover, but on doing this, loses him.

In assessing Swift's view of women, we may also take into account a group of poems including *Strephon and Chloe*, *Cassinus and Peter*, *A Beautiful Young Nymph Going to Bed*, and also *The Lady's Dressing Room*. These represent what Norman O. Brown characterized as the excremental vision in the work of Swift. *Strephon and Chloe* (1731) tells how Strephon is unable to consummate his marriage with the spotless Chloe until he hears her urinate. *Cassinus and Peter* (1731) describes how a student is driven into withdrawal and depression by discovering his mistress's secret; "Nor wonder how I lost my wits / Oh Celia Celia Celia sh**s."

The other two poems are poems about the disgust aroused by the sight of a woman's dirty body and dirty linen, and are frankly voyeuristic.

In these cloacal poems, the anal fixation prevents a fully adult sexual relationship and substitutes a relationship built on elements of aggression and punishment, directed both to the self and the partner. The poet first of all foregrounds the tokens of the infantile exchange—feces and urine, their color, smell, and sound; this embodies the infantilization of the relationships with women. Secondly, he is concerned to stereotype women. They must join in this infant world (Chloe ends by warming the seat of the commode for Strephon). Yet when they do so, they disqualify themselves as subjects for adult love: "O Strephon, e'er that fatal day / Had you but through a cranny spied / On house of ease your future bride . . . / Your heart had been as whole as mine" (p. 461).

Such features enable a reduction of relationships to simple economic transaction. Feminist studies emphasize that such transactions in Swift's time tended to destroy the autonomy of women. It was impossible for them to enjoy economic independence. Instead they were forced into the role of mothers, cherished as producers of children for work in the growing imperialist framework but disabled as independent earners in their own right.

Vanessa in turn can never teach Cadenus the meaning of adult love. The infantilization of this relationship (as of the relationship with Stella) shows in the way it is displaced on to a tutor-pupil relationship. The older man is always safe—society will always support his refusing a full relationship because of the gap in ages. Only a Mrs. Harris might constitute a real threat, so she must be assaulted through humor. Of course *Cadenus and Vanessa* is unresolved; Swift's fixation is itself unresolved.

To balance this, however, such critics as Margaret Anne Doody suggest a different feminist view. Doody points out that Swift enjoyed warm relationships with a number of women he encouraged in their own poetic writing, so much so that one of them, Mary Leapor, was influenced in choice of form and content, taking up Swift's interest in the labor of women, especially in the kitchen. He writes of himself making butter in the dairy in a relaxed poem, *A Panegyric on the Dean in the person of a Lady of the North* (1730). Doody reads *Cadenus and Vanessa* as sympathetic to the position of women, allowing Vanessa without reproach to exercise the power of a

seducer and allowing the "unhandsome" Cadenus in turn to experience a relationship where he is not forced into conventional phallic certainty. As she points out, there can be no resolution to the poem because there is no social role available to Vanessa that leaves her autonomous.

CONCLUSION

SWIFT was an angry, unhappy, paradoxical man. Unquestioningly committed to the Church in Ireland, one of the major instruments of oppression in that country, he was yet remembered by ordinary Irishmen for two hundred years after his death as a voice on their behalf for independence of feeling and action. A believer in the education of women, whom he did much to encourage intellectually, he also wrote some vicious documents which diminished them. Above all, he is both contemptuous of political power and eager for it. The strength of some of his best work is that he does not blur the contradictions, but leaves them in contention and unresolved.

SELECTED BIBLIOGRAPHY

I. COLLECTED WORKS. Contemporary edition: Jonathan Swift (as "J. S." or "Lemuel Gulliver"), *The Works of J. S., D.D, D.S.P.D.* (Jonathan Swift, Doctor of Divinity, Dean of St. Patrick's Dublin), 4 vols. (Dublin, November 1734 to January 1735; dated 1735, substantially rev. 1746). Vol. 1, Prose; Vol. 2, Poems; Vol. 3 (with pastiche title page and frontispiece, internally signed "J. S.") is "Lemuel Gulliver," *Travels into Several Remote Nations of the World (Gulliver's Travels)*; Vol. 4, Prose and Supplement of additional poems.

Modern editions: Harold Williams, ed., *The Poems of Jonathan Swift*, 3 vols. (Oxford, 1937; 2nd ed. 1958); Herbert Davis, ed., *The Prose Works of Jonathan Swift*, 14 vols. (Oxford, 1939–1968); P. Rogers, ed., *Complete Poems* (Harmondsworth, U.K., 1983).

Selections: Useful working texts with selections of both prose and verse are Roger A. Greenberg and William B. Piper, eds., *The Writings of Jonathan Swift: A Norton Critical Edition* (New York, 1973), with texts, background contemporary writing, modern criticism, bibliography; includes *Gulliver's Travels*; Angus Ross and David Woolley, eds., *The Oxford Authors: Jonathan Swift* (Oxford, 1984), with texts, notes, glossary, bibliography; excludes *Gulliver's Travels*.

II. MAJOR ALLEGORIES. *The Battle of the Books, A Tale of a Tub, and Mechanical Operation of the Spirit* (1704, rev. 1710); *Travels into Several Remote Nations of the World*

(*Gulliver's Travels*) (1726, rev. 1735). An essential working text is Christopher Fox, ed., *Jonathan Swift Gulliver's Travels* (Boston, 1995), with text, introduction, and substantial critical items.

III. COMIC PARODY. *Predictions for the Ensuing Year, by Isaac Bickerstaff and Vindication (The Bickerstaff Papers)* (1708); *Meditation upon a Broomstick* (1710); *Complete Collection of Polite and Ingenious Conversation* (1738); *Directions to Servants* (written 1731, pub. posthumously 1745).

IV. POLITICAL WRITING. *A Short Character of T[homas] E[arl] of W[harton], L[ord] L[ieutenant] of I[reland]* (1710); *The Conduct of the Allies and Some remarks on the Barrier Treaty* (1711); *Advice . . . to members of the October Club* (1712), against extreme Tories; *Importance of the Guardian Considered* (1713), against Addison and Steele's Whig journal of that name; *The Public Spirit of the Whigs* (1714); *Some Free Thoughts upon the Present State of Affairs* (1714); *History of the Four Last Years of the Reign of Queen Anne* (1758).

V. PAMPHLETS ON THE CONDITION OF IRELAND. *Proposal for the Universal Use of Irish Manufacture* (1720); *The Drapier's Letters* (1724); *A Short View of the State of Ireland* (1728); *A Modest Proposal* (1729).

VI. RELIGIOUS WRITING. *Argument Against Abolishing Christianity* (1708); *Letter concerning the Sacramental Test* (1708); *A Letter to a Young Gentleman, Lately Entered into Holy Orders* (1721); *Sermons* (1744).

VII. ON LANGUAGE. *Proposal for Correcting, Improving and Ascertaining the English Tongue* (1712).

VIII. POETRY. Political satire: *The Virtues of Sid Hamet the Magician's Rod* (1710), against Godolphin; *An Excellent New Song* (1711), for the peace; *The Windsor Prophecy* (1711), against duchess of Somerset; *A Satirical Elegy on the Death of a Late Famous General* (written 1722, pub. 1764), against Marlborough; *Wood, an Insect* (1725), against the Wood of Wood's Halfpence; *Traulus* (1730), against Lord Allen; *A Character of the Legion Club* (1736), against the Irish Parliament.

Poems of landscape and country life: *Verses from Quilca* (1725); *A Pastoral Dialogue between Richmond Lodge and Marble Hill* (1727); *On Cutting Down the Old Thorn at Market Hill* (1728); *Drapier's Hill* (1729); *A Pastoral Dialogue* (1729); *A Panegyric on the Dean* (1730).

Poems of the excremental vision: *The Lady's Dressing Room* (1731); *A Beautiful Young Nymph Going to Bed* (1731); *Strephon and Chloe* (1731); *Cassinus and Peter* (1731).

Others: *Mrs Harris's Petition* (1700); *Baucis and Philemon* (1708–1709); *Description of the Morning* (1709); *Description of a City Shower* (1710); *Cadenus and Vanessa* (1712–1713); *Stella's Birthday,* five poems from various years (1719, 1721, 1723, 1725, 1727); *Verses on the Death of Dr Swift* (1731).

IX. PERIODICAL JOURNALISM. *The Examiner* (Swift's first number: 2 November 1710); *The Intelligencer,* with Thomas Sheridan, Sr. (from 11 May 1728). Modern collection: James Wooley, ed., *The Intelligencer* (Oxford, 1992).

X. CORRESPONDENCE. *Journal to Stella* (1710–1713). Modern edition: H. Williams, ed., *Journal to Stella,* issued as Vols. 15 and 16 of H. Davis, *The Prose Works of Jonathan Swift* (Oxford, 1948, repr. 1975); H. Williams, ed., *The Correspondence of Jonathan Swift,* 5 vols. (Oxford, 1963–1965).

XI. BIOGRAPHIES OF SWIFT. Contemporary memoirs: Laetitia Pilkington, *Memoirs of L[a]etitia Pilkington, Written by Herself, with Anecdotes of Dean Swift,* Vol. 1 (1748); Deane Swift, *An Essay upon the Life, Writings and Character of Dr Jonathan Swift* (1755); Thomas Sheridan, Jr., *The Life of the Reverend Dr Jonathan Swift* (1784).

Modern critical biographies: Irvin Ehrenpreis, *Swift: The Man, His Works, and the Age.* Vol. 1, *Mr Swift* (1962), Vol. 2, *Dr Swift* (1967), Vol. 3, *Dean Swift* (1983) (Cambridge, Mass.); David Nokes, *Jonathan Swift: A Hypocrite Reversed* (Oxford, 1985).

XII. CRITICAL STUDIES. Kathleen Williams, *Jonathan Swift and the Age of Compromise* (Lawrence, Kans., 1958); Norman O. Brown, *Life Against Death: The Psychoanalytical Meaning of History* (Middletown, Conn., 1959).

A. Norman Jeffares, *Fair Liberty Was All His Cry* (New York, 1967); Miriam Kosh Starkman, *Swift's Satire on Learning in* A Tale of a Tub (New York, 1968).

Kathleen Williams, *Swift: The Critical Heritage* (New York and London, 1970); James L. Clifford, "Gulliver's Fourth Voyage: 'Hard' and 'Soft' Schools of Interpretation," in Larry Champion, ed., *Quick Springs of Sense: Studies in the Eighteenth Century* (Athens, Ga., 1974); Clive T. Probyn, *Jonathan Swift: The Contemporary Background* (Manchester, 1978).

Carole Fabricant, *Swift's Landscape* (Baltimore, Md., 1982); Felicity Nussbaum, *The Brink of All We Hate: English Satires on Women, 1660–1750* (Lexington, Ky., 1984); Ellen Pollak, *The Poetics of Sexual Myth: Gender and Ideology in the Verse of Swift and Pope* (Chicago, 1985); Margaret Anne Doody, "Swift Among the Women," in *Yearbook of English Studies* 18 (1988) (also in Nigel Wood, 1999).

Laura Brown, "Reading Race and Gender: Jonathan Swift," in *Eighteenth-Century Studies* 23 (1990); Frederik N. Smith, *The Genres of Gulliver's Travels* (Newark, Del., 1990); Richard Rodino, " 'Splendide Mendax': Authors, Characters, and Readers in *Gulliver's Travels,*" in PMLA 106 (1991) (also in Nigel Wood, 1999); Christopher Fox and Brenda Tooley, eds., *Walking Naboth's Vineyard* (Notre Dame, 1995); Robert Phiddian, *Swift's Satire* (New York, 1995); Aileen Douglas, Patrick Kelly, and Ian Campbell Ross, eds., *Locating Swift* (Dublin, 1998); Nigel Wood, ed., *Jonathan Swift,* Longman Critical Readers Series, (London, 1999).

Frank Boyle, *Swift as Nemesis: Modernity and its Satirist* (Stanford, 2000).

XIII. OTHER AUTHORS. Giovanni Boccaccio, *Decameron* (1350, English trans. 1620; modern trans., J. Usher and G. Waldman, Oxford 1993); François Rabelais, *Gargantua and Pantagruel* (1542, English trans. 1653, 1693–4; modern trans., J. H. Cohen, Harmondsworth, U.K.,

1955); Thomas Hobbes, *Leviathan* (1668), ed. by C. B. Macpherson (Harmondsworth, U.K., 1968); Samuel Johnson, *Lives of the English Poets* (1779–1781), ed. by G. B. Hill, 3 vols. (Oxford, 1905);

Introduction L. Archer-Hind, 2 vols (London, Everyman, 1925)

James Boswell *Life of Samuel Johnson* (1791), ed. by B. Hill (Oxford 1877, repr. 1998), for Johnson's resentment of Swift see under 1738; Mikhail Bakhtin, *Rabelais and his World,* trans. by H. Iswolsky (Cambridge, Mass., 1968).

JOHN MILLINGTON SYNGE

(1871–1909)

Scott Ashley

JOHN MILLINGTON SYNGE was born on 16 April 1871 into a family that had provided the human foundations of the Protestant Anglo-Irish ascendancy in the shape of churchmen and landowners from the seventeenth century. Among his ancestors had been five bishops of the Church of Ireland, and when Synge's great-grandfather died in 1831 the family firmly controlled large estates built up through marriage, inheritance, and purchase in the mountains of County Wicklow, centered on the ugly neo-gothic Glanmore Castle. But the future playwright was born into a world that offered few of the gilded opportunities that had existed less than half a century earlier. Grandfather John "Pestalozzi" Synge, blessed with a religious zeal that far outshone his financial sense, found that declining rents and profits from agriculture were inadequate to maintain an affluent lifestyle; he borrowed vast amounts that he was unable to repay, and in 1845 the inevitable crash came.

Although Glanmore Castle was saved, John Pestalozzi's sons had to go out and make their own way in the world. The youngest of these sons was John Hatch Synge, a lawyer, who in 1856 married Kathleen Traill, the daughter of the Reverend Robert Traill. The Reverend Traill was a hellfire preacher from Ulster who had devoted his life to the ending of Roman Catholicism in Ireland but had met his own end when he caught a fever from a famine-stricken Catholic peasant in County Cork in 1847. John Hatch and Kathleen Synge had four surviving children, a daughter and three sons, when their last child, Edmund John Millington Synge, was born. Before he was a year old, domestic disaster struck when his father died of smallpox, and the years of Synge's childhood were ones of suburban, essentially middle-class living on the outskirts of Dublin in a staunchly Protestant Christian (and rather anti-intellectual) household. Through family holidays to Wicklow, sometimes accompanied by a visit to his father's brother, Uncle Francis, at Glanmore Castle, the young Johnnie (the name Edmund was never used) was brought up keenly aware of how, if they were not exactly poor, his junior branch of the once great Synge clan were now living in sorely reduced circumstances.

A sickly child, Synge chose youthful intellectual pursuits rather than physical endeavors, and he developed an early interest in natural history, an interest that he was later to recall caused him a severe religious crisis at the age of fourteen, when he read Charles Darwin's *Descent of Man* (1871). But in his mid-teens he turned to a passionate involvement in music and literature with a patriotic tinge, exchanging, as he put it years later, the Kingdom of God for the Kingdom of Ireland. When he entered the conservative intellectual environment of Trinity College, Dublin, in 1888, probably following vague family expectations that he might become a clergyman, it was the violin and the antiquities of Ireland that dominated his mind.

Given such a clear antagonism between private enthusiasms and public conformity, it is perhaps unsurprising that Synge's undergraduate career at Trinity proved to be undistinguished. Despite winning college prizes for achievement in the Hebrew and Irish languages, he graduated with a poor degree in 1892. It was increasingly clear to Synge's family that a clerical career was not to be viewed as an option, and music occupied more and more of his time. It was this passion that led him to leave Ireland in the summer of 1893 with his cousin Mary Synge to study the violin in Germany. Despite her serious disapproval of such frivolous ambitions, Kathleen Synge had agreed to fund her son's travels. Unfortunately, what had originally been planned as a short (and, as Mrs. Synge hoped, unsuccessful) trip proved anything but brief, and despite extended trips back to Ireland (some of which had momentous consequences, as we shall see) the prodigal son was not to return for good until 1903.

Within months of Synge's death in 1909 the poet W. B. Yeats was creating an image of the dead playwright as a man rooted in the soil of Ireland, as an artist who had found his subject in the people, landscapes, and languages of the nation. While there is a large element of truth in this, it is also true that it was his time spent in Europe, and especially in Paris, that determined the kind of Irish writer Synge would become. After spending eighteen months in Germany, wandering between the pious Von Eiken sisters (four conventionally Protestant but intellectual friends of cousin Mary Synge) in the Rhineland and the more cosmopolitan delights of the city of Würzburg, he finally set out for the French capital on 1 January 1895. By that time literature had effectively replaced music as Synge's touchstone, as he despaired of ever overcoming an aversion to public performance. Having enrolled himself for lectures in comparative Celtic linguistics and folklore at the Sorbonne, he seemed to be carving out a literary role for himself as a translator and scholar. Indeed, it was as a young student of Irish and Breton culture that Synge was introduced in the winter of 1896 to Yeats, who was then in Paris to sample bohemian living and to continue his hopeless pursuit of his beloved Maud Gonne, Yeat's poetic muse and radical Irish nationalist. Although Synge quickly declined to have anything to do with Gonne's radical nationalist political movement—and while it would take several years for the acquaintance to mature—the momentous contact had been made.

Unknown to Yeats, Synge already had started composing more literary essays alongside his scholarly notes, and there survive fragments of several semi-autobiographical pieces, obviously influenced by the canons of French decadent and symbolist writing. Reading such contemporary classics as those written by Charles Baudelaire, Stéphane Mallarmé, Émile Zola, and Joris-Karl Huysmans, Synge, it seemed, was about to fall into the trap of becoming a second-hand fin de siècle Frenchman. In May 1898, however, he made a decision that precipitated his accelerated rise to becoming a major literary force: he decided to go and spend two months on the Aran Islands off the west coast of Ireland. Why Synge chose to go to live on three Irish-speaking and largely poverty-stricken islands remains one of the several biographical mysteries surrounding his life. In later years Yeats liked to flatter himself that he had focused his young protégé's eyes westward, back toward Ireland,

famously recalling in 1905 that he had said to Synge in 1896, "Give up Paris. You will never create anything by reading Racine, and Arthur Symons will always be a better critic of French literature. Go to the Aran Islands. Live there as if you were one of the people themselves; express a life that has never found expression" (Yeats, p. 299).

Few critics and biographers have allowed Yeats his self-appointed role as mentor, pointing out that even if this advice was indeed given, it matured very slowly; an eighteen-month gap separated that Parisian meeting and Synge's arrival on the islands. Equally, Synge little needed Yeats's (minimal) knowledge of Aran, for from 1851 to 1855 the Protestant minister on Inis Mór, the largest of the Aran Islands, had been Synge's uncle, the Reverend Alexander Synge, a fact remembered well in family lore. And as a serious student of Celtic languages and literature, Synge knew that the Aran Islands had been elevated during the nineteenth century into sites of uncontaminated Gaelic culture, attracting scholars, tourists, and pilgrims from Germany, Denmark, and the United States as well as from Ireland and Britain.

Finally, Synge may have had a very personal reason for wanting to escape into isolation. His emotional life through the entire decade had been intimately bound up with a young woman from a family of Plymouth Brethren, Cherrie Matheson, whose parents had been near neighbors of the Synges since 1890. She became something of a muse figure for Synge, and he had unsuccessfully proposed marriage to her in 1896. Visiting his sick mother in Dublin in the spring of 1898, he tried again, only to be left disappointed and humiliated. Two weeks after this second approach to Cherrie's family, Synge was on a train heading for Aran. If Yeats's words did indeed influence that fateful decision, then it seems unlikely to have been the defining factor but only one among several.

THE BIRTH OF TRAGEDY: THE ARAN ISLANDS

IN the last year of his life Synge wrote in his notebook about "our quite modern feeling for the beauty and mystery [of] nature," identifying "an emotion that has gradually risen up as religion in the dogmatic sense has gradually died. Our pilgrimages are not to Canterbury or Jerusalem, but to Killarney and Cumberland and the Alps" (*Collected Works*, vol. 2, p. 351). Like all pilgrimages, religious or secular, the intensity of the experience far outweighs the temporal duration of the journey, and Synge's visits to the Aran Islands are no exception. Each of the five annual expeditions to the islands between 1898 and 1902 lasted no more than six to eight weeks and often was rather less. Yet it is no exaggeration to say that without the emotional and intellectual shock of his encounter with the land-scapes, lives, and languages he encountered there, Synge would not be the major force in Irish and world drama that he is today. It was on the islands that he heard the tales that would provide him with the plots for most of his major plays, including the story of the man who killed his father with a spade—this man became Christy Mahon in *The Playboy of the Western World*. It was on the islands that he lived among and listened to the Irish and Hiberno-English speakers who would provide him with so much of the violent and vibrant language that so scandalized and electrified those first audiences in Dublin, New York, and London. And it was on the islands and in the composition of his first finished work, his autobiographical prose masterpiece *The Aran Islands*, written in 1901 but unpublished until 1907, that Synge was to recognize the basic themes of his short, productive life.

If it is true that in *The Aran Islands* Synge record-ed the tremendous mental shock (the word is his own term) of his first days among a people whose "life is perhaps the most primitive that is left in Europe" (*Collected Works*, vol. 2, p. 53), it is equally true that he was not unprepared to be shocked. Despite their isolation and poverty, the three islands already had inspired a small library of scholarly and imaginative literature by 1898. It was not uncommon to find academic linguists, Irish- language enthusiasts, folklorists, spiritual-ists, archaeologists, anthropologists, and the odd future revolutionary sliding over the wet rocks and poking about the turf-smoke-filled cottages. Although *The Aran Islands* is now established as the acknowledged classic of the islands, Synge was, in fact, something of a latecomer to Aran.

Antiquarians had been regularly extolling the history of the islands since the 1820s. The German Celtic scholar Heinrich Zimmer was there in 1880, supporting the islanders in their campaigns for land reform. Lady Gregory, who later became co-director with Synge of the Abbey Theatre, had first gone to the north island of Inis Mór as early as 1889, had traveled to the south island of Inis Oirr in 1893, and was on Inis Mór again collecting folklore when Synge arrived in May 1898. The

Irish writer Emily Lawless had published an Aran novel, *Grania: The Story of an Island*, in 1892, although Synge professed to find it inauthentic. Yeats had gone there in 1896 to research the back-ground for his own unfinished novel, *The Speckled Bird*, and to keep a weather eye out for any pass-ing fairies. When Synge moved to the middle island of Inis Méain at the end of May and took lodging at the cottage of the MacDonnacha family, his bed quite likely was still warm from the previ-ous occupant, a young Patrick Pearse, who later, in 1916, led the sacrificial Easter Rising against British rule. In other words, Synge arrived not in a new world but in terrain that had been imagina-tively mapped for the best part of a century. If Aran came as a revelation (which it did), it was a revelation mediated through books and the expe-riences of others. But in *The Aran Islands* and in his plays, Synge was to express things that had never found expression in the works of his predecessors; he was to remain true to the spirit of Yeats's famous words to him in Paris.

Synge seems originally to have been influenced in the writing of his own book by the French nov-elist Pierre Loti, whose works Synge carried to Aran in 1898 and whose novel of Breton fishing life, *Pêcheur d'Islande* (1886), offered a vision of an analogous community: primitive, Celtic-speaking, living and dying on the sea. Loti's hold weakened early, however, and the critic Declan Kiberd has suggested that the finished work bears the imprint of the poet-critic Arthur Symons' essay "The Isles of Aran," published in the *Savoy* maga-zine in 1896. Symons had been on Aran with Yeats in 1896, and there are certainly verbal and themat-ic resemblances between his essay and *The Aran Islands*. The latter book, however, develops and complicates the language and themes so thor-oughly that it seems fair to describe Symons' work more as a starting point or inspiration than as a template. Indeed, rather than looking for any one particular source for *The Aran Islands*, scholar-ly research has revealed the eclecticism of Synge's worldview, taking in philosophy, anthropology, folklore, political theory, and natural history as well as literature, all of which contributed to the rich mix. Friedrich Nietzsche, James Frazer, the Brothers Grimm, William Morris, and Charles Darwin are just a few of the perhaps unlikely names that need to be set alongside those of Loti and Symons, Yeats and Lady Gregory, as the pre-siding genii of Synge's Aran Islands.

Synge's rejection of the novelistic models of Emily Lawless and Pierre Loti reflects the kind of book *The Aran Islands* became. Although the book is, in theory, "about" the author's experiences during his first four trips to Aran between 1898 and 1901, there is no immediate plot that reveals itself to the first-time reader. Despite the fact that the book is autobiographical in origin, Synge does not offer much analysis of his reasons for traveling to the islands or of their effects on his future life and work. He comes and he goes; what happens elsewhere is largely incidental. And these ruthless exclusions run into the heart of the book. Despite Synge's knowledge of the history of the islands and the hopes and fears he had for their future, which are revealed in his notebooks, *The Aran Islands* itself begins by announcing how uninterested Synge is in historical change. Inis Mór has become modern and homogeneous: "The other islands are more primitive, but even on them many changes are being made, that it was not worth while to deal with in the text" (*Collected Works,* vol. 2, p. 47). The islands are divided immediately between the primitive and real and the modern and inauthentic. Synge makes it clear in the preface and in the first section of the book that it is to the primitive and real that his gaze will be directed.

In fact, it is precisely this quality of change that Synge so clearly declares will not concern him that provides one of the central plotlines of the book. The first part of *The Aran Islands* covers Synge's visit of 1898 and resolutely strives to uncover the primitive, essential aspects of island life. Synge tells how he quickly moves on from the modernized Kilronan (the main village of Inis Mór) to the middle island of Inis Méain, where he experiences "a moment of exquisite satisfaction to find myself moving away from civilisation" (*Collected Works,* vol. 2, p. 57). On Inis Méain, Synge describes with anthropological precision what he takes to be a primitive peasant society, learning Irish, elucidating folk customs with the (unacknowledged) help of James Frazer's *Golden Bough* (1890), presenting himself as constantly observing, constantly listening. The predominant tone of these pages is a bewildered delight at the medieval strangeness and simplicity of the islanders and an intense excitement, as Synge, like a snake casting off its worn-out skin, rediscovers the "natural" life.

Something of the qualities of this enraptured prose is best demonstrated by quotation. The Aran islanders traditionally wore not shoes but cowhide slippers known as pampooties, which were kept in water and worn damp over woolen socks. Synge's first experiences with pampooties prompted him to pen this famous passage:

The absence of the heavy boot of Europe has preserved to these people the agile walk of the wild animal, while the general simplicity of their lives has given them many other points of physical perfection. Their way of life has never been acted on by anything much more artificial than the nests and burrows of the creatures that live round them, and they seem in a certain sense to approach more nearly to the finer types of our aristocracies—who are bred artificially to a natural ideal—than to the labourer or citizen, as the wild horse resembles the thoroughbred rather than the hack or cart-horse. Tribes of the same natural development are, perhaps, frequent in half-civilised countries, but here a touch of the refinement of old societies is blended, with singular effect, among the qualities of the wild animal.

(*Collected Works,* vol. 2, p. 66)

Yet if romantic and patronizing primitivism defined the book, then *The Aran Islands*, in all likelihood, would be little more than a minor period piece today, a precursor to a major career rather than that career's first masterwork. For even as Synge hymns the sunlit primitive life of Inis Méain, darker and more troubling elements begin to brim over the horizon. Literally so in the first part of the book, for a "week of sweeping fogs," Synge notes, "has passed over and given me a strange sense of exile and desolation" (*Collected Works,* vol. 2, p. 72). The harshness of island life is revealed to him, with all its isolation and the psychological pressures it imposes. After sharing the islanders home-distilled alcohol, he notes how "their grey poteen, which brings a shock of joy to the blood, seems predestined to keep sanity in men who live forgotten in these worlds of mist" (*Collected Works,* vol. 2, p. 73).

He sounds for the first time a tragic note that increasingly comes to dominate the book, the recognition of the unbridgeable gap between the outsider and the people among whom he lives. The islanders will not follow his own idealized vision of what they should be like, preferring to talk of the tides, fish, and the price of kelp in Connemara than the ancient folktales and poetry that Synge has come to uncover. As his understanding of the islands deepens, Synge undermines his own primitivist assumptions, revealing Inis Méain as a deathly place, filled with the bodies of the drowned, and as a world on the verge of extinction. These intimations of mortality assume greater significance if we look for reasons why Synge fled to Aran when he did, for he had undergone an operation to remove swollen glands in his neck in December 1897. Although he was not told at the time, Synge may well have realized that the cancer to which he eventually succumbed had attacked his body for the first time. It was not just the culture of Inis Méain that was dying, but Synge himself who teetered on the verge of extinction.

Synge had little faith in the ability of cultural nationalism, and particularly of the Gaelic League (founded in 1893 to protect and revive the Irish language), to preserve the traditions of a place like Aran in the face of the modern world. Perhaps the most famous passage from *The Aran Islands* concerns the attempted eviction of island families by police from the mainland, a scene that Synge dramatizes as a contrast between the "mechanical police, with the commonplace agents and sheriffs, and the rabble they had hired" and the natural "islandmen, who walked up and down as cool and fresh-looking as the sea-gulls" (*Collected Works*, vol. 2, pp. 89, 91). But that dichotomy is immediately blurred by the fact that the bailiff in charge of the eviction is himself an islander, a man symbolic of the falling away of ancient loyalties in the face of change. Although no explicit attention is drawn to the fact, Synge himself was implicated in these processes of social and economic violence: his elder brother Edward was a land agent in County Mayo and had supervised many such evictions. The family income that allowed him to live in Paris and Aran depended on rents from their remaining estates, as Synge admitted to himself in one of his notebooks: "To the little Irish pigs that have eaten filth all their lives to enable me to wander in Paris these leaves are dedicated with respect and sympathy" (*Collected Works*, vol. 2, p. 138, note 1).

As it progresses, *The Aran Islands* increasingly draws attention to these processes, as Synge notes the decay of the Irish language in the face of English, the longing of the younger people of the islands to escape their traditional culture, and the spread of modern patterns of work and social organization, especially in Inis Mór and Inis Oirr. The tension between the older (what Synge terms "primitive") communal values of the islands and the new individualist spirit of the nineteenth century comes to dominate the book and provides it with a central drama that Synge was to carry forward into his work for the theater. He develops a romantic image (or character) for himself in the book as a lone wanderer, seeking some kind of empathy with the islanders, fantasizing about abandoning the atomized bourgeois world of Paris or Dublin for the peasant community of the west. Yet Synge's desire to scrub away all the unnatural accretions that the modern world has coated him with, and to give himself wholeheartedly to a selfless, classless communitarian world, is balanced against an acute recognition of what that would mean. He would lose his identity; he would stop being John Synge. But could he possibly be anyone else? Hidden within *The Aran Islands* lies the message that no one can evade his or her origins. No matter how hard people try, they must wrestle with being themselves rather than try to escape into fantasy.

As soon as Synge steps off the boat at Kilronan, he is recognized as the descendant of the Reverend Alexander Synge. He remains for the islanders a *duine uasal*, the Irish for "honourable person," someone above them in the social hierarchy to whom they offer welcome out of deference rather than love. Although the biographical details are never articulated anywhere in his published work, Synge returned again and again to the theme of eviction, of being an outsider, of exile. He could never escape his fate as a decayed aristocrat whose inheritance had been taken away and as a member of a family that lived by taking away the inheritance of others. By the end of *The Aran Islands*, Synge presents himself as in a kind of existential crisis of exile and loss: "I became indescribably mournful, for I felt that this little corner on the face of the world, and the people who live in it, have a peace and dignity from which we are shut for ever" (*Collected Works*, vol. 2, p. 162). But he has at last come to recognize that the gulf is there and cannot be bridged. In the book at least, he leaves the islands abruptly and without a backward glance. If it is melancholy to contemplate living outside Eden, to exist after the Fall (the Protestant child proved to be a father to the man), it is also painfully impossible to give up being himself.

This seems to be the message in one of the most enigmatic passages in *The Aran Islands*, when he records a dream he experienced on Inis Méain. Hearing strange music, he is overcome by the need to dance to it, only to find himself in "an ecstasy where all existence was lost in a vortex of movement" (*Collected Works*, vol. 2, p. 100). Trying to stop the dance, he finds that he can only keep on, though he feels both agony and rage. At last he manages to drag himself awake. In his dream the seductive qualities of the music, tempting him into identifying himself with a rhythm not of his own making, leads only to a loss of freedom of will. If one yields to the primitive, giving up the self, Synge seems to be saying, only pain and anger will follow.

Although there is no direct evidence, it seems likely that Synge recently had read Friedrich Nietzsche's *Birth of Tragedy* (1872), with its association between the Dionysian spirit of music, with its annihilation of selfhood, and the beginnings of tragic drama among the ancient Greeks. If the student of Synge's work is often driven to wonder how a talented but essentially unsuccessful music student could transform himself into a truly original dramatist in little more than five years, then the theoretical underpinnings of that transition can be found in large part in Nietzsche's little book. Rather than following Nietzsche's belief in tragedy as a necessary self-oblivion, however, Synge resisted his dream music and, while suffering, found in lonely individuality his true strength. That was the result of those months he spent largely isolated on the Aran Islands. The time provided him with the intellectual vision that sustained his drama throughout the decade of life that was left to him.

Between 1898 and early 1903 the Aran Islands and Paris constituted the major imaginative axis along which Synge shuttled back and forth. Yet new places and new friendships were being added to his world. Lady Augusta Gregory and Synge had eyed each other suspiciously on Aran in 1898, but at Yeats's instigation Synge was invited to break his journey from the islands at the Gregorys' house, Coole Park in County Galway. For the first time Synge became involved in the Irish cultural renaissance at its highest levels, as Yeats, Lady Gregory, and Edward Martyn, another Galway landowner, planned to found the Irish Literary Theatre. Synge's emotional life was in no better shape, however, and on returning to Paris he proposed marriage to Margaret Hardon, an American art student, only to be rejected. Synge continued to live largely between France and Ireland in these years, continuing to work on an abortive essay, "Étude Morbide; or, Imaginary Portrait," full of clichéd fin de siècle self-dramatization.

His Celtic interests were beginning to take over, however, and, along with his continued trips to Aran, he visited Brittany in the spring of 1899 and began to put together *The Aran Islands.* By early 1901 the first three sections of that book were complete, and Synge left his manuscript at Coole Park with Yeats and Lady Gregory when he made his fourth visit to Aran in September. While the book generally met with their approval, both Yeats and Gregory advised Synge to include more fairy lore and less concrete detail, encouraging him to aim for a dreamy quality in his work. By the end of the year Synge had written a fourth part to his book, following the advice emanating from Coole Park in adding more island fairy tales but retaining all the geographical specificity. His first mature work complete, Synge was to endure frustration and heartache over *The Aran Islands* as publisher after publisher returned his manuscript. But the extraordinary creativity that had been seeking an outlet ever since his student days at Trinity had been let loose and could not be dammed.

THEATER BUSINESS: IN THE SHADOW OF THE GLEN *TO* THE WELL OF THE SAINTS

IT can sometimes seem as if Synge sprang forth as a dramatist fully formed in 1902, without preliminaries and almost without warning. To contemporaries, seeing this unknown springing on the world of mysterious and profoundly disturbing plays, it must have appeared little short of miraculous. Of course, nothing is quite so simple or so attractive. There are dramatic fragments and drafts dating back as early as 1894 and an almost but never quite completed play, *When the Moon Has Set*, that Synge had begun in 1900. This play, set in a decaying country house and dealing with issues of hereditary madness and sexual passion, clearly was influenced by the work of Henrik Ibsen. It has received serious and perceptive criticism, but was never produced after being rejected by Lady Gregory and Yeats, although Synge kept working at it until 1903. *The Aran Islands* demonstrates that the intellectual vision of the plays, certain elements of the plots, and something of the plays' distinctive language had been worked out in the years since 1898. There is, then, a definite context for Synge's emergence as a playwright; it is worth recording, however, that in 1902 a kind of strange chemistry transmuted these false starts and uncertain directions into original and mature works of art. Few theatrical debuts have been as distinguished or abiding as *In the Shadow of the Glen* and *Riders to the Sea,* both published in 1905.

Although both plays were written at Tomrilands House in County Wicklow, to which the Synge family had decamped for the summer of 1902, the two one-act plays constitute different aspects of Synge's vision of Ireland. Although he had heard the basis for the plot of *In the Shadow of the Glen* on Inis Méain in 1898, the play is set in the Wicklow mountains, its characters the small farmers, shepherds, and tramps whom Synge had met on the roads and hills of his native county. By contrast, *Riders to the Sea* is set on Inis Méain itself and portrays the tragic and morbid quality of life experienced by the fishermen and women of the islands that Synge already had placed center stage in *The Aran Islands.* While the Wicklow play is comic in tone and ends on a note of vigor, *Riders to the Sea* is essentially tragic in mood and contemplates death and dissolution. Yet both works are bound together by a concern with the relationship between the individual and the community in which that individual exists, linking these first dramatic works with *The Aran Islands* and demonstrating their common roots.

In the Shadow of the Glen is set in an isolated farmstead in one of the great sheep-rearing valleys of Wicklow. A tramp calls at the farm to find the man of the house, Dan Burke, lying dead and his widow, Nora, sitting over him. When Nora leaves the tramp to find her neighbor, the dead man rises from beneath his shroud: he is testing his wife and her fidelity by feigning death. Returning with Nora, it becomes clear that the neighbor, Michael Dara, has designs on her and her property. Dan Burke "recovers" and banishes his wife from his house. She leaves, not with Michael Dara but with the silver-tongued tramp, while the more prosaic farmers, in a moment of black irony, are left toasting each other's health and fortune.

The dead play a major role in *Riders to the Sea* too, but there is no faking or testing in that play, and an air of the supernatural hangs over the stage. It opens with another Nora bringing into her family's Aran cottage a bundle of clothing belonging to a drowned man whose body has been found floating off the coast of Donegal. She fears that the clothes will prove to be those of her brother Michael, lost at sea. But before Nora and her sister, Cathleen, can investigate, they are interrupted by their old mother, Maurya, and their living brother, Bartley, who is preparing to sail to Galway to sell horses at the fair. Maurya fears that Bartley is to be drowned on this trip, and when she fails to offer him her blessing, her daughters send her off to intercept him and rectify her temptation of fate. While she is gone, they untie the bundle and find that it is indeed Michael's shirt and stockings. Maurya suddenly returns, having seen a vision of the dead Michael riding behind Bartley on his way down to the sea. Maurya's ghostly premonition proves all too true when Bartley is thrown from his horse into the sea and drowned. The play ends with the stoical Maurya lamenting that all her menfolk have been claimed by the ocean.

Although the plotlines of the two plays bear little immediate relationship to each other, both are stamped with Synge's interest in the heroic individual who, despite the prospect of suffering, ennobles and to some extent redeems the harsh world through poetic language. Nora Burke and the tramp in *In the Shadow of the Glen* look for a kind of fulfilment alone on the road, away from the petty jealousy of Dan Burke, who suspects his wife of infidelity whenever she talks to another man, and from the materialism of Michael Dara, who understands only financial, never emotional, security. The poverty that the pair can expect is never ignored by Synge (the semimythic shepherd Patch Darcy, who went mad and died on the mountainside, is a leitmotif in the play), but he insists that it be accompanied by a spiritual freedom such as Nora could never find in her marriage:

TRAMP: . . . it's fine songs you'll be hearing when the sun goes up, and there'll be no old fellow wheezing the like of a sick sheep close to your ear.

NORA: I'm thinking it's myself will be wheezing that time with lying down under the Heavens when the night is cold, but you've a fine bit of talk, stranger, and it's with yourself I'll go.

(*Collected Works,* vol. 3, p. 57)

Physical discomfort and social ostracism is a price worth paying for a life freed from the constraints of a loveless marriage lived in isolation, "seeing nothing but the mists rolling down the bog, and the mists again, and they rolling up the bog" (*Collected Works*, vol. 3, p. 49). It was this conclusion that was to land Synge in the middle of vicious controversy when *In the Shadow of the Glen* was introduced to Dublin audiences.

Riders to the Sea offers no such optimistic message, no matter how qualified, but the same themes are to the fore. Like Patch Darcy, Michael is already dead when the play opens, but he and his brother, Bartley, are types of the individual who leaves behind hearth and home and ignores the earnest pleas of their mother, Maurya, to stay behind. Unlike the tramp and Nora in *In the Shadow of the Glen*, however, Bartley is driven onto the sea by the hope of commercial gain, by the modern desire to make money by selling his horses. Synge's perception that archaic communal values were being eroded on the Aran Islands by the spread of capitalist social and economic customs is dramatized in the tension between Bartley's modern desire to amass riches and Maurya's primitive recognition of an unrelenting fate that destroys or protects regardless of human agency or of Christian faith. "They're all gone now," says Maurya as Bartley's body is returned to the cottage, "and there isn't anything more the sea can do to me" (*Collected Works*, vol. 3, p. 23). In the final moments of the play, Maurya achieves tragic nobility, recognizing the impersonal and cruel world around her and accepting the suffering to which it has condemned her:

MAURYA: Michael has a clean burial in the far north, by the grace of the Almighty God. Bartley will have a fine coffin out of the white boards, and a deep grave surely. . . . What more can we want than that? . . . No man at all can be living for ever, and we must be satisfied.

(*Collected Works*, vol. 3, p. 27)

Irony is added to Maurya's final speech by the fact that her prayers have been proved ineffectual time and again. (*Riders to the Sea* is a play that refuses to acknowledge the efficacy of Christianity.) Cathleen remembers that there are no nails with which to make Bartley's coffin. But Maurya's words seek to wrench the tragedy of human existence into some kind of transcendental meaning, not to respond to the cold realities and impoverishments of peasant life. Synge offers us again a suffering individual, freed from the rituals of daily life by the death of her husband and all her sons, trying to find her small portion of bitter peace.

Synge had completed both plays by the autumn of 1902 when he left his manuscripts at Coole Park with Yeats and Lady Gregory while he set out for the fifth and last time to the Aran Islands. Both plays went into production with the Irish National Theatre Society, and on 8 October 1903 *In the Shadow of the Glen* opened in Dublin. A storm of controversy broke over Synge's head as members of the company refused to play in it, the actors were hissed by sections of the audience, and nationalist critics denounced the play as a slur on the virtues of Irish womanhood. No real Irish woman would leave her husband to run off with a tramp as Nora Burke had done. Both W. B. Yeats and his father, John Butler Yeats, put up spirited public defenses of the play; Synge himself remained silent. But early the next year he gave his opinion of the controversy in a letter to his old friend from Paris, Stephen MacKenna: "On the French stage the sex-element of life is given without the other ballancing [sic] elements; on the Irish stage the people you agree with want the other elements without sex. I restored the sex-element to its natural place, and the people were so surprised they saw the sex only" (*Collected Letters*, vol. 1, p. 74). Irish audiences were, in Synge's view, not yet sophisticated enough to cope with his disturbing material.

The controversy soon blew over, but it had two important consequences. John Millington Synge was now, after the production of only one one-act play, someone in the Irish literary world. More important, he had made enemies among Ireland's nationalist circles, enemies who would not forgive and forget but would become only more violent in their responses to his work. On 25 February 1904, *Riders to the Sea* premiered in Dublin to a grudgingly positive reaction, with even those who had most hated *In the Shadow of the Glen* admitting a tragic beauty in it. It was to be only a temporary respite, for by then it was plain to everyone that Synge was working on new plays guaranteed to upset Dublin's volatile nationalist audiences.

The astonishing burst of creativity that had seen Synge complete *The Aran Islands* and write the one-act dramas also had produced another play set in Wicklow, *The Tinker's Wedding*. Although it was published in 1907, the play was not acted in Synge's lifetime; it finally premiered in London in November 1909. Yeats and Synge both considered it as too dangerous to be staged in Ireland after the critical mauling Synge's new play, *The Well of the Saints*, had received early in 1905. One can only concur with their judgment, as *The Tinker's Wedding* is Synge's most deliberate attempt to ridicule the Catholic Church as spiritually empty and materialistic when, by the beginning of the twentieth century, to be a Roman Catholic was firmly identified as an integral part of what it meant to be Irish and national.

As published, the play is in two acts and concerns a group of three tinkers, or traveling beggar-craftsmen—Michael Byrne; the mother of his children (but, crucially, not his wife), Sarah Casey; and his mother, Mary Byrne. Sarah has decided that she wants to be married to Michael, and so they have camped by a church in the Wicklow mountains and plan to persuade the priest to perform the ceremony for less than the recognized fee. He reluctantly agrees, but the drunken Mary Byrne steals the tin can that is to be part of the fee to buy beer. When the theft is discovered on the wedding day, the priest scorns the tinkers, who bind him up and mock him, forcing him to swear an oath that he will not inform on them to the police. He calls down a Latin curse on the tinkers, who flee, perhaps in terror, perhaps in jest.

The opposition in Synge's earlier plays between a life-denying conformity and an affirmative individualism are central to *The Tinker's Wedding*, though, it must be admitted, with little of the subtlety or passion of *In the Shadow of the Glen* or *Riders to the Sea*. Here conformity rests in the figure of the priest and the system of Christian ethics that forces men and women into marrying and then demands money for performing that service. The freedom the tinkers have achieved is summarized by Michael and Mary Byrne as they mock the priest:

MARY: . . . it's little need we ever had of the like of you to get us our bit to eat, and our bit to drink, and our time of love when we were young men and women, and were fine to look at.
   MICHAEL: Hurry on now. He's a great man to have kept us from fooling our gold; and we'll have a great time drinking that bit with the trampers on the green of Clash.

(*Collected Works*, vol. 4, p. 49)

For a Protestant (no matter how lapsed) Anglo-Irishman, who already had been accused of impugning Irish morals in *In the Shadow of the Glen*, to suggest that the money of the poor might be better spent on alcohol than on the Catholic rites of passage was deliberately inflammatory. *The Tinker's Wedding* was not to be produced in Ireland until the centenary of Synge's birth in 1971.

The decision not to proceed with a production of *The Tinker's Wedding* was made as a result of the reception of Synge's most recent play, *The Well of the Saints*, which he had been working on since 1903 and which had premiered in Dublin in February 1905. The central figures in the story are two blind beggars, Martin and Mary Doul, who have their sight restored to them by a holy man, only to find that they are far from being the handsome pair they believed themselves to be. Facing the mockery and empty piety of the villagers around them, Martin and Mary prefer to return into darkness and the clarity of their dreams, rather than remain among the emotionally and aesthetically blind community around them. *The Well of the Saints* thus can stand as the quintessence and greatest achievement of the first stage of Synge's dramatic career, which ran from the composition of *In the Shadow of the Glen* and *Riders to the Sea* and reached maturity with this play. The spiritually emaciated community represented by the coquettish Molly Byrne and the stolid, unimaginative Timmy the smith offers the semblance of security and comfort to the two Douls, flattering the beggars' blind pride with tales of their physical beauty. But once the beggars are cured, that same community insists that the Douls follow their values of conformity and productivity, looking to suppress Martin and Mary's poetic, as opposed to material, sense of reality.

Through the second and third acts of the play, Synge returns repeatedly to the idea that Martin Doul sees more clearly than those who have been sighted all their lives. He recognizes both the beauty of Molly Byrne and, at the end, the lies and hypocrisy of the villagers through intensely poetic language that already looks forward to that of Christy Mahon in *The Playboy of the Western World*:

I'm thinking by the mercy of God it's few sees anything but them is blind for a space. It's few sees the old woman rotting for the grave, and it's few sees the like of yourself, though it's shining you are, like a high lamp, would drag in the ships out of the sea.

(*Collected Works*, vol. 3, p. 117)

Like Nora Burke and the tramp, like Maurya, and like the tinkers, at the end of the play the

Douls walk off out of the drama into their own brighter (though literally darker) world:

MARTIN DOUL: Isn't it finer sights ourselves had a while since and we sitting dark smelling the sweet beautiful smells do be rising in the warm nights and hearing the swift flying things racing in the air, till we'd be looking up in our own minds into a grand sky, and seeing lakes, and broadening rivers, and hills are waiting for the spade and plough.

(*Collected Works,* vol. 3, p. 141)

Although the play is influenced by contemporary Continental drama, perhaps most immediately by the Belgian dramatist Maurice Maeterlinck's *Les Aveugles* (1890), and by Synge's hard reading in early Irish literature, *The Well of the Saints* brought to the stage all of the hard-won conclusions Synge had taken from the Aran Islands about the most healthy relationship between individuals and their environment and about the power of language to create alternative worlds, perhaps better, but never romanticized. As the couple wander out of the play and back into their dark daydreams, Mary Doul recognizes that by rejecting settled life, they can look forward to being constantly cold and wet, with no respite until their deaths. There is no evasion of harsh reality in Synge; none of the characters who break the communal bonds think that they are making an easy or a pleasant choice. As Mary Byrne says in *The Tinker's Wedding,* however, as she anticipates blows when her theft of the tin can is discovered, "What's a little stroke on your head beside sitting lonesome on a fine night, hearing the dogs barking, and the bats squeaking, and you saying over, it's a short while only till you die" (*Collected Works,* vol. 4, p. 27).

The nationalist press that had disliked *In the Shadow of the Glen* was guaranteed to hate *The Well of the Saints,* and the attacks came thick and fast after the opening night at the newly opened Abbey Theatre in Dublin. The play was denounced as blasphemous, as un-Irish, and as deeply unsympathetic to the country people it attempted to represent. Synge himself was accused of being mad. After a holiday in Donegal he soon shrugged off these attacks and set out for Connemara and County Mayo to write on social conditions for the liberal newspaper the *Manchester Guardian* in the company of W. B. Yeats's younger brother, the painter Jack.

Aside from this nascent journalistic career, however, Synge's life had changed remarkably in the previous four years. He had finally given up his room in Paris in early 1903 and returned to Ireland for good, only to head out to the western islands again, though this time it was not to Aran but to the Blasket Islands off the coast of County Kerry (about which he wrote a series of articles published in 1907). Despite the criticisms of Dublin audiences, his plays had been lauded in London, and successful tours had been undertaken through Britain. His plays were being translated into several European languages, including German and Czech. Synge was now one of the Irish National Theatre Society's most successful and certainly most notorious playwrights. In the autumn of 1905 he became a co-director of the society, along with Yeats and Lady Gregory. His personal life had been transformed as well, by a young actress called Molly Allgood, who, after a walk-on role in *The Well of the Saints,* was given the important role of Cathleen in a revival of *Riders to the Sea* in 1906. By then Synge had fallen in love with her.

"A JOY AND TRIUMPH TO THE ENDS OF LIFE AND TIME": THE PLAYBOY OF THE WESTERN WORLD *AND* DEIRDRE OF THE SORROWS

"AUDIENCE broke up in disorder at the word shift." This is probably the most famous telegram in literary history, sent from Lady Gregory to W. B. Yeats on 26 January 1907, the opening night of the Abbey Theatre's latest production, *The Playboy of the Western World.* Synge's new play about a young man who kills his father, only to be praised rather than condemned by the emotionally and physically desiccated Mayo village to which he escapes, already had provoked serious nerves among actors and directors, but at the interval everything seemed to be going well. Lady Gregory sent off her first telegram to Yeats, lecturing in Scotland: "Play great success." But as things resumed and the humor darkened and the language and actions became more violent, the audience became uneasy. Yells and hisses were heard. Then, with the hero, Christy Mahon, in sore danger of being lynched by the villagers, came the fateful lines: "It's Pegeen I'm seeking only, and what'd I care if you brought me a drift of chosen females, standing in their shifts itself maybe, from this place to the Eastern World?" (*Collected Works,* vol. 4, p. 167).

The image of the women of Ireland standing in their shifts, or underwear, was too much for part of the audience, who prided themselves on a prim adherence to correct morals. Synge already was identified as casting gross slurs against the sexual conduct of Irish womanhood; Willie Fay, the actor playing Christy, added to the insult by fluffing his lines, substituting "Mayo girls" for "chosen females" and thereby making the image all too specific, all too real. There was uproar, and the last minutes of the play were drowned out in boos, groans, and shouts.

For a week the violence that nightly was played out on the stage flowed into and through the audience at the Abbey Theatre and out again into the Dublin streets. The police were called in by Lady Gregory and Synge to deal with an increasingly organized, nationalist opposition determined to render the play inaudible. By the third night Yeats had returned to Ireland but made things worse by inviting some Trinity College students into the theater to prevent violence, only to see them arrive drunk and begin fistfights. Clearly on the edge of nervous collapse, Synge claimed not to "care a rap!" (Kilroy, 1971, p. 25) for the audience reaction and helped the police evict troublemakers, who promptly began brawling outside the theater. Throughout, the shell-shocked actors stood in front of the yelling, stamping, screaming audience mouthing their lines into the din. By the end of the week a kind of order had been restored inside the theater, but only by filling the auditorium with police and by appearing to put what claimed to be an Irish *national* theater under the protection of the British state. The press continued to be hostile, forthcoming scripts were withdrawn from the Abbey in protest, and Irish nationalist groups in Ireland and England censured the work, while Yeats enthusiastically took up the gauntlet by defending the play in public. As for Synge himself, he retired to bed physically and mentally exhausted.

What was it about *The Playboy of the Western World* that caused such an extreme reaction in 1907 and which continues to unsettle audiences up to the present day? Even a bare outline of the plot can suggest a few answers. A young man, Christy Mahon, who claims to have killed his cruel father with a blow from a spade, walks into a County Mayo shebeen (a rough, unlicensed bar) kept by the fiery Pegeen Mike and her father. A fine and poetic talker and an accomplished sportsman, Christy proves both fascinating and sexually attractive to the bored and degenerate villagers. Christy's position in the vil-

lage collapses, however, when his father, wounded rather than killed by the blow, hunts down his son and exposes him as a timid fool. Thinking to restore his heroic self-image and cement his love with Pegeen, Christy seemingly kills his father in front of the villagers, who find that while they can stomach no end of violence when it is described in stories, they have no taste for the real thing. While the crowd attempts to lynch Christy, his father, still alive but driven completely mad by the blow, crawls into the shebeen, taking Christy off with him to "have great times from this out telling stories of the villainy of Mayo and the fools is here" (*Collected Works*, vol. 4, p. 173). Pegeen remains, bewailing her fate and having lost her chance of life and vigor; she is left condemned to a sterile marriage with the weakling Shawn Keogh.

The Freudian-oedipal character of *The Playboy of the Western World*, which has as its hero a man who kills his father, is obvious and needs little belaboring. The fact that this "murderer" proves sexually attractive and a potential husband for both Pegeen Mike and the cunning Widow Quin clearly disgusted many among the original audience, who were convinced that any criminal would be rejected by the virtuous Irish peasants of their imagination. The fact that Synge heard the real-life story that provided the basis for *The Playboy of the Western World* on the Aran Islands counted for little among those persuaded that the play grossly and deliberately insulted the western peasant. With comedy and extreme violence in the form of beating, biting, and burning standing shoulder to shoulder in the play, the audience is constantly challenged in its reactions. Are we meant to be horrified or amused by Christy's desperate outburst as his father, covered in blood, crawls onstage: "Are you coming to be killed a third time or what ails you now?" (*Collected Works*, vol. 4, p. 171).

Ambiguity is at the very heart of the play, with tragedy and comedy, repulsion and attraction, laughter and horror, truth and fiction constantly battling for our attention. The rioting of those first Dublin audiences in 1907 can be viewed as an attempt, albeit an extreme one, to resolve the deep psychic tensions in the play by trying to fix it as immoral, false, and literally not worth listening to. A group claiming to speak for the community, or in this case the nation, by attempting to stifle individual dissent through the use of force had unwittingly acted out and validated the dramatic vision forged by Synge on the Aran Islands.

The Playboy of the Western World is generally felt by critics and modern audiences to be Synge's masterpiece, an epithet it fully deserves by being a clear dramatic and intellectual advance on his earlier work. The clash between the enervated community and the alienated individual, the material calculations underpinning sexual desire, and the profoundly poetic language that constantly seeks to negotiate between a better world existing in the imagination and the harshness that reality constantly thrusts on us are all familiar from *In the Shadow of the Glen* onward. But the occasional stiffness of characterization that is sometimes apparent in the earlier plays, the sense that for all their beauty of language old Maurya or Martin Doul are as much symbols as they are human beings, is dissipated in *The Playboy of the Western World.* The strange rhythms of Synge's language, the rhythms of a peasantry speaking English but still using the syntax and intonation of Irish, are on brilliant display throughout, spoken by what we feel to be real people.

It is in the social vision of *The Playboy of the Western World,* however, that Synge's arrival as a mature writer is most clearly displayed. In *The Aran Islands* and the earlier plays, heroic individuals like Nora Burke and the tramp, Michael Byrne and Sarah Casey, Martin and Mary Doul, even Synge himself, leave settled life behind for a difficult but more free existence on the road. Christy and old Mahon seem to fit this pattern, the former expressing the joys of his newfound freedom in a famous speech: "Ten thousand blessings upon all that's here, for you've turned me a likely gaffer in the end of all, the way I'll go romancing through a romping lifetime from this hour to the dawning of the judgment day" (*Collected Works,* vol. 4, p. 173). Yet, at the end, Synge introduces into the play a new and more disillusioned note. For if Christy looks forward to a "romping lifetime from this hour," it is possible only by exploiting the labor of his mad father: "Go with you, is it! I will then, like a gallant captain with his heathen slave. Go on now and I'll see you from this day stewing my oatmeal and washing my spuds, for I'm master of all fights from now" (*Collected Works,* vol. 4, p. 173).

In 1910 Yeats claimed that "Synge seemed by nature unfitted to think a political thought" (Yeats, p. 319). By the end of *The Playboy of the Western World,* however, Synge's reading in Paris of Marxist and anarchist classics a decade earlier bore belated fruit by providing him (despite Yeats) with a genuine politics: to rise to freedom in this world Christy has to push someone else down. Individual and, by implication, national independence can be achieved only by dominating others, be they crazed parents, recalcitrant poets and playwrights, or those of the "wrong" religion, politics, or background. To claim that liberation comes without a cost is exposed as a delusion. It is little wonder that the most extreme opposition to *The Playboy of the Western World* came from precisely those groups who claimed to be working disinterestedly for an independent Ireland.

By the time Molly Allgood played Pegeen Mike (the role had been specially written for her) in January 1907, she and Synge had been having a clandestine relationship for the best part of a year. She was about as unsuitable a match as an intellectual of an evangelical Protestant, patrician family approaching middle age could hope to make, being not only an actress (and, hence, intrinsically sinful in the eyes of Synge's family) but a Roman Catholic of poor background. Only eighteen years of age when Synge became infatuated with her, Molly often was more concerned with having fun than with the feelings of her rather jealous lover; the relationship was predictably stormy.

Despite the emotional tumults of his relationship with Molly and of the *Playboy* riots, Synge's literary career continued to prosper. *The Aran Islands* finally was published in April 1907, and the next month the Abbey Theatre took *The Playboy of the Western World* on tour to England, where it achieved resounding success in both Oxford and London. But his body was in decline. He had been ill for several months after the rioting in January. His neck glands, which had first been operated on a decade earlier, swelled again, and he was forced into a second operation in September 1907. By the end of the year he was experiencing severe pains in his side. Although plans to marry Molly went ahead in the teeth of opposition from the Synge family, he seems to have realized he was dying. He had begun writing poetry again and was to have a collection ready for publication by late 1908. Many of the poems are explicitly concerned with the realization that death was approaching:

And so when all my little work is done
They'll say I came in Eighteen-seventy-one,
And died in Dublin. . . . What year will they write
For my poor passage to the stall of Night?
(Collected Works, vol. 1, p. 33)

But even with Synge's temper clouded by thoughts of death and strained to breaking by Molly, by his family, and by Yeats and the Abbey company (he felt he was asked to take on too much of the daily grind, while his plays were deliberately underperformed by a company nervous of new riots), he continued to work. Through the winter of 1907 and into 1908 he was writing a new play, *Deirdre of the Sorrows*. With the title role to be played by Molly, this elegiac story of a doomed love may have had its roots in ancient Irish legend, but it also is resolutely autobiographical. As Robin Skelton notes, Deirdre's great final lament at the end of the play is also "Synge's lament for his own death, and also, perhaps, a speech he wished Molly herself to make over him" (Skelton, *J. M. Synge and His World*, p. 125).

In *Deirdre of the Sorrows*, Synge looked backward to his scholarly interests in archaic Irish history and legend pursued at Trinity College and in Paris and to the stately, classical quality he had perfected in *Riders to the Sea*. He also looked forward by abandoning the vigorous, colloquial tragicomedy of *The Playboy of the Western World* for something more mournful and obviously serious in tone, creating a mood in keeping with that of a man who knew his end was fast approaching. A brooding sense of coming dissolution hangs over the play from its opening scenes, as Deirdre's nurse, Lavarcham, and an old woman anxiously look into the twilight, fearing for their charge's safety: "The Sons of Usna, Naisi and his brothers, are above chasing hares for two days or three, and the same a while since when the moon was full" (*Collected Works*, vol. 4, p. 183). Betrothed to the aged king of Ulster, Conchubor, Deirdre also has been prophesied as fated to bring destruction on the royal halls at Emain Macha with aid of the sons of Usna. Conchubor's sudden arrival at Lavarcham's house to wed Deirdre only encourages her to elope to Britain with Naisi and his brothers.

The second act opens seven years later in Alban (modern-day Scotland), where Deirdre and Naisi have been living in the woods in an almost paradisiacal happiness. But with the arrival of Conchubor's envoy, Fergus, who aims to bring them back to Ireland, Deirdre begins to fear not the death she foresees back in Emain Macha but the loss of youth and love if Naisi and she are left to grow old together in Alban:

DEIRDRE: There are as many ways to wither love as there are stars in a night of Samhain; but there is no way to keep life or love with it a short space only. . . . It's for that there's nothing lonesome like a love is watching out the time most lovers do be sleeping. . . . It's for that we're setting out for Emain Macha when the tide turns on the sand.

NAISI: You're right maybe. . . . It should be a poor thing to see great lovers and they sleepy and old.
(*Collected Works*, vol. 4, p. 233)

Returning to Ireland, Deirdre and Naisi find nothing but treachery from a vengeful Conchubor, "ready to destroy mankind, and skin the gods to win her" (*Collected Works*, vol. 4, p. 243). With the honorable Fergus delayed in the north, Naisi and his brothers are killed by Conchubor's soldiers. Fergus arrives and burns Emain Macha and fulfils the prophesies spoken at Deirdre's birth. "I have put away sorrow like a shoe that is worn out and muddy," says Deirdre, who, stabbing herself, finally escapes Conchubor (*Collected Works*, vol. 4, p. 267). The king, now shown as nothing but an old and weak man, is led offstage as Emain Macha burns and Lavarcham bewails the fate of Deirdre and Naisi.

Although the play is complete, *Deirdre of the Sorrows* never was truly finished, and Synge was revising and reworking it until he became too ill to write. The broad outlines of his vision are clear, however. As in *The Playboy of the Western World*, Synge darkens and makes more complex the ideas behind the early plays and *The Aran Islands* by focusing on the *return* of Deirdre and Naisi to Ireland and their expected social positions rather than on their leaving. The act of return is itself part of the greater escape—not this time an escape from the trammels of a brutal marriage or the ugliness of the body and the world but a metaphysical jailbreak out of the inevitable decline of life through a clear-eyed acceptance (on Deirdre's part at least) of death. "It is not a small thing to be rid of grey hairs and the loosening of the teeth," she announces in her final keen for herself and Naisi (*Collected Works*, vol. 4, pp. 267).

It is in this seeking for solace in the face of imminent death that *Deirdre of the Sorrows* takes on its air of intimate autobiography. The latest extant revisions to the play date from January 1909, and by that time death was staring Synge directly in the face. He had undertaken a trip to Germany in October 1908, revisiting (as he probably knew) for the last time the Von Eiken sisters and the

Rhineland, where his European adventure had begun fifteen years earlier. While he was in Germany his mother died; he could not bring himself to return to Ireland for the funeral. As his letters to Molly from this time make plain, the loss was too much. Despite the fact that Synge rejected her religious and moral principles, mother and son had remained emotionally bonded to the last. By early 1909 he was preparing for his own death, working hard at *Deirdre of the Sorrows,* correcting proofs of his *Poems and Translations,* and putting his papers and monetary affairs in order. On 31 January he entered the Elpis Nursing Home, suffering from terminal cancer; on 24 March 1909 he died at the age of thirty-seven. At the funeral the Synge family, formal and reserved, stood apart from Yeats and the company from the Abbey Theatre, their disapproval of their most famous kinsman's vocation absolute even in death. For reasons of her own, Molly Allgood did not attend. *Deirdre of the Sorrows* was first performed at the Abbey on 13 January 1910, directed by and starring Molly. Perhaps she paid her final respects there: "It is a pitiful thing, Conchubor, you have done this night in Emain, yet a thing will be a joy and triumph to the ends of life and time" (*Collected Works,* vol. 4, p. 269). It was a fitting epitaph.

SELECTED BIBLIOGRAPHY

I. COLLECTED WORKS. *The Works of John M. Synge,* 4 vols. (Dublin, 1910); *The Plays and Poems of J. M. Synge* (London, 1963), ed. by T. R. Henn; *Collected Works,* comprising *Poems* (London, 1962), ed. by Robin Skelton; *Prose* (London, 1966), ed. by Alan Price; *Plays, Book 1* (London, 1968), ed. by Ann Saddlemyer; *Plays, Book 2* (London, 1968), ed. by Ann Saddlemyer; *Plays, Poems and Prose,* ed., with an intro and notes, by Alison Smith (London, 1992).

II. PLAYS. The Shadow of the Glen *and* Riders to the Sea (London, 1905); *The Well of the Saints* (London, 1905); *The Playboy of the Western World: A Comedy in Three Acts* (Dublin, 1907); *The Tinker's Wedding: A Comedy in Two Acts* (Dublin, 1907); *Deirdre of the Sorrows: A Play* (Dublin, 1909); *The Playboy of the Western World* (London, 1975), ed. by Malcolm Kelsall; *The Well of the Saints* (Washington, D.C., 1982), ed., with an intro. and notes, by Nicholas Grene; *The Playboy of the Western World and Other Plays* (Oxford, 1995), ed. by Ann Saddlemyer.

III. OTHER WORKS. *The Aran Islands* (Dublin and London, 1907), autobiography; *Poems and Translations* (Dublin, 1909); *The Aran Islands* (Oxford, 1979), ed. by Robin Skelton; *The Aran Islands* (Harmondsworth, U.K., 1992), ed., with an intro., by Tim Robinson.

IV. LETTERS. *Theatre Business: The Correspondence of the First Abbey Theatre Directors—William Butler Yeats, Lady Gregory and J. M. Synge* (Gerrards Cross, 1982), selected and ed. by Ann Saddlemyer; *The Collected Letters of John Millington Synge,* vol. 1: *1871–1907* (Oxford, 1983), ed. by Ann Saddlemyer; *vol. 2: 1907–1909* (Oxford, 1984), ed. by Ann Saddlemyer.

V. BIBLIOGRAPHIES. Nicholas Grene, ed., *The Synge Manuscripts in the Library of Trinity College, Dublin: A Catalogue Prepared on the Occasion of the Synge Centenary Exhibition, 1971* (Dublin, 1971); Paul Michael Levitt, ed., *J. M. Synge: A Bibliography of Published Criticism* (Dublin, 1974); E. H. Mikhail, ed., *J. M. Synge: A Bibliography of Criticism* (London and Totowa, N.J., 1975).

VI. BIOGRAPHICAL STUDIES. Lady Gregory, *Our Irish Theatre: A Chapter of Autobiography* (New York and London, 1914); Samuel Synge, *Letters to My Daughter: Memoirs of John Millington Synge* (Dublin, 1932); David H. Greene and Edward M. Stephens, *J. M Synge, 1871–1909* (New York, 1959); W. B. Yeats, "Preface to the First Edition of *The Well of the Saints,*" and "J. M. Synge and the Ireland of His Time," in his *Essays and Introductions* (New York, 1961); Robin Skelton, *J. M Synge and His World* (London, 1971); Edward Stephens, *My Uncle John: Edward Stephens's Life of J. M. Synge,* (London, 1974), ed. by Andrew Carpenter; E. H. Mikhail, ed. *J. M. Synge: Interviews and Recollections* (London, 1977); David M. Kiely, *John Millington Synge: A Biography* (Dublin, 1994); W. J. McCormack, *Fool of the Family: A Life of J. M. Synge* (London, 2000).

VII. CRITICAL STUDIES. Maurice Bourgeois, *John Millington Synge and the Irish Theatre* (London, 1913); Daniel Corkery, *Synge and Anglo-Irish Literature* (Cork, Ireland, 1931); Alan Price, *Synge and Anglo-Irish Drama* (London, 1961); Donna Lorine Gerstenberger, *John Millington Synge* (New York, 1964; rev. ed., Boston, 1990); Thomas R. Whitaker, ed., *Twentieth-Century Interpretations of* The Playboy of the Western World (Englewood Cliffs, N.J., 1969).

James Francis Kilroy, *The "Playboy" Riots* (Dublin, 1971); Robin Skelton, *The Writings of J. M. Synge* (London, 1971); Lilo Stephens, ed., *My Wallet of Photographs: The Collected Photographs of J. M. Synge* (Dublin, 1971); S. B. Bashrui, ed., *A Centenary Tribute to John Millington Synge, 1871–1909: Sunshine and the Moon's Delight* (Gerrards Cross and New York, 1972); Maurice Harmon, ed., *J. M. Synge: Centenary Papers, 1971* (Dublin, 1972); Nicholas Grene, *Synge: A Critical Study of the Plays* (Basingstoke, 1975); Robert Hogan and James Kilroy, *The Abbey Theatre: The Years of Synge, 1905–1909* (Dublin, 1978); Katharine Worth, *The Irish Drama of Europe from Yeats to Beckett* (London, 1978);

Declan Kiberd, *Synge and the Irish Language* (2nd ed., London, 1993); Weldon Thornton, *J. M. Synge and the Western Mind* (Gerrards Cross, 1979); George J. Watson, *Irish Identity and the Literary Revival: Synge, Yeats, Joyce* and O'Casey (London, 1979, and Washington, D.C., 1994).

Toni O'Brien Johnson, *Synge: The Medieval and the Grotesque* (Gerrards Cross, 1982); Mary C. King, *The Drama of J. M. Synge* (London, 1985); Simon Williams, "John Millington Synge: Transforming Myths of Ireland," in *Facets of European Modernism: Essays in Honour of James McFarlane* (Norwich, England, 1985), edited by Janet Garton; John Wilson Foster, *Fictions of the Irish Literary Revival: A Changeling Art* (Syracuse, N.Y., 1987); Edward A. Kopper, Jr., ed., *A J. M. Synge Literary Companion* (London and New York, 1988); Declan Kiberd, "Synge, Symons and the Isles of Aran," in *Notes on Modern Irish Literature*, vol. 1 (Fenelton, Penn., 1989).

Deirdre Toomey, "Killing the Da: Synge and *The Golden Bough*," in *Sir James Frazer and the Literary Imagination: Essays in Affinity and Influence* (Basingstoke, U.K., and New York, 1990), ed. by Robert Fraser; Ronald Ayling, ed., *J. M. Synge: Four Plays: A Casebook* (Basingstoke, U.K., 1992), including *Riders to the Sea*, *The Well of the Saints*, *The Playboy of the Western World*, *Deirdre of the Sorrows*; Deborah Fleming, *"A Man Who Does Not Exist": The Irish Peasant in the Work of W. B. Yeats and J. M. Synge* (Ann Arbor, Mich., 1995); Alexander G. Gonzalez, ed., *Assessing the Achievement of J. M. Synge* (London and Westport, Conn., 1996); Declan Kiberd, *Inventing Ireland: The Literature of the Modern Nation* (London, 1996); R. F. Foster, *W. B. Yeats: A Life*, vol. 1: *The Apprentice Mage, 1865–1914* (Oxford, 1997); Donald Davie, "The Poetic Diction of John M. Synge," in his *With the Grain: Essays on Thomas Hardy and Modern British Poetry* (Manchester, England, 1998), ed. by Clive Wilmer; Robert Welch, *The Abbey Theatre, 1899–1999: Form and Pressure* (Oxford, 1999); Nicholas Grene, ed., *Interpreting Synge: Essays from the Synge Summer School, 1991–2000* (Dublin, 2000).

VIRGINIA WOOLF

(1882–1941)

Jane Goldman

LIFE

THE ART OF biography is for Virginia Woolf "that queer amalgamation of dream and reality, that perpetual marriage of granite and rainbow," which corresponds to the combination of "truth" and "personality," and allows us access to "not only the outer life of work and activity but the inner life of emotion and thought," and is concerned as much with the "uneventful lives of poets and painters" as with "the lives of soldiers and statesmen" ("The New Biography," in Leonard Woolf, ed., *Collected Essays*, p. 474). Her dualism, "granite and rainbow," has been helpful as a critical tool for reading her work (which so often engages in dualisms, contraries, and oppositions), and heeded—to varying degrees—as a guide for writing her life. It is worth noting how her biography (more accurately, biographies) has enormously influenced the reception of her work and our cultural preconceptions about her person. There have been numerous, often competing, biographies of Woolf. The standard authority remains Quentin Bell's excellent 1972 biography of his aunt, but this is probably best read alongside Hermione Lee's already classic *Virginia Woolf* (1996), which offers a wealth of new insight and material. Whereas Bell's biography is told very much from the perspective of his mother and Woolf's sister, Vanessa Bell, Lee's biography tends to orient Woolf's life more sympathetically from the standpoint of her husband, Leonard Woolf. *Moments of Being*, a collection of Woolf's autobiographical reflections, published posthumously, is also an important source, along with the many published volumes of her diaries, journals, and letters.

Woolf's public and inner lives, then, are well documented. In her diaries, letters, and notebooks, we can read both granite and rainbow. There are entertaining and moving accounts of her social engagements and encounters (she seems to have known or met nearly everyone of importance in her day) as well as of her intimate personal relationships, insightful notes on her vast reading (she seems to have read nearly everything), and illuminating discussions of her works in progress (she attempted most genres: novels, reviews, essays, articles, short stories, pamphlets, biographies, translations, even the odd poem).

One aspect of biography that Woolf's "granite and rainbow" theory perhaps does not adequately explore or anticipate, however, is the potentially turbulent and proliferating iconic cultural afterlife of the subject. In other words, as well as the facts and personality and imaginative and creative life, there is also the ongoing cultural production of the subject to consider, and this is crucial to any consideration of Virginia Woolf's life and work. Brenda Silver, in her brilliant and timely *Virginia Woolf Icon* (1999), remarks on how, "in the popular realm, continual enactments and reenactments of Virginia Woolf as name, image, spectacle, fashion, or performance have become the norm" (p. xvii). She traces the "multiple, contradictory sites [Woolf] occupies in our cultural discourses: British intellectual aristocrat, high modernist, canonical author, writer of best-sellers, Bloomsbury liberal, Labour Party socialist, feminist, sapphist, acknowledged beauty, suicide, and woman" (p. 11). She comments on the cultural phenomenon whereby people who have never knowingly read a word by Virginia Woolf can confidently relate (while fatuously citing the title of Edward Albee's play, *Who's Afraid of Virginia Woolf?*) that she was mad, a snob, and committed suicide.

It here seems necessary (even now) to modify these observations by noting that although Woolf endured a number of episodes of insanity, she seems to have enjoyed a full and productive creative and social life with long periods free of illness; that she was capable of sending up her own snobbery ("I am not only a coronet snob; but also a lit up drawing room snob; a social festivity snob" (*Moments of Being*, p. 210); and that her suicide was not as youthful as Sylvia Plath's, occurring when she was nearly sixty years old (and no longer much resembling the young beauty of the famous G. C. Beresford photograph in the National Portrait Gallery), at a harrowing time of national emergency (German bombardment in World War II). Putting aside the cultural wars over her iconic persona, it may still be acknowledged that Woolf's literary reputation rests on her innovative work as a writer of experimental fiction and, posthumously, as a central and virtuoso diarist and letter writer of the Bloomsbury Group. But she was also (from a young age) a professional reviewer, a biographer, an accomplished and innovative essayist, an impressive polemicist and political organizer (in the socialist and women's movements), and not least, along with her husband, a successful and influential publisher.

It is a terrifying responsibility to relate even the bare facts of Woolf's life, given the explosively divergent accounts of it in circulation. The Woolf scholar Jane Marcus has argued bitterly and publicly with Woolf's nephew and biographer, Quentin Bell, who insisted "Woolf wasn't a feminist and wasn't political," that Woolf's work is in fact Marxist and feminist (Homans, p. 7). Feminist scholarship has done much to counter such venomous demolitions of Woolf as the poet and critic Tom Paulin's notorious 1991 British television broadcast, *J'Accuse.* But feminist scholarship has also occasionally unleashed its own dangerous stereotypes of Woolf, for example, as "guerrilla fighter in a Victorian skirt" (Marcus, *New Feminist Essays*), or as suicide case and victim of childhood sexual abuse (DeSalvo). Here, then, are the facts.

Virginia Woolf was born Adeline Virginia Stephen on 25 January 1882. Her father was the distinguished author, critic, and Alpinist, Leslie Stephen (1832–1904), editor of the *Cornhill Magazine* (1871–1882), the *Dictionary of National Biography* (1882–1890), and the *Alpine Journal* (1868–1872). Her mother was Julia Prinsep Stephen (1846–1895), widow of Herbert Duckworth, with whom she had three children, George, Stella, and Gerald. Leslie Stephen, also widowed, had one child, Laura, by his first marriage to Minny, the daughter of William Makepeace Thackeray. Virginia was the third of four children born to Leslie and Julia. The eldest, Vanessa (Bell), became an important avant-garde artist; the second, Thoby, died tragically young; and the youngest, Adrian, became a psychoanalyst and prominent pacifist.

Virginia and Vanessa were not schooled like their brothers but educated at home. Woolf later recalled the formative influence of having "free run of [her father's] large and unexpurgated library" (*Essays,* vol. 4, p. 79). She also met many of the period's most notable intellectuals, artists, and writers, who were often visitors to the Stephen household. She enjoyed idyllic family holidays in St. Ives, Cornwall, reading, talking, and playing. The Stephen children produced their own family newspaper, *The Hyde Park Gate News* (now in the British Library). When her mother died in 1895, Woolf suffered her first breakdown, and the family endured an unhappy period of mourning, further exacerbated by the death of Woolf's half-sister, Stella, in 1897. Woolf's childhood and adolescence were also marred by sexual abuse at the hands of her half-brothers, a matter of incendiary concern for some biographers (see DeSalvo). While Thoby, and later, Adrian, went to Trinity college, Cambridge, Vanessa undertook training in the visual arts (attending the Slade School of Fine Art for a while), and Woolf pursued a writer's education and trained in classical Greek (at King's College in Kensington, and later with Clara Pater and then Janet Case). The sisters visited Cambridge a number of times to meet Thoby, whose friends there included Clive Bell, Lytton Strachey, Leonard Woolf, and Saxon Sydney-Turner.

Leslie Stephen died in 1904. That year his children took a retreat in Wales for a period and then traveled in Italy. Vanessa and Virginia went on to Paris, where they met up with Clive Bell. On returning to London, Woolf suffered a severe, suicidal breakdown. But several positive changes also occurred. During her convalescence, Vanessa moved the Stephen household to Gordon Square, Bloomsbury, a move that ushered in a new period of freedom and independence, particularly for the sisters. In the same year, Woolf assisted F. W. Maitland with a biography of her father, and her first (anonymous) review appeared in the *Guardian.* In 1905 Woolf began work as teacher of literature at Morley College, and traveled to Portugal. Thoby began hosting "Thursday Evenings" in the Bloomsbury house, and Vanessa founded the Friday Club, a society where young, and at first, female, artists could meet, debate, and exhibit work. After an ill-fated family visit to Greece in 1906, Thoby died of typhoid. Vanessa married Clive Bell in 1907. Woolf moved with Adrian to Fitzroy Square, where they continued hosting "Thursday Evenings."

Apart from Woolf, other members of the Bloomsbury Group as it strengthened in the following years included the art critics Roger Fry and Clive Bell, the artists Duncan Grant and Vanessa Bell, the economist Maynard Keynes, the critic Lytton Strachey, the novelist E. M. Forster, the society hostess Lady Ottoline Morrell, and the political journalist and publisher Leonard Woolf, formerly in the Colonial Service. They were a liberal, pacifist, and at times libertine intellectual enclave of Cambridge-based privilege. Woolf's aesthetic understanding was in part shaped by, and at first primarily interpreted in terms of, (male) Bloomsbury's dominant aesthetic and philosophical preoccupations, rooted in the work of G. E. Moore, and culminating in Fry's and Clive Bell's differing brands of pioneering aesthetic formalism (see Johnstone; McLaurin). But increasing awareness of Woolf's feminism and of the influence on her work of other women artists, writers, and thinkers has meant that these points of reference, though of importance, are no longer considered adequate in approaching Woolf's work (see Marcus; Gillespie; Carpentier).

The year 1910 was significant for Woolf and Bloomsbury. In February she took part in the notorious *Dreadnought* hoax. Woolf and her brother Adrian, Duncan Grant, Horace Cole, and others, masquerading as the emperor of Abyssinia and entourage, conned their way past naval high security into a guided tour of the warship HMS *Dreadnought*. Bloomsbury notoriety was compounded in November of that year with the opening of Roger Fry's groundbreaking exhibition "Manet and the Post-Impressionists," the first major showing in Britain of the work of Van Gogh, Gauguin, Cezanne, and other avant-garde continental artists. It met with huge public and critical outrage. Woolf and Vanessa Bell masqueraded as "Gauguin girls" at the Post-Impressionist Ball. She also joined the suffrage movement in 1910. By 1912 Vanessa Bell and Duncan Grant were among those representing the English artists converted to the new avant-garde aesthetic, in the Second Post-Impressionist Exhibition.

The year 1912 also saw the marriage of Leonard and Virginia Woolf. They were advised against having children because of Virginia's recurring depressive illness, a cause of some regret to her, and a point of much heated debate among her later biographers. She suffered another breakdown soon after her marriage and again after the publi-

cation of her first novel, *The Voyage Out* (1915), which was published by her half-brother, Gerald Duckworth. The Woolfs moved to Hogarth House, London, in 1915, and began the Hogarth Press in 1917. Their first publication was *Two Stories* (1917) by Leonard and Virginia Woolf—"Three Jews" and "The Mark on the Wall," respectively.

During this period Woolf attended the 1917 Club, a left-wing political society founded by Leonard, and was organizer of her local Women's Co-Operative Guild. Woolf's second novel, *Night and Day*, was published by Duckworth in 1919. Thereafter the Hogarth Press published all her work. Her first set of experimental short stories, *Monday or Tuesday*, was published in 1921. Woolf's control over the production of her own work is a significant factor in her genesis as a writer. The Hogarth Press became an important and influential publishing house in the decades that followed. It was responsible, for example, for the first major works of Freud in English and published significant works by key modernist writers such as T. S. Eliot and Gertrude Stein (see Willis). Woolf herself set the type for the Hogarth edition of Eliot's *The Waste Land* (1923). In 1919 the Woolfs acquired Monk's House in Rodmell, Sussex, where they spent nearly every summer until her death. They moved their London residence from Hogarth House to Tavistock Square in 1924, and to Mecklenburgh Square in 1939.

By the time *Jacob's Room* (1922) was published, Woolf's reputation was consolidating as an avant-garde writer and important literary critic. *Jacob's Room* was the first in a sequence of formally experimental, increasingly lyric novels including *Mrs. Dalloway* (1925), *To the Lighthouse* (1927), *Orlando: A Biography* (1928), and *The Waves* (1931). Woolf's highly influential modernist and feminist literary theories were expounded in *Mr. Bennett and Mrs. Brown* (1924), and *A Room of One's Own* (1929). She also published two collections of essays, *The Common Reader* (1925) and *The Common Reader: Second Series* (1932). In the early 1920s she met and fell in love with the writer Vita Sackville-West, wife of Harold Nicolson, and the development of their close relationship, which does not seem to have undermined either woman's marriage, coincided with Woolf's most productive years as a writer. In June 1927 Woolf joined Vita, Harold, Leonard, and other friends on an expedition to Yorkshire to witness (along with twenty thousand others) the first total eclipse of the sun to be visible from Britain in several hundred years. It had a momentous influence on Woolf. She recorded it in her diary, drew upon it for her influential essay "The Sun and the Fish" (1928), and rewrote it (in many drafts) for her closing meditation on "the world seen without a self" in *The Waves* (pp. 310ff). This was a period of increasing commercial success for Woolf in which she took great pride as writer *and* publisher. *To the Lighthouse*, for example, was awarded the Prix *Femina* in 1928, and sold 3,873 copies in its first year. Woolf splurged on a new car in the summer after its publication. *The Waves* too sold very well.

In the 1930s Woolf's work became more overtly political. The (draft) essay-novel *The Pargiters* (published posthumously in 1978), was an ambitious project conceived to combine critical and political argument with fictional narrative, which Woolf eventually divided for publication into two works, the epistolary antifascist, pacifist polemic *Three Guineas* (1938) and the more conventional novel *The Years* (1937). During this period the composer Ethel Smythe eclipsed Vita Sackville-West as the center of Woolf's affections. Woolf's experiments in biography continued with *Flush: A Biography* (1933), a fictional and satirical portrait of the poet Elizabeth Barrett-Browning's spaniel; and with the more serious, straightforward (and for Woolf, more difficult to write) biography, *Roger Fry* (1940). Bloomsbury lost Fry and Lytton Strachey to early deaths in the 1930s. But the death of Woolf's nephew Julian Bell in the Spanish Civil War was perhaps the bitterest blow. The Woolfs retreated to Monk's House during the early bombardments of World War II. She was in the process of finalizing her last novel, known in draft as *Pointz Hall*, when on 28 March 1941, fearing a return of her insanity, she committed suicide by drowning herself in the river Ouse. *Between the Acts* was published posthumously in July 1941.

CRITICAL WRITINGS AND
THE MODERNIST AESTHETIC

WOOLF was not only a writer of avant-garde, experimental fiction, whose reputation stands alongside canonical high modernists such as James Joyce and T. S. Eliot, she was also a centrally important theorist of modernist writing and of feminist aesthetics. Her criticism has shaped many of the fundamental ideas and debates of literary criticism and theory concerned with modernism, feminism, and even postmodernism. It also provides a framework for understanding Woolf's own fiction. It seems sensible, therefore, to discuss as fully as possible the key issues in her critical works before turning to her fiction.

Although she did not write in the style of high theoretical discourse, Woolf has been recognized for her experimentalism with, and transformation of, critical writing itself. Her criticism is discussed below in terms of modernism and feminism.

"Modern Fiction," first published in April 1919 (as "Modern Novels") and revised for the first *Common Reader* (it is the revised, 1925, version—often dated 1919—that is commonly anthologized and cited here), is perhaps Woolf's best known and most frequently quoted essay. Woolf here distinguishes between the outmoded "materialism" of the Edwardian novelists H. G. Wells, John Galsworthy, and Arnold Bennett, and the more "spiritual" and experimental writing of her Georgian contemporaries. The tyranny of plot and characterization afflicts Bennett's work, she contends, along with the obligation "to provide comedy, tragedy, love interest, and an air of probability embalming the whole so impeccable that if all his figures were to come to life they would find themselves dressed down to the last button of their coats in the fashion of the hour." Such writing fails to capture "life," as Woolf's most famous and most quoted passages of criticism explains:

Look within and life, it seems, is very far from being "like this." Examine for a moment an ordinary mind on an ordinary day. The mind receives a myriad impressions—trivial, fantastic, evanescent, or engraved with the sharpness of steel. From all sides they come, an incessant shower of innumerable atoms; and as they fall, as they shape themselves into the life of Monday or Tuesday, the accent falls differently from of old; the moment of importance came not here but there; so that, if a writer were a free man and not a slave, if he could write what he chose, not what he must, if he could base his work upon his own feeling and not upon convention, there would be no plot, no comedy, no love interest or catastrophe in the accepted style, and perhaps not a single button sewn on as the Bond Street tailors would have it. Life is not a series of gig lamps symmetrically arranged; life is a luminous halo, a semi-transparent envelope surrounding us from the beginning of consciousness to the end. Is it not the task of the novelist to convey this varying, this unknown and uncircumscribed spirit, whatever aberration or complexity it may display, with as little mixture of the alien and external as possible?

(*Essays*, vol. 4, pp. 160–161)

Woolf's story "The Moment: Summer's Night" (c.1929), offers a closer, equally lyrical account of a luminous moment and is often cited in conjunction with this passage (see Guiguet; Richter). In advocating subjective, fleeting, interior experience as the proper stuff of fiction along with the abandonment of conventional plot, genre, and narrative structure, this passage of "Modern Fiction" has become one of the standard critical sources in the discussion of modernist literary qualities—particularly "stream-of-consciousness"—not least because it is followed by a (not uncritical) defense of James Joyce's work. Woolf cites his *Portrait of the Artist as a Young Man* (1916) and the extracts from *Ulysses* (1922) that had been recently published in the *Little Review* (1918) to exemplify the new "spiritual" writing. Joyce, she argues, is "concerned at all costs to reveal the flickerings of that inmost flame which flashes its messages through the brain" (*Essays,* vol. 4, p. 161). Woolf's alchemical imagery here owes much to Walter Pater's aesthetics (see Meisel), and her concern with subjective temporality—the epiphanic "moment"—to the philosophy of Henri Bergson (see Kumar). Although Woolf identifies a fragment of *Ulysses* ("Hades") as a "masterpiece" for "its brilliancy, its sordidity, its incoherence, its sudden lightning flashes of significance," she nevertheless finds that it "fails to compare" with the work of Joseph Conrad or Thomas Hardy "because of the comparative poverty of the writer's mind" (p. 161). Woolf is less generous to Joyce in private. On reading *Ulysses* she notoriously captures him in her diary as "a queasy undergraduate scratching his pimples" (*Diary,* vol. 2, p. 188). "Modern Fiction" nevertheless stands as an early and significant defense of his work, and as a manifesto of modernism.

"Mr. Bennett and Mrs. Brown" (first published in 1924 as "Character in Fiction"), like many of Woolf's essays, evolved from a speech (in this instance to the Cambridge Heretics Society), and many of its rhetorical features survive in the published text. Here Woolf continues her assault on the Edwardians, Wells, Galsworthy, and Bennett, for their materialist conventions, as well as her uneven defense of the Georgians, Joyce, Eliot, Forster, Strachey, and D. H. Lawrence, whose work, she declares, must make us "reconcile ourselves to a season of failures and fragments" (*Essays* , vol. 3, p. 435). The essay's title is derived from its central, virtuoso conceit whereby Woolf illustrates the inadequacies of the Edwardian novelists as she makes a number of attempts, using their "tools," to construct a fictional narrative about the character of "Mrs. Brown," a stranger encountered on a train. The essay also contains one of Woolf's most famous and most quoted assertions, that "on or about December 1910 human character changed" (p. 421). This has come to represent for many cultural commentators the cataclysmic moment of modernity, the inception of the avant-garde, the shock of the new. In the context of the essay, it marks the shift from the Edwardian to the Georgian era, when "all human relations have shifted—those between masters and servants, husbands and wives, parents and children. And when human relations change there is at the same time a change in religion, conduct, politics, and literature" (p. 422). But Woolf is not arguing that literature merely changes in terms of subject matter to reflect new, modern experience, but that literary form itself undergoes radical and turbulent transformation: "And so the smashing and the crashing began. . . . Grammar is violated; syntax disintegrated" (p. 434).

The work of Joyce, Eliot, and Strachey illustrate the point that modern literature has necessarily become caught up in the business of finding new form. Readers must "tolerate the spasmodic, the obscure, the fragmentary, the failure" (p. 436). The self-reflexive, fragmentary, subjective, and momentary qualities of modernist writing are, of course, acknowledged and celebrated by Woolf's avant-garde contemporaries, but her own particular aesthetic was anathema to some. Woolf's "luminous halo" metaphors, for instance, "imply an art that rejects precise statement and moral certainty," according to M. H. Levenson, "in favour of the suggestiveness and imprecision usually associated with symbolism or Impressionism. [Ezra] Pound on the other hand, opposed all 'mushy technique' and 'emotional slither,' preferring a poetry 'as much like granite as it could possibly be' " (pp. 154–155). Levenson alerts us to the critical ruptures of the period. Yet there is common ground between Woolf and Pound. Eliot, who owed much to Pound, for example, was also championed by Woolf.

FEMINISM AND A ROOM OF ONE'S OWN

IT was not only her choice of metaphor that could distance Woolf from her male contemporaries, but her feminism. "There are spots of it all over her work," according to her friend Forster, "and it was constantly in her mind" (p. 34). But even he acknowledged *A Room of One's Own* (1929), as "brilliant" (p. 34). Woolf's feminist tract, undoubtedly her most important contribution to literary criticism and theory, famously blurs the boundaries between critical and fictional discourses. It is regarded as a founding text for feminist aesthetics, not least because it is also a source of many, often conflicting, theoretical positions. *A Room of One's Own* is cited as locus classicus for a number of important modern feminist debates concerning gender, sexuality, materialism, education, patriarchy, androgyny, subjectivity, the feminine sentence, the notion of "Shakespeare's sister," the canon, the body, race, class, and so on. The title alone has had enormous impact as cultural shorthand for a modern feminist agenda, while the book itself is widely regarded as "the first book of feminist literary criticism" and "the founding text of Anglo-American feminist literary theory" (Gallop, pp. 77, 145). Woolf developed the text from two lectures, to Cambridge women students, and an essay version, on "Women and Fiction"; and although much revised and expanded, the final version significantly retains the original's sense of a woman speaking to women.

Woolf again adopts fictional narrative strategies and shifting narrative personae to present her argument. She anticipates postmodernist, post-Lacanian theoretical concerns with the constitution of gender and subjectivity in language when she begins by declaring that " 'I' is only a convenient term for somebody who has no real being . . . (call me Mary Beton, Mary Seton, Mary Carmichael or by any name you please—it is not a matter of any importance)" (p. 5). Woolf here invokes the Scottish ballad "The Four Marys," and ventriloquizes much of her argument through the voice of her own "Mary Beton" (Marcus, p. 197). In the course of the book she encounters the other Marys—Mary Seton has become a student at "Fernham" college, and Mary Carmichael an aspiring novelist—and it has been suggested that Woolf's opening and closing remarks may be in the voice of Mary Hamilton (the narrator of the ballad). This multivocal strategy, along with the text's multitude of other citations, has encouraged later feminists, following Julia Kristeva, to celebrate *A Room of One's Own* as a dialogical text. The intertext with the Scottish ballad feeds a subtext in Woolf's argument concerning the suppression of

the role of motherhood—Mary Hamilton sings the ballad from the gallows where she is to be hung for infanticide. (Marie Carmichael, furthermore, is the nom de plume of the contraceptive activist Marie Stopes, who published a novel, *Love's Creation*, in 1928.) Woolf further insists, in her later essay "Professions for Women" (1931), on the woman writer's necessary suppression of a traditionally submissive—and domestic—feminine role, encapsulated in Coventry Patmore's 1856 poem *Angel in the House*: "Had I not killed her she would have killed me. She would have plucked the heart out of my writing. . . . Killing the Angel in the House was part of the occupation of a woman writer" (*Essays*, vol. 4, p. 153).

Woolf's main subject in *A Room of One's Own*, as her earlier title indicates, is "Women and Fiction," and her main argument is that "a woman must have money and a room of her own if she is to write fiction" (p. 4). Woolf's contempt for the "materialism" of the Edwardian novelists seems forgotten here, as the narrator begins by recounting her experience at Oxbridge where she was refused access to the library and goes on to compare in some detail the splendid opulence of her lunch at a men's college with the austerity of her dinner at a more recently established women's college (Fernham). This account is the foundation for the book's main, materialist, argument: "intellectual freedom depends upon material things" (p. 141). Woolf extends this line of argument in her later essay "The Leaning Tower," a paper she read to the Workers' Educational Association, to discuss the class alignments of writing. She claims that "all writers from Chaucer to the present day . . . come from the middle class" and "were educated at public schools and universities" (p. 165). D. H. Lawrence is her only exception. She rallies her working class audience by insisting, "we are not going to leave writing to be done for us by a small class of well-to-do young men who have only a pinch, a thimbleful of experience to give us. We are going to add our own experience, to make our own contribution" (p. 178).

If the categorization of middle-class women like herself with the working classes seems problematic here, Woolf has already proposed, in *A Room of One's Own*, that women be understood as a separate class altogether. Here is the nub of contention in feminism's encounters with Marxism. Yet the alignment of women and the working class is hardly exclusive to Woolf. *A Room of One's Own* was published in the year after the full enfranchisement of women and ten years after the enfranchisement of working-class men along with middle-class, propertied women over thirty years of age. Woolf's point concerns the exclusion of women and the working classes from material resources and education. In "Memories of a Working Women's Guild" (1931) she explores the complexities of her position as an educated and privileged middle-class woman aligned with working-class women in organized feminist politics. In *Three Guineas*, Woolf's counterblast to fascism (which she aligns with patriarchy), she more radically separates off the category of women as, paradoxically, transcending all boundaries, including national ones: "As a woman, I have no country. As a woman I want no country. As a woman my country is the whole world" (p. 313).

Woolf puts forward, in *A Room of One's Own*, a sophisticated and much-quoted simile for the material basis of literary production when she begins to consider the apparent dearth of literature by women in the Elizabethan period. She submits that

fiction is like a spider's web, attached ever so lightly perhaps, but still attached to life at all four corners. Often the attachment is scarcely perceptible; Shakespeare's plays, for instance, seem to hang there complete by themselves. But when the web is pulled askew, hooked up at the edge, torn in the middle, one remembers that these webs are not spun in mid-air by incorporeal creatures, but are the work of suffering human beings, and are attached to grossly material things, like health and money and the houses we live in.

(pp. 62–63)

Feminist scholarship has since corrected the view of a singularly male Elizabethan literary canon, while feminist literary theory has claimed "Virginia's web" as a defining figure for writing by women. The passage offers a number of different ways of understanding literary materialism. Firstly, it suggests that writing itself is physically made, and not divinely given or unearthly and transcendent. Woolf seems to be attempting to demystify the romantic figure of the (male) poet or author as magically singled out, or divinely elected, but this idea is also connected to a strand of modernist aesthetics concerned with writing as a self-reflexive object and to a more general sense of the materiality of the text—the concreteness of words, spoken or printed. Secondly, the passage

suggests writing as somatic process or bodily production. The material status of the body is far from stable here, and the figure of the spider suggests a gendered somatic model of writing. Thirdly, writing as "the work of suffering human beings" suggests that literature is produced as compensation for, or in protest against, existential pain and material lack. Finally, moving from this general sense of connection with human lived experience to a more specific one, in proposing writing as "attached to grossly material things, like health and money and the houses we live in," Woolf is delineating a model of literature as grounded in the "real world," that is, in the realms of historical, political, and social experience.

This latter position may be broadly associated with Marxist literary theory, but Woolf's work cannot very readily be reconciled to this category per se, and it is possible to understand, in any case, this sense of materialism as not, strictly speaking, Marxist. It should be noted that *A Room of One's Own*, experimental in form, appeared before the Soviet and Marxist antimodernist strictures of the 1930s, after which social(ist) realism was the dominant Marxist aesthetic; this has some bearing on later feminist debate centering on this work (see Marcus; Michèle Barrett). It is not merely Woolf's avant-garde aesthetic, however, that problematizes this work's relationship to Marxism, but—more significantly—her feminism. Attempts to "marry" Marxism and feminism, in short, arose from the desire to correct and supplement a historical and class-based analysis of literature with a gender-based one, and vice-versa. Materialist feminism, although sometimes a more polite term for Marxist feminism, may also be understood as the issue borne of that well-documented "unhappy marriage" (see Sargent). Woolf's work remains an important focus for both Marxist and materialist feminist literary theory.

The narrator shifts scene, in *A Room of One's Own*, to the British Museum (also a significant location in *Jacob's Room*) where she researches "Women and Poverty" under an edifice of patriarchal texts, concluding that women "have served all these centuries as looking glasses . . . reflecting the figure of man at twice his natural size" (p. 45). Here Woolf touches upon the forced, subordinate complicity of women in the construction of the patriarchal subject. Later in the book Woolf offers a more explicit model of this when she describes the difficulties for a woman reader encountering the first-person pronoun in the novels of "Mr. A": "a shadow seemed to lie across the page. It was a straight dark bar, a shadow shaped something like the letter 'I'. . . . Back one was always hailed to the letter 'I'. One began to tire of 'I'. . . . In the shadow of the letter 'I' all is shapeless as mist. Is that a tree? No it is a woman" (p. 130).

This displacement of the feminine in the representation and construction of subjectivity not only points up the alienation experienced by women readers of male-authored texts but also the linguistic difficulties for women writers in trying to express feminine subjectivity. It certainly explains Woolf's sliding and elliptical use of the first person throughout her argument. But Woolf's idiosyncratic narrative strategies in *A Room of One's Own* have also been regarded as detracting from her feminist message. The American feminist Elaine Showalter notably takes Woolf to task for the book's "playfulness [and] conversational surface" (p. 282). Toril Moi, in her introduction to *Sexual/Textual Politics*, claims to "rescue" Woolf's text from such criticism by showing how its very playfulness is in fact a feminist strategy that anticipates the deconstructive and post-Lacanian work of the French feminists Julia Kristeva, Hélène Cixous, and Luce Irigaray (broadly associated with the idea of "*écriture feminine*"). Moi's reading of Woolf's writing as radically feminist by virtue of its textuality, although helpful to her basic introduction to French feminism, is dismissive of the latent humanism and Marxism in much "Anglo-American" feminist criticism and makes no account of such aspects in the argument, however circumlocutionary or playful, of *A Room of One's Own*, which nevertheless puts forward a strong materialist and historicist approach to women's writing.

The narrator discovers a significant discrepancy between women in the real world and "woman" in the symbolic order:

Imaginatively she is of the highest importance; practically she is completely insignificant. She pervades poetry from cover to cover; she is all but absent from history. She dominates the lives of kings and conquerors in fiction; in fact she was the slave of any boy whose parents forced a ring upon her finger. Some of the most inspired words, some of the most profound thoughts in literature fall from her lips; in real life she could scarcely spell, and was the property of her husband.

(p. 56)

Woolf here points up not only the relatively sparse representation of women's experience in historical records, but also the more complicated business of how the feminine is already caught up in the conventions of representation itself; how women may be represented at all when "woman," in poetry and fiction, is already a signifier in patriarchal discourse, functioning as part of the symbolic order: "It was certainly an odd monster that one made up by reading the historians first and the poets afterwards—a worm winged like an eagle; the spirit of life and beauty in a kitchen chopping suet. But these monsters, however amusing to the imagination, have no existence in fact" (p. 56). Woolf converts this dual image to a positive emblem for a feminist writing:

What one must do to bring her to life was to think poetically and prosaically at one and the same moment, thus keeping in touch with fact—that she is Mrs Martin, aged thirty-six, dressed in blue, wearing a black hat and brown shoes; but not losing sight of fiction either—that she is a vessel in which all sorts of spirits and forces are coursing and flashing perpetually.

(pp. 56–57)

This dualistic model, contrasting prose and poetry, is of central importance to Woolf's modernist aesthetic, encapsulated in the phrase "granite and rainbow." In the essay "Poetry, Fiction and the Future" (1927; also known as "The Narrow Bridge of Art"), Woolf acknowledges the different tasks each traditionally performs but is interested in creating a new form of writing that marries prose and poetry: "[Poetry] has always insisted on certain rights, such as rhyme, metre, poetic diction. She has never been used for the common purpose of life. Prose has taken all the dirty work on to her own shoulders; has answered letters, paid bills, written articles, made speeches, served the needs of business men shopkeepers, lawyers, soldiers, peasants" (*Essays*, vol. 4, p. 434). She anticipates a new form of writing in a "prose which has many of the characteristics of poetry," asking whether prose can "chant the elegy, or hymn the love, or shriek in terror, or praise the rose" (p. 436). This is a celebration of the new lyrical prose of modernism—and indeed of her own novel, *To the Lighthouse*, which she famously christened an elegy (see *Diary*, vol. 3, p. 34). But *A Room of One's Own* explores the gender implications of this new form of writing and puts it forward as a feminist tool—just as *To the Lighthouse*, in exploring the social politics surrounding the execution of a painting by a woman artist, is simultaneously a high modernist and a feminist text.

Yet it is still considered controversial, in some quarters, to talk of Woolf's writing as feminist. The source of the confusion may well be the much-cited passage in *A Room of One's Own* where it is declared that "it is fatal for anyone who writes to think of their sex" (p. 136), and a model of writerly androgyny is put forward, derived from Samuel Taylor Coleridge's work:

It is fatal to be a man or woman pure and simple; one must be woman-manly or man-womanly. It is fatal for a woman to lay the least stress on any grievance; to plead even with justice any cause; in any way to speak consciously as a woman. And fatal is no figure of speech; for anything written with that conscious bias is doomed to death. It ceases to be fertilized. . . . Some collaboration has to take place in the mind between the woman and the man before the art of creation can be accomplished. Some marriage of opposites has to be accomplished.

(p. 136)

Woolf's theory of androgyny has been interpreted as positioning her argument beyond feminist concerns, yet it is conceived in the context of her analysis of women and fiction and is proposed as a goal not yet attained by most of her contemporaries because of inequalities between men and women. Shakespeare, the poet playwright, is Woolf's ideal androgynous writer. She lists others—all men—who have also achieved androgyny (Keats, Sterne, Cowper, Lamb, and Proust—the only contemporary). Carolyn G. Heilbrun and Nancy Topping Bazin were the first critics to explore Woolf's theory of androgyny. Showalter's attack on it, in her famous chapter "Virginia Woolf and the Flight into Androgyny," marks the start of continuing ferocious theoretical debate on the subject (See also DiBattista; Jacobus; Moi). For critics like Moi, Woolf's theory of androgyny anticipates the French feminist concept of *"différance."*

A Room of One's Own culminates in the prophesy of a woman poet to equal or rival Shakespeare—"Shakespeare's sister." But in collectively preparing for her appearance, women writers need to develop in several respects. In predicting that the aspiring novelist Mary Carmichael "will be a poet . . . in another hundred years' time" (p. 123), Mary Beton seems to be suggesting that prose must be explored and exploited in certain ways by women

writers before they can be poets. She also finds fault with contemporary male writers—such as Mr A, who is "protesting against the equality of the other sex by asserting his own superiority" (p. 132). She sees this as the direct result of women's political agitation for equality: "The Suffrage campaign was no doubt to blame" (p. 129). She raises further concerns about politics and aesthetics when she comments on the aspirations of the Italian Fascists for a poet worthy of fascism: "We may well join in that pious hope, but it is doubtful whether poetry can come out of an incubator. Poetry ought to have a mother as well as a father. The Fascist poem, one may fear, will be a horrid little abortion such as one sees in a glass jar in the museum of some county town" (p. 134). Yet if the extreme patriarchy of fascism cannot produce poetry because it denies a maternal line, Woolf argues that women cannot write poetry either until the historical canon of women's writing has been uncovered and acknowledged. Nineteenth-century women writers experienced great difficulty because they lacked a female tradition: "For we think back through our mothers if we are women" (p. 99). They therefore lacked literary tools suitable for expressing women's experience. The dominant sentence at the start of the nineteenth century was "a man's sentence. . . . It was a sentence that was unsuited for women's use" (pp. 99–100).

Woolf's assertion here, through Mary Beton, of gendered syntax, and that "the book has somehow to be adapted to the body" (p. 101)—again anticipating the libidinal writing projects of French feminism—seems to contradict the declaration that "it is fatal for anyone who writes to think of their sex." She identifies the novel as "young enough" to be of use to the woman writer:

No doubt we shall find her knocking that into shape for herself when she has the free use of her limbs; and providing some new vehicle, not necessarily in verse, for the poetry in her. For it is the poetry that is still the denied outlet. And I went on to ponder how a woman nowadays would write a poetic tragedy in five acts. Would she use verse?—would she not use prose rather?

(pp. 100–101)

Woolf seems to confirm this theory of gendered aesthetic form in her earlier review (1923) of Dorothy Richardson's novel, *Revolving Lights*: "She has invented, or, if she has not invented, developed and applied to her own uses, a sentence which we might call the psychological sentence of the feminine gender. It is of a more elastic fibre than the old, capable of stretching to the extreme, of suspending the frailest particles, of enveloping the vaguest shapes" (*Essays*, vol. 3, p. 367) But, acknowledging that men too have constructed similar sentences, she points out that the difference lies with content rather than form:

Miss Richardson has fashioned her sentence consciously, in order that it may descend to the depths and investigate the crannies of Miriam Henderson's consciousness. It is a woman's sentence only in the sense that it is used to describe a woman's mind by a writer who is neither proud nor afraid of anything that she may discover in the psychology of her sex.

(p. 367)

This assertion of woman as both the writing subject and its object is reinforced in *A Room of One's Own*: "above all, you must illumine your own soul" (p. 117), Mary Beton advises. The "obscure lives" (p. 116) of women must be recorded by women.

Mary Carmichael's novel in fact explores women's relationships with each other. *A Room of One's Own* was published shortly after the obscenity trial of Radclyffe Hall's *The Well of Loneliness* (1928), and Woolf flaunts in the face of this a blatantly lesbian narrative: "if Chloe likes Olivia and Mary Carmichael knows how to express it she will light a torch in that vast chamber where nobody has yet been" (p. 109). Her refrain, "Chloe likes Olivia," has become a critical slogan for lesbian writing. Woolf's own fictive celebration of her lesbian lover, Vita Sackville-West, in the satirical novel, *Orlando* (1928), escaped the censure directed at Hall's work. In *A Room of One's Own*, Woolf calls for women's writing to more openly explore lesbianism and for the narrative tools to make this possible. Lesbian writing certainly was widely published in the decades following, but it wasn't until the later part of the twentieth century that lesbian criticism of Woolf's own work began to flourish (see Barrett and Cramer).

A Room of One's Own has not always been regarded positively by feminists, as Showalter's work has shown, but it has become a touchstone for most feminist debates. One of the most controversial passages, for example, concerns Woolf's positioning of black women. Commenting on the sexual and colonial appetites of men, the narrator concludes: "It is one of the great advantages of being a woman that one can pass even a very fine negress without wishing to make an Englishwoman of her" (65). In seeking to distance women from colonial practices, Woolf disturbingly excludes black women here from the very category of women. This has become the crux of much contemporary feminist debate concerning the politics of identity. The category of women both unites and divides feminists: white middle-class feminists, it has been shown, cannot speak for the experience of all women; and reconciliation of universalism and difference remains a key issue. "Women—but are you not sick to death of the word?" Woolf retorts in the closing pages of *A Room of One's Own*. "I can assure you I am" (p. 145).

The category of women is not chosen by women, it represents the space in patriarchy from which women must speak and which they struggle to redefine. Woolf's ambition for the coming of Shakespeare's sister has been taken up by feminist critics and anthologizers. "Judith Shakespeare" stands for the silenced woman writer or artist (see Ezell; Modleski; Smith). But to seek to mimic *the* model of the individual masculine writing subject may also be considered part of a conservative feminist agenda. On the other hand, Woolf seems to defer the arrival of Shakespeare's sister in a celebration of women's collective literary achievement: "I am talking of the common life which is the real life and not of the little separate lives which we live as individuals" (pp. 148–149). Shakespeare's sister is a messianic figure who "lives in you and in me" (p. 148) and who will draw "her life from the lives of the unknown who were her forerunners" (p. 149), but has yet to appear. She may be the common writer to Woolf's "common reader" (a term she borrows from Samuel Johnson), but she has yet to "put on the body which she has so often laid down" (p. 149). The sense of a collective authorial voice here, along with the multivocal narrative of *A Room of One's Own*, has been seen to anticipate Woolf's more formally stylized and poetic multivocal novel *The Waves* (1931). But while writing *The Waves*, Woolf was also composing her introduction to another, perhaps more prosaic multivocal text, *Life as We Have Known It*, a collection of letters by members of the Working Women's Guild (Goldman, *Feminist Aesthetics*, p. 192).

Woolf puts forward a collective and nontranscendent sense of the writing subject in her memoir "A Sketch of the Past" (c. 1939), in the posthumously published collection of autobiographical writings *Moments of Being*. She explains her "philosophy" in terms of epiphanic moments, maintaining:

> that behind the cotton wool is hidden a pattern; that we—I mean all human beings—are connected with this; that the whole world is a work of art; that we are parts of the work of art. *Hamlet* or a Beethoven quartet is the truth about this vast mass that we call the world. But there is no Shakespeare, there is no Beethoven; certainly and emphatically there is no God; we are the words; we are the music; we are the thing itself. And I see this when I have a shock.
>
> (p. 72)

This vision, more radical than Eliot's theory of impersonality, and anticipating in some respects Roland Barthes' idea of "death of the author," seems to move beyond questions of gender and feminism to a sense of an ungendered collective aesthetic. Yet it appears in the context of Woolf's account of her experience of childhood sexual abuse by her brother and of the domestic tyranny of her father. Having recalled these unhappy auto-biographical details, she goes on to consider how memory operates; and to record three particular epiphanic "moments of being," triggered by physical shocks. Woolf's "moments of being" have been likened to Henri Bergson's idea of the *durée*—subjective, nonspatial temporality—but they are also rooted in, record, and resonate with, the historical and material. Her aesthetic attempts both to record the real, including the interior lives of women, and to imagine life and art beyond such concerns.

FIRST NOVELS: THE VOYAGE OUT
AND NIGHT AND DAY

THE *Voyage Out* (1915), Woolf's first novel (*Melymbrosia* in draft), is a conventionally written Conradian narrative with many of the features of a bildungsroman, or "künstlerroman" (since it charts the life of a musician). It is set in 1905 and concerns the journey that Rachel Vinrace, a musically talented but socially isolated and motherless young woman, takes to South America on her father's boat, the *Euphrosyne* (which not only refers to the Greek goddess the Grace of Joy but is also Woolf's dig at the privately published collection of rather bad poetry that appeared under this title in 1905 by Clive Bell, Leonard Woolf, Lytton Strachey, and others). Richard and Clarissa Dalloway (who reappear in Woolf's fourth novel) join the boat for a while and the naive Rachel is greatly disturbed by Richard Dalloway's sexual advances to her. Clarissa Dalloway exhibits a startling ignorance of classical literature, which early reviewers attributed to Woolf herself rather than to her satirical commentary.

Under the wing of her aunt, Helen Ambrose, wife of a classical scholar, Rachel's social horizons are broadened by her stay in South America. There she meets two somewhat patronizing young Englishmen of intimidating intellect, St. John Hirst and Terence Hewet. The novel is peppered with allusions to canonical literature (including Sophocles, Hakylut, Shakespeare, Milton, Wordsworth, Scott, and Conrad). Rachel falls in love with and becomes engaged to Hewet, an aspiring writer, whose ambition it is to "write a novel about Silence" (p. 204). Rachel falls into a silent and fatal swoon while listening, in the heat of the sun, to her fiancé read Milton's *Comus* (such is the power of poetry!). In the deathbed scene, Terence seems sinisterly to celebrate Rachel's death as a perfection of their love, and he does so with her very dying breath: "she had ceased to breathe. So much the better—this was death. It was nothing; it was to cease to breathe. It was happiness, it was perfect happiness" (p. 334). This scene may be understood as the fatal culmination of Terence's contemptuous and smothering attitude to Rachel's own creativity (as a musician), and it is an indictment of patriarchal marriage as the crushing end for women's artistic potential. Interestingly, Woolf dedicates the novel to her husband. Rachel's sorry fate is contrasted in the novel to the enthusiasm and optimism of a minor character, the left-wing suffragist and aspiring revolutionary Evelyn Murgatroyd, who dodges several marriage proposals and is intent on traveling to Moscow at the close of the novel.

Clive Bell commented on a draft version's rather schematic characterization of "subtle, sensitive, tactful, gracious, delicately perceptive, & perspicacious women" and "obtuse, vulgar, blind, florid, rude, tactless, emphatic, indelicate, vain, tyrannical, stupid men" (Bell, *Virginia Woolf*, vol. 1, p. 209), and something of this schema survives in the final version. *The Voyage Out* is nevertheless an impressive first novel and has attracted a range of critical readings from feminist to postcolonial; its dense allusiveness and intertextuality are still to be more thoroughly probed. Several drafts of this novel survive, and there has been important comparative scholarly examination of these (see DeSalvo; Heine; Schlack). It should also be noted that the 1920 American edition differs significantly from the 1915 first edition, and both versions have been in circulation. Scholarly preference lies with the 1915 edition. C. Ruth Miller and Lawrence Miller's Shakespeare Head Press edition (1993) gives all variants.

Night and Day (1919) is also conventional in form. Woolf regarded this romantic comedy as another apprentice piece, a means of learning "what to leave out: by putting it all in" (*Letters*, vol. 6, p. 216). It seems to mimic nineteenth century realism even as it outlines the passing of all things Victorian. The heroine is Katharine Hilbery, the daughter—like Woolf—of an upper-middle-class intellectual household. She is assisting her mother in writing the biography of her grandfather, a famous poet. She is also a closet mathematician-astronomer, who enjoys a secret "unwomanly" nocturnal life of rationalism: "She would not have cared to confess how infinitely she preferred the exactitude, the star-like impersonality, of figures to the confusion, agitation, and vagueness of the finest prose" (p. 40).

Katharine becomes involved in an emotional triangle with Ralph Denham, a lawyer who writes for the *Critical Review*, and Mary Datchet, a suffragist undergoing difficulties with "The Cause," who is attracted to Katharine and in love with Ralph (and responsible for educating him in radical politics). After the usual obstacles, mistaken pairings, and misunderstandings, Katharine and Ralph become engaged at the close of the novel. Katharine's joy in things rational is used subversively throughout *Night and Day*, and most effectively in love scenes as, for example, when Ralph ("a person who feels") proposes: "If Denham could have seen how visibly books of algebraic symbols, pages all speckled with dots and dashes and twisted bars, came before her eyes as they trod the Embankment, his secret joy in her attention might have been dispersed" (pp. 316–17). The novel's solar imagery implicitly reminds us that daylight, and by association the solar light of masculinity, prevents other stellar worlds from being visible at all. Woolf's imagery here anticipates the solar imagery of Mr A's first person overshadowing the woman reader in *A Room of One's Own*. If the light of the man's world is regarded as obscuring Katharine's true self, then it is certainly with irony that one reads of Ralph's sudden realization "that he had never seen her in the daylight before" (p. 246). Such engagements in the novel with the gender and hierarchy of traditional dualisms and oppositions have encouraged critics to read it in terms of Woolf's theory of androgyny (see Richter; Marder; Lee). More recently, the imperial subtexts of *Night and Day* have been pointed up (see Phillips).

JACOB'S ROOM *AND* MRS. DALLOWAY

JACOB'S Room (1922), the first of her novels to be published by the Hogarth Press, with a Vanessa Bell dust jacket, was a turning point for Woolf: "There's no doubt in my mind that I have found out how to begin (at 40) to say something in my own voice" (*Diary*, vol. 2, p. 186). Critically acclaimed as Woolf's first high-modernist novel, it is an avant-garde bildungsroman (see Fleishman), charting the life of Jacob Flanders, a privileged and educated young man who, as his surname suggests, dies before his time in the Great War like so many of his generation (see Handley). The tightly constructed, self-reflexive narrative draws Jacob largely as an absence in the lives of others (the short text is teeming with characters touching upon Jacob's life), and his life is given as a montage of moments rather than a coherent narrative progression. Jacob is seen in many contexts, including with family, friends, at study, on a trip to Greece, and in a brothel.

The novel critiques imperial patriarchal culture at the same time as it explores the construction of subjectivity (see Bishop). The final single-page chapter shows Jacob's room, empty of Jacob, in which his friend cries out for him in lyric despair, and his mother asks: " 'What am I to do with these, Mr. Bonamy?' She held out a pair of Jacob's old shoes" (p. 155). Her question not only speaks movingly to the lacunae left by the war dead but also raises the problem of gender, class, and subjectivity in the context of the postwar extension of the franchise to working-class men and partial enfranchisement of women. Can women occupy the same subjective space as men, or must identity, and narratives of identity, be reinvented to accommodate the feminine?

As the name of the eponymous heroine of her fourth novel, *Mrs. Dalloway* (1925), suggests, women's identity remains for Woolf circumscribed by men. *Mrs. Dalloway* (in draft, *The*

Hours) is a seamless account (there are no chapters) of one June day in London 1923, and the parallel experiences of two figures, Clarissa Dalloway, society hostess and politician's wife, and Septimus Warren Smith, a shell-shocked young war veteran. In keeping with Woolf's theory of androgyny, a double narrative unfolds in which we follow Clarissa, haunted by a refrain from *Cymbeline*, in the preparations for her party, to be attended by various friends from her past as well as the prime minister, alongside Septimus' mental decline toward suicide in the company of his despairing wife, Rezia. Clarissa's sexuality is a point of considerable critical interest. She is visited by an old suitor, Peter Walsh, whom she remembers for interrupting "the most exquisite moment of her whole life" (p. 52), when the friend she was in love with, Sally Seton, kissed her. This sympathetically drawn Sapphic moment contrasts with Woolf's rather crude portrayal of the lesbian Doris Kilman, tutor to Clarissa's daughter. Septimus' mental illness has attracted many biographically based critical approaches to the novel, showing how Septimus' appalling medical treatment parallels Woolf's own.

Both Clarissa's and Septimus' narratives are elliptically conjoined at Clarissa's party when Sir William Bradshaw, the specialist seen by Septimus earlier in the day, tells of his suicide to Richard Dalloway, who is working on a parliamentary bill on shell shock. The narration shifts almost imperceptibly between the two parallel strands and uses a number of the day's passing events held in common for transition between them. For example, the opening passage in which Clarissa is described buying flowers switches to Septimus' narrative perspective by virtue of the description of an official car backfiring outside the shop she is in: the "violent explosion . . . made Mrs. Dalloway jump." A passerby identifies it as the prime minister's car, and "Septimus Warren Smith, who found himself unable to pass, heard him" (p. 11).

Woolf's free-indirect technique allows the narrative subtly to shift interior focus between characters, creating a collective discursive continuum. The structural parallels with *Ulysses* (which similarly takes place on one June day, in Dublin 1916), have encouraged critics (erroneously) to liken this method of shifting and collective free-indirect discourse in *Mrs. Dalloway* to Joyce's "stream-of-consciousness." A skywriting plane, the song of a flower-seller, and the striking of Big Ben are among the novel's other points of transition between different consciousnesses (see Bazin). *Mrs. Dalloway* has also been read with Eliot's *Waste Land* in mind, but like other women writers of the period, Woolf departs from his apocalyptic dread of the "unreal city" and celebrates the urban scene of London as at times a powerful and liberating feminine space, for all that it is haunted by the specters of war.

TO THE LIGHTHOUSE

To the Lighthouse (1927) remains the most widely read and critically scrutinized of Woolf's novels and has been examined in relation to every modern phase of literary criticism from formalism to postmodernism and postcolonialism (see Goldman, *Icon*). It constitutes a significant breakthrough for Woolf, as her diary famously records: "(But while I try to write, I am making up "To the Lighthouse"—the sea is to be heard all through it. I have an idea that I will invent a new name for my books to supplant "novel". A new — by Virginia Woolf. But what? Elegy?)" (*Diary*, vol. 3, p. 34). In her early formulations she envisages the work as an elegy on her parents (*Diary*, vol. 3, pp. 18–19), leading many later critics to understand the novel as "frankly biographical" (Love, p. 70). On the other hand, the aesthetic formalism of *To the Lighthouse* also has engaged a good deal of formalist criticism (see McLaurin). More conventional, novelistic interpretation, and interest in stable meaning, are certainly subsumed to formal concerns in the kind of critical response Woolf herself outlines to her friend Roger Fry, the influential theorist of formalism in the visual arts: "I meant *nothing* by The Lighthouse. One has to have a central line down the middle of the book to hold the design together. I saw that all sorts of feelings would accrue to this, but I refused to think them out, and trusted that people would make it the deposit for their own emotions" (*Letters*, vol. 3, p. 385). This statement has encouraged numerous readings of the novel and its imagery as enigmatic, mystical, and nebulously symbolic.

Highly poetic and densely allusive, *To the Lighthouse* is also a self-reflexive, feminist künstlerroman. Woolf conceived its triadic structure as "two blocks joined by a corridor" (Dick, pp. 44–45): part one, "The Window" is linked via part two, "Time Passes," to part three, "The Lighthouse." Each part is subdivided into numbered sections varying in length. Arnold Bennett, Woolf's literary sparring partner, mordantly sums up, in his *Evening Standard* review, her sacrifice of plot to the poetic: "A group of people plan to sail in a small boat to a lighthouse. At the end some of them reach the lighthouse in a small boat. That is the externality of the plot" (Majumdar and McLaurin, pp. 200–201).

Set in a holiday house on the Hebridean island of Skye, part one examines the domestic, sexual, political, philosophical, and aesthetic tensions in the lives of Mr. and Mrs. Ramsay, a philosopher and his wife of renowned beauty, and their numerous children and guests, as they take their holiday one summer around 1910. It culminates in a banquet to celebrate the engagement of two guests, Paul and Minta. Part three returns to the house during a summer after the Great War, when the certainties and pleasures of the prewar world have crumbled (along with Paul and Minta's marriage). In each summer one of the guests, Lily Briscoe, hemmed in by patriarchal contempt for women's artistic abilities, and by Mrs. Ramsay's forceful marital ideology, attempts a painting, which serves as self-reflexive reference point for the novel itself. Indeed, it closes with an account of her final visionary brushstroke in an elegiac moment of lyric consolation. Lily's rejection of Mr. Ramsay's amorous approaches, combined with his children's defiance, suggest an unsettling, if not an overcoming, of (his) patriarchy.

The middle section, "Time Passes," covers the intervening years, focusing on the object world of the house and its environs, in decline and under repair, as a metaphor for the losses and changes in personal terms for the individuals in the novel as well as in wider social and political terms. Written by Woolf during the General Strike of 1926 (see Flint), this highly experimental piece of writing, published separately to begin with (see Haule), has been understood to reflect on the social and political upheavals occurring during the war period through the lens of further turbulence in the 1920s. Shockingly, major events, such as the death of Mrs. Ramsay, the central figure in part one, and the deaths of her son in the war and her daughter in childbirth, are communicated in brief, stylized, parenthetical statements inserted into Woolf's sustained lyrical description of time passing in the house. Woolf's theory of androgyny has been pressed into critical service for readings of this part of the novel, where the Great War's unset-

tling of gender politics is suggested by a cataclysmic "down-pouring of immense darkness" (p. 195) in which "not only was furniture confounded; there was scarcely anything left of body or mind by which one could say 'This is he' or 'This is she' "(p. 196). We might ask of this writing Erich Auerbach's simple but perceptive question (directed at an earlier passage): "Who is speaking in this paragraph?" Woolf has pushed free-indirect discourse to the limits in describing the forces at work in an empty house.

Auerbach's impressive reading of a section of *To the Lighthouse* (in terms of point-of-view, narrative voice, time, interior and exterior consciousness, epistemology, and fragmentation) closes his classic critical work on representation and narrative in Western literature from Homer to the twentieth century *Mimesis: The Representation of Reality in Western Literature* (1946). This reading is possibly responsible for securing the reputation of *To the Lighthouse* as a (if not *the*) major twentieth-century work of fiction. Auerbach makes the point that modern philologists (himself included) share the very technique of modern writers (Woolf's in particular) that his final chapter explores. This technique is encapsulated by Lily Briscoe: "The great revelation perhaps never did come. Instead there were little daily miracles, illuminations, matches struck unexpectedly in the dark; here was one" (p. 249).

ORLANDO

ORLANDO: A Biography (1928), "the longest and most charming love letter in literature" (Nicolson, *Portrait*, p. 202), is dedicated to Woolf's lover Vita Sackville-West and tells the story of Orlando, perennial heir to Knole, the Sackville stately home, who at the start of the book is a young nobleman and aspiring poet of the Elizabethan period. After a few hundred years of literary, amorous, and heroic adventures and encounters with nearly all the great literary canonical figures through the ages, by the close of the novel on "Thursday, the eleventh of October, Nineteen Hundred and Twenty-eight" (p. 329) (the day of *Orlando's* publication), Orlando is a successful *woman* poet. Her book, *The Oak Tree*, hundreds of years in gestation, wins a literary prize and critical acclaim. Orlando changes sex in the middle of the novel during a tour of duty as Charles II's ambassador to Constantinople. But gender expectations are further complicated when as a man Orlando masquerades as a woman and as a woman masquerades as a man.

This mock biography perhaps takes a swipe at other Bloomsbury biographical innovators such as Lytton Strachey and Vita's husband, Harold Nicolson, in a review of whose work Woolf coined her famous phrase, "granite and rainbow." *Orlando* mockingly sports a preface, illustrations (including elaborately staged photographs), and an index. It may also be seen as a satirical künstlerroman, exploring the gender politics of poetics and subjectivity across the ages. Evading the censorship that Radclyffe Hall's notorious lesbian novel, *The Well of Loneliness* (1928), met with in the same period, *Orlando* has since attracted many readings concerned with Woolf's theories of androgyny and, latterly, lesbian aesthetics (see Barrett and Cramer). Woolf conceived of it as "an escapade after these serious poetic experimental books": "Sapphism is to be suggested. Satire is to be the main note— satire & wildness. . . . My own lyric vein is to be satirised" (*Diary*, vol. 3, p. 131). She memorably sends up the "Time Passes" part of *To the Lighthouse* when she helps the reader of *Orlando* reach a "conclusion which, one cannot help feeling, might have been reached more quickly by the simple statement that 'Time passed' (here the exact amount could be indicated in brackets) and nothing whatever happened" (p. 91).

THE WAVES

THE Waves (1931, in draft "The Moths"), was envisioned by Woolf as she wrote the closing passages of *To the Lighthouse*, when she glimpsed "a fin passing far out . . . a fin rising on a wide blank sea" (*Diary*, vol. 3, pp. 113, 153); and a "fin in a waste of waters" punctuates the final text (pp. 189, 245, 273, 284). As this imagistic inception suggests, *The Waves* is Woolf's most stylized, poetic work. Conceived as "prose yet poetry; a novel & a play" (*Diary*, vol. 3 p. 128), and as "an abstract mystical eyeless book: a play-poem" to reconcile her "mystical feelings" (*Diary*, vol. 3, p. 203), she considered it "my first work in my own style" (*Diary*, vol. 4, p. 53). It comprises nine italicized pastoral "interludes" describing the progress of the sun across a seascape and landscape, interwoven with nine multivocal sections of interrelated soliloquies by six characters, Bernard, Jinny, Louis, Neville, Rhoda, and Susan, from childhood to maturity. Percival, the seventh character, who dies in youth,

is the voiceless center of their circle. Rhoda, the most alienated of the group, commits suicide, a fact communicated in the last soliloquy, Bernard's final summing up.

Woolf's own private review of *The Waves*, having "netted that fin in the waste of waters which appeared to me over the marshes out of my window at Rodmell when I was coming to an end of *To the Lighthouse*," is couched in terms of a new, poetic sense of freedom in her handling of formal, aesthetic elements. She comments on

the freedom & boldness with which my imagination picked up used & tossed aside all the images & symbols which I had prepared . . . —not in set pieces, as I had tried at first, coherently, but simply as images; never making them work out; only suggest. Thus I hope to have kept the sound of the sea & the birds, dawn, & garden subconsciously present, doing their work under ground.

(*Diary*, vol. 4, pp. 10–11)

The lyricism of the work similarly dominates critical responses. Embodying a more fully sustained attempt at the lyric prose promised in some of the flights of language in *To the Lighthouse*, it is, in the words of Harold Nicolson, "a literary sensation," taking to the brink Woolf's experimentalism in plot, lyric, and character into the realms of the "antiphonal, sacerdotal, vatic" (Majumdar and McLaurin, p. 266). His wife, Vita Sackville-West, on the other hand, to Woolf's great delight, considered *The Waves* "so bad that only a small dog that had been fed on gin could have written it" (*Letters*, vol. 4, p. 401).

Woolf's sister, Vanessa Bell, responded to the more personal aspects of its elegiac dimension, for the novel is in part an elegy on their brother Thoby, as Woolf's diary entry on the completion of the manuscript reveals: "Anyhow it is done; & I have been sitting these 15 minutes in a state of glory, & calm, & some tears, thinking of Thoby & if I could write Julian Thoby Stephen 1881-1906 on the first page. I suppose not" (*Diary*, vol. 4, p. 10). Woolf resists this temptation, but the novel is still often read as (auto)biographical. Woolf's organization of *The Waves* into subjective passages by six soliloquists, punctuated by objective, pastoral passages without a marked narrator, suggests a concern both with subjectivity (individual and collective) and phenomenology, with subjective engagement and objective detachment, with processes of the self as well as absence of the self.

"I did mean that in some vague way we are the same person, and not separate people," she tells G. Lowes Dickinson:

The six characters were supposed to be one. I'm getting old myself. . . . and I come to feel more and more how difficult it is to collect oneself into one Virginia; even though the special Virginia in whose body I live for the moment is violently susceptible to all sorts of separate feelings. Therefore I wanted to give the sense of continuity, instead of which most people say, no you've given the sense of flowing and passing away and that nothing matters.

(*Letters, vol.* 4, p. 397)

Vanessa Bell's response has come to dominate interpretations—after being "completely submerged in The Waves" she finds herself "gasping, out of breath, choking, half-drowned . . . so overcome by the beauty" (*Selected Letters*, p. 361). Mystical and aesthetic analogies abound in criticism of *The Waves* (see Moore; Stewart), along with a dominant and lasting strand of Bergsonism; more recent feminist and postcolonial readings have focused on its feminine textuality and opened up its anti-patriarchal, lesbian, suffragist, and anti-imperial subtexts (see Minow-Pinkney; Oxindine; Goldman; and Marcus, "Brittania"). Leonard Woolf had Bernard's final words in *The Waves* engraved on a tablet marking his wife's ashes buried beneath elms in their garden: "Against you I will fling myself, unvanquished and unyielding, O Death!" (Lee, *Virginia Woolf*, p.766).

FLUSH, THE YEARS, *AND* BETWEEN THE ACTS

FLUSH: A Biography (1933), a comedic, fictional account of the life of Elizabeth Barrett-Browning's spaniel, with ten illustrations including four drawings by Vanessa Bell, was for Woolf another spree, a relief between more serious projects. It was rapidly a best-seller, and as such considered a fall from highbrow grace by some contemporary reviewers and most subsequent Woolf critics. It has more recently been read as an allegory of Woolf's affair with Vita Sackville-West (Vanita), and as a feminist narrative anticipating *The Years* (Squiers). *Flush*'s very transgression and destabilization of the categories of "high" and "low" art make it, for Caughie, "an allegory of canon formation" (p. 146). It is clearly ripe for more sustained critical attention.

The Years (1937, in draft the novel-essay *The Pargiters*), returns to a more conservative novelistic form, consisting of a chronological account of the middle-class Pargiters from 1880 to "the present day." It is presented in eleven chapters, each allocated a sample, apparently arbitrary, year, and each opens with a descriptive passage on the elements and the seasons. No one character is central, and the lives of its various characters, Eleanor, Kitty, Rose, Martin, Sara, Peggy, and North, are seen caught up in, and pitted against, the social, imperial, and martial forces and institutions of patriarchal capitalism. Woolf envisioned "a curiously uneven time sequence—a series of great balloons, linked by straight narrow passages of narrative" (*Diary*, vol. 4, p. 142), and her ambition, in the midst of proofing *Flush*, was to

be bold & adventurous. I want to give the whole of the present society—nothing less: facts, as well as the vision. And to combine them both. I mean, The Waves going on simultaneously with Night & Day. Is this possible?. . . . And its to end with the press of daily normal life continuing. And there are to be millions of ideas but no preaching—history, politics, feminism, art, literature—in short a summing up of all I know, feel, laugh at, despise, like, admire hate & so on.

(*Diary*, vol. 4, pp. 151–152)

After lengthy compositional agonies her double vision for this project eventually diverged into two books, her feminist and pacifist tract *Three Guineas* (1938) and "that misery The Years" (*Diary*, vol. 5, p. 340). The draft's more propagandist and overtly political elements are missing from, or diluted, in the novel (see Radin). But it remains a radical feminist critique of its time, examining women's negotiation of domestic and public spheres. *The Years* combines Woolf's interest in visionary and mythic matriarchal sources, identified by a number of critics (see Marcus; Cramer) in the work of the Cambridge classicist Jane Harrison, along with her materialist feminist social analysis. In retrospect Woolf saw the novel as an effort to "give characters from every side; turn them towards society, not private life; exhibit the effect of ceremonies" and to "shift the stress from present to future; and show the old fabric insensibly changing without death or violence into the future—suggesting that there is no break, but a continuous development, possibly a recurrence of some pattern." But she concludes: "Of course I completely failed, partly through illness . . . partly through sheer incompetence. The theme was too ambitious. . . . I expect I muted down the characters too much, in order to shorten and keep their faces towards society; and altogether muffed the proportions" (*Letters,* vol. 6, p. 116).

Between the Acts (1941, in draft *Pointz Hall*), published shortly after Woolf's death, returns to a more stylized and streamlined form and seems to achieve her ambition for a lyric novel-drama. She conceived of it as an exploration of collective subjectivity: " 'I' rejected: 'We' substituted: to whom at the end there shall be an invocation? 'We' . . . composed of many different things . . . we all life, all art, all waifs & strays . . . & people passing—& a perpetual variety & change from intensity to prose. & facts—& notes" (*Diary,* vol. 5, p. 135). Chapterless and sectionless, *Between the Acts* comprises a sequence of scenes from an English village on a summer's evening in the Oliver family house, Pointz Hall, and on the day following, when the annual pageant takes place. Many of the villagers participate in this satirical romp through the history of England in various kinds of theatrical tableaux, under the direction of the eccentric Miss La Trobe.

The novel bristles with the menace of incipient fascism and impending war. The main characters are depicted in action and dialogue interwoven with the italicized passages of the pageant's performance, itself punctuated by various incidental, natural, and man-made events such as a sudden downpouring of rain, the flitting of birds, and the flight of military planes, all of which complicate the boundaries between art and life. In the interstices the marital tensions between Isa and Giles Oliver are explored. Isa, a closet poet, disillusioned with her husband, is attracted to Rupert Haines, a married gentleman farmer; Giles becomes enamored of the exotic urbanite Mrs Manresa, who is accompanied by William Dodge, a homosexual whom he scathingly terms a "half-breed" (p. 61). Giles's contempt and self-loathing culminate in a horrific apocalyptic moment of domestic—and biblical—patriarchal fascism when, discovering the "monstrous inversion" of a snake choking on a toad, he "stamp[s] on them": "The mass crushed and slithered. The white canvas on his tennis shoes was bloodstained and sticky. But it was action. Action relieved him" (p. 119).

The pageant formally closes with an avant-garde gesture when the actors assemble onstage turning mirrors of all sizes on the audience, and a voice "from the bushes—megaphontic, anonymous, loud-speaking affirmation" addresses them: *"All you can see of yourselves is scraps, orts and fragments? Well then listen to the gramophone affirming . . ."* (pp. 218, 220). The novel closes with the ambivalent passions of Giles and Isa in confrontation, encapsulated by two brief but powerful sentences: "Then the curtain rose. They spoke."

Critical responses to *Between the Acts* were at first colored by the aftermath of Woolf's suicide at a low point in the war: Mitchell Leaska referred to its draft as "the longest suicide note in the English language" (*Pointz Hall,* p. 451). Sophisticated readings have since developed of Woolf's polyphonic technique, which is seen as both unifying (Kelley) and endlessly transgressive and open (Bowlby; Caughie). The mythic and pre-historic subtexts of *Between the Acts* have yielded psychoanalytical, political, and feminist readings (Pawlowski; Beer; Eileen Barrett). Isa's reading of a newspaper account of a rape of a girl by soldiers (a real report taken by Woolf from the *Times*), has been interpreted by Jane Marcus ("Liberty, Sorority, Misogyny") in terms of the classical myth of Procne and Philomela, a recurrent motif in Woolf's work. This typifies Woolf's technique of collapsing history, politics, and feminism into densely allusive, highly charged imagistic prose, to which all semblance of plot is sacrificed. Readers of Woolf should heed Isa's observations on Miss La Trobe's theatrical practice: "Don't bother about the plot: the plot's nothing" (p. 109).

SELECTED BIBLIOGRAPHY

I. NOVELS. *The Voyage Out* (London, 1915); *Night and Day* (London, 1919); *Jacob's Room* (London, 1922); *Mrs. Dalloway* (London, 1925); *To the Lighthouse* (London, 1927); *Orlando: A Biography* (London, 1928); *The Waves* (London, 1931); *Flush: A Biography* (London, 1933); *The Years* (London, 1937); *Between the Acts* (London, 1941).

II. SHORT STORIES AND DRAMA. *Two Stories* (London, 1917); *Monday or Tuesday* (London, 1921); *A Haunted House and Other Short Stories,* ed. by Leonard Woolf (London, 1944); *Mrs. Dalloway's Party: A Short Story Sequence by Virginia Woolf,* ed. by Stella McNichol (London, 1973); *Freshwater: A Comedy,* ed. by Lucio Ruotolo (London, 1976); *The Complete Shorter Fiction of Virginia Woolf,* new edition (London, 1989).

III. NONFICTION. *The Common Reader* (London, 1925); *A Room of One's Own* (London, 1929); *The Common Reader: Second Series* (London, 1932); *Three Guineas* (London, 1938); *Roger Fry: A Biography* (London, 1940*)*; *The Death of the Moth and Other Essays,* ed. by Leonard Woolf (London, 1942); *The Moment and Other Essays,* ed. by Leonard

Woolf (London, 1948); *The Captain's Death Bed and Other Essays*, ed. by Leonard Woolf (London, 1950); *Granite and Rainbow*, ed. by Leonard Woolf (London, 1958); *Collected Essays*, 4 vols., ed. by Leonard Woolf (London, 1966–1967); *Books and Portraits*, ed. by Mary Lyon (London, 1977); *Virginia Woolf: Women and Writing*, ed. by Michèle Barrett (London, 1979); *Moments of Being*, ed. by Jeanne Schulkind, 2d edition (London, 1985); *The Essays of Virginia Woolf*, vols. 1–4 (of 6), ed. by Andrew McNeillie (London, 1986–1994).

IV. HOLOGRAPH AND DRAFT EDITIONS. *The Pargiters: The Novel-Essay Portion of* The Years, ed. by Mitchell A. Leaska (London, 1978); *Melymbrosia: An Early Version of* The Voyage Out, ed. by Louise DeSalvo (New York, 1982); *Pointz Hall: The Earlier and Later Typescripts of* Between the Acts, ed. by Mitchell A. Leaska (New York, 1982); *To the Lighthouse: The Original Holograph Draft*, ed. by Susan Dick (Toronto and London, 1983); *The Waves: The Two Holograph Drafts*, ed. by J. W. Graham (London, 1983); *Women & Fiction: The Manuscript Versions of* A Room of One's Own, ed. by S. P. Rosenbaum (Oxford, 1992); *Orlando: The Original Holograph Draft*, ed. by Stuart N. Clarke (London, 1993); *Virginia Woolf's "The Hours": The British Museum Manuscript of* Mrs. Dalloway, ed. by Helen M. Wussow (New York, 1996); *Virginia Woolf's "Jacob's Room": The Holograph Draft*, ed. by Edward Bishop (New York, 1998).

V. DIARIES, JOURNALS, LETTERS. *The Letters of Virginia Woolf(1888–1941)*, 6 vols., ed. by Nigel Nicolson and Joanne Trautman (London, 1975–1980); *The Diary of Virginia Woolf* (1915–1941), 5 vols, ed. by Anne Olivier Bell and Andrew McNeillie (London, 1977–1984); *Virginia Woolf's Reading Notebooks*, ed. by Brenda Silver (Princeton, N.J., 1983); *A Passionate Apprentice: The Early Journals, 1897–1909*, ed. by Mitchell A. Leaska (London, 1990).

VI. ARCHIVE MATERIAL. An annually updated guide to library special collections is published by the *Woolf Studies Annual*. Among the major Woolf archives are: the Beinecke Rare Book and Manuscript Library, Yale University Library; Henry W. and Albert A. Berg Collection of English and American Literature, New York Public Library; British Library Manuscript Collection, London; Harry Ransom Humanities Research Center, University of Texas at Austin; King's College Archive Centre, Cambridge; Monks House Papers/Leonard Woolf Papers/Charleston Papers/Nicolson Papers, University of Sussex Library; and Library of Leonard and Virginia Woolf, Washington State University Libraries. Much archive material, including holograph material, is available in electronic form online or CD-ROM: see *Major Authors on CD-ROM: Virginia Woolf*, ed. by Mark Hussey.

VII. BIBLIOGRAPHY. B. J. Kirkpatrick and Stuart N. Clarke, *A Bibliography of Virginia Woolf*, 4th ed. (Oxford and New York, 1997).

VIII. BIOGRAPHIES. Quentin Bell, *Virginia Woolf: A Biography*, 2 vols. (London, 1972); Phyllis Rose, *Woman of Letters: A Life of Virginia Woolf* (London, 1978); Louise DeSalvo, *Virginia Woolf: The Impact of Childhood Sexual Abuse on Her Life and Work* (London and Boston, 1989); Jane Dunn, *A Very Close Conspiracy: Vanessa Bell and Virginia Woolf* (London, 1990); John Mepham, *Virginia Woolf: A Literary Life* (London, 1991); James King, *Virginia Woolf* (London, 1994; New York, 1995); Roger Poole, *The Unknown Virginia Woolf*, 4th edition (Cambridge and New York, 1995); Hermione Lee, *Virginia Woolf* (London, 1996); Panthea Reid, *Art and Affection: A Life of Virginia Woolf* (New York, 1996); Mitchell Leaska, *Granite and Rainbow: The Hidden Life of Virginia Woolf* (New York, 1998).

IX. CRITICAL STUDIES. Erich Auerbach, *Mimesis: The Representation of Reality in Western Literature* (1946), trans. by Willard R. Trask (Princeton, N.J., 1953); J. K. Johnstone, *The Bloomsbury Group: A Study of E. M. Forster, Lytton Strachey, Virginia Woolf, and Their Circle* (London, 1954); Shiv K. Kumar, *Bergson and the Stream of Consciousness Novel* (London and Glasgow, 1962); Carolyn Heilbrun, *Towards Androgyny: Aspects of Male and Female in Literature* (London, 1963; 1973); Herbert Marder, *Feminism and Art: A Study of Virginia Woolf* (Chicago, 1968).

Jean O. Love, *Worlds in Consciousness: Mythopoetic Thought in the Novels of Virginia Woolf* (Los Angeles and Berkeley, Calif., and London, 1970); Harvena Richter, *Virginia Woolf: The Inward Voyage* (Princeton, 1970); Nancy Topping Bazin, *Virginia Woolf and the Androgynous Vision* (New Brunswick, N.J., 1973); Allen McLaurin, *Virginia Woolf: The Echoes Enslaved* (Cambridge, 1973); Robin Majumdar and Allen McLaurin, eds., *Virginia Woolf: The Critical Heritage* (London and Boston, 1975); Hermione Lee, *The Novels of Virginia Woolf* (London, 1977); Elaine Showalter, *A Literature of Their Own: British Women Novelists from Brontë to Lessing* (Princeton, N.J., 1977); Michèle Barrett, "Introduction," in Michèle Barrett, ed., *Virginia Woolf: Women and Writing* (London, 1979); Elizabeth Heine, "The Earlier *Voyage Out*: Virginia Woolf's First Novel," in *Bulletin of Research in the Humanities* 82 (Autumn 1979); Beverly Ann Schlack, "The Novelist's Voyage from Manuscripts to Text: Revisions of Literary Allusions in *The Voyage Out*," in *Bulletin of Research in the Humanities* 82 (autumn 1979).

Louise DeSalvo, *Virginia Woolf's First Voyage: A Novel in the Making* (Totowa, N.J. 1980); Maria DiBattista, *Virginia Woolf's Major Novels: The Fables of Anon* (New Haven, Conn., 1980); Perry Meisel, *The Absent Father: Virginia Woolf and Walter Pater* (New Haven, Conn., 1980); Jane Marcus, ed., *New Feminist Essays on Virginia Woolf* (Lincoln, Neb., and London, 1981); Jane Marcus, "Thinking back through our mothers," in Jane Marcus, ed., *New Feminist Essays on Virginia Woolf* (Lincoln, Neb., 1981); Grace Radin, *Virginia Woolf's* The Years: *The Evolution of a Novel* (Knoxville, 1981); Jane Marcus, ed., *Virginia Woolf: A Feminist Slant* (Lincoln, Neb., 1983); M. H. Levenson, *A Genealogy of Modernism: A Study of English Literary Doctrine, 1908–1922* (Cambridge, 1985); Toril

Moi, *Sexual/Textual Politics: Feminist Literary Theory* (London and New York, 1985).

Kate Flint, "Virginia Woolf and the General Strike," in *Essays in Criticism* 36 (1986); Mary Jacobus, *Reading Woman: Essays in Feminist Criticism* (New York, 1986); Eileen Barrett, "Matriarchal Myth on a Patriarchal Stage: Virginia Woolf's *Between the Acts*," in *Twentieth Century Literature* 33 (1987); Jane Marcus, ed., *Virginia Woolf and Bloomsbury: A Centenary Celebration* (Bloomington, Ind., 1987); Jane Marcus, *Virginia Woolf and the Languages of Patriarchy* (Bloomington, Ind., 1987); Diane Filby Gillespie, *The Sisters' Arts: The Writing and Painting of Virginia Woolf and Vanessa Bell* (Syracuse, N.Y., 1988); James M. Haule and Philip H. Smith, Jr., *Concordance to The Voyage Out by Virginia Woolf* (Ann Arbor, Mich., 1988); Jane Marcus, *Art and Anger: Reading Like a Woman* (Columbus, Ohio, 1988); Tania Modleski, "Some Functions of Feminist Criticism, or The Scandal of the Mute Body," *October* 49 (summer 1989).

Margaret J. M. Ezell, "The Myth of Judith Shakespeare: Creating the Canon of Women's Literature," *New Literary History* 21 (spring 1990); William R. Handley, "War and the Politics of Narration in *Jacob's Room*," in Mark Hussey, ed., *Virginia Woolf and War* (Syracuse, N.Y., 1991); Edward Bishop, "The Subject in *Jacob's Room*," in *Modern Fiction Studies* 38 (spring 1992); Jane Gallop, *Around 1981: Academic Feminist Literary Theory* (New York, 1992); Jane Marcus, "Britannia Rules *The Waves*," in Karen Lawrence, ed., *Decolonizing Tradition: New Views of Twentieth-Century "British" Literary Canons* (Urbana, Ill., 1992); J. H. Willis, Jr., *Leonard and Virginia Woolf as Publishers: The Hogarth Press, 1917–1941* (Charlottesville, Va., 1992); Vanessa Bell, *Selected Letters of Vanessa Bell*, ed. by Regina Marler (New York, 1993); Margaret Homans, ed., *Virginia Woolf: A Collection of Critical Essays* (Englewood Cliffs, N.J., 1993); Annette Oxindine, "Sapphist Semiotics in Woolf's *The Waves*: Untelling and Retelling What Cannot Be Told," in Vara Neverow-Turk and Mark Hussey, eds., *Virginia Woolf: Themes and Variations: Selected Papers from the Second Annual Conference on Virginia Woolf* (New York, 1993); Suzanne Raitt, *Vita & Virginia: The Work and Friendship of V. Sackville-West and Virginia Woolf* (New York, 1993); Susan Bennett Smith, "Gender and the Canon: When Judith Shakespeare At Last Assumes Her Body," in Vara Nevarow-Turk and Mark Hussey, eds, *Virginia Woolf:*

Themes and Variations. (New York, 1993); Eleanor McNees, ed., *Virginia Woolf: Critical Assessments*, 4 vols. (New York, 1994); Kathy J. Phillips, *Virginia Woolf Against Empire* (Knoxville, Tenn., 1994); Mark Hussey, *Virginia Woolf A to Z: A Comprehensive Reference for Students, Teachers, and Common Readers to Her Life, Work, and Critical Reception* (New York, 1995).

Gillian Beer, *Virginia Woolf: The Common Ground* (Edinburgh and Ann Arbor, Mich., 1996); Judy S. Reese, *Recasting Social Values in the Work of Virginia Woolf* (London and Selinsgrove, Penn.,1996); Eileen Barrett and Patricia Cramer, eds., *Virginia Woolf: Lesbian Readings* (New York, 1997); Rachel Bowlby, *Feminist Destinations and Further Essays on Virginia Woolf* (Edinburgh, 1997); Leila Brosnan, *Reading Virginia Woolf's Essays and Journalism* (Edinburgh, 1997); Juliet Dusinberre, *Virginia Woolf's Renaissance: Woman Reader or Common Reader?* (Iowa, 1997); E. M. Forster, "Virginia Woolf," Rede Lecture, in Jane Goldman, ed., *Icon Critical Guide: Virginia Woolf* (Cambridge, 1997); Jane Goldman, ed., *The Icon Critical Guide to Virginia Woolf* (Cambridge, 1997); Regina Marler, *Bloomsbury Pie: The Making of the Bloomsbury Boom* (New York, 1997); Beth Carole Rosenberg and Jeanne Dubino, eds., *Virginia Woolf and the Essay* (New York, 1997); Marta C. Carpentier, *Ritual, Myth, and the Modernist Text: The Influence of Jane Ellen Harrison on Joyce, Eliot, and Woolf* (Amsterdam, 1998); Jane Goldman, *The Feminist Aesthetics of Virginia Woolf: Modernism, Post-Impressionism, and the Politics of the Visual* (Cambridge, 1998); Ellen Tremper, *"Who Lived at Alfoxton?": Virginia Woolf and English Romanticism* (London and Lewisburg, Penn., 1998); Karen L. Levenback, *Virginia Woolf and the Great War* (Syracuse, N.Y., 1999); Brenda R. Silver, *Virginia Woolf Icon* (Chicago, 1999).

Ann Banfield, *The Phantom Table: Woolf, Fry, Russell, and the Epistemology of Modernism* (Cambridge, 2000); Eleanor Gualtieri, *Virginia Woolf's Essays: Sketching the Past* (New York, 2000); Sue Roe and Susan Sellers, eds., *The Cambridge Companion to Virginia Woolf* (Cambridge, 2000); Anna Snaith, *Virginia Woolf: Public and Private Negotiations* (New York, 2000).

X. JOURNALS. Pace University Press has published selected papers from the first ten annual International Virginia Woolf Conferences (1990–2000) and publishes the *Woolf Studies Annual* (1995–).

W. B. YEATS

(1865–1939)

Neil Powell

THE STORY OF W. B. Yeats seems symbolically to begin and end at Drumcliffe, County Sligo: "Under bare Ben Bulben's head / In Drumcliff churchyard Yeats is laid. / An ancestor was rector there / Long years ago, a church stands near, / By the road an ancient cross" (*CP*, p. 400; *YP*, p. 451).

But, like so much about Yeats, this is not quite what it seems. His great-grandfather, the Reverend John Yeats (1774–1846), was indeed the rector of Drumcliffe (usually spelt with the final "e") from 1811 until his death. The great-grandson, however, was buried in France, at Roquebrune, on 30 January 1939, and it is not entirely certain that he was re-interred at Drumcliffe, according to his wishes, after the war. That final ambiguity is an apt enough emblem for the life, shrouded in ambiguities, of a poet addicted to emblems.

It was to the town of Sligo itself that a Dublin law student called John Butler Yeats went in 1862: his purpose was to visit his friend George Pollexfen, but he ended up proposing to, and the following year marrying, George's sister Susan. Unlike the scholarly, clerical Yeats clan, the Pollexfens were solid west-coast business people; except that their businesses were in decline and their Irishness stretched back only a couple of generations, when they had arrived from Devon. John Butler Yeats, meanwhile, had no sooner secured his bride than he abandoned his legal career to become a painter; before long he would take the family—including their first two children, William Butler Yeats (born in Dublin on 13 June 1865) and Susan Mary Yeats (born in Sligo on 25 August 1866)—to London, eventually settling in the new "artistic" suburb of Bedford Park. In short, this was a marriage in which neither side was quite what it seemed and neither got quite what it was bargaining for. Moreover, the rootless, often impoverished existence of the unsuccessful painter and his disappointed, increasingly distant wife meant that the education their children received was disjointed and eccentric.

This matters, because during the years in which young Willie Yeats might have been discovering the literature in which he himself would play such a prominent part, he was doing no such thing: his report cards from Godolphin School, Hammersmith, are unenthusiastic, and in 1879—at an age when literary talent often declares itself—he was actually bottom of his class in English; he would never master spelling and grammar, and may have suffered from dyslexia. Back in Dublin in 1881, he enrolled at the High School and cut a rather different figure: odd but popular, intellectual rather than academic, he was, according to a contemporary, W. K. Magee, "an unusually well-read young man of about nineteen with a conscious literary ambition" (quoted in R. F. Foster, *W. B. Yeats: A Life*, 1, p. 33) by the time he left school. John Butler Yeats would have liked his wayward, gifted son to follow the orthodox academic career at Trinity College, Dublin, that he himself had so conspicuously rejected; however, in May 1884, Willie chose to instead enroll at the Metropolitan School of Art.

The two consequences of this—an eccentric friendship and an esoteric belief—would recur repeatedly over the next thirty years. The friend was his fellow-student George Russell (Æ) and the belief, Esoteric Buddhism, led to the formation in June 1885 of the Dublin Hermetic Society; the following year, he joined the recently founded Dublin Theosophical Lodge. At the same time, a very different kind of society, the Contemporary Club, fostered his interest in Irish politics and introduced him to the fifty-five-year-old Fenian writer John O'Leary (who in turn persuaded Yeats to join the Young Ireland Society), while through the Contemporary Club's organizer, Charles Oldham, he met lastingly influential friends such as Douglas Hyde and Katharine Tynan. He was also working on a verse drama, *The Island of Statues,* and on his first long poem, *The Wanderings of Oisin.* Still in his early twenties, Yeats was leading a busy and complicated life, typically uniting three strands—mystical, political, and literary—and making connections in a way which a later, more cynical age would call "networking"; but such practical considerations as earning a living so far played almost no part in his plans.

That had to change. In 1887, impoverished by declining revenue from family properties and by J. B. Yeats's legendary inability to finish or sell his paintings, the Yeatses moved back to London—first to Earls Court, then more permanently to Bedford Park, where Susan Yeats, suffering from depression and a stroke, was to become virtually housebound. Willie hated London, but he began to pursue an energetic career as a literary reviewer (despite his inability to produce grammatical or accurately spelled copy) and, characteristically, was soon meeting almost everyone worth meeting: William Morris, George Bernard Shaw, Oscar Wilde. Assuming him to be a young Irish writer on his own in London, Wilde invited Yeats to dinner on Christmas Day 1888; his acceptance of the invitation, evidently without enlightening his host, is a perfect example of behavior that may either be charmingly vague or calculatingly shrewd. With Ernest Rhys, later the editor of Dent's Everyman's Library, he founded the Rhymers' Club in 1890: just as in Dublin, when he was not joining influential circles he was inventing them.

The most important encounter of his life, however, occurred on 30 January 1889, when Maud Gonne called at Bedford Park. Yeats, at once bowled over, swiftly agreed to write *The Countless Cathleen* for her; the long-term hopelessness of his love for Maud—they would eventually have an affair in 1908–1909 and his intermittent proposals of marriage would continue until as late as July 1916—would be matched by her equally enduring influence on his poetry. (Her marriage to John MacBride, on 21 February 1903, effectively lasted only two years; MacBride was executed after the Easter Rising of 1916.) During the 1890s, Maud Gonne's impact on Yeats was rivaled, though seldom eclipsed, by two other extraordinary women: the actress Florence Farr, his Bedford Park neighbor and fellow-member of the Order of the Golden Dawn, for whom he would write *The Land of Heart's Desire*; and the novelist Olivia Shakespear, with whom he had an affair in 1896–1897, shortly after his move to the rooms at 18 Woburn Buildings which were to remain his London home until 1919.

Meanwhile, Yeats was also busily involved with Irish political and cultural organizations such as the Young Ireland League and the Irish Literary Society, the latter prompting a characteristic schism between conservative and modern literary tastes over a planned Irish Library. In 1895 he joined the Irish National Alliance. He visited Paris in 1894, when he met Paul Verlaine, and again in 1896, when he met J. M. Synge (whom he persuaded to join a Young Ireland Society), although his main purposes were to establish an Order of Celtic Mysteries and to visit Maud Gonne. As usual with Yeats, elements of experience that might ordinarily seem distinct and even contradictory—politics, mysticism, literature—become inextricably fused.

In the mid-1890s he was writing plays, essays, journalism, and working on a novel to be called *The Speckled Bird,* though producing relatively few poems. One partial explanation is that his passionate interest in Irish culture was both naive and deracinated: he neither understood the likely consequences of his political ideas nor did he have a base in Ireland where he could think and write. This began to change after the Dublin riots which accompanied Queen Victoria's Diamond Jubilee in 1897: precipitated by Maud Gonne's speech to the crowd, they left 200 people injured and Yeats in a state of shocked bewilderment. He went first to his uncle George Pollexfen at Sligo, then to Edward Martyn at Tulira Castle, and finally to Coole Park, which he had visited briefly a year earlier; there, he said, "I found at last what I had been seeking always, a life of order and of labour" (quoted by R. F. Foster, *W. B. Yeats: A Life,* 1, pp. 181–182). He had also found the second of the three important women in his life, Lady Augusta Gregory.

Born in 1852, Augusta Persse married a wealthy and much older husband, Sir William Gregory, who had been governor of Ceylon; he died in 1892, leaving her with a son, Robert, and a fine estate, Coole Park. For Yeats she became surrogate mother, patroness, adviser, and example; moreover, she was an enthusiastic supporter of his latest project, an Irish theater. One day during the summer of 1897, she took him to visit an old friend, Count Florimond de Basterot, at his house in Galway: "In his garden, under his friendly eyes, the Irish National Theatre, though not under that name, was born" (*Autobiographies*, p. 398). It was to need all the friendly eyes it could find, for its early years were stormy—predictably so, given the ultimately irreconcilable tension between politicized nationalists such as Maud Gonne and those (including Yeats and Lady Gregory) whose main ambition was for a professional company with the highest standards of stagecraft. The intervention in 1904 of a second benefactor, Annie Horniman, who offered £5,000 towards the conversion and upkeep of buildings in Abbey Street, Dublin, seemed decisively to tilt the balance towards professional stability; but the Abbey Theatre was never far from controversy, notably during and after the first performances of J. M. Synge's *The Playboy of the Western World* in January 1907.

Coole had become for Yeats a sanctuary and a second home, but the first decade of the twentieth century found him traveling far afield. In 1903–1904, happy to escape from the factional infighting which afflicted many of his projects in Ireland and England, he undertook his first American lecture tour; while in 1907, in a more leisurely spirit, he toured Italy with Lady Gregory and her son. These excursions seem to have left him feeling, not quite paradoxically, less like a Dubliner and more like an Irishman. He temporarily withdrew from the Abbey Theatre and its wrangles, most urgently to work on the eight-volume *Collected Works,* published in 1908 with financial backing from Annie Horniman. In the same year he embarked on an affair with Mabel Dickinson—a relationship which, unusually for Yeats, was wholly physical rather than in any sense spiritual: it seemed unlikely to last, but continued on and off until 1913.

The Abbey Theatre remained an abiding and time-consuming interest. In 1910, Annie Horniman offered to sell the theater to its remaining directors, Yeats and Lady Gregory (the third director, Synge, had died a year earlier); the transition might have proceeded amicably had not the theater, almost certainly due to a genuine misunderstanding, remained open when all others closed on the day of King Edward VII's funeral, infuriating the very English Miss Horniman. To raise funds and to supplement the Abbey company's regular and successful visits to England, an American tour was arranged; Yeats and Lady Gregory accompanied successive stages of it. Then, a parallel cause was added to the perennially embattled affairs of the Abbey when the Dublin Corporation refused to finance a gallery to house the fine collection of paintings left to them by Lady Gregory's nephew, Hugh Lane. And, as if the crises of Dublin political and cultural life were not enough,

complications were brewing in Yeats's London circle. One was the arrival of Ezra Pound who, much to Olivia Shakespear's displeasure, had become friendly with her daughter Dorothy, whom he would eventually marry (he also served for a time as Yeats's secretary). The other was a chance meeting at the British Museum in 1911 with the step-daughter of Olivia's brother Harry Tucker: Georgie Hyde Lees. Yeats appears not to have been swept off his feet by her—and perhaps, bearing in mind the failure of his continuing infatuation with Maud Gonne to develop into a permanent relationship, this was a good omen. For he had met the third important woman in his life.

Almost everything in Yeats's world would alter over the next few years, with the momentous consequence that, as we shall see later, he at last became a mature and indeed a major poet. The outbreak of World War I was profoundly unsettling for everyone caught in the conflict of Anglo-Irish allegiances. The Easter Rising of 1916 resulted in the execution of some of his oldest nationalist friends (and at least one enemy): after that, all was "changed, changed utterly." Such plentiful evidence of things falling apart could only serve to emphasize Yeats's own lack of stability: in his early fifties, he had neither a permanent home nor a wife. In April 1917, almost exactly two decades after his first summer at Coole, he acquired the derelict castle and cottage nearby at Ballylee: he paid £35 for the freehold. It was uninhabitable at first but rich in history and in symbols: it would become in every sense the basis of his greatest poetry. Six months later, in October 1917, he married Georgie—usually called, by her own preference, George—Hyde Lees.

The marriage was almost a fiasco: no sooner had the couple set off on their honeymoon than Yeats realized that he was still incurably in love with Maud Gonne. His wife reacted with extraordinary tact, inspiration, and (as Brenda Maddox makes clear in her book *George's Ghosts*) shrewdness. Yeats's fascination with spiritualism was undiminished, though wavering between extremes of skepticism and gullibility; astonishingly, within a week of their marriage, George discovered a facility for "automatic writing" through which over the coming years she would convey a huge amount of information and instruction to her husband, including the esoteric theories which form the basis of *A Vision* (1925). "We have come to give you metaphors for poetry," the script announced, though it would no less usefully manage to give him a good deal of frank advice about the conduct of his married life. It is scarcely an exaggeration to say that George's ingenuity both saved the marriage and made the poet.

Although George's "communicators" had rashly promised a son, in February 1919 she gave birth to a daughter, Anne Butler Yeats; later that year, the Yeatses moved their English base from London to Oxford. Work on Thoor Ballylee was progressing well, but money was still needed to complete the roof; so Yeats set off, with his wife, on another American lecture tour early in 1920, during which he met Junzo Sato (the Japanese Consul at Portland, Oregon), who presented him with a five-hundred-year-old ceremonial sword. On their return, George soon became pregnant again and this time—in August 1921—she did produce the son and heir so long anticipated by the dynastic side of Yeats's personality.

Despite the escalating violence as Ireland descended into civil war, the Yeatses bought a house in Merrion Square, the best address in Dublin. Conventional success had come late to Yeats, but now it arrived resoundingly: he had an affectionate and resourceful wife, a daughter, a son, a house in town, and a castle (albeit a small one) in the country. In 1922 he became a member of the Irish Senate, while the following year he was awarded the Nobel Prize for Literature: accepting it, he invoked the imaginary presences, standing each side of him, of Lady Gregory and John Synge. He was now, as he said, "A sixty-year-old smiling public man." As a senator, he proved to be independent and outspoken, authoritarian on matters of public order but liberal on issues such as censorship and divorce. And he was producing his finest work—the poems which would be included in *The Tower* (1928) and *The Winding Stair* (1933). He ought to have been content.

But his health was starting to deteriorate and cultural life in Dublin continued to be marred by such dispiriting events as the riots that greeted Sean O'Casey's *The Plough and the Stars* at the Abbey Theatre in 1927, an almost exact replica of the *Playboy* affair twenty years earlier. The long Mediterranean holiday which he and George took in the winter of 1924–1925 was the precursor of their semi-permanent move to Rapallo, where Ezra and Dorothy Pound were at the heart of a lively circle, in 1928: there, the first year went well, but for most of the second winter Yeats was feverishly and irascibly ill. The house in Merrion Square had been sold; so returning to Dublin meant a return to rented accommodation—a flat in Fitzwilliam Square, followed by a house on the coast south of the city. He was delighted by the award of an honorary Oxford D. Litt. in 1931—honors and ceremonies always gave him pleasure—but this was soon overshadowed by news of Lady Gregory's final illness: although Yeats spent months with her at Coole, he was in Dublin when she died in May 1932.

Hoping to re-create something of Coole's atmosphere on a smaller scale, the Yeatses took a thirteen-year lease on a country house at Riversdale, Rathfarnham. Despite his precarious health, Yeats's passionate involvement in his long-standing causes remained undiminished: partly in response to Ireland's increasingly theocratic censorship, in September 1932 he founded the Irish Academy of Letters (though Joyce and Shaw declined to join); censorship was also at the heart of continuing conflict between the authorities and the Abbey Theatre (whose 1932 tour of the United States had once again proved controversial); and a meeting with Shri Purohit Swami led to literary collaborations and ultimately farcical travels (the Swami and his mistress, Gwyneth Foden, are justly described by Brenda Maddox, on p. 291 of *George's Ghosts*, as "two dubious characters who might have come from a Marx Brothers comedy").

The most literal aspect of Yeats's elderly rejuvenation occurred in April 1934 when he underwent the Steinach operation for "rejuvenation by experimental revitalization of the ageing puberty gland": it did nothing for his sexual performance but provided a psychological boost, as if he needed it, for his persona as a lecherous old fool. During his remaining years he would be involved in four affairs: with Margot Ruddock, a competent actress and incompetent poet, eventually driven to attempted suicide by Yeats's frank assessment of her work; Ethel Mannin, a novelist and member of the Sexual Reform League; the aristocratic poet Dorothy Wellesley; and the journalist Edith Shackleton Heald. These last two hold special places in the roll call of Yeats's extraordinary and often brilliant women friends: Dorothy Wellesley was, unusually, an able and sympathetic poet, to whom Yeats wrote remarkable letters on poetry; while Edith Shackleton Heald was the woman with whom George shared both Yeats's affections and the chores of looking after him until the very end.

Yeats's last years were as busy as ever. He continued to write prolifically. He bustled about between Dublin, the English homes of his lady-friends, and Monte Carlo. He edited the *Oxford Book of Modern Verse* (1936) and enjoyed broadcasting for the BBC, giving their National Lecture in 1936. In November 1938, George met him in London (he had been staying with Edith in Sussex) and they set off for the Hotel Idéal-Séjour at Menton; there—surrounded by George, Dorothy, and Edith, who had arrived that day for a planned month's stay—he died on 28 January 1939. "O all the instruments agree," wrote W. H. Auden, the major poet who learned most from him, "The day of his death was a dark cold day" ("In Memory of W. B. Yeats," *The English Auden*, p. 242).

This brief biographical introduction is a necessarily selective sketch of an enormously complex life—one that is exhaustively explored in innumerable books on Yeats, including the three standard biographies by Joseph Hone, A. Norman Jeffares, and R. F. Foster. The remainder of this essay will focus on the poems that most clearly illustrate Yeats's development as a major poet.

EARLIER POEMS

"HE hangs in the balance between genius & (to speak rudely) fool," wrote Edward Dowden of Yeats in 1886—a judgment that might plausibly have been uttered at any time during the first half of Yeats's literary career. Two mildly iconoclastic general points need to be made about the earlier poetry, by which I mean (following for convenience the arrangement of the familiar 1950 *Collected Poems*) the contents of Yeats's collections from *Crossways* (1889) to *Responsibilities* (1914): one is that an astonishing amount of it is feeble and silly; the other is that for most of this time Yeats, busy as he was in all sorts of literary-cultural ways, was unprolific as a lyric poet, often producing only a piece or two a year until a striking acceleration in his creativity occurred in 1912. Had he died in 1910, at the not terribly youthful age of forty-five, he would have been remembered as an energetic figure in the Anglo-Irish literary scene, an eccentric playwright, and a very minor poet.

The problem was cheerfully stated by Yeats himself: "The mystical life is the centre of all that I do & all that I think & all that I write" (*Collected Letters*, 1, p. 303). It is this "mystical life," crowding out any other sort of life, which clogs the early poems with supernatural exotica, and the reader accordingly looks for premonitions of the more mature and solidly based poet. Paradoxically, the first poem to provide this is "The Stolen Child" (*CP*, pp. 21–22; *YP*, pp. 53–54), which anchors its "faery" imagery in a very specific landscape north of Sligo, beside Lough Gill: "Where the wandering water gushes / From the hills above Glen-Car." Moreover, the famous and eerily evocative refrain seems to carry unexpected literary echoes: "Come away, O human child! / To the waters and the wild / With a faery, hand in hand, / For the world's more full of weeping than you can understand."

The presence of Irish folk song is unmistakable; but so too is the resonance of a different kind of metaphysical song, John Donne's "Goe, and catche a falling starre, / Get with child a mandrake roote . . . ." To mention so apparently different a poet as Donne is to be sharply reminded that the young Yeats is not a writer to be easily pigeonholed with a phrase such as "Celtic twilight."

Equally familiar, and equally surprising when read afresh, is "The Lake Isle of Innisfree," which appears to be "about" one of the islands in Lough Gill. But that landscape, despite its putative clay-and-wattle cabin and "Nine bean-rows" (and these, after all, are items which Yeats proposes to supply when he gets there), remains mistily elusive; the poem's most enduring image is, on the contrary, that of the poet staring miserably into a shop window on a London street:

> I will arise and go now, for always night and day
> I hear lake water lapping with low sounds by the
>   shore;
> While I stand on the roadway, or on the pavements
>   grey,
> I hear it in the deep heart's core.
>
> (*CP*, p. 44; *YP*, p. 74)

In other words, the underlying theme of the poem, and the reason for its haunting memorability, is not so much a remembered landscape as the experience of urban alienation. Similarly, in Yeats's version of a Ronsard sonnet, "When You Are Old" (*CP*, p. 46; *YP*, p. 76), the poem's peculiar force springs from a juxtaposition of the specific— Maud Gonne's rejection of him—with the universal, in this case the mutating effect of time on memory.

To notice this is to reaffirm a truism: that the successful lyric poem is likely to occur at the junction of two disparate impulses. Mere description is seldom enough, and mere whimsy, however colorfully dressed, never is; which is why the perfect lyric "He Wishes for the Cloths of Heaven" (*CP*, p. 81; *YP*, p. 108)—its haunting conclusion, "I have spread my dreams under your feet; / Tread softly because you tread on my dreams," becomes lovelier still in Thomas Dunhill's setting, which the tone-deaf Yeats could not have fully appreciated—remains a minor poem. So too does "The Lover Tells of the Rose in his Heart," though the plangent beauty of the verse is indisputable:

> All things uncomely and broken, all things worn out
>   and old,
> The cry of a child by the roadway, the creak of a
>   lumbering cart,
> The heavy steps of the ploughman, splashing the
>   wintry mould,
> Are wronging your image that blossoms a rose in the
>   deeps of my heart.
>   (*CP*, p. 62; *YP*, p. 90)

These potentially vigorous and affecting images are so generalized that they might as well be abstractions. The much-needed qualities of concreteness and directness are more likely to find their way into Yeats's early poetry when he confronts the problematical aspects of Irish culture and politics: *The Rose* (1893) ends with a heavily revised manifesto-poem, "To Ireland in the Coming Times" (*CP*, pp. 56–58; *YP*, pp. 85–86), which attempts a three-way fusion of spiritual past ("Ah, faeries, dancing under the moon, / A Druid land, a Druid tune!"), cultural history ("Nor may I less be counted one / With Davis, Mangan, Ferguson . . ."), and political destiny. The insistent italics signal, as they often do in Yeats, a determination to be both serious and memorable: "Know, that I would accounted be / True brother of a company / That sang, to sweeten Ireland's wrong, / Ballad and story, rann and song. . . ."

Yet even here, Yeats remains aware of his ambiguous status as a semi-outsider: he cannot say that he "is" of this company, only that he "would accounted be . . . ," which is a more cautiously conditional proposition; the idea of being simultaneously historian, chronicler, and prophet will recur much later on, in "Sailing to Byzantium."

The central uncertainty of "To Ireland in the Coming Times" is more swiftly resolved, though not until what the Contents in the *Collected Poems* call the "Introductory Rhymes," otherwise untitled and once again italicized, of *Responsibilities*. Here Yeats invokes his actual Irish ancestors, the "old fathers" to whom he now applies for forgiveness:

> Pardon that for a barren passion's sake,
> Although I have come close on forty-nine,
> I have no child, I have nothing but a book,
> Nothing but that to prove your blood and mine.
>   (*CP*, p. 113; *YP*, p. 197)

This bracing candor and scaled-down rhetoric mark a radical transformation of Yeats's style, which is made possible by his newfound ability to incorporate his own history, with its often bitter memories, into his work. He has lived enough to become part of his own subject matter. Nowhere is this transformation clearer than in the acerbic opening of "September 1913":

> What need you, being come to sense,
> But fumble in a greasy till
> And add the halfpence to the pence
> And prayer to shivering prayer until
> You have dried the marrow from the bone?
> For men were born to pray and save:
> Romantic Ireland's dead and gone,
> It's with O'Leary in the grave.
>   (*CP*, pp. 120–121; *YP*, p. 210)

It need hardly be said that this stanza could not have occurred in any of Yeats's previous collections. The poem appeared, with the more informative though ludicrously cumbersome title "Romance in Ireland (On reading much of the correspondence against the Art Gallery)," in the *Irish Times* on 8 September 1913; but it outgrew its original context (and title) to become the first of Yeats's major poems on the condition of Ireland. In it he found the voice that characterizes his political poetry.

Yeats knew what he was doing in *Responsibilities*: in "A Coat" (*CP*, p. 142; *YP*, p. 230), a tiny poem near the end of the book, he explicitly rejects his earlier poetry as "a coat / Covered with embroideries / Out of old mythologies / From heel to throat," a style borrowed and degraded by "fools"; "For there's more enterprise," he concludes, "In walking naked." It was a brave resolution, if not a foolish one, for a poet who was then approaching his fiftieth birthday; shrewdly, or fortuitously, Yeats would appear to keep it while actually doing something rather different.

THE WILD SWANS AT COOLE

AN unwary reader, supposing that Yeats's poetry provides at least an approximate biography, might be forgiven for thinking that from about 1915 onwards his life was centered on Lady Augusta Gregory's estate at Coole Park and the nearby tower, Thoor Ballylee, which he bought in 1917. The biographies tell a rather more complicated story, but it is the story the poetry tells which matters. As Yeats himself would later write: "The intellect of man is forced to choose / Perfection of the life, or of the work" ("The Choice," *CP*, p. 278; *YP*, p. 362).

Not only does *The Wild Swans at Coole* (1919) open with two magnificent poems; their magnificence is of a kind that could not have easily been foretold from his earlier books. The new note is one of elegiac restraint, held in place by the metrical subtlety of verse in which end-stopping is interspersed with suspended lines of almost unbearable poignancy:

> The trees are in their autumn beauty,
> The woodland paths are dry,
> Under the October twilight the water
> Mirrors a still sky;
> Upon the brimming water among the stones
> Are nine-and-fifty swans.
>> (*CP*, pp. 147–148; *YP*, p. 233)

Yeats takes his time preparing the ground for his central image: the swans, carefully counted—as, he tells us, he has counted them for the past nineteen years; at the end of the poem he will envisage the appalling prospect of waking one day to find them gone. For on one level, this is that very Yeatsian thing, a poem about time past, present, and future; but it is also perhaps the first of his poems fully to vindicate his later description of himself as one of "the last Romantics," for its use of an exactly realized place as the basis for reflections on time and mortality is a technique which would have been perfectly familiar to Wordsworth or Coleridge.

"In Memory of Major Robert Gregory" (*CP*, pp. 148–152; *YP*, pp. 234–237) is also in a recognizable Romantic-elegiac tradition, but here Yeats adds a notably audacious touch by casting his elegy for Lady Gregory's son (killed in action in World War I) within a more general recollection of "the friends that cannot sup with us," including the poet and critic Lionel Johnson, the playwright John Synge, and his uncle George Pollexfen—Robert Gregory does not make his appearance until the sixth stanza. Far from diminishing the main subject, as one might have expected, this unconventional approach has quite the opposite effect: Gregory's renaissance talents—"Our Sidney and our perfect man"—seem all the more notable for their association with Yeats's valued friends of earlier generations. In the final stanza, Yeats seems about to introduce a further selection of dead friends and relations, "but a thought / Of that late death took all my heart for speech"—a brilliant conclusion if a pardonably inexact one, since he has already managed ninety-six lines of eloquence. By comparison, the shorter elegy in the form of a first-person monologue that immediately follows, "An Irish Airman Foresees His Death" (*CP*, p. 152; *YP*, p. 237), though serviceable enough, reverts to a style of Yeatsian rhetoric that the poet seems quite suddenly to have outgrown.

The change in style implies a corresponding change in his relationship with his readers. Although never in any formal or technical sense a modernist, Yeats was steadily moving away from a quasi-populist position with its roots in legend and folk song and towards T. S. Eliot's view that the poet should "address the one hypothetical Intelligent Man who does not exist and who is the audience of the artist" (*The Athenaeum*, 9 May 1919). In "The Fisherman," he tries to have the best of both worlds by giving his ideal reader, his "wise and simple man," "grey Connemara clothes" and a "sun-freckled face," while admitting—in words which are very close to Eliot's—that he is "A man who does not exist, / A man who is but a dream. . . ." The resolve that he states at the poem's conclusion only looks like a paradox: "Before I am old / I shall have written him one / Poem maybe as cold / And passionate as the dawn" (*CP*, pp. 166–167; *YP*, pp. 251–252).

Cold *and* passionate: it is exactly the balance he has so finely achieved in "The Wild Swans at Coole." It is also, no less remarkably, just how Lady Gregory herself was recalled by an old Galway acquaintance: "the most complicated woman I can think of. . . . Loving—cold" (quoted in R. F. Foster, *W. B. Yeats: A Life*, 1, p. 168).

MICHAEL ROBARTES AND THE DANCER

IN a less turbulent political time Yeats might now have become a rather stately poet celebrating the big houses and cultural continuities of Ireland. But

Michael Robartes and the Dancer, though its title incorporates the name of one of Yeats's invented Irish archetypes, is primarily notable for poems connected with the Easter Rising of 1916: passionate but far from cold. "Easter 1916" will at once remind us of "September 1913," although the earlier poem's four-stress line has been tightened to a three-stress line in which urgency and weariness strangely coexist:

> I have met them at close of day
> Coming with vivid faces
> From counter or desk among grey
> Eighteenth-century houses.
> I have passed with a nod of the head
> Or polite meaningless words,
> Or have lingered awhile and said
> Polite meaningless words . . .
> (*CP*, pp. 202–205; *YP*, pp. 287–289)

This is one of the inimitable notes in twentieth-century poetry: to so commanding an extent that the only possible imitation is in a spirit of conscious homage, as in W. H. Auden's "September 1, 1939" ("I sit in one of the dives / On Fifty-Second Street . . ."). Yeats's opening lines are designed to emphasize the ordinariness of the executed revolutionary leaders; these are people he was accustomed to bump into in the street, transformed by their grotesque and disproportionate fate: "All changed, changed utterly: / A terrible beauty is born." Just as in "In Memory of Major Robert Gregory," Yeats prefaces his elegiac gravity with a gentler piece of scene setting, as if to insist that the tragic takes places within the context of the everyday. His allusive roll call evenhandedly embraces enemies as well as friends: the "drunken, vainglorious" John MacBride "had done most bitter wrong / To some who are near my heart" through his disastrous marriage to Maud Gonne. But the poem is all about transformation beyond the "casual comedy" of ordinary life, and the closing lines magnanimously unite the protagonists:

> And what if excess of love
> Bewildered them till they died?
> I write in out in a verse—
> MacDonagh and MacBride
> And Connolly and Pearse
> Now and in time to be,
> Wherever green is worn,
> Are changed, changed utterly:
> A terrible beauty is born.
> (*CP*, pp. 202–205; *YP*,
> pp. 287–289)

"Easter 1916" is so inevitable a poem, and so justly admired, that it may seem churlish to point out that it doesn't quite make sense—and to add that one of Yeats's paradoxical strengths is his ability to make a resonant phrase override meaning. For it is by no means self-evident that the Easter revolutionaries were driven by "excess of love," nor that such an excess, if its consequence is civil disorder, can be excused by a simple "what if": the poet's head and heart are in unresolved conflict here, and the phenomenon is worth pointing out because we shall come across it again.

Indeed, we almost at once encounter a comparable problem, in "The Second Coming," which readers tend to view either as a great and memorable poem or as a piece of irredeemable mumbo-jumbo. It is both. Like *Hamlet*, it has the disconcerting air of being made almost entirely of quotations. "Things fall apart; the centre cannot hold"; "The ceremony of innocence is drowned"; "The best lack all conviction, while the worst / Are full of passionate intensity": all these occur in the first eight lines, and the poem ends with the unforgettable image of the "rough beast, its hour come round at last" which "Slouches towards Bethlehem to be born" (*CP*, pp. 210–211; *YP*, pp. 294–295). Few poems in the language begin to convey so intense a feeling of universal chaos and collapse. Yet at the same time it is the first of Yeats's major poems to depend unavoidably on one of his most eccentric ideas: the gyres.

It is hard for the skeptical reader to understand quite why Yeats, who may have been eccentric but who was not stupid, should have become so devoted to this complicated image of the blindingly obvious. He himself, in *A Vision*, and countless writers since have struggled to make sense of the things: as lucid as any is John Unterecker, who calmly explains that the gyres are "a pair of interpenetrating cones" which "represent the antithetical elements in every man's, nation's, and era's nature" (*A Reader's Guide to W. B. Yeats*, p. 25). All opposites thus coexist in differing proportions at different points: the lessening of one (e.g., "objective") implies the increase of the other (e.g., "subjective"), and one need only substitute the words "thesis" and "antithesis" to see how close we are to the familiar, comprehensible idea of the dialectic. But Yeats had worked out the symbolic paraphernalia of his gyres with obsessive care, and "The Second Coming" is on one level an exact account of what must follow when "Turning and turning in the widening gyre, / The falcon cannot hear the falconer . . ." On another and more manageable level, it is a powerful metaphorical response to World War I and the threat to cultural continuity as Ireland drifted into civil war.

"A Prayer for My Daughter," written soon after "The Second Coming" in early 1919, offers a more practical response to the same circumstances: the paternal wishes—that Anne "be granted beauty and yet not / Beauty to make a stranger's eye distraught," "chiefly learned" in "courtesy," and spared "intellectual hatred"—are those of a father who foresees bad times ahead, in which to "become a flourishing hidden tree" may be the best, safest, and happiest course; the implicit comparison is with the turbulent, self-destructive life of Maud Gonne. At the same time, the poem is locked firmly into Romantic tradition, alluding in its opening lines ("half hid / Under this cradle-hood and coverlid / My child sleeps on") to the "Dear Babe, that sleepest cradled by my side" in Samuel Taylor Coleridge's "Frost at Midnight"; but whereas the Coleridgean night was cold and still, for Yeats "the storm is howling":

I have walked and prayed for this young child an
   hour
And heard the sea-wind scream upon the tower,
And under the arches of the bridge, and scream
In the elms above the flooded stream;
Imagining in excited reverie
That the future years had come,
Dancing to a frenzied drum,
Out of the murderous innocence of the sea.
         (*CP*, pp. 211–214; *YP*, pp. 295–297)

Despite the "great gloom" he professes, his exhilaration is plain: "excited reverie," as potent an oxymoron as "passionate and cold," fairly sums up his reaction to the next few years.

THE TOWER

"SAILING to Byzantium" (*CP*, pp. 211–214; *YP*, pp. 295–297), which opens *The Tower* (1928), is a poem which must always be read as if for the first time; for only then will its first sentence—"That is no country for old men"—seem properly enigmatic. Which country? And who are these old men? Yeats, aged sixty-two, was certainly oldish when he wrote "Sailing to Byzantium," but the poem's location remains unresolved for sixteen lines. In the first stanza, "That" country is vividly though unhelpfully portrayed as a place of youthful plenty and thoughtlessness: "The young / In one another's arms, birds in the trees / —Those dying generations—at their song. . . ." The difficulty for Yeats is that this "sensual music," which fatally neglects "Monuments of unageing intellect," is also enormously attractive: the tone is again that of "excited reverie," as in "A Prayer for my Daughter," in which apprehension and admiration merge. Moreover, as the second stanza tells us, the "aged man," "A tattered coat upon a stick," has the worst of both worlds; since he can be neither a hedonistic youth nor a timeless artifact, he has decided to transport himself imaginatively to a world of monumental grandeur: "And therefore I have sailed the seas and come / To the holy city of Byzantium." Those lines ought to jolt us with a shock of dislocation, partly because so much hangs, and so tenuously, on that "therefore," and partly because the syntax seems suddenly at odds with the title: for "Sailing to Byzantium" suggests that the poem's subject is to be the journey itself, whereas now we discover that Yeats has already arrived there and is looking back at "That" abandoned country of Ireland.

Byzantium attracted Yeats for several reasons: it had conveniently flourished towards the midpoint of the two thousand-year time span which defined the beginning and end of modern civilization; it was, he thought, a society which successfully fused religious, aesthetic, and practical life (as Ireland plainly did not) and in which artist and artifact enjoyed a perfect coexistence, like the dancer and the dance; moreover, it was sufficiently distant to be peopled by emblematic beings such as the "sages standing in God's holy fire" who appear in the third stanza and are then required to "perne in a gyre"—or more prosaically "spin in a cone"—before becoming "the singing-masters of my soul" and gathering "me / Into the artifice of eternity." The poem is dense with paradox: in this world of eternal artifacts, eternity itself is an "artifice." In the last stanza, Yeats's transmogrification is complete:

Once out of nature I shall never take
My bodily form from any natural thing,
But such a form as Grecian goldsmiths make
Of hammered gold and gold enamelling
To keep a drowsy Emperor awake;
Or set upon a golden bough to sing

To lords and ladies of Byzantium
Of what is past, or passing, or to come.
(*CP*, pp. 211–214; *YP*, pp. 295–297)

This too has its paradoxes: to be a golden bird (and, what is more, one that can sing) is surely to take one's "bodily form" quite specifically from a "natural thing"; while preventing an emperor from nodding off is a surprisingly modest ambition for a poet, or a bird, whether or not he is made of gold. But the final resonant assertion of timelessness triumphs over the poem's characteristically contorted logic.

The three great, flawed sequences that immediately follow "Sailing to Byzantium" in the *Collected Poems* actually precede it chronologically: they deal with different aspects of the Ireland that prompts Yeats's imaginary emigration. Indeed, "The Tower" (*CP*, pp. 218–225; *YP*, pp. 302–307) opens with an image close to the "tattered coat upon a stick": here, "Decrepit age" is an "absurdity" "that has been tied to me / As to a dog's tail" (though at *this* time of writing the poet was only just sixty: Yeats, like Robert Frost, did well out of pretending to be immensely old before his time). In the second part of "The Tower" he employs the now-familiar strategy of invoking a series of characters who in various ways raged against their predicaments: one, Mrs. French, sent a servant to clip a neighboring farmer's ears and bring them to her "in a little covered dish," a small-scale variation on the Salome theme which prompts him to a rare joke when he describes Mrs. French as "Gifted with so fine an ear." But "The Tower" is for the most part a grimly acidic poem, and Yeats signals as much when in the third part he returns to the somber three-stress meter of "Easter 1916":

It is time that I wrote my will;
I choose upstanding men
That climb the streams until
The fountain leap, and at dawn
Drop their cast at the side
Of dripping stone; I declare
They shall inherit my pride . . .
(*CP*, pp. 218–225; *YP*, pp. 302–307)

This, then, is a symbolic, poetic "will" in which the chief legacy is to be "pride" (Yeats has by now a family to inherit his more tangible assets); and the chosen inheritor turns out to be very like the fisherman who was his ideal audience. For all the pent-up passion, there is an inescapable sense of the poet retreading familiar ground.

"Meditations in Time of Civil War" (*CP*, pp. 225–232; *YP*, pp. 308–314) is another matter. Its fine opening section, "Ancestral Houses," is in that stately iambic pentameter shared with Romantic poems of place such as William Wordsworth's "Tintern Abbey"; this is the form, and the tone, which was to shape many of Yeats's most impressive later poems. There is from the start—"Surely among a rich man's flowering lawns . . ."—an atmosphere of rueful lament; the fountain, symbol of cultivated life, has been supplanted by an "empty sea-shell" that "Shadows the inherited glory of the rich." We seem to have come a long way from qualified endorsement of the Easter Rising and its civic vandalism: one simple explanation for this is that Yeats has in the meantime become a husband, a father, and a country property-owner. But he has also come to recognize that artistic creation depends on continuity and on patronage: "The sweetness that all longed for night and day" is the result of one "violent bitter man," the landowner, summoning others, "architect and artist," to produce it. The dialectical relationship between bitterness and sweetness is reinforced in the closing lines of each of the last two stanzas, and it will be echoed in the sixth section, when Yeats invites honeybees to occupy the empty starling's nest outside his window.

From the generalized "Ancestral Houses" we zoom in on the particular, first to "My House" and then to "My Table." The house is plentifully provided with Yeatsian symbols—rose, elms, thorns, water-hen—and its winding staircase leads to a candlelit room; here the poet claims a new spiritual ancestor in the man-at-arms who "spent his days / In this tumultuous spot." The five-hundred-year-old Japanese ceremonial sword, the present from Junzo Sato that occupies his table, is also a link with the heroic past as well as being a changeless artifact of exactly the sort found in "Sailing to Byzantium." After these three sections dealing with aspects of ancestry, he turns to "My Descendants" and to the appalling possibility that they might squander their inheritance of his "vigorous mind" "Through too much business with the passing hour, / Through too much play or marriage with a fool"; if so, he wishes, with King Lear-like violence, that his tower may become "a roofless ruin"— although in truth its state was fairly ruinous when he took it over. In any case, he relents, recalling the consolations of love and friendship:

For an old neighbour's friendship chose the house
And decked and altered it for a girl's love,
And know whatever flourish and decline
These stones remain their monument and mine.
                    (*CP*, pp. 225–232; *YP*, pp. 308–314)

This is an elegant recasting of the similarly benign epigram "To be Carved on a Stone at Thoor Ballylee," which concludes *Michael Robartes and the Dancer*:

I, the poet William Yeats,
With old mill boards and sea-green slates,
And smithy work from the Gort forge,
Restored this tower for my wife George;
And may these characters remain
When all is ruin once again.
                    (*CP*, p. 214; *YP*, p. 298)

But the stones are now under a threat more immediate than that of neglectful descendants, from both sides in the Irish conflict: in "The Road at My Door" an "affable Irregular" arrives joking about the civil war, followed by a "brown Lieutenant" to whom Yeats complains, in a variation of his recurrent scarecrow image, of "A pear-tree broken by the storm."

"Meditations in Time of Civil War" ends on a strained, apocalyptic, visionary note: a mutinous self-destructive mob, "cloud-pale unicorns," and "brazen hawks" resolve into "innumerable clanging wings that have put out the moon"—thereby destroying cosmological order. Turning away and closing the door on his vision, Yeats seeks reassurance: "The abstract joy, / The half-read wisdom of daemonic images, / Suffice the ageing man as once the growing boy."

This Wordsworthian cadence may sound convincing, but the reversion to youthful occultism is perverse: concreteness, not abstraction, is what gives these later poems their unmistakable strength.

"Nineteen Hundred and Nineteen" (*CP*, pp. 232–237; *YP*, pp. 314–318) confirms this: despite its references to Yeatsian mythography, it is a startlingly physical poem, both in its distant and immediate images, the Byzantine "golden grasshoppers and bees" and the all-too-close "drunken soldiery." Its note is one of plangent sorrow: "Man is in love and loves what vanishes, / What more is there to say?" As elsewhere in this group of poems, archetypal images (for instance, the swan as solitary soul) are set against the destructive violence of a world in which "All

break and vanish, and evil gathers head"; the poem, returning to the visionary horror of "The Second Coming" ends in pure nightmare.

"But is there any comfort to be found?" Yeats asks earlier in "Nineteen Hundred and Nineteen." There is, though it is of a qualified kind. In "Among School Children" (*CP*, pp. 242–245; *YP*, pp. 323–325), the "sixty-year-old smiling public man" finds himself surrounded by representatives of the next generation: children who may grow up to create rather than to destroy. Anticipating the later and more concise "Long-Legged Fly" (*CP*, pp. 381–382; *YP*, p. 463), the poem is founded on a sequence of trinities (infant, child, "scarecrow"; lover, nun, mother; Plato, Aristotle, Pythagoras) that culminate in the famous image of the chestnut tree:

Labour is blossoming or dancing where
The body is not bruised to pleasure soul,
Nor beauty born out of its own despair,
Nor blear-eyed wisdom out of midnight oil.
O chestnut-tree, great-rooted blossomer,
Are you the leaf, the blossom or the bole?
O body swayed to music, O brightening glance,
How can we tell the dancer from the dance?
                    (*CP*, pp. 242–245; *YP*, pp. 323–325)

In a great and wayward misreading of this poem, Yvor Winters (whose objections to Yeats's historical inaccuracies and "concern with his uninteresting relatives and ancestors" are not without foundation) angrily argued that the body is "always bruised to pleasure soul" and wisdom "always born out of midnight oil"; the "question addressed to the tree is preposterous" and "if the dancer and the dance could not be discriminated in fact, the dancer could never have learned the dance" (*Forms of Discovery*, p. 220). Everything Winters says is true on his own terms, and yet it curiously fails to diminish the poem. This blossoming and dancing innocence, where pleasure and wisdom occur without their adult cost in human damage, marks an implicit return to the "long schoolroom," the "wonder" of the schoolchildren who give the poem its title. In claiming that the tree is more than the sum of its parts, Yeats is reaffirming his faith in natural creativity, while in stressing the inseparable unity of dancer and dance (one might insist, *contra* Winters, that without the dance there could be no dancer) he restates the synthesis of artist and artifact from "Sailing to Byzantium": all is not lost.

THE WINDING STAIR

"I AM content," says Yeats—twice—in "A Dialogue of Self and Soul" (*CP*, pp. 265–267; *YP*, pp. 348–350), a poem which revisits images from the *Tower* sequences, such as Sato's sword and the winding stair itself, but which arrives at a startlingly affirmative, Wordsworthian conclusion: "We must laugh and we must sing, / We are blest by everything, / Everything we look upon is blest."

This note of benign reconciliation, as characteristic of *The Winding Stair* as rancorous despair was of *The Tower*, is evident above all in two tributes to Augusta Gregory and her estate, "Coole Park, 1929" (*CP*, pp. 273–275; *YP*, pp. 357–358) and "Coole Park and Ballylee, 1931" (*CP*, pp. 275–276; *YP*, pp. 358–360). The first of these is a meditation "Upon an aged woman and her house," in which "house" takes on its dynastic connotation, naming Lady Gregory's relatives (John Shawe-Taylor, Hugh Lane) as well as her literary visitors (Douglas Hyde, John Synge): they were like swallows, the image which opens the poem and returns midway through it, who came and went but loyally returned. These visitors form themselves into yet another trinity—"traveller, scholar, poet"—which echoes and modifies the "Soldier, scholar, horsemen" of "In Memory of Major Robert Gregory"; but it is the travelers, scholars, and poets of the future who are urged to return there, when Coole Park would be "a shapeless mound," to dedicate "A moment's memory to that laurelled head."

Fine as "Coole Park, 1929" is, "Coole Park and Ballylee, 1931" is the incomparably finer poem of the pair: it is one of those relatively rare pieces in which the disparate elements of Yeats's complex imagination mesh in perfect harmony. It begins at Thoor Ballylee, from where the racing waters, with their otters and moor-hens (favorite symbols but also very real creatures), run underground to reappear at Coole to feed the lake: "What's water but the generated soul?" This lake is bordered by a wood, "Now all dry sticks under a wintry sun," in keeping both with the poet's advancing age and his elegiac mood ("For Nature's pulled her tragic buskin on"), and it is also home to the wild swans, so memorably adopted as a symbol over a dozen years earlier. In three stanzas, Yeats has reached the house itself; in the fourth, he enters it and notices a single sound, exactly as one does when entering an otherwise silent place:

Sound of a stick upon the floor, a sound
From somebody that toils from chair to chair;
Beloved books, that famous hands have bound,
Old marble heads, old pictures everywhere;
Great rooms where travelled men and children found
Content or joy; a last inheritor
Where none has reigned that lacked a name and fame
Or out of folly into folly came.
(*CP*, pp. 275–276; *YP*, pp. 358–360)

Introduced by the touchingly low-key image of Lady Gregory's walking-stick as she "toils from chair to chair," these notably plain and understated lines provide an elegant summary of the views on cultural continuity which resonate through the accumulated body of Yeats's work. He is well aware that the poem exists at a pivotal moment. The diminished future, "Where the swan drifts upon a darkening flood," is now faced with stoical calm, as the departing age is memorialized: "We were the last romantics—chose for theme / Traditional sanctity and loveliness. . . ." There are possible objections to this—that literary romanticism still had more life in it than Yeats could have guessed, that in his earlier work he chose rather different themes—but he is surely right to align his work explicitly with that of his great predecessors.

Coleridge, indeed, springs usefully to mind when we come to "Byzantium" (*CP*, pp. 280–281; *YP*, pp. 363–364), which Yeats wrote while recovering from his feverish illness in 1930: it is his "Kubla Khan." Unlike its predecessor, "Sailing to Byzantium," it contains no retrospective glance back at an abandoned Ireland: its world is circumscribed by the "great cathedral gong" which begins to strike midnight in the first stanza and which will end the poem. Within this frame there appears a series of visions—of "Hades" "bobbin bound in mummy-cloth," of the golden bird, and of an eternal fire—all of which are in different ways time-defying and self-generating: "These images that yet / Fresh images beget, / That dolphin-torn, that gong-tormented sea."

"Byzantium" is a strange and powerful poem. It has its admirers, but it seems to me decisively less successful than its predecessor: its rhetoric is too strident and loud, an unrelieved fortissimo; despite its furious energy, it remains paradoxically static, for it lacks the tension between Ireland and Byzantium that so effectively powers the earlier poem. There is also a sense in which raw passion is becoming unseemly for the "ageing man"; and that is why, in the sequence "Words for Music

Perhaps" (*CP*, pp. 290–307; *YP*, pp. 371–384), he diverts his extreme feelings into two new characters, Crazy Jane and Mad Tom. Madness, *in propria persona*, must wait a little longer.

LATER POEMS

"WHY should not old men be mad?" asks Yeats, in the poem of that title (*CP*, pp. 388–389; *YP*, p. 443), which originally prefaced his not entirely sane pamphlet *On the Boiler* (1938); he gives various instances of promising lives ruined, concluding that the old man who has observed all this (and read books which confirm the nature of human folly) has every reason to be mad. But this won't quite do, as he well knows, not least because madness must be countered by a stronger allegiance to wisdom: "That civilisation may nor sink, / Its great battle lost, / Quiet the dog, tether the pony / To a distant post...."

These are the opening lines of "Long-Legged Fly" (*CP*, pp. 381–382; *YP*, p. 463), perhaps the most compact and mysterious of Yeats's later poems. It is a trinity, providing in its three stanzas three paradigms of civilization: the great soldier, Caesar; the beautiful woman, Helen of Troy; and the supreme artist, Michelangelo. Each, in the poem's hauntingly elliptical refrain, is "Like a long-legged fly upon the stream"; in each case, his or her "mind moves upon silence." The image cannot be paraphrased, but it is very clear that for Yeats true greatness demands an engagement with the quiet depths rather than with the noisy surfaces of life. Something comparable happens in another beautifully enigmatic poem, "Lapis Lazuli," where archetypal instances of human passion—"Hamlet rambles and Lear rages"—give way to this image of the still center:

> Two Chinamen, behind them a third,
> Are carved in lapis lazuli,
> Over them flies a long-legged bird,
> A symbol of longevity;
> The third, doubtless a serving-man,
> Carries a musical instrument.
> (*CP*, pp. 338–339; *YP*, pp. 412–413)

Apart from forming yet another trinity, these three Chinamen embody quiet purposefulness; being carved, they are of course motionless, but in the final stanza Yeats delightedly imagines them, having climbed their mountain, surveying the scene while listening to "mournful melodies."

Old men, then, should ideally be wise and calm rather than mad, yet nagging doubts inescapably remain. In "What Then?" in which he again reverts to his earlier practice of including an italicized refrain, Yeats surveys his successful life and the fulfillment of "his happier dreams." He should, he acknowledges, be content:

> The work is done, grown old he thought,
> According to my boyish plan;
> Let the fools rage, I swerved in naught,
> Something to perfection brought;
> *But louder sang that ghost, "What then?"*
> (*CP*, pp. 347–348; *YP*, p. 420)

It is surely no accident that this poem, with its unanswerably discontented question, should be followed by "Beautiful Lofty Things" (*CP*, p. 348; *YP*, p. 421); one hints at unattainable goals beyond human experience, the other regrets the passing of those unique elements which make up human experience. It is a familiar Yeatsian roll-call: John O'Leary, Lady Gregory, "Maud Gonne at Howth station waiting a train": each of them worthy of memorial, each "a thing never known again." As he had written earlier, in "Nineteen Hundred and Nineteen": "Many ingenious lovely things are gone / That seemed sheer miracle to the multitude...."

The paradox, of course, is that it is exactly this sense of loss that supplies the creative energy for Yeats's finest late poems. When, in "The Municipal Gallery Revisited," he finds himself surrounded by "the images of thirty years" (the first painting he notices is of "An ambush," but the slyly ambiguous syntax admits the sense of the poet himself being ambushed), the irony is brilliantly compounded: here, once more, are the familiar figures of his life, memorialized as art—which is, of course, precisely what he has been doing to them for years in his poetry. Though the poem somewhat rashly claims a unique significance for the trinity of John Synge, Augusta Gregory, and Yeats himself, it moves to a conclusion that would have been intolerably bombastic if it were not so self-evidently true:

> You that would judge me, do not judge alone
> This book or that, come to this hallowed place
> Where my friends' portraits hang and look thereon;
> Ireland's history in their lineaments trace;
> Think where man's glory most begins and ends,

And say my glory was I had such friends.
(*CP*, pp. 369–370; *YP*, pp. 438–440)

If "The Municipal Gallery Revisited" is Yeats's grand valediction to his friends, "The Circus Animals' Desertion" is his grand valediction to his images. Here are Oisin and Cuchulain, *The Countess Cathleen*, the Fool and the Blind Man, "masterful images" which were nevertheless founded on the detritus of ordinary life: "Old kettles, old bottles, and a broken can, / Old iron, old bones, old rags. . . ." These belong to the same world as the scarecrow images which recurred in *The Tower,* but even the scarecrow is now broken and recumbent: "I must lie down where all the ladders start, / In the foul rag-and-bone shop of the heart" (*CP*, pp. 391–392; *YP*, pp. 471–472).

That, too, is a partial truth, though hardly the whole truth. In the event, the scarecrow remains defiant to the end, and in "Under Ben Bulben" (*CP*, pp. 397–401; *YP*, pp. 449–452), not in fact Yeats's last poem (it is dated "September 4, 1938") but the poem which concludes the *Collected Poems,* he issues a series of clear instructions for cultural regeneration: "Poet and sculptor, do the work . . ."; "Irish poets, learn your trade, / Sing whatever is well made. . . ." He also leaves instructions, more easily obeyed, of a more personal sort. This essay began with the five lines that open the sixth and final section of "Under Ben Bulben," and it is now time to complete that quotation:

No marble, no conventional phrase;
On limestone quarried near the spot
By his command these words are cut:
Cast a cold eye
On life, on death.
Horseman, pass by!
(*CP*, pp. 397–401; *YP*, pp. 449–452)

CONCLUSION: THE LAST ROMANTIC?

IN a letter to Dorothy Wellesley (8 September 1935), Yeats wrote: "The correction of prose, because it has no fixed laws, is endless, the poem comes right with a click like a closing box" (*Letters on Poetry from W. B. Yeats to Dorothy Wellesley,* p. 22). Not all poems are like that, but Yeats's best poems are: they click with a rightness and an inevitability which is unmistakable.

But what sort of a poet is he? Rereading the major poems suggests that the answer to this question is not quite the one supplied by popular reputation. His eccentric beliefs are neither as important nor as obstructive as they at first appear; the uncertainties of tone and rhetoric which trouble his earlier work have very little to do with the mature style. And this style is formed by the convergence of two distinct but compatible impulses. One is occasional and political: these poems record events in contemporary Irish history in a verse which is somber, direct, and typically in Yeats's unmistakable three-stress line; the outstanding example is "Easter 1916." The other is the memorializing of people and places: more expansive, meditative, and associative, often though not always in iambic pentameters, these poems form the stabilizing core of Yeats's work from "In Memory of Major Robert Gregory" onwards. The two strands most spectacularly converge when political urgency is added to the great, grounded themes of place and friendship in the sequences from *The Tower;* here and in his later work, a remarkable number of the indisputably major poems are those centered on places—essentially, Thoor Ballylee and Coole Park—and their past or present inhabitants.

So Yeats is above all a great memorializer, whose true literary ancestors are the major Romantic poets. "We were the last romantics," he wrote, in the poem which most eloquently defines his cultural values, "Coole Park and Ballylee, 1931"; and, though he was arguably wrong about "last," he was absolutely right to claim such a distinguished lineage.

SELECTED BIBLIOGRAPHY

I. POETRY[1] *The Poems of W. B. Yeats* (London, 1949); The *Collected Poems* of W. B. Yeats (London, 1950); *The Variorum Edition of the Poems of W. B. Yeats,* ed. by Peter Allt and Russell K. Alspach (New York and London, 1957); *The Poems of W. B. Yeats: A New Edition,* ed. by Richard Finneran (London and New York, 1983); *Yeats's Poems,* ed. by A. Norman Jeffares (London, 1989).

II. PLAYS. *Collected Plays* (London, 1952); *The Variorum Edition of the Plays of W. B. Yeats,* ed. by Russell K. Alspach (London, 1966).

[1] The original volume-by-volume publication of Yeats's poetry, particularly the earlier work, is a complicated affair that does not always match the familiar divisions of the *Collected Poems.* The following list contains only the most authoritative collected editions, while the text provides page references for both *Collected Poems* (1950) [*CP*] and *Yeats's Poems* (1989; third ed., 1996) [*YP*].

III. PROSE. *Autobiographies* (London, 1955); *Mythologies* (London, 1959); *Essays and Introductions* (London, 1961); *Explorations,* selected by Mrs. W. B. Yeats (London, 1962); *A Vision* (London, 1962); *Uncollected Prose,* Vol. 1, ed. by John P. Frayne (London, 1970); *Memoirs,* ed. by Denis Donoghue (London, 1972); *Uncollected Prose,* Vol. 2, ed. by John P. Frayne and Colton Johnson (London, 1975); *W. B. Yeats: Prefaces and Introductions,* ed. by William H. O'Donnell (London, 1988).

IV. LETTERS. *The Letters of W. B. Yeats,* ed. by Allan Wade (London, 1954); *Letters on Poetry from W. B. Yeats to Dorothy Wellesley* (New York, 1940; rev. ed., London, 1964); *The Collected Letters of W. B. Yeats,* Volume 1, ed. by John Kelly and Eric Domville (Oxford, 1986); *The Collected Letters of W. B. Yeats,* Volume 3, ed. by John Kelly and Ronald Schuchard (Oxford, 1994); *The Collected Letters of W. B. Yeats,* Volume 2, ed. by Warwick Gould, John Kelly, and Deirdre Toomey (Oxford, 1997).

V. AS EDITOR. *A Book of Irish Verse Selected from Modern Writers* (London, 1895); *The Oxford Book of Modern Verse 1892–1945,* chosen by W. B. Yeats (Oxford, 1936).

VI. BIOGRAPHICAL AND CRITICAL STUDIES. Joseph M. Hone, *W. B. Yeats, 1865–1939* (London, 1943); Richard Ellman, *Yeats: The Man and the Masks* (New York and London, 1948); A. Norman Jeffares, *W. B. Yeats, Man and Poet* (London, 1949); T. R. Henn, *The Lonely Tower: Studies in the Poetry of W. B. Yeats* (London, 1950); Richard Ellmann, *The Identity of Yeats* (London, 1954); Frank Kermode, *Romantic Image* (London, 1957); John Unterecker, *A Reader's Guide to W. B. Yeats* (New York and London, 1959); A. G. Stock, *W. B. Yeats: His Poetry and Thought* (Cambridge, 1961); Jon Stallworthy, *Between the Lines: Yeats's Poems in the Making* (Oxford, 1963); Peter Ure, *Yeats* (Edinburgh, 1963); Yvor Winters, *Forms of Discovery* (Chicago, 1967);

Harold Bloom, *Yeats* (New York, 1970); A. Norman Jeffares, *The Circus Animals: Essays on W. B. Yeats* (Stanford, 1970); Denis Donoghue, *Yeats* (London, 1971); A. Norman Jeffares, *A New Commentary on the Poems of W. B. Yeats* (London, 1975); Frank Tuohy, *Yeats: An Illustrated Biography* (East Meredith, N.Y., and London, 1976); A. Norman Jeffares, *W. B. Yeats: A New Biography* (London, 1988); David Pierce, *Yeats's Worlds: Ireland, England, and the Poetic Imagination* (New Haven and London, 1995); R. F. Foster, *W. B. Yeats: A Life.* Vol. 1, *The Apprentice Mage* (Oxford, 1997); Brenda Maddox, *George's Ghosts: A New Life of W. B. Yeats* (London, 1999), published in U.S. as *Yeats's Ghosts: The Secret Life of W. B. Yeats* (New York, 1999).

MASTER INDEX

The following index covers the entire British Writers series through Retrospective Supplement I. All references include volume numbers in boldface Roman numerals followed by page numbers within that volume. Subjects of articles are indicated by boldface type.

"Bull: A Farce" (Self), **Supp. V:** 405–406

"Bull That Thought, The" (Kipling), **VI:** 189, 190

"Bulldog" Drummond series (Sapper), **Supp. IV:** 500

Bullett, Gerald, **V:** 196, 199, 200

Bulwer–Lytton, Edward, **III:** 340, 345; **IV:** 256, 295, 311; **V:** 22, 47

Bundle, The (Bond), **Supp. I:** 423

Bundle of Letters, A (James), **VI:** 67, 69

Bunting, Basil, **Supp. VII: 1–15**

Bunyan, John, **I:** 16; **II: 240–254; III:** 82; **V:** 27

Buoyant Billions: A Comedy of No Manners in Prose (Shaw), **VI:** 127, 129

Burbidge, Thomas, **V:** 159

Burckhardt, Jakob, **V:** 342

"Burden of Itys, The" (Wilde), **V:** 401

"Burden of Ninevah, The" (Rossetti), **V:** 240, 241

Bürger, Gottfried August, **IV: 44, 48**

Burger's Daughter (Gordimer), **Supp. II:** 225, 228, 230, 231, 232, **234–237**, 241, 242, 243

Burgess, Anthony, **Supp. I: 185–198; Supp. IV:** 4, 13, 234, 449

"Burghers, The" (Hardy), **Retro. Supp. I:** 120

"Burial of the Rats, The" (Stoker), **Supp. III:** 382

Buried Alive (Bennett), **VI:** 250, 252, 257, 266

Buried Day, The (Day Lewis), **Supp. III:** 116, 128

"Buried Life, The" (Arnold), **V:** 210

Burke, Edmund, **III:** 185, **193–206**, 274; **IV:** xii–xvi, 54, 127, 130, 133, 136–138, 271, 275; **VI:** 356; **Supp. III:** 371, 467, 468, 470

Burke, Kenneth, **Supp. IV:** 114

Burke and Bristol, 1774–1780 (Barker), **III:** 196

"Burleigh" (Macaulay), **IV:** 279

Burlington Magazine, **Supp. IV:** 121

"Burma Casualty" (Lewis), **VII:** 447

Burmann, Peter, **III:** 96

Burmese Days (Orwell), **VII:** 276, 278

Burn, The (Kelman), **Supp. V:** 243, 249, 250–251

Burne–Jones, Edward, **IV:** 346; **V:** 236, 293–296, 302, 318n, 355; **VI:** 166; **Supp. V:** 98, 99

Burney, Charles, **Supp. III:** 65–67

Burney, Frances, **Supp. III: 63–78**

Burning Cactus, The (Spender), **Supp. II:** 488

Burning of the Brothel, The (Hughes), **Supp. I:** 348

"Burning Want" (Murray), **Supp. VII:** 283–284

Burning World, The (Ballard), **Supp. V:** 24

Burnshaw, Stanley, **Supp. IV:** 460, 473

Burnt Ones, The (White), **Supp. I:** 131, 136, 143

Burnt–Out Case, A (Greene), **Supp. I:** 7, 13, 15, 16, 18

Burroughs, William S., **Supp. V:** 26

Busconductor Hines, The (Kelman), **Supp. V:** 242, 246–247

Business of Good Government, The (Arden), **Supp. II:** 29

Busker, The (Kelman), **Supp. V:** 256

Busman's Honeymoon (Sayers), **Supp. III:** 335, 336, 347–348

"Busted Scotch" (Kelman), **Supp. V:** 249

"Busy" (Milne), **Supp. V:** 302

"But at the Stroke of Midnight" (Warner), **Supp. VII:** 381

...but the Clouds (Beckett), **Retro. Supp. I:** 29

Butcher's Dozen (Kinsella), **Supp. V:** 267

Butler, Samuel, **Supp. II: 97–119**

Butor, Michel, **Supp. IV:** 115

"Butterflies" (McEwan), **Supp. IV:** 391

"Buzzard and Alder" (Stevenson), **Supp. VI:** 261

"By Achmelrich Bridge" (MacCaig), **Supp. VI:** 182

"By the burn" (Kelman), **Supp. V:** 250–251

By Jeeves (Ayckbourn and Webber), **Supp. V:** 3

By Night Unstarred (Kavanagh), **Supp. VII:** 189

By the Line (Keneally), **Supp. IV:** 345

By Way of Introduction (Milne), **Supp. V:** 300

Byatt, A. S. (neé Antonia Drabble), **Supp. IV: 139–156,** 229

Bye–Bye, Blackbird (Desai), **Supp. V:** 55, 60–62

"Byre" (MacCaig), **Supp. VI:** 188, 190, 194

Byron, George Gordon, Lord, **III:** 329; **IV:** x, xi, 46, 61, 91, 129, 132, 168, **171–194,** 198–199, 202, 206, 215, 281, 299; **V:** 111–112, 247, 324; **Supp. III:** 356, 365; and Coleridge, **IV:** 46, 48; and Hazlitt, **IV:** 129; and Shelley, **IV:** 159, 172, 176–177, 179, 181, 182, 198–199, 202, 206; **Retro. Supp. I:** 250–251; and Southey, **IV:** 61, 184–187; literary style, **III:** 336, 337–338; **IV:** viii, ix, xi, 129, 281; **V:** 17, 116; **VII:** xix

"Byron" (Durrell), **Supp. I:** 126

"Byron" (Macaulay), **IV:** 281

Byron, Robert, **Supp. IV:** 157

Byron and the Ruins of Paradise (Gleckner), **IV:** 173, 194

Byron in Italy (Quennell), **IV:** 194

Byron: The Years of Fame (Quennell), **IV:** 194

Byronic Hero, The Types and Prototypes (Thorslev), **IV:** 173, 194

Byron's Conspiracy (Chapman), **I:** 249–251

Byron's Tragedy (Chapman), *see Tragedy of Byron, The*

"Byzantium" (Yeats), **VI:** 215; **Retro. Supp. I:** 336–337

C. G. Jung's First Years" (Kinsella), **Supp. V:** 269

Cab at the Door, A (Pritchett), **Supp. III:** 311, 312

Cabinet of Dr. Caligari, The (film), **III:** 342

Cadenus and Vanessa (Swift), **III:** 18, 31, 35; **Retro. Supp. I:** 283–284

Cage Without Grievance (Graham), **Supp. VII:** 105, 107–109, 112

"Caedmon" (Nicholson), **Supp. VI:** 216

Caesar and Cleopatra (Shaw), **VI:** 112

Caesar and Pompey (Chapman), **I:** 252–253

Caesar Borgia (Lee), **II:** 305

Caesar's Fall (Drayton, Middleton, Munday, Webster, et al.), **II:** 68, 85

Caesar's Wife (Maugham), **VI:** 369

"Cage of Sand" (Ballard), **Supp. V:** 24

Cagliostro, Alessandro di, **III:** 332

Cahier d'un retour au pays natal (Césaire), **Supp. IV:** 77

Cain (Byron), **IV:** xviii, 173, 177, **178–182,** 193

Cakes and Ale (Maugham), **VI:** 367, 371, 374, 377

Calderón de la Barca, Pedro, **II:** 312n, 313n; **IV:** 206, 342, 349

Caleb Williams (Godwin), *see Adventures of Caleb Williams, The*

Caledonia (Defoe), **III:** 13

Calendar of Love, A (Brown), **Supp. VI:** 64

Calendar of Modern Letters (periodical), **VII:** 233

"Calenture" (Reid), **Supp. VII:** 328

"Caliban upon Setebos" (Browning), **IV:** 358, 364, 370, 372

"Calidore" (Keats), **IV:** 214

Caliph's Design, The (Lewis), **VII:** 72, 75n

Call for the Dead (le Carré), **Supp. II:** 299, **305–307,** 308, 311

Called to Be Saints (Rossetti), **V:** 260

Call–Girls, The (Koestler), **Supp. I:** 28n, 32

Callista: A Tale of the Third Century (Newman), **Supp. VII:** 299

"Calmative, The" (Beckett), **Supp. I:** 50, 59; **Retro. Supp. I:** 21

Calvin, John, **I:** 241

Calvino, Italo, **Supp. IV:** 558

"Camberwell Beauty, The" (Pritchett), **Supp. III:** 312, **327–328,** 329

Camberwell Beauty and Other Stories, The (Pritchett), **Supp. III:** 313, 327

Cambises (Preston), **I:** 122, 213–214

"Cambridge" (Ewart), **Supp. VII:** 36

Cambridge (Phillips), **Supp. V:** 380, 386, 388–390

Cambridge Bibliography of English Literature, **III:** 51, 52

Cambyses (Preston), *see Cambises*

Camden, William, **Retro. Supp. I:** 152–153

Cameron, Norman, **VII:** 421, 422, 426

Camilla; or, A Picture of Youth (Burney), **Supp. III:** 64, 65, 68, 72, 73–75, 76

Cammaerts, Emile, **V:** 262, 274

Camp, The (Sheridan), **III:** 253, 264

Campaign, The (Addison), **III:** 46

Campaspe (Lyly), **I:** 198, 199–200

Mighty and Their Full, The (Compton–Burnett), **VII:** 61, 62

Mighty Magician, The (FitzGerald), **IV:** 353

Miguel Street (Naipaul), **Supp. I:** 383, 385–386

"Mike: A Public School Story" (Wodehouse), **Supp. III:** 449

Mike Fletcher (Moore), **VI:** 87, 91

"Mildred Lawson" (Moore), **VI:** 98

Milestones (Bennett), **VI:** 250, 263, 264

Milford, H., **III:** 208*n*

"Milford: East Wing" (Murphy), **Supp. V:** 328

Military Memoirs of Capt. George Carleton, The (Defoe), **III:** 14

Military Philosophers, The (Powell), **VII:** 349

Mill, James, **IV:** 159; **V:** 288

Mill, John Stuart, **IV:** 50, 56, 246, 355; **V:** xxi–xxii, xxiv, 182, 279, 288, 343

Mill on the Floss, The (Eliot), **V:** xxii, 14, 192–194, 200; **Supp. IV:** 240, 471

Millais, John Everett, **V:** 235, 236, 379

Miller, Arthur, **VI:** 286

Miller, Henry, **Supp. IV:** 110–111

Miller, J. Hillis, **V:** 147

Miller, Karl, **Supp. IV:** 169

"Miller's Daughter, The" (Tennyson), **IV:** 326

Miller's Tale, The (Chaucer), **I:** 37

Millet, Jean François, **Supp. IV:** 90

Millett, Kate, **Supp. IV:** 188

Millionairess, The (Shaw), **VI:** 102, 127

"Millom Cricket Field" (Nicholson), **Supp. VI:** 216

"Millom Old Quarry" (Nicholson), **Supp. VI:** 216

Mills, C. M., pseud. of Elizabeth Gaskell

Millstone, The (Drabble), **Supp. IV:** 230, 237–238

Milne, A. A., **Supp. V:** 295–312

"Milnes, Richard Monckton" (Lord Houghton), *see* Monckton Milnes, Richard

Milton (Blake), **III:** 303–304, 307; **V:** xvi 330; **Retro. Supp. I:** 45

Milton (Meredith), **V:** 234

"Milton" (Macaulay), **IV:** 278, 279

Milton, Edith, **Supp. IV:** 305–306

Milton in America (Ackroyd), **Supp. VI:** 11–12, 13

Milton, John, **II:** 50–52, 113, **158–178,** 195, 196, 198, 199, 205, 206, 236, 302; **III:** 43, 118–119, 167*n*, 211*n*, 220, 302; **IV:** 9, 11–12, 14, 22, 23, 93, 95, 185, 186, 200, 205, 229, 269, 278, 279, 352; **V:** 365–366; **Supp. III:** 169

Milton's God (Empson), **Supp. II:** 180, **195–196**

Milton's Prosody (Bridges), **VI:** 83

Mimic Men, The (Naipaul), **Supp. I:** 383, 386, 390, 392, 393–394, 395, 399

"Mina Laury" (Brontë), **V:** 122, 123, 149, 151

Mind at the End of Its Tether (Wells), **VI:** xiii; **VI:** 228, 242

Mind Has Mountains, The (Jennings), **Supp. V:** 213, 215–216

Mind in Chains, The (ed. Day Lewis), **Supp. III:** 118

Mind of the Maker, The (Sayers), **Supp. III:** 345, 347

Mind to Murder, A (James), **Supp. IV:** 319, 321, 323–324

"Mine old dear enemy, my froward master" (Wyatt), **I:** 105

"Miner's Hut" (Murphy), **Supp. V:** 328

"Miners" (Owen), **VI:** 452, 454

Ministry of Fear, The (Greene), **Supp. I:** 10–11, 12

Minor Poems of Robert Southey, The (Southey), **IV:** 71

Minpins, The (Dahl), **Supp. IV:** 204, 224

Minstrel, The (Beattie), **IV:** 198

Minstrelsy of the Scottish Border (ed. Scott), **IV:** 29, 39

"Mint" (Heaney), **Retro. Supp. I:** 133

Mint, The (Lawrence), **Supp. II:** 283, **291–294**

Minute by Glass Minute (Stevenson), **Supp. VI:** 261

Minute for Murder (Day Lewis), **Supp. III:** 130

Minutes of the Negotiations of Monsr. Mesnager, . . . (Defoe), **III:** 13

"Mirabeau" (Macaulay), **IV:** 278

"Miracle Cure" (Lowbury), **VII:** 432

Miracles (Lewis), **Supp. III:** 248, 255, 258–259

Mirèio (Mistral), **V:** 219

Mirour de l'omme (Gower), **I:** 48, 49

Mirror for Magistrates, The, **I:** 162, 214

"Mirror in February" (Kinsella), **Supp. V:** 262

Mirror of the Sea: Memories and Impressions, The (Conrad), **VI:** 138, 148

Mirror Wall, The (Murphy), **Supp. V:** 313, 329–330

Mirrour; or, Looking–Glasse Both for Saints and Sinners, A (Clarke), **II:** 251

Misadventures of John Nicholson, The (Stevenson), **V:** 396

Misalliance (Shaw), **VI:** xv, 115, 117, 118, 120, 129

Misalliance, The (Brookner), **Supp. IV:** 129

Misanthrope, The (tr. Harrison), **Supp. V:** 149–150, 163

"Misanthropos" (Gunn), **Supp. IV:** 264–265, 268, 270

Miscellanea (Temple), **III:** 40

Miscellaneous Essays (St. Évremond), **III:** 47

Miscellaneous Observations on the Tragedy of Macbeth (Johnson), **III:** 108, 116, 121

Miscellaneous Poems (Marvell), **II:** 207

Miscellaneous Studies (Pater), **V:** 348, 357

Miscellaneous Works of the Duke of Buckingham, **II:** 268

Miscellaneous Works . . . with Memoirs of His Life (Gibbon), **III:** 233

Miscellanies (Cowley), **II:** 198

Miscellanies (Pope and Swift), **II:** 335

Miscellanies (Swinburne), **V:** 332

Miscellanies; A Serious Address to the People of Great Britain (Fielding), **III:** 105

Miscellanies, Aesthetic and Literary . . . (Coleridge), **IV:** 56

Miscellany (Tonson), **III:** 69

Miscellany of New Poems, A (Behn), **Supp. III:** 36

Miscellany Poems (Wycherley), **II:** 321

Miscellany Tracts (Browne), **II:** 156

Mischmasch (Carroll), **V:** 274

"Mise Eire" (Boland), **Supp. V:** 45–46

Miser, The (Fielding), **III:** 105

"Miserie" (Herbert), **II:** 128–129

Miseries of War, The (Ralegh), **I:** 158

Misfortunes of Arthur, The (Hughes), **I:** 218

Misfortunes of Elphin, The (Peacock), **IV:** xviii, 163, 167–168, 170

Mishan, E. J., **VI:** 240

"Misplaced Attachment of Mr. John Dounce, The" (Dickens), **V:** 46

"Miss Brill" (Mansfield), **VII:** 175

Miss Gomez and the Brethren (Trevor), **Supp. IV:** 507, 508–509

"Miss Gunton of Poughkeepsie" (James), **VI:** 69

Miss Herbert (The Suburban Wife) (Stead), **Supp. IV:** 473, 476

"Miss Kilmansegg and Her Precious Leg" (Hood), **IV:** 258–259

Miss Lucy in Town (Fielding), **III:** 105

Miss Mackenzie (Trollope), **V:** 101

Miss Marple's Last Case (Christie), **Supp. II:** 125

Miss Ogilvy Finds Herself (Hall), **Supp. VI:** 120–121, 128

"Miss Ogilvy Finds Herself" (Hall), **Supp. VI:** 121

"Miss Pulkinhorn" (Golding), **Supp. I:** 78–79, 80

"Miss Smith" (Trevor), **Supp. IV:** 502, 510

"Miss Tickletoby's Lectures on English History" (Thackeray), **V:** 38

"Miss Twye" (Ewart), **Supp. VII:** 36

"Missing, The" (Gunn), **Supp. IV:** 276

"Missing Dates" (Empson), **Supp. II:** 184, 190

Mistake, The (Vanbrugh), **II:** 325, 333, 336

Mistakes, The (Harris), **II:** 305

Mr. A's Amazing Mr. Pim Passes By (Milne), **Supp. V:** 299

"Mr. and Mrs. Dove" (Mansfield), **VII:** 180

"Mr. and Mrs. Frank Berry" (Thackeray), **V:** 23

"Mr. Apollinax" (Eliot), **VII:** 144

Mr. Beluncle (Pritchett), **Supp. III:** 311, 313, 314–315

Mr. Bennett and Mrs. Brown (Woolf), **VI:** 247, 267, 275, 290; **VII:** xiv, xv

"Mr. Bennett and Mrs. Brown" (Woolf), **Supp. II:** 341; **Retro. Supp. I:** 309

"Mr. Bleaney" (Larkin), **Supp. I:** 281

"Mr. Bodkin" (Hood), **IV:** 267

My Lady Ludlow (Gaskell), **V:** 15

"My Last Duchess" (Browning), **IV:** 356, 360, 372

"My Life up to Now" (Gunn), **Supp. IV:** 255, 265, 266, 268, 269, 273

"My love whose heart is tender said to me" (Rossetti), **V:** 251

"My lute awake!" (Wyatt), **I:** 105–106

My Man Jeeves (Wodehouse), **Supp. III:** 455

"My Mother" (Kincaid), **Supp. VII:** 221

"My own heart let me more have pity on" (Hopkins), **V:** 375–376

"My Own Life" (Hume), **Supp. III:** 229

"My pen take pain a little space" (Wyatt), **I:** 106

"My Picture Left in Scotland" (Jonson), **Retro. Supp. I:** 152

My Sad Captains (Gunn), **Supp. IV:** 257, 262–264

"My Sad Captains" (Gunn), **Supp. IV:** 263–264

My Sister Eileen (McKenney), **Supp. IV:** 476

"My Sister's Sleep" (Rossetti), **V:** 239, 240, 242

"My Sister's War" (Thomas), **Supp. IV:** 492

My Son's Story (Gordimer), **Supp. II:** 233, 240–242

"My Spectre" (Blake), **V:** 244

"My spirit kisseth thine" (Bridges), **VI:** 77

"My true love hath my heart, and I have his" (Sidney), **I:** 169

My Uncle Oswald (Dahl), **Supp. IV:** 213, 219, 220

My Very Own Story (Ayckbourn), **Supp. V:** 3, 11, 13

My World as in My Time (Newbolt), **VI:** 75

My Year (Dahl), **Supp. IV:** 225

Myer, Valerie Grosvenor, **Supp. IV:** 230

Myers, William Francis, **VII:** xx, xxxviii

Myles Before Myles, A Selection of the Earlier Writings of Brian O'Nolan (O'Nolan), **Supp. II:** 322, 323, 324

Myrick, K. O., **I:** 160, 167

"Myself in India" (Jhabvala), **Supp. V:** 227, 229–230

Myself When Young: Confessions (Waugh), **Supp. VI:** 270

Mysteries, The (Harrison), **Supp. V:** 150, 163

Mysteries of Udolpho, The (Radcliffe), **III:** 331–332, 335, 345; **IV:** xvi, 111; **Supp. III:** 384

Mysterious Affair at Styles, The (Christie), **Supp. II:** 124, 129–130

"Mysterious Kôr" (Bowen), **Supp. II:** 77, 82, 93

Mystery of Charles Dickens, The (Ackroyd), **Supp. VI:** 13

Mystery of Edwin Drood, The (Dickens), *see Edwin Drood*

"Mystery of Sasaesa Valley" (Doyle), **Supp. II:** 159

Mystery of the Blue Train (Christie), **Supp. II:** 125

Mystery of the Charity of Charles Péguy, The (Hill), **Supp. V:** 189, 196–198

Mystery of the Fall (Clough), **V:** 159, 161

Mystery of the Sea, The (Stoker), **Supp. III:** 381

Mystery Revealed: . . . Containing . . . Testimonials Respecting the . . . Cock Lane Ghost, The (Goldsmith), **III:** 191

Mystic Masseur, The (Naipaul), **Supp. I:** 383, 386, 387, 393

"Mysticism and Democracy" (Hill), **Supp. V:** 192–193

Myth of Modernism (Bergonzi), **Supp. IV:** 364

"Mythical Journey, The" (Muir), **Supp. VI:** 206

Mythologiae sive explicationis fabularum (Conti), **I:** 266

"Mythological Sonnets" (Fuller), **Supp. VII:** 73

"Mythology" (Motion), **Supp. VII:** 266

N.

'n Droë wit seisoen (Brink), **Supp. VI:** 50

'n Oomblik in die wind (Brink), **Supp. VI:** 49

"Naaman" (Nicholson), **Supp. VI:** 216

"Nabara, The" (Day Lewis), **Supp. III:** 127

Nabokov, Vladimir, **Supp. IV:** 26–27, 43, 153, 302

Nacht and Traüme (Beckett), **Retro. Supp. I:** 29

Nada the Lily (Haggard), **Supp. III:** 214

Nadel, G. H., **I:** 269

Naipaul, V. S., **VII:** xx; **Supp. I:** **383–405; Supp. IV:** 302

Naive and Sentimental Lover, The (le Carré), **Supp. II:** 300, **310–311,** 317

Naked Warriors (Read), **VI:** 436

Name and Nature of Poetry, The (Housman), **VI:** 157, 162–164

Name of Action, The (Greene), **Supp. I:** 3

Name of the Rose, The (Eco), **Supp. IV:** 116

"Naming of Offa, The" (Hill), **Supp. V:** 195

"Naming of Parts" (Reed), **VII:** 422

Nannie's Night Out (O'Casey), **VII:** 11–12

Napier, Macvey, **IV:** 272

Napoleon of Notting Hill, The (Chesterton), **VI:** 335, 338, 343–344

Napoleon III in Italy and Other Poems (Browning), *see Poems Before Congress*

Narayan, R. K., **Supp. IV:** 440

"Narcissus" (Gower), **I:** 53–54

Nares, Edward, **IV:** 280

Narrative of All the Robberies, . . . of John Sheppard, A (Defoe), **III:** 13

"Narrative of Jacobus Coetzee, The" (Coetzee), **Supp. VI:** 76, **79–80**

Narrow Corner, The (Maugham), **VI:** 375

Narrow Place, The (Muir), **Supp. VI:** 204, **206**

"Narrow Place, The" (Muir), **Supp. VI:** 206

Narrow Road to the Deep North (Bond), **Supp. I:** 423, 427, 428–429, 430, 435

"Narrow Sea, The" (Graves), **VII:** 270

"Narrow Vessel, A" (Thompson), **V:** 441

Nashe, Thomas, **I:** 114, 123, 171, 199, 221, 278, 279, 281, 288; **II:** 25; **Supp. II:** 188; **Retro. Supp. I:** 156

Nation (periodical), **VI:** 455

Nation Review (publication), **Supp. IV:** 346

National Observer (periodical), **VI:** 350

National Standard (periodical), **V:** 19

National Tales (Hood), **IV:** 255, 259, 267

"National Trust" (Harrison), **Supp. V:** 153

Native Companions: Essays and Comments on Australian Literature 1936–1966 (Hope), **Supp. VII:** 151, 153, 159, 164

"Natura Naturans" (Clough), **V:** 159–160

Natural Causes (Motion), **Supp. VII:** 254, 257–258, 263

Natural Curiosity, A (Drabble), **Supp. IV:** 231, 249–250

Natural History and Antiquities of Selborne, The, (White), **Supp. VI:** 279–284, **285–293**

Natural History of Religion, The (Hume), **Supp. III:** 240–241

"natural man," **VII:** 94

"Natural Son" (Murphy), **Supp. V:** 327, 329

Naturalist's Calendar, with Observations in Various Branches of Natural History, A (White), **Supp. VI:** 283

Naturalist's Journal (White), **Supp. VI:** 283, 292

"Naturally the Foundation Will Bear Your Expenses" (Larkin), **Supp. I:** 285

Nature of a Crime, The (Conrad), **VI:** 148

Nature of Blood, The (Phillips), **Supp. V:** 380, 391–394

Nature of Cold Weather, The (Redgrove), **Supp. VI: 227–229,** 236

"Nature of Cold Weather, The" (Redgrove), **Supp. VI:** 228,237

"Nature of Gothic, The" (Ruskin), **V:** 176

Nature of History, The (Marwick), **IV:** 290, 291

Nature of Passion, The (Jhabvala), **Supp. V:** 226

"Nature of the Scholar, The" (Fichte), **V:** 348

Nature Poems (Davies), **Supp. III:** 398

"Nature That Washt Her Hands in Milk" (Ralegh), **I:** 149

Natwar–Singh, K., **VI:** 408

Naufragium Joculare (Cowley), **II:** 194, 202

Naulahka (Kipling and Balestier), **VI:** 204

"Naval History" (Kelman), **Supp. V:** 250

"Naval Treaty, The" (Doyle), **Supp. II:**
169, 175

Navigation and Commerce (Evelyn), **II:**
287

"Navy's Here, The" (Redgrove), **Supp.
VI:** 234

Naylor, Gillian, **VI:** 168

Nazarene Gospel Restored, The (Graves
and Podro), **VII:** 262

Nazism, **VI:** 242

Neal, Patricia, **Supp. IV:** 214, 218, 223

Near and Far (Blunden), **VI:** 428

"Near Lanivet" (Hardy), **VI:** 17

"Near Perigord" (Pound), **V:** 304

Necessity of Art, The (Fischer), **Supp. II:**
228

Necessity of Atheism, The (Shelley and
Hogg), **IV:** xvii, 196, 208; **Retro.
Supp. I:** 244

"Necessity of Not Believing, The"
(Smith), **Supp. II:** 467

Necessity of Poetry, The (Bridges), **VI:**
75–76, 82, 83

"Necessity's Child" (Wilson), **Supp. I:**
153–154

"Neck" (Dahl), **Supp. IV:** 217

"Ned Bratts" (Browning), **IV:** 370

Ned Kelly and the City of the Bees
(Keneally), **Supp. IV:** 346

"Ned Skinner" (Muldoon), **Supp. IV:**
415

"Need to Be Versed in Country Things,
The" (Frost), **Supp. IV:** 423

Needham, Gwendolyn, **V:** 60

Needle's Eye, The (Drabble), **Supp. IV:**
230, 234, 241, 242–243, 245, 251

"Neglected Graveyard, Luskentyre"
(MacCaig), **Supp. VI:** 182, 189, 194

Neizvestny, Ernst, **Supp. IV:** 88

"Nelly Trim" (Warner), **Supp. VII:** 371

Nelson, W., **I:** 86

Nerinda (Douglas), **VI:** 300, 305

Nero Part I (Bridges), **VI:** 83

Nero Part II (Bridges), **VI:** 83

Nesbit, E., **Supp. II:** 140, 144, 149

"Nest in a Wall, A" (Murphy), **Supp. V:**
326

*Nest of Tigers, A: Edith, Osbert and
Sacheverell in Their Times*
(Lehmann), **VII:** 141

Nether World, The (Gissing), **V:** 424, 437

Netherwood (White), **Supp. I:** 131, 151

"Netting, The" (Murphy), **Supp. V:** 318

Nettles (Lawrence), **VII:** 118

"Netty Sargent's Copyhold" (Hardy),
VI: 22

"Neurotic, The" (Day Lewis), **Supp. III:**
129

Neutral Ground (Corke), **VII:** 93

"Neutral Tones" (Hardy), **Retro. Supp.
I:** 110, 117

New Age (periodical), **VI:** 247, 265; **VII:**
172

New and Collected Poems 1934–84
(Fuller), **Supp. VII:** 68, 72, 73, 74,
79

New and Collected Poems, 1952–1992
(Hill), **Supp. V:** 184

*New and Improved Grammar of the Eng-
lish Tongue, A* (Hazlitt), **IV:** 139

New and Selected Poems (Davie), **Supp.
VI:** 108

New and Useful Concordance, A (Bunyan), **II:** 253

New Apocalypse, The (MacCaig), **Supp.
VI:** 184

New Arabian Nights (Stevenson), **V:**
384n, 386, 395; **Retro. Supp. I:** 263

New Atlantis (Bacon), **I:** 259, 265,
267–269, 273

"New Ballad of Tannhäuser, A" (David-
son), **V:** 318n

New Bath Guide (Anstey), **III:** 155

New Bats in Old Belfries (Betjeman), **VII:**
368–369

New Bearings in English Poetry (Leavis),
V: 375, 381; **VI:** 21; **VII:** 234,
244–246

"New Beginning, A" (Kinsella), **Supp.
V:** 270

New Belfry of Christ Church, The (Carroll), **V:** 274

New Characters . . . of Severall Persons . . .
(Webster), **II:** 85

"New Cemetery, The" (Nicholson),
Supp. VI: 219

*New Cratylus, The: Notes on the Craft of
Poetry* (Hope), **Supp. VII:** 151, 155

New Country (ed. Roberts), **VII:** xix, 411

"New Delhi Romance, A" (Jhabvala),
Supp. V: 236–237

New Discovery of an Old Intreague, An
(Defoe), **III:** 12; **Retro. Supp. I:** 67

New Dominion, A (Jhabvala), **Supp. V:**
230–231

"New Drama" (Joyce), **Retro. Supp. I:**
170

New Dunciad, The (Pope), **III:** 73, 78;
Retro. Supp. I: 238

"New Empire Within Britain, The"
(Rushdie), **Supp. IV:** 436, 445

"New England Winter, A" (James), **VI:**
69

New Essays by De Quincey (ed. Tave); **IV:**
155

New Ewart, The: Poems 1980–82 (Ewart),
Supp. VII: 34, 44, 45

New Family Instructor, A (Defoe), **III:** 14

"New Forge" (Murphy), **Supp. V:** 328

*New Form of Intermittent Light for Light-
houses, A* (Stevenson), **V:** 395

New Grub Street (Gissing), **V:** xxv, 426,
427, 429, 430, 434–435, 437; **VI:**
377; **Supp. IV:** 7

"New Hampshire" (Reid), **Supp. VII:**
326

New Inn; The Noble Gentlemen (Jonson),
II: 65; **Retro. Supp. I:** 165

New Journey to Paris, A (Swift), **III:** 35

"New King for the Congo: Mobutu and
the Nihilism of Africa" (Naipaul),
Supp. I: 398

New Light on Piers Plowman (Bright), **I:** 3

New Lines (Conquest), **Supp. IV:** 256

New Lives for Old (Snow), **VII:** 323

New Love–Poems (Scott), **IV:** 39

New Machiavelli, The (Wells), **VI:** 226,
239, 244

New Magdalen, The (Collins), **Supp. VI:**
102

New Meaning of Treason, The (West),
Supp. III: 440, 444

New Men, The (Snow), **VII:** xxi, 324,
328–329, 330

New Method of Evaluation as Applied to π,
The (Carroll), **V:** 274

New Monthly (periodical), **IV:** 252, 254,
258

"New Novel, The" (James), **VI:** xii

New Numbers (periodical), **VI:** 420;
Supp. III: 47

New Oxford Book of Irish Verse, The (Kinsella), **Supp. V:** 274

New Poems (Arnold), **V:** xxiii, 204, 209,
216

"New Poems" (Bridges), **VI:** 77

New Poems (Davies), **Supp. III:** 398

New Poems (Fuller), **Supp. VII:** 76–77

New Poems (Kinsella), **Supp. V:** 266, 274

New Poems (Thompson), **V:** 444, 446,
451

*New Poems by Robert Browning and Eliza-
beth Barrett Browning* (ed. Kenyon),
IV: 321

*New Poems Hitherto Unpublished or
Uncollected . . .* (Rossetti), **V:** 260

New Quixote, The (Frayn), **Supp. VII:** 57

New Review (periodical), **VI:** 136

New Rhythm and Other Pieces, The (Firbank), **Supp. II:** 202, 205, 207, 222

New Satyr on the Parliament, A (Defoe),
Retro. Supp. I: 67

New Selected Poems (Heaney), **Retro.
Supp. I:** 131

New Signatures (Day Lewis), **Supp. III:**
125

New Signatures (ed. Roberts), **VII:** 411;
Supp. II: 486

"New Song, A" (Heaney), **Supp. II:** 273

New Statesman (periodical), **VI:** 119, 250,
371; **VII:** 32; **Supp. IV:** 26, 66, 78,
80, 81

New Stories I (ed. Drabble), **Supp. IV:**
230

New Territory (Boland), **Supp. V:** 35, 36

New Testament in Modern English
(Phillips), **I:** 383

New Testament in Modern Speech (Wey-
mouth), **I:** 382

New Voyage Round the World, A (Dampi-
er), **III:** 7, 24

New Voyage Round the World, A (Defoe),
III: 5, 13

New Weather (Muldoon), **Supp. IV:**
412–414, 416

"New Weather" (Muldoon), **Supp. IV:**
413

New Witness (periodical), **VI:** 340, 341

New Worlds for Old (Wells), **VI:** 242

New Writings of William Hazlitt (ed.
Howe), **IV:** 140

New Year Letter (Auden), **VII:** 379, 382,
388, 390, 393; **Retro. Supp. I:** 10

"New Year Wishes for the English"
(Davie), **Supp. VI:** 110